Museums in the Material World

Museums in the Material World seeks to both introduce classic and thought-provoking pieces and contrast them with articles which reveal grounded practice. The articles are selected from across the full breadth of museum disciplines and are linked by a logical narrative, as detailed in the introductions.

The choice of articles reveals how the debate has opened up on disciplinary practice, how the practices of the past have been critiqued and in some cases replaced, how it has become necessary to look beyond and outside disciplinary boundaries and how old practices can in many circumstances continue to have validity.

Museums in the Material World clarifies and expands the horizons of material culture studies as they pertain to museums and opens the eyes of students from a range of disciplines to a much broader understanding of the complexities and subtleties of the museum engagement with the material world. Museums in the Material World is about broadening horizons and moving museum studies students, and others, beyond the narrow confines of their own disciplinary thinking or indeed any narrow conception of collections. In essence, this is a book about the practice of interpretation and will therefore be of great use to those students of museums and museum practitioners.

Simon J. Knell is Head of Department of Museum Studies at the University of Leicester, UK.

Leicester Readers in Museum Studies
Series editor: *Professor Simon J. Knell*

Museum Management and Marketing
Richard Sandell and Robert R. Janes

Museums in the Material World
Simon J. Knell

Museums and their Communities
Sheila Watson

Museums
in the Material
World

Edited by

Simon J. Knell

Routledge
Taylor & Francis Group

LONDON AND NEW YORK

First published 2007
by Routledge
2 Park Square, Milton Park, Abingdon, Oxon OX14 4RN

Simultaneously published in the USA and Canada
by Routledge
270 Madison Ave, New York, NY 10016

Routledge is an imprint of the Taylor & Francis Group, an informa business

Transferred to Digital Printing 2008

© 2007 Department of Museums Studies, University of Leicester for editorial
matter and selection; individual contributions, the contributors

Typeset 11.5/12.5pt Perpetua by Graphicraft Limited, Hong Kong
Printed and bound in Great Britain by Cpod, Trowbridge, Wiltshire

British Library Cataloguing in Publication Data
A catalogue record for this book is available from the British Library

Library of Congress Cataloging-in-Publication Data
Knell, Simon J.
Museums in a material world / Simon Knell.
p. cm.
"Simultaneously published in the USA and Canada by Routledge"—T.p. verso.
1. Museum techniques. 2. Museums—Collection management. 3. Material culture—
Conservation and restoration. 4. Cultural property—Protection. 5. Museums—Study
and teaching (Higher) 6. Museums—Philosophy. I. Title.
AM111.K58 2007
069—dc22
2007015694

ISBN10: 0-415-41698-1 (hbk)
ISBN10: 0-415-41699-X (pbk)
ISBN10: 0-203-94685-5 (ebk)

ISBN13: 978-0-415-41698-6 (hbk)
ISBN13: 978-0-415-41699-3 (pbk)
ISBN13: 978-0-203-94685-5 (ebk)

For Sue Pearce

Contents

Series preface

Leicester Readers in Museum Studies provide students of museums – whether employed in the museum, engaged in a museum studies programme or studying in a cognate area – with a selection of focused readings in core areas of museum thought and practice. Each book has been compiled by a specialist in that field, but all share the Leicester Department's belief that the development and effectiveness of museums relies upon informed and creative practice. The series as a whole reflects the core Leicester curriculum which is now visible in programmes around the world and which grew, 40 years ago, from a desire to train working professionals, and students prior to entry into the museum, in the technical aspects of museum practice. In some respects the curriculum taught then looks similar to what we teach today. The following, for example, was included in the curriculum in 1968: history and development of the museum movement; the purpose of museums; types of museum and their functions; the law as it relates to museums; staff appointments and duties, sources of funding; preparation of estimates; bye-laws and regulations; local, regional, etc., bodies; buildings; heating, ventilation and cleaning; lighting; security systems; control of stores, and so on. Some of the language and focus here, however, indicates a very different world. A single component of the course, for example, focused on collections and dealt with collection management, conservation and exhibitions. Another component covered 'museum activities' from enquiry services to lectures, films, and so on. There was also training in specialist areas, such as local history, and many practical classes which included making plaster casts and models. Many museum workers around the world will recognise these kinds of curriculum topics; they certainly resonate with my early experiences of working in museums.

While the skeleton of that curriculum in some respects remains, there has been a fundamental shift in the flesh we hang upon it. One cannot help but think that the museum world has grown remarkably sophisticated: practices are now regulated by equal opportunities, child protection, cultural property and wildlife conservation laws; collections are now exposed to material culture analysis, contemporary documentation projects, digital capture, and so on; communication is now multimedia, inclusive, evaluated and theorised. The museum has over that time become intellectually fashionable, technologically advanced and developed a new social relevance. *Leicester Readers in Museum Studies* address this change. They deal with practice as it is relevant to the museum today, but they are also about expanding horizons beyond one's own experiences. They reflect a more professionalised world and one that has thought very deeply about this wonderfully interesting and significant institution. Museum studies remains a vocational subject but it is now very different. It is, however, sobering to think that the Leicester course was founded in the year Michel Foucault published *The Order of Things* – a book that greatly influenced the way we think about the museum today. The writing was on the wall even then.

Simon J. Knell
Series Editor 2007

Preface

This Reader situates the museum in the material world by examining and inter-relating four quite distinct aspects of its engagement. The first is the museum in its traditional role as repository of facts. The second concerns the democratisation of museum interpretation and the admission of subjective meanings which resulted from the museum's examination under the lenses of postmodernism. The third area of engagement places the museum in a social world of ubiquitous consumption, and in the fourth, the very act of keeping – so integral to the concept of the museum – is questioned. This book follows a change of intellectual focus from object to subject, from fixity to fluidity. In order to reveal this change, I have adopted a historical approach, selecting articles from key moments or relating to important issues, although I have not attempted to construct a history. I believe it is important for the student of the museum to understand this change and yet also understand that the change is not what it seems: we have not abandoned object-oriented, reality-centred, practice in order to pursue dreams and myths. Rather, the changes suggested here are about re-evaluation and cumulative diversification. In order to do the 'new', we need to preserve old values but also better understand them. This is, then, not a material culture reader in the traditional sense, and there is currently no book in the museological literature that does what this Reader attempts to do.

A casual glance at the readings in this book might suggest that this is not a book about practice – but it is, indeed, I would suggest it discusses the most fundamental of all museum practices. Essentially this book is about understanding why and how museums engage with the world through objects. How should museum people think about objects? What do objects contain? How can they be used? At the heart of these questions is the issue of interpretation – how we read and communicate using material things. This lies at the heart of decision-making when using collections or managing museums in such actions as collecting and disposal, outreach and education sessions, gallery interpretation, and so on. In order to work, this book should ideally be read from beginning to end. In selecting a range of disciplinary perspectives it is not my intention that scientists dip into the science, and archaeologists into the archaeology. The real story here cuts across the disciplines, so the art historian, for example, can consider some of the issues of connoisseurship and cultural debate that have surrounded his or her discipline, but yet also ponder if paintings are 'vouchers', how consumption practices play a role, how interpretation can shape or dissolve notions of authenticity. The introductory chapter attempts to give a sense of this complex, pluralistic and changing engagement.

In making the selections for this volume, I have been resolute in attempting to capture the essence of this period of change. I have not attempted to corral the great and the good – there are many Readers, for example, collecting together Foucault and his contemporaries. I have exercised a preference for those works where individuals have engaged with issues on the ground using their discipline, rather than including museological syntheses. I have tried to steer clear of areas covered by other Readers in this series but this has not resulted in any major omission: there are articles on interpretation and exhibition here, but a Further Reader is also planned. The ownership of the material culture of other societies is discussed here but will be treated more fully in a collections management Reader. There is also a more object-oriented material culture reader planned, but many of these ideas are introduced here. I have not discussed museum collecting in any detail as the topics discussed here really inform collecting activity. I have dealt with museum collecting more extensively in *Museums and the Future of Collecting* (2nd edn, Ashgate, 2004).

Simon J. Knell

Acknowledgements

The literature reviewed in order to make this selection was vast and would not have been possible without some help. Mike Taylor has for many years sent me a great deal of useful material on natural history museums and science context. Magnus Gestsson and Anastasia Filippopouliti located a number of useful references as part of a department-wide bibliographic project. Further material has arisen from working with Sandra Dudley and Katy Garfitt on the Interpretive Studies programme. The two readers of the book proposal, Julian Thomas at the University of Manchester and Bob Frost at the University of Michigan, also made many very helpful suggestions. In particular, I must thank Bob for permitting me to access materials used in his own excellent curriculum which added further to my selection. I am most grateful for all their help and hope that the book that has transpired meets their expectations.

Cato, Paisley S. 1991. The value of natural history collections in Latin American Conservation, in Mares, M.A. and Schmidly, D.J. (eds) *Latin American Mammology: History, Biodiversity and Conservation*, Copyright © 1991 by the University of Oklahoma Press, Norman, Publishing Division of the University, pp. 416–429. Reprinted with permission.

Lee, Welton L., Bell, Bruce M., and Sutton, John F. (eds) 1982. *Characterization of voucher specimens: Guidelines for Acquisition and Management of Biological Specimens*, Association of Systematics Collections, Museum of Natural History, University of Kansas, Kansas.

Stavenow-Hidemark, Elisabet. 1985. *Home Thoughts From Abroad: An Evaluation of the SAMDOK Homes Pool*, Nordiska Museet, Stockholm. Reproduced by permission of the author and SAMDOK.

Frank, Barbara E. 2000. Ceramics as testaments of the past: field research and making objects speak, in Ardouin, Claude Daniel and Arinze, Emmanuel (eds), *Museums and History in West Africa*, West African Museums Programme/Smithsonian Institution,

Washington, 93–104. Reprinted by kind permission of the author and WAMP www.wamponline.org

Carrier, David. 2003. In praise of connoisseurship, *The Journal of Aesthetics and Art Criticism*, 61, 2, 159–69. Blackwell Publishing. Reprinted with permission of the publisher.

Shanks, Michael and Tilley, Christopher. 1987. Chapter 4: Material culture, *Social Theory and Archaeology*, Polity Press, Cambridge, 79–117. Reprinted with permission.

Weil, S.E. 1995. On a new foundation: the American art museum reconceived, *A Cabinet of Curiosities: Inquiries into Museums and their Prospects*, Smithsonian Institution Press, Washington, 81–123.

Preziosi, Donald. 1998. The art of art history, in Preziosi, Donald (ed.) *The Art of Art History: A Critical Anthology*, Oxford UP US, 507–68. By permission of Oxford University Press and the author.

Berlo, Janet Catherine and Phillips, Ruth B. 1995. Our (museum) world turned upside down: re-presenting Native American Arts, *The Art Bulletin*, LXXVII, 6–10. Reproduced by kind permission of the authors.

Alan Munslow. 1997. History as deconstruction, *Deconstructing History*, Routledge, Abingdon, 58–75.

Shanks, Michael and Hodder, Ian. 1995. Processual, postprocessual and interpretive archaeologies, in Ian Hodder, Michael Shanks, Alexandra Alexandri, Victor Buchli, John Carman, Jonathan Last and Gavin Lucas (eds) *Interpreting Archaeology*, Routledge, Abingdon, pp. 3–29.

Miller, Daniel. 1994. Artefacts and the meaning of things, in Ingold, Tim (ed.) *Companion Encyclopedia of Anthropology*, Routledge, Abingdon, pp. 396–419.

Bourdieu: Distinction, extract, Routledge, Abingdon.

Chong, Derrick. 2005. Stakeholder relationships in the market for contemporary art, in Iain Robertson (ed.) *Understanding International Art Markets and Management*, Routledge, Abingdon, 84–102.

Vickery, J. 2006. Organising art: constructing aesthetic value, *Culture and Organization*, 12: 51–63. Taylor & Francis, London.

McVeigh, Brian J. 2000. How Hello Kitty commodifies the cute, cool and camp, reproduced with permission from *Journal of Material Culture*, 5(2), 225–245. Copyright © Sage Publications 2000, by permission of Sage Publications Ltd.

Colin Campbell. 1995. The sociology of consumption, in Miller, D. (ed.) *Acknowledging Consumption: A Review of New Studies*, Routledge, Abingdon, 96–126.

Weiner, Annette B. 1985. Inalienable wealth, *American Ethnologist*, 12, 210–227. Copyright 1985 by American Anthropological Association (J). Reproduced with permission of American Anthropological Association (J) in the format Other Book via Copyright Clearance Center.

Knell, Simon J. 2000. Consuming fossils, geology and museums in the nineteenth-century, retitled edited extract from Knell, S.J. *The Culture of English Geology 1815–1851: A Science Revealed Through Its Collecting*, Ashgate. Reprinted by kind permission of the publisher.

Morell, Virginia. 1992. Dustup in the bone pile: academics v. collectors, *Science*, 258, 391–2. Copyright © 1992 AAAS. Reprinted with permission.

Gulliford, Andrew. 1996. Bones of contention: The repatriation of native American human remains, *The Public Historian*, 18(4), 119–143. University California Press. Copyright 1996 by University of California Press–Journals. Reproduced with permission of University of California Press—Journals in the format Other Book via Copyright Clearance Center.

Trachtenberg, Alan. 1991. Contesting the West, originally published in *Art in America*, 79(9), 118–23, September 1991. Brant Publications, Inc. Reprinted with permission.

Bruner, E.M. 1994. Abraham Lincoln as authentic reproduction: a critique of post-modernism, *American Anthropologist*, 96 (New Series): 397–415. Copyright 1994 by American Anthropological Association (J). Reproduced with permission of American Anthropological Association (J) in the format Other Book via Copyright Clearance Center.

Gable, E. and Handler, R. 1996. After authenticity at an American heritage site, *American Anthropologist*, 98: 568–78. Copyright 1996 by American Anthropological Association (J). Reproduced with permission of American Anthropological Association (J) in the format Other Book via Copyright Clearance Center.

Dudley, Sandra. 2002. Diversity, identity and modernity in exile: 'traditional' Karenni clothing, in Green, Alexandra and Burton, T. Richard (eds) *Burma: Art and Archaeology*, British Museum, London, 143–151. Reprinted by permission of the publisher.

Collins, Glen. 2002. Tangible reminders of Sept. 11, *The New York Times*, September 5. Copyright © 2002 by The New York Times Co. Reprinted with permission.

Doughty, Philip S. 1980. On the rocks. *Museums Association Conference Proceedings*, 1980, pp. 12–14. Museum Association London. Reprinted with kind permission of the author.

Geist, Valerius. 1992. Endangered species and the law, *Nature*, 357, 274–6. Copyright 1992 by Nature Publishing Group. Reproduced with permission of Nature Publishing Group in the format Other Book via Copyright Clearance Center.

Alberch, Pere. 1993. Museums, collections and biodiversity inventories, reprinted from *Trends in Ecology and Evolution*, 8(10), 372–5. Copyright © 1993 with permission from Elsevier.

Chapter 1

Museums, reality and the material world

Simon J. Knell

'I have a question for you,' he said, taking out of his pocket a crumpled piece of paper on which he had scribbled a few key words. He took a breath: 'Do you believe in reality?' 'But of course!' I laughed . . . Has reality truly become something people have to believe in, I wondered, the answer to a serious question asked in a hushed and embarrassed tone? Is reality something like God, the topic of a confession reached after a long and intimate discussion? Are there people on earth who *don't* believe in reality? . . . his relief proved clearly enough that he had anticipated a *negative* reply, something like 'Of course not! Do you think I am that naïve?' This was not a joke, then: he really was concerned.

(Bruno Latour 1999: 1–2)

IN THE CLOSING DECADES of the twentieth century, scientists found themselves at war, embroiled in disputes over method, authority, the sanctity of evidence, the hand of God, and even the certainties of reality. Bruno Latour, in this opening passage from *Pandora's Hope*, knew well enough the propaganda and misinformation which confused both sides in the Science Wars; despite his indignation he knew that the 'highly respected psychologist' who asked him this question was not alone in being unsure about the level of subjectivity and relativism the other side was willing to admit. Some had certainly denied a knowable reality. Scientists, however, remained resolute in their methods and beliefs. Once wholly scientific, many anthropologists were by then taking large doses of such mind-altering drugs as feminism and postcolonialism, in an attempt to destroy their inner devils: objectification, homogenization, exoticization (Heshusius and Ballard 1996; Rapport and Overing 2000: 98). 'The history of ethnography', Roth (1989: 556) claimed, 'is one of successive constitution and dissolution of "modes of ethnographic authority"'; Herzfeld (1997: 302) called it a 'crisis of representation'. Such were the maladies of archaeologists, as they made their 'New Archaeology' old, that they were willing to take any drug they could lay their hands on. 'How do we do archaeology at all?' they exclaimed as they strove to establish their own disciplinary identity beyond the natural sciences, anthropology and history (Hodder and Hutson 2004: 4). Historians, who once considered their own discipline scientific, now found themselves rematerialised in a world of relativistic constructivism. What point was there to history if any possibility of reconstruction was an illusion? In Australia particularly, but also elsewhere, a 'postcolonial breeze' began to alter interpretations of the past, forcing historians into wars of their own (Macintyre and Clark 2003). In contrast, historians of art for the most part seemed as sure of their field as the scientists, although some were, they felt, staring into the face of disciplinary oblivion: 'Is the undoing of modernity the end of art history as we know it?' Preziosi (1998: 277) asked. The artist was now playing with the art world. Anthropologist Alfred Gell (1996) saw the rise of conceptual art as 'the final convergence of art-making, art history, art philosophy and art criticism' – the replacement of aesthetics with reactionism; art was now an 'evocation of complex intentionalities'. While some, as they climbed into Tracey Emin's bed, saw the traditions of still life and classical sculpture in Damien Hirst's 'over-exposed' shark, *The Physical Impossibility of Death in the Mind of Someone Living* (1991), others saw Hirst's pickled fish as the embodiment of the postmodern condition: cynical and mocking through the very objects and institutions which underpinned modernity and permitted his work to be displayed as art (Spring 1997).

Onlookers, like Latour's psychologist, might well have believed that the intellectual world had been consumed in a pandemic of politicised subjectivity which saw former authorities rise up, zombie-like, with the single aim of destroying their structured and empirical existence. They might also have imagined – had not museums already slipped into the intellectual backwater, residues of a modernity now surpassed in the relentless pursuit of progress – that these institutions, the icons of Enlightenment thinking, would be the first port of call for the angry mob. A few, it is true, charged around the galleries, smashing cases with barbed words, in old neglected galleries which still promoted a nineteenth-century racism or modern ones which discussed the atom bomb, slavery or living 'Others' without recognising a new need for inclusive engagement. But others, on opening the doors to the museum, were amazed to find, in the smell of wood polish, among the serried rows of fossils, in the photograph that sat beside the weaving frame and in the lever waggling interactive placed beneath the ceiling-hung aeroplanes, a treasure house of a rather different kind. Not one of a million ordered facts or of a chaos of curiosities, but rather the very essence of everything that was 'modern' in buildings that also spoke of modernity's antiquity. Many of those who made this discovery were not strangers to the museum at all: they had lived their lives there as professionals or as museum studies academics, but suddenly they found a veil had been lifted and the museum had changed.

Others slipped in sideways, opening a side door in such disciplines as sociology, history and anthropology, to discover the museum's strange practices, hidden powers, and extraordinary collections for the first time. If the museum was a physical embodiment of Enlightenment thinking, it was now also the subject of a new enlightenment, that of postmodernism. For one could now annotate the institution, its position in society, its processes, values, and so on with the labels of that penetratingly cynical mode of thinking – identity, power, legitimisation, subjugation, representation, construction – and diagrammatically show the nebulous and reflexive structure of postmodernism itself. The museum revealed a new kind of order; the latest phase in a history of ordering: postmodernism's body, apparently composed of nebulous doubting subjectivity, had buried within it its own universal anatomy – an anatomy no less judgmental, authoritative and pervasive as the metanarratived modernism which some wished to render dead.

The museum became what it had rarely been: delightfully contentious. Gone, so it seemed, was any notion of the museum as trusted purveyor of knowledge and learning – 'disinterested' and apolitical; who now could claim anything as neutral? The annotations of postmodernism soon became a political agenda for actual change. The museum was to be a place of pluralism and inclusion. The broadcasting of supposedly unmediated and objective facts was to be replaced by opportunities for 'meaning making'. History was now identity, to be democratised and performed in a 'dreamspace' where one's very being could be re-invented and mythologised. Eilean Hooper-Greenhill's (2000: 152–3) notion of the 'post-museum' saw a future less concerned with the tangible, which was unbounded (both physically and intellectually) in the experiences it could offer. More radical still was the proposed 'feminisation' of the museum: 'Rather than upholding the values of objectivity, rationality, order and distance, the post-museum will negotiate responsiveness, encourage mutually nurturing partnerships, and celebrate diversity.' Hooper-Greenhill noted that this new kind of museum was not likely to emerge in those Western centres of the 'modernist museum' but elsewhere. Fearing the force of repatriation in postmodernism's postcolonial backwash, the most powerful museums then turned the manly universalism of Enlightenment to political effect: the 'Enlightenment museum' was to be reinvented as the 'museum of everyman', democratised, worldly and inclusive. The material world, so carefully bottled and boxed in a museum history stretching over centuries, now had its own 'home guard'; and it now had more politics than it ever cared to know.

Museum Studies, once a vehicle for the training of students in established professional practices and standards (Singleton 1966), had become, in the process, an intellectual playground. Only vaguely bounded, it claimed an interest in all societies, in most disciplines, in the material world in totality, and most aspects of education and communication. In the true sense of architectural postmodernism, museum studies became eclectic and fostered illusions. Those who did not enter it believed it was simply a place where people learned how to accumulate things and put them in glass cases; those who did take a look inside, however, now found a discipline debating representation and censorship or social practice and the Enlightenment mission, and relating these to thoughtful practices that would indeed support the diverse needs of disciplinary knowledge, inclusive societies and cultural preservation. Some mockingly suggested that this was an indulgence in theory, but they failed to see that the field had grown sophisticated and more responsive. One could not continue thinking old thoughts and doing old things, at least not without asking 'why?' It wasn't that museums needed a revolution, they simply needed understanding. Only then could their future be assured, nurtured by a creative and responsive workforce.

The subjective world: politics, culture, interpretation

This is, admittedly, an impressionistic picture of intellectual change as the tide of postmodernism swept through. It took a while for people to get to grips with relativism, to understand that it too was relative, and sometimes relatively unimportant. As with Latour's psychologist, the change simultaneously confused and liberated, its nebulous form often polarising thought. The museum, as with all public and many private institutions, changed, though that change was driven as much by the faltering rise of liberal politics as it was by the intellectual shift that rise engendered. But was this really a moment as extraordinary for museums as it was for museum studies?

We should perhaps take a moment to consider a longer period and, as we travel from then to now, do what the historian of museums can often fail to do, that is look outside and observe the changing museum context. We need not go too far back, two hundred years will do. And so as not to over-generalise, we shall travel through the English landscape. The journey itself, if an overall impression of the evolving landscape could be captured, would reveal a broad trend of liberalisation accompanying the development of the modern museum, not just over the past 40 years but over the whole period.

Two hundred years ago, the birth of Britain's provincial museums drew upon an emergent middle class, which included many who had risen on enterprise and now demanded the rights and freedoms previously reserved for those of the state religion and in possession of land. Although exclusive to modern eyes, the (learned) societies which built these museums exploited exclusivity to foster inclusivity: the society and its museum became a means of social adjustment, which helped, to some degree, prevent the new bourgeoisie from leading their riotous underlings in revolution (Knell 2000). Population growth, industrialisation and mass urbanisation produced social and intellectual conditions of revolutionary potential across Europe. But while much of the rest of that continent realised that potential in the middle of that century, Britain managed to avert calamity. A series of major political reforms in the 1830s helped make this possible, but we should not forget the role played by museums. Nearly every major industrial town established or possessed a philosophical society in the 1820s where politically and religiously neutral topics – such as the 'brand new' and fashionable science of geology (which had less religious opposition than is traditionally thought) – were discussed. In so doing, these societies performed acts of social adjustment which overcame political and religious difference and which brought together new blood with blue blood. These acts of inclusive engagement made the societies, and the museums they fostered, tick. It gave them social relevance.

However, by the middle of the century, social commentators were criticising the elitism of these societies and their museums having rather forgotten their necessity, 30 years earlier, as 'local parliaments'. Now social change and the push for a democratic and educated society called for greater inclusion and the throwing open of museum doors to the masses. The museum was to be reinvented in this era of mechanics institutes – institutions aimed at a different social class but remaining largely middle-class inventions and manipulations. Educational opportunity was progressively filtering down in society, slowly permitting the eradication of the social imprisonments of class, race and gender. Only through education could an individual realise his or her potential; but also, so it was thought (and the argument was still being made by Public Understanding of Science advocates in the 1980s), only through education could the citizen become an informed democrat rather than a subjective political anarchist. Those who made museums in the 1870s did so in a rather different context of mixed gender field clubs of a kind that would have seemed quite alien to the gentlemen who made their local parliaments a half century before. Accompanying and following the field clubs, the notion of the 'educational museum' took hold, with that at Haslemere in Surrey acting as an exemplar. It offered a more inclusive view of education; the museum was now more inclusively inclusive.

Had a field of museum studies accompanied these social changes of the nineteenth century, its theoretical framework would have had to have shifted quite drastically at least every 30 years; as it was, ideas about museums changed continually, though there were, indeed, also periods of revolt as I have indicated. They were also not immune from relentless technological 'progress'. Today, from my office in the UK, I can visit a museum in New Zealand, virtually, in a second or so – something I could not do when I moved to this university in 1992. But this is little different from the Victorian scientist who could in 1842 catch an 'extravagantly cheap' train into the distant wilds of England, collect some key objects and return home in time for supper. Previously such activity was far more expensive both in time and cost. Charles Dickens captured this change perfectly in *Bleak House*:

> Railroads shall soon traverse all this country, and with a rattle and a glare the engine and train shall shoot like a meteor over the wide night-landscape, turning the moon paler; but as yet such things are non-existent in these parts, though not wholly unexpected. Preparations are afoot, measurements are made, ground is staked out. Bridges are begun, and their not yet united piers desolately look at one another over roads and streams like brick and mortar couples with an obstacle to their union; fragments of embankments are thrown up and left as precipices with torrents of rusty carts and barrows tumbling over them; tripods of tall poles appear on hilltops, where there are rumours of tunnels; everything looks chaotic and abandoned in full hopelessness. Along the freezing roads, and through the night, the post-chaise makes its way without a railroad on its mind. (Dickens 1853)

Dickens began writing *Bleak House* in 1851, the year the Great Exhibition opened in London, a moment when the British public's sense of self and world utterly changed. Dickens's sketch, similarly, describes the moment before a revolution which many of his readers had experienced. Here distances measured by post-chaise were to shrink under locomotive wheels; the interpretive frame by which people understood the world was about to expand. Simultaneously, the English rural idyll was to be hopelessly displaced by noisy, smoky machines; normality had shifted and what was there before now seemed increasingly worthy of museum preservation. Towns and museums once out of reach were now simply an affordable day trip away, and if museums really were nodes on a nationwide network of knowledge, as was claimed in the 1820s, then the Victorians had now learned to surf. And as they surfed into these museums, their heads conceiving an already shrinking world, they would look through eyes that were also changed in other ways, perhaps also altered by Dickens's cynical contempt for social injustice.

So, before we begin to consider the relationship of the museum to the modern material world, we must put aside any notion that we exist in an era unlike any other in terms of experiencing change or changing ways of seeing. We don't see as our predecessors did, but nor did they as theirs did. To see postmodernism as the rail buffers into which 'the Enlightenment project' crashed is to suffer delusions. A little cynicism never hurt anyone, and through it society puts in place the checks and balances it feels it needs. In our time, museums have responded with pluralism to counter inequality and localism to defend against the homogenising influence of globalism, identity to foster personal conceptions of value and democracy to check the power of privilege. These don't seem particularly peculiar or threatening actions. To a liberal mind, they seem right. But are these postmodernist or postcolonial outcomes so vastly different from the humanism for which Dickens was admired?

Postmodernism has been about adjusting the interpretive frame, about questioning and exposing our *modern* interpretive workhouses. It has been about making the implicit explicit. For those concerned with culture, postmodernism, and the plethora of philosophies and ideologies it has hidden beneath its umbrella, represented a big and pervasive change of interpretive frame. If the museum founders' formational dance of patronage and membership of nearly two centuries ago was performed to the music of contemporary expectation, music everyone understood but few articulated (Bulwer-Lytton 1830), some thirty years later its elitist heart was exposed. Today, we have no difficulty in exposing that social underbelly; postmodernism has ensured that we have all become sociologists. So if we see postmodernism as an interpretive frame, then we can relate it to other such frames, or ways of seeing. Science, like all disciplines, changes its interpretive frameworks all the time, generally in piecemeal fashion but also by revolution. For example, if, to evolutionists, Darwin was alive in the late nineteenth century, he was 'dead' in the early twentieth (at least in the USA), but reincarnated in the middle of that century (Simpson 1978: 114; Larson 2004: 224); a catastrophic view of the formation of the Earth was abandoned in the 1820s, but reawakened in 1980; in the 1990s catastrophism was shaping evolutionary thinking. Darwin would have understood both concepts but would have been extraordinarily surprised by this turn of events.

Postmodernism as an interpretive shift was no respecter of disciplinary boundaries; it seemed to challenge everything, even disciplinarity itself. Interpretation, that central act of 'reading' and 'presenting' performed in all museum actions, was built around that disciplinarity, but postmodernism — and particularly postcolonialism (broadly defined) — challenged its absolute right to dominate museum making and museum practice. Postmodernism, as with every other interpretive frame, placed spectacles before the eyes of the interpreter giving visual acuteness to those things considered important and throwing out of focus things that now became superfluous and irrelevant 'noise'. This wearing of different spectacles opens the mind, and one feels compelled to try others. Many modern students of the material world, for example, have been quick to pick up the antique spectacles of such late nineteenth- and early twentieth-century workers as Mauss and Simmel, and their resulting work has revealed the utility of changing one's glasses from time to time, and, indeed, that sometimes it is useful to combine new minds with old 'specs'. This book, then, is a book of spectacles: spectacles to look through and spectacles to look at. It is an opportunity to see things differently and to question what is implicit in the lenses of our own interpretive glasses.

Museums and material culture studies

So is the museum a cathedral to materialism, to Enlightenment knowledge, to modernity? The buildings and ordered collections that we have inherited speak of such things, but they do so because we can no longer see the makers, only the made. It is easy as a result to adopt a view that presupposes a museum engagement with the material world which had the abstract sterility of the science laboratory. The science laboratory, of course, was long ago debunked as a place of scientific purity and there really is no reason to perpetuate this myth of museums either. The museum has always had that same mix of intellectual (in startlingly varying degrees) aspiration and social politics. The supposedly objective collection conceals irrational passions, poetry, debts, claims, and so on, mixed with all those museum inadequacies and vices: neglect, territorialism, bias, poverty, ignorance, and misunderstanding. And while we rightly push objects and collections to the fore as the distinguishing features of museums, we need to remember that if those objects *are* 'made to speak', they do so through a human act of authorship with all its editing, contextual manipulation, and censorship. This combines in an interpretive coupling of speaker and listener where both are manipulating meaning, often unknowingly. But in this 'conversation', is the object active or passive? Does it embody and communicate some aspect of ourselves or is it simply a slave to our words and thoughts?

Perhaps the answer lies not in the setting of the museum exhibition, but behind the scenes where some museum workers use objects to make knowledge. Natural scientists, archaeologists and art historians, in some respects, share a similar engagement with objects: they build whole subjects from material things. Their disciplines are largely shaped by rules of engagement with the material world, but, rather curiously, the uniting discipline of the museum is history, for in its keeping the museum makes things old and creates a past. But why have I not listed history amongst these disciplines? Thirty years ago, historian Cary Carson pondered this question in the American context and concluded:

> No matter what standard measure objective scholars use they can hardly avoid the conclusion that the study of artifacts has contributed to the *main themes* of American history almost not at all. Yes, of course, historians use artifacts all the time to *teach* . . . But the monumental fact remains unbudged that *things* have seldom been a source of *ideas* for historians. (Carson 1978: 42)

Carson recalled how seminal art historian Rudolf Wittkower, when asked what he thought of the Winterthur Museum in Delaware, remarked: 'An unmatched collection . . . of anthropological curiosities' (Carson 1978: 44). So history cannot claim the same intellectual relationship to the museum as, say, biology or archaeology or the history of art? The answer is rather more opaque than that. In some respects history is all about objects – Dickens's historical sketch above, for example, is just that.

It is true, however, that this was pretty much the relationship between 'history proper' and museum history in Carson's time. However, consider Carson's dismissal of a queen's, or a tollbooth's, receipts, or a list of the identifying marks of royal swans:

> It is not that these documents are beneath historical notice; but until historians find something to do with them, they languish in a mass of unenfranchised facts. Facts do not become historical evidence until someone thinks up something for them to prove or disprove.

Museums are full of such things, but at the time of Carson's comments, they were not calling to the historian for attention. Since then, however, the academic field has continued to swell (not least in the number of active academics attempting to make their intellectual mark) and with it has grown an interest in the unfashionable and obscure. Increasingly it has become possible to ask questions of these once peculiar things and to derive perspectives far exceeding mere object description. However, it is an illusion to believe that these new perspectives have been won by the analysis of objects alone. My own historical studies of the uses of fossils in the making of museums, society and science, for example, in which fossils are not so far removed from tollbooth receipts, drew heavily on contemporary documents, and not on the fossils themselves. One reason is that decades or even centuries of resource-starved keeping and 'miscuration' can leave just about any collection of objects decontextualised and historically unreliable. By contrast, the meaning of seemingly more fragile collections of words on paper in archives and libraries (and museum files) survives abuse far more readily. The fossils – provided they could still be located – gave useful insights into what my actors saw and acquired, but all else relied upon what my actors *wrote*. As recorded and purposeful communications they are less ambiguous, more easily interpreted and directly quotable. Using these kinds of materials, historians believe they can permit their actors to speak with their own words and thus recover something of the truth of the past. Whether we study the objects themselves in museums or the words written about them, these are both what are termed 'material culture studies'.

I should perhaps explain the term 'material culture' here, as some have used it in a restricted sense to mean man-made artefacts. Today it tends to be used to refer to all 'things' people come to know and possess, and indeed make – intellectually if not physically – including fossils, blue tits, landscapes and paintings. (A later contribution to this series of Readers will engage more fully with material culture studies and consider the place of other objectified 'things' such as concepts, songs, dances and memories, and debate the often overstated differences between the tangible and intangible.)

Some historians did attempt to utilise objects in their work. In the vanguard was Thomas Schlereth (1982, 1985), who initially sought appropriate methods in anthropology and archaeology, drawing upon their functionalist, behaviourist and environmental schools. In doing so, Schlereth was not aiming merely to describe objects:

> [W]e must always remember that it is the culture, rather than the material, that should interest the material culture researchers. As Brooke Hindle reminds his fellow historians: 'It is the spatial and analytical understanding offered by artifacts, not the things themselves, that is the historian's goal. He has to see through the objects to the historical meaning to which they relate.' (Schlereth 1985: 23)

Schlereth understood that simple object fetishism led nowhere. It was a key point also long understood by those other more object-oriented disciplines, but which was so rarely understood by museum makers. Through Schlereth's work, history now legitimately joined these other disciplines in perceiving collections as factual repositories useful to the derivation of knowledge. Though, to this day and for reasons Carson fully understood, they remain relatively weak resources for constructing history because history is about actions and to extract these from objects requires far greater interpretation and thus invokes far more debatable 'truths'. One only need see an archaeologist's joy at locating an object containing a written word (as I did in my last museum) to understand how envious that discipline is of its literature-rich sister subject.

Nevertheless, archaeology and the sciences, and historians of art, technology and design, do make use of objects and these rather disparate disciplines have established rather similar ways to establish reasonably reliable interpretations, at least at a fundamental level. We should take a moment to consider some of them and demonstrate that, in the museum, even the arts and sciences are joined at the hip.

The objective world: reality, context, expertise

The key attribute of the object, giving it both intellectual and poetic possibilities, is a relationship to the external world, to an original context. The gathering of an object is an act of gathering a piece of that context. Note the object is not surrounded by 'context' but part of it. For this reason, the natural and medical sciences incorporated the museum into their disciplinary make-up from the very beginning. Here natural objects were given names, and particular examples given status as name carriers, known as holotypes. The names themselves were opinions and tied to a literature of images and descriptions which captured the author's own scholarship, preferences and biases (McOuat 2001). However, it was the object, and not the published description, that was the final authority; the object was the reality, the only truth. Thus science understood that truth was only inadequately captured in language.

This idea that objects were a material embodiment of the real world meant that science could progress even before it had established the basics of language and concept. Again this can be seen in the British case where a preoccupation with fossils accompanied the birth of the modern museum. In the early nineteenth century, it was recognised that there was a consistent natural order or sequence to rocks and that each had its own peculiar fossils. However, few fossils or rocks had reliable names. They acquired them through an act of collecting and by reproducing the order of the natural world in the arrangement of the museum collection (Knell 2000). The fossils were literally 'hard facts', and became the foundations of interpretations which made these objects active, experimental and newsworthy. The structure and nomenclature of the lithological world were by this means established, and they became sufficiently stable to be considered universal and long term: the plastic in our computers, the metals that make up our jewellery, the petrol in our cars, all owe a debt to this museum effort.

This embodiment of truth within collections becomes apparent if one examines those moments of interpretive revolution, such as when Darwin saw the monkey in us. It had always been a fairly straightforward matter to see rational order in the natural world, right back to Aristotle's 'Great Chain of Being', which locked species into a hierarchical 'chain' stretching from the inorganic world to the perfection of God, and which included such natural things as angels and demons. By the early nineteenth century, European museums were moving beyond this simple classification but yet many still believed they were engaged in an activity to discover a divine plan which might reveal something of their Christian God. It was as if the divine plan was fact and could be pieced together from the multitude of smaller facts that composed it. Natural systems of classification, which seemed to reflect creation, had been perfected a century earlier, by Swedish naturalist Carl Linnaeus who published his *Systema Naturae* in 1735. Linnaeus's ideas gave science a simple, universal and commonsensical language for naming animals and plants, which included in its logic a means to represent the order and relationships of the natural world. The museum was able to realise this order with physical examples, but it was also engaged in collecting examples supporting the diversifying interests of science including variants and freaks, reproductive and growth stages, biological dependences and geographical distributions. Collections of natural objects became multidimensional embodiments of the real ordered by contemporary knowledge, which for many favoured the hand of God to some degree. By the middle of the nineteenth century, however, this exploration of the natural world required and saw no divine being. Time now extended back beyond human comprehension and theories of evolution and extinction revealed a world where revolution was natural and the constancy of the status quo unthinkable. The interpretive frame that had shaped the first phases of collecting had led to knowledge that meant the collections themselves required complete reinterpretation. But this is the critical point, for it was the interpretation and not the collection that was changed. As embodiments of reality, how could they be changed? They were, after all, the final tests of theory, and while they could be called upon to play a role in theory as 'evidence' – that is data marshalled into argument – those theories only really existed in the communications of scientists, they were never an inherent part of the objects and collections themselves. Thus, the collection as final test, sat quietly as an unarticulated argument, only to be read and called to support or oppose a view when technology and intellect permitted.

Changing explanations, which continued to accommodate the truth of the collection, assured museums that the material world was finite and knowable. The collection could thus also be finite, and by the 1870s, after half a century of collecting, many British museums felt they had moved to the final stages of gap filling in the natural sciences. By the mid-century archaeology had found its science and overtook the now professionalised science of geology as the height of intellectual fashion. New civic museums also began to collect art, which had previously been locked away in private estates along with valuable antiquities. Later still, museums would notice the disappearance of the everyday world and gather the artefacts of vanishing trades and crafts either as anthropologists or social historians. In every case – whether painting or plough – the collecting served the same purpose: to keep in order to understand; to preserve a moment, a fugitive context. Collecting followed the pattern of the natural sciences. Each object was, at one level, a fact or piece of data which had a relationship to other data from its original context whether also collected or recorded in notebooks or on film. Measurement, drawing and photography were the preferred supplements to collecting as they too ensured supposedly interpretation-free data gathering. Thus, the object was part of a dataset. Yet, examining the object in greater detail reveals that the object itself can be conceived as a container of information (the various characteristics of the object) and was thus a dataset. Thus each object maintains a complex of data. To consider it as a single piece of the real or a thing set in a context is rather to underestimate the extent and complexity of its baggage.

Aside from the factual qualities associated with the object as a captured context, the object in the museum also develops a more theoretical relationship to those concepts the museum constructs in its drawers, display cases and exhibition galleries such as in a classification of furniture. This adds still further to the things the object carries, though here we enter, more obviously, the world of interpretation and we already understand from our previous discussion that these interpretations do not reside in the object in the same way as those things which define it as context. There is a relationship, however. Some of the information derived from context and also present as inherent qualities of the object itself, such as ornament, is useful for such things as placing a Japanese chest in a furniture history. It permits the object to be the subject of formal 'stylistic analysis' (Prown 1993: 4). Other characteristics, such as where it was used or who used it, might assist a museum in deciding whether it has relevance to that museum's own peculiar objectives but have little role to play in these more abstract intellectual concepts, such as classification. Other characteristics still, such as the colour of the wood from which the chest is made, may perform aesthetically – simply adding values which act on our more subjective tastes.

The valuing of each different 'character' and the recognition of its various 'states' (possibilities of form) in such a thing as a classification of furniture is a matter of choice, a reflection of scholarship and experience which we might better know as expertise or connoisseurship. Objects under the action of expertise can be organised, with judgements shaped by the 'resolution' of perception. Resolution defines the degree to which the viewer focuses in on and takes account of, or even perceives, detail. Those who select, sort, organise, and give meaning, aim also to generalise and group. Low resolution analysis results in large heterogeneous groups: at low resolution all chairs are chairs. At higher resolution, groups become more numerous and each more homogeneous: chairs can be divided by material, maker, era, style, and so on. (Another way to look at grouping is to consider it as the construction of boundaries or discontinuities between things.) The result of all this museological activity is a hierarchical grouping of things which relies upon these things being pieces of context (that is having a relationship to the real — the real within (the object) and without (its original place in the world)). Hierarchies and groups permit museums to act rationally in collecting, managing and exhibiting the world. They make it possible for one thing to speak for many, thus one of Monet's haystack paintings can be made to 'represent' the whole series, Impressionism, or even French painting.

But before we become too comfortable with this clean and logical system, we should consider how securely we know these things in collections. We now have all kinds of ideas and data attached to objects and we can soon begin to lose sight of which bits we can trust and which we cannot. Here we must introduce 'probability', a quality of interpretation that attempts to move from subjectivity to a possible truth. Science knows this as 'degrees of confidence', a statistical term. Take, for example, a piece of nineteenth-century pottery with maker's name and a serial number stamped on its base which links it directly to a documentary record giving the date and place of manufacture. As a collected piece of reality we could desire little more. What then of an unmarked pot with identical glaze and style excavated at the site of one of the old kilns, or a mere fragment of a very similar pot found on a rubbish dump 200 miles away? All these things might find their way into museums, all might be given the same identification and attached to a raft of secondary data relating to that particular ceramics company, but clearly they are all rather different in terms of their reliability. All three objects are understood by a process of interpretation, but one of these objects, we would hopefully agree, has a greater chance of being correctly interpreted, and another I would be more than happy to countenance as likely true; the third, however, depends far more on expertise and in that regard I would look at the interpreter far more than the object before accepting a judgement! In museums — as in all other places of interpretation (newspapers, television, academic research) — people are pushed to interpret, to draw conclusions, to make decisions, to go that one stage beyond. In such circumstances, one can easily lose sight of an essential 'might' and replace it with certainty. In the museum, then, object–context–meaning associations can become thrown into a black box. Recorded contexts can become confused with interpreted contexts, and the truth of the collection as a result can become compromised. It is so easily done, and in Britain presented a particularly grave risk as Victorian collections were called upon to supply data for the information age ideal of comprehensive computer catalogues. How well I remember the dataless collection of specimens in a small museum which became data rich during cataloguing as the inexperienced operatives interpreted the examples given in identification manuals as offering a singular truth which could then be imposed on the objects themselves. Or indeed the helpful volunteer who threw away those useless old Victorian labels as he modernised the collection. A day, a week, a decade later, who would know the trueness of the reality now contained in those collections? Experience has told me to interpret the neglected collection as perhaps holding a more probable truth than a recently established neat and tidy store, though in doing so I realise I am exploiting my own subjective (and perhaps unjustifiable) connoisseurship.

For the museum, as for scientific method more generally, repeated observation, triangulation of information, and good record keeping can often resolve these kinds of issues by revealing those objects that appear to lie. But one cannot discount connoisseurship as a vitally important curatorial attribute which is rather irrationally undervalued these days. Connoisseurship grows from these notions of classification, object characters, and collections as real and true; connoisseurship is not restricted to those who deal in 'antiques', it is the most essential of curatorial traits, not as a 'high art' but merely as a reflection of experience. To some degree we are all connoisseurs of something: chocolate, wine, cars, music or video games. And in suggesting this, I would not wish to confuse this with mere taste. My children, for example, believe they can distinguish fake, authentic and rare pokémon figures and cards but they also have favourite pokémon. Connoisseurs, it is believed, can recover missing information, such as in the case of our collected pottery. A connoisseur might on the basis of experience conclude that the ceramic from the dump truly is a production of this company. He or she may believe they have seen every type of pot that might be confused with such items. This expertise may as a result be able to completely eradicate doubt or merely contribute an authoritative view. Such expertise is, of course, fallible, not least because connoisseurs can sometimes believe they know more than they do. In its worst excesses, connoisseurship is little more than social posture; a good connoisseur should be disinterested and cautious.

So given its logic and framing constraints, has this form of collecting and keeping really served any larger purpose? Can we justify the museum's peculiarly objective engagement with the material world? A reader of this book, who has most likely already made, at very least, an intellectual commitment to the museum, will have already answered this question I suspect, but evidence for confidence in the museum project is not hard to find. A classic example concerns the peregrine falcon, a bird edging towards extinction in the early 1960s. Research, however, revealed that parents crushed their eggs prior to hatching. Comparison with museum specimens showed that this was a new phenomenon and that the egg shells had thinned and that this thinning could be associated with the introduction of the persistent pesticide DDT (Ratcliffe 1967). At the top of the food chain, falcons, hawks and eagles were concentrating pesticide residues from seed dressings consumed by their grain-eating prey. The celebrated eradication of this pesticide has seen the recovery of these bird populations and, in this, museum egg collections – so often the product of collector avarice rather than scientific investigation (but yet real things all the same) – proved of key importance. Similarly, museum specimens of moss have, rather surprisingly, provided evidence of changing levels of lead in the environment, and contributed to arguments to have this health-damaging substance removed from petrol.

One final proof of the validity of the museum in this regard concerns the role of specimens as 'vouchers', that is things that vouch for the correctness of a statement and permit verification. When discovered in 1913, a skull and jaw permitted the construction of a hominid which filled a gap in the fossil record between apes and humans. In 1953, fluorine tests raised questions of authenticity. Re-examination revealed the jaw to be that of an orang-utan and the skull to be that of a man, both from the Middle Ages. The Piltdown Man was, as a result, no more, but the specimens remain important vouchers now verifying a rather different interpretation.

This empirical tradition continues in museums today, indeed, it absolutely dominates museum engagement with the material world. Without it, museums could make no claims to do with reality and all would be aesthetics. This museum tradition, then, permits us to see, make and represent a structured world (a world that is structured in reality by nature and manufacture) — this structure is vital to rationalism, policy-making, interpretation, commerce. It also provides us with a language through which we can communicate and extend knowledge, while maintaining a secure reality to which we can return for verification or testing. This requires the preservation of context — indeed, seeing the object as a piece of context — so it is always more than its material self. The approach permits us to utilise representatives, to permit one to speak for all, to seek generalisation. All these things work together and reflect wider social and cultural desires. Often funded from the public purse, museums were to be apolitical purveyors of truth and for this reason they have become institutions that generally steer clear of controversy. Their aim and their implicit claim are objectivity, and the rejection of the interestedness of personal, party or commercial politics.

However, rarely did these objects exist as purely intellectual entities; collections invariably required an emotive response, objects had a poetry and people engaged for individualistic reasons and sought progress and social positioning through participation. One cannot presume that the museum achieved its rational goals with the purity and simplicity method alone seems to suggest. It is time to return to our earlier theme and put real people back in the picture.

The subjective world revisited

Since the mid-1960s there has been a challenge to this uncomplicated view of knowledge building and that challenge has really come about by a change of focus, from object to interpreter. Michel Foucault's *The Order of Things* (1966) and *The Archaeology of Knowledge* (1969) made knowledge, understanding, meaning, value, and the material fabric of society, a product of local circumstance in time and space. What we value, such as the word of science, has been determined by society, not by God or natural law. With everything man-made, universal truth ceased to exist; truth was determined by systems of value existing at a particular time and place. Why, then, it could be argued, should a White Christian Enlightenment truth be any more valid than one produced in an entirely different culture a world away? In terms of conducting one's life, one's values and making sense of the world, the imposition of such an external view is nothing less than cultural imperialism. Reason and truth were now not to be understood as objective but rather at the command of the powerful. This was as true of the production and interpretation of the past as it was of other cultures. It invoked a postcolonial perspective which today is forming a new disciplinary locus, and especially so for museum studies.

This democratising thrust, as it pushed the object into the background, also reconstituted the public as individuals and social groups far beyond the divisions of class which had previously permitted the analysis of a visiting public. This increased sense of audience focus has permitted museums to step away from a rigorous and controlled engagement of the type discussed above and value the more subjective qualities of objects. This subjective engagement, however, still relied upon an underlying truth held within collections; it was simply another interpretive frame. As Prown (1993: 4–5) remarked: 'A chair is Philadelphia of the 1760s because it embodies elements of what was believed in Philadelphia in the 1760s, and that formal pattern is what enables an analyst to determine the truth of the chair.' For Prown, the assumptions and beliefs of a moment of creation are captured in the 'style' of the chair. These are unarticulated things but available for extraction:

> Perhaps if we had access to a culture's dream world, we could discover and analyze some of these hidden beliefs. In the absence of that, I suggest that some of these beliefs are encapsulated in the form of things, and there they can be discerned and analyzed.

From these beginnings in empirical representation, then, Prown moves on to consider the more subjective, metaphorical and poetic meanings one might attribute to objects through material culture analysis, in the hope that one might 'see with their eyes and touch with their hands' (Prown 1993: 17). It seems improbable that we can recover these things, but nevertheless we might see and we might believe, and that might be enough. By this means we can engage with the object at a more powerful level, perhaps far more powerful than the historian's rigorously researched narrative. It is here in a dimension beyond what we see, and about which we have difficulty articulating questions, that objects can reveal what the museum really possesses. Here we move beyond the written record, beyond the boundaries of literacy or literary expediency, beyond the read and enter the real of the sensed. Here history takes on a vivid reality.

To admit such things is not to move from our objective museum world into a world of fiction. Certainly museums can be places of fictional engagement, but here the truth of the object as a piece of real-world context remains – regardless of whether we can ever extract it. It is simply a change in the way we see; much as with the Darwinian revolution, the collection and the processes by which it is formed remain largely unchanged. Asante objects on display at the American Museum of Natural History or on show at the living museum in Kumasi, Ghana, are valid for the same reason: their authenticity. That the American audience might engage with these objects through the disciplinary eyes of anthropology and the Asante with an awareness of things in life, does not remove the need for the objects to be real and true. What it does change, however, are perceptions of the context of which the object is part. If Western museums admit other valid engagements with the real world, then they must at very least respect them and reflect them in their perception of context, and if they intend to collect them, then they will need to understand them, and that may require further changes in terms of who collects or interprets, and how. This applies not just to objects in alien societies but also to the understanding of objects in the everyday life of our own societies. It places disciplinary engagement in a real world, and admits that such things as science or art are messy, that the objective and subjective generally work together: the scientist who never visualises *T. rex* as anything more than a heap of bones is never really going to achieve much in science. This brief discussion naturally brings us into the source of our accepting and valuing subjective things, the social world which might be best understood as a world of consumption. This forms the third section in this book.

The consumed world: society, belief, identity

The things of the world are incorporated into social interaction and provide an embodiment of social structures reflecting back the nature and form of our social world . . . All objects are social agents in the limited sense that they *extend human action* and *mediate meanings* between humans.

(Dant 1999: 2, 13)

We engage with the material world from the moment we are born, we learn intuitively what it is, we make it physically, we shape it emotionally, we create meanings, consume objects and meanings together, and even give those objects, and perhaps even those meanings, to others. This is a world of objects participating in lives, rather than simply in ideas, and it has been a particularly keen area of interest for anthropologists, sociologists and historians for the past two decades. It is important to the museum professional for fairly obvious reasons as museum visitors engage in the socialised world of objects far more than they do in a world of disciplinary abstraction. Anthropologists, in particular, have been keen to see the present era as one defined by the consumption of material culture: never has society been so enabled to consume. Initially, this interest in consumption focused particularly on consumerism and comparing, contrasting and even uniting such work with other long-established interests in object exchange, particularly gift giving. Increasingly, consumption became a far broader concept to the point that everything could be seen in a world of consumption. We consume through purchase, through the receipt of gifts, but also through looking, visiting, engaging – museums are consumed and museums consume. Consumption became one of the grand structuring concepts of postmodernism and it had a natural twin in another: identity. Indeed, much of this work has centred on the construction and reinforcement of identities. Museums were quick to pick up on this and now history can be consumed in an act of community identity-making. But one needs to be careful not to lose the specificity here. Identity-making happens all the time, as indeed does consumption; to use identity as a bland notion to justify museums is a risky strategy. When I walk into my local city centre with its mix of architectures and monuments, with their origins stretching back centuries, the very environment seems to conjure up pasts that speak of my youth in the brutalist world of *Get Carter* (1971) and a deep-rooted Englishness in the city's castle mound (c.1068) and Guildhall (c.1390) which seem to belong to that Romantic England of Walter de la Mare poetry and *Greensleeves* (c.1580) which children are exposed to in primary education. Museums cannot really compete with this engagement with real things in the real places where real events really occurred. Buildings collected and preserved in heritage parks are the architectural equivalent of the museum, claiming an authenticity of materials but not of location or interrelationship; a pastiche not so far removed from the film set of *Pride and Prejudice* (this is discussed in rich detail by Gable and Handler in Chapter 25 in this book; see also Bruner, Chapter 24). That is not to deny the power of such places, but it is also to fear the intrusion of illusion – an illusion more starkly demonstrated in many a modern shopping mall where all is imitation – architectural signification of a purely superficial kind. What the museum has, in this world of meaning making, is authenticity but that authenticity – as in the heritage park – needs careful understanding and control; authenticity is a fugitive quality easily lost.

One cannot, then, blandly claim the museum as a special place of meaning making through material things. Consumption and identity creation are implicit in the human condition and museums will only ever play a tiny role. Similarly, meaning making, more generally, and learning are ubiquitous and interrelated because we cannot know the world by any other means, and without further qualification, the terms themselves become meaningless. As spectacles they are undoubtedly useful for looking at things differently, but they do not displace the contextual necessities of museum things; they still require objects to be bits of the real maintained by disciplinary rigour and integrity.

That is not, however, to suggest unchanging disciplinarity. What we consider rigorous or appropriate at the moment is rather different from how things seemed in the past. Consider, for example, the entry of identity into the museum consciousness. Identity became a key aspect of British museum engagement as historians adopted the new history of the French Annales School back in the 1960s and 1970s. The resulting rise of social history transformed objects previously classified as 'folk life', giving them historiographic context, disciplinary credibility, and a politics of interpretation slightly to the left. It made historians increasingly aware of contemporary society and the role of history in its shaping. There was now new interest in representing working lives and so, in a Britain entering a post-industrial phase, mills and factories were converted into museums, manufacturing narratives which spoke of skill, dedication, community and hardship. These were sometimes 'living museums' but at other times sobering war memorials to those who had given their lives in the trenches of industrialisation. Britain was by then actively preserving the houses and estates of the aristocracy, and permitting the majority to view the opulence of the minority and believe it was theirs too. Access had been driven by changes to the British tax system, which led the assault on wealth, privilege and power dating back to the Norman Conquest nearly a millennium before. The industrial museums were in many regards about redressing the balance, a counterweight to a portrayal of British society as gentrified. By the early 1990s, the social historians were turning to living popular culture, and museums across Britain opened 'People's Shows', which exhibited the collections of ordinary people. In some respects these were unproblematic as museums could claim that collectors were part of a shared community of practice in which the museum had a senior role. They could also be justified as an act of democratisation when such notions seemed far less complicated: exhibitions of the people, for the people, though often not by the people. Such shows repeated today might draw a rather different reaction, for if one did not visit out of consumer or collector empathy, then the sight of someone fetishising porcelain figures and cuddly toys risks objectifying individuals as exotic and weird in a fashion once popular in London's Egyptian Hall nearly two centuries ago. The industrial museums were rather different: people were the blood that flowed through industrial heritage in the form of oral histories and images. They were doing what they had to do; museums were not exposing their foibles. The problem for the museum engaging in the contemporary, however, is that it joins the ranks of the mass media. It is not dealing with an objectified past (which has by this means been neutralised), but a political present. Though what this means in terms of museum representation is quite uncertain. Museums require, at very least, consent, and hopefully full engagement, but such considerations have given us *Big Brother, Pop Idol*, Spencer Tunick's massed nudes and Gunther von Hagen's *Body Worlds*. People are thirsty for celebrity, even if they become manipulated and manufactured, objectified and exhibited. People as much as objects now ask to be consumed, they have become indistinguishable in a world of consumption. (Although even 200 years ago people wished to be consumed as heroic, cultured, savants – the phenomenon is not as new as it sometimes seems, it simply reaches deeper into society.)

As museum historians' interests moved from objects to their more natural subjects (that is, people) many people-centred academics were looking in the opposite direction: increasing their focus on objects and their consumption. Their work opened up new ways for museums to think about objects and contexts. Take, for example, a simple purse with a Hello Kitty motif. Typical museum practice would perceive this as a late twentieth-century costume accessory which might be collected systematically recording individual and moment but never really thinking beyond that local context. For an adolescent girl, however, buying such a purse might also permit her to enter into a circle of friends. It also places her in a world-wide community of owners who share a relationship with this motif, and it also places her in a relationship to an older generation who are now courted by fashion houses using the motif to evoke nostalgia. If Hello Kitty becomes associated with a distinctive social group, then in a reflexive way it becomes representative of that group, and as a commodity it is surely then far more complex than the object a museum professional might perceive. The shops which sell these objects might also gain meaning and status (identity) in this object-centred world – mere shops they are not.

Marketing now not only sells such things but attempts to sell by gaining sociological understanding of its audience. So what does a museum collect if it collects the purse? Just to collect it as an example of 'today' is to get drawn into an unacknowledged illusion. The owner of the purse is in fact part of global business, her tastes captured and reflected. Consumption here represents a sophisticated symbiosis between identity and big business. Like *The Fashion System* exposed by Roland Barthes in 1967, this whole business is built around mythology; not pointless mythology but mythology which permits society to function as a social entity. Thus, the association between the thing and its owner is not as museums tend to read it. (Hello Kitty is explored in Chapter 17 in this book). Similarly, Shove and Southerton's (2000) investigation of the domestic freezer showed how the object's changing form reflected not just technological change or fashion but a fundamental change in the place of this object in lives during its period of adoption and integration: from food glut handling, to household management, to time management. In this last phase, the freezer adopted a critical twin – the microwave – which, from a museum perspective, demonstrates the continuing validity of Susan Pearce's (1992: 171) interpretive idea (which draws upon a structuralist literature) that objects can be more effectively communicated if we understand their natural relationships. In a structuralist sense, objects work together to form communication, much as words, governed by rules, form effective sentences.

In this world of consumption, it is frequently noted that free choice is an illusion. Daniel Miller, for example, noted that Britain's social housing – the council house – was regarded as standing for the identity of the country's lower classes. He pointed out, however, that the council house is a middle-class invention, a thing given by the empowered rather than a thing representing working-class desires. Nevertheless, this is where working-class and lower middle-class lives shaped their own environment. Ironically, with the selling off of the housing stock, and rising house prices, many (former) council houses are now home to that middle class which designs and manages our social housing. The problem, of course, is that one cannot chase out middle-class intervention in the production of goods: by definition, it is the middle classes who design, manage and sell. Museums are encapsulations of middle class values – the relationship is axiomatic.

Consumption, then, produces a world of interrelatedness and reflexivity shaped by the production, possession and movement of people and things. Indeed, objects acquire values simply by moving between people. This is often more important to the object's purpose or meaning than any implicit qualities it might have. Research has shown that those who buy things construct themselves by that act (Miller 1998; Miller et al. 1998). Those who collect similarly construct and display themselves; they bring order to their lives and build homes (Pearce 1998). And outside of Western societies objects are involved in acts of gifting and exchange which construct identities and distribute power, perhaps by a process of indebtedness or through complex interlocking networks that see transactions repeated year after year. Objects exist in socialised worlds, interwoven into the fabric of place, and shaped by societies' interconnectivity.

By this means, these worlds of consumption – which involve movements of things in which values of various kinds are created and manipulated – can become structured and formalised, and draw in the museum as a major participant. The art world, whether conceived as having theoretical, commercial or sociological interconnectivity, is the most studied example of such a structure. In this world, artists shape the objects at its heart. Only for them, it might seem, is there truly a relationship between person and the materiality of the thing. But if the artist desires success, then he or she must offer some form of engagement with the art world. The paradoxical aspect of this engagement, however (if they are to avoid that jobbing life which once paid the way for the Victorian portrait painter) is that they must offer up a degree of resistance. One cannot begin an artistic career on the artistic edge, one must be beyond it, a node on a trajectory of art history which only becomes apparent through the production of the work and its 'discovery'. Its acceptance is possible only through an act of legitimising consumption whether by dealer, collector, critic or museum. It is a kind of courtship, where disdain can be a useful affectation. The aim, however, is intimate engagement: radicalism accepted on its own terms, not through compromise on the part of the artist, yet accepted nonetheless. Legitimising consumption is an act of admittance whether an intellectual acquisition in response to art historical theory, as suggested by Danto, or admittance by entry into an institution of art, as discussed by Dickie, or simply a product of a powerful individual exercising taste politically, as proposed by Bourdieu.

It was Pierre Bourdieu (1984) who most forcibly drove a stake into the heart of art world judgement in a book that at first sight seems only concerned with that seemingly innocuous social attribute, 'taste'. In Bourdieu's study, taste unifies social groups and excludes others; it legitimises particular objects and practices, and by this means forges identities. In his view, it was by this means that museums came to represent the tastes of the educated and wealthy. Patronage and social power turn things into symbols which conspicuously radiate qualities that socially position participants. It is a form of conspicuous consumption of a kind Veenis (1999: 102) recognised in the former East Germany, where participants understood its superficiality but could not withdraw. Of course, it is the idea that this is a purely superficial engagement which is an illusion – conspicuous consumption has real social (political) depth (though clearly appearing ridiculous to those outside that social group).

The art museum likes to believe it exists outside this world of personal interest and the marketplace, but it cannot escape its influence on perceptions of value and price. Art museums legitimise old works as well as new. As one art curator put it: 'I find it exciting to bet on a young and undiscovered artist, to know my backing may help him' (Walker 1974: xvii). Greenfeld (1989: 96) found that, like critics, curators believed they were creative, that they were not there to satisfy the aesthetic needs of the public but to create new needs by exercising their judgement (and power). However, the problem for the curator acquiring or showing contemporary art is the lack of objective or rational criteria (on which, see Vickery in Chapter 16 in this book) – they might instead need to rely upon their own subjective tastes. Some have suggested waiting 50 years, and then deciding whether an artwork should be kept, but this presupposes a fairly objective art historical process, uninfluenced by museum possession or the 'serious speech acts' of the institutionally empowered expert (Bundgaard 1999; Dreyfus and Rabinow 1983: 48). Museums need to believe that such things are possible – that the reflexive and interconnected world of value creation has no perverting effect. But that art world includes value-creating organisations and individuals that are entirely self-interested: art dealers attempting to make a living; wealthy collectors, but self-confessed art novices, like Charles Saatchi; auction houses with their chandelier bids, dominated by the recently indicted Sotheby's and Christie's; governments defining and protecting a country's national heritage; and fakers and thieves who distort and corrupt. The art museum must believe it can extract itself from all of these influences for to do otherwise is, perhaps, to take that suicidal leap that Donald Preziosi ponders in Chapter 9 in this book. That the art museum cannot entirely disentangle itself from this world may not matter, however. Science sometimes finds itself in a similar tangle – the best example being the scandal surrounding the *T. rex* skeleton named 'Sue'. Here political aspiration, Native American land rights, dealer identity, corporate and national interest, and museum desire, all conspired to create a modern sensation of extraordinary proportions (Fiffer 2000). The object which ended up in the museum was by that time no less contentious than the Parthenon Marbles, but yet still sufficiently intact to be transferred into a world of rational science. Now the object begins a process of naturalisation, as occurs with the painting on the art museum wall, where the history of its selection and acquisition is progressively lost. Like money laundering, the museum makes cultural objects legitimate.

In recent years, the hidden politics and judgements behind museum things have called into question museum practices in a number of areas, but these are matters which must be defined by professional integrity, from which one must disentangle the rationale for intellectual engagement. While many would debate the British Museum's retention of the Parthenon Marbles, few would object to that museum's recognition that these are objects worthy of museum possession and public engagement. That is not to suggest that the intellectual and political entanglement is so easily unravelled. Consider Berlo and Phillips's Chapter 10 in this book which calls for an elevation in the status of Native American arts in museums and academic art history courses, while delineating all the impropriety which has created collections of these materials in the past. They do not, however, see the task as insurmountable: the intellectual desire is unwavering, but the means by which this can be most effectively and appropriately achieved requires new levels of professionalism and inclusive practice. The power given to the curator – beyond the ethical issues which professional organisations seek to manage through codes of conduct – results from an appointment made by society for the purposes of developing expertise and utilising judgement for the public good. This isn't the role of a mere functionary but one reliant on creativity in order to provide a paying (whether by entrance fee or taxation) public with visual and intellectual delights and challenges. Curators should not be defensive about their empowerment but simply understand the professional responsibilities and risks which come with it. As Alan Trachtenberg discusses in an exhibition review in Chapter 23 in this book, curators must be permitted such freedoms even if they pay the price of bad review.

The opposite side of this empowerment and acquisition is potential disenfranchisement and loss. The act of selecting one thing is always accompanied by a sister act of rejecting countless others. Loss is an inevitability of acquisition in a multitude of ways. It is a process very much at the heart of museums, though one frequently overlooked. It forms the final theme in this chapter and book.

The transient world: keeping, losing, changing

Loss is pervasive, an inevitable product of change, and change is implicit in consumption. As Daniel Miller (1987) noted, people and things interact to create identities; neither are something but are becoming and developing each other. In a world of consumption, people and things are in constant movement, and meanings in a constant state of flux.

> Within each local circumstance, specific meanings will be mobilised that have provisional significance within the site concerned. These meanings may change radically as the object is moved from one site of semiosis to another. As the moves take place in time, and across space, earlier meanings may be lost or recovered, overlaid by new significations, or reinterpreted by different interpreters. (Hooper-Greenhill 2000: 153)

What, then, of the museum as a place of keeping, is it immune from this constancy of change, can it really keep vouchers or preserve keepsakes? The presumption we began with is that if things seem to speak the truth of reality, then knowledge and identity can depend upon their keeping. But loss is not simply an accident of change or misadventure; it is an act of Nature. Indeed, like gravity, it is governed by a natural law which ensures us of its inevitability. Museums cannot evade it.

It is said that this law was in Charles Dickens's mind when he came to write *Bleak House* (1853). Indeed, the whole novel is a metaphor for the law as, in a legal battle over a property, the property's value is consumed in legal fees. But even the opening page, which mentions that other novelty of the moment – the museum reconstruction of life-sized dinosaurs – describes a city's order transformed by the advancing chaos of Nature. It is one of the most celebrated opening pages of any English novel:

> London. Michaelmas term lately over, and the Lord Chancellor sitting in Lincoln's Inn Hall. Implacable November weather. As much mud in the streets as if the waters had but newly retired from the face of the earth, and it would not be wonderful to meet a Megalosaurus, forty feet long or so, waddling like an elephantine lizard up Holborn Hill. Smoke lowering down from chimney-pots, making a soft black drizzle, with flakes of soot in it as big as full-grown snowflakes – gone into mourning, one might imagine, for the death of the sun. Dogs, undistinguishable in mire. Horses, scarcely better; splashed to their very blinkers. Foot passengers, jostling one another's umbrellas in a general infection of ill temper, and losing their foot-hold at street-corners, where tens of thousands of other foot passengers have been slipping and sliding since the day broke (if this day ever broke), adding new deposits to the crust upon crust of mud, sticking at those points tenaciously to the pavement, and accumulating at compound interest.
>
> Fog everywhere. Fog up the river, where it flows among green aits and meadows; fog down the river, where it rolls deified among the tiers of shipping and the waterside pollutions of a great (and dirty) city. Fog on the Essex marshes, fog on the Kentish heights. Fog creeping into the cabooses of collier-brigs; fog lying out on the yards and hovering in the rigging of great ships; fog drooping on the gunwales of barges and small boats. Fog in the eyes and throats of ancient Greenwich pensioners, wheezing by the firesides of their wards; fog in the stem and bowl of the afternoon pipe of the wrathful skipper, down in his close cabin; fog cruelly pinching the toes and fingers of his shivering little 'prentice boy on deck'. Chance people on the bridges peeping over the parapets into a nether sky of fog, with fog all round them, as if they were up in a balloon and hanging in the misty clouds.

The law – grandly titled 'The Second Law of Thermodynamics' – is one of three which concern the relationship between energy, work and heat (wasted energy). The second law tells us that all systems left to themselves tend to disorder or chaos; order requires work – the expenditure of energy. The law was articulated by German physicist Rudolf Clausius in 1850 and by William Thomson (later Lord Kelvin) in

1851. It gave chaos a natural inevitability which must have altered perceptions of the world: disorder could no longer be blamed on slovenliness alone.

In Dickens's time, the museum stood as a perfect illustration of the law, for those who had created museums in the first part of the century had believed they could simply gather and arrange, but, as any curator knows, collecting and use requires disorganising acts of insertion. As Henry Jelly wrote in 1833, on the premature death of a curator friend,

> no one, who has not experienced it, can form an adequate conception of the labour of reducing into system and method the chaos of a newly-established museum, into which contributions are unceasingly flowing, and where there is as yet no adequate provision made for placing them away. (Knell 2000: 103–4)

Few museums could afford paid curators, and the unpaid honorary curators seldom had time or interest to indulge in the dull drudgery of maintaining collections. In the language of the law, effort (acquisition and ordering) – the expenditure of energy – always generates heat or wasteful side effects (such as further disorder). The law states that one cannot convert one form of energy into another without losing some: turn electricity into light in an ordinary domestic light bulb and most of that electricity will be wasted producing heat!

However, let's put that piece of science to one side, accepting loss's inevitability, and consider the insidiousness of that loss in the museum collection. Figure 1.1 shows this inevitability from an interpretive perspective. In this diagram the angled line represents social change over time (it does not infer that this is linear or shaped by 'progress'). In this diagram a collection is formed at a moment in society, and embodies contemporary social aspirations, characteristics and values. Society, however, continues to change. The collection too might change. Rather than the simple horizontal line indicating 'collection state 1', it might attempt to keep pace with social change. However, in order for this to occur, there would need to be considerable museum effort, and collections – by their size, by the complexities of arrangement, use and curatorial process, by the sheer repetitive drudgery of certain tasks, and by the endless calls on staff time – inevitably have inbuilt inertia. Over time an 'interpretive tension' develops between the values enshrined in the collection and the requirements of modern society. For example, a costume

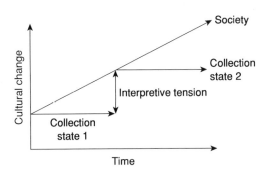

Figure 1.1   Loss as a result of social change

collection that privileged White middle-class female dress might, in a modern British city, rightly be considered unrepresentative. Its use could only ever encapsulate past interpretive values. This can be countered, however, by further collecting and some 'rationalisation'. By this means, the museum can create a rather different collection which is also altered by modern expectations in terms of documentation and notions of context and inclusive involvement, and perhaps a greater valuing of subjective and personal contexts over attributes that might lead to a design history or categorised social history. Even as the collection is refurbished, however, society is changing and growing yet another tension between what it has created and what it needs. Over long periods of time such collections can be perceived as irrelevant and suffer disposal by direct means or by stealth (neglect). Alternatively, the collection might be perceived as a 'time capsule': its shortcomings reduced in the aurora of rare survival.

But loss is so insidious that even virtuous acts of renovation result in loss. In making new we always destroy aspects of the old: perhaps things implicit in the collection's former arrangement have become invisible to us and are thus easily lost. It is because so much resides in minds, and not on paper, that curators end up examining handwriting and label designs so as to recover pasts lost as the collection has passed into the present.

But museum workers also know that inactivity can result in loss. Agents of deterioration wait menacingly in the wings, there to take advantage of a momentary lapse in appropriate humidity levels, blind control or the screening of vents and chimneys. Many materials are only too willing to fall into decay, but this enactment of Nature's law is unsurprising to us; indeed, it has fascinated authors and poets for centuries. Daniel Defoe, for example, in his *Tour of the Eastern Counties of England* (1722), considered the heritage of the 'wonderful' coastal town of Dunwich which was then threatened with a 'fatal immersion'.

> From Aldborough to Dunwich there are no towns of note; even this town seems to be in danger of being swallowed up, for fame reports that once they had fifty churches in the town; I saw but one left, and that not half full of people. This town is a testimony of the decay of public things, things of the most durable nature; and as the old poet expresses it,
>
> 'By numerous examples we may see,
> That towns and cities die as well as we.'

He continued,

> this, I must confess, seems owing to nothing but to the fate of things, by which we see that towns, kings, countries, families, and persons, have all their elevation, their medium, their declination, and even their destruction in the womb of time, and the course of nature.

Such things are obvious to us even if we did not know they had the certainty of natural law. They are an inevitability of time which affects history in all its guises.

Disciplines and people change, and in doing so their interpretations change, and thus, for them, objects and collections change. The means by which we interpret things is not unaffected by this incessant erosion of resources. Consider, for example, television histories of the Second World War, which in my lifetime always drew on the testimony of those who were there, who could articulate authentically what they saw, what they decided, what they felt. Tears were real tears. Inevitably, these days there is a shortage of veterans for such histories, and television producers have turned to actors and re-enactment to fill this gap. Now actors run across imaginary minefields, to a backdrop of sound-alike sounds, or talk to the camera in imitation of the veteran but with blood still on their faces just moments after the imaginary fight, their words perhaps juxtaposed with images of real conflict and sounds which, although possibly authentic, were probably recorded at another time and place. Here the ravages of time, and consequent loss, are everywhere, and what remains of an authentic truth exists in another of those interpretive pastiches so inevitable in the museum. And beyond this hodgepodge of fiction and fact, drama and event, is a creative intention which melds music, word and image in an attempt to shape our mood and our understanding, or which more cynically constructs a saleable product or attempts to elevate viewing figures.

Yet, to aspire to an ideal beyond this, is perhaps to have idle dreams and to underestimate the viewer's powers of disentanglement and interrogation. Museums can handle these complications and do so from the moment they consider acquiring an object. As a captured fragment of context, we understand its imperfections but counter these with a belief that in capturing the thing we also hold something of untapped and unrecognised potential. In other words, we have collected less than was there, but we have also collected more than we know! However, almost immediately we begin to lose what we have acquired as the object becomes naturalised within its new museum context: 'A naturalized object has lost its anthropological strangeness. It is in that narrow sense desituated – members have forgotten the local nature of the object's meaning or the actions that go into maintaining and recreating its meaning' (Bowker and Star 1999: 299). The losses we are willing to accept in our 'museumisation' of things are quite remarkable: the electric guitar's chords, harmonies and riffs lost as the object becomes a piece of design, an icon of popular culture; the bright-eyed and acrobatic squirrel, similarly, becomes an inanimate corpse valued for its morphological characteristics. But to believe we can collect and keep without loss is to suffer an illusion, even if we don't kill and stuff the object or put it in a museum. Consider a 'wild' Spitfire, still able to fly and entertain air show crowds. We might feel we can sense something of a war fought long ago in the purr of the Merlin engine and in that aeroplane's graceful curves but what is it that forms in our minds that makes us think this is so? The hard realities of noise, shape and aerial manoeuvrability combine with film, history, and fiction to create an image that is sufficiently real, even if only imperfectly so. The object as objectively understood (form, model, history, etc.), works with its subjective relations (heroic iconography, wartime propaganda, patriotism, etc.), and with its socialised contexts (air show culture, family history, sense of nation, sense of place, memorabilia markets, etc.), and all are shaped in their various ways by factors causing loss and change. What we know is what we believe, and while we have established ways to increase knowing over mere believing, the two are always companions.

Similarly, the things museums keep, are both real and illusion. It is those things which most fundamentally belong to the object — those objective characteristics discussed above which seem to belong to an earlier era of curatorship — that museums *can* collect and keep. These are not, however, things that drive interpretation in the modern museum; museum audiences are much more interested in the dynamics of things in life, not in serial numbers, models, and materials. As Schlereth noted above, for the most part our engagement with objects is to understand wider things. However, despite Schlereth's best efforts, objects remain weak repositories of information about processes, actions and relationships but that was never really the intention in keeping them. That kind of information exists in archives and libraries and not, in the narrowest sense, in museums. Although Samdok was established to tackle the impossibilities of collecting contemporary society, it implicitly recognised that museum labels and documents, rather than the objects themselves, were the true resource that permitted our valuing and interpretation of those material things. Museum objects themselves are never entirely mute because our heads are never entirely empty: they can speak to us through a language of signs we have already learned. If we educate or familiarise ourselves, then these objects might say 'Picasso' and 'Braque' and much more besides, rather than simply: 'old', 'cute', 'complicated', 'beautiful', 'like my mother's'. Objects also affect our emotions in ways it is impossible to articulate: how do we describe the wonder of standing next to a real thing centuries old? But yet, while the psychological effect is undeniable, we might well question if the object itself is wholly responsible; most of us cannot know the object's antiquity or authenticity without being told.

The museum object is reliant upon labels: whether in the form of context gathering notes, interpretive exhibition panels or the labels located in a visitor's or expert's head, acquired through learning. Museums have frequently believed that objects can do more than this, that objects can, for example, tell stories or speak, though postcolonial sensitivity should really have dispelled such illusions. Beyond engagement which is only concerned with constructing fictions, the object's active role, even in the most mythologising acts of identity-making, is dependent upon it being real and authentic. Such notions are not simply dependent on good curatorial practice; they more critically depend upon the rigour of disciplinary expertise, something in Britain we have rather forgotten. It is expertise — with all the risks of bias — which breathes life into the corpse-like object, by shaping the labels in drawers, exhibits and heads. The object inevitably performs in the pastiche that is museum interpretation, its meaning not wholly dependent on its material preservation of a context for it cannot retain that world around it. Rather the object's success is dependent upon how well the museum can take these remnants of the real and suffuse them with socialised and subjective things, only by this means can the everyday and beyond notice justify a place on the museum pedestal. Thus if museums necessarily turn the reality of the material world into a pastiche in their collections and exhibitions, it is not something in which they have any choice, nor is it a negative attribute, nor, indeed, does it mean that they cannot work with, understand and communicate that reality which so deeply worried Latour's psychologist. It is simply that reality really is something in which one has to believe.

References

Bourdieu, P. (1984) *Distinction: A Social Critique of the Judgement of Taste*, Cambridge, MA: Harvard University Press.

Bowker, G. and Star, S.L. (1999) *Sorting Things Out: Classification and its Consequences*, Cambridge, MA: MIT Press.

Bulwer-Lytton, E. ([1830] 1970 facsimile) *England and the English*, Shannon: Irish University Press.

Bundgaard, H. (1999) 'Contending Indian art worlds', *Journal of Material Culture*, 4: 321–37.

Carson, C. (1978) 'Doing history with material culture', in Quimby, I.M.G. (ed.) *Material Culture and the Study of American Life*, New York: Norton, 41–64.

Dant, T. (1999) *Material Culture in the Social World: Values, Activities, Lifestyles*, Buckingham: Open University Press.

Dreyfus, H.L. and Rabinow, P. (1983) *Michel Foucault: Beyond Structuralism and Hermeneutics*, 2nd edn, Chicago: University of Chicago Press.

Fiffer, S. (2000) *Tyrannosaurus Sue*, New York: W.H. Freeman.

Foucault, M. ([1966] 2001) *The Order of Things*, London: Routledge.

Foucault, M. ([1969] 2002) *The Archaeology of Knowledge*, London: Routledge.

Gell, A. (1996) 'Vogel's net: traps as artworks and artworks as traps', *Journal of Material Culture*, 1: 15–35.

Greenfeld, L. (1989) *Different Worlds: A Sociological Study of Taste, Choice and Success in Art*, Cambridge: Cambridge University Press.

Herzfeld, M. (1997) 'Anthropology: a practice of theory', *International Social Science Journal*, 153: 301–18.

Heshusius, L. and Ballard, K. (eds) (1996) *From Positivism to Interpretivism and Beyond: Tales of Transformation in Educational and Social Research*, New York: Teachers College Press.

Hodder, I. and Hutson, S. (2004) *Reading the Past: Current Approaches to Interpretation in Archaeology*, 3rd edn, Cambridge: Cambridge University Press.

Hooper-Greenhill, E. (2000) *Museums and the Interpretation of Visual Culture*, London: Routledge.

Knell, S.J. (2000) *The Culture of English Geology, 1815–1851: A Science Revealed Through Its Collecting*, Aldershot: Ashgate.

Larson, E.J. (2004) *Evolution: The Remarkable History of a Scientific Theory*, New York: The Modern Library.

Latour, B. (1999) *Pandora's Hope: An Essay on the Reality of Science Studies*, Cambridge, MA: Harvard University Press.

Macintyre, S. and Clark, A. (2003) *The History Wars*, Melbourne: Melbourne University Publishing.

McOuat, G. (2001) 'Cataloguing power: delineating "competent naturalists" and the meaning of species in the British Museum', *British Journal for the History of Science*, 34, 1–28.

Miller, D. (1987) *Material Culture and Mass Consumption*, London: Blackwell.

Miller, D. (1998) *A Theory of Shopping*, Cambridge: Polity Press.

Miller, D., Jackson, P., Thrift, N., Holbrook, B. and Rowlands, M. (1998) *Shopping, Place and Identity*, London: Routledge.

Pearce, S.M. (1992) *Museums, Objects and Collections*, London: Leicester University Press.

Pearce, S.M. (1998) *Collecting in Contemporary Practice*, London: Sage.

Preziosi, D. (1998) 'Modernity and its discontents', in Preziosi, D. (ed.) *The Art of Art History: A Critical Anthology*, Oxford: Oxford University Press, 277–80.

Prown, J.D. (1993) 'The truth of material culture: history or fiction?', in Lubar, S. and Kingery, W.D. (eds) *History from Things: Essays on Material Culture*, Washington, DC: Smithsonian Institution Press.

Rapport, N. and Overing, J. (2000) *Social and Cultural Anthropology: The Key Concepts*, London: Routledge.

Ratcliffe, D.A. (1967) 'Decrease in eggshell weight in certain birds of prey', *Nature*, 215: 208–10.

Roth, P.A. (1989) 'Ethnography without tears', *Current Anthropology*, 30: 555–69.

Schlereth, T.J. (1982) *Material Culture Studies in America*, Nashville, TN: American Association for State and Local History.

Schlereth, T.J. (ed.) (1985) *Material Culture: A Research Guide*, Lawrence, KS: University Press of Kansas.

Shove, E. and Southerton, D. (2000) 'Defrosting the freezer: from novelty to convenience', *Journal of Material Culture*, 5: 301–19.

Simpson, G.G. (1978) *Concession to the Improbable: An Unconventional Autobiography*, New Haven, CT: Yale University Press.

Singleton, R. (1966) 'The Leicester course', *Museums Journal*, 66: 135–8.

Spring, C. (1997) 'Slipping the net: comments on Gell (1996)', *Journal of Material Culture*, 2: 125–31.

Veenis, M. (1999) 'Consumption in East Germany: the seduction and betrayal of things', *Journal of Material Culture*, 4: 79–112.

Walker, J. (1974) *Self-portrait with Donors: Confessions of an Art Collector*, Boston: Little, Brown and Co.

Simon Knell is Professor of Museum Studies, and Director and Head of the Department of Museum Studies, University of Leicester. His books include *The Culture of English Geology 1815–1851: A Science Revealed Through Its Collecting* (2000) and *Museums and the Future of Collecting* (1999, 2004). He is a museologist and cultural historian of science with particular interests in museums, objects, collecting and geology.

PART ONE

The Objective World

Introduction to Part One

Simon J. Knell

THIS FIRST GROUP of readings concerns the museum's empirical engagement with the material world. Paisley Cato's succinct summary of the methods and values of natural history collecting and collections maps out this classic museum engagement. Something similar is found in all other museum disciplines; in the museum, seemingly disparate disciplines have surprising commonality. All are in some respects engaged in a fact-collecting exercise, a broadly Baconian mode of knowledge production or world representation. Disciplinarity ensures informed engagement and rigour, and has proven a critical interface between museums and the exterior world – even if that disciplinarity preaches rationalism rather than an objective ideal. In the next section this negotiated sense of the objective is discussed in more detail with regard to changing archaeological practices. In this section, what matters for all these authors is that the object is an embodiment of the real and true. All disciplines establish practices of recording, management and authentication to ensure these objects have integrity – that the truth is not compromised (however, many later readings will introduce doubts about this museum view). The Association of Systematics Collections' guidelines produced by Welton Lee, Bruce Bell and John Sutton discuss these kinds of controls as they pertain to natural history specimens. Science likes system but, knowing that it exists in a world of self-interest not so far removed from the art world, it also puts in place its laws and policemen to ensure the integrity of its materials and practices. Many scientific journals, for example, require cited specimens to be deposited in public collections.

An act of recording is central to the natural science methodology discussed by Cato and became a prominent component in Samdok's approach to collecting contemporary Swedish society. As is apparent from Elisabet Stavenow-Hidemark's now classic introduction to the work of this organisation, there are parallels here with habitat recording undertaken by natural history museums. Samdok's approach is very scientific. Note also that this science can result in the collection of surrogate objects identical to those possessed by the household. As such, the objects collected are types and classes with all the universality and objectivity of species and none of the direct personal associations we usually enshrine in social history collections. But could Samdok really study a house and then strip it of all the things that made it a home? In the past, collectors had no hesitation is taking this rather questionable step, as we shall see in various chapters later on.

Eva Fägerborg of the current Samdok Secretariat told me at the time of compiling this book that that even after three decades of operation the organisation remains robust and relevant. After a period of reinvention in 1998, the pools remain a key innovation ensuring focus and collaboration. They are governed by their own policies, encourage the involvement of external expertise, and organise training. Most importantly they ensure that the museum project is a socialised activity. 'Samdok's primary mission was to direct part of the museums' object collecting to the present, to save ''today for tomorrow'' through planned and active collecting, effective use of resources and shared responsibility. The early visions can be characterised by the key words systematic and rational. The original idea soon expanded to a much broader task, ''contemporary documentation'', understood as ethnological fieldwork – recording the present day in the form of interviews, observations, photography, sound and video recordings, objects and documents.' It remains the model of thoughtful, richly contextualised, museum collecting.

Barbara Frank's engagement with Mali ceramics has that same – Samdok-like – desire to document and record. While techniques and objectives are different, there is much here that is like the voyage of discovery, where discovery exists at those boundaries which lie between civilisations. Here disciplinary methodologies are used to recover data-rich objects. Clearly, the art museum collects its 'vouchers' in the same manner as its natural history counterpart, and it applies similar kinds of expertise or connoisseurship in order to reveal the underlying abstract truth of the object. One might compare Frank's ceramic empiricism with countless anthropological investigations of similar contexts, which although focused on objects are never purely so. In these, the subject of investigation may remain the material object but anthropology's overriding concern is with people and with objects as lived and socialised things. Each is wearing different interpretive spectacles. Frank's engagement is that of an art specialist and in the world of craft pottery there has long been cultural exchange regarding techniques, styles and other ideas. While the anthropologist starts by locating difference in order to establish an appropriate interpretive strategy, Frank's engagement is in one respect that of perceiving a sisterhood of potters – the craft unites – and in another that of the well-meaning medical practitioner in possession of arcane knowledge.

These various disciplinary engagements inevitably grow connoisseurship which, as David Carrier explains, is a notion that has been under assault in recent years as a display of exclusive power. However, as Carrier shows, it is only by this means that the 'honest' object is separated from its lying imitators; connoisseurship is implicit in the notion of authenticity and authenticity is critical to the validity of the museum. Connoisseurship is built from experience: it includes empirical knowledge shaped by a disciplinary framework and judgements about objects which sometimes appear indistinguishable from these more secure facts. Connoisseurship internalises these things, shaping values and beliefs that often make its judgements controversial but not invalid.

This section ends with Michael Shanks and Christopher Tilley's discussion of material culture from their classic analysis of social theory in archaeology at a time in the late 1980s when structuralism had not breathed its last. Unlike the chapters which began this section and which exploited, professionalised and concretised a traditional approach, Shanks and Tilley are here trapped in the emerging postprocessual caverns of archaeological practice, shining their torches into the darkness of known routes and unexplored passages looking for signs to indicate a new interpretive framework for archaeological engagement with the material world. In this chapter we can see archaeology rejecting a pure scientism and recognising the object in a structured and socialised world of signification. Conceptions of the material world were now becoming more complex, but not necessarily any clearer, and many museum disciplines – indeed, all which made human activity their subject – now found scientific explanation or justification politically, socially and intellectually inadequate. While anthropologists were already becoming well adjusted to seeing as their subjects did and permitting their subjects a voice, the archaeologists had to marry this expanded world of meaning and interpretation with artefacts of long extinguished peoples. While this problem of interpreting things from the deep past was shared with the geologists, the latter could, in a Nature which lacked self-determination, call upon the principle of uniformitarianism to argue that the present was the key to the past. Any problems this caused could be ironed out progressively without offending anyone other than fellow scientists who had signed up to the same disciplinary charter. Archaeologists, too, looked to the present to understand the past, but they were already abandoning any notion of reconstructed pasts. In the next section, as we shall see, Shanks and Hodder, eight years later, have emerged from a 15-year birth, now seemingly able to clearly articulate an archaeology beyond the 'New'.

Chapter 2

The value of natural history collections in Latin America conservation

Paisley S. Cato

Theoretical basis for development of a systematics collection

Sample characteristics

A SYSTEMATICS COLLECTION of Recent mammals contains a sample of mammalian species collected over both time and space. This sample documents exact localities of occurrence of species as well as variation in individuals relative to a particular date of collection and/or geographic location. In addition, the specimens may be preserved in a variety of physical forms which determine, in part, the nature of information that is preserved. Considered together, these features create a matrix which represents the characteristics of the samples that comprise a systematics collection. The data contained in a sample are dependent on both the sampling methodologies and the method of specimen preparation.

The sampling methods used to collect specimens have historically been determined primarily by the needs of individual research projects. The initial scientific approach to a region for which the fauna was unknown was generally a systematic survey to locate and identify as broad a sample of species as possible. This was followed by systematic surveys of small portions of the region for one of several reasons: economic importance of the area; economic importance of the fauna suspected to be in the region; unusual characteristics of the ecosystem; unusual characteristics of the taxa; or geopolitical considerations. Additional collecting followed to obtain particular taxa for specific research projects; rarely were systematic surveys repeated at later dates for an entire region.

Unfortunately, in practice collecting has rarely been as thorough as sampling theory would predict. The purposes of each project, as well as practical constraints, influence sampling methodology. For example, many of the early biological and geological surveys in the United States were instigated to determine the extent of natural resources for agriculture and mining. Other early surveys were carried out by individuals assigned to U.S. border surveys or military explorations. Therefore, regions covered by faunal surveys were often dictated by economic or military considerations, rather than a scientific, systematic collecting plan. As a result, there were gaps in the geographic and taxonomic information of species represented by museum specimens. Even if those gaps were filled by later surveys or research projects, the temporal gap persists forever – only a time machine would allow us to return to the 1830s to collect species that were missed in an earlier survey.

Other practical considerations which may affect sampling methodology include inclement weather, inhospitable terrain (Wemmer and Watling 1986), a university time schedule (Stangl and Jones 1987), and a time limit on funding for a project. As a result, strengths and gaps may exist in the geographic, taxonomic, and temporal contents of a collection, and even the aggregate of series of specimens contained in many collections.

The uneven representation of a collection's contents does not necessarily diminish the value of the whole, but it must be taken into consideration by researchers developing, managing, and using collections. Consider the following: the presence of a specimen in a collection provides physical evidence of the existence of a species at a particular location at a specific time in the history of that environment. It provides a point for comparison to other times and locations, and removes an element of speculation. However, the existence in a collection of individuals of a species may or may not reflect the relative abundance of the species in its environment, and does not preclude the existence of the species in other regions. These factors may be addressed only in light of the sampling methods followed by the individual researchers (as might be documented in field notes or publications), and the information contained in other systematic collections. The needs of individual research projects as well as practical considerations also determine the manner in which specimens are prepared and data recorded. The type of preparation, in turn, affects the precise characteristics of and the extent to which genotypic [relating to an organism's genetic makeup] and phenotypic [relating to an organism's appearance, behaviour and other observable characteristics] variables are documented in collection specimens. Clearly, a variety of preparation types are essential if the collection is to serve various research needs.

Preparation types for mammals can be grouped most simply into three categories: (1) traditional materials including skins, skulls, skeletons, and fluid-preserved specimens (Alberch 1985; Anderson 1965; Hafner et al. 1984; Hall 1962; Jones and Owen 1987; Nagorsen and Peterson 1980; Quay 1974); (2) non-traditional or ancillary preparations including frozen tissues, blood, cell lines; and phalli (Barrowclough 1985; Dessauer and Hafner 1984; Johnson et al. 1984); and (3) associated materials including skin tags, field notes, computerized data bases, photographs of habitats and chromosome spreads, and similar materials.

These three categories store information in different formats. Traditional materials have provided the basis for a morphological approach to questions of taxonomy and diversity. Fluid-preserved specimens have provided access to internal organs and muscles, complementing studies on external and skeletal characteristics.

Ancillary preparations have made it possible to approach many of the same questions from different perspectives depending on the precise nature of the preparation. A major focus with these preparations is on comparative studies of molecular structures of animal tissues.

The materials associated with both traditional and non-traditional specimens include data and observations obtained when the specimen was collected. These data are the primary source for locality information and date of collection as well as observations pertaining to reproductive, ecological, and behavioural characteristics. The amount and quality of data recorded by the collector in the field directly affect how the specimens might be used in various research projects.

Each preparation type stores data which must be extracted by a researcher for analysis. The datasets obtained from these three basic groups may be used independently or in combination to look for answers to a variety of complex questions, both within and between various levels of organization: individual organisms, populations, species, communities, and ecosystems. However, it is evident that gaps in a specific preparation type within or among collections may affect the completeness of the data available to researchers concerning certain taxa or groups of taxa (Baker 1985; Zink 1983; Zusi 1969; Zusi et al. 1982).

In order to minimize gaps in available data and to maximize the completeness and value of samples stored in collections, it is important to recognize the need for cooperation among researchers and collectors (Barrowclough 1985; Foster 1982; Genoways et al. 1982). Systematic sampling of fauna from a broad region is beyond the capabilities of any single researcher or institution. The costs in money, time, and personnel are too great for such projects to be accomplished effectively. Cooperative efforts can alleviate and often solve many of the problems involved with developing adequate faunal samples from a region.

Cooperative efforts to improve the value of data available in collections include projects by professional societies to list currently available collection resources. Listings such as those compiled by the American Society of Mammalogists (Yates et al. 1987), Genoways and Schlitter (1981), and Dessauer and Hafner (1984) facilitate survey efforts by researchers of existing collections to determine the representation of species according to locality and preparation type. Such information is essential for guiding new sampling in order to improve the total sample available in collections for research purposes. Computerized inventories of the holdings of several North American collections compiled by members of the American Ornithologists' Union Committee on Collection Inventories are especially useful for planning collecting activities relative to avian skeletal and spirit specimens (Jenkinson and Wood 1985; Wood et al. 1982a, 1982b; Zusi et al. 1982). These inventories facilitate collection surveys and the development of collections, and are valuable projects to undertake for other vertebrate groups.

Cooperative efforts also facilitate the collecting process. Projects such as those of the Suriname expeditions (Genoways et al. 1982) make it possible to: (1) sample a greater diversity of taxa; (2) sample a larger geographic region; (3) obtain a greater variety of preparation types; and (4) develop a representative systematics collection for regions which do not already maintain such a database. These joint projects serve to increase both the quantity and the quality of the data available in collections. (...)

The value of collections in conservation

A systematics collection serves as a powerful database for us in a wide variety of basic and applied research. Such collections act as a source of data for current research as well as serving as a mechanism to monitor changes by storing data for the future. Specimens in collections store information that is not available elsewhere. As with any resource, they do not provide all the answers but must be combined with information available from other sources in order to present a more accurate solution to a problem. The value of collections in biological research has been extensively argued by numerous authors (Banks 1979; Barlow and Flood 1983; Dessauer and Hafner 1984; Foster 1982; Miller 1985; Parkes 1963; Zusi 1969). (...)

Identification of species

'Systematically organized collections will always be at the cutting edge of biological research, yet not always obviously so, but there of necessity because if you don't name it correctly, you don't know what you are talking about' (Edwards 1985: 7). Specimens in collections are invaluable for making accurate identifications of organisms under study in almost any research field of conservation biology – behaviour, genetics, reproduction, physiology, ecology, endocrinology. The validity of many of these studies depends on the accuracy with which the subjects have been identified.

Compared to insects and plants, mammalian species are relatively well known. Yet knowledge of mammalian taxonomy is far from complete. Many tropical regions and underdeveloped countries support faunas which have not been systematically studied and which are relatively unknown and undocumented (Mares and Braun 1986; Pine 1982; Wilson 1985). Pine (1982) reports that the mammals of the South American continent are probably the most poorly known in the world, and Mares (1986) emphasizes that one of the primary factors affecting the conservation situation in South America is the lack of a solid database about the environment and its biotic components. Evidence of the lack of data is the paucity of available literature pertaining to Latin American mammals (Mares and Braun 1986).

Basic faunal surveys and the development of systematics collections are necessary components to the growth of a database on which to make conservation and management decisions. Faunal surveys provide the raw material of data in the form of specimens for extraction and analysis by researchers. The initial results generally appear as species lists, descriptions, and field guides (for example, compare Mares *et al.* 1981, 1989). However, these are all essential precursors to the growth of taxonomic knowledge and therefore the ability to identify accurately organisms that are the focus of other types of research and management decisions.

In spite of the taxonomy of mammals in developed countries being well studied, there remain unanswered taxonomic questions for taxa which belong to groups for which the taxonomy is unstable or unclear. Conclusions about topics such as adaptive radiation, competition among species, interbreeding, and community structure depend on accurate identifications, as well as accurate characterizations of the systematics of the species in question. As knowledge of the relationships among species changes, conclusions about the ecology, behaviour, and management of the species will also change.

Taxonomically difficult species exemplify the need for voucher specimens, that is, specimens which are deposited in a collection to document a specific study (Lee *et al.* 1982). Voucher specimens circumvent some, though not all, of the problems of a dynamic classification system. A research project carried out with species identified according to current taxonomic knowledge does not necessarily lose its validity if the taxonomy of that species changes, as long as vouchers are retained permanently. In the event of a taxonomic revision, it is generally possible to reanalyze voucher specimens, update their classification, then determine how such a revision affects the conclusions of the original study.

Identification of organisms plays an important role in a variety of issues facing conservationists. One of these questions concerns species composition of a particular community or ecosystem. Observation data are insufficient to verify identifications for most species, and accurate identifications generally require the collection of specimens. One method for identifying components of systems is through the identification of animal remains found in stomach contents, pellets and faeces (Pearson and Pearson 1982). Other methods rely on systematic surveys to sample individual systems. Regardless of how the sample is acquired, an initial mis-identification of taxa or lack of accurately identified reference samples can result in mistaken conclusions about community structure. As a result, the validity of the entire project may be questioned (Lee 1977).

Another critical area for identification is the accurate classification of individuals as members either of an endangered taxon or of a more abundant, unprotected relative. To make such a distinction, accurate characterizations and discrimination between the protected and common taxa are essential, and the latter is rarely accomplished without museum specimens. A recent example of this problem is the status of bobcats in Texas. The question arose as to whether in fact Texas bobcats belonged to a subspecies identified as threatened, *Felis rufus baileyi*, or a more common subspecies, *F. r. texensis*. Schmidly and Read (1986) relied extensively on museum specimens in order to analyze non-geographic and geographic variation in Texas bobcats and arrive at a characterization of *F. r. texensis*.

The issue of introduced species also relies on data extracted from systematics collections. Species of unknown origin can be identified based on specimens already contained in collections. An accurate identification makes it possible to determine the natural requirements of the species, knowledge that is essential if it is necessary to develop a plan to control the introduced species (Banks 1979). A decision to transplant species from one region to another must be based on accurate identifications of the populations considered as well as accurate characterizations of the taxa involved (Aldrich 1946).

Another important use of collections for identification purposes is the enforcement of laws designed to present trafficking in native fauna. Law enforcement agents cannot be taxonomic specialists; they must rely on services provided by collection personnel to identify confiscated materials accurately. The only way to ensure accurate identifications is for a collection to maintain a complete and accurate sample of regional fauna, because often collection personnel will be presented with only parts of an organism – skins, hair, ivory, bones, or merely tissue or blood (Dessauer and Goddard 1984; Genoways *et al.* 1976).

Distributional patterns

Specimens in museum collections provide data concerning the distribution and ranges of species. As noted previously, the existence of a specimen in a collection documents the existence of that species at a particular time and place. By compiling records from a number of collections, it is possible to develop an initial distribution map for a species. For many regions, this initial dataset must be augmented by faunal surveys to obtain a more accurate representation of a species' distribution (Genoways et al. 1982; Mares et al. 1981).

Accurate distribution data play an important role in ecological studies such as in biogeography (Mares et al. 1985), assessment of causes of extinction (Patterson 1984), and studies directly applied to potential reserve sites. Diamond (1980) stresses that because of the patchiness of the geographic distribution of some species, it is not sufficient to assume species exist in the habitats where they are supposed to occur. Instead, species inventories may be necessary to verify species distributions in areas proposed as reserves.

Distribution data available from museum specimens are also used to determine the status of potentially threatened taxa. Wemmer and Watling (1986) relied on museum specimens, records written by collectors, and field observations to determine the status of the Sulawesi palm civet (*Macrogalidia musschellbroekii*). Their study refuted the earlier belief that the species was rare. Similar studies to determine the status of potentially endangered taxa are routine at both the state and federal level in the United States.

Genetic diversity

Many systematics collections now contain the raw material for a variety of types of genetic research which, in turn, provide basic knowledge essential for the conservation of diversity. This raw material is in the form of frozen tissues, and, if properly frozen and maintained, a high percentage of macromolecules are stable for extended periods of time (Dessauer and Menzies 1984).

The resources maintained in frozen tissue collections can be used to determine the genetic nature of individuals and populations. Six questions were cited by Dessauer et al. (1984) as ones which may be solved with the increase in available genetic evidence: (a) the genetic uniqueness of the individual; (b) breeding patterns within a population; (c) the genetic parameters that describe the population; (d) the magnitude and nature of genetic interactions in contact zones between members of different populations; (e) the identification of sibling species; and, (f) the estimation of the magnitude of genetic divergence between groups of closely related organisms. Answers to these basic questions make it possible to address issues such as how genetic thresholds determine minimum viable populations (Gilpin and Soulé 1986), how inbreeding affects natural populations of birds and mammals (Ralls et al. 1986), and how outbreeding and heterozygosity affect viability and fitness (Allendorf and Leary 1986; Ledig 1986; Templeton 1986). These issues are among many of central importance to conservation.

Another important use of frozen tissue collections relates to zoo-based research for identifying and maintaining genetic diversity, especially in rare and endangered species. In addition to basic studies in population genetics, systematics and evolutionary biology, applied studies rely on evidence obtained from frozen tissue collections. Among the studies cited by Ryder and Benirschke (1984) are studies documenting the loss of genetic variation in *Equus przewalskii*, and studies to identify the ancestry of individuals in order to assist with breeding programmes of rare species, such as with the two subspecies of *Pongo pygmaeus* at the San Diego Zoo. Studies such as these may affect how rare species are managed in the wild.

Zoos are also actively involved in gene pool preservation through programmes to collect and preserve spermatozoa (Gee 1984; Ryder and Benirschke 1984). Active programmes to maintain frozen spermatozoa help breeding programs of rare species to avoid the effects of inbreeding, as well as serving as a bank of genetic diversity for basic research. Zoos have the opportunity to preserve samples of genetic diversity to which most researchers do not have access in the species' native environments.

Environmental assessment

One of the potentially most valuable uses of a systematics collection is to monitor changes in ecosystems over time. Living organisms reflect, to varying degrees, their environments. Thus, many can indicate changes in the environment and document the biological effects of change (Brinkhurst 1985; Committee 1986; George 1987). These changes might range from a natural ecosystem succession to the introduction of pollutants or exotic species to the drastic modification of an environment by man or natural causes. In order for a collection to be a useful tool for monitoring changes, however, there must be a baseline sample of accurately identified specimens both from the location of interest as well as from other well characterized localities for comparisons (Barlow and Flood 1983; Brinkhurst 1985; Committee 1986; Lee 1977; Smith and Hafner 1984).

Probably the most famous of such studies are those which documented the effect of DDT on eggshell thickness (for example, Cooke 1979). Other examples include studies to monitor mercury residues in fish (Kelly *et al.* 1975), and the effects of thermally altered environments on largemouth bass (Smith *et al.* 1983). Zink (1983) reported morphometric variation in fox sparrows (*Passerella iliaca*) over a 50-year interval at two California sites, and noted that this was most likely the result of environmental changes. However, these and similar studies are impossible without archival samples such as those found in systematic collections, whether traditional preparations such as skeletons (Zink 1983), frozen tissues (Lewis *et al.* 1984; Smith and Hafner 1984) or eggs (Klaas *et al.* 1974). Some recent projects designed to show the effect of environmental change have, in fact, been invalidated because of the lack of a sample of accurately identified specimens from the environment in question (Lee 1977).

The value of collections as a tool for monitoring environmental change emphasizes the need for conservationists and allied researchers to be concerned with the development and management of systematics collections. Knowledge about the environmental effects of waste disposal sites, industrial plants and their pollutants, pesticide treatments, and other intrusive activities on living organisms depends on the thorough collection of a representative sample of individuals to serve as a source of baseline data – a sample which must predate the intrusive agent.

Education

An important component of a successful conservation programme is the education of a region's populace concerning the basics of conservation and the need for and value of a conservation programme (Mares 1986; Soulé 1986). This educational effort must proceed at two levels: an advanced level for training researchers, wildlife officers, forest and faunal managers, law enforcement officers and bureaucrats; and a popular level for the general public. Collections play an important role in this educational process by providing direct access to many of the materials that are the subjects of conservation programmes.

Systematics collections provide students of biology and wildlife science with the tools for learning the taxonomy and natural history of species as well as techniques for research. They provide specimens which serve as the focus of programmes and exhibits for the general public as well as reference material for artistic renderings to accompany field guides. Thus, systematics collections serve the dual educational functions of providing specialized training and the translation of specialized knowledge into a popular format.

References

Alberch, P. (1985) 'Museum collections and the evolutionary study of growth and development', in Miller, E.H. (ed.) *Museum Collections: Their Roles and Future in Biological Research*, British Columbia Provincial Museum, Occasional Papers, 25, 29–42.

Aldrich, J.W. (1946) 'Significance of racial variation in birds to wildlife management', *J. Wildlife Management*, 10: 86–93.

Allendorf, F.W. and Leary, R.F. (1986) 'Heterozygosity and fitness in natural populations of animals', in Soulé, M.E. (ed.) *Conservation Biology: The Science of Scarcity and Diversity*, Sunderland, MA: Sinauer Assoc., 57–76.

Anderson, R.M. (1965) 'Methods of collecting and preserving vertebrate animals', *Bull. Natl. Mus. Canada*, 69 (Biol. Series. No. 18): 1–99.

Baker, A.J. (1985) 'Museum collections and the study of geographic variation', in Miller, E.H. (ed.) *Museum Collections: Their Roles and Future in Biological Research*, British Columbia Provincial Museum, Occasional Papers, 25, 55–78.

Banks, R.C. (ed.) (1979) *Museum Studies and Wildlife Management*, Washington, DC: Smithsonian Institution Press.

Barlow, J.C. and Flood, N.J. (1983) 'Research collections in ornithology – a reaffirmation', in Brush, A.H. and Clark, G.A. (eds) *Perspectives in Ornithology*, New York: Cambridge University Press, 37–54.

Barrowclough, G.F. (1985) 'Museum collections and molecular systematics', in Miller, E.H. (ed.) *Museum Collections: Their Roles and Future in Biological Research*, British Columbia Provincial Museum, Occasional Papers 25, 43–54.

Brinkhurst, R.O. (1985) 'Museum collections and aquatic invertebrate environmental research', in Miller, E.H. (ed.) *Museum Collections: Their Roles and Future in*

Biological Research, British Columbia Provincial Museum, Occasional Papers, 25, 163–98.

Committee on the Applications of Ecological Theory to Environmental Problems, Commission on Life Sciences, National Research Council (1986) *Ecological Knowledge and Environmental Problem-Solving*, Washington, DC: National Academy Press.

Cooke, A.S. (1979) 'Changes in eggshell characteristics of the Sparrowhawk *(Accipiter nisus)* and Peregrine *(Falco peregrinus)* associated with exposure to environmental pollutants during recent decades', *J. Zool.*, 187: 245–63.

Dessauer, H.C. and Goddard, K.W. (1984) 'Value of frozen tissue collections for forensic studies', in Dessauer, H.C. and Hafner, M.S. (eds) *Collections of Frozen Tissues: Value*, Lawrence, KS: Association of Systematics Collections, 12–13.

Dessauer, H.C. and Hafner, M.S. (eds) (1984) *Collections of Frozen Tissues: Value*, Lawrence, KS: Association of Systematics Collections.

Dessauer, H.C., Hafner, M.S. and Goodman, M. (1984) 'Value of frozen tissue collections for studies in evolutionary biology', in Dessauer, H.C. and Hafner, M.S. (eds) *Collections of Frozen Tissues: Value*, Lawrence, KS: Association of Systematics Collections, 3–5.

Dessauer, H.C. and Menzies, R.A. (1984) 'Stability of macromolecules during long term storage', in Dessauer, H.C. and Hafner, M.S. (eds) *Collections of Frozen Tissues: Value*, Lawrence, KS: Association of Systematics Collections, 17–20.

Diamond, J.M. (1980) 'Patchy distributions of tropical birds', in Soulé, M.E. and Wilcox, B.A. (eds) *Conservation Biology: An Evolutionary-Ecological Perspective*, Sunderland, MA: Sinauer Assoc., 57–74.

Edwards, R.Y. (1985) 'Research: a museum cornerstone', in Miller, E.H. (ed.) *Museum Collections: Their Roles and Future in Biological Research*, British Columbia Provincial Museum, Occasional Papers, 25, 1–12.

Foster, M.S. (1982) 'The research natural history museum: pertinent or passe?', *Biologist*, 64: 1–12.

Gee, G.F. (1984) 'Value of frozen tissue collections for gene pool preservation', in Dessauer, H.C. and Hafner, M.S. (eds) *Collections of Frozen Tissues: Value*, Lawrence, KS: Association of Systematics Collections, 14–16.

Genoways, H.H. and Schlitter, D.A. (1981) 'Collections of Recent mammals of the world, exclusive of Canada and the United States', *Ann. Carnegie Mus.*, 50: 47–80.

Genoways, H.H., Reichart, H.A. and Williams, S.L. (1982) 'The Suriname small mammal survey: a case study of the cooperation between research and national conservations needs', in Mares, M.A. and Genoways, H.H. (eds) *Mammalian Biology in South America*, Linesville, PA: Univ. Pittsburgh, Pymtuning Lab. Ecol., Spec. Publ. No. 6, 491–504.

Genoways, H.H., Choate, J.R., Pembleton, E.F., Greenbaum, I.F. and Bickham, J.W. (1976) 'Systematists, other users, and uses of North American collections of Recent mammals', *Museology, Texas Tech Univ.*, 3: 1–87.

George, S.B. (1987) 'Specimens as bioindicators of environmental disturbance', in Genoways, H.H., Jones, C. and Rossolimo, O.L. (eds) *Mammal Collection Management*, Lubbock, TX: Texas Tech Univ. Press, 65–73.

Gilpin, M.E. and Soulé, M.E. (1986) 'Minimum viable populations: processes of species extinctions', in Soulé, M.E. (ed.) *Conservation Biology: The Science of Scarcity and Diversity*, Sunderland, MA: Sinauer Assoc., 19–34.

Hafner, D.J., Hafner, J.C. and Hafner, M.S. (1984) 'Skin-plus-skeleton preparation as the standard mammalian museum specimen', *Curator*, 27: 141–6.

Hall, E.R. (1962) *Collecting and Preparing Study Specimens of Vertebrates*, Mus. Nat. Hist., Univ. Kansas, Misc. Publ., 30.

Jenkinson, M.A. and Wood, D.S. (1985) 'Avian anatomical specimens: a geographic analysis of needs', *Auk*, 102: 587–99.

Johnson, N.K., Zink, R.M., Barrowclough, G.F. and Martin, J.A. (1984) 'Suggested techniques for modern avian systematics', *Wilson Bull.*, 96: 543–60.

Jones, E.M. and Owen, R.D. (1987) 'Fluid preservation of specimens', in Genoways, H.H., Jones, C. and Rossolimo, O.L. (eds) *Mammal Collection Management*, Lubbock, TX: Texas Tech Univ. Press, 51–63.

Kelly, T.M., Jones, J.D. and Smith, G.R. (1975) 'Historical changes in mercury contamination in Michigan walleyes *(Stizostedion vitreum vitreum)*', *J. Fish. Res. Board Canada*, 32: 1745–54.

Klaas, E.E., Ohlendorf, H.M. and Heath, R.G. (1974) 'Avian eggshell thickness: variability and sampling', *Wilson Bull.*, 86: 156–64.

Ledig, F.T. (1986) 'Heterozygosity, heterosis, and fitness in outbreeding plants', in Soulé, M.E. (ed.) *Conservation Biology: The Science of Scarcity and Diversity*, Sunderland, MA: Sinauer Assoc., 77–104.

Lee, W.L. (1977) 'The San Francisco Bay Project: a new approach to using systematics', *Assoc. Syst. Coll. Newsl.*, 5: 15–17.

Lee, W.L., Bell, B.M. and Sutton, J.F. (eds) (1982) *Guidelines for Acquisition and Management of Biological Specimens*, Lawrence, KS: Association of Systematics Collections.

Lewis, R.A., Stein, N. and Lewis, C.W. (1984) *Environmental Specimen Banking and Monitoring as Related to Banking*, Boston: Martinus Nijhoff.

Marcs, M.A. (1986) 'Conservation in South America: problems, consequences, and solutions', *Science*, 233: 734–9.

Mares, M.A. and Braun, J.K. (1986) 'An international survey of the popular and technical literature of mammalogy', *Ann. Carnegie Mus.*, 55: 145–205.

Mares, M.A., Ojeda, R.A. and Barquez, R.M. (1989) *Guide to the Mammals of Salta Province, Argentina*, Norman, OK: University of Oklahoma Press.

Mares, M.A., Ojeda, R.A. and Kosco, M.P. (1981) 'Observations on the distribution and ecology of the mammals of Salta Province, Argentina', *Ann. Carnegie Mus.*, 50: 151–206.

Mares, M.A., Willig, M.R. and Lacher, Jr., T.E. (1985) 'The Brazilian Caatinga in South American zoogeography: tropical mammals in a dry region', *J. Biogeogr.*, 12: 57–69.

Miller, E.H. (ed.) (1985) *Museum Collections: Their Roles and Future in Biological Research*, British Columbia Provincial Museum, Occasional Papers, 25: 1–219.

Nagorsen, D.W. and Peterson, R.L. (1980) *Mammal Collector's Manual*, Toronto: Royal Ontario Mus., Life Sci. Misc. Publ.

Parkes, K.C. (1963) 'The contribution of museum collections to knowledge of the living bird', *Living Bird*, 2: 121–30.

Patterson, B.D. (1984) 'Mammalian extinction and biogeography in the southern Rocky Mountains', in Nitecki, M.H. (ed.) *Extinctions*, Chicago: University of Chicago Press, 247–64.

Pearson, O.P. and Pearson, A.K. (1982) 'Ecology and biogeography of the southern rainforests of Argentina', in Mares, M.A. and Genoways, H.H. (eds) *Mammalian Biology in South America*, Linesville, PA: Univ. Pittsburgh, Pymtuning Lab. Ecol., Spec. Publ. No. 6, 129–42.

Pine, R.H. (1982) 'Current status of South American Mammalogy' in Mares, M.A. and Genoways, H.H. (eds) *Mammalian Biology in South America*, Linesville, PA: Univ. Pittsburgh, Pymtuning Lab. Ecol., Spec. Publ. No. 6, 27–38.

Quay, W.B. (1974) 'Bird and mammal specimens in fluid – objectives and methods', *Curator*, 17: 91–104.

Ralls, K., Harvey, P.H. and Lyles, A.M. (1986) 'Inbreeding in natural populations of birds and mammals', in Soulé, M.E. (ed.) *Conservation Biology: The Science of Scarcity and Diversity*, Sunderland, MA: Sinauer Assoc., 35–56.

Ryder, O.A. and Benirschke, K. (1984) 'The value of frozen tissue collections for zoological parks', in Dessauer, H.C. and Hafner, M.S. (eds) *Collections of Frozen Tissues: Value*, Lawrence, KS: Association of Systematics Collections, 6–9.

Schmidly, D.J. and Read, J.A. (1986) 'Cranial variation in the bobcat *(Felis rufus)* from Texas and surrounding states', Texas Univ., Occasional Papers, Mus., 101: 1–39.

Smith, M.H. and Hafner, M.S. (1984) 'Value of frozen tissue collections for environmental monitoring and retrospective studies', in Dessauer, H.C. and Hafner, M.S. (eds) *Collections of Frozen Tissues: Value*, Lawrence, KS: Association of Systematics Collections, 10–13.

Smith, M.H., Smith, M.W., Scott, S.L., Liu, E.H. and Jones, J.C. (1983) 'Rapid evolution in a post-thermal environment', *Copeia*, 1983: 193–7.

Soulé, M.E. (1985) 'What is conservation biology?' *BioScience*, 35: 727–34.

Soulé, M.E. (1986) 'Conservation biology and the "real world"', in Soulé, M.E. (ed.) *Conservation Biology: The Science of Scarcity and Diversity*, Sunderland, MA: Sinauer Assoc., 1–12.

Stangl, F.B., Jr. and Jones, E.M. (1987) 'An assessment of geographic and seasonal biases in systematic mammal collections from two Texas universities', *Texas J. Sci.*, 39: 129–37.

Templeton, A.R. (1986) 'Coadaptation and outbreeding depression', in Soulé, M.E. (ed.) *Conservation Biology: The Science of Scarcity and Diversity*, Sunderland, MA: Sinauer Assoc., 105–16.

Wemmer, C. and Watling, D. (1986) 'Ecology and status of the Sulawesi palm civet *Macrogalidia musschenbroekii* Schlegel', *Biol. Conserv.*, 35: 1–18.

Williams, S.L., Laubach, R. and Genoways, H.H. (1977) *A Guide to the Management of Recent Mammal Collections*, Pittsburgh: Carnegie Museum of Natural History, Special Publication 4, 1–105.

Wilson, E.O. (1985) 'The biological diversity crisis', *BioScience*, 35: 700–6.

Wood, D.S., Zusi, R.L. and Jenkinson, M.A. (1982a) *World Inventory of Avian Skeletal Specimens*, Norman, OK: American Ornithological Union and Oklahoma Biol. Survey.

Wood, D.S., Zusi, R.L. and Jenkinson, M.A. (1986b) *World Inventory of Avian Spirit Specimens*, Norman, OK: American Ornithological Union and Oklahoma Biol. Survey.

Yates, T.L., Barber, W.R. and Armstrong, D.M. (1987) 'Survey of North American collections of Recent mammals', *J. Mamm.*, 68(2, Suppl.): 1–76.

Zink, R.M. (1983) 'Evolutionary and systematic significance of temporal variation in the fox sparrow', *Syst. Zool.*, 32: 223–38.

Zusi, B.L. (1969) 'The role of museum collections in ornithological research', *Proc. Biol. Soc. Washington*, 82: 651–61.

Zusi, R.L., Wood, D.S. and Jenkinson, M.A. (1982) 'Remarks on a world-wide inventory of avian anatomical specimens', *Auk*, 99: 740–57.

Edited extract from Cato, P.S. (1991) 'The value of natural history collections in Latin American conservation', in Mares, M.A. and Schmidly, D.J. (eds) *Latin American Mammology: History, Biodiversity and Conservation*, Norman, OK: University of Oklahoma Press, 416–29. Paisley Cato is currently Curator of Collections Care and Conservation at San Diego Natural History Museum. She is a prominent figure in natural history circles in the USA, where she has made significant contributions nationally to the use, care and development of collections.

Chapter 3

Characterization of voucher specimens

Welton L. Lee, Bruce M. Bell and John F. Sutton

A VOUCHER SPECIMEN IS ONE which physically and permanently documents data in an archival report by:

1   verifying the identity of the organism(s) used in the study; and,
2   by so doing, ensures that a study which otherwise could not be repeated can be accurately, reviewed or reassessed.

Kinds and numbers of voucher specimens adequate to document such a report should be determined jointly by participating investigator/collector(s) and repository institution(s) at the onset of the project.

Identification of organisms is the first step in communicating an investigator's results in any report involving any biological entities (Carriker 1976; Hedgpeth 1961; Heppell 1979). As noted in an earlier report (Lee *et al.* 1978):

> In all biological studies concern must be given to the accurate identification of the organisms under investigation, for this is the key to all past and future reference to data derived from the study. Given the often extreme variations in tolerances, biochemical and behavioral adaptations, and responses at all levels to normal and abnormal perturbations found between related but distinct species, genera, etc., accurate identification represents the only key to repeatability in the laboratory or the field. As such, it represents one of the foundations of the scientific approach and of its often extolled objectivity.

Voucher specimens ensure that identification of organisms studied can be verified and corrected if necessary even in cases where a study cannot or will not be repeated, such as before and after environmental studies, ecological studies, large faunal or floral surveys, or such studies as biochemical investigations where research involves destruction of the study specimen. They are the sole means to verify the data documented in a report and to make historical comparison possible. In addition, they provide critical information for future investigations of, for example, biochemical properties, demography, and geographic distribution. These properties make voucher collections unique resources that must be carefully protected.

The three categories of voucher specimens are:

1   type specimens, upon which names of taxonomic units are based;
2   taxonomic support specimens (specimens of primary importance in taxonomic studies other than nomenclatural studies, such as range extensions, life-history studies and morphological variability); and,
3   biological documentation specimens (representative organisms derived from studies or projects other than primarily taxonomic).

Voucher specimens are required in any study in which:

1   verification of experimental results can be accomplished only through reassessment or re-evaluation of existing data, and where the species involved may not be unequivocally identified without access to samples taken in the original study;
2   the nature of the study brings about alteration of specimens such that future re-identification or verification is made impossible;
3   diversity of taxa under study is so great or the systematics so complex that all species involved probably will not be identified accurately;
4   taxonomic groups are not yet known accurately to species level; or,
5   the nature of the study is strictly systematics.

Studies requiring voucher specimens can be characterized as:

A.   *Space/time specific studies.* Such studies determine organisms in a given location at a given time and include ecological base-line studies and environmental impact statements. The fact that populations fluctuate over generations, move, and become extinct are basic phenomena pertinent to such studies.
B.   *Disciplinary studies.* These address phenomena characteristic of levels of biological organization ranging from molecular to ecosystem (e.g. chemicals produced by particular cells, physiology of particular organ systems, behaviour of particular organisms, and patterns of population distribution and dynamics).
C.   *Experimental studies.* These studies emphasize extraction, characterization, or manipulation of components or contents of organisms, or responses of organisms to stimuli. This is a special case where verification can only be achieved through vouchers. Without voucher specimens, such studies cannot be reproduced or critically evaluated, since the organisms utilized are destroyed through the experimental process or experimental organisms are returned to their environment.
D.   *Systematic studies.* These studies deal with problems of speciation, phylogeny and classification.

Voucher specimens may be:

1   *The actual organism* (part or whole) that is studied, observed or treated.
2   *A sample* of one or more individuals (part or whole) from a population that is studied, observed, or treated.
3   *A representation of the organism(s)* or its characters (e.g. sound recordings, photographs, fossils, etc.) that is studied, observed, or treated. However, these representations are usually not adequate as a substitute for voucher specimens and should be used only when the organisms themselves are impractical or illegal to collect.
4   *An associated specimen* that is biologically or functionally related (e.g. stomach contents, parasites, pollen preparations, etc.) to the organism that is studied, observed, or treated.
5   *A corroborative specimen* that provides additional data or character (e.g. from the same population or individual but a different time or stage of the life cycle) to a previously collected voucher specimen (categories 1–4).

To fulfil its function, a voucher specimen must:

1   Have recognized diagnostic characters that are appropriate to the level of identification in the report. Specific life stages or body parts may be required.
2   Be preserved in good condition by the investigator/collector according to acceptable practice.
3   Be thoroughly documented with field and/or other relevant reports.
4   Be maintained in good condition and be readily accessible in suitable repository institution(s).

(…)

Selection of a repository for voucher specimens

A suitable repository is an institutional collection serving two basic functions:

1   preserving specimens and related information; and,
2   making it easy for people to find and use them later. A good repository does these things well; a poor one does not.

Planning ahead

The person, group or agency seeking a future repository for voucher specimens should carefully consider the following questions as early as possible before collection begins:

1   What will be the nature and quantity of material and data collected?
2   Where is the material likely to be of greatest future use?
3   Where are the biological specialists who might help in the present study or use the materials in the future?

4   Are identifications expected? If so, to what level?

5   What will be the scheduling and terms of the deposit of such materials?

6   How should specimens be processed prior to deposition?

7   Are there to be any restrictions on future use?

8   Can the specimens be integrated into the general collection or must they be kept separately?

9   Are supporting funds available for costs of processing, future care, or other services?

10   Will the institution you have in mind as a repository accept your collection? Remember that although the initial selection of a repository is the investigator's/ collector's responsibility, final decision on acceptance of material must remain with the institution. It is not obligated to take all materials that might be sent.

(...)

Criteria for repository designation

Professional persons, institutions, disciplinary groups, umbrella organizations, or other reference sources will recommend or suggest possible repositories. Actual selection of a repository should be made by the depositor after discussion of detailed terms of the deposit with curators of the potential recipient institution.

In selecting a repository, a potential depositor should be aware of and should apply the criteria listed below rather than rely upon uncritical advice. The reason for this is that people who planned the study that produced the voucher material conducted the field work, prepared the specimens, and used the newly gained information in preparing reports, understand the ramifications of their information system better than anyone else. These ramifications should be discussed with the relevant curator at potential recipient institutions. These curators may have ideas for optimizing future values of the material, ideas that have not occurred to the originators, hence the desirability of such collaboration.

Characteristics of a suitable repository

A.   The collection is administered by a non-profit public or private institution.

B.   The collection has at least one curator who is directly responsible for it.

C.   The collection is housed in a building that provides adequate protection from fire, water, dust, excessive heat or light, and other physical hazards. Important permanent records (such as catalogues and field notes) should be kept in a fireproof or fire retardant safe or its equivalent.

D.   Specimens are stored in containers appropriate to the discipline and nature of the specimen.

E.   Specimens are periodically inspected and maintained in accordance with accepted procedures.

F.   Specimens are prepared and processed in a manner that insures their present and future utility.

G.   Specimens are arranged according to a specific plan that is recorded and, preferably, posted.

H.   Field notes and ancillary data are preserved as a part of the permanent record for each specimen or lot.

I.   Data on specimen labels, in field notes, in permanent catalogues, and wherever else data are recorded in the collection are accurate and original labels are available to investigators.

J.   The collection is accessible to all qualified users. Qualified users are those with demonstrated ability to handle material properly, and a specific purpose for so doing.

K.   Accessibility to collections by unqualified persons is restricted. We recommend formation of separate teaching collections for use in basic courses, and restriction of other materials to research use.

L.   Loans to other institutions are handled and packaged in an appropriate and legal manner. When material is kept alive and propagation is possible, the repository agrees to provide subcultures, progeny, or seeds to qualified researchers.

M.   Type specimens are identified as such, segregated and marked accordingly, and made accessible only to qualified scientists. Loans, if made, are considered and handled with special care.

N.   The institution has the stated intent to continue support of the collection at least at a level necessary to maintain these standards. Should institutional priorities change, the institution will transfer the collection to an appropriate institution which will insure its perpetual maintenance.

O.   Specimens are acquired and possessed in accord with federal and state regulations pertaining thereto.

P.   A written policy exists for collection management, including acquisition, preservation and de-accessioning.

References

Carriker, M.R. (1976) 'The crucial role of systematics in assessing pollution effects on the biological utilization of estuaries, in USEPA Office of Water Planning and Standards', *Estuarine Pollution Control and Assessment, Proceedings of Conference*, Washington, DC: US Government Printing Office, 487–506.

Hedgpeth, J.W. (1961) 'Taxonomy: man's oldest profession', Eleventh Annual University of the Pacific Faculty Research Lecture, May 22, 1961.

Heppell, R. (1979) 'Biological collections, systematics and taxonomy', *Museums Journal*, 79(2): 75–7.

Lee, W.L., Devaney, D.M., Emerson, W.K., Ferris, V.R., Hart, C.W., Kozloff, E.N., Nichols, F.H., Pawson, D.L., Soulé, D.F. and Woolacott, R.M. (1978) 'Resources in invertebrate systematics', *American Zoologist*, 18(1): 167–85.

Edited extract from Lee, W.L., Bell, B.M. and Sutton, J.F. (eds) (1982) *Guidelines for Acquisition and Management of Biological Specimens*, Lawrence, KS: Association of Systematics Collections, 5–7, 19–22. This report arose from a conference on voucher specimen management.

Chapter 4

Home thoughts from abroad
An evaluation of the SAMDOK Homes Pool

Elizabet Stavenow-Hidemark

Guidelines for the Homes Pool

THE HOMES POOL STARTED in 1978, and in summary its guidelines for the first working period are as follows. The Homes Pool shall consist of five museums with a geographical distribution throughout Sweden. Together they will be responsible for the documentation of the contemporary household environment by means of collecting in objects and recording information of those objects and their surroundings. Documentation will take place through the recording of representative type households. The work shall be undertaken in consultation with the SAMDOK Secretariat and in accordance with the following guidelines on which the Homes Pool has agreed.

The following museums have taken upon themselves to participate in work in the Homes Pool: Hälsinglands museum, Hudiksvall (regional museum); Nordiska museet, Stockholm (national museum); Jämtlands läns museum, Ostersund (county museum); Göteborgs historiska museum, Göteborg (regional museum); Kulturen, Lund (regional museum); Torekällbergets museum, Södertälje (local museum which joined the Pool in 1982).

Each museum that joins the Homes Pool will research a type household every five years. In this way one type household will be researched every year. The scheme will start in 1978 in Hudiksvall. In between these research projects of type households, which includes the taking in of objects, each museum shall take on a lesser research project of a different type of household, whereby the acquisition of objects shall be limited to objects which are specific to them.

The type household shall be chosen in consultation with the SAMDOK Secretariat and the Home Pool. The type households should have a good social and geographical spread. They should be distributed in accordance with a rough scheme which the Department of Field Research and Archives of the Nordiska museet has drawn up and used. The households should be of different sizes and combinations of age groups, live in different types of homes and in different types of area, in the country and in the town.

For the research a model will be followed which was worked out by the Department of Field Research and Archives at the Nordiska museet in Stockholm: the home shall be photographed. All the rooms, including the store and service rooms shall be photographed. The cupboards, wardrobes, etc., shall be opened and photographed. Plans of the dwelling shall be drawn up and also a plan made of the way the furniture is placed. The holding of the household's objects shall be catalogued. All the objects, with a description and information about where they came from shall be catalogued room by room on punch-cards with the following headings:

> Household members
> Relatives
> Immediate environment and close contacts
> Distant environment and distant contacts
> Timetable
> Environment round building
> Outdoor area
> Description of the building
> Fixtures and fittings and technical equipment
> Vehicles owned
> Furniture
> Textiles
> Electrical fittings
> Wall decorations
> Ornaments
> Work and hobby equipment
> Plants
> Contents of cupboards and drawers

The family shall be interviewed about personal data and for an account of their lifestyle, work, education, working routine, food habits, hygiene, economy, and leisure-time. The family shall be offered payment by the hour for their trouble.

A special list shall be drawn up of the acquisitions of the household during the previous calendar year. In accordance with the Homes Pool's original scheme the museum doing the research shall acquire the objects the household has itself acquired during the previous year. Items similar to those acquired by the household shall be acquired by the museum on the open market. Those items one cannot buy shall be acquired where possible from the household itself.

The museum undertaking the research shall be free to complement the above acquisitions with the further acquisition of something in its totality, e.g. the furnishings of a room or part of a room. Identical objects shall be acquired so that one can furnish and equip a kitchen or living room from a household, for example. The family's everyday clothing, a set of bedclothes, a week's advertising material put through the door and a week's packaging materials, are examples of the collecting done in Hudiksvall. The choice of room and collection in totality should be made in consultation with the SAMDOK Secretariat, but should at least in part be able to be acquired at second-hand afterwards. In part such items have already been collected by specialised museums. With the acquisition of larger and more expensive items in mind the advice of the Secretariat should be sought, so that no unnecessary duplication occurs. Items which are not acquired shall be recorded by the use of photographs, department store catalogues, etc.

The museums undertaking the research shall be answerable for the care and conservation of the objects. The museum should place those collections connected with the contemporary documentation of the home at the disposal of other museums for the purpose of research and display.

Five research projects

Hälsinglands museum, 1978

The research criteria for choice were the following:

> The household should be living in a rented flat in one of the larger residential areas.
> At least one of the income earners should be working in a typical Hudiksvall industry.
> The woman in the household should work at least part-time.
> One of the partners should be born in one of the communities immediately outside Hudiksvall and have moved into the town in adulthood.

The museum looked for a suitable family by putting out an appeal through the letterboxes of 2-bedroomed flats in a modern tower-block on the outskirts of Hudiksvall. 34 households received the circular, 19 of them were visited to make short structured interviews, 8 households fulfilled the demands listed above, 2 were positive about taking part, 1 of them was chosen. The job of finding a family took a week. In the light of further experience this is unusually speedy.

The family: the man was a stevedore, the woman worked as a health service ancillary, nights only. The woman also did office-cleaning work. The three children went respectively to secondary, primary and nursery schools. The couple came from a community outside Hudiksvall and moved into the town as adults.

They set up house in 1959, and moved to this particular flat in the 70s. The place has two bedrooms and a total living space of 80 square metres. The living room furnishings include a bed-sofa, a large coffee table and two armchairs. There is also in this room a colour T.V. and a large aquarium. The parents and the youngest daughter sleep in the main bedroom. The boy and girl share the other bedroom. There are bunk-beds there and another aquarium. The walls are almost completely covered with posters including sportsmen such as Ingemar Stenmark and Björn Borg.

In the flat there is a big walk-in storage area for clothes, within the building there is a cellar and garage space. The kitchen is the room which is used most, all the meals are taken there, and parties, and the wife does all her sewing there. The living room is always available for the children and their friends. The family is happy with their living area. They often have contact with the older generation of the family out in the country and at the husband's mother's they grow their whole consumption of potatoes for the year. To some extent there is some remaining self-sufficiency. With the help of a deep freeze berry-fruit and fish are preserved. The wife bakes all the bread. The family often visit their relatives, and have coffee with friends but they do not have a lot of friends. The wife likes working at various handicrafts, while the husband's great hobby is fishing.

At the time of the research project the family owned some 2,420 objects. About 2,000 were kept in cupboards, drawers and on shelves — of those, 600 were in the kitchen. Of the 420 items set out in the flat, not less than 160 were there as ornaments, which means more than one-third of all the items that were visible to the eye. Among these are included watercolours, drawings, reproductions, posters, stickers, ornamental plates, animal figures, ceramic tiles, trolls, miniature bottles, etc. The large number of items was mainly because of the children's freedom to put up pictures all over the flat. The cataloguing of pictures and ornaments clearly makes it possible to interpret and analyse this type of more or less conscious message.

This research project was done in such a way as to make it a model for the future.

Nordiska museet, 1979

The Nordiska museet looked for a family with children in a suburb, preferably one living in a terrace house. The wife would be a child-minder, the husband a white-collar worker. A one-time neighbour of one of the research team answered this description and the family came forward. The husband is an officer in military service. The wife looks after four children. They have three children of their own and live in a terrace house. The terrace house consists of a hall, living room, kitchen-cum-dining area, with a laundry room and toilet all on the ground floor, there is a landing, three bedrooms and a bathroom on the first floor. The kitchen is the most frequently used room in the house. All meals are taken here, and all the ironing is done here. The dining table doubles also as a writing and sewing table. The children staying here during the day play in the kitchen, and the family often sit here in the evening when they are not watching T.V.

The T.V. stands in the living room, and this is where the family gather. The family's own children and the children who are minded are allowed here but not with toys. The smallest child who is minded sleeps here after lunch.

The parents give priority to being with their children over and above seeing relations and friends. The husband likes carpentry and making improvements around the house. His wife likes doing handicrafts. The family is happy with its housing and the area as a whole, except that the house could do with an extra room.

The museum collected in everything from the boys' room including a fitted carpet and wardrobes. Certain certificates and drawings which the boys were keen to keep were photographed both in colour and in black-and-white.

Jämtlands läns museum, 1980

The museum looked for a family where one of the partners worked in tourism, which is financially speaking the most important industry in the county. The family was to be one living in one of the county's bigger tourist areas in the westerly sparsely populated region.

After a number of difficulties and with the help of a hotel organization a family was found. The couple, who are in their thirties, run a village of cottages for tourists; the husband hires out skis and his wife works part-time in the bank. They have a large number of relations living in the area. The farm where they live is a family one on the husband's side. They married in 1966 when their second daughter was born. They moved into the husband's childhood home in 1978.

The relatives within the family see a lot of each other. The couple get help with their family or do things with the older generation, for instance with baby-sitting, or doing a big batch of baking, but also with hunting and slaughtering, long-term boiling of meat, and the preserving of berry-fruit.

The house they live in was built in 1942–43. It has twice been modernised, the last time in 1978. On the ground floor there is an entrance-way, a hall, kitchen, living room, office and bathroom, on the first floor the family have two bedrooms, each with a landing.

Noteworthy for this couple is that apart from their work they have quite a circle of friends and bottle parties are organized at home where people also bring food. They also go out to restaurants with these friends.

Once or twice a week friends come in, in the evening, for coffee. The group consists of five couples who have stuck together for some time. These parties necessarily also entail rather better clothes, and are stretched out over the whole year in a prescribed pattern.

The wife helps her aunt to drive the cows up to the summer pasture farm. She and her husband go to Rhodes and Malta, she makes a paella for her husband's thirtieth birthday party. So the old style of Swedish farm-life is blended with a modern and international style of life.

The collecting in of objects was directed towards illustrating the different basic functions in the life of the family. The starting point was the family's acquisitions from the previous year and the collecting was structured along the lines of a number of different themes, e.g. eating, playing, etc. A newly made peasant cupboard had symbolic importance (connection with the area, the feeling for wood and for the crafts involved) while clothes were an illustration of everyday life but also of an outward-going lifestyle.

During the research project three new aspects were particularly followed: 1) How and where the family did their shopping; 2) How and from where the members of the family got the ideas and impulses which had an influence on their lifestyle; 3) Hopes and dreams for the future.

Göteborgs historiska museum, 1981–82

The museum in Gothenburg chose to document a dockworker's home in connection with a research and recording project which was already under way on the crisis-ridden docks industry. After contacts with business management and trade unions, appeals in staff newspapers, leaflets and then new union contacts nine families were eventually found, who were willing to come forward. Eight of them became reference families. The family chosen lived in a comparatively newly built suburb at Hisingen, where some 45% of the dockworkers in fact live. The husband was a plater at the Arendal Dock, the wife a child-minder. They have two boys. At the time of the documentation project they were living in an owner-occupied flat.

This consisted of a living room, kitchen, 3 bedrooms, bathroom and hanging space for clothes, hall and cloakroom with separate W.C. i.e. an area of altogether approximately 93.5 square metres. The family live a very active life in their spare time. The husband is trainer to the boys' handball and football teams to which his sons belong. The wife does jogging and is a woodland study leader with organized groups of small children. Her main hobbies are weaving, sewing, vegetable-dyeing and other handicrafts. The spare-time activities of the family were followed in much greater detail than in the other research projects. Their places of work were also documented, as was also done in other research projects, e.g. at Hudiksvall.

The taking in of objects was directed towards the items that were visible in the kitchen. Since the family moved house immediately after the documentation project this facilitated the acquisition of the fittings and fixtures in the kitchen.

Objects in cupboards and drawers which illustrate such functions as baking, and also everyday clothes, were collected.

Kulturen, Lund, 1983

Lund is a university town and the Cultural Historical Museum looked for a student family in Lund, who lived in one of the Academic Association's (A.F.) student flats, with furniture either from the Association or from the family itself. One of the adults in the family was to be actively involved in university studies.

It was actually difficult to find a family who lived in this way and who were also willing to come forward. Neither was it as usual as one had imagined for student families to live in A.F. flats.

Three months were set aside for the whole project, including the writing up of the report and the collecting in of objects. A fortnight was taken up with finding a family.

The family: The husband is busy with university studies, which are partially financed by two days a week part-time work; the wife, trained as a nurse, is now at home to look after the two small children, of whom the elder had a third birthday during the research project, while the younger was still being breast-fed.

They live in an area of low-level buildings, which were finished in 1966, quite near the town centre in Lund. The flat, which covers an area of 69 square metres consists of four rooms plus a little kitchen without any dining area, a bathroom, clothes-hanging space and large balcony.

Both partners have a non-conformist religious background and are deeply committed Christians. Their home is full of souvenirs from two long journeys to mission-stations in far-off countries. The flat is adapted to the children, except for the best room, where they are not allowed in.

The report and the interviews give an excellent picture of an active and open family, but for the sake of the integrity which was demanded the material cannot be used at the moment.

Kulturen's collecting in took the form of visible objects in the living room, which for the most part the family simply relinquished. The things they wanted to keep, souvenirs and wall decorations, records and books, were photographed carefully. A certain amount of everyday clothes for use inside the house were taken in, door-to-door advertising material and packaging material for a week were documented.

Collecting objects

The aim of the SAMDOK research projects even right from the start was to make an adequate collection of contemporary objects. In connection with these research programmes the Homes Pool has now taken in over 1,100 items. These should be seen as a common resource, not only for the five museums involved, but also for the other cultural museums in Sweden as a whole. With this collection we have lifted the responsibility off the shoulders of the others. The objects will obviously be available for loan for temporary exhibitions on the same terms as for ordinary loans.

Here follows a table where the material collected in has been divided up according to different uses and groups of objects. Those objects which are in brackets are the ones which have several different uses and can also be found under another and more primary use.

Complete rooms

The following complete rooms have been collected in:

> 1 living room (Hälsinglands museum)
> 1 boys' room (The Nordiska museet)
> 1 kitchen (Göteborgs historiska museum)
> 1 open-plan (all-purpose) room (Kulturen, Lund)

During their research project at Ljusnedal Jämtlands läns museum did not take in any complete room. By agreement with the Homes Pool the collecting in was spread out so that basic functions were comprehensively covered without any problematic duplication. One might say that clothes were possibly over-represented, which is quite natural when each research project chose to document 'their' people. Clothes certainly give identity, and form a kind of skin. Ways of dressing are particularly connected with time and at least on an everyday scale are quite independent of economic, social and geographical factors. So the material collected is too similar. Jeans are quite clearly over-represented, with 12 pairs.

Certain functions have been left out or are poorly covered. Under cleaning there are only buckets and cloths and empty packaging for cleaning liquid. There is no vacuum-cleaner, brush and dustpan, window-cleaning equipment, etc. There are just a few things to illustrate sewing or handicrafts, in spite of the fact that a number of women in various research projects said that they spent a lot of time on this sort of activity. There is nothing on home carpentry. Hobbies and leisure-time activities are poorly covered. There is no sports equipment except sporting clothes and nor are there any gardening tools. Music, radio and T.V. are not well illustrated, but one can complete this area later. Pets were not often around in these families, and this was an influential factor in collecting, but Göteborgs historiska museum acquired a bird-cage.

Thematic displays

The objects collected in have the potential to illustrate very well how the families who were researched lived, or at least some important area of their lives. These objects can also be used loose from their context in thematic displays. If one puts together all the clothes that were collected in they show how adults and children dressed c. 1980, in terms of party-wear, everyday and sports-wear. The material which was catalogued and photographed plus the interviews form a good comple-ment. The packaging which was taken in with the photographs of the insides of cupboards is suitable for display on that subject. Posters and stickers can go into a display on young people's culture. Here is a resource, available for loan to all cultural history museums. If the collection of objects is structured so that basic functions in the home can be illustrated, the potential for use of such objects in thematic displays will be increased enormously.

An old-age pensioner uses mostly things he or she has had for a number of years. A collection of objects only bought in during the previous year would be misleading as far as his/her lifestyle is concerned.

Six criteria

In the English version of the first report on *Contemporary Documentation, Today for Tomorrow* (1980) the principles for selection are summarized according to six selection criteria:

1   Frequency – the most commonly occurring, or the most sold object.
2   Ladder – innovations and phases of development.
3   Representativity – carriers of symbolic function.
4   Domain – the personal, the simple and typical object.
5   Appeal – objects which have connections with famous people or with his-torically important events.
6   Form – variations in form and style.

The importance of collecting in totality is emphasised in the report. Totalities have been collected in four out of five of the household research projects: the contents of a room, for instance. That which is simple and typical has been provided for by the taking in of IKEA (good design/popular prices) and similar furniture, clothes, posters, and packaging.

It was not one of our specific aims to cover the development of products or innovations, the ladder criterion, but since we have taken in contemporary objects this side of things should more or less subconsciously have been provided for. Symbolic functions have been given too little attention. The appeal criterion is not relevant in this context.

These six points are related generally to the collecting in of objects in cultural history museums and are not specially directed at the contemporary scene, even if they can also quite well be used in this context.

Souvenirs and inherited objects

It has proved easier than we thought to acquire objects that have been in family use. Several families have been stimulated by the money they received to change their furnishings, textiles and clothes for completely new different things and have themselves organized the buying in of replacements. On the other hand families have often chosen to hold on to ornaments and souvenirs. When it came to acquiring such items the museums were very careful in the photography so that a reproduction might be made or so that they could try to find a similar item. Acquisition of inherited objects has not so far come up, but it is reckoned that museums can find something similar in their own collections.

Reference

Rosander, G. (1980) *Today for Tomorrow: Museum Documentation of Contemporary Society in Sweden by Acquisition of Objects*, Stockholm: SAMDOK Council.

Source: Stavenow-Hidemark, E. (1985) *Home Thoughts from Abroad: An Evaluation of the SAMDOK Homes Pool*, Stockholm: Nordiska museet/samdok, 5. Samdok was founded in 1977 as a voluntary association which includes nearly every Swedish museum of cultural history — about 85 members. Pools currently cover Leisure, Domestic Life, Local and Regional Spheres, Management of Natural Resources, Politics and Society, Manufacture and Services, Saami Life, and Cultural Encounters.

Chapter 5

Ceramics as testaments of the past
Field research and making objects speak

Barbara E. Frank

MUSEUMS WORLDWIDE FACE similar challenges of making objects speak. Far too often, however, objects enter into museum collections surrounded by silence, their stories lost to an unknown past. Museum professionals are somehow expected to produce the words to tell of their place in history.

As an art student, I was trained to think of art objects as things that speak directly by visual means. Great art has what Robert Plant Armstrong has called an 'affecting presence': the power to move one's emotions, to communicate an aesthetic charge without words. The phrase suggests that great art is timeless.

However, as an art historian and educator, I recognise that great art exists within and because of a larger social and historical context. I encourage my students to look for subtle variations in style and iconography that might suggest change over time and space, thus revealing the interaction of peoples and ideas. We explore a broad range of quality and character in the arts of a particular culture or moment in time. It is much easier to grasp what art has to say if we understand something of the circumstances surrounding its creation and use.

My point is that, in order to make the objects in museum collections speak, we must attempt to reconstruct their histories. Field research focused on objects already in collections as well as combined collection and documentation projects are essential to the success of this endeavour. Museum professionals, archaeologists, art historians and others need to use the strengths of their respective disciplines and collaborate with each other toward this goal.

I would like to illustrate these ideas with several examples from my research and from a collaborative collection and documentation project undertaken by myself and a team from the National Museum of Mali. My own fieldwork has dealt with two quite different domains among the Mande-speaking peoples of Mali. In 1982–84 my research focused on Mande leatherworking traditions. I returned to the field in 1991 and 1992 to work with women potters. Although each project was carried out in similar ethnic and geographic contexts, and although my focus in both instances was on historical reconstruction, the nature of the data available presented very different challenges.

My research on Mande leatherwork began with a review of the literature. I found very little in terms of written documentation on the objects or technology of Mande leatherwork. What there was on the social identity and history of leather-workers tended to be limited and, as I later realised, misinformed. In contrast to the dearth of published information, however, there are literally thousands of examples of West African leather bags, pouches, sandals, powder horns, and sword and knife sheaths in the ethnographic museums of the United States and Europe, many of them dating from the nineteenth century (when warfare and slave raiding caused increased demand for leather goods, which were also collected by colonial military officers). Unfortunately, the vast majority of these objects are silent – without provenance, context, or voice. Some came into museum collections as curiosities, souvenirs of the travels of colonial officers, their origin recorded as 'Soudan' or 'Mandingue'. Others entered without any attribution and at some later point were catalogued as Hausa or Tuareg simply because published accounts attribute leatherworking skills to those two major groups.

However, there are a select but nevertheless important number of leather objects with solid documentation. These were usually collected as part of museum expeditions whose purpose was to amass a full picture of material culture from particular settings. When located within a comparative framework that is both geographic and ethnic, these objects become testaments of the past.

As a result of museum research, supported by limited field examples, I was able to define a regional Mande style of leatherwork as distinct from that of the Hausa, Tuareg and other West African leatherworking traditions (Frank 1998). Characteristics of this style include a preference for red-brown or maroon leather with geometric black painted designs, wide bands with incised and peeled patterns, leather moulded over raised ridges, and embroidery with palm fibres. The geographical extent of this style led me to explore through field interviews the notion that Mande leatherworkers may have been part of the well known diaspora of Mande traders and clerics beginning as early as the fall of the empire of Ghana. I would not have been able to reach or support such a conclusion had I not found solid field documentation associated with particular objects in museum collections. My field research on oral traditions concerning the history of leatherworking and the identity of leatherworkers was equally important. In short, it was the combination of collection information and fieldwork that allowed me to construct a framework for the history of Mande leatherworking.

The challenge I faced with my subsequent research on Mande ceramic traditions was somewhat different. There is an extensive body of literature on ceramics – especially associated with archaeological research and a series of ongoing ethno-archaeological projects in the inland Niger Delta region of Mali. However, there are very few ceramic objects clearly identified as Mande in American museum collections, and very little on the social identity of Mande women potters in the literature. I based my field research in the Mande heartland region – in the towns of Kangaba, Bamako, Kolokani and Banamba – where I worked with Bamana and Maninka potters. I observed and photographed all aspects of the technology of pottery production, conducted interviews on individual, family and regional history, and documented other aspects of the lives and identities of the potters as the wives of blacksmiths.

In 1991 I went with a team from the Musée national in Bamako on a ceramic collection and documentation mission to the region of Kadiolo in southern Mali, near the border with Côte d'Ivoire. The potters in this region identify themselves as Mande, or more precisely as Dyula, distinct from the Senufo-speaking majority. Unlike their Bamana-Maninka counterparts to the north, they are the wives not of blacksmiths but of *griots* (or bards) who bear the classic Mande *griot* patronyms of Kouyaté and Diabaté. They say that their distribution of selected ceramic ancestors left the village of Kaaba (Kangaba) at some point in the distant past and travelled south by way of Sikasso eventually to settle in their present location.

Despite their claims to a Mande heritage, our research suggested that, whatever the origin of the men may have been, the potters and their artistry were descendants of a quite different tradition from that of the Bamana and Maninka women of the Mande heartland. While our first clue was the significant departure from the Mande model in terms of identities and craft specialisation, a comparison of object styles and types, and of the technology of their manufacture, lends support to this theory.

I would like to provide some background on the mission, our methods and the kind of information we sought to record. I will then suggest how the contemporary data we collected may contribute to a more complete understanding of the history of the region, and where the Kadiolo potters fit within the complex panorama of ceramic traditions in West Africa.

Our first trip was a brief reconnaissance mission undertaken by Mamadou Samaké, researcher and audio-visual technician, Oumar Traoré, chauffeur, and myself. Our goals were to identify the most important centres of ceramic production in the region; to explain the nature of our mission to local leaders and solicit their support; and to establish contact with potters in these villages and ascertain when the next firing would be likely to take place so that we could plan accordingly. Upon arrival in Kadiolo we were told that in addition to Sissingue (32 km north-west of Kadiolo) there are two other villages in the region where women engage in pottery production on a large scale: Doguélédougou (4–5 km south-east of Kadiolo) and Dioumaténé (about 15 km west of Kadiolo). We visited all three villages and found women active in various stages of pottery production. In addition, we witnessed a spectacular communal firing at Doguélédougou before returning to Bamako.

On the second mission we were joined by Mme Dia Oumou Dia, researcher, museum documentalist and *chef du mission*, and Youssouf Kalapo, draughtsman, from the Institut des sciences humaines in Bamako. Because our time was limited to fifteen days we chose to concentrate our efforts on the villages of Sissingué and Doguélédougou, where it seemed there were more potters working more frequently with better-quality results. During the time we spent in each village we observed and photographed most phases of the process, from the pounding of fired clay and broken pots for temper and mixing the clay to forming, decorating, burnishing, and colouring. We documented tool forms as well as the marks or signatures each woman uses to distinguish her pots from those of others. We attended several communal firings ranging from about 800 to well over 1,000 pieces at a time. This represented about three weeks of pottery making during the height of the dry season.

We also completed inventories of all the ceramic pieces in several households, obtaining information on when, how and from whom each piece was acquired, names in Senufo and Dyula, as well as intended and actual uses. I was particularly struck by just how precise our informants were able to be about the makers of the vessels and the circumstances of their acquisition. These pieces were photographed and then measured and drawn by Kalapo.

We conducted interviews with selected potters (and, in some cases, their husbands) concerning the process of pottery production, changes over time, as well as individual and family histories. The women provided information concerning prohibitions formerly adhered to, sacrifices once practised, as well as qualities in the different types of clay available. Most of our information on local history came from discussions with village elders.

During the course of the mission we purchased just over thirty pieces, including newly fired examples as well as older ones still in use and some now abandoned. In addition, we acquired examples of tools and a variety of materials, and pots at various stages of production. With the assistance and advice of our hosts, the pots were carefully loaded into and on top of the museum vehicle and secured for the ride back to Bamako. These pieces are now in the collections of the National Museum, accompanied by solid field documentation.

The challenge was then to think about the implications of the data we had collected. What could the information tell us about the history of this tradition, and of the women who were keeping it alive and vital? What could objects reveal about the past? In examining the repertoires of different potter groups, one finds certain basic shapes and functions common to virtually all ceramic traditions throughout the region. Cooking pots and water jars are ubiquitous, though variations in proportions, decorative detail, and shape suggest distinct styles. Thus while Bamana and Maninka pots tend to be robust in form, with bold, simple designs, those of the Kadiolo potters are smaller, with more delicate proportions, thinner rims, and multiple layering of decorative surface details.

A closer examination of the distribution patterns of objects that are distinctive in either form or function might reflect alternative shared histories of producers and patrons. For example, Bamana and Maninka potters produced large bowl forms known as *faga*, traditionally used for washing clothes, indigo dyeing and tanning. Consistent with the stylistic characteristics mentioned above, the ones from the Mande heartland are large, low, and wide, with a few lines impressed into the rim. They are treated to a vegetal bath direct from the firing that renders their surfaces a mottled black.

The Kadiolo potters also produced a vessel they call a *faga* (or *fagaba*, meaning 'large *faga*') but of a quite different style. These have taller, more slender proportions, with tiny feet, and often a surface textured with roulette patterns. In addition to the stylistic variance there is also an important difference in the uses to which such vessels are put by their respective patrons. In the Kadiolo area, while they may be used in a domestic context, their most important use is that of closing off the shafts of tombs in non-Moslem cemeteries. This association was very strong in the minds of several elderly Senufo women we interviewed. They claimed that the potters quietly but maliciously sing the Senufo widow's song when they begin making such a vessel, in anticipation of a quick sale. (The potters, of course, deny it.) As yet I have not found any references to any such use elsewhere, though ceramic vessels are often among burial goods and may serve as grave markers. Documenting this kind of use and association is especially urgent because as Islam becomes more and more established in rural areas these funerary practices will surely disappear. (...)

Reference

Frank, B.E. (1998) *Mande Potters and Leatherworkers: Art and Heritage in West Africa*, Washington, DC: Smithsonian Institution.

Edited extract from Frank, B.E. (2000) 'Ceramics as testaments of the past: field research and making objects speak', in Ardouin, C.D. and Arinze, E. (eds) *Museums and History in West Africa*, Washington, DC: West African Museums Programme/Smithsonian Institution, 93–104. Barbara Frank is Associate Professor of Art History and Director of Graduate Studies at the State University of New York, Stony Brook, where she continues to pursue her interests in the arts of Mali.

Chapter 6

In praise of connoisseurship

David Carrier

One might say, I have invented Poussin. I frequently think this is the chief function of the art historian, to synthesise, to concentrate, to *fix* his subject, to pull together into a unity all the disparate strands of character and inspiration and achievement that make up this singular being . . . After me, Poussin is not, cannot be, what he was before me.

(Banville 1997: 343)

Recent methodological studies tend to be highly critical of connoisseurs. 'Lacking a social conscience, Bernard Berenson sought perfection of self in aesthetic sensibility' (Brown 1979: 2). What more damning judgment of the most famous American connoisseur? And this by a sympathetic commentator. Connoisseurs are often thought to be but servants of the art dealers. This critical view is entirely mistaken. Connoisseurship is a great intellectual achievement, but in order to understand what connoisseurs do, it is necessary to link their interests with the broader concerns of art historians (see, for example, Wollheim 1987; 1973).

I start with the well-known argument of Nelson Goodman's (1976) in *Languages of Art* regarding 'Art and Authenticity' (Carrier 1979). I am not concerned with the debates about the details of his claims, nor the relationship of his discussion of connoisseurship to his more general aesthetic, or his nominalism. For my present purposes, Goodman's account provides a useful starting point for a general account of connoisseurship, and its place within art history. Goodman's argument has been much discussed by philosophers, mostly without reference to the concerns of connoisseurs, which has made it difficult to see why his claims are relevant to art historians. Place side by side two objects that appear visually indistinguishable. Even if initially the objects appear visually indiscernible, X-rays, special photography, or historical investigation may lead us to tell them apart. Any visual differences, even those initially indiscernible, may be of great aesthetic significance. (As the literal uses of the word 'see' indicate, connoisseurs are logocentric thinkers. They think it possible to *see* the visual qualities they articulate).

Because Caravaggio's early works quickly became very famous, copies were made. Then when his reputation was long eclipsed, some paintings disappeared, so identifying the originals can now be extremely difficult. *The Boy Bitten by a Lizard*, now in the National Gallery, London, has at least one very serious rival, the version of the painting acquired by Roberto Longhi, the Italian art historian who played a key role in the revival of this artist's fortunes. The Metropolitan catalogue of the 1985 *The Age of Caravaggio* exhibition, after surveying the literature, makes elaborate comparisons between those two objects. Mina Gregori writes:

> The youth's expression . . . is less savage – although it is still horrific – than in the Longhi version. In X-rays, the whites of the shirt bear comparison with passages in X-rays of the Doria *Magdalen* . . . and there are small pentimenti in the drapery around the boy's right shoulder and in the leaves of the flowers in the vase – whereas X-rays of the Longhi version show virtually no pentimenti. The execution of the Longhi picture . . . seems more incisive and cursory, and, in fact, almost aggressive in the handling and consistency of the paint the present picture differs from other securely youthful works of Caravaggio.

Describing a thought experiment like Goodman's, the catalog adds:

> The exclusion here of the [Longhi] version in the Fondazione has denied us a unique occasion for the sort of comparisons that would permit a better perhaps a definitive evaluation of the two pictures.

Goodman discussed only this special kind of forgeries, near indiscernibles. He was not really interested in connoisseurship for its own sake, for his goal is to motivate the distinction between allographic and autographic art, and so to develop a semiotic theory of visual art. In distinguishing the genuine Caravaggio, *The Boy Bitten by a Lizard*, from its near-discernible twin, the connoisseur's aim is to identify one of the group of works made by a great artist. Connoisseurs seek a systematic analysis. We value original Caravaggios highly because these paintings are made by an artist with a highly distinctive style (Gilmore 2000; Carrier 2002b). The ultimate goal is to build up a picture of the body of art made by Caravaggio. The word 'style' has become controversial in art history, for it is often associated with all the conservative aspects of connoisseurship. For my present purposes, 'style' refers to the identifiably individuating features of an artist's work, or the work of a school of artists. Just as 'red' identifies all and only red things, so 'the style of Caravaggio' identifies all and only the paintings by him. To speak of the style of Caravaggio's paintings is to assert that these are distinctive objects made by him, as distinguished from copies, forgeries, and imitations. But whereas the extension of the colour term 'red' can be independently specified, the art historian may have no practical way of providing necessary and sufficient conditions explicitly identifying the style of Caravaggio's paintings.

Although most forgeries are not near-indiscernibles such as the two versions of *The Boy Bitten by a Lizard*, Goodman's argument can be developed to provide a general characterization of connoisseurship. Giorgione's *Madonna with St. Francis and St. Liberle* (1505; Castelfranco) and Giovanni Bellini's *Madonna with Saints* (1505; Venice, S. Zaccaria) both show the enthroned Virgin at the centre, with saints on either side. Contrasting these objects is not unlike comparing the two versions of *The Boy Bitten by a Lizard*. Given two similar-looking things, the connoisseur verbalizes differences. But the goal has shifted. We now articulate, by comparison, the contrasting styles of two different artists.

Sydney J. Freedberg (1971: 79–80) argues that these paintings present quite different visual conceptions:

> In the Giorgione altar there are elements that assert existence, and convince of it, more than in the Bellini; and even more, there are elements that assert a principle of order. Both the existence and the order are, however, differently conceived. For example, in the Giorgione the shapes and stance of figures imply a heaviness of presence that is more than in Bellini, and their clothing has texture that conveys physical and optical effects like those of reality.

These differences are best understood by contrasting these two Venetian paintings:

> The imitative truth of parts of the Giorgione altar may resemble Bellini's, but the facts are related by a different principle. This is evident in the single figures, where Giorgione has connected parts he may have described precisely into an arbitrary smoothed pattern to make a purified and artificial whole.

And that contrast leads Freedberg to make some further distinctions:

> Giorgione's picture affirms a sensuous existence more compelling than in Bellini, but this existence is at the same time reformed towards an abstracting purity of shapes, of whole pictorial structure, of situation, of human types, and of their state of mind.

His aim is to place Giorgione (and the Venetian tradition) in relation to the High Renaissance. What in large part defines the style of the young Giorgione is his opposition to Bellini.

One goal of the connoisseur is to make attributions, separating the genuine paintings of an artist from early copies, works by followers, and forgeries; another is to place the genuine works in proper chronology. To reliably attribute individual works, we need a complete picture of an artist's development. We seek as complete a picture as is possible to construct from the surviving works, an account that almost everyone involved will be prepared to accept when they match the visual reasoning against the pictures. In comparing the would-be Caravaggios, the connoisseur sought to articulate differences between similar-looking paintings to attribute those paintings to different artists. The goal was to identify the style of

Caravaggio, Giorgione, and Giovanni Bellini as manifest in those works. Now the aim is to enunciate the development of the style of one artist. This too requires verbalizing relevant differences between two paintings.

Nicolas Poussin's early development is hard to reconstruct, for a number of his paintings have controversial dates and recently a number of debatable attributions have been made (Carrier 1993). Denis Mahon (1962: 76–7) argues against the view of Anthony Blunt that Nicolas Poussin's *The Inspiration of the Poet* and *Martyrdom of St. Erasmus* were done at nearly the same time:

> Certainly the placing of the forms in relation to each other is quite strikingly different, with the angular and abrupt recessional superimpositions of the one (*St. Erasmus*) contrasting forcibly with the balanced harmonies within the plane which are typical of the other . . . but in addition the individual forms themselves are conceived in a different way . . . In the *Inspiration* the light hovers gently over the forms, caressing them; a passage lit with such delicacy as that centering round Apollo's lyre is not to be found in the *St. Erasmus*, where the light strikes forcefully, often bringing out brilliant chords of colour. The scrupulous care taken to articulate the draperies of the Muse in the *Inspiration*, in which the lighting plays so helpful a part, finds no echo in the *St. Erasmus*.

Mahon's detailed comparison of these two paintings needs to be placed in context of his discussion of Poussin's stylistic development.

Unlike the two versions of *The Boy Bitten by a Lizard*, *The Inspiration of the Poet* and *Martyrdom of St. Erasmus* are very easy to tell apart. Given these two paintings have different subjects, Mahon is asking what can we infer about when they were made. Suppose a connoisseur believed that the paintings were made at about the same time. Then the differences between them would be due completely to the different subjects. If, however, the two paintings were made at different times, then there would be a second cause of their different appearances: Poussin's stylistic development. How can we distinguish between these two causes of the differences between *The Inspiration of the Poet* and *Martyrdom of St. Erasmus*? The subjects are different; they were painted at different times by an artist whose style was developing. Poussin sees art, reflects on his goals, reads, and paints. And so, as his style changes, he develops new ways of painting his subjects and identifies new subjects as paintable in his style. If we can know his development in sufficient detail, then we can determine whether he painted *The Inspiration of the Poet* and *Martyrdom of St. Erasmus* at nearly the same time, or whether the differences in those paintings are due in part also to his stylistic development. Knowing Poussin's style, we should be able to *see* the temporal relationship between these paintings.

Connoisseurs are thought to be methodologically conservative, and so too, it is said, are formalists. And so, sometimes connoisseurs are identified as formalists. But our examples from the writings of Freedberg and Mahon show that this identification of connoisseurs as formalists is mistaken. These writers say much about the content of the art they analyze. To understand Poussin, Mahon repeatedly claims, we must know how that artist adapts his style to a particular subject. Nor is there any reason in principle to link connoisseurs and formalists. A formalist could take little interest in attributions, and a connoisseur might reject formalism.

Traditional connoisseurs assume it is possible to reconstruct the development of an artist with an individual style. When Mahon sees the development of Poussin differently than Blunt, we need to choose between their claims. Noting that other experts agree with one connoisseur merely postpones the problem. If we are unsure whether the order one person sees exists, why should the fact that several people claim to see this order make the situation any better? Just as we envisage someone calling out numbers in sequence 2, 4, 6, going further because they obey a rule, so we imagine Poussin to paint additional works in his style, which thus has a rule-like generality.

It would be possible to find more than one system of rules describing all the actual paintings by Poussin. How, then, in this inevitably circular process in which the theory influences how we read the evidence, would it be possible to choose between those systems? Richard Wollheim argues that style has psychological reality. The painter worked according to the conception of style the connoisseur presents; it is not merely the invention or discovery of the connoisseur. When you count, 2, 4, 6, and so on, I plausibly infer that you know the rule, n, n + 2. But in art history, appeal to psychological reality merely postpones the problems. Mahon and Wollheim describe Poussin's paintings very differently from the artist's contemporaries. And so how, apart from looking, can we identify Poussin's style? The connoisseur, we may reasonably think, should be prepared to make new attributions. Otherwise, if we recover the concept 'Poussin style' only when we have identified independently all of the paintings, then the concept is merely empirical, and cannot be generalized. Nothing is gained by appeals to psychological reality, for that amounts to saying that the artist must have had something like our analysis in his mind. But either our analysis is visually convincing, in which case appeal to psychological reality is redundant; or it is not visually convincing, in which case appeal to psychological reality will not support the analysis. Wollheim's claim adds nothing to the defence of connoisseurship.

We can better understand this reasoning process by examining another related way that historians of art make visual comparisons. Connoisseurship of quality, as I shall call this common procedure, involves making comparisons of paintings to identify the greater work.

Comparing the versions of *Self-Portrait for Van Gogh* by Emile Bernard and Paul Gauguin (both 1888, Stedelijk Museum, Amsterdam), two roughly similar paintings, Mark Roskill (1970: 101–2) focuses on stylistic differences that come to define, also, major differences of quality:

> The most distinctive and imposing feature of the imagery in the Gauguin is the counterpoint between his fierce-eyed, full-blooded countenance and the background of flowered wall-paper . . . The whole relationship between head and background, then, suggests fierceness and primitiveness of character operating in a context of purity . . . There is no such counterpoint between images in the Bernard *Self-portrait*. The most that can be said of the relationship between Bernard's own features and the Gauguin self-portrait . . . is that the spectator is introduced to this image of Gauguin in an implied spirit of respect and defense on the part of Bernard himself . . . this is a much more timid picture than the Gauguin.

The cumulative effect is to identify enormous differences between the same subject done by two artists in contact with each other, working at exactly the same time. These two paintings with similar subjects are of very different quality.

More typically, such quality judgments involve elliptical comparisons among paintings. After identifying Willem de Kooning as 'one of the four or five most important painters in the country', in his review of that painter's first show published in *The Nation*, April 24, 1948, Clement Greenberg (1986a: 228–9) offers an elaborate historical analysis.

> A draftsman of the highest order, in using black, gray, tan and white preponderantly he manages to exploit to the maximum his lesser gift as a colorist. For de Kooning black becomes a color . . . a hue with all the resonance, ambiguity, and variability of the prismatic scale . . . de Kooning, along with Gorky, Gottlieb, Pollock, and several other contemporaries, has refined himself down to black in an effort to change the composition and design of post-cubist painting and introduce more open forms, now that the closed-form canon-the canon of the profiled, circumscribed shape-as established by Matisse, Picasso, Mondrian and Miro seems less and less able to incorporate contemporary feeling. The indeterminateness or ambiguity that characterizes some of de Kooning's pictures is caused, I believe, by his effort to suppress his facility.

Greenberg celebrates de Kooning, arguing that he thus goes beyond Matisse, Picasso, Mondrian, and Miro. Juxtaposing this de Kooning with Matisses, Picassos, Mondrians, and Miros would permit spelling out this judgment that de Kooning can better incorporate contemporary feeling.

To move from distinguishing near-indiscernibles, comparing paintings by different artists, and describing the stylistic development of one painter to this connoisseurship of the quality may seem to change the direction of analysis rather drastically. Certainly the goals change, but in these commentaries on Caravaggio, Giorgione and Bellini, and Poussin, it would be difficult to make a hard and fast distinction between description and evaluation. Contrasting two almost-indiscernible Caravaggios; comparing the Giorgione and Bellini; setting Poussin's paintings in order; this involves comparisons such as those of Roskill between Bernard and Gauguin, and Greenberg's praise of de Kooning.

Much recent analysis of connoisseurship involves hostile discussion of the most famous American connoisseur, Bernard Berenson. No doubt he was, as any reader of his lesser books or his biographies will realize, 'human, all too human.' And yet, when Greenberg (1986b: 247) describes him as 'one of America's most signal contributions to European culture . . . Mr. Berenson has brought greater clarity to a larger and essential part of the surviving past', surely that is correct. Berenson was but one of many people making such attributions; that he became the most famous, and so had his grand social role, is a great tribute to his visual and verbal skills. Art writing very often is involved, ultimately, with the art market. The net effect of much politically radical art writing – Meyer Schapiro in his early Marxist phase, or Tim Clark and Thomas Crow today – is, like Berenson's activity, inseparable from the acquisition of market value.

Crow (1996: 53) writes:

> Each of Andy Warhol's *Marilyn Diptychs* (1962) lays out a stark and
> unresolved dialectic of presence and absence, of life and death . . . The
> left-hand side is a monument; color and life are restored, but as a
> secondary and unchanging mask added to something far more fugitive.
> Against the quasi-official regularity and uniformity of the left panel, the
> right concedes the absence of its subject, openly displaying the elusive
> and uninformative trace underneath.

His distinction in kind between Warhol's early art, which 'fosters critical or subversive apprehension of mass culture and the power of the image as commodity'
(Crow 1996: 49), like Mahon's account of Poussin, sets individual pictures in a
narrative about an artist's development. In arguing for the superiority of Warhol's
early paintings, Crow, as much as Greenberg, is involved in that making of distinctions that I call connoisseurship of quality. 'Style' is a word sometimes associated in narrow ways with traditional connoisseurship. Whatever word be used, what
is required is some way of describing this circular movement back and forth from
evaluation of particular works to the body of an artist's production.

To get us to properly see the individual picture, the connoisseur may need to
draw our attention to other artworks, and to the artist's culture. His or her concerns are, thus, closely linked to those of art historians in general. When in his
justly famous account of Manet's *A Bar at the Folies-Bergère* Tim Clark (1985: 250)
writes the following, then his descriptive techniques are the same as a connoisseur's:

> The girl in the mirror does seem to be part of some . . . facile narrat-
> ive . . . But that cannot be said of the 'real' barmaid, who stands at
> the centre, returning our gaze with such evenness, such seeming lack
> of emotion or even interest . . . There is a gentleman in the mirror
> . . . Who is this unfortunate, precisely? Where is he? Where does he
> stand in relation to her, in relation to us?

Sydney Freedberg (1950) describes another picture with a mirror, the Parmigianino
Self-Portrait in Convex Mirror (1524, Vienna):

> Into this demonstration of illusionistic realism, and actually dominating
> its effect, are intermingled other motives . . . There is the very fact that
> he has chosen, as the basis for this scientific demonstration, an extreme
> complication of a problem in realistic representation . . . It is true that
> Francesco has counterfeited a real image on his panel, and that he has
> done so with remarkable scientific truth. But though the counterfeit is
> visually exact as a rendering of a thing seen, the thing seen is not in
> itself an ordinary image, but a singular distortion of objective normalcy.

Like Clark, Freedberg brings individual pictures into a cultural history. Freedberg
is said to be a formalist; but when he introduces Venetian art by noting the following, then he, as much as Clark, places the art in its larger setting.

The modern traveler still knows the maze-like illogic of the city and
the swift changes of sensation that are offered by its variety of direction, of size and shape of space, of brilliances and darkness, of silence
and sound. (Freedberg 1971: 77)

Commentary dealing with these concerns appears in the writings of modernist art
historians who would perhaps be surprised to think of themselves as connoisseurs.
In her imaginatively aggressive analysis of Alberto Giacometti's *Suspended Ball*
(1930–1931, Giacometti Foundation, Kunstmuseum, Basel) Rosalind E. Krauss (1985:
57–8; see also Carrier 2002c) argues:

An erotic machine, *Suspended Ball* is, then, like Duchamp's *Large Glass*,
an apparatus for the disconnection of the sexes, the nonfulfillment of
desire. But *Suspended Ball* is more explicitly sadistic . . . the sliding action
that visibly relates the sculpture's grooved sphere to its wedge-shaped
partner suggests not the act of caressing but that of cutting . . . In this
double gesture incarnating love and violence simultaneously one can locate
a fundamental ambiguity with regard to the sexual identity of the
elements of Giacometti's sculpture.

This comparison leads her to relate *Suspended Ball* to another Giacometti made immediately before it, *The Hour of the Traces* (whereabouts unknown):

The two sculptures are structurally connected by virtue of their shared
play with a pendant element swung from a cagelike structure . . . They
are both assimilable to Giacometti's fully elaborated accounts of his own
thoughts of sadism and violence.

And to place it in a more general account of his career:

In 1935 Giacometti's art changed abruptly . . . rejecting . . . not simply surrealism or a related connection to tribal art. At a deeper, structural level, he renounced the horizontal and everything it meant . . .
From 1935 on, he devoted himself to vertical sculpture.

Once you make allowance for the obvious differences between Giacometti's art
(and culture) and Poussin's, Krauss's procedure is very similar to Mahon's and
Roskill's. Offering a theory of Giacometti's development, she argues that *Suspended
Ball* is a better work of art than his later sculptures.

All of these accounts employ what I call interpretation by description (Carrier
1996: 97–102). Persuasively describing how he or she sees a picture, the art writer
evaluates that work of art. When, to give another example, Bernard Berenson says
of Caravaggio's *Madonna di Loreto* that 'she stoops' toward the pilgrims 'but seems
to feel the burden of the Holy Child's weight as He blesses', I count this as such
an interpretation (Berenson 1953: 27). When in the next three sentences Berenson
compares this image to paintings by Murillo and Velazquez, this seemingly unassuming account carries real art historical weight. Similarly, when in a review of a

Richard Diebenkorn retrospective I wrote, 'Diebenkorn's relation to his subjects resembles a conversation between two friends, who repeatedly re-establish a trusting relationship', I too seek to suggest how these paintings should be seen. The sense of my elliptical phrase might be spelled out by contrasting other paintings that do not establish such a relation with their subjects (Carrier 1997: 900).

In thus identifying interpretation by description, I offer no necessary and sufficient conditions. For my present purposes, it suffices to observe that art historians readily talk in these terms. Most of what is said by art writers, Alberti in the fifteenth century and critics writing in *Artforum*, is interpretation by description. Almost any art-historical description, short of identification of obviously visible physical qualities, is interpretation by description. Noting that the Parmigianino *Self-Portrait in Convex Mirror* is round, or that *A Bar at the Folies-Bergère* depicts a woman would be redundant. Everyone can see that. Explaining how these paintings use mirrors, as Freedberg and Clark do, is to interpret by description, for these art writers get us to see these artefacts in original ways. Interpretation by description essentially involves calling attention to novel ways of seeing. The dividing line between bare description and interpretation by description changes over time. When an interpretation by description becomes well enough known, as is now the case with Clark's account of this Manet, then it may seem so obvious as to constitute a mere description. But the history of interpretation of *A Bar at the Folies-Bergère* reveals that the painting was not always seen as Clark describes it. Clark's very success makes it difficult for younger readers to realize how original his analysis was.

The specialized interests of the traditional connoisseur in making attributions are pursued using the same literary skills as the art historian who writes a stylistic history, gets us to see works according to an interpretation, or offers perhaps controversial judgments of quality. Connoisseurship, thus, is an integral part of art history. When, for example, Gary Schwartz (1985: 42) describes Rembrandt's *Christ Driving the Money-changers out of the Temple* (1626, Pushkin Museum, Moscow) in the following way, he is (among other things) explaining why it is a Rembrandt.

> One of the few early history paintings with an easily identifiable subject, but so jarring in composition and colour that several art historians vehemently deny that Rembrandt could have painted it . . . Apparently in an attempt to see how far he could go compressing figures and motifs into a confined space, Rembrandt oversteps the bounds of artistic propriety.

Traditional connoisseurship and art-historical interpretation, in general, I have claimed, are the same activity, for they both involve interpretation by description. But that is not the whole story. The traditional connoisseur uses interpretation by description to get us to see the artwork a certain way. But perhaps the connoisseur need not employ interpretation by description, for in some cases it is possible to base attributions upon documentary evidence. New technologies may make it possible to change the practice of connoisseurship (Carrier 1990). Let us consider the philosophical implications of this change.

Attributions concern matters of fact. Either Caravaggio painted the London *The Boy Bitten by a Lizard* or he did not; either Poussin's *The Inspiration of the Poet* and

Martyrdom of St. Erasmus were done at nearly the same time, or they were not. Gregori and Mahon get us to see these pictures a certain way. If their claims are right, then they are true to the facts. But in general, art-historical interpretation does not involve straightforward truth to the facts. Freedberg, Clark, Crow, and Krauss are major art writers because their accounts are original and suggestive. Interpretation by description makes claims about the appearance of artworks. If we see the paintings they describe as they would have us see them, then we judge their accounts to be convincing, plausible, and suggestive. Freedberg, Clark, Crow, and Krauss are trying to get us to see paintings and sculptures certain ways. But it is not a matter of fact that their interpretations by description are true or false. It is not a fact that the girl in the mirror in Manet's *A Bar at the Folies-Bergère* is part of some facile narrative or that *Suspended Ball* is an apparatus for the disconnection of the sexes. Nor is it a matter of fact that Roskill and Greenberg correctly identify the quality of the pictures they describe.

Good interpretations, thus, are like successful jokes and convincing metaphors. Jokes and metaphors are not true or false, but they are successful or not, and original or clichéd. Interpretation by description that fails is like a joke that is not funny, or a metaphor that is unilluminating. But there are limits to these suggestive parallels. When feminist or Marxist art historians call attention to facts that were not previously properly attended to, then we see art differently. Quintilian remarks that the orator's aim is not merely to assert the facts, but to display them 'in their living truth to the eyes of the mind' (Butler 1976: 245). Deeply original art-historical analysis involves a more radical revision of our previously held ideas (Carrier 1991: 2002a).

Our analysis points to a deep difference between traditional connoisseurship and art-historical interpretation. There is a difference in kind between matters of fact and questions of appearance. If a man is generally thought attractive, then he is, for in matters of appearances there is no distinction between how things seem to be and how they actually are. But if a woman is thought to be born in Berlin, it is possible, still, that she really was born in London, for the fact of the matter may not be generally known. Interpretation by description involves getting people to see things a certain way. The successful art writer is a master of rhetoric. But, unlike interpretations, attributions cannot be judged in literary terms. Gregori's and Mahon's attributions are true or not, though it is of course possible that we may never know enough to be sure of the facts. Interpretation by description is a plausible way of making attributions because often the appearance of an object permits us to infer who made it. The appearance of Caravaggio's paintings identifies them as Caravaggios. But there is another way of making attributions, tracing the physical history of the artwork. The appearance of the painting at best provides a good guide to the facts about its origin. If in making an attribution, there is a conflict between appearances and the facts, then a judgment based on the facts always takes priority.

Traditional connoisseurs tend to believe that every object made by a major artist who has found his or her style is visually distinctive. That claim involves two nontrivial assumptions. Connoisseurs distinguish major artists from minor figures who work in an eclectic mixture of styles (only major artists are able to form a highly distinctive personal style). And they allow that major artists make prestylistic works, while looking for their style and may, if they lose that style, make poststylistic art. Connoisseurship traditionally has employed both interpretation by description and documentary information. If many of the Italian old master paintings of interest to Berenson did not have secure attributions, it would have been impossible for him to plausibly judge those works whose attribution was controversial. On one extreme view, the claim of traditional connoisseurship is that the eyes alone suffice to make judgments.

> *Thesis 1*: The direct visual evidence is sufficient alone to establish attributions and sequence of making.

In imagining that someone could make attributions, or place artworks in the correct sequence of making, using merely visual evidence, I leave aside the role of any source of information not derived simply from looking at those artworks. The visual identity and order of what an artist makes are self-evident. Identifying the exact conditions of such looking is not important so long as we can make a distinction in kind between secondary evidence, which may inform looking, and direct visual inspection.

Were Thesis 1 correct, then it would be possible to make attributions purely visually, without additional information. We would be able to identify all of the genuine Caravaggios and Poussins, and set them in the order of making, without appeal to documentary evidence. Since that extreme view is unlikely to be found convincing, connoisseurs might fall back on a weaker claim:

> *Thesis 2*: Given help with evidence from physical testing, it is possible to make attributions and establish sequences of making that are visually convincing.

In practice, many works by most famous artists have reliable attributions and datings, so much of the argumentation among connoisseurs involves sorting out a relatively small percentage of difficult cases. With Poussin, for example, the more difficult problems of attribution arise mostly with early paintings. Many canonical paintings have quite uncontroversial dating.

But perhaps Thesis 2 also is too strong and the connoisseur should settle for a much weaker claim:

> *Thesis 3*: The only reliable basis for attributions is documentary evidence — the history of a picture together with physical information not itself initially viewable under normal gallery viewing conditions.

Were traditional connoisseurship replaced by such testing, we would have something like the transition from astrology to astronomy, a movement from pseudo-science to testable techniques.

In his published commentaries, Schwartz argues that documentation evidence should be a corrective to visual impressions. That claim leaves undecided the crucial question: Must such documentation ultimately be manifest visually? In our unpublished dialogue, he took a harder line. Responding to a draft of this essay, he said:

> You completely ignore what to my mind is the essential point: that con-
> noisseurship, in contrast to criticism, lays a claim to establishing his-
> torical facts concerning the origins and authorship of the work. The
> question is: What is the relation between the kind of observations you
> quote and reliable historical reconstruction? If you cannot demonstrate
> that, you should not be pretending to be writing an apology of con-
> noisseurship.

When I questioned Schwartz about two painters he has written books about,
Pieter Saenredam and Rembrandt, he replied that they posed essentially different
problems:

> Everything makes Saenredam into a low risk case . . . He had only two
> pupils, neither of whom became a painter. For twenty-five years he was
> the only painter in Holland doing his kind of work.

Rembrandt, by contrast,

> documented nothing, did not even leave drawings for his compositions;
> he had lots of pupils whose work, according to the Rembrandt
> Research Project, he was capable of signing with his own monogram
> or signature; he practiced modes that were very popular then and later.

Knowing the appearance of Saenredam's paintings permits making good attributions; knowing the appearance of Rembrandt's pictures does not. Late Poussin,
a relatively isolated artist, was like Saenredam; no contemporary was making
similar pictures. Young Poussin, experimenting with the rich stylistic possibilities
available in Rome in the 1620s was akin to Rembrandt. If in many cases connoisseurship is replaced by appeal to historical facts, then how we understand art will
change dramatically. We might identify the works made by an artist without claiming that visual inspection permits us to see who made them.

A homely analogy suggests what might happen if visual traditional connoisseurship
were replaced by physical testing. An observer can reliably guess lengths only with
a certain precision. If we need more accurate measurements, a ruler is required.
Analogously, in looking at would-be Rembrandts or Poussins, a certain limited precision is obtained; greater accuracy may be provided with physical testing. But whether
reliable attributions can be made merely by looking depends upon the accuracy of
the needed distinctions. If, as with Saenredam, there is no need for fine accuracy,
then attributions can be made by looking. But when, as with Rembrandt and early
Poussin, adequate precision is unlikely, then only physical testing can give reliable
results.

Experts cultivate a certain mystique, but unless they make plausible testable
claims, traditional connoisseurship based primarily upon direct visual evidence will
be replaced by more accurate physical testing. Such a change is not simply the replacement of a rudimentary technology with a better technique accomplishing the same
goal. The art dealer Richard Feigen has recently displayed what the Poussin bio-
grapher Jacquest Thuillier (1995) claims is a very early painting. If given the right

information, we cannot *see* that this is one of Poussin's prestylistic paintings, then what aesthetic value could it have? If only some physical test could show that this is a Poussin, then the painting is a kind of relic, something we would value in the way that we value furniture from his studio. Could we not see the difference between a Poussin and copies or forgeries? Then why value that painting *as* an artwork?

Sometimes critics of connoisseurship appeal to Michel Foucault's famous account of the death of the author (for example, Wilson 1985). My argument takes no stand on that debate. Given that an individual produces distinctive artifacts, it is an open question whether those objects can be identified purely on the basis of their visual properties. If the objects an artist makes can only be identified by laboratory testing, using evidence that does not enter our direct visual experience, then why should we value them? A minor early Rembrandt is a fetish, for the value of such a work depends mostly upon the attribution. Connoisseurship plays a role of especial economic importance with such otherwise marginal works; paintings not visibly in a famous artist's style gain great value if the attribution is accepted. If *The Night Watch* or *The Arcadian Shepherds* are reattributed tomorrow, they still are major art, but if the Feigen Poussin loses its attribution, it likely will go back to the storeroom.

In thus explaining how traditional connoisseurship works, I cannot predict whether that technique might be replaced by physical testing. But I can explain the relationship of these techniques of making attributions to the broader goals of art historians. If the only way to measure lengths is to use intuitive visual tests, then such judgments will be subjective. Imagine a culture that only measured lengths of things some distance away, and did not juxtapose them to check judgments. If these people discovered how to make rulers, they might plausibly conclude that the nature of such judgments had changed. They would think that the old techniques, which merely judged appearances, had been replaced by ways of discovering the facts. Their judgments would not just be more accurate. Rather, their ideal of accuracy itself would change drastically. Instead of speaking of the appearance of the length of rulers, they would talk about matters of fact about the actual length of rulers.

My aim has been to open up discussion, showing how philosophy can contribute to discussion among art historians. I have raised more questions than can in this essay be fully or satisfactorily answered. In making attributions, as in life in general, the reasonable goal is to do the best that we can.

References

Banville, J. (1997) *The Untouchable*, New York: Knopf.

Berenson, B. (1953) *Caravaggio: His Incongruity and His Fame*, London: Chapman & Hall.

Brown, D.A. (1979) *Berenson and the Connoisseurship of Italian Painting*, Washington; DC: National Gallery.

Butler, H.E. (trans.) (1976) *The Institutio Oratoria of Quantilian*, Cambridge, MA: Harvard University Press and William Heinemann.

Carrier, D. (1979) 'Recent Esthetics and the Criticism of Art', *Artforum*, 18: 41–7.

Carrier, D. (1990) 'A. Brainerd, *The Infanta Adventure and the Lost Manet* (review)', *Arts* (February 1990): 112.

Carrier, D. (1991) *Principles of Art History Writing*, Philadelphia, PA: Pennsylvania State University Press.

Carrier, D. (1993) *Poussin's Paintings: A Study in Art Historical Methodology*, Philadelphia, PA: Pennsylvania State University Press.

Carrier, D. (1996) *High Art: Charles Baudelaire and the Origins of Modernism*, Philadelphia, PA: Pennsylvania State University Press.

Carrier, D. (1997) 'Whitney: Richard Diebenkom', *The Burlington Magazine*, December 1997.

Carrier, D. (2002a) 'Deep Innovation and Mere Eccentricity: Six Case Studies of Innovation in Art History', in Mansfield, E. (ed.) *Art History and Its Institutions*, New York: Routledge.

Carrier, D. (2002b) *Art and its Literature: The Philosophy of Artwriting*, New York: Allworth.

Carrier, D. (2002c) *Rosalind Krauss and American Philosophical Art Criticism: From Formalism to beyond Postmodernism*, Westport, CT: Greenwood/Praeger.

Clark, T.J. (1985) *The Painting of Modern Life: Paris in the Art of Manet and His Followers*, New York: Knopf.

Crow, T. (1996) *Modern Art in the Common Culture*, New Haven, CT: Yale University Press.

Freedberg, S.J. (1950) *Parmigianino: His Works in Painting*, Cambridge, MA: Harvard University Press.

Freedberg, S.J. (1971) *Painting in Italy 1500 to 1600*, Harmondsworth: Penguin.

Gilmore, J. (2000) *The Life of a Style: Beginnings and Endings in the Narrative History of Art*, Ithaca, NY: Cornell University Press.

Goodman, N. (1976) *Languages of Art*, Indianapolis: Hackett.

Greenberg, C. (1986a) *The Collected Essays and Criticism*, Vol. 2: *Arrogant Purpose, 1945–1949*, O'Brian, J. (ed.) Chicago: University of Chicago Press.

Greenberg, C. (1986b) *The Collected Essays and Criticism*, Vol. 3: *Affirmations and Refusals, 1950–1956*, O'Brian, J. (ed.) Chicago: University of Chicago Press, 228–9, 247.

Krauss, R.E. (1985) *The Originality of the Avant Garde and Other Modernist Myths*, Cambridge, MA: MIT Press.

Mahon, D. (1962) 'Poussiniana: Afterthoughts Arising from the Exhibition', *Gazette des Beaux-arts*, 2: 76–7.

Roskill, M. (1970) *Van Gogh, Gauguin and the Impressionist Circle*, Greenwich, CT: New York Graphic Society.

Schwartz, G. (1985) *Rembrandt: His Life, His Paintings*, New York: Viking.

Thuillier, J. (1995) *Poussin before Rome 1594–1624*, trans. Allen, C., London: Richard L. Feigen.

Wilson, J.C. (1985) 'Adriaen Isenbrant and the Problem of His Oeuvre', *Oud Holland* 109: 1–17.

Wollheim, R. (1973) *On Art and the Mind: Essays and Lectures*, London: Allen Lane.

Wollheim, R. (1987) *Painting as an Art*, Princeton, NJ: Princeton University Press.

Edited version of Carrier, D. (2003) 'In praise of connoisseurship', *The Journal of Aesthetics and Art Criticism*, 61: 159–69. David Carrier is the Champney Family Professor at Case Western Reserve University, Cleveland, Ohio, and the Cleveland Institute of Art where he is currently working on his next book, on the philosophy of the art museum.

Chapter 7

Material culture

Michael Shanks and Christopher Tilley

Types, culture and cognition

IN TRADITIONAL ARCHAEOLOGY the question of the relationship between material culture and society was addressed in a fairly limited fashion and was very closely bound up with considerations of artefact classification and the establishment of typological sequences. The attempt to establish a spatio-temporal systematics for the pigeon-holing of artefacts formed the backbone of research in Anglo-American archaeology until the relatively recent rise of the new archaeology.

Given that artefacts exhibited demonstrable variation across both time and space, one of the primary aims of traditional archaeology was to bring order to this variability by stipulating redundancies in the form of classificatory schemes often explicitly modelled on the basis of biological analogies in which artefacts were to be sorted and 'identified' in a manner equivalent to plants, animals, or mushrooms and toadstools. For example, the 1930 Pecos Conference concerned with the formulation of procedures for classifying American south-western ceramics adopted the following scheme: 'Kingdom: artefacts; Phylum: ceramics; Class: pottery; Order: basic combination of paste and temper; Ware: basic surface colour after firing; Genus: surface treatment; Type or Subtype' (Hargrave 1932: 8 cited in Hill and Evans 1972: 237). Clark notes that 'the fact that industrial and art forms are subject to evolutionary processes is a great aid when it comes to arranging them in sequence . . . [The problem is] to determine the direction in which the development has proceeded, to determine in other words whether one is dealing with progressive evolution or with a series of degeneration' (Clark 1972: 134–6, cf. Kreiger 1944: 273). One task of the archaeologist was to determine *types*, usually descriptively labelled according to the locality where first identified (e.g. Flagstaff red pottery; Folsom point; Peterborough Ware), or presumed function, or a mixture of the two (e.g. La Tène fibulae). Artefacts could then, ideally, be assigned to these type groupings on the basis of perceived similarities and differences. Different groups of artefacts, associated together in hoards, burials, settlements, votive deposits etc., could be grouped together in more inclusive entities, 'cultures'. But what did the 'types' and the 'cultures' mean in social terms?

Meaning and artefact types

Traditional archaeology provided three main answers to this question. The first largely evaded the question of social meaning altogether. Types were developed as purely classificatory devices to bring order to the immense range of archaeological materials discovered and to facilitate comparison of specimens and expedite field recording and cataloguing (Kreiger 1944: 275).

The second answer was that the types defined by the archaeologist were expressions of the 'mental templates' of their makers. (...) Rouse (1939: 15) writes: 'Types are stylistic patterns, to which the artisan tries to make his completed artefacts conform'. Compare Gifford (1960: 341–2): 'When entire cultural configurations are taken into account certain regularities are discernible that are due to the interaction of individuals and small social groups within a society, and these are observed as types. Types in this sense are material manifestations of the regularities of human behaviour (...).' The third answer, very closely related to the second, was that types and cultures primarily had meaning as historical indicators of temporal and spatial relationships between human groups. (...) The ideas of artefacts as 'types' reflecting basic ideas, mental images; preferences or culturally prescribed ways to do things, and of regularly occurring patterns of different material items as representing peoples or ethnic groups, formed the interpretative basis for assigning meaning to material culture and the archaeological record. It is represented perhaps most succinctly in the 'type-variety' concept developed in the US, initially for classifying ceramics.

European and American prehistory was, in essentials, written as the history of cultural continuity and change of types and cultures. A number of assumptions underpinned such an approach. Learning formed the basic means for cultural transmission between generations in any particular cultural group, while diffusion of ideas between discrete non-breeding populations accounted for cultural similarities and differences. This cultural transmission of ideas took place in inverse proportion to the degree of physical or social distance between them. Concomitantly spatial discontinuities in culture resulted from either natural boundaries to interaction or social value systems inhibiting the acceptance or adoption of new ideas. Internal cultural change was deemed to be essentially slow and incremental resulting either from an inbuilt dynamic or 'drift' away from previously accepted norms governing artefact production, vagaries of fashion, or technological innovation. Alternatively, obvious discontinuities in the archaeological record were explained as resulting from the development of exchange networks with other groups; migration or invasion of populations; or diffusion of radically new and powerful ideas, for example religious cults. (...)

Artefact classification

One idea underlying the development and refinement of the classificatory schemes was that the act of classification was usually held to be a neutral device and independent of theory. Classification followed data collection and once carried out could lead to inferences being made from the materials thus sorted. Material culture had a meaning or significance inherent in itself and the task of the archaeologist was to extract this meaning which was restricted, i.e. each artefact retained within itself one or a few meanings. Much debate centred on how artefacts might be *best* classified (e.g. Rouse 1960; Sears 1960) and whether these classifications were 'real' or 'ideal', i.e. whether they actually reflected the ideas of prehistoric artisans which were then discovered, or were imposed by the archaeologist (Ford 1954a, 1954b; Spaulding 1953, 1954). Because many of the typologies obviously worked, at least as limited temporal indicators, they were assumed to be in essentials correct and the 'types' and 'cultures' became canonized in the literature as *the* types and *the* cultures: 'pottery types are not primarily descriptive devices but are refined tools for the elucidation of space-time problems' (Sears 1960: 326).

As we have mentioned above, the meaning of archaeological data was its supposed direct relationship to cognitive structures collectively held by peoples or ethnic groups; but despite this interest traditional archaeology never really developed such concerns because to identify types, cultures and spatio-temporal relationships between them became ends in themselves. This was coupled with a pessimism in which it was claimed that little could be known beyond the realms of technology and the economy (Hawkes 1954; Piggott 1959: 9–12).

The cognitive and social reality of artefact taxonomies and cultures has been much disputed during the last 25 years. As regards artefact classification, it has begun to be recognized that classification is not independent of theory (Dunnell 1971; Hill and Evans 1972) and that there is no such thing as a 'best' classification. All classifications are partial and select from observed features of the data set. Attempts to create some kind of 'natural' classification, good for all purposes, and dealing with all possible variation within the data set studied is simply unattainable. Any form of classification involves the definition of significant criteria (significant to the classifier) to be used in the process of forming classes. This may involve the arrangement of these criteria in some order of importance which depends on theory or what we know or want to know. The link between classificatory systems and theoretical knowledge of the data universe to be studied is insoluble. Classifications are dependent on and derived from theory; they are not in some sense independent formal schemes which may be considered to be more or less convenient or useful. An infinite number of different classificatory systems may be developed for the same data set and there is no automatic obligation for the archaeologist to model, or attempt to model, his or her taxonomic systems on the basis of those utilized by prehistoric artisans.

Cognition and the past

Archaeological taxonomies and descriptions of the past may tell us a great deal about the manner in which the archaeologist thinks about past socio-cultural systems, but is there any reason to think that they tell us anything about the manner in which prehistoric social actors thought about their culture? Is this irrelevant anyway? One answer is provided by Eggert (1977) who makes four points:

1   A native people's way of thinking about and explaining their world should represent a starting rather than an end point for inquiry and this inquiry has to be undertaken from another (scientific) frame of reference.

2   Material forms not explicitly devised for communicative purposes, unlike language, are too ambiguous to reflect in an unequivocal manner the ideas embodied in them.

3   Cognitive systems are abstractions of the anthropologist. They are idealized and tend to subsume or ignore the considerable degree of individual variability in action sequences and thought.

4   People's conceptions of what they do and how they should act may differ markedly from their actual practices.

Eggert concludes that any attempt on the part of the archaeologist to study or infer or attempt to model taxonomic systems in terms of prehistoric cognitive systems is fundamentally misguided.

Some ethnoarchaeological studies, on the other hand, have attempted to demonstrate that cognitive systems are embodied in material culture and cannot be ignored by the archaeologist if he or she wishes to arrive at an adequate under-standing of that being investigated (e.g. Arnold 1971; Friedrich 1970; Hardin 1979, 1983). (...) Arnold's study attempts to demonstrate a clear relationship between the cognitive ethnomineralogical system used by potters in Ticul, Yucatan, and verbal, non-verbal and material aspects of processes involved in selecting and using raw materials for making pottery. He finds a correlation between certain emic ethnomineralogical categories of raw materials used to make pottery (clays, temper, etc.) and actual (etic) composition as determined by X-ray diffraction studies. However, studies such as those by Arnold and Hardin seem to fall rather short of mapping a cognitive *system* in terms of material culture patterning.

Even if an archaeologist were able to reproduce an exact replica of a prehis-toric taxonomic system, how much would this tell us? It appears to be insufficient to regard such an attempt at a reconstruction of the 'templates' of prehistoric artisans as providing an *explanation* of material culture patterning. An archaeologist duplicating a prehistoric taxonomic system would be arriving at a *description* of that system, but such a description of the manner of ordering and thinking about arte-facts is itself in need of explanation or further description in relation to social strat-egies and practices. Material culture should be regarded as not merely a *reflection* of cognitive systems and social practices but actively involved in the formation and structuring of those practices. So, we are never likely to be dealing with a simple correspondence relationship between idea and/or action and material culture form but a situation in which material culture actively mediates ideas and practices. The fact that material culture differs from language in its communicative form and effect does not require that we evaluate the communicative intent of material culture negatively, in terms of its difference from language, and conclude that material cul-ture as a communicative form is too ambiguous to repay study. Cognitive systems are, of course, attributed by the anthropologist or the archaeologist to ethnic groups and material culture patterning. Such systems are constructs; but this in no way implies that they do not exist or that the actions of individuals might be contra-dictory or variable. (...)

Style and function

In much of the literature post-dating the mid-1960s the notion of material culture as more or less directly relating to cognition or peoples was challenged or abandoned by many. A realization developed that archaeological cultures could simply not be correlated in any direct or immediate manner with ethnicity and there were in fact multiple factors affecting the nature of distributions of material culture items perceived in the archaeological record (e.g. Hodder 1978). The interpretative basis of the meaning of material culture provided by traditional archaeology was undermined. Instead, material culture was granted a fresh significance which became grafted in terms of the opposition between two dichotomous terms: style and function. Much of the debate which has taken place during the last 15 years about the relationship between material culture and the social hinges on the definition and use of these terms and whether primacy can (or should) be granted to one or the other in an understanding of the past.

Material culture: system and adaptation

(...) Binford (1962), following White (1959), redefined culture as an extrasomatic means of adaptation. Consequently the primary meaning of material culture was its role as an interface between people, the environment, and interactions of individuals regarded as components of social systems. Culture was no longer to be regarded as something shared by people but as participated in differentially. (...)

As Binford regarded material culture as an extrasomatic means of adaptation it was entirely consistent that he should regard it in wholly functional terms. (...) Binford (1965) redefined artefacts as possessing primary (utilitarian) and secondary (stylistic) functions cross-cutting morphological and decorative variation (in the case of ceramics). Primary functional variation referred to utilitarian use (e.g. the difference between a drinking vessel and a plate). Secondary functional variation referred to the social context of the production and use of material culture: 'this variation may arise from a traditional way of doing things within a family or a larger social unit, or it may serve as a conscious expression of between-group solidarity' (Binford 1972: 200). (...)

In all accounts, function has either been privileged in relation to style or style has been explained away as existing because of an inherent social function. However, specifying a social function for stylistic aspects of material culture patterning tells us virtually nothing about its specificity, for example all the multitudes of different chair forms, past or present, their shapes, decorative features, arrangements in different rooms or types of rooms. The general conclusion that may be drawn is that the term function is virtually redundant.

When we are dealing with material culture we are analysing a world of stylistic form and conceptual choice, creating things in one way rather than another. The corollary is that the archaeological record is a record of form according to specific cognitive orientations toward the world. The first stage in trying to understand material culture is to accept it as a stylistic cultural production. The second stage is to make full use of the range of variability in the material culture patterning apparent to us and not to subsume this variability under high-level generalizations. Exploiting the variability in material culture patterning is of vital importance: it gives us clues on which to hinge our statements and ensures we realize the full potential of the archaeological record.

Place a brick somewhere in London. Imagine that London represents the totality of the social relations and practices existing in a prehistoric society. The brick represents the archaeological evidence from which we have to extrapolate to come to an understanding of that past-social totality. Obviously the variability in the brick is of vital importance if we are going to understand anything at all. However, for many archaeologists, it appears as if even our solitary brick in the centre of London is too variable and complicated, so much so that high-level generalizations must be employed to further reduce the brick to a few fragments via the operation of certain methodological hammers. One of the most powerful of these hammers – the hammer of function – has already been discussed above, and is often combined with another even more powerful tool, the sledge hammer of cross-cultural generalization (e.g. Arnold 1985), which finally manages to reduce our brick to fine particles of dust. London appears to be lost.

History, structure and material culture

Perception, history and material culture

(...) All communicative media from the patterns on a pot to television and video not only transmit information but also form, package and filter it. If the medium doesn't actually constitute the message, it certainly alters it. Historically, media for communication have changed dramatically, from oral cultures in which there was no written language, script or text, to cultures where writing was the preserve of an elite minority, to the introduction of print and an increase in literacy, to the mass media electronic communicative forms of today. (...) In an oral culture it would seem to be quite plausible to regard material culture as a communicative medium of considerable importance for transmitting, storing and preserving social knowledge and as a symbolic medium for orientating people in their natural and social environment because of the relative permanence of material culture *vis à vis* speech acts. So material culture can be regarded in oral societies as a form of writing and discourse inscribed in a material medium in just the same way as words in chirographic and typographic cultures are inscribed on a page. It is then possible to go on to suggest that as a communicative discourse material culture becomes successively transformed in importance with the advent and spread of communicative media directly related to spoken language writing, printing and the mass media of today, which do not transcribe speech but actually transmit it.

With the development of mass industrial production as opposed to craft production, the role of material culture as an active symbolic transformative intervention in the social world is certainly altered. In a world capitalist economy we may be wearing jeans at the same time as a Lebanese gunman. The material form – in this case jeans – remains the same but its meaning will alter according to the context. Jeans will be consumed in different ways, appropriated and incorporated into various symbolic structures according to historical tradition and social context. In a prehistoric situation not only will the meanings differ but so will the particularity of the material form. Consequently it is possible to argue that there is likely to be a closer relationship between material form and meaning content than exists today.

Material culture, the individual and society

In considering the nature of material culture as communication, as a form of writing and silent discourse, we need some perspective on the relationship between the individual subject and society. (...) We should insist, therefore, on the logical priority of the social and the structuring of social relations in accounting for all social practices including material culture production. Material culture is in no sense to be regarded as a product of unmediated individual intentionality but as a production of the intersubjective social construction of reality. Individuals are structured in terms of the social and, concomitantly, material culture is socially rather than individually structured. (...)

Material culture and structure

(...) Saussure, the father of contemporary structuralism, in his *Course in General Linguistics* (1978), regarded the study of linguistics as one day forming part of a general science of signs. This would seem to suggest that language forms one sign system among many and that there might be a relative autonomy among different semiotic systems. Barthes, in his *Elements of Semiology* (1967), strongly criticized such a view regarding all sign systems as part of language. For him there could be no non-linguistic semiotic system. Rather than adhering either to Saussure or Barthes' position it would seem best to regard material culture as forming a system of discourse which has a relative degree of autonomy from a language, a second order type of writing which shares some essential features with linguistic systems while at the same time not being directly assimilable to, or reducible to, language. So, in what manner does material culture as a signifying system have a relative autonomy from language and what features does it share with language? The answer to this question depends, of course, on how we regard language as a signifying system.

Saussure in his *Course* viewed language as a system of signs which must be studied synchronically rather than diachronically. Each sign is made up of a signifier (sound-image or graphic equivalent) and a signified (a concept or meaning). According to Saussure the relationship between the signifier and that signified was entirely arbitrary, a matter of cultural or historical convention. Each sign in a system only had meaning by virtue of its difference from other signs. For example, badger has meaning because it is not rat, dog or pig; but its relationship with the four-legged, black and white striped creature is entirely arbitrary, a matter of convention. In Saussure's conception of a linguistic system emphasis is placed therefore on relational difference. Meaning does *not* inhere in a sign in itself but by virtue of its difference from other signs. Saussure was not particularly interested in actual speech (*parole*) but with objective structures making speech possible (*langue*), i.e. the rules underlying and structuring any particular real speech act in the world. The nature of *langue* as a system of rules lies underneath and governs the relative superficiality of day-to-day speech. If language is an exchange of messages constituted in their difference, governed by an underlying system of grammatical rules and is taken as a paradigm for social and cultural analysis, then the move made by Lévi-Strauss (1968) to view kinship as a structured exchange of mates within the confines of an abstract system of underlying unconscious rules, the economy an exchange of goods and services, politics an exchange of power and so on, is quite easy to understand. But what of material culture? If language is an exchange of messages, then material culture might be thought to act as a kind of second level back-up, mirroring in some sense this message exchange and reinforcing it by virtue of its very materiality and relative permanence.

There are two major problems with this structuralist perspective. First it systematically diverts attention from history, the manner in which people have altered and do alter their objectifications of the social. A structuralist perspective concentrates on the synchronic investigation of order, the codes underlying the order, and the significance of the experience of the order.

In archaeology formal analysis of pattern in material culture is now well established. The aim has been to investigate pattern, to establish the logic behind the patterning and establish rules for constructing the patterns. Washburn (1978, 1983) has used symmetry (repetition, rotation, reflection of a design element) as a logic lying beneath pottery decoration. Hodder (1982: 174–81) has claimed a generative grammar for the decoration of calabashes among the Sudanese Nuba, a system of rules operating on an originary cross motif, which can generate a wide variety of actually occurring calabash designs. (...)

In addition to attempts to identify rules of symmetry and design combination and space syntax, analysis of pattern or structure in archaeology has employed the use of binary oppositions such as bounded/unbounded, horizontal/vertical, left/right, hierarchical/sequential. (...) A structuralist position privileges language and this may hinder the recognition of the importance of non-verbal signifying systems. Granting priority to the verbal, and suggesting that non-verbal forms of communication merely directly mirror (inadequately) linguistic structures and forms of signification is, as Rossi-Landi (1975: 20–1) points out, 'rather like asserting the priority of digestion upon breathing (...)'.

Material culture as a coded sign system constitutes its own 'material language', tied to production and consumption. It does not simply reflect the significative structures of language in another form. Like language it is itself a practice, a symbolic practice with its own determinate meaning product which needs to be situated and understood in relation to the overall structuration of the social.

If for Saussure the relationship between the signifier and that signified is entirely arbitrary within the context of an overall system of difference, then for Derrida (1976, 1978), the later work of Barthes (1977) and for Foucault (1981) this difference can be extended infinitely. If meaning is a matter of difference and not identity, taken to its logical conclusion language cannot be held to constitute a stable closed system. Meanings of signs are always elusive, for if a sign is constituted by what it is not, by difference from other signs, there can be no final relationship between one signifier and something that is signified, as the signified is always already the signifier of another signified. Meaning is then the result of a never-ending play of signifiers rather than something that can be firmly related to a particular referent. The meaning of one sign depends on that of another; signifieds keep on changing into signifiers and vice versa. Signs confer value as much by virtue of what they are not as what they are. The concomitant of this position is that meaning in language is floating rather than fixed, dispersed along whole chains of signifiers as each becomes in effect a residue of others, a trace of language. For signs to have any capacity for meaning they must be repeatable or reproducible: something that occurs only once cannot count as a sign. The reproduction of signs constitutes part of their identity and difference but the very fact of their reproduction entails a lack of any unitary meaning or self-identity because they can always be reproduced in different contexts, changing their meaning. Signifieds always become altered by the chains of signified–signifiers in which they become embroiled through usage.

Material culture, language and practice

We want to suggest that material culture can be considered to be an articulated and structured silent material discourse forming a channel of reified expression and being linked and bound up with social practices and social strategies involving power, interests and ideology. As a communicative signifying medium material culture is quite literally a reification when compared with the relatively free-flowing rhythms of actions of individuals in the world and the spontaneity of spoken language. If we take up Saussure's notion of the diacritical sign – i.e. the sign whose value is independent of denoted objects and rests upon its insertion in a system of signs, and Derrida's deconstruction of the notion of the sign as possessing a plenitude of meaning by virtue of its relation to other signs – we arrive at what might be termed the *metacritical* sign: the sign whose meaning remains radically dispersed through an essentially open chain of signifieds–signifiers. If we conceive of material culture as embodying a series of metacritical signs then we must regard the meaning of the archaeological record as being always already irreducible to the elements which go to make up and compose that record, characterized as a system of points or units. What we will be involved with will be a search for the structures, and the principles composing those structures, underlying the visible tangibility of the material culture patterning. Our analysis must try to uncover what lies beneath the observable presences, to take account of the absences, the co-presences and co-absences, the similarities and the differences which constitute the patterning of material culture in a particular spatial and temporal context. The principles governing the form, nature and content of material culture patterning are to be found at both the level of micro-relations (e.g. a set of designs on a pot) and macro-relations (e.g. relationships between settlement and burial), but they are irreducibly linked, each forming a part of the other; hence any analysis which restricts itself to just considering one feature of the archaeological record such as an isolated study of pot design is bound to be inadequate.

Material culture can be considered to be constituted in terms of a spiralling matrix of associative (paradigmatic) and syntagmatic relations involving parallelism, opposition, linearity, equivalence and inversion between its elements. Each individual act of material culture production is at the same time a contextualized social act involving the relocation of signs along axes which define the relationships between signs and other signs. The meaning of these signs is constituted in their lateral or spatial and horizontal or temporal relations. The signs reach out beyond themselves and toward others and become amplified in specific contexts or subdued in others. Material culture does not so much signify a relationship between people and nature, since the environment is itself socially constituted, but relationships between groups, relationships of power. The form of social relations provides a grid into which the signifying force of material culture becomes inserted to extend, define, redefine, bolster up or transform that grid. The social relations are themselves articulated into a field of meaning partially articulated through thought and language and capable of reinforcement through the objectified and reified meanings inscribed in material culture. The material logic of the relationships involved in the contextual patterning of material culture may run parallel to, subvert or invert the social logic or practices involved at the sites of the production, use, exchange or destruction of artefacts. Material culture as constituted by chains of signifiers–signifieds should not be treated in a simplistic fashion as necessarily representing anything in particular, such as red ochre or use of red as symbolizing blood or pots of shape X as signifying male and pots of shape Y as signifying female, *on its own*. The signifying force of material culture depends on the structure of its interrelations, and the signification of any particular artefact or item can be seen as being intersected by the meanings of other items. So, particular objects form nodes in a grid of other objects. This follows from a view of material culture as being constituted in an open field rather than as a closed system of signs. The material culture record is a set of conjunctions, repetitions and differences, and meaning shifts across from context to context, level to level, association to association. Despite that, material culture forms part of the encoding and decoding strategies involved in the active social construction of reality helping to constitute a common cultural field and tradition along with action and speech. It would be naive to suppose that material culture expresses exactly that which might be expressed in language but in a different form. The importance of material culture as a signifying force is precisely its difference from language while at the same time being involved in a communication of meanings. Material culture forms part of the social construction of reality in which the precise status of meaning becomes conceptually and physically shifted from one register to another: from action to speech to the material. Meaning can be communicated in all these areas but the medium alters the nature and effectiveness of the message. The depth of social meaning in the world derives partly from the use of multiple channels for its transmission. Material culture constitutes an external field to the intersubjectivity of social relations and is dialectically related to them, its signifying relations affecting the constitution and transformation of the social.

Material culture may be regarded as revealing its structure and the principles which underlie it through its repetition. This is why, as has long been recognized, consistent patterning in the archaeological record is so important for understanding its nature. Material culture as a communicative discourse solidifies, encodes and reifies the social relations in which it is embedded and from which it is derived. Social action is the product of discourse and from this discourse both action and material culture arise. Material culture plays less the role of signifying social relations than acting in terms of established and fixed relations.

We can argue, therefore, that artefacts constitute a code of signs that exchange among themselves. The production, utilization and consumption of material culture on the part of the individual agent can be regarded as an act of *bricolage*. Material culture is used to organize the existence of agents and invest this existence with meaning and significance. The *bricoleur*, or handyman (Lévi-Strauss 1966, 1969), who uses odd scraps of wood, a bent saw or whatever, to do a reasonable patching up job, cannot by the nature of his or her situation create something entirely new, but is trapped by the 'constitutive sets' from which the elements came. The bricoleur is never fully in control or master of the situation with which he or she is confronted. Similarly, the agent produces and uses material culture, but is never aware of the entire system of material significations. The agent lives through the world metonymically. That which is being utilized, produced and consumed is never the individual artefact or object (although it may appear as such), but rather the entire symbolic structured system of objects or artefacts of which it forms a part; the use and production of artefacts is simultaneously the use and reproduction of the system of which they form a part.

The primary significance of material culture is not pragmatic, its utilitarian or technological use-value, but its significative exchange value. In our argument, we agree with Baudrillard (1981: 63) in suggesting that a theory of material culture simply cannot be established in terms of biological needs and their satisfaction, but must be based on a theory of signification and regarded as a symbolic production, part of the social constitution of reality:

> the empirical 'object,' given in its contingency of form, colour, material, function and discourse . . . is a myth. How often it has been wished away! But the object is *nothing*. It is nothing but the different types of relations and significations that converge, contradict themselves, and twist around it, as such – the hidden logic that not only arranges this bundle of relations, but directs the manifest discourse that overlays and occludes it.

We need to analyse artefacts in terms that go entirely beyond them, in relation to meaning structures and the social strategies to which they are related, to determine what specific place in the social is occupied by material culture as part of an overall pattern of significations. (...)

Studying material culture

Material culture and the archaeological record

We have argued for a view of material culture as a constructed network of significations, linking this position with some recent studies. Considered in terms of the archaeological record material culture obviously has boundaries and thresholds in terms of its content and internal structure. It is not reducible to, nor deducible from, a universal code because material culture is intimately linked with social praxis and it is through praxis that it comes into being as an objectification and in an objectified form. Material culture is structured in relation to a specific social totality and is historically and spatially constituted.

Individual material culture items are concrete and particular. They are, after all, empirical objects. At the same time material culture items in the archaeological record are meaningfully constituted and linked in structural relationships underlying their physical presence, forming a network of cross-references. The individual item forms part of the totality and the totality in part serves to constitute the nature of the individual artefact, its value and significance. The interrelatedness of the meaning of material culture in the archaeological record refers to the intersubjectivity of human actions. Material culture production, in any particular context, is not an isolated act but is always already established as a juncture: a relation to the material culture which already exists in a cultural tradition both spatially and temporally. Any fresh or novel material culture production is always a response to an established tradition. The space and time of material culture patterning is charged through with the space and time of the social relations to which it refers and relates. This is not quantitative space and time but lived human space and time. Meaning is distributed across space and time through repetition and difference, contextualized parallels, associations, inversions and so on. While the meaning of material culture is relatively fixed as compared with the nuances of speech, i.e. it is likely to possess fewer syntactic links, and differences between right and wrong are likely to be more clear cut than in speech, the meaning of material culture can by no means be regarded as stable. It can possess different meanings at different times and in different locations. A large tomb such as a megalith is unlikely to possess exactly the same meaning 1,000 years after it was first constructed and this point leads us on to a consideration of how we, as archaeologists, go about interpreting material culture.

Translating material culture

The past is not an eternally open site in which the archaeologist rambles around conferring meaning and significance at will. Regarding material culture as meaningfully constituted forming a signifying field inevitably involves the archaeologist in a complex process of interpretation, decoding or translation. The single most important feature of material culture is that while it is irreducibly polysemous with an indeterminate range of meanings we can't just ascribe any old meaning to it. Material culture patterning is not a reality to be questioned in the way in which a hypothethico-deductive analysis might suggest but a reality that has to be constructed in the process of translative, interpretative analysis. Gaining a representation of the significance of material culture forms a process in which the significance is achieved by making visible or drawing out certain features of the data rather than others.

In translating from the past to the present we are not trying to convey exactly the form and meaning of artefacts in terms of their significance for prehistoric social actors. They had their point of view; we have ours. Is one any better than the other? Are our categories their categories? Much archaeological discussion, particularly that concerned with erecting typologies, has concerned itself, as we discussed earlier in this chapter, with this distinction. Our present analysis of the archaeological record provides one perspective on that record, and as all material objects have to be interpreted, whether they exist in the present or the past, we cannot restrict ourselves to some arcane attempt at a recovery of original meaning for there is no such thing as original meaning given the intersubjective context of the production and use of material culture. In this the position of the archaeologist is no different from an anthropologist faced with an essentially alien culture. So we are not trying to convey form and meaning from an original, somehow untainted past context into a present-day context as accurately as possible. Such a perspective would find it hard to define the nature of its own accuracy and, therefore, could shed no light on what actually is important in the process of translating the past. In the act of translating the past we change it just as we change a text in translation from one language into another. No translation or conceptually mediated intervention would be possible if it strove for an absolute degree of identity with the original (see Benjamin 1970). Translation is always active, it changes the past while being constrained by that being translated, the foreignness, the otherness. Translation is a mode of recovering the meaning in the past, an active remembering on the part of the archaeologist. The past does not somehow form a slate which we can wipe clean since materiality is inscribed or written into it. No interpretation can ever be complete or whole or exhaust the meaning of the past because of the polysemous nature of the structured series of metacritical signs that compose it. Content and form in the past form a whole, like a banana in its skin. Our interpretations can either envelop the past like a gigantic octopus with ample tentacles to suck it in or, alternatively, can try to come to terms with the otherness through a theory-data dialectic in which we allow the data to challenge our presuppositions while at the same time not privileging that data as in standard empiricist approaches. This is in part a realization that all archaeology is essentially derivative, derived from that which it studies.

The artefact constitutes both a point of departure and a point of return. The point of return is a translation of the archaeological record into a fresh constellation. Truth does not reside in a recovery or reproduction of some supposed original meaning but in the process of the transformation of the past. The difference between a translation of the past and the empirically perceived past indicates the similarities and not vice versa. Because material culture relates to and was produced in a past social context we should not think of it as being mute and enclosed in an isolation which can only be broken by an infusion of our present consciousness. The past still speaks in its traces, in the signifying residues of the texture of the social world in which it was once located. It is up to us to articulate that past in our own speech, to come to terms with it as a vast network of signifying residues, to trace the connections down the signifying axes and place them back in our present.

Conclusion

In this paper we have argued that to try and explain material culture in functionalist terms or subsume it under cross-cultural generalizations is entirely unsatisfactory.

Instead we should be thinking in terms of human potentialities linked with social constraints rather than the asocial and the environmental. Material culture forms a set of resources, a symbolic order in practice, something drawn on in political relations, activated and manipulated in ideological systems. In other words, material culture is actively involved in the social world. We have suggested that material culture should be regarded as a social production rather than an individual creation. Conceived as a form of communication it constitutes a form of 'writing' and is located along structured axes of signification. We are not attempting to argue that material culture, in a manner analogous to language, directly represents things, features or concepts in the social world, but that it is ordered in relation to the social. The structure of this ordering is of vital significance. Material culture is polysemous, located along open systems of signified–signifiers or metacritical signs. This means that we can never exhaust or pin down its meaning once and for all. Material culture in the archaeological record consists of a set of conjunctions and repetitions with meaning shifting between different levels and contexts. Interpreting material culture might be regarded as a kind of translation which is essentially transformative and does not aim at a recovery of original meaning. Given the intersubjective context of the production and use of material culture there is no original meaning to be recovered as the meaning depends on the structured and positioned social situation of the individual.

References

Arnold, D. (1971) 'Ethnomineralogy of Ticul, Yucatan potters: ethics and emics', *American Antiquity*, 36: 20–40.

Arnold, D. (1985) *Ceramic Theory and Cultural Process*, Cambridge: Cambridge University Press.

Barthes, R. (1977) *Image, Music, Text*, New York: Hill and Wang.

Baudrillard, J. (1981) *For a Critique of the Political Economy of the Sign*, St. Louis, MO: Telos Press.

Benjamin, W. (1970) 'The task of the translator', *Illuminations*, London: Fontana.

Binford, L. (1962) 'Archaeology as anthropology', *American Antiquity*, 28: 217–25.

Binford, L. (1965) 'Archaeological systematics and the study of culture process', *American Antiquity*, 31: 203–10.

Binford, L. (1972) *An Archaeological Perspective*, London: Seminar Press.

Clark, J.G.D. (1972) *Archaeology and Society*, London: Methuen.

Derrida, J. (1976) *Of Grammatology*, Baltimore, MD: Johns Hopkins University Press.

Derrida, J. (1978) 'Structure, sign, and play in the discourse of the human sciences', *Writing and Difference*, London: Routledge and Kegan Paul.

Dunnell, R. (1971) *Systematics in Prehistory*, New York: Free Press.

Eggert, M. (1977) 'Prehistory, archaeology and the problem of ethnocognition', *Anthropos*, 72: 242–55.

Ford, J. (1954a) 'The type concept revisited', *American Anthropologist*, 56: 42–54.

Ford, J. (1954b) 'Comment on A. C. Spaulding, "Statistical techniques for the discovery of artefact types"', *American Antiquity*, 19: 390–1.

Foucault, M. (1981) 'The order of discourse', in Young, R. (ed.) *Untying the Text*, London: Routledge and Kegan Paul.

Friedrich, M. (1970) 'Design structure and social interaction: archaeological implications of an ethnographic analysis', *American Antiquity*, 35: 332–43.

Gifford, J. (1960) 'The type-variety method of ceramic classification as an indicator of cultural phenomena', *American Antiquity*, 25: 341–7.

Hardin, M. (1979) 'The cognitive basis of productivity in a decorative art style: implications of an ethnographic study for archaeologists' taxonomies', in Kramer, C. (ed.), *Ethnoarchaeology: Implications of Ethnography for Archaeology*, New York: Columbia University Press.

Hardin, M. (1983) 'The structure of Tarascan pottery painting', in Washburn, D. (ed.), *Structure and Cognition in Art*, Cambridge: Cambridge University Press.

Hargrave, L. (1932) 'Guide to forty pottery types from the Hopi country and the San Francisco mountains', *Museum of Northern Arizona Bulletin*, No. 1, Arizona.

Hawkes, C. (1954) 'Archaeological theory and method: some suggestions from the old world', *American Anthropologist*, LVI: 55–68.

Hill, J. and Evans, R. (1972) 'A model for classification and typology', in Clarke, D. (ed.), *Models in Archaeology*, London: Methuen.

Hodder, I. (ed.) (1978) *The Spatial Organization of Culture*, London: Duckworth.

Hodder, I. (1982) *Symbols in Action*, Cambridge: Cambridge University Press.

Kreiger, A. (1944) 'The typological concept', *American Antiquity*, 9: 271–88.

Lévi-Strauss, C. (1966) *The Savage Mind*, London: Weidenfeld and Nicolson.

Lévi-Strauss, C. (1968) *Structural Anthropology*, London: Allen Lane.

Lévi-Strauss, C. (1969) *Totemism*, Harmondsworth: Penguin.

Piggott, S. (1959) *Approach to Archaeology*, London: A. and C. Black.

Rossi-Landi, F. (1975) *Linguistics and Economics*, The Hague: Mouton.

Rouse, I. (1939) *Prehistory in Haiti: A Study in Method*, New Haven, CT: Yale University Publications in Anthropology, No. 21.

Rouse, I. (1960) 'The classification of artifacts in archaeology', *American Antiquity*, 25: 313–23.

Sears, W. (1960) 'Ceramic systems and eastern archaeology', *American Antiquity*, 25: 324–9.

Spaulding, A. (1953) 'Statistical techniques for the discovery of artefact types', *American Antiquity*, 18: 305–13.

Spaulding, A. (1954) 'Reply to Ford', *American Antiquity*, 19: 391–3.

Washburn, D. (1978) 'A symmetry classification of pueblo ceramic design', in Grebinger, P. (ed.) *Discovering Past Behaviour*, New York: Gordon and Breach.

Washburn, D. (1983) 'Symmetry analysis of ceramic design: two tests of the method on neolithic material from Greece and the Aegean', in Washburn, D. (ed.) *Structure and Cognition in Art*, Cambridge: Cambridge University Press.

White, L. (1959) *The Evolution of Culture*, New York: McGraw-Hill.

Edited extract from Shanks, M. and Tilley, C. (1987) *Social Theory and Archaeology*, Cambridge: Polity Press, 79–117. Michael Shanks is at Stanford University where he is Director of Metamedia Lab and Stanford Humanities Lab. Professor Chris Tilley is located at the Department of Anthropology at University College London. He has written a large number of books including *Material Culture and Text* and *Metaphor and Material Culture*. The two authors also collaborated on *Re-constructing Archaeology*.

PART TWO

The Subjective World

Introduction to Part Two

Simon J. Knell

THE READINGS IN THIS second section explore the fragmenting of the certainties of museum disciplines, collections, practices and purposes which arose with the entry of postmodernism and social theory into the museum conscience. Steve Weil, for example, and in typical fashion, ponders the vacuum that seemed to appear in the art world if artistic genius was denied. What is important here is the role of artistic quality – the notion that this can be discerned and that it is a distinguishing characteristic of the art museum. But, as he reveals, in this regard, the art museum itself was far from beyond question. For Weil, then, the museum was a starting point – accepted if not unquestioned in its values and practices; in contrast, Donald Preziosi takes one further step away from any certainty by more fundamentally questioning art and its institutions. In the extract included here, he draws a critical symbiosis between the museum and discipline. Both now appear conspiratorial as Preziosi claims a world of fictions, inventions, illusions and mythologies that captures the very essence of the contestable museum. One can almost imagine the look of puzzlement on the museum's previously self-assured face; it was as if it had woken up in another world where all its virtuous and civilising values were suddenly revealed to be the most hideous of socially unacceptable vices.

The museum did indeed find itself in another world, though the change was by no means as immediate as waking up. Museums had long been exposed to liberalising forces, and from the 1960s, one can trace the seeds of postcolonial sensibility permeating into its sensibility; indeed, if we don't attempt to homogenise the past into something fake and oppositional, these seeds of course go far back. For culture, however, postcolonialism certainly did become the most important social and intellectual change of recent decades, fundamentally affecting attitudes to collections and interpretive practices. It was accompanied by similar social changes elsewhere in society which pushed, for example, for the acceptance of multiculturalism and social inclusion. Janet Catherine Berlo and Ruth Phillips's particular contribution is one of a number in this book which reveal the impact of postcolonial attitudes on perceptions of Native American objects and communities in the United States. Here, museums were not only required to alter their beliefs and begin to deepen their understanding of the museum's intrusion into other cultures – it is not just a taking of things that matters here – they also needed to fundamentally alter their practices. Postcolonialism also fed into wider debates about cultural dispossession and repatriation. It is a project which is far from complete, and which logically must pursue a course from education of those who own the material of the dispossessed, to inclusive representation to self-determination. However, there remains a great deal of debate about the detail and the projected ideal. History and political context shape local agenda and possibilities, while global communication permits precedents to become models; together they provide museums with an ethical means to engage with a difficult inheritance as well as shape more appropriate professional practices.

In some parts of the world, postcolonialism impacted upon histories which suddenly took on a political aspect. That these histories could do so was partly a result of change that had taken place in history itself. History could no longer be seen as purely objective or factual. This change is the subject of Alan Munslow's chapter, which does not engage in a discussion of history in museums but rather ponders the role of evidence and reconstruction – surely implicit in museum representations of the past. Indeed, in the museum, as in popular and amateur history writing and television, history can be seen as unproblematic, a discipline available to anyone and not just the trained historian. No one is unaware of science's peculiar form of engagement – even if they do not understand it – but in the 'anyone can write history' world we live in it is easy to believe we can live without historiography. Munslow sees history as situated and authored, reliant not just on the marshalling of evidence but on language, objectification, culture, and so on. The 'real' is here challenged, and 'narrative' – that favourite of museum interpretation – problematic. Deconstructive or post-empiricist history fundamentally alters the historian's relationship to the past, and sees interpretation as considerably more complex and impure. This theme is further explored in later sections in critiques of American historic heritage sites and exhibitions.

It is a rather different kind of history that concerns Michael Shanks and Ian Hodder who take the practice of interpretation and disentangle its complexity. They hope that the pragmatic and inclusive will prevail over the narrow, politicised and contentious. Although focused on archaeology, interpretative practices are central to museum activity, and are invoked during collecting, management, conservation, exhibition and disposal. Shanks and Hodder's contribution is particularly useful for its clarity and utility – it ultimately aims to inform practice and to do so through a process of demystification. Unlike earlier contributions to this section, theirs is not a problematic step into the subjective but one that permits the subjective to inform and reformulate the objective. By this means they do not plummet into that pit of relativism many of their contemporaries feared: such notions are judged and managed succinctly and simply. Their handling of objectivism, for example, might be usefully compared with the critiques of Bruner, and Gable and Handler in the final section of this book, where objectivity and authenticity become complexities in historical interpretation and 'reconstruction'.

The final contribution to this section is Daniel Miller's overview of material culture studies which essentially confronts the same world facing Samdok but raises a raft of anthropological complexities in terms of objects and meanings, and more specifically ordering, tradition, materiality, symbolism, and so on. Like Shanks and Hodder, Miller encapsulates much of the philosophy which informs this Reader and which is explored further in later sections. An evangelist for the anthropological study of modern consumption and for the reinvigoration of a multidisciplinary field of material culture studies, Miller here really only uses the notion of a museum of contemporary things in order to ponder the 'farcical nature' of such an enterprise. Of course, museums have worried about this for a long time, though never seeing a farce, only lost and unfathomable opportunity. Samdok's contemporary documentation programme, however, took the bull by the horns and turned the impossible into an empirical project which categorises society and its practices. Without invalidating Samdok's documentation project, Miller's discussion illustrates how far the study of objects in society – at least as seen through anthropological eyes – has moved since the 1970s. But, Samdok had not stood still. Ensuring its validity meant that it needed to be wise to social and intellectual change, yet also, wisely, to respect the organisation's unique strengths. Eva Fägerborg, again: 'As the work became more oriented to phenomena in society, increasing efforts were made to relate it to current academic research. Theoretically, Samdok's work today reflects a movement away from the positivism behind the idea of systematic "data-catching" towards a view of the world as socially and culturally constructed. This, in turn, has shed new light on the museums' power to select and legitimate what is to be included in the collective memory of society as well as consider the role of cultural heritage in society. Consequently, collecting activities are now more influenced by reflexivity and discussions regarding how cultural heritage is produced and used.' Miller's article naturally leads us into the next section of the book.

Chapter 8

On a new foundation

The American art museum reconceived

Stephen E. Weil

IF THE ROMANTIC VISION of the artist as autonomous genius is no longer viable as one of the art museum's supporting premises, what then of the work of art itself? Putting aside the threshold question as to whether any object truly exists as a work of art in itself or simply becomes regarded as a work of art by its deliberate insertion into an 'art world' context – the question that Duchamp raised when he first began to exhibit his 'readymades' in 1916 – there still remain the questions of how such a work is to be evaluated and to what public purpose it might be put (Camfield 1989). Can the art museum – as a concept – still be supported by the interlocking premises that some works of art may be distinguished from others for their superior artistic quality, that the museum has the expertise to identify, as well as the duty to collect and/or display, these higher-quality works of art, and that such a display simply, in and by itself, may constitute a public good? Once again, each of these premises is today under fire.

One of the places where the battle has been most fiercely joined is over the issue of artistic quality. Is 'quality' an inherent characteristic of a work of art or, like beauty, does it lie not merely in the eye but ultimately in the mind – and, possibly, even in the entire social experience – of the beholder? Perhaps nobody in recent years has made the traditional case that artistic quality is a property intrinsic to works of art in more unequivocal terms than Lorenz Eitner, for many years the Chair of the Art Department at Stanford University. 'Quality resides in the object,' he said, 'and it endures as long as its physical substance' (Eitner 1975: 78). To the suggestion that artistic quality may be relative either to the time and place in which a work of art was created or to the circumstances in which the work is being perceived, Eitner responded by arguing that such quality is universal and absolute:

> The quality in a work of art is unaffected by the shifting cultural and social conditions that surround it. It may remain unrecognized over long

spans of time, but where it lives in a work of art it is forever ready to communicate itself to a beholder who comes to it with unobstructed senses . . . Quality differences intersect the varieties of content, style, and technique developed by the different cultures and periods. They have nothing to do with conformity to rules of art or standards of taste. They are unaffected by social relevance. Their durability . . . rests on the fundamental permanence of the human sensory constitution. For the experience of quality is not, I believe, a divine gift or the stirring of some mysterious special organ, but a very human response to arrangements in the work of art that are calculated by the artists, guided by age-long wisdom, to accommodate and stimulate the senses.

Eitner leaves us with this difficulty, though: neither he nor anybody else has yet been able to propose a formulation that would successfully capture what he or she means by quality (Dickie 1989). Acknowledging this, Eitner's long-time Stanford colleague Albert Elsen has suggested that, in its verbally elusive but nonetheless (to him) palpable reality, 'quality' might well be likened to obscenity in that – as Supreme Court Justice Potter Stewart observed about the latter – without being able to define it he would still know it when he saw it. Lest this might tempt one to think, however, that quality might be instantly perceptible, Elsen also suggested – the point is one on which a good number of other commentators agree – that quality must be determined over time. A work of art of quality is one, he said, with 'aesthetic durability', one that does not wear out 'its intellectual and emotional welcome' (Elson 1990: 9). In a similar vein, Meyer Shapiro noted that 'the best in art can hardly be discerned through rules; it must be discovered in a sustained experience of serious looking and judging' (Shapiro 1978: 232).

For those who hold this view, the primary role of the art museum is clear. As noted earlier, it is to distinguish works of art of greater quality from those of lesser and to make these greater-quality works accessible to the public. The late Alfred H. Barr, Jr., who all but single-handedly created the Museum of Modern Art in New York, once described the day-to-day work of the art museum in just such terms. It consisted, he said, of 'the conscientious, continuous, resolute distinction of quality from mediocrity' (Oldenburg 1977: ix). Expanding on this, the critic Hilton Kramer identified the art museum's principal purposes as twofold: first, in its role as collector, 'distinguishing and preserving what informed judgment found to be the best in art, the highest accomplishments of their kind', and second, in its role as educator, 'to aid us in understanding this distinction and in making the highest of these accomplishments a permanent part of our existence' (Kramer 1991). For a more rarefied vision of the art museum's purpose, see Marc Fumaroli (1992: 288) who saw the original purpose of the museum as 'the awakening of artistic genius through contact with works of genius, and the development of artistic taste through the careful comparison of masterpieces'.

Once more, not everybody still believes this. Some of those who doubt it argue that such an emphasis on quality is simply an extension of the nineteenth-century rationalization that an art that served no other purpose might still be of value for its own sake alone. At its most intense, they charge, this concentration on art-for-art's-sake can only lead toward a sterile formalism through which art becomes wholly divorced from life. The contemporary artist Hans Haacke (1986: 66) put it this way:

> The gospel of art for art's sake isolates art and postulates its self-sufficiency, as if art had or followed rules which are impervious to the social environment. Adherents of the doctrine believe that art does not and should not reflect the squabbles of the day. Obviously they are mistaken in their assumption that products of consciousness can be created in isolation.

By way of a necessary correction, proponents of this view urge that museums and their publics ought to concentrate not on whether a work of art is well or poorly made but on what it is about — its content or subject matter — as well as on the social conditions attendant to its production and to its public display. By no means clear, however, is the basis on which the museum would select which of many competing works of content-heavy art it ought to exhibit to the public. Would, for example, a poorly executed work that could be understood to advocate the favoured side of a political or ideological dispute be deemed preferable for public display to a better-executed work that advocated the contrary position? If so, who gets to decide which position is favoured, and what happens to the continuity of value when one decision-maker replaces another?

At an even further remove from any focus on quality is the argument that art ought not be judged merely by the acceptability of the ideology it advocates but by the degree to which it proves itself effective in translating that ideology into constructive social action. In short, does it work as an instance of agit-prop? Thus, the West Coast art magazine *High Performance*, published in association with the California Institute of the Arts, announced in an editorial in the summer of 1992 that it would no longer carry reviews of art exhibitions and performances because such reviews ultimately tend to emphasize critical determinations (i.e. critical judgments as to the work's artistic merit or quality) rather than explore the work's success or failure in terms of the artist's activist intentions. No matter how 'well done' it may be, a work of art that fails to accomplish such intentions can scarcely be said to be successful.

> There is growing feeling amongst artists and a broad range of cultural critics that it is no longer sufficient for art to express the artist's inspired creativity if that work fails to resonate beyond the art world. It is no longer enough for the work to succeed in art world terms if it fails to have relevance to the broader context in which that work is created. The artist as iconoclast is being replaced by the artist as citizen.

At its most extreme, this rejection of quality as a principal consideration in the evaluation of works of art goes beyond questioning what weight it should be given to question whether the concept is itself in any way meaningful. To the critic Benjamin H. D. Buchloh, for example, quality is fundamentally a social issue rather than an aesthetic one. The 'abstract concept' of quality, he wrote, is 'the central tool which bourgeois hegemonic culture (that is, white, male, Western culture) has traditionally used to exclude or marginalize all other cultural practices' (*Art in America*, May 1989).

In July 1990, the *New York Times'* then-critic Michael Brenson published a widely discussed article that exposed this debate over quality to a larger than art world public (Brenson 1990). In it he suggested that it was primarily those on the political left who rejected the notion of 'quality' in the visual arts while those on the political right tended to 'embrace it.' That seems, however, too simple.

Although there are undoubtedly conservative critics who have made quality central to their approach to art – the previously quoted Hilton Kramer is certainly one – the politicians of the right have been no less zealous than the artists of the left in singling out content or subject matter rather than any evaluation of quality to be the predominant element of the art that they find abhorrent. This was certainly the case in the recent controversies over the work of Andres Serrano and Robert Mapplethorpe. That Serrano's photograph *Piss Christ* might have been an image of great formal appeal availed naught in the eyes of its critics. The obscenity charges that arose from showing Mapplethorpe's photographs, likewise, were all content-based. If we look to an earlier time – back, for example, to that most deliciously ludicrous of all descriptions of modern art that Michigan's art-bashing Congressman George A. Dondero gave to the press some forty years ago – we will still find that same narrow focus on content. Listen carefully to Dondero's words:

> Modern art is Communistic because it is distorted and ugly, because it does not glorify our beautiful country, our cheerful and smiling people, and our material progress. Art which does not glorify our beautiful country in plain, simple terms that everyone can understand breeds dissatisfaction. It is therefore opposed to our government, and those who create and promote it are our enemies. (quoted in Hauptman 1973: 48)

This is scarcely the position of somebody for whom questions of artistic quality are central or even interesting. That it so faithfully parallels and almost exactly reproduces the antiformalist stance of Dondero's principal nemesis, the Stalinist Soviet Union, is, to say the least, deeply ironic (see Lehmann-Haupt 1973: 231–5). Brenson to the contrary, left and right seem indistinguishable in their insistence that works of visual art ought to be judged by what they say rather than how they say it.

Closely linked to this issue of quality is that of taste – the ability to distinguish, as Barr put it, 'quality from mediocrity.' Indeed, in the small world of the art museum, an individual may sometimes achieve considerable renown for being thought to have what is colloquially called an 'eye' – the instinctive ability to recognize in advance qualities in a work of art that those without such an eye will only much later discern. Something of the same sort happens at the institutional level. The public's perception of a particular museum's excellence will vary with what it believes to be the ability of the museum's staff to separate out, from the great mass of art that it confronts, those few examples that embody the greatest artistic value. This notion, too, has recently been challenged.

Of particular interest is a line of inquiry that was initiated by Duchamp's comment that 'taste' was really nothing more than 'a habit. The repetition of something already accepted' (Cabanne 1971: 48). If so, what would it then mean to be considered by one's peers to be a person of superior taste, to have an eye? The critic Thomas McEvilley (1991: 68) suggested an answer. If the canons of taste are 'not . . . eternal cosmic principles, but . . . transient cultural habit formations', then for somebody to be considered to be a person of superior taste, he said, would be 'for that person to sense and exercise the communal habit-system with unusual attention and sensitivity'.

Curiously, it was the economist John Maynard Keynes (1936: 156) who left us a clue as to how such a line might be taken still a step farther. In a well-known passage dealing with professional investment, Keynes likens the successful investor's choice among competing possibilities to

> those newspaper competitions in which the competitors have to pick out the six prettiest faces from a hundred photographs, the prize being awarded to the competitor whose choice most nearly corresponds to the average preferences of the competitors as a whole; so that each competitor has to pick, not those faces which he himself finds prettiest, but those which he thinks likeliest to catch the fancy of the other competitors, all of whom are looking at the problem from the same point of view. It is not a case of choosing those which, to the best of one's judgment, are really the prettiest, nor even those which average opinion genuinely thinks the prettiest. We have reached the third degree where we devote our intelligences to anticipating what average opinion expects the average opinion to be.

Is there not possibly some rough analogy here to the situation of those museum workers reputed to have so special an eye? Might it not be the case that what is actually special about them is their ability to anticipate an emerging habit-system before it becomes evident to their less sensitive and less far-sighted colleagues? Might it not even be the case that they sometimes participate in the shaping of such an emerging habit-system? These may be no less impressive talents than to be blessed with some optical superiority, but they are most certainly different ones.

The notion that mere exposure to works of art can, in and of itself, confer a moral benefit on the viewer has by now fallen to such low repute that we can pass it by with only a brief comment. Suffice it to say that such a view was still widely held in the mid-nineteenth century when the first American art museums were established. Robert Hughes quoted the following from an 1855 editorial in *Crayon*, one of the leading art magazines of its day: 'The enjoyment of Beauty is dependent on, and in ratio with, the moral excellence of the individual. We have assumed that Art is an elevating power, that it has in *itself* a spirit of morality.' Hughes's reaction to this seems exactly on point. 'We know, in our hearts,' he wrote, 'that the idea that people are morally ennobled by contact with works of art is a pious fiction. The Rothko on the wall does not turn its lucky owner into Bambi' (Hughes 1986: 220).

Moving on from these quarrels about artists and art, about taste and moral uplift, to the other category of charges to be examined – questions about the art museum itself and doubts about its importance as an institution – we find a similarly troubling erosion of what once seemed a solid cluster of premises about the museum's objectivity, value, and purpose.

Some of the accusations against the art museum will scarcely be surprising. Over the past several decades, it has been charged with being racist, sexist, elitist, largely

Eurocentric, an instrument of capitalist exploitation, and a good deal more (Berger 1990; Duncan and Wallach 1980; Chapin and Klein 1992). It is not to be expected that any enterprise of such visibility, wealth, patrician bearing, and apparent authority – an enterprise, moreover, so deeply interwoven with other aspects of American life – might be spared such charges. Neither is it to be expected that the art museum will, with respect to such matters as race and gender, in fact differ very much more than marginally from the surrounding community from which, necessarily, it draws much of its staff, many of its board members, all its volunteers, and the bulk of its financial support.

In a like manner, it is charged that the art museum is not now nor has ever been the neutral and disinterested institution that it claims to be. Notwithstanding its claims to be pure, autonomous, and beyond worldly things, it cannot be otherwise than deeply coloured by its social, economic, and political setting. Again, the artist Hans Haacke:

> Irrespective of the 'avant-garde' or 'conservative,' 'rightist' or 'leftist' stance a museum might take, it is, among other things, a carrier of socio-political connotations. By the very structure of its existence, it is a political institution . . . The question of private or public funding of the institution does not affect this axiom. The policies of publicly financed institutions are obviously subject to the approval of the supervising governmental agency. In turn, privately funded institutions naturally reflect the predilections and interests of their supporters. (quoted in Harrison and Wood 1992: 904)

Addressing the American Association of Museums' Midwest Museum Conference in September 1986, the University of Chicago's Neal Harris observed that the 'museum's voice is no longer seen as transcendent. Rather it is implicated in the distribution of wealth, power, knowledge and taste shaped by the larger social order.'

These, however, are but general charges that might be and have been made with equal validity against any large institution – certainly, for example, against the university. The art museum, however, is also charged with many more specific failings. One of the most serious of these is that it allegedly destroys – at least in aesthetic terms – the very works of art for the preservation and appreciation of which it was putatively established in the first instance. In an essay entitled 'The Problem of Museums', the poet Paul Valéry, after acknowledging that he was 'not overfond' of such institutions, laid this charge out in some detail.

The finer a work of art might be, Valéry argued, the more distinct an object it must be. It is a rarity whose creator envisioned it to be unique. To jumble such works of art together in the galleries of a museum, he said, is the equivalent of having ten orchestras playing at the same time:

> Only an irrational civilization, and one devoid of the taste for pleasure, could have devised such a domain of incoherence . . . Egypt, China, Greece, in their wisdom and refinement, never dreamed of this system of putting together works which simply destroy each other: never arranged units of

incompatible pleasure by order of number, and according to abstract principles.

This same point about the jangling interaction of the works of art gathered together in the museum's collection was made earlier in the Futurist Manifesto of 1909. Comparing the museum to a cemetery, F.T. Marinetti had suggested that they were 'identical, surely, in the sinister promiscuity of so many bodies unknown to one another. Museums: public dormitories where one lies forever beside hated or unknown beings. Museums: absurd abattoirs of painters and sculptors ferociously slaughtering each other with colour-blows and line-blows.'

While the late American artist Robert Smithson was to draw virtually the same parallel between museums and cemeteries – actually, he described museums as 'grave-yards' and 'tombs' – it was because he thought that removing works of art from the context for which they were originally created destroyed whatever vitality they might once have possessed. He wrote in 1967:

> Visiting a museum . . . is a matter of going from void to void. Hallways lead the viewer to things once called 'pictures' and 'statues'. Anachronisms hang and protrude from every angle. Blind and senseless, one continues wandering around the remains of Europe, only to end in that massive deception 'the art history of the recent past' . . . Museums are tombs . . . Painting, sculpture and architecture are finished, but the art habit continues. (Smithson 1979: 58)

In a 1972 text, Smithson again addressed what he perceived to be the devastating impact that the art museum has on a work of art:

> A work of art when placed in a [museum] gallery loses its charge, and becomes a portable object or surface disengaged from the outside world . . . Once the work of art is totally neutralized, ineffective, abstracted, safe, and politically lobotomized it is ready to be consumed by society. All is reduced to visual fodder and transportable merchandise. (Smithson 1979: 132)

In Europe, an astonishingly eclectic range of commentators have taken more or less the same position. They range from Pablo Picasso – 'Museums are just a lot of lies, and the people who make art their business are mostly impostors . . . We have infected the pictures in our museums with all our stupidities, all our mistakes, all our poverty of spirit. We have turned them into petty and ridiculous things' (quoted in Barr 1946: 274) – to the journalist/novelist Bruce Chatwin (1988: 20): 'An object in a museum case must suffer the de-natured existence of an animal in the zoo. In any museum the object dies of suffocation and the public gaze . . . Ideally, muse-ums should be looted every fifty years and the collections returned to civilization'; to the Frankfurt School critic Theodor W. Adorno. Commenting on the negative overtones of the adjective 'museumlike', Adorno (quoted by Crimp 1983: 43) observed that it is used to describe 'objects to which the observer no longer has a vital rela-tionship and which are in the process of dying. They owe their preservation more to historical respect than to the needs of the present. Museum and mausoleum are connected by more than phonetic association. Museums are the family sepulchres of works of art.'

A different twentieth-century variation on this theme is the notion that, regardless of whether they enter the museum or not, works of visual art by their very nature lose their vitality over time. The French wine merchant turned artist Jean Dubuffet (1987: 33) once likened art products to Beaujolais: 'I don't think they have a bouquet unless drunk during their first year . . . Away with all those stale canvases hanging in dreary museums . . . They *were* paintings: they no longer *are*. What is the life expectancy of an art product? Ten years? Twenty, thirty? Certainly never longer.' Dubuffet's compatriot Marcel Duchamp held a similar view. 'I think painting dies,' he said. 'After forty or fifty years a painting dies, because its freshness disappears . . . Men are mortal, pictures too' (Cabanne 1971: 67).

All these attacks on the museum and its underlying premises appear, however, as so much nit-picking in comparison with that first launched nearly a quarter-century ago and sustained ever since by the eminent French sociologist Pierre Bourdieu. Although Bourdieu's principal target has been the continental European art museum and although Bourdieu himself acknowledges that the situation may be different elsewhere, there is no question but that his charges have at least some relevance to museums in this country as well as to those on the continent.

To Bourdieu, the art museum functions principally – and he takes this to be the case as well for other institutions of high culture, including the university – as a means by which the existing class structure is reproduced in each successive generation. 'Art and cultural consumption', he wrote, 'are predisposed, consciously and deliberately or not, to fulfil a social function of legitimating social differences' (Bourdieu 1984: 7). They do so by providing occasions around which such notions as taste, inherent sensibility, and aesthetic discernment can be organized. In so doing, they participate in what Bourdieu termed the 'consecration of the social order.'

Bourdieu did not simply argue that works of art – independent of their intrinsic value – are susceptible to use by the dominant classes as a means to maintain their political and economic position. What he argued is that these works may not, in fact, have any fundamental value apart from such a use. What is designated to be art or not art, what is judged to be good art or bad, may not even be matters of taste or habit. They might, instead, be wholly arbitrary. No more may be required for a work of art to be deemed of artistic quality than that a well-educated elite is able to agree that such a value ought to be assigned to it. The critic Fredric Jameson (1986: 44) has called this aspect of Bourdieu's work 'one long implacable assault on the very rationalizations and self-justifications of culture itself.'

For Bourdieu, in the end, the point of the art museum is neither to educate and preserve (as the museum itself would traditionally claim) nor to bestow value on the art it chooses to display (as its public might think to be the case). From his survey data identifying those who do and do not visit art museums and his investigations of how those who do visit such museums respond to their visits, he concluded with some combination of bitterness and irony that the 'true function' of the museum in no way resembles what the museum claims it to be. Based on the effect that it actually produces on its visitors, the art museum's 'true function', he said, is to 'reinforce for some the feeling of belonging and for others the feeling of exclusion'.

It may be responded that Bourdieu's analysis is too reductive. The art museum is not so limited in its range of functions as he described it. Neither is the art that it exhibits. Although both may sometimes serve the purposes he proposed – nobody familiar with the American art museum can possibly deny that it may frequently serve as a site for snobbish display and social ambition – both the museum and its art can and do function in a variety of other and more important ways as well. Moreover, Bourdieu's proposition that the value to be found in art may be imputed rather than inherent need not necessarily be fatal to art's claims on public attention. The everyday life that each of us lives is laced throughout and around by any number of values that, when closely scrutinized, may prove to be nothing more than social constructs but that we nevertheless continue to find rewarding, sustaining, and even essential.

References

Barr, A.H., Jr. (1946) *Picasso: Fifty Years of His Art*, New York: The Museum of Modern Art.

Berger, M. (1990) 'Are art museums racist?' *Art in America*, 78 (September): 69–71.

Bourdieu, P. (1984) *Distinction: A Social Critique of the Judgment of Taste*, Cambridge, MA: Harvard University Press.

Brenson, M. (1990) 'Is "quality" an idea whose time has gone?', *The New York Times*, July 22.

Cabanne, P. (1971) *Dialogues with Marcel Duchamp*, New York: The Viking Press.

Camfield W.A. (1989) *Marcel Duchamp: Fountain*, Houston, TX: Houston Fine Arts Press.

Chapin, D. and Klein, S. (1992) 'The epistemic museum', *Museum News*, 71: 60–1.

Chatwin, B. (1988) *Utz*, New York: Viking Press.

Crimp, D. (1983) 'On the museum's ruins', in Foster, H. (ed.) *The Anti-Aesthetic: Essays on Postmodern Culture*, Port Townsend, Wash.: Bay Press.

Dickie, G. (1989) *Evaluating Art*, Philadelphia, PA: Temple University Press.

Dubuffet, J. (1987) 'Author's forewarning', in Dubuffet, J. and Glimcher, M. (eds) *Jean Dubuffet: Toward an Alternative Reality*, New York: Pace Publications and Abbeville Press.

Duncan, C. and Wallach, A. (1980) 'The universal survey museum', *Art History*, 3.

Eitner, L. (1975) 'Art history and the sense of quality', *Art International*, 19: 78.

Elson, A. (1990) Essay in *Bruce Beasley: An Exhibition of Bronze Sculptures* [catalogue], Sonoma, CA: Sonoma State University.

Fumaroli, M. (1992) 'What does the future hold for museums?', in *Masterworks from the Musée des Beaux-Arts, Lille*, New York: Metropolitan Museum of Art/Abrams.

Haacke, H. (1986) 'Museums, managers of consciousness', in Wallis, B. (ed.) *Hans Haacke: Unfinished Business*, New York; The New Museum of Contemporary Art.

Harrison, C. and Wood, P. (eds) (1992) *Art in Theory, 1900–1990: An Anthology of Changing Ideas*, Oxford: Blackwell.

Hauptman, W. (1973) 'The suppression of art in the McCarthy decade', *Artforum* 12.

Hughes, R. (1986) 'Afterword: art and politics', in Hobbs, R. and Woodward, F. (eds) *Human Rights, Human Wrongs: Art and Social Change*, Iowa City: University of Iowa.

Jameson, F. (1986) 'Hans Haacke and the cultural logic of postmodernism', in Wallis, B. (ed.) *Hans Haacke: Unfinished Business*, New York: The New Museum of Contemporary Art.

Keynes, J.M. (1936) *The General Theory of Employment, Interest and Money*, New York: Harcourt, Brace & World, Inc.

Kramer, H. (1991) 'The assault on the museums', *New Criterion*, 9.

Lehmann-Haupt, H. (1973) *Art under a Dictatorship*, New York: Octagon Books.

McEvilley, T. (1991) *Art and Discontent: Theory at the Millennium*, Kingston, NY: McPherson & Co.

Oldenburg, R.E. (1977) 'Foreword', in Barr, A.H. Jr., *Painting and Sculpture in the Museum of Modern Art*, New York: Museum of Modern Art.

Shapiro, M. (1978) *Modern Art: 19th and 20th Centuries*, New York: George Braziller.

Smithson, R. (1979) *The Writings of Robert Smithson: Essays with Illustrations*, New York: New York University Press.

Extract from Weil, S.E. (1995) 'On a new foundation: the American art museum reconceived', in *A Cabinet of Curiosities: Inquiries into Museums and Their Prospects*, Washington, DC: Smithsonian Institution, 81–123. Stephen Weil (1928–2005) was a specialist in art law and a senior scholar at the Smithsonian Institution's Center for Museum Studies. Possessing the lawyer's mind for penetrating the assumptions in arguments, Weil excelled as a teacher. His skills in locating debate and applying lateral thought are apparent in his books: *Rethinking the Museum and Other Meditations*, *Beauty and the Beasts*, *A Deaccession Reader* and *Making Museums Matter*.

Chapter 9

The art of art history

Donald Preziosi

THE MODERN PRACTICES of museology – no less than those of the museum's auxiliary discursive practice, art history (let us call this here *museography*) – are firmly rooted in an ideology of representational adequacy, wherein exhibition is presumed to 'represent' more or less faithfully some set of extra-museological affairs; some 'real' history which, it is imagined, pre-exists its portrayal; its re-presentation, in exhibitionary space. (...)

This essay is a meditation or reflection (the use of such words is inescapably part of that long tradition) upon the broad architectonic parameters, distinctive features, or systemic structures underlying the historical formation of art history and museology. In particular, it is an 'attempt to articulate what characterizes the *storied space* of museology in a manner which may help shed light on what may have been at stake in the origins of art history, itself a facet of a broader discursive field that might possibly be termed "museography"'. (...)

The evolution of the modern nation-state was enabled by the cumulative forma-tion of a series of cultural institutions which pragmatically allowed national mytholo-gies, and the very myth of the nation-state as such, to be vividly imagined and effectively embodied. As an imaginary entity, the modern nation-state depended for its existence and maintenance on an apparatus of powerful (and, beginning in the eighteenth century, increasingly ubiquitous) cultural fictions, principal amongst which were the *novel* and the *museum*. The origins of the professional discipline of art history, it will be argued here, cannot be understood outside of these comple-mentary developments.

The new institution of the museum in effect established an imaginary space-time and a storied space: a historically inflected or *funeous* site [a place incorporat-ing its entire history or ontogeny in its very structure]. It thereby served as a *disciplinary* mode of knowledge-production in its own right, defining, formatting, modelling, and 're-presenting' many forms of social behaviour by means of their products or relics. Material of all sorts was recomposed and transformed into component parts of the stage-machinery of display and spectacle. These worked to establish by example, demonstration, or explicit exhortation, various parameters for acceptable relations between subjects and objects, among subjects, and between subjects and their personal histories, that would be consonant with the needs of the nation-state. To be seen in the storied spaces of the museum were not only objects, but other subjects viewing objects, and viewing each other viewing. And the smile of the Mona Lisa appearing not to smile for thee.

Museums, in short, established exemplary models for 'reading' objects as traces, representations, reflections, or surrogates of individuals, groups, nations, and races and of their 'histories'. They were civic spaces designed for European ceremonial engagement with (and thus the evocation, fabrication, and preservation of) its own history and social memory (see, for examples, Mitchell 1988; Celik 1992). As such, museums made the visible *legible*, thereby establishing what was worthy to be seen, whilst teaching museum users how to read what is to be seen: how to activate social memories. Art history becomes one of the voices – one might even say a major popular historical novel – *in and of* museological space. In a complementary fashion, art history established itself as a window onto a vast imaginary universal museum, encyclopaedia, or archive of all possible specimens of all possible arts (Preziosi 1994), in relation to which any possible physical exhibit, collection, or museum would be itself a fragment or part.

Since its invention in late eighteenth-century Europe as one of the premier epistemological technologies of the Enlightenment, and of the social, political, and ethical education of the populations of modernizing nation-states, the modern museum has most commonly been constructed as an evidentiary and documentary artefact. At the same time, it has been an instrument of historiographic practice; a civic instrument for *practising* history. It constitutes in this regard a particular mode of fiction: one of the most remarkable genres of imaginative fiction, and one which has become an indispensable component of statehood and of national and ethnic identity and heritage in every corner of the world. In no small measure, *modernity itself is the museum's collective product and artefact; the supreme museographic fiction.*

What can it mean, then, to be a 'subject' in a world of 'objects' where some are legible or construed as *representative* of others because of their physical siting in the world, or the manner in which they are staged or framed? What constitutes such 'representation'? What exactly makes this possible or believable? The possibilities of representation in the modern world are grounded in much more ancient philosophical and religious traditions of thought regarding the nature of the relations between character and appearance. Nevertheless, as we shall see, there are aspects of civic and secular forms of representational adequacy and responsibility that are specific to the syntheses of modernity, being closely tied to what is made possible by the system of cultural technologies in service to, and simultaneously enabling, the nation-state.

We live in a world in which virtually anything can be staged or deployed *in* a museum, and in which virtually anything can be designated or serve *as* a museum. Although in the last two decades of the twentieth century there has appeared an immense and useful literature on museums and museology, it has also become clear that significant progress in understanding the remarkable properties, mechanisms, and effects of museological practice remains elusive. In fact it is clear that nothing less is demanded than a major rethinking of not a few historical and theoretical assumptions, and modes of interpretation and explanation. The position taken here is that the Enlightenment invention of the modern museum was an event as profound and as far-reaching in its implications as the articulation of central-point perspective several centuries earlier (and for not dissimilar reasons).

That this was truly a revolutionary social invention is increasingly clear. It was achieved abruptly in some places, and more gradually in others, as was the case with the European social revolutions that the new institution was designed to serve. The museum crystallized and transformed a variety of older practices of knowledge-production, formatting, storage, and display into a new synthesis that was commensurate with the eighteenth-century development of other modern forms of observation and discipline in hospitals, prisons, and schools (Foucault 1970, 1972; Reiss 1982). In this regard, the museum will most usefully be understood as a primary site for the manufacture of that larger synthesis constituting modernity itself; it simultaneously stands as one of its most powerful *epitomes*. (...)

Museology and museography

I identify myself in language, but only by losing myself in it like an object.

(Jacques Lacan 1977: 86)

1. Museums do not simply or passively reveal or 'refer' to the past; rather they perform the basic historical gesture of *separating out of the present* a certain specific 'past' so as to collect and recompose (to re-member) its displaced and dismembered relics as elements in a *genealogy* of and for the present. The function of this museological past sited within the space of the present is to signal alterity or otherness; to distinguish from the present an Other which can be reformatted so as to be legible in some plausible fashion as generating or *producing* the present. What is superimposed within the space of the present is imaginatively juxtaposed to it as its prologue (Certeau 1986: 3–16, 1988; Schleifer, Davis and Mergler 1992: 1–63).

This museological 'past' is thus an *instrument* for the imaginative production and sustenance of the present; of modernity as such. This ritual performance of commemoration is realized through disciplined individual and collective use of the museum, which, at the most basic and generic level, constitutes a choreographic or spatiokinetic complement or analogue to the labour of reading a novel or newspaper, or attending a theatre or show.

2. The elements of museography, including art history, are highly coded rhetorical tropes or linguistic devices that actively 'read', compose, and allegorize the past. In this regard, our fascination with the institution of the museum – our being drawn to it and being held in thrall to it – is akin to our fascination with the novel, and in particular the 'mystery' novel or story. Both museums and mysteries teach us how to solve things; how to think; and how to put two and two together. Both teach us that things are not always as they seem at first glance. They demonstrate that the world needs to be coherently pieced together (literally, re-membered) in a fashion that may be perceived as rational and orderly: a manner that, in reviewing

its steps, seems by hindsight to be natural or inevitable. In this respect, the present of the museum (within the parameters of which is also positioned our identity) may be staged as the inevitable and logical outcome of a particular past (that is our heritage and origins), thereby extending identity and cultural patrimony back into a historical or mythical past, which is thereby recuperated and preserved, without appearing to lose its mystery.

In essence, both novel and museum evoke and enact a desire for panoptic or panoramic points of view from which it may be seen that all things may indeed fit together in a true, natural, real, or proper order. Both modes of magic realism labour at convincing us that each of us could 'really' occupy privileged synoptic positions, despite all the evidence to the contrary in daily life, and in the face of domination and power.

Exhibition and art historical practice (both of which are subspecies of museography) are thus genres of imaginative fiction. Their practices of composition and narration constitute the 'realities' of history chiefly through the use of prefabricated materials and vocabularies – tropes, syntactic formulas, methodologies of demonstration and proof, and techniques of stagecraft and dramaturgy (White 1978). Such fictional devices are shared with other genres of ideological practice such as organized religion and the entertainment – that is, the containment – industries.

3. The museum is also the site for the imaginary exploration of linkages between subjects and objects; for their superimposition by means of juxtaposition. The art museum *object* may be imagined as functioning in a manner similar to an *ego:* an object that cannot exactly coincide with the subject, that is neither interior nor exterior to the subject, but is rather a permanently unstable *site* where the distinction between inside and outside, subject and object, is continually and unendingly negotiated (Butler 1993: 57–91; Grosz 1995). The museum in this regard is a stage for socialization; for playing out the similarities and differences between an *I* (or eye) confronting the *world* as object, and an *I* (or eye) confronting *itself* as an object among objects in that world – an adequation, however, that is never quite complete. See also (8) below.

4. In modernity, to speak of things is to speak of persons. The *art* of art history and aesthetic philosophy is surely one of the most brilliant of modern European inventions, and an instrument for retroactively rewriting the history of all the world's peoples. It was, and remains, an organizing concept which has made certain Western notions of the subject more vividly palpable (its unity, uniqueness, self-sameness, spirit, non-reproducibility, and so on); in this regard it recapitulates some of the effects of the earlier invention of central-point perspective.

At the same time, the art of art history came to be the paradigm of all production: its ideal horizon, and a standard against which to measure all products. In a complementary fashion, the producer or artist became the paragon of all agency in the modern world, 'As ethical artists of our own subject identities, we are exhorted to compose our lives as works of art, and to live *exemplary* lives: lives whose works and deeds may be legible as representative artefacts in their own right.'

Museography in this regard forms an intersection and bridge between religion, ethics, and the ideologies of Enlightenment governance, wherein delegation and exemplarity constitute political representation.

5. Art is both an *object* and an *instrument*. It is thus the name of what is to be *seen*, read, and studied, and the (often occluded) name of the *language* of study itself;

of the artifice of studying. As with the term 'history', denoting ambivalently a disciplined practice of writing and the referential field of that scriptural practice, *art* is the metalanguage of the history fabricated by the museum and its museographies. This instrumental facet of the term is largely submerged in modern discourse in favour of the 'objecthood' of art (Fried (1980) [1967]; Danto (1980) [1973]. What would an art historical or museological practice consist of which was attentive to this ambivalence?

As an organizing concept, as a method of organizing a whole field of activity with a new centre that makes palpable certain notions of the subject, art renarrativizes and recentres history as well. As a component of the Enlightenment project of commensurability, art became the universal standard or measure against which the products (and by extension the people) of all times and places might be envisioned together on the same hierarchical scale or table of aesthetic progress and ethical and cognitive advancement. To each people and place its own true art, and to each true art its proper position on a ladder of evolution leading towards the modernity and presentness of Europe. Europe becomes not only a collection of artworks, but the organizing *principle of collecting:* a set of objects in the museum, and the museum's vitrines themselves.

As Sir John Summerson astutely observed during his inaugural lecture at the University of Hull in 1960:

> New art is observed as history the very moment it is seen to possess the quality of uniqueness (look at the bibliographies on Picasso or Henry Moore) and this gives the impression that art is constantly receding from modern life – is never possessed by it. It is receding, it seems, into a gigantic landscape – the landscape of ART – which we watch as if from the observation car of a train . . . in a few years [something new] is simply a grotesque or charming incident in the whole – that whole which we see through the window of the observation car, which is so like the *vitrine* of a museum. Art is behind glass – the history glass.

Art, in short, came to be fielded as central to the very machinery of historicism and essentialism; the very *esperanto* of European hegemony. It may be readily seen how the culture of spectacle and display comprising museology and museography became indispensable to the Europeanization of the world: for every people and ethnicity, for every class and gender, for every individual no less than for every race, there may be projected a legitimate 'art' with its own unique spirit and soul; its own history and prehistory; its own future potential; its own respectability; and its own style of representational adequacy. The brilliance of this colonization is quite breathtaking: there is no 'artistic tradition' anywhere in the world which today is not fabricated through the historicisms and essentialisms of European museology and museography, and (of course) in the very hands of the colonized themselves.

In point of fact, art history makes colonial subjects of us all.

In other words, the Enlightenment invention of the 'aesthetic' was an attempt to come to terms with, and classify on a common ground or within the grid of a common table or spreadsheet, a variety of forms of subject-object relationships observable (or imagined) across many different societies. As object and instrument, this art is simultaneously a kind of thing, and a term indicating a certain relativization of things. *It represents one end in a hierarchized spectrum from the aesthetic to the fetishistic*: an evolutionary ladder on whose apex is the aesthetic art of Europe, and on whose nadir is the fetish-charm of primitive peoples.

6. Taking up a position from within the museum makes it natural to construe it as the very summa of optical instruments, of which the great proliferation of tools, toys, and optical games and architectural and urban experiments of the eighteenth and nineteenth centuries might then be understood as secondary servo-mechanisms and anecdotal emblems. The institution places its users in anamorphic positions 'from which it may be seen that a certain historical dramaturgy unfolds with seamless naturalism; where a specific teleology may be divined or read in geomantic fashion as the hidden figure of the truth of a collection of forms; and where all kinds of genealogical filiations may come to seem reasonable, inevitable, and demonstrable. Modernity itself as the most overarching form of identity politics.'

It is the most extraordinary of 'optical illusions' that museological space appears baldly Euclidean in this anamorphic dramaturgy. The museum appears to masquerade (but then there's no masquerade, for it's all masquerade) as a heterotopic lumber-yard or department store of alternative models of agency that might be taken up and consumed, meditated upon, imagined, and projected upon oneself or others. What one is distracted from is of course the larger picture and the *determinations* of these storied spaces: the overall social effects of these ritual performances, which (a) instantiate an ideology of the nation as but an individual subject writ large, and (b) reduce all differences and disjunctions between individuals and cultures to variations on the same; to different but commensurate versions of the same substance and identity. In such a regime, we are all relatives in this Family-of-Man-and/as-Its-Works.

7. Within the museum, each object is a trap for the gaze (Lacan 1977: 91–104). As long as our purview remains fixed in place at the level of the individual specimen, we may find it comfortable or pleasing to believe in an individual 'intentionality' at play in the production and appearance of things, as its significant and determinate, and even final, cause. Intentionality becomes the vanishing point, or explanatory horizon, of causality. It is a catalyst of the ubiquitous museological exhortation, 'let the work of art speak directly to you with a minimum of interference or distraction' (Finn 1985: 1; critiqued by Derrida 1984 and Grosz 1995: 9–24; Preziosi 1996a, 1996b).

8. The museum may also be understood as an instrument for the production of *gendered* subjects. The topologies of imaginary gender positions are among the institution's effects: the position of the museum user or operator (the 'viewer') is an unmarked analogue to that of an unmarked (usually, but not necessarily, male) heterosocial pose or position. But as an object of desire, the staged and storied museum artefact is simultaneously a simulacrum of an agental being or subject (usually, but not necessarily female) with whom the viewing subject will bond, or by whom he/she will be repelled.

In short, the superimposition of subjects and objects within the storied space of the museum creates the conditions for a blurring or complexifying of male–female gender distinctions: the museum object, in other words, is gender-ambiguous. Such an ambiguity creates the need for more distinct gender-framing. What becomes clear in the process is that all art is drag, and that *both* hegemonic and marginalized sexualities are themselves continual and repeated imitations and reiterations of their own idealizations. Just as the viewer's position in exhibitionary space is always already prefabricated and bespoken, so too is all gender (a) drag (Butler 1993; Grosz 1995).

Museology and museography are instrumental ways of distributing the space of memory. Both operate together on the relationships between the past and present, subjects and objects, and collective history and individual memory. These operations are in aid of transforming the recognized past *in* the present into a storied space wherein the past and present are imaginatively *juxtaposed*, where their virtual relationships cannot *not* be construed as succession and progression; cause and effect. Where, in other words, the illusion that the past exists in and of itself, immune from the projections and desires of the present, may be sustained.

Progress in understanding the museographical project, as well as the museology which is one of its facets, would entail taking very seriously indeed the paradoxical nature of that *virtual* object (what I elsewhere called the *eucharistic* object (Preziosi 1989: 80–121)) that constitutes and fills that space. The art of art history and its museology became an instrument for thinking representationally and historically; for imagining a certain kind of historicity commensurate with the (now universally exported) nationalist teleologies of European modernity.

References

Butler, J. (1993) *Bodies that Matter*, New York: Taylor and Francis.

Celik, Z. (1992) *Displaying the Orient: The Architecture of Islam at Nineteenth-Century Worlds Fairs*, Berkeley, CA: University of California Press.

Certeau, M. de (1986) *Heterologies: Discourse on the Other*, Minneapolis, MN: University of Minnesota Press.

Certeau, M. de (1988) *The Writing of History*, New York: Columbia University Press.

Danto, A. (1980 [1973]) 'Artworks and real things', in Philipson, M. and Gudel, P. (eds) *Aesthetics Today*, New York: Peter Smith, 322–36.

Derrida, J. (1984) *Signeponge/Signsponge*, New York: Seuil.

Finn, D. (1985) *How to Visit a Museum*, New York: Harry N. Abrams.

Foucault, M. (1970) *The Order of Things: An Archaeology of the Human Sciences*, New York: Tavistock Publications.

Foucault, M. (1972) *The Archaeology of Knowledge*, New York: Vintage Books.

Fried, M. (1980 [1967]) 'Art and objecthood', in Philipson, M. and Gudel, P. (eds) *Aesthetics Today*, New York: Peter Smith, 214–39.

Grosz, E. (1995) *Space, Time, and Perversion*, New York: Taylor and Francis.

Lacan, J. (1977) *Ecrits: A Selection*, New York: Norton.

Mitchell, T. (1988) *Colonising Egypt*, Berkeley, CA: University of California Press.

Preziosi, D. (1989) *Rethinking Art History: Meditations on a Coy Science*, New Haven, CT: Yale University Press.

Preziosi, D. (1994) 'The question of art history', in Chandler, J., Davidson, A. and Harootunian, H. (eds) *Questions of Evidence: Proof, Practice, and Persuasion across the Disciplines*, Chicago: University of Chicago Press.

Preziosi, D. (1996a) 'Brain of the earth's body', in Duro, P. (ed.) *The Rhetoric of the Frame*, Cambridge: Cambridge University Press.

Preziosi, D. (1996b) 'Museums/collecting', in Nelson, R. and Schiff, R. (eds) *Critical Terms for Art History*, Chicago: Chicago University Press.

Reiss, T.J. (1982) *The Discourse of Modernism*, Ithaca, NY: Cornell University Press.

Schleifer, R., Davis, R. Con and Mergler, N. (1992) *Culture and Cognition: The Boundaries of Literary and Scientific Inquiry*, Ithaca, NY: Cornell University Press.

White, H. (1978) *Tropics of Discourse: Essays in Cultural Criticism*, Baltimore, MD: Johns Hopkins University Press.

Edited extract from Preziosi, D. (1998) 'The art of art history', in *The Art of Art History: A Critical Anthology*, Oxford: Oxford University Press, 507–68. Donald Preziosi is Professor of Art History at UCLA where he has published extensively on the nature of art history and museums.

Chapter 10

Our (museum) world turned upside down

Re-presenting Native American arts

Janet Catherine Berlo and Ruth B. Phillips

> Our aim is the complete u'*mista* or repatriation of everything we lost when our world
> was turned upside down.
>
> (Gloria Cranmer Webster 1992)

THE VAST MAJORITY of Native American objects in private and public
collections are the legacy of the high period of colonialism that lasted from
about 1830 to 1930 (which corresponds closely with what Sturtevant (1969) called
'The Museum Age'). In the subfield of art history devoted to the arts of Native North
America, the most urgent issues surrounding the collecting and display of these objects
arise directly from the imperialist histories of their formation. Prodded by Native
American activists and academic theorists, historians and curators of Native American art are today rethinking the most fundamental questions: Who has the right
to control American Indian objects, many of which are thought by their makers
not to be art objects but instruments of power? Who has access to knowledge (even
simply the knowledge gained from gazing upon an object of power), only those
who have been initiated, or all who pass through the doors of a cultural institution?
Who has the right to say what the objects mean, and whether and how they are
displayed? And how will Native Americans, as they assume increasingly authoritative roles in museum representation, remake the museum as an institution?

Native American arts are still radically underrepresented in arts institutions,
both academic and museological, perhaps because they are less easily aligned with
Western fine-art media and genres than African, Oceanic, or Pre-Columbian objects.
Even more than other 'tribal' objects, Native American arts have largely fallen within
the domain of anthropology. The manner in which we have framed the preceding
statements, however, indicates key discursive conventions that need to be interrogated at the start of this discussion. The paradigms of art and artefact, spawned
respectively by art history and anthropology, have structured most past discussions

of collecting and display. They have been constructed as a binary pair of opposites comprising a closed system. Discussions of their problematics have tended to begin and end with the evaluation of their respective merits as representation (Phillips 1993, 1994a).

The tendency of poststructuralist and postcolonial critiques of the museum (a notable feature of which has been a focus on the representation of non-Western cultures) has been to flatten out the distinction between art and artefact. Recent critiques privilege the importance of the systemic and intertextual relationships between ethnography and art history, *both* of which were engaged by the imperialist project of inscribing relationships of power (Clifford 1988; Stocking 1985; Pearce 1992; Karp and Lavine 1991). The 'relic room' of the amateur collector of Native American archaeology, with its quilt-like arrangements of 'frames' of arrowheads, the spacious, evenly lit installation of the art gallery, the exhibition hall of a world's fair, and anthropology halls of the early twentieth century are increasingly seen as intersecting spaces for the display of objects. All invoke formal, aesthetic, and intellectual templates that are equally arbitrary in relation to other cultural systems of priority and prerogative; all privilege the sense of sight over other modes of knowing; all make captured objects available to our surveillance (Alpers 1991).

To a postcolonial sensibility, the difference between the jeweller's case and the specimen case seems, ultimately, of less significance than the wholesale historical appropriations of patrimonies and of voice that have led to the presence of these objects in Western collections. Both art-historical and anthropological practices of collecting and display have proceeded from the same tragically misconceived set of assumptions about the nature of progress and the inevitability of assimilation. They have both been forms of mortuary practice, laying out the corp(u)ses of the Vanishing American for post-mortem dissection in the laboratory, for burial in the storage room, and for commemoration in the exhibition.

On collecting

> Dollar bills cause the memory to vanish, and even fear can be cushioned by the application of government cash. I closed my eyes . . . and I saw this: leaves covering the place where I buried Pillagers, mosses softening the boards of their grave houses, once so gently weeded and tended . . . I saw the clan markers [Fleur] had oiled with the sweat of her hands, blown over by wind, curiosities now, a white child's toys.
>
> (Louise Erdrich, *Tracks*)

During the century from about 1830 to 1930, an extraordinary quantity of objects became 'toys of the white child', to be rearranged according to the taxonomies of science, or admired as objects of the aestheticizing gaze (Sturtevant 1969). One explorer, reporting in 1880 to the Department of the Interior about a Yup'ik Eskimo graveyard in southwest Alaska, announced that he had found 'a remarkable collection of grotesquely carved monuments and mortuary posts [which] would afford a rich harvest of specimens to any museum' (Petroff 1884: 133).

A few figures, chosen almost at random, indicate the astonishing scale and rapidity of this 'harvest', as it occurred inexorably across the continent. Between 1879 and 1885 the Smithsonian collected over 6,500 pottery vessels made by Pueblo women from Acoma and Zuni, villages of just a few hundred inhabitants (Batkin 1987: 16). Between 1888 and 1893 George Emmons sold over 4,000 pieces of Tlingit art to the American Museum of Natural History, including 'hundreds of supernaturally potent artworks' belonging to Tlingit shamans (Jonaitis 1988; Cole 1985). The numbers grew more staggering and more wildly disproportionate in relation to the demography of Native American communities. By 1911 Stuart Culin returned from his collecting expeditions to the West with over 9,000 artefacts for the Brooklyn Museum, including Zuni kachina masks and War God figures from sacred shrines (Fane, Jacknis and Breen 1991).

The vacuum sweep of Native American objects into public and private collections was prosecuted with a systematic thoroughness that routinized what amounted to the rape of entire cultural patrimonies. In sheer volume, the greatest collector of all was George Heye, founder of the Museum of the American Indian, the largest single repository of aboriginal objects from the Americas, with holdings numbering over a million items (renamed the National Museum of the American Indian in 1989 when it became part of the Smithsonian, where it is directed by a Native American staff (West 1993, 1994)). A journalist, describing Heye's mode of collecting, reported (only slightly tongue in cheek) that 'what George enjoyed most on his automobile trips was hunting up Indian reservations.' He was so obsessive that 'he felt that he couldn't conscientiously leave a reservation until its entire population was practically naked' (Wallace 1960).

Great violence has been done to Native American communities in the names of salvage anthropology and, since the early twentieth century, primitivist art collecting. During campaigns against Plains Indians in the second half of the nineteenth century, military officers had their Indian scouts strip the corpses of the men, women, and children they had just killed. Moccasins, drawings, and weapons became personal trophies, some of which were later sent to the Smithsonian Institution and other museums. (The traffic in personal items was not entirely one-way, however. To cite just one example of the multiple exchanges of objects between cultures: a small notebook kept by a member of the 7th Cavalry in the 1870s was captured by a Cheyenne warrior named High Bull who pulled it from its owner's dead body at the Battle of Little Big Horn in 1876. High Bull turned it into a drawing book. A few months later, High Bull was killed in battle by U.S. soldiers, who reclaimed the notebook. It came to rest in George Heye's collection.) In an (in)famous incident in British Columbia in 1922, Kwakwaka'wakw (Kwakiutl) participants in a banned potlatch were blackmailed with the threat of imprisonment into surrendering most of their ceremonial regalia to government officials. Kwakwaka'wakw anthropologist Gloria Cranmer Webster (1992: 35), daughter of one of the chiefs involved, writes: 'Those who were charged under the potlatch law did not have to serve their gaol sentences if their entire villages agreed to give up their ceremonial gear, including masks, rattles, whistles, and coppers. The federal government paid the owners a total of $1,450.50 for several hundred objects, which were crated and shipped to Ottawa. There, what came to be known as the Potlatch Collection, was divided between the Victoria Memorial Museum (later the National Museum of Man and now the Canadian Museum of Civilization) and the Royal Ontario Museum. Thirty-three artifacts were purchased by George Heye.'

Although the history of Native American art collecting is marked by many such episodes of plunder and seizure, cash transactions were most common. They cloaked the process of appropriation in a normalizing fiction. (Native American artists were also engaged in the large-scale production of objects for sale to outsiders. These objects have often been regarded as 'inauthentic' by both art and anthropology collectors (Phillips 1994b)). Acts of purchase not only ensured peaceful surrenders; they also reassured buyers of the progress Native Americans were making toward assimilation through their participation in the rituals of commodity exchange.

In the late twentieth century an official ethos of multiculturalism and pluralism has replaced assimilationism. It is cultural evolutionist ideology, not Native Americans, that has vanished. We are left, however, with vast hoards of objects acquired under what can be considered, at best, mistaken assumptions and, at worst, outright coercion. The consequences of the wholesale removal of objects have been particularly serious in North America. The totalizing construct of 'primitive art' obscures differences among colonized peoples that are worth remembering. The demographic and political imbalances affecting internally colonized minorities such as Native Americans allow the institutions of the dominant culture to exert even more effective hegemonic control than is the case in 'third-world' countries of Africa and other regions. Extensive missionization, the residential schooling system, and the pervasive reach of the media of mass communication inscribed stereotypes of 'Indianness' and led many aboriginal people to accept the myth that their very existence constituted an anachronism.

Many individual Native people were led by this process to collaborate in the process of collecting, believing that the museum was the only place in which a record of aboriginal cultures would eventually be preserved. Yet, as Edward Said has pointed out, in the imperial encounter, 'there was *always* some form of active resistance, and in the overwhelming majority of cases, the resistance finally won out' (Said 1993: xii). Although the collaborations of Native Americans facilitated anthropological collecting projects, they can also be considered a form of resistance to the nihilism that threatened. There were more overt acts of resistance as well. During Culin's 1902 trip to Zuni, for example, a village crier circulated through the town, warning people, upon pain of death, not to sell sacred objects to him (Fane, Jacknis and Breen 1991: 60).

On display

The hand that collects the basket, displays the cloth and photographs the weapon is removed from the hand that wove the basket, wore the cloth or wielded the weapon.
(Loretta Todd 1993)

The interventions of art history and art criticism in the representation of Native American objects occurred several decades later than those of anthropology, and their impact has been more evident in practices of display than in those of collecting (Berlo 1992; Rushing 1992; Rubin 1995; Rushing 1995). The paradigm of 'primitive art', no less than that of the scientific specimen, trains the gaze on the object; the museum, as Svetlana Alpers has argued, is first and foremost a way of seeing

(Alpers 1991). Yet pluralism invokes emic (indigenous) perspectives on objects. For many aboriginal peoples the most important thing about an object may be the way in which it restricts the gaze. The vision-inspired paintings on Plains shields, among the most visually attractive and tautly designed examples of Plains graphic art, were sacred to their owners; though displayed on stands, they were normally hidden by a painted cover. Many Pueblo figural paintings and sculptures were sequestered in the semisubterranean kiva, a space often restricted to initiated males.

Part of the postcolonial Native American agenda has been the outright removal of certain classes of objects from the kind of democratic exposure enjoined by the art gallery or museum. The most well-known case is the repatriation of Zuni *Ahayu:da* (war-god images). These simple, abstract male figures have a visual eloquence that has appealed to many twentieth-century artists (Rubin 1985: 29–32); more import-ant, they are among the most sacred of Zuni religious icons, and their place is in remote open-air hillside shrines where they are supposed to weather and return to the elements. (There, the Zuni say, their power works for all humankind (Ferguson and Martza 1990; Merrill, Ladd and Ferguson 1993).) Since the historic moment in 1978 when the Zuni Tribal Council prevented Sotheby Parke Bernet from auc-tioning one of these sacred figures, more than fifty *Ahayu:da* have been repatriated to the Zuni people from collections as diverse as the Denver Art Museum, the Smithsonian, the University of Maine, some private collections, and the Brooklyn Museum. The idea of the removal of significant art objects from museums, where they have resided for perhaps a century, strikes terror into the hearts of some curators and art historians. Yet, as Zuni councilman Barton Martza has observed, 'white society must learn that some of our traditional culture is for Zunis only' (Ferguson and Martza 1990: 11). Although this is perhaps the hardest lesson for the dominant culture to accept, it is by no means an isolated example. The same message emerges from the interventions of a number of Iroquois faith keepers and political leaders in relation to *Hadui* (False Face) masks worn by traditional Iroquois healers. These masks, regarded as the most important sculptural products of Iroquois carvers, have long been identified by scholars as canonical objects of Iroquois 'art'. Many contemporary Iroquois object strenuously to their presence in public museum displays and have successfully called for their removal to restricted storage areas.

On addressing the problematics

> But they can't fool me. In those basement rooms without windows or in spacious labs with bright lights, when no one is looking, they throw their heads back, eyes close and fingers touch; fragile threads, polished stone and massive masks. For a moment their hands – the collector, the cataloger, the curator, the anthropologist – have become the hands before, the hands that shaped and prayed.
>
> (Loretta Todd 1993)

Michael Baxandall has described the museum exhibition as a field in which at least three agents are independently in play – makers of objects, exhibitors of made objects, and viewers of exhibited made objects. He observes that each of the three agents is playing a different game in the field (Baxandall 1991). Yet an observant ethnographer of Native American art history and museology today, trying to track the rules of representation as we move toward the end of the century, would certainly discover that there are, in fact, many more players than this, and the number of rule books has proliferated well beyond Baxandall's estimate. In Native American art-historical practice, the makers of objects and the exhibitors of objects increasingly will find themselves at odds if long-term and meaningful collaboration on every level of the curatorial process does not take place, and if they cannot redefine their legitimate common interest in objects. This has been occurring in many places with results that may disturb the comfortable routines of the museum but that will ultimately offer new and stimulating perspectives on objects that museums hold.

The history of violence done to Native American communities by the collecting projects of our forebears, whether in the name of science, art, or sentimental commemoration, informs almost the entire corpus of Native American objects on which art-historical study has depended. Far-reaching new policies and legislative acts that regulate museum practice and allow Native Americans to reclaim or otherwise gain access to much that was removed from their communities are now in force in the United States and Canada. At this moment it is urgent that we consider the benefits of empowerment and of collaboration as much as the difficulties, for this historical unfolding, unless scholars can address it honestly and constructively, has the potential to silence art-historical work. We have to accept, first of all, that scholars and aboriginal people will not always agree in their readings of objects, that different forms of authority will be recognized and different facts privileged. Access to objects will also change, not always in conformity with late twentieth-century Western standards of equity (Nicks 1992). But, as the return of collections and individual objects proceeds, a different kind of access will become available. When art-historical researchers revisit objects in Native American communities, they will find them differently presented, embedded in different texts from which much can be learned. The community perspective may well be more continuous with the historical and cultural truths that originally shaped the objects (Clifford 1991; Jonaitis and Inglis 1994).

Objects matter in cultural process, especially among peoples who have not relied on written texts for the recording of knowledge. Stripped bare of their traditional objects of use, beauty, and power, Native American communities have suffered interruptions of historical memory, paralysing failures in the generational transfer of political and sacred power, and the cessation of organic growth in many ancient stylistic and iconographic traditions (McMaster and Martin 1992). Gloria Cranmer Webster's words, with which we opened this essay, link the past with the future:

> We do not have a word for repatriation in the Kwak'wala language. The closest we come to it is the word u'mista, which describes the return of people taken captive in raids. It also means the return of something important. We are working towards the u'mista of much that was almost lost to us. The return of the potlatch collection is one u'mista. The renewed interest among younger people in learning about their cultural history is a kind of u'mista. The creation of new ceremonial gear to replace that held by museums is yet another u'mista. We are taking back, from many sources, information about our culture and our history, to help

us rebuild our world which was almost shattered during the bad times. Our aim is the complete *u'mista* or repatriation of everything we lost when our world was turned upside down, as our old people say. (Webster 1992: 11)

The *u'mista* of confiscated Kwakwaka'wakw art remains one of the most important contemporary examples of the re-emplacement in a Native American community of objects displaced earlier in the century. In their new locations at the U'mista Centre at Alert Bay, British Columbia, and at the Cape Mudge Museum on nearby Vancouver Island, they are presented in ways that differ not only from standard, non-Native museums but also from the way they would have been seen in these communities in the 1920s (for example, they are not in glass cases, and they are grouped according to the order in which they appear in a potlatch, rather than according to Western taxonomies. In other words, today aboriginal people often 'museumize' their objects too.) At the Cape Mudge Museum, masks and other objects are periodically removed and refurbished so that they can be worn in potlatches. The incremental changing of the objects that occurs as a result of use – anathema to Western conservation practices – are acceptable because Kwakwaka'wakw beliefs locate ownership primarily in the mental concept behind the object and in rights of reproduction, and only secondarily in the object itself. Nevertheless, the repatriation of historical objects has been an essential step in permitting the rearticulation of such principles of indigenous knowledge, many of which are in danger of being forgotten. It has also set in motion a new cycle of artistic production and reproduction (Ostrowitz 1993). The insights gained from this process, both by Native and non-Native parties to it, have already resulted in the re-presentation of Kwakwaka'wakw objects in urban museums serving largely non-Native audiences that more accurately reflect the ways in which contemporary Native Americans understand their own heritage (Jonaitis 1991). The dismantling of the imperialist legacy of collecting and display has only just begun, but it is already clear that the old illusion of ideal panoptical vision has been shattered. The partial views that replace it offer insights into the meanings of objects that more accurately reflect the multiple ways of knowing that are emerging in the late twentieth century.

References

Alpers, S. (1991) 'The museum as a way of seeing', in Karp, I. and Lavine, S.D. (eds) *Exhibiting Cultures: The Poetics and Politics of Museum Display*, Washington, DC: Smithsonian Institution Press, 25–32.

Batkin, J. (1987) *Pottery of the Pueblos of New Mexico, 1700–1940*, Colorado Springs: Taylor Museum of the Colorado Fine Arts Center.

Baxandall, M. (1991) 'Exhibiting intention: some preconditions of the visual display of culturally purposeful objects', in Karp, I. and Lavine, S.D. (eds) *Exhibiting Cultures: The Poetics and Politics of Museum Display*, Washington, DC: Smithsonian Institution Press, 33–41.

Berlo, J.C. (1992) 'Introduction: the formative years of Native American art history', in Berlo, J.C. (ed.) *The Early Years of Native American Art History*, Seattle: University of Washington Press, 1–21.

Clifford, J. (1988) 'On collecting art and culture', *The Predicament of Culture*, Cambridge: Cambridge University Press.

Clifford, J. (1991) 'Four northwest coast museums: travel reflections', in Karp, I. and Lavine, S.D. (eds) *Exhibiting Cultures: The Poetics and Politics of Museum Display*, Washington, DC: Smithsonian Institution Press, 212–54.

Cole, D. (1985) *Captured Heritage: The Scramble for Northwest Coast Artifacts*, Seattle: University of Washington Press.

Fane, D., Jacknis, I. and Breen, L. (1991) *Objects of Myth and Memory: American Indian Art at the Brooklyn Museum*, Seattle: Brooklyn Museum.

Fenton, W. (1989) 'Return of eleven Wampum belts to the Six Nations Iroquois Confederacy on Grand River, Canada', *Ethnohistory*, 36: 392–410.

Ferguson, T.J. and Martza, B. (1990) 'The repatriation of Zuni *Ahayu:da*', *Museum Anthropology*, 14(2): 7–15.

Jonaitis, A. (1988) *From the Land of the Totem Poles: The Northwest Coast Indian Art Collection at the American Museum of Natural History*, New York: American Museum of Natural History.

Jonaitis, A. (ed.) (1991) *Chiefly Feasts: The Enduring Kwakiutl Potlatch*, New York: American Museum of Natural History.

Jonaitis, A. and Inglis, R. (1994) 'Power, history, and authenticity: the Mowachat whalers' Washing Shrine', in Torgovnick, M. (ed.) *Eloquent Obsessions: Writing Cultural Criticism*, Winston-Salem, NC: Duke University Press, 157–84.

Karp, I. and Lavine, S.D. (eds) (1991) *Exhibiting Cultures: The Poetics and Politics of Museum Display*, Washington, DC: Smithsonian Institution Press.

Merrill, W.L., Ladd, E.J. and Ferguson, T.J. (1993) 'The return of the *Ahayu:da*: lessons for repatriation from Zuni Pueblo and the Smithsonian Institution', *Current Anthropology*, 34: 523–67.

Nicks, T. (1992) 'Partnerships in developing cultural resources: lessons from the Task Force on Museums and First Peoples', *Culture*, 12: 87–94.

Ostrowitz, J. (1993) 'Trailblazers and ancestral heroes: collaboration in the representation of a native past', *Curator*, 36: 50–65.

Pearce, S.M. (1992) *Museums, Objects and Collections: A Cultural Study*, Washington, DC: Leicester University Press.

Petroff, I. (1884) *Report on the Population, Industries, and Resources of Alaska*, Tenth Census (1880) Washington, DC: US Department of the Interior.

Phillips, R.B. (1993) 'How museums marginalise: naming domains of inclusion and exclusion', *Cambridge Review*, 64: 6–10.

Phillips, R.B. (1994a) 'Fielding culture: dialogues between art history and anthropology', *Museum Anthropology*, 63: 39–46.

Phillips, R.B. (1994b) 'Why not tourist art?: Significant silences in Native American museum collections', in Prakash, G. (ed.) *After Colonialism: Imperial Histories and Post-Colonial Displacements*, Princeton, NJ: Princeton University Press, 98–125.

Powell, P. (1975) 'High Bull's victory roster', *Montana: The Magazine of Western History*, 25: 14–21.

Rubin, W. (ed.) (1995) *'Primitivism' in Twentieth Century Art: Affinity of the Tribal and the Modern*, New York: Museum of Modern Art.

Rushing, W.J. (1992) 'Marketing the affinity of the primitive and the modern: René d'Harnoncourt and "Indian Art of the United States"', in Berlo, J.C. (ed.) *The Early Years of Native American Art History*, Seattle: University of Washington Press, 191–236.

Rushing, W.J. (1995) *Native American Art and Culture and the New York Avant-Garde, 1910–1950*, Austin, TX: University of Texas Press.

Said, E. (1993) *Culture and Imperialism*, New York: Vintage.

Stocking, G. (ed.) (1985) *Objects and Others: Essays on Museums and Material Culture*, Madison, WI: University of Wisconsin Press.

Sturtevant, W. (1969) 'Does anthropology need museums?', *Proceedings of the Biological Society*, 82: 619–50.

Todd, L. (1993) 'Three moments after "Savage Graces"', *Harbour*, 3: 57–62.

Wallace, K. (1960) 'A reporter at large: Slim-Shin's monument', *New Yorker*, Nov. 19: 106.

Webster, G.C. (1992) 'From colonization to repatriation', in McMaster, G. and Martin, L. (eds) *Indigena: Contemporary Native Perspectives*, Hull, Quebec: Canadian Museum of Civilization.

West, W.R., Jr. (1993) 'Research and scholarship at the National Museum of the American Indian: the new inclusiveness', *Museum Anthropology*, 17: 5–8.

West, W.R., Jr. (1994) 'Cultural resources center to house NMAI collection', *Native Peoples*, 7: 66.

First published as Berlo, J.C. and Phillips, R.B. (1995) 'Our (museum) world turned upside down: re-presenting Native American Arts', *The Art Bulletin*, 77: 6–10. Janet Catherine Berlo is currently Professor of Art History and Visual and Cultural Studies at the University of Rochester where her interests include museum representations of indigenous peoples and Native North American visual cultures. Ruth Phillips holds the Canadian Research Chair in Modern Culture at Carlton University, Ottawa, where she studies culture contact and colonization in order to contribute to new museological and academic representations of First Nations art.

Chapter 11

History as deconstruction

Alun Munslow

THE HISTORY PROFESSION is not starkly divided between deconstruction-ists and the reconstructionist/constructionist mainstreams, not least because, as we have seen, there are active debates that cut across all positions, and most historians presuppose the use of narrative at least as the vehicle for conveying historical knowledge if not for creating it. But it is on this very point that there is still a broad division between those who think self-consciously about the nature and particular role of narrative in the practice of the craft, what I have designated as the deconstructive consciousness, and those who view the reconstruction of the past as primarily a skilled engagement with the evidence and who think, therefore, that there is little to dispute about its written form as history. As I have indicated, this division focuses on how content and form relate, specifically the extent to which historical knowledge and explanation are the function primarily of evidence placed in context or the aesthetics and structure of narrative discourse.

Conservative reconstructionist historians do not accept empiricism as only one of several competing modes of knowing the past. They reject all other methods of historical interpretation, especially those that smack of an ideology of which they disapprove, e.g. Marxism, cultural materialism, Hegelianism, bourgeois liberalism, or whatever. Historians in the mainstreams prefer to view history as primarily a *practice* – the craft of history (Poster 1982: 120; Goldstein 1994; Dean 1994). It is perceived as a technique of non-ideological discovery (Megill 1979: 451). What is challenged by the deconstructive historical consciousness is this belief that historical investigation can offer a peculiarly empiricist historical litmus test of knowledge, emphasising instead the belief that the past is only ever accessible to us as a textual representation – 'the past' translated into 'history'. From a deconstructive perspective on the significance of language and narrative structure, I will now address each of the four questions in turn.

Epistemology

As a consequence of the post-structuralist challenge to empiricism and the correspondence theory of meaning we are confronted by what, at first blush, appears to
be the discomforting notion that there is no access to knowledge except through
the murky and dangerous waters of language. Historians as a group respond to this
by refusing to explore its implications. In spite of Derrida's and Barthes' warnings,
historians generally continue to rely on the commonsense notion that they will locate
the knowable external presence to the text in the context. This is the investment
the discipline has in referentiality – a referent for each word and consequently a
precise meaning to be discovered. The problem is that such a fixation makes it very
difficult to view narratives for what they are: meaningful historical explanations
in themselves, rather than plain *vehicles* with which to explain the past as it actually
happened. In order to pursue this we need to know more about how narrative works
in epistemological terms.

This opening up of historical analysis to questions of rhetoric is found in the
work of Hayden White and other philosophers and historians like F.R. Ankersmit,
Hans Kellner, Jörn Rüsen and Keith Jenkins. The deconstructive historical consciousness suggests that history written by working historians should explicitly acknowledge and, when appropriate, explore its emplotted or prefigured form. What is
argued for is that the analysis of style, genre and narrative structure, more usually
associated with fictional literature, be applied to the understanding of the historian's
sources *and* written interpretations. Although this approach emerges from structuralism's early concern with the arbitrary nature of language, history produced
within the deconstructive consciousness has a much wider range of concerns.
Reconstructionist historians choose, however, to keep both structuralism and historical deconstruction at arm's length by regarding the written form of the past as
somehow not especially relevant to the reconstruction and explanation of the past
as it actually was. Although they applaud precision in the use of language and recognise its limitations, the importance of language-use in its broadest explanatory sense
remains secondary to the discovery of true origins, causal analysis and contextualism.

As I have already indicated, the early seventeenth-century positivist legacy of
Francis Bacon has remained the controlling metaphor of twentieth-century historical study even at the practical realist centre. History becomes genuinely problematic
only when historians draw untenable inductive inferences, shape history for their
ideological/political purposes or, what for a few is worse, dabble in the nether world
of hypothesis-making. History should be *like* science to the extent that science is
the study of the real world 'out there', is factual not speculative, empirical rather
than *a priori*, verifiable, anti-hypothetical, ideologically neutral and, above all, non-
impositionalist and objective. Consequently, the fundamental implication of the
theories of postmodernism for history – its demise as a legitimate discipline – is
unacceptable.

Questioning history as an empirical project ought not, in fact, be a problem
for historians. If we accept that there are no master narratives – such as history
proper assumes itself to be – then, as Lyotard says, there is no inside track to reality. Questioning the epistemological basis of history, however, cuts deep into the
mind of historians. It concerns the objectivity with which the historian deals with

sources and then writes up a disinterested interpretation tracing and explaining origins and causes. While most historians would not argue that historical method is scientific, there remains this strong sense of being rationally and objectively in touch with a potentially understandable, causally 'analysable and truthful past' (Beard 1934, 1935). To argue otherwise is simply to cease to be a historian.

The leading critic of what we might loosely call traditional history is Michel Foucault. In accepting the German philosopher Friedrich Nietzsche's reaction against the certainty of the empiricism of the second half of the nineteenth century, Foucault's attack on history is less directed towards the post-structuralist indeterminacy of language, but rather more against the manner in which historians believe in the recovery of the truth of the past (Koshar 1993). Foucault challenges the belief that historians can effectively step outside history, capture the context, and be object-ive – arguing instead that all written history is an act of creation through the narrative impositionalism of the historian as he/she emplots the data, and this act is to some degree the ideological product of the age in which he/she lives.

Foucault's critique of history as a legitimate discipline is paralleled by the French cultural critic Roland Barthes. Building on the distinction between *histoire*, in which events seemingly tell themselves without the intrusion of a narrator, and *discourse*, which is overtly self-conscious and authorial, in his essay 'The discourse of history' Barthes contests history's dependence on the correspondence between evidence, the designation of historical facts and the 'reality effect' of 'objective' history as created in the historian's written interpretation (Barthes 1967). Barthes suggests that written history is only another narrative, effectively collapsing the story dis-course distinction. As Barthes' interpreter Stephen Bann comments, the 'rhetorical analysis of historical narrative . . . cannot grant to history, *a priori*, the mythic status which differentiates it from fiction' (Bann 1981: 5).

In his defence of narrative in 'The discourse', Barthes strikes at the very exist-ence of history as an epistemology. History, he notes, is usually 'justified by the principles of "rational" exposition' but he asks 'does this form of narration really differ, in some specific trait, in some indubitably distinctive feature, from imagin-ary narration, as we find it in the epic, the novel, and the drama?' (Barthes 1967: 7). He goes on to challenge the authority of the historian based on his/her access to the sources by emphasising that the real work of history resides in their translation (Barthes describes this as utterance) into a narrative of historical interpretation. Barthes' challenge takes the shape of a critique of the structure of the historian's discourse. The examples he offers include the historian's traditional deployment of lots of detail amid the minutiae of events. In the history of art this is the *trompe l'œil* principle whereby fine detail is intended to create a sense of reality. Barthes' challenge also extends to how historians complicate chronology by compressing time in a few pages, flipping back and forward through the past. Barthes' further probes the historian's unspoken claim to omniscience – the process; whereby the historian absents him/herself from the discourse to create the impression of realism through direct access to the referent – from where, as Barthes says,

> there is in consequence a systematic deficiency of any form of sign refer-
> ring to the sender of the historical message. The history seems to be
> telling itself all on its own. This feature . . . corresponds in effect to

the type of historical discourse labelled as 'objective' (in which the historian never intervenes) . . . On the level of discourse, objectivity – or the deficiency of signs of the utterer – thus appears as a particular form of imaginary projection, the product of what might be called the referential illusion, since in this case the historian is claiming to allow the referent to speak all on its own. (Barthes [1967] 1981: 11)

The epistemological status of historical discourse is thus conventionally affirmed and asserted. The historical fact is privileged by being placed in the specially reserved position of a superior claim to truthfulness, as warranted by both a plain language and an independent research methodology and as supported in the notes and references – the scaffolding of proper historical methodology. Barthes goes on to suggest that this illusory correspondence between plain language, historical evidence and historical truth is also to be found in realist novels which similarly appear objective because they too have suppressed the signs of the 'I' in their narrative.

Barthes is claiming that historians play a confidence trick because of the way in which we use the trope of the real – in effect the Elton method – to wring historians out of history and presume to get to the reality of the past. Barthes is suggesting that history is performing an epistemological trick through which the referent is placed in a privileged world of the real beyond arbitrary signification. As he says, 'The historian is not so much a collector of facts as a collector and relator of signifiers; that is to say, he organises them with the purpose of establishing positive meaning' (Barthes 1981: 16). While most mainstream historians accept an organising role for the historian, they draw the line at this deconstructive vision which holds that there can be no objectivity in selection of material, and that all judgements about what to include or exclude are based on ideology, preferred narrative structures, and the limitations of the signifier–signified–sign relationship. Barthes' deconstructionist point is that the historian deliberately confuses or conflates the signified with the referent, producing a signifier–referent correspondence, hence Barthes' warning that 'in "objective history" the "real" is never more than an unformulated signified, sheltering behind the apparently all-powerful referent. This situation characterises what we might call the *realistic effect*' (Barthes [1967] 1981: 16). This is similar to Foucault's idea that all discourses are at best perspectives that produce *truth effects*. This is not so much anti-referentialism as a recognition of referentialism's boundaries.

Most historians refuse to view the real as only a truth-effect, given the profession's continuing investment in the independence of the discipline and the traditional Western belief in reason and rationality (logocentrism). In so doing we fail to acknowledge that the narrative description of historical facts is integral to our proof of those facts. Barthes comments that by instituting 'narration as the privileged signifier of the real', historical truth emerges as the composite of 'careful attention to narration', and the 'abundance of . . . "concrete details"'. He concludes that 'Narrative structure, which was originally developed within the cauldron of fiction (in myths and the first epics) becomes at once the sign and the proof of reality' (Barthes [1967] 1981: 18). These are concerns that influenced Hayden White, among others, to explore the rhetorical dimension to writing history, and have posed a question mark over narrative structure and the impositions it makes on writing history (White 1984). Regardless of Barthes' argument that history is at best a fudged-up performative and unavoidably ideological, mainstream historians still insist that they work in a discipline that aspires to a high degree of correspondence with the past as it actually was and that narrative is a vehicle for report rather than the primary (if flawed) medium of explanation. Deconstructionist historians, however, are driven to ask what kind of epistemological status can the sorts of stories historians tell have, and what have they the right to claim, by virtue of their narrative form (Norman 1991)?

Evidence

There are two related questions raised by deconstructionist history about historical evidence. How can we discover the intentionality in the mind behind the source, and how much reliance can we place on the reconstructionist's contextualisation of events as a form of explanation? It is here that we come across the apparently strange notion of the death of the author/subject. For Barthes, the importance of the author of historical evidence is diminished in as much as he/she is perceived as representative of further texts and ideological positions rather than as the originator of meaning. Evidence does not refer to a recoverable and accurately knowable past reality but represents chains of interpretations, that is, we have no master or transcendent signifiers. In the sense that we as historians cannot know what were the intentions of the author of the source, to suggest that we look to those intentions as a means to interpret the evidence is only to invite yet further textual investigation. This contradicts Lemon's view that narrative's power to explain emerges from its tracking of the historical agent's intentional and intelligible response to their context. Barthes maintains that

> The names of authors or of doctrines have here no substantial value.
> They indicate neither identities nor causes. It would be frivolous to think
> that 'Descartes,' 'Leibniz,' 'Rousseau,' 'Hegel,' etc., are names of authors,
> of the authors of movements or displacements that we thus designate.
> The indicative value that I attribute to them is first the name of a problem.
> (Barthes quoted in Harlan 1989: 585)

The inevitable rejection by empiricists of this position is founded on the belief that the historian and the evidence are separate entities – a further re-stating of the traditional distinction between knower and known – and this gap permits historians to stand back and see the origins of meaning in the evidence.

F.R. Ankersmit (1989: 146) describes what he calls the postmodernist historian's perception of evidence as a tile, not to be picked up to see what is underneath it, but as something which the historian steps on in order to move on to other tiles: horizontally instead of vertically. For Hayden White (1987: 192), this perspective (stepping from tile to tile) has further significance for the constitution of meaning because of what it says about ideology. The real problem with historical evidence for White is not Barthes' unending roundabout of meanings, but the inevitable ideological dimension to the interpretation of evidence.

The idea of historical interpretation being influenced by ideological considerations seems wrong to reconstructionist historians. Elton, for example, rejects any ideological impositionalism of the historian of the kind acknowledged by White because it produces 'uncertainty around historical truth'. The 'true view of the past' emerges instead for Elton (1991: 49) from 'the deficiencies of the evidence and the problems it poses, rather than from the alleged transformation of events in the organising mind of the historian'. White opposes this, persevering with the argument that

> there is no such thing as a *single* correct view of any object under study but . . . there are *many* correct views, each requiring its own style of representation. For we should recognise that *what constitutes the facts themselves* is the problem that the historian, like the artist, has tried to solve in the choice of metaphor by which he orders his world, past, present, and future. (White 1978: 47)

Any crossing of the boundary between the observer and that which is to be observed, through the choice of metaphor, thus clearly contravenes one of the most basic 'rules' of traditional historical analysis because it threatens Elton's ideal of objectively dealing with the evidence. Because objectivity is the central metaphor of empiricism, the ideological meshing of historian and his/her sources starkly presents the danger of subjectivity and eventual corruption of history. Even R.G. Collingwood's (1994) interventionist historical method, 'that the historian must re-enact the past in his own mind', presupposes a minimum level of objectivity. I have already pointed out how this also prompts the argument that, by a thorough knowledge of the facts, the reconstructionists reject the folly of social science model-making as applied to history, notably the use of social theory and the appeal to covering laws. While the question of subjectivity in dealing with the evidence is at the heart of the long contested issue of covering laws in history, it is also a debate that is important for the deconstructive consciousness. It further opens up the epistemological foundation of narrative as a legitimate type of explanation in distinction to, among other things, overt social theorising.

Theories of history: constructing the past

To his own question, 'Of what can there be historical knowledge?', Collingwood's (1994: 302) reply, 'Of that which can be re-enacted in the historian's mind', remains a problem for many reconstructionists because it is not based upon their method of historical analysis. Collingwood elaborated, 'Of that which is not experience but the mere object of experience, there can be no history' (see also Elton 1991: 43). To overcome the lack of direct experience in historical explanation Collingwoodian historians like E.H. Carr plunge themselves in the evidence and experience the past as best they can – by rethinking it. Although crude empiricists like Geoffrey Elton believe this to be a quite wrong-headed method believing instead in maintaining the distinction of knower and known – they would generally agree with Collingwood that, whatever method is used, historians must avoid the more grievous error of appealing to a universal explanatory social theory that is usually just a fancy cloak for personal bias or the methodological dead-end of covering law positivism. The framing of laws in the form of a proposition suggesting why an event occurred in order to yield causal connections is taken not to be history (Hempel (1942) in Gardiner 1959). But, as Callinicos suggests from his constructionist Marxist standpoint, the study of how humans relate to their contexts necessitates a social theory. For Callinicos, all history must attempt to discover some pattern in the transformations in human society.

As we have already noted, covering law theory is unpopular among those who judge it to be founded on a model or historical explanation acquired from science. For others, its unpopularity stems from its relegation of the power of narrative to explain the past. Consequently, few historians have employed what Hempel designated in the early 1940s as covering law theory. Some fifty years before, one of the most influential pieces of written history – Frederick Jackson Turner's work on the role of the frontier in American history – illustrates positivism's limited influence. While denying the existence of general laws in history, Turner was largely alone in using them in practice. By borrowing from the social and the natural sciences, Turner (1920; 1935) became one of the leading historians of his generation by inferring the existence of a general law that applied directly to American historical experience (see also Ridge 1988; Munslow 1992; Faragher 1993; Stoneley 1994). He argued in his famous lecture before the American Historical Association gathered in Chicago in 1893 that 'The existence of an area of free land, its continuous recession and the advance of American settlement westward explain American development' (Turner 1920: 2–3). For Turner, this law of westward movement accounted for American history. Turner's approach made him one of the leading social scientists of his time. However, the reaction against positivism in historical explanation emerged in the interwar years, led by two more American historians, Carl Becker and Charles Beard. Derived again from a Nietzschean position, but specifically under the influence of Italian historian Benedetto Croce, Beard and Becker challenged any objectivist history that saw itself as above the concerns of the present (Croce 1995). Endorsing this relativist line, Becker (quoted in Novick 1988: 98) asserted that 'Historical thinking . . . is a social instrument, helpful in getting the world's work more effectively done.' Most historians by today have accepted relativism at least to the extent that they continue to reject absolutist covering laws, but still refuse to accept that there may be more fiction in history than positivists admit (Popper 1959).

For deconstructionist historians, the rehearsing of these arguments for or against constructionism is a rather meaningless exercise if one entertains doubts about the truth-value of textual evidence and the interpretation built upon it. Debating covering law theory is irrelevant if the whole empiricist model of induction and inductive inference is flawed, because facts neither measure nor produce the kind of historical knowledge that mainstream historians claim. Most mainstream historians ignore the implications of this, preferring instead to concentrate on the sources, endorsing Collingwood's description of the historical method as the objective analysis of sources into their component parts to distinguish which are the more trustworthy. However, Collingwood (1994: 130) also acknowledged the role of the historian in construing historical accounts. As he argued, historians know how to do their own work in their own way and should no longer run the risk of being misled by try-ing to assimilate scientific method into history. The almost universal rejection of positivist constructionism rests, however, on the doubtful belief of most historians that historical explanation is really objective interpretation cast in a narrative form. The deconstructive argument holds instead that our sources are never transcendent signifieds because they have a pre-figured historical status by being already recounted in chronicles, diaries, legends, memories and interpretations, even before another generation of historians go to work on them again.

The deconstructive critique of empiricist representation and referentiality effectively asks: does knowledge emerge through social being and/or language-use? Although as a form of representation, narrative always fails the correspondence test, it remains of crucial importance in the reconstruction/construction of the past. It is worth considering at this point that the effort to find out truth in the past may be less about the rules of evidence, covering laws and even narrative, but is per-haps about the will to gain power. For Foucault there is a fundamental chasm between language and reality. The only reality is found when language produces a meaning. We use language but language also uses us (Ross 1995). Consequently, narrative is a discourse, the currency of which is power. That power may well be used to create a usable past for a nation. Narrative may, therefore, be viewed as a discurs-ive formation that exists in the present and is not a simple and uncomplicated reference to the past (Tilley 1990). The accretion of historical knowledge – 'know-ing the past' – often justifies the present, or some preferred version of it, and this is the motivating force that drives the historian as a professional. Accordingly, Foucault argues that all historians, because we are attached to a profession and a discipline, have a vested interest – usually ideologically framed – in maintaining the import-ance of the myth of the objective search for truth, whether reconstructionist or constructionist in orientation. The worst offenders, in Foucault's eyes are liberal bourgeois empiricists who believe that they have a control over their ideology that allows them objective access to the essential past. The point of deconstructionist history is the challenge it throws down to the idea, which reaches its ultimate expres-sion in hard-core constructionism, especially of the statistical variety, that there are essential (true) patterns 'out there' to be discovered in the past.

The deconstructive consciousness assumes that the treatment of the evidence in the historical narrative deals mainly in verisimilitude and coherence rather than objective explanation. This does not mean that we are all extreme relativists. White, for example, rejects extreme scepticism about the epistemological value of narrative, in fact putting it at the centre of what history is really about. 'As thus envisaged, the "content" of the discourse consists as much of its form as it does of whatever information might be extracted from a reading of it' (White, quoted in Norman 1991: 130). White (1984: 19) concludes that a discourse should be regarded as an 'apparatus for the production of meaning rather than as only a vehicle for the transmission of information about an extrinsic referent'. In acknowledging the cog-nitive importance of narrative, White does not suggest that it can recover the past as it actually was any more than can positivism. Deconstructionist history's suspicions about referentiality and representation in the reading of sources, and the writing of history, doubts about recovering the intentions of the author, construc-tionist theorising, and the often hidden agenda of power not only mean questioning the claims of the mainstream, but also attest to the need to address more fully the shortcomings, as well as the potential, of historical narrative as a means of explanation.

History as narrative

The impact of the deconstructive consciousness means not only questioning historical interpretation as an objective avenue to the past as it actually was, but also entails exploring the explanatory or story-telling power of narrative. If historical writing is the analysis of complex, pre-existing chains of interpretation, whereby documents do not guarantee authorial meaning and signifiers create only more signifiers, then discussion of content in history must begin with an understanding of its linguistic and story form. Historians are increasingly encouraged to think not only about researching the past, but also about how to express *and* undertake that research. Thinking about the form will make us think about how to deal with its content. To what extent then is the form of written history as significant as its factual content?

W.H. Dray (1970) summarised the various positions that can be held on the importance of narrative to historical explanation, namely that

> history simply *is* narrative; or that it is *essentially* narrative; or that a history must contain *some* narrative elements; or that *one form* of history, at any rate, and perhaps the most important one, narrates. It has been held, too, that it is through narration that historians achieve whatever is specifically historical about historical understanding; or that historical explanations get their distinctive structure by reason of their occurring in the course of historical narratives. It has even been held that narratives can themselves be explanatory in a special way; or that narrative is *per se* a form of explanation, if not indeed self-explanatory.

The functioning of narrative is thus a dilemma for historians. Narrative claims to represent the complexities and realities of the past, but because it is a story form it must be the creation of the historian's imagination. Can it therefore entertain any claim to being a true representation of what actually happened? Narrative, Louis Mink suggests, is the product of an 'imaginative construction which cannot defend its claim to truth by any accepted procedure of argument or authentication' (quoted in Norman 1991: 117). This means that historians unavoidably impose themselves on the past by inventing narratives as they try to explain what the past 'really meant', what the source-text 'really says', what the author's intentions 'really were' (Harlan 1989: 600).

As we know, for most historians narrative is the unquestioned *form* of history. Although a number of philosophers of history have argued narrative to be the essential and distinguishing feature of history, most practitioners fail to grasp its practical methodological significance, still regarding it as only a casual stylistic property that some essays possess and others do not. Like most things, whether narrative is explanatory or not comes down to how we define it. The debate on it as a legitimate form of historical explanation has produced anti-narrativists, among them philosophers of history Maurice Mandelbaum and Leon Goldstein, who claim that although narrative is an element of historical study, not all history has to be framed in the narrative form, and the discipline has other prior and more important methodological claims. Then there are pro-narrativists like philosophers Frederick A. Olafson, David Carr, William Gallie, Arthur Danto and A.R. Louch (1969) who insist there is a strong correspondence between the past as lived, and history as written. Then there are those pro-narrative but determined anti-deconstructionists like J.H. Hexter and Lawrence Stone, who do not accept that language must always fail the correspondence test. Finally, there are those of a broadly defined deconstructive turn like Hayden White, Dominick LaCapra, F.R. Ankersmit, Hans Kellner and David Harlan, who view narrative as the essential but largely misunderstood feature of historical explanation – a misunderstanding that among many other things permits history a claim to a spurious epistemological legitimacy through its favourite metaphor of objectivity.

Maurice Mandelbaum, in observing the general relevance of narrative, suggests that historians write it while keeping their 'eyes on higher things' – the prize of historical truth (Goldstein 1976: 140, quoting Dray). Like Arthur Marwick, philosopher of history Leon Goldstein cannot understand the fuss made over history's narrative form, what he calls the superstructure of history. Its real business is research on archival sources, the infra-structure. For Goldstein, history is 'a technical discipline', one that uses methods that are peculiarly its own: 'History is a way of knowing, not a mode of discourse' (Goldstein 1976: xix). He concludes, 'What we know about the historical past we know only through its constitution in historical research' (Goldstein 1976: xx–xxiii). The deconstructive turn counters this by declaring that the past exists as history only because a narrative or story structure has been imposed by the historian on the evidence.

Because the historical text consists of a narrative that purports to describe and evaluate past reality, what is at issue is the power to explain of story-form narrative. As we have seen, structuralist and post-structuralist literary theory has thrown open the question of how historians employ narrative as a way to fix historical know-ledge as unique to itself, and consequently divide history from other kinds of writing (Gallie 1968; Lemon 1995). In support of a pro-narrativist position, M.C. Lemon argues that the logic of life is replicated in narrative. As he says, the lesson is that 'there are, "out there", amidst a virtual infinity of occurrences real stories to be truly told and their telling must conform to the logic of narrative explanation' (Lemon 1995: 133). Lemon's view is shared by Dominick LaCapra, Hayden White and Paul Ricoeur, who maintain that because of its essential narrative form, history cannot be categorised as anything other than a kind of literature, but that this does not devalue its significance or explanatory power. The consequence is, in fact, a recast-ing of its character and functioning. As Paul Ricoeur (1981: 275) says, history must possess an 'irreducibly narrative character' in the same way that human existence does. Its function is to describe the process in which people construe themselves and their culture through the production of language. This emphasis on the cognit-ive value of narrative does not of course mean that we now suddenly have *the* access to the past as it actually was – we only have *a* story version of it. Narrative can explain the past, but not guarantee that its explanations are truthful.

Deconstructionist historians approach this issue through the following thinking. The past as it actually was, and the individual historical statements composing its narrative, can never coincide precisely. The problem is that we cannot verify the past by the evidence. Evidence is not past reality because our access to it must be through many intermediaries — absence, gaps and silences, the contrived nature of the archive, signifier-referent collapse, the historian's bias and, not least, the structure of the historian's imposed and contrived narrative argument. It is probably best to view historical narratives as propositions about how we *might* represent a past reality, suggestions of *possible* correspondences rather than *the* correspondence. Hayden White (1995) endorses philosopher Arthur Danto's view that historical facts are really only events under a description. It follows that, as events under a description, these narrative proposals/suggestions are the result of individual historians' interpretations and compete for acceptance in those terms. History results not from the debate about past reality as such, but from competing narrative proposals about the nature and possible meanings of past events. Of course, once a narrative proposal has achieved a more or less universal acceptance (like 'the Cold War' or 'the Industrial Revolution'), it becomes concretised as past reality. It is no longer a narrative proposal, but has become *the* past. This makes it impossible, in effect, to distinguish between language-use and past reality. It is at this point that empiricism notches up another success.

What is undeniable is that it is historians who construct narratives through which historical knowledge is acquired and disseminated. How is it possible for us to distinguish between the narrative proposals of different historians, between those likely to be *right* and those *wrong*? How can we tell *good* history from *bad* history? This is not too hard to do for reconstructionists. They judge the degree to which the narrative lacks structure, unity and/or coherence in its congruence or correspondence with its contextualised sources. The most convincing historians are those who write narratives possessing this in full measure. Unity and cohesion are found in the intelligible and reasonable relationship established between individual statements and the sources, but even more importantly the narrative *as a whole* possesses an informing structure of argument — the article, essay or book is not waffly or rambling. In 'good history' the informing narrative argument will contain a clear and upfront statement as to how the past actually was — the coherence of form coming from the overarching social theory deployed, or the fact that they have got the story/theory straight according to the evidence.

What is 'good' or 'bad' history for the deconstructionist? Hopefully the narrative in a deconstructionist essay will be coherent and sensible, but it will not be epistemologically self-assured. This lack of certainty arises because of the doubts harboured about correspondences. How can we readily differentiate truth-effect plausibility from fact? How may we disentangle social theory arguments from low-level descriptions of events? How can we unpick ideologically inspired gaps and silences or unravel the collapsed signifier-referent? For every history that aims to get at the past as it actually happened, there is always another version, which, like the first, is by definition another fiction. As to what constitutes good history, then, it is that which is self-reflexive enough to acknowledge its limits, especially aware that the writing of history is far more precarious and speculative than empiricists usually admit. Deconstructionist history openly accepts a dissenting role for the historian as someone who must challenge the established notions of authority within contemporary society by refusing to 'tidy up' the past by ascribing origins and causes with the claim to evidentially certified truth. What does this mean in more practical terms, and what are its implications for history as narrative?

We have now arrived at two conclusions about history: first, all composed, written narratives *are* supported by a philosophy or ideology, often buried so deeply that no amount of conscious historical awareness can eliminate it; and second, because it relates stories about real past events in the evidence, deconstructionist history is not a fictional narrative. But, as a form of representation, all historical narrative proposals are shaped by the conventions of rhetoric and language-use – emplotment, argument and other culturally provided constraints, both material and ideological. This relationship between narrative form and historical content is explored by Hayden White in his study of historical interpretation, which in turn owes much to the investigation of language and representation undertaken by Roland Barthes, Paul Ricoeur and Michel Foucault (White 1984: 1). For the anti-narrativist White, the essence of history is that it is a literary enterprise, and we 'know the past' through the narrative design we impose on it, which, as Ankersmit (1994: 83) agrees, 'acquires a substantiality of its own'. Both White and Ankersmit request that before historians can embrace the true character of historical explanation through a figurative narrative, we must resist the temptation of keeping up our pretence to objectivity, and turn instead to a richer understanding which is to be gained through an appreciation of history as literature. In his 1973 text *Metahistory*, White argued that all history writing is basically a linguistic and poetic act. Facts are not discovered, they are actually sources interpreted according as much to literary as any other criteria. Consequently, if we approach history as literature we may even write better history, as we deploy an additional range of critical apparatuses to the established rules of contextualised evidence. By recognising its literary form we are not constrained to present it as mainstream history would have it done.

Because written history is a literary artefact, White claims that historians share the same formal narrative structures used by writers of realist story literature based on the main categories of figurative language – the tropes – what White calls tropicropic prefiguration. White uses something like a base–superstructure metaphor himself to explain how this works. Historians construct narratives (stories) to produce explanations employing three superstructural strategies of explanation, viz., explanation by emplotment, explanation by formal argument and explanation by ideological implication. These strategies of explanation are the surface features of the narrative, with White suggesting a deep or infrastructure of consciousness (operating at the level of the tropes) that ultimately determines how historians elect to explain the facts explored in their narratives. Extending the base–superstructure metaphor, White argues that language is not to be located in the economic base of society, nor the social superstructure, but is prior to both.

Next, White carries forward the analysis from the level of rhetoric to that of the historical by borrowing Michel Foucault's concept of the episteme – a way of describing how a culture in each age acquires and uses its knowledge as embedded in figurative language. White suggests that it is possible for historians to interpret the culture of any historical period with reference to its ascendant tropic prefiguration (White 1974). White proposes that as the tropes organise the deep structures of human thought in de Saussure's sense of constituting meaning through binary opposition – the idea of otherness, or difference in any historical period – tropes lie at the core of every society's and every historian's historical imagination. White has explored the literary theory of tropes as a way of distinguishing the dominant modes of the historical imagination in nineteenth-century Europe, and by extension to the cultural level his model allows the identification of the deep and surface structures of the historical imagination.

It is important to note that the key to this narrative model of cultural change is White's conjecture that ideology and the exercise of power are ultimately settled by the cardinal text, yet operate in the real world of social relationships (White 1987). In moving from the rhetorical level to that of the material context, White is describing the writing of history as an intertextual and material act, with history as a conforming or dissenting voice. This he attempts to demonstrate in his analysis of E.P. Thompson's *Making of the English Working Class*, claiming that like all history it is a necessarily fabricated work because of its inevitable dependence on the tropic model of historical explanation. Thompson is in the business of metaphorically 'making' the English working class for overtly ideological reasons. According to White, 'The pattern which Thompson discerned in the history of English working class consciousness was perhaps as much imposed upon his data as it was found in them.' But White goes on to make an even more telling point: 'the issue here surely is not whether some pattern was imposed, but the tact exhibited [by Thompson] in the choice of the pattern used to give order to the process being represented'. As White says, the 'planned or intuitive' tropological pattern Thompson selected for the English working class is the movement from a 'naive (metaphorical) to a self-critical (ironic) comprehension of itself' (White 1978: 19). What is significant for historians in White's analysis of history is his questioning of the relationship between the trope and social and cultural practice. In his work *Mythologies*, Roland Barthes (1972: 129) also interprets language as being assembled by one social group to be consumed by another as ideology. With others like the anthropologist Clifford Geertz and cultural critic Michel Foucault, White has constantly reviewed the representational and ideological status of the tropes (metaphor) in forming the social institutions of power and consciousness (Geertz 1973).

White is fully aware of another central problem raised by his rhetorical approach to the study of history, and that is the fear of extreme interpretative relativism. This can threaten a 'free play' of interpretative fantasy that may take us further from, rather than closer to, the origin and subject of the evidence. White accepts that we have here a division between the historian who wants to 'reconstruct' or 'explain' the past and one who wishes to interpret it or use it as 'the occasion for his own speculations on the present and future' (White 1987: 188). In following Foucault's logic on the text–context relationship, White does draw a line at the argument of Jacques Derrida that there is only figuration and hence no meaning in and through language (White 1978). The deconstructive historian need not be trapped in a forlorn snarl of rhetorical relativism. White believes, along with Foucault, that we can actually know many things about the real world despite the limitations of language. But withal there remains his warning about the power of language:

> The use of a technical language or a specific method of analysis, such
> as, let us say, econometrics or psychoanalysis, does not free the histor-
> ian from the linguistic determinism to which the conventional narrative
> historian remains enslaved. On the contrary, commitment to a specific
> methodology . . . will close off as many perspectives on any given
> historical field as it opens up. (White 1978: 117)

The charge of rhetorical relativism, with its descent into moral decline and the sink
of ideology, is countered by White's claim that all languages — whether the language of supposed objective history, or of the poet — are equally relativistic, and
equally limited by the language chosen 'in which to delimit what it is possible to
say about the subject under study' (ibid.). When the historian interprets the past
he/she is not inventing it, or producing a fictionalised version that plays with the
real events and real lives of the past. The historian is rather imposing a narrative
structure that has coherence and unity, endowing the past 'experience of time with
meaning' (White 1987: 188). It is far from a descent into rhetorical relativism (and
the moral turpitude, as Saul Friedlander suggests, that would deny events like the
Holocaust) to recognise that the past is intervened in when emplotted by historians,
or, as Ricoeur (1981: 279) puts it, 'the narrative art [that] characteristically links
a story to a narrator'. What White is saying is that it is the function of the historian to explore the emplotments that may already exist in the past:

> The meaning of real human lives . . . is the meaning of the plots . . .
> by which the events that those lives comprise are endowed with the aspect
> of stories having a discernible beginning, middle, and end. A meaningful
> life is one that aspires to the coherency of a story with a plot. Historical
> agents prospectively prefigure their lives as stories with plots. (White
> 1987: 173)

This daring vision of the historical enterprise necessitates rather than denies the kind
of attention to the evidence that all empiricists and contextualists would applaud.
The logic of this argument is that we historians, while we tell stories, have little
of the imaginative freedom exercised by writers of fiction because we are in the
business of the retrospective emplotment of historical events and narratives. While
the historical account is a figurative exercise in the sense of being a product of the
literary imagination, its relativism remains limited by the nature of the evidence.

Conclusion

The deconstructive consciousness raises several fundamental questions about the character of history defined as the reconstruction of the past according to the available
sources, and the construction of the past by the imposition of explanatory frameworks. The empiricist argument that our knowledge of the past is derived through
the painstaking study and interpretation of fragmentary and partial evidence, and
that the sheer professionalism of the working historian will overcome the problems of bias, ideology and the many other obstacles to historical understanding, is

countered by the proposal that history is instead a recognition of the intimacy exist-ing between content and form. In other words, we remind ourselves that history is not only about the sifting of evidence and constitution of facts, and that inter-pretation itself is an act of linguistic and literary creation.

This approach to historical analysis suggests that that which we call 'the his-torical' cannot be understood in all its fullness by *a priori* logic, positivism, or by the painstaking reconstructionist analysis and constitution of facts alone. Instead we may grasp more of the richness of historical analysis by incorporating into the study of the past the intertextual nature of history as a discourse. The truth found in histories, White suggests, 'resides not only in their fidelity to the facts of given individual or collective lives' but 'most importantly in their faithfulness to that vision of human life informing the poetic' (White 1987: 181). It is by recognising the expressive and figurative content of historical narrative, 'the content of its form', that the historian contributes to our understanding of the past. This does not mean that we historians only examine the purely figurative or metaphorical level of the discourse of history, but we intervene in the past by actively extrapolating from the literal to the symbolic level of understanding, from the present to the past.

Perhaps the central point about the deconstructive turn is the recognition that narrative upsets the assumed balance between language and reality. Historical lan-guage (Ankersmit's narrative proposal) becomes the primary vehicle for understanding. We should abandon the traditional empiricist epistemology in favour of a radical new hermeneutic or interpretative approach to the generation of knowledge about the past. I will elaborate on this significant suggestion later in my more detailed study of Foucault and White. For now I will repeat that we must examine the figur-ative use to which the historian puts the literal sense of meaning he/she has sup-posedly discovered in his/her research. This applies not only to the interpretations of historians but also to our sources. Consequently, every history is always some-thing more than the events described. The historian represents the past rather than reclaims it as it really was. It is the deep suspicion, generated by this emphasis upon narrativisation and presentism, that motivates the empiricist critique of the decon-structive consciousness. Deconstructionists, it is claimed, forget the sources, the problems of research, and assume that ideology must unavoidably colour our his-torical descriptions.

References

Ankersmit, F.R. (1989) 'Historiography and postmodernism', *History and Theory*, 28(2): 146.

Ankersmit, F.R. (1994) *History and Tropology: The Rise and Fall of Metaphor*, Berkeley, CA: University of California Press.

Bann, S. (1981) 'Introduction', *Comparative Criticism: A Yearbook 3*, University Park: Pennsylvania University Press, 3–20.

Barthes, R. (1972) *Mythologies*, London: Cape.

Barthes, R. (1981 [1967]) 'Discourse of history', *Comparative Criticism: A Yearbook 3*, University Park, PA: Pennsylvania University Press.

Beard, C. (1934) 'Written history as an act of faith', *American Historical Review*, 39: 219–31.

Beard, C. (1935) 'That noble dream', *American Historical Review*, 41: 74–87.

Collingwood, R.G. (1994) *The Idea of History*, Oxford: Oxford University Press.

Croce, B. (1995) *Aesthetics as Science of Expression and General Linguistics*, New Brunswick, NJ: Transaction Publishers.

Dean, M. (1994) *Critical and Effective Histories: Foucault's Methods and Historical Sociology*, London: Routledge.

Dray, W.H. (1970) 'On the nature and role of narrative in historiography', *History and Theory*, 10: 153–71.

Elton, G.R. (1991) *Return to Essentials*, Cambridge: Cambridge University Press.

Faragher, J.M. (1993) 'The frontier trail: rethinking Turner and re-imagining the American West', *American Historical Review*, 98(1): 106–17.

Gallie, W. (1968) *Philosophy and the Historical Understanding*, 2nd edn, New York: Schocken Books.

Geertz, C. (1973) *The Interpretation of Cultures*, New York: Basic Books.

Goldstein, J. (1994) *Foucault and the Writing of History*, Oxford: Basil Blackwell.

Goldstein, L. (1976) *Historical Knowing*, Austin, TX: University of Texas Press.

Harlan, D. (1989) 'Intellectual history and the return of literature', *American Historical Review*, June, 585.

Hempel, C.G. (1959 [1942]) 'The function of general laws in history', in Gardiner, P. (ed.) *Theories of History*, New York: Free Press, 344–56.

Koshar, R. (1993) 'Foucault and social history: comments on "combined under development"', *American Historical Review*, 98: 354–63.

Lemon, M.C. (1995) *The Discipline of History and the History of Thought*, London: Routledge.

Louch, A.R. (1969) 'History as narrative', *History and Theory*, 8: 54–70.

Megill, A. (1979) 'Foucault, structuralism, and the ends of history', *Journal of Modern History*, 51: 451.

Munslow, A. (1992) *Discourse and Culture: The Creation of America, 1870–1920*, London: Routledge.

Norman, A.P. (1991) 'Telling it like it was: historical narratives on their own terms', *History and Theory*, 30(2): 119–35.

Novick, P. (1988) *That Noble Dream: The Objectivity Question and the American Historical Profession*, Cambridge: Cambridge University Press.

Popper, K. (1959) *The Logic of Scientific Discovery*, London: Hutchinson.

Poster, M. (1982) 'Foucault and history', *Social Research*, 49: 120.

Ricoeur, P. (1981) *Hermeneutics and the Human Sciences*, Cambridge: Cambridge University Press.

Ridge, M. (1988) 'Frederick Jackson Turner, Ray Allen Billington, and frontier history', *Western Historical Quarterly*, 19 (January): 5–20.

Ross, D. (1995) 'Grand narratives in American historical writing: from romance to uncertainty', *American Historical Review*, 100: 651–77.

Stoneley, P. (1994) 'Signifying frontiers', *Borderlines*, 1(3): 237–53.

Tilley, C. (ed.) (1990) *Reading Material Culture*, Oxford: Basil Blackwell.

Turner, F.J. (1935 [1906]) 'Rise of the New West, 1819–1829', in *The American Nation; The United States, 1830–1850: The Nation and Its Sections*, New York: H. Holt & Co.

Turner, F.J. (1962 [1920]) *The Frontier in American History*, New York: Holt, Rinehart & Winston.

White, H. (1978) 'The burden of history', in *Tropics of Discourse: Essays in Cultural Criticism*, Baltimore, MD: Johns Hopkins University Press.

White, H. (1984) 'The question of narrative in contemporary historical theory', *History and Theory*, 23(1): 1–33.

White, H. (1987) 'The context in the text: method and ideology in intellectual history', in *The Content of the Form; Narrative Discourse and Historical Representation*, Baltimore, MD: Johns Hopkins University Press.

White, H. (1995) 'Response to Arthur Marwick', *Journal of Contemporary History*, 30: 233–46.

White, H. (1974) 'Structuralism and popular culture', *Journal of Popular Culture*, 7: 759–75.

First published as Munslow, A. (1997) 'History as deconstruction', in *Deconstructing History*, London: Routledge, 58–75. Alun Munslow is Professor of History at Staffordshire University, UK. He is editor of the journal *Rethinking History*, and widely regarded for his analyses of the postmodern engagement with history. His other books include *The Routledge Companion to Historical Studies* and *The New History*.

Chapter 12

Processual, postprocessual and interpretive archaeologies

Michael Shanks and Ian Hodder

Pᴿᴏᴄᴇꜱꜱᴜᴀʟ ᴀʀᴄʜᴀᴇᴏʟᴏɢʏ ɪꜱ the orthodoxy which emerged after the reaction, beginning in the 1960s and calling itself 'new archaeology' (Trigger 1989a; Willey and Sabloff 1980; Renfrew and Bahn 1991), against traditional culture-historical and descriptive approaches to the material past. Its characteristics are as follows: archaeology conceived as anthropological science rather than allied with history; explanation of the past valued over description; explanation via the incorporation of particular observations of the material past into cross-cultural generalisations pertaining to (natural and social) process (hence the term 'processual'); explanation via explicit methodologies modelled on the hard sciences; an earlier interest in laws of human behaviour has shifted to an interest in formation processes of the archaeological record – regularities which will allow inferences about processes to be made from material remains.

For many, processual archaeology is a good means, if not the best, of acquiring *positive knowledge* of the archaeological past. Positive archaeological knowledge is *of the past*, which means that it aspires to objectivity in the sense of being neutral and, indeed, timeless (the past happened in the way it did; that much at least will not change). Under a programme of positive knowledge, archaeologists aim to *accumulate* more knowledge of the past. The timeless and objective quality of knowledge is important if the aim is to accumulate and build on what is already known; it would be no good building on facts which cannot be relied upon, because they might change. The aspiration to timeless and value-free knowledge also enables high degrees of specialisation, knowledges isolated in their own field and disconnected from the present. The cultural politics of the 1990s does not affect what happened in prehistory, it is held. The archaeologist can live with one while quite separately gaining knowledge of the other.

To secure this timeless objectivity is the task of method(ology), and in processual archaeology this may be described as coming down to reason or rationality working objectively upon data or the facts. Reason is that cognitive processing which is divorced from superstition, ideology, emotion, subjectivity – indeed, anything which compromises the purity or neutrality of logical calculation. To attain object-ivity means carefully relying on those faculties which allow access to the past parti-cularly observation, controlled perception of those empirical traces remaining of what happened. Theory-building may be involved in moving from the static archaeological record of the present to past social dynamics (Binford 1977), but to move beyond controlled observation is to speculate and to invite bias and subject-ivity, contamination of the past by the present.

These aspirations to positive scientific knowledge, neutrality, and reliance on controlled observation of facts have led to processual archaeology being described as positivist and empiricist (Shanks and Tilley 1987a).

Processual archaeology is anthropological in the sense of being informed by an interest in social reconstruction of the past. The following form the main outlines of processual conceptions of the social as they developed from the late 1960s: soci-ety is essentially composed of patterned sets of behaviours; material culture and material residues, the products of processes which form the archaeological record, *reflect* the patterned behaviours which are society, or they are the result of natural processes which can be defined scientifically (the decay of organic materials; the corrosion of metals); society is a mode of human adaptation to the social and natural environment; accordingly, explaining social process means focusing on those fea-tures of the society which most relate to adaptation to environments – resources, subsistence and economic strategies, trade and exchange, technology – attention has, however and more recently, turned to symbolism and ritual; the interest in cross-cultural generalisation and patterning is expressed in societal typing (identi-fying a particular society as band, lineage-based, chiefdom, state, etc.) and schemes of cultural evolution.

Postprocessual archaeology, as the label implies, is something of a reaction and supersession of this processual framework (Hodder 1982; Hodder 1985, 1986). Since the late 1970s issue has been taken with most of these tenets of processual archae-ology: the character of science and aims of objective explanation; the character of society; and the place of values in archaeology, the sociopolitics of the discipline, its contemporary location as a mode of cultural production of knowledges.

Doubt, from theoretical and empirical argument, has been thrown on the possibility of an anthropological science, based upon observation of residues of patterned behaviours, detached from the present and aspiring to value-freedom (as positive knowledge). So the processual-postprocessual debate has centred upon the forms of knowledge appropriate to a *social* science, how society may be conceived (reconciling both patterning or structure and individual action, intention and agency), and upon the workings of the discipline of archaeology, its ideologies and cultural politics, its place in the (post)modern present.

The debate has tended towards a polarisation of positions, and it is this which has led to an obscuring of the issues. Postprocessual has come to be seen by some as anti-science, celebrating subjectivity, the historical particular in place of gener-alisation: the cultural politics of the present displacing positive knowledge of the past. Above all, the authority of a scientific and professional knowledge of the past is posited against particular and subjective constructions, a pluralism of pasts appropriate each to their own contemporary constituency: science is pitted against relativism (Yoffee and Sherratt 1993; Trigger 1989b; Watson 1990).

We refer to an obscuring of the issues because this polarisation is unnecessary, indeed, damaging. We are proposing that a consideration of the character and scope of interpretation may help overcome the polarisations. And, to begin, a renaming may be appropriate. The label 'postprocessual' says nothing about what it stands for, other than a relative position in respect of processual archaeology. If we are to use interpretation as an epithet, *interpretive archaeologies* may be used as a more positive label, perhaps, for many of those approaches which have been called post-processual. These are archaeologies (the plural is important, as will become clear) which work through interpretation. And we hope it will become clear that a careful consideration of interpretation entails abandoning the caricatures of science versus relativism, generalisation versus the historical particular, and the objective past versus the subjective present.

The main aspects of archaeologies termed interpretive might be summarised as follows: foregrounded is the person and work of the interpreter. Interpretation is practice which requires that the interpreter does not so much hide behind rules and procedures predefined elsewhere, but takes responsibility for their actions, their interpretations; archaeology is hereby conceived as a material practice in the present, making things (knowledges, narratives, books, reports, etc.) from the material traces of the past – constructions which are no less real, truthful or authentic for being constructed; social practices, archaeology included, are to do with meanings, making sense of things – working, doing, acting, making are interpretive; the interpretive practice that is archaeology is an ongoing process – there is no final and definitive account of the past as it was; interpretations of the social are less concerned with causal explanation (accounts such as 'this is the way it was' and 'it happened because of this') than with *understanding* or *making sense* of things which never were certain or sure; interpretation is consequently multivocal – different interpretations of the same field are quite possible – we can therefore expect a plurality of archaeological interpretations suited to different purposes, needs, desires; interpretation is thereby a creative but none the less critical attention and response to the interests, needs and desires of different constituencies (those people, groups or communities who have or express such interests in the material past).

To interpret, the act of interpretation: what do the words mean and imply?

We particularly stress the active character of interpretation: one is an interpreter by virtue of performing the act or practice of interpreting. An interpreter is a translator, an interlocutor, guide or go-between.

Meaning

To interpret something is to figure out what it means. A translator conveys the sense or meaning of something which is in a different language or medium. In this way interpretation is fundamentally about meaning. Note, however, that translation is not a simple and mechanical act but involves careful judgement as to appropriate shades of meaning, often taking account of context, idiom and gesture which can seriously affect the meaning of words taken on their own.

Dialogue

A translator may be an interlocutor or go-between. Interpretation contains the idea of mediation, of conveying meaning from one party to another. An interpreter aims to provide reciprocity of understanding, overcoming the lack of understanding or semantic distance between two parties who speak different languages or belong to different cultures. Interpretation is concerned with dialogue, facilitating and making easier.

In a good dialogue or conversation one listens to what the other says and tries to work out what they mean, tries to understand, to make sense. Translation may be essential to this, performed either by a separate interpreter or by the parties of the dialogue themselves. Further questions might be asked and points put forward based on what has already been heard and understood. The idea is that dialogue moves forward to a consensus (of sorts) which is more than the sum of the initial positions. This *fusion of horizons* (a term taken from hermeneutics, the philosophy of interpretation, discussed below) is potentially a learning experience in which one takes account of the other, their objections and views, even if neither is won over.

It is not a good and open dialogue if one party simply imposes its previous ideas, categories and understandings upon the other. Preconceptions are simply confirmed. It is not good if the interpreter does not recognise the independence of the interpreted, their resistance to control and definition. A good conversation is one perhaps which never ends: there is always more to discover.

What might be a dialogue with the past? One where the outcome resides wholly in neither side but is a product of *both* the past and the present. Archaeological interpretation here resides in the gap between past and present. Such a dialogue is also ongoing. We will take up these points again below.

Uncertainty

Interpretation involves a perceived gap between the known and the unknown, desire and a result, which is to be bridged somehow. There is thus uncertainty, both at the outset of interpretation (what does this mean?) and at the end of the act of interpretation. It could always have been construed in a different way, with perhaps a different aspect stressed or disregarded. Although we might be quite convinced by an understanding we have managed to achieve, it is good to accept fallibility and not to become complacent. Is this not indeed the character of reason? Rationality is not an abstract absolute for which we can formulate rules and procedures, but is better conceived as the willingness to recognise our partiality, that our knowledge and reasoning are open to challenge and modification. Final and definitive interpretation is a closure which is to be avoided, but suspected at the least.

Exploration and making connections

Interpretation implies an extension or building from what there is here to something beyond. We have already mentioned that interpretation should aspire to being open to change, exploring possibility. Exploration of meanings is often about making different connections.

Here can be mentioned the structuralist argument that meaning, if it is to be found at all, resides in the gaps between things, in their interrelationships. A lone signifier seems empty. But once connected through relations of similarity and difference with other signifiers it makes sense. In deciphering a code different permutations of connections between the particles of the code are explored until meaning is unlocked.

Judgement

A sculptor or woodcarver might examine their chosen material, interpret its form and substance, taking note of grain and knots of wood, flaws and patterning in stone, and then judge and choose how to work with or against the material. An archaeologist may examine a potsherd, pick out certain diagnostic traits and judge that these warrant an identification of the sherd as of a particular type: they choose an identification from various possibilities. Interpretation involves judgement and choice: drawing sense, meaning and possibility from what began as uncertainty.

Performance

In this way interpretation may refer to something like dramatic performance, where a particular interpretation of a dramatic text is offered according to the judgement of performers and director. The text is worked with and upon. Focus is drawn to certain connections within the characters and plot which are judged to be significant. Interpretation is here again reading for significance, where significance is literally making something a sign.

Dramatic interpretation has further dimensions. A text is read for significance and courses of action inferred. A past work (the text of a play) is acted out and in so doing it is given intelligible life. Now, there is no need here to take a literal line and think that archaeological interpretation involves those experimental reconstructions of past ways of life that are familiar from television programmes and heritage parks (though there is here a serious argument for experimental archaeology). We would rather stress that interpretation is in performance an *active apprehension*. Something produced in the past is made a presence to us now. It is worked upon actively. If it were not, it would have no life. An unread and unperformed play is dead and gone. Analogously an archaeological site which is not actively apprehended, worked on, incorporated into archaeological projects, simply lies under the ground and decays. The questions facing the actor-interpreters are: How are the characters to be portrayed? What settings are to be used? What form of stage design? What lighting, sound and ambience? Simply, what is to be made of the play? (Pearson 1994).

Courses of action inferred, projects designed: these are conditions of interpretation.

Critique

Judgement here involves taking a position, choosing how to perform, what to do, which meanings to enact or incorporate. Involved is a commitment to one performance rather than another. Any interpretation is always thus immediately critical of other interpretations. Performance is both analytic commentary on its source, the written play, but also critical in its choice of some meanings and modes and not others.

The ubiquity of interpretation forgotten in black boxes

Interpretation is insidiously ubiquitous. There are always choices and judgements being made even in the most mundane and apparently empirical activities. Describing and measuring an artefact, for example, always involves acts of interpretation and judgement. Which parts of a stone axe-blade are to be measured, for example, and from where to where?

But some interpretation is often overlooked when people accept certain interpretive conventions. So, for example, plants are most often described according to scientific species lists. But these species lists are not 'natural': they are the result of scientific interpretation concerning the definition and classification of plants and creatures. Such interpretation may have occurred a while ago now, and be more of interest to historians of science, but it should be recognised that the choice or judgement is made to accept that interpretation. Interpretations such as this concerning the classification of plants are often worth following simply because so much work would be required, starting almost from first principles, to redesign natural history. The idea of a species is tied into so many other things: evolutionary theory and ecology, botany and zoology, etc.

When an interpretation or set of interpretations is accepted, treated as uncontroversial and no longer even seen for what it is, the term *black-boxed* can be used. Interpretation is made, accepted and then put away, out of sight and often out of mind, in a black box. It allows us to live with the world more easily; we would otherwise be as infants, asking whether this thing in front of us really could be interpreted as a table with a box (a computer) upon it.

Indeed, all archaeology is hereby interpretive, concerned intimately with the interpretation of things. However, some archaeologists refuse to accept this, or choose to overlook or black-box acts of interpretation. Excavation, for example, is so thoroughly interpretive. Many students on their first dig find the uncertainty very disturbing. Where does one layer end and another begin? How can you tell? How can it be ascertained that this scatter of traces of holes in the ground was once a wooden house? Yet this pervasive interpretive uncertainty is the construction of 'hard' facts about the past.

Hermeneutics

The theoretical and philosophical field of interpretation, the clarification of meaning and achievement of sense and understanding, is covered by *hermeneutics*. Hermeneutics addresses the relationship between interpreter and interpreted when that which is to be interpreted is not just raw material to be defined and brought under technical control, but *means* something. The term is traditionally applied to the reading of texts and the understanding of historical sources: Is the source authentic? What does it mean? What were the author's intentions? We do not propose a simple import of hermeneutic principles into archaeology, but note their relevance. Having unpacked the idea of interpretation, we will now develop some of the observations.

Uncertainty

Interpretation is rooted in a world which cannot be tied down to definitive categories and processes. Consider classification. Articles are grouped or a group divided according to their similarities. Each class or taxon contains those articles judged the same. There are two fields of remaindering or possible foci of uncertainty where judgement is required. First, it may not be absolutely clear where a particular article belongs, particularly if the criteria for inclusion in a class are not specific, if an article is approaching the edges, the margins of a taxon, or if it is somehow incomplete. Second, there is always a remainder after classification. Classification never completely summarises. There are always aspects or attributes of an article which are disregarded and which remain outside taxa, embarrassing classification.

Classification operates under a 'rule of the same'. Taxa are characterised by relative *homogeneity*. This is a legitimate strategy for coping with the immense empirical variety and particularity that archaeologists have to deal with. However, we should be clear that classification does not give the *general* picture; it gives the *average*. It is not a general picture because there is no provision in classification for assessing the norm, the taxa (where do they come from; they are supplemental or external to the classification), nor the variations within a class, nor the variability of variability. Classification is less interested in coping with particularity: Why are the members of a class of pots all in fact slightly different?

Things are equivocal. A pot can be classified according to its shape and decoration as of a particular type. But thin-sectioned under a polarising microscope it explodes into another world of micro-particles and mineral inclusions. The pot is not just one thing which can be captured in a single all-encompassing definition. There is always more that can be said or done with the pot. A single pot is also multiple. It depends on the trials we make of it, what we do with it, how we experience it — whether we attend to surface and shape or slice it and magnify it.

Instead of smoothing over, we can also attend to that which does not fit, to the rough and irregular, to the texture of things. Everyday life is not neat and tidy. History is a mess. We can attend to the equivocal, to the absences in our understanding, focus on the gaps in neat orders of explanation. Conspicuously in archaeology there can be no final account of the past — because it is now an equivocal and ruined mess, but also because even when the past was its present it was to a considerable extent incomprehensible. So much has been lost and forgotten of what never was particularly clear. Social living is immersion in equivocality, everyday uncertainty. What really is happening now? There are no possible final answers.

Uncertainty and equivocality refer to the difference of things: they can be understood according to a rule of the same, but difference escapes this rule, escapes homogeneity. Because an attention to texture which escapes classification is outside of qualities of sameness (the homogeneity of what is contained within the class), the term *heterogeneity* may be used. To attend to difference is to attend to heterogeneity – the way things escape formalisation, always holding something back.

Nietzsche's and Foucault's projects of *genealogy* involve difference and discontinuity; heterogeneity in what was taken to be homogeneous and continuous. Nietzsche (1967) reveals the 'uncertain' origins of morality. Sexuality is shown to be far from a biological constant by Foucault (1979, 1984a, 1984b).

The social world is thoroughly *polysemous*. This is another concept which can be related to uncertainty. That a social act or product is polysemous means that it can always be interpreted in various ways. Meanings are usually negotiated: that is, related to the interpersonal practices, aspirations, strategies of people. We repeat the classic example of the safety pin, the meaning of which was radically renegotiated by punk subculture in the 1970s (Hebdige 1979). (...)

When the uncertainty of an interpretation declines it is black-boxed and need no longer be subject to suspicion and negotiation. The controversy over an interpretation is settled and closed. (...)

Creativity and the technology that is archaeology

The equivocality, heterogeneity or multiplicity of the material world means that choices must be made in perception and to what we attend. The archaeological record is an infinity in terms of the things that may be done with it and in terms of how it may be perceived. Which measurements are to be made? Are some aspects of an artefact to be disregarded in coming to an understanding? How is justice to be done to the empirical richness of the past? (...)

Archaeological interpretation requires that some things be connected with others in order to make sense of what remains of the past. Circular features in earth of contrasting colour are associated with removed wooden stakes, and then in turn associated with other post-holes to trace the structural members of a building. To interpret is in this way a creative act. Putting things together and so creating sense, meaning or knowledge.

We are concerned to emphasise that the person of the archaeologist is essential in coming to understand the past. The past is not simply under the ground waiting to be discovered. It will not simply appear, of course, but requires work. Consider discovery. Discovery is invention. The archaeologist uncovers or discovers something by coming upon it. An inventor may be conceived to have come upon a discovery. Discovery and invention are united in their etymology: *invenire* in Latin means to come upon, to find or invent. Invention is both finding and creative power. The logic of invention, poetry and the imaginary is one of conjunction, making connections. It is both/and, between self and other; not either/or. The pot found by the archaeologist is both this and that (surface decoration and mineral inclusions). A castle is both technical drawing and romantic painting. It is there in the land-scape and here in a painting. It is both of the past and of the present. Archaeology's poetry is to negotiate these equivocations and make connections. It is the work of imagination.

This is to deny the radical distinction of subjectivity and objectivity in that the subjective is simply the form that the objective takes.

Foregrounding the creativity of the interpreting archaeologist is to hold that archaeology is a mode of production of the past (Shanks and McGuire 1991; Shanks 1992). This would seem to be recognised by those many archaeologists and text-books which talk at length of archaeological techniques – archaeology seen as technology. The past has left remains, and they decay in the ground. According to their interest an archaeologist works on the material remains to make something of them. So excavation is invention/discovery or sculpture where archaeologists craft remains of the past into forms which are meaningful. The archaeological 'record' is, concomitantly, not a record at all, not given, 'data', but made. 'The past' is gone and lost, and *a fortiori*, through the equivocality of things and the character of society as constituted through meaning, never existed as a definitive entity 'the present' anyway. An archaeologist has a raw material, the remains of the past, and turns it into something – data, a report, set of drawings, a museum exhibition, an archive, a television programme, evidence in an academic controversy, and perhaps that which is termed 'knowledge of the past'. This is a mode of production.

To hold that archaeology is a mode of production of the past does not mean that anything can be made. A potter cannot make anything out of clay. Clay has properties, weight, plasticity, viscosity, tensile strength after firing, etc., which will not allow certain constructions. The technical skill of the potter involves working with these properties while designing and making. So there is no idealism here which would have archaeologists inventing whatever pasts they might wish. (...)

Expression and taste

The expressive, aesthetic and emotive qualities of archaeological projects have been largely down-played or even denigrated over the last three decades as archaeolo-gists have sought an objective scientific practice. In popular imagination the archae-ological is far more than a neutral acquisition of knowledge; the material presence of the past is an emotive field of cultural interest and political dispute. The prac-tice of archaeology also is an emotive, aesthetic and expressive experience. This affective component of archaeological labour is social as well as personal, relating to the social experiences of archaeological practice, of belonging to the archaeological community and a discipline or academic discourse. Of course such experiences are immediately political (Shanks 1992).

The essentially creative character of production is also one of expression: taking purpose, assessing viability, working with material, and expressing interpretation to create the product that retains traces of all these stages. This expressive dimen-sion is also about pleasure (or displeasure) and is certainly not restricted to the intellectual or the cognitive. Pleasure is perhaps not a very common word in academic archaeology, but an interpretive archaeology should recognise the role of pleasure and embody it in the product made. This means addressing seriously and with imagination the questions of how we write the past, our activities as archaeologists and how we communicate with others.

In archaeological interpretation the past is designed, yet is no less real or objective. (We can expect some to dispute the reality of a past produced by such an interpretive archaeology which realises the subjective and creative component of the present: such a product cannot be the 'real' past, it might be said, because it has been tainted by the present and by the person of the archaeologist. This is precisely like disputing the 'reality' of a television set. Here is a technological product which looks like a television set. To ask whether it is real is a silly question. A far better question, and one that applies to the product of archaeological interpretation, is: Does it do what is required of it – does it work?) The question of archaeological design is: What kind of archaeology do we want?

A product of technology is both critique and affirmation; it embodies its creation, speaks of style, gives pleasure (or displeasure) in its use, solves a problem perhaps, performs a function, provides experiences, signifies and resonates. It may also be pretentious, ugly or kitsch, useless, or untrue to its materials and creation. In the same way each archaeology has a style; the set of decisions made in producing an archaeological product involves conformity with some interests, precepts or norms, and not with others. As with an artefact, the judgement of an archaeological style involves multiple considerations, many summarised by the term 'taste'. We need to consider its eloquence: that is, how effective and productive it is. We should also make an ethical appraisal of its aims and purposes and possible functions. Technical matters are implicated, of course, including how true it has been to the material past, the reality and techniques of observation that it uses to construct facts. Judgement refers to all these aspects of archaeological production: purpose, viability and expression. (...)

Context and dialogue

A pot without provenance is of limited value to archaeological interpretation. It has long been recognised that placing things in context is fundamental to understanding the past. Much of conventional archaeological technique is about establishing empirically rich contexts of things.

A 'contextual archaeology' makes much of the associations of things from the past (Hodder 1986, 1987). Meanings of things can only be approached if contexts of use are considered, if similarities and differences between things are taken into account. It is often argued that, since the meanings of things are arbitrary, archaeologists cannot reconstruct past symbolism. There are two ways in which archaeologists avoid this impasse. First, artefacts are not like words in that they have to work in a material way and are subject to universal material processes. Thus, an axe used to cut down a tree must be made of rock of a certain hardness and the cutting action will leave wear-traces. An axe made of soft chalk and without wear-traces can thus be identified, on universal criteria, to be of no use for tree-cutting

— an aspect of its meaning has been inferred. Archaeologists routinely think through why prehistoric actors built this wall, dug this trench, using common-sense arguments based on universal criteria. In all such work universal characteristics of materials are linked to specific contexts to see if they are relevant. Interpretation and uncertainty are involved in deciding which aspects of the materials are useful in determining meaning. Hence, and second, the archaeologist turns not to universal characteristics of materials but to internal similarities and differences. Thus, perhaps the chalk axes are found in burials with female skeletons, while the hard stone axes are found in male burials. Such internal patterning not only supports the idea that stone hardness is relevant to meaning in this case, but it also adds another level of meaning — gender. (...)

It is important to recognise that a contextual emphasis does not mean that archaeologists can interpret without generalisation. It is impossible to approach the data without prejudice and without some general theory. But the interpretive challenge is to evaluate such generality in relation to the contextual data. So much of what archaeologists assume in a general way is 'black-boxed'. But even terms like 'pit', or 'ditch' or 'wall' or 'post-hole' should be open to scrutiny to see if they are relevant in each specific context. (...)

Archaeologists, working in their own contexts, are likely to pick out certain types of context in the past and look for patterning in relation to them (...). Interpretation, in its concern with context, can also be described as being to do with *relationality* — exploring connections in the way we have been describing. (...)

Involved here is the context (historical, social, ethical, disciplinary, whatever) of interpretation itself. In coming to understand we always begin with presuppositions. There can be no pure reception of a raw object of interpretation. We begin an interrogation of an historical source with an awareness of its historical context — we view it with hindsight; the flows and commixtures of earths, silts and rubbles in the archaeological site are understood as layers. As interpreters we have to start from somewhere; what we wish to interpret is always already understood *as* something. This is prejudgement or prejudice. And it is essential to understanding. Prejudgement and prejudice are legitimate in that they furnish the conditions for any real understanding.

Another aspect of this is that the acts of looking, sensing and posing questions of things always involve intentional acts of giving meanings. These meanings (rubble as layers, for example) derive from the situation of the interpreter. So the archaeological past is always *for* something. At the least an archaeological site under excavation is part of an archaeological project, and, as we have just argued, *would not exist for us* if it were not. It is understood in terms of its possible applications and relevances in the present. So the 'prejudice' of the interpreting archaeologist's position (ranging from social and cultural location to disciplinary organisation to personal disposition) is not a barrier to understanding, contaminating factors to be screened out; prejudice is the very medium of understanding indeed, *objective* understanding.

Prejudgement and prejudiced assumptions regarding what it is we seek to understand bring us to the hermeneutic circle. Realising that interpretation is about establishing connections and contexts involves realising interpretation as dialogic in character.

This is partly recognised by the idea of *problem orientation*, strongly supported by processual methodology. This maintains that research projects, archaeological observation and study should be designed around meaningful questions to be posed of the past. The correct methodological context is one of question and answer. (...)

But we hope that the notion of interpretation as dialogue suggests a more sensitive treatment and awareness of the relationship between interpreter and interpreted. There is much more to interpretive context. First, the interpreted past is more than something which exists to supply responses to questions deemed meaningful by male and middle-class academics of twentieth-century Western nation states (as most processual archaeologists are). The past has an independence of research design, procedures of question-and-answer (this independence is accommodated in the notion of heterogeneity). It overflows the questions put to it by archaeologists. It may be recognised (Charles Redman, in discussion) that strict problem orientation may miss a great deal, and that simply being open to what may happen to turn up in an excavation is a quite legitimate research strategy. There is nothing wrong with sensitive exploration, being open to finding out.

Second, the past is constituted by meanings. By this is meant that the past is not just a set of data. Some archaeologists have responded to the Native American request for respect for the spiritual meanings of their material pasts with a cry 'They are taking away our database.'

This relates closely to our third and most important point: a dialogue with the material past is situated in far more than *methodological* context. The means of archaeological understanding include everything that the interpreting archaeologist brings to the encounter with the past. The context includes method, yes; but also the interests which brought the archaeologist to the past, the organisation of the discipline, cultural dispositions and meanings which make it reasonable to carry out the investigations, institutional structures and ideologies. We repeat that the archaeological past simply could not exist without all this, the heterogeneous networking of archaeological projects.

Meaning and making sense

Interpretation may suggest meanings for things from the past. A sociological argument is that social practice is to do with interpreting the meanings of things and actions; society is constituted through meanings ascribed and negotiated by social agents (Giddens 1984). So an understanding of the past presupposes that interpretation is given of past meanings of things.

Meaning is a term which requires examination. For example, archaeologists have tried to distinguish functional from symbolic meanings, primary from secondary, denotative from connotative (Shanks and Tilley 1987a; Conkey 1990). In practice, however, it is difficult to separate functional, technological meanings from the symbolic realm, and conversely symbols clearly have pragmatic social functions. In the material world function contributes to abstract symbolic meaning. Much symbolism is entirely ingrained in the practices of daily life, in the rhythms of the body and the seasons, and in the punctuated experience of time. The notion of abstract symbolic code, arbitrarily divorced from practice, has little role to play in current understanding of meaning and its interpretation. There has been a gradual shift in archaeology from a consideration of material culture as language, to a concern with material culture as text and then to an emphasis on practice.

It thus often becomes difficult to ask 'What does this pot mean?', since it may not 'mean' in a language-type way. There may be no signifieds tied to the signifier in a code. Rather it may be the case that, even if people cannot answer what the pot means, they can use the pot very effectively in social life. This practical knowledge of 'how to go on' may be entirely ingrained in practices so that the meanings cannot be discussed verbally with any readiness — the meanings are *non-discursive*. This does not, of course, preclude verbal meanings being construed by an outside interpreter. And at other times — for example, in conflicts over uses and meanings — non-discursive meanings may be brought into 'discursive consciousness', although in doing so actors often embellish and transform. (...)

There is also the question: Whose meanings? (...)

Pluralism and authority

A guide interpreting a map and the land can follow equally feasible paths which may offer different returns or benefits, different vistas. There are different ways of achieving the same ends. Interpretations may vary according to context, purpose, interest or project. Interpretation, we have argued, implies a sensitivity to context. With the equivocality and heterogeneity of things and the underdetermination of interpretation, there are many arguments for pluralism.

But pluralism introduces the problem of authority. On what grounds are different interpretations of the same field to be judged? The problem arises because finality and objectivity (residing in and with the past itself) have been abandoned for an attention to the *practice* of interpretation (making sense of the past as it presents itself to us now). Charges of relativism have been made (Trigger 1989b). Relativism is usually held not to be a good thing. If interpretations of the past depend on present interests and not on objectivity, then there is no way of distinguishing a professional archaeological explanation from the crazed views of cranks who may interpret archaeological remains as traces of alien visitors (Renfrew 1989).

The real issue in the debate over pluralism and relativism is that of *absolutes*. Truth and objectivity are not abstract principles inherent in the past, but have to be worked for. That Anglo-Saxon cemetery in the countryside will not excavate itself. It needs the archaeologist's interest, efforts, management skills, excavation teams, finds laboratories and publisher to be made into what we come to call the objective past.

There are very important issues here to do with the value of interpretation in relation to what science is commonly taken to be. Relativism has not been adequately dealt with, so we present some possible lines which can be taken regarding judgement, authority, objectivity and science.

Objectivity

It is argued that objectivity is not an absolute or abstract quality towards which we strive. Objectivity is constructed. This is not to deny objectivity, but rather, ironically, to make it more concrete. So let it be agreed that an objective state-ment is one which is, at the least, strong; and that, indeed, we would wish our interpretations to be full of such strong statements. What makes a statement strong? The conventional answers are that strength comes from logical coherence, or because the statement corresponds with something out there, external to the statement, or because of some inherent quality called objectivity. But who decides on how coher-ent a statement must be? How exact must correspondence be? And in historical and sociological studies of scientific controversies there appear many other sources of strength such as government or religious support, good rhetoric in convincing others, even financial backing.

We have been arguing that the archaeological past will not excavate itself but needs to be worked for. If objectivity is an abstract quality or principle held by reality, how does it argue for itself, how does it display its strength? No, people are needed, their projects. Gravity does not appear to all and everyone on its own. Microbes needed the likes of Pasteur (Latour 1988). So a statement about the archae-ological past is not strong because it is true or objective, but because it holds together when interrogated; it is then described as objective. What, then, does a statement hold on to, whence does it derive strength, if not from objectivity? There is no necessary answer. It can be many things. An objective statement is one that is con-nected to anything more solid than itself, so that, if it is challenged, all that it is connected to threatens also to fall.

An archaeological report usually aims to present data as objectively as pos-sible, as a strong basis for subsequent inference. Its strength comes from all those diagrams and photographs, the many words of detailed description, the references to comparative sites and materials which give further context to the findings. These all attest to the actual happening of the excavation and to the trustworthiness of the excavation team. Where otherwise is the quality of objectivity? Because the report is coherent and reads well (no contradictions betraying lies and artifice), and the photographs witness things actually being found, because its style and rhetoric are found acceptable, because it delivers what is required (from format to types of information), it is described as sound. Objectivity is what is held together. If a report holds together, it is considered objective.

Challenge a fact in the report and you have to argue with all of this, with the happening of the excavation, that great heterogeneous assemblage of people, things and energies. Ultimately the only way to shake its strength is to excavate another similar site, mobilising another army of resources and people. The skill of crafting objectivity is heterogeneous networking – tying as many things together as possible.

Relativism

If the abstract and independent principle of objectivity is denied, relativism is held to result. Here an important distinction is between *epistemic* and *judgemental* relativism (Bhaskar 1979). Epistemic relativism, which we follow, holds that know-ledge is rooted in a particular time and culture. Knowledge does not just mimic things. Facts and objectivity are constructed. Judgemental relativism makes the *additional* claim that all forms of knowledge are equally valid. But judgemental relativism does not follow from epistemic relativism. To hold that objectivity is constructed does not entail that all forms of supposed knowledge will be equally successful in solving particular problems. Epistemic relativism simply directs attention to the reasons why a statement is held to be objective or strong; it directs attention to the heterogeneous assemblages of people and things and interests and feelings, etc., mobilised in particular projects. To argue a relativism which maintains objectivity is socially constructed is to argue simply for *relationality*. (...)

The reality of the past

But what is the *real* past? Reality is what resists, and trials test its resistance. (...) It has to be specified which trial has been used to define a resistance and hence a *specific* reality. Look at a ceramic thin section down a microscope and there is a reality different from that of its surface decoration. Reality is plural; the artefact is a multiplicity. It depends on what 'work' is done upon and with it. (...) [But] maintaining an absolute objectivity makes it impossible to understand the reasons for there being different versions of the past. (...) There still remains the issue that the past happened when it did. If it is argued that archaeology is a mode of cultural production of the past, does this mean that things did not exist before they were so constructed? Was the Bronze Age hut circle not there before being excavated? (...) Here it is important not to confuse *existence* and *essence*. Existence is when you specify times and settings; it is historical and local. Essence makes no reference to time and space. If something exists at time 1 (the excavated cemetery), can we conclude that it *always* existed, even at time 2 (i.e. in essence)? (...) The specific realities of the past are now historically connected with those of archaeologists in particular projects. (...) How could Star Carr be defined and pictured before Grahame Clark? Perhaps we should apply Clark's excavation retrospectively and suppose that the site was there all along. It is quite legitimate to believe this, but how could it be proved? There is no time machine to take archaeologists back to 1182 or 431 to check that Star Carr was there then, albeit perhaps less decayed. Rather than jumping to conclusions about total existence or non-existence – essences – why not stick with reality defined as that which resists particular trials made of it? The confusion of existence and essence is a damaging one.

A site such as Star Carr does not have an abstract essence or timeless objectivity. We argue that its objective existence has a history. Clark is part of the reality of Star Carr, just as the excavations at Star Carr are part of the biography of Grahame Clark. (...)

Critique

Another aspect of judging the relative value and worth of different interpretations of the same field is critique (see Connerton 1976; Held 1980, Kellner 1989; Leone, Potter and Shackel 1987; Olsen 1986; Shanks and Tilley 1987a, 1987b). Awareness of the dialogues at the heart of interpretation requires self-reflexivity regarding the situated and contextualised interpreters and interpretands. Vital here is the project of ideology critique, now well established in archaeology. Ideology may hinder or make impossible the project of making good sense of the past.

Another dimension of critique is rooted in the heterogeneity, otherness and consequent independence of the material past. The past may become grounds for a critique of the present in that its forms and meanings may defamiliarise and throw into contingency what is taken in the present to be natural or unchanging.

The terms 'equivocality' and 'heterogeneity' were introduced to describe how something always escapes its classification, there always being more to say and consider. The old pot found by an archaeologist is equivocal also because it belongs both to the past and to the present. This is its history; it has survived. And the equivocality confers upon the pot an autonomy because it is not limited to the moment of its making or use, or to the intentions of the potter. It goes beyond. The archaeologist can look back with hindsight and see the pot in its context, so time reveals meanings which are accessible *without* knowledge of the time and conditions of its making. The pot transcends. In this it has qualities which may be called timeless.

Here also historicism (understanding in historical context) must be denied, otherwise we would only be able to understand a Greek pot by reliving the reality of the potter, a reality which anyway was indeterminate and equivocal. We would be fooling ourselves in thinking that we were appreciating and understanding the art and works of other cultures.

Pots are often used as a means to an end by archaeologists. They are used for dating a context; they may be conceived as telling of the past in different ways. Historicist interpretation reduces the significance of a cultural work to voluntary or involuntary *expression*: the pot expresses the society, or the potter, or the date. This is quite legitimate. But there is also the pot itself, its equivocal materiality, its mystery and uncertainty, which open it to interpretation.

The pot does indeed preserve aspects of its time and it can be interpreted to reveal things about the past. So the integrity and independence of the pot does not mean that it does not refer outside of itself. It means that no interpretation or explanation of a pot can ever be attached to the pot for ever, claiming to be integral or a necessary condition of experiencing that pot. The autonomy of the pot is the basis of opposition to totalising systematics: systems of explanation or understanding which would claim closure, completeness, a validity for all time. We must always turn back to the pot and its particularity. This autonomy brings a source of authority to interpretation, if it is respected.

The autonomy of the past is also the reason why archaeological method has no monopoly on the creation of knowledges and truths about the material past. Does a painting of a castle by Turner reveal no truths of its object in comparison with archaeological treatment? Were there no truths about the material past before the formalisations of archaeological method from the late nineteenth century onwards?

There is a gap between the autonomy and dependency of the pot. If we were back in the workshop where the pot was made, we might have a good awareness of its meaning. If we were the one who actually made the pot, then it would very much be dependent upon us. But its materiality, equivocality, heterogeneity always withhold a complete understanding: the clay is always other than its maker; the pot is always more than its classification. People may interpret it in all sorts of different ways. The material world provides food for thought, for negotiation of meaning, as we have already indicated.

So the tension within the pot between dependency and autonomy is a tension between its expressive (or significative) character and its materiality. It is a gap between, for example, an image (which has an autonomous existence) and its meanings. Or between the sound of a word and its meaning to which it cannot be reduced. To bridge these gaps requires effort, work, the time of interpretation. This work is one of reconstruction and connection, putting back together the pieces which have been separated.

When a pot becomes part of the ruin of time, when a site decays into ruin, revealed is the essential character of a material artefact – its duality of autonomy and dependency. The ruined fragment invites us to reconstruct, to exercise the work of imagination, making connections within and beyond the remnants. In this way the post-history of a pot is as indispensable as its pre-history. And the task is not to revive the dead (they are rotten and gone) or the original conditions from whose decay the pot remained, but to understand the pot as ruined fragment. This is the fascination of archaeological interpretation.

Commentary and critique

The tension within the (temporality of an) artefact between past and present, between autonomy and dependence upon its conditions of making, corresponds to the complementarity of critique and commentary. Commentary is interpretation which teases out the remnants of the time of the artefact, places it in historical context. Critique is interpretation which works on the autonomy of the artefact, building references that shift far beyond its time of making. It may be compared artistically with artefacts from other times and cultures in critical art history. Critique may consider different understandings of the artefact in our present. Critique may use the integrity of the artefact as a lever against totalising systems, undermining their claims to universality.

Both are necessary. Commentary without critique is empty and trivial information with no necessary relation to the present. Critique without commentary may be a baseless and self-indulgent appreciation of the aesthetic achievements of the past, or a dogmatic ideology, an unedifying emanation of present interests.

Commentary is made on the dependency of things upon their time of making, fleshing out information of times past. But the flesh needs to be brought to life, and this is the task of critique: revealing heterogeneity, yoking incongruity, showing the gaps in the neat orders of explanation, revealing the impossibility of any final account of things. This is a living reality because it is one of process rather than of arrest. It is the ongoing dialogue that is reasoned interpretation.

Designed pasts: discourse and writing

Archaeology is a practice in which language plays a dominant part. The archaeologist comes literally to the site with a coding sheet, labelled with words, to be filled in. In addition there is a large implicit 'black-box' coding sheet, never discussed, which defines walls, pits, sections, layers and so on. If the excavation process starts with language, so, too, it finishes with language. The events which take place in practice on an archaeological excavation are contingent and they are experienced differently by different participants. Interpretations are continually changed and contested. But in the end a report has to be written, the diversity and contingency subsumed within an ordered text. A story has to be told which not only describes what happened on the site (usually a minor part of the report) but also describes how the layers built up, when and perhaps why the walls were constructed, and so on. The story has to be coherent, with a beginning, a middle and an end. The site has to be moulded into a narrative using rhetoric which makes the story persuasive. A practice has been translated into words and narrative.

Archaeology, like any other discipline, constructs its object past through the workings of *discourse* (see Foucault 1972, 1981; Macdonell 1986; Tilley 1989, 1990a, 1990b, 1993). This is a key concept in directing attention not so much to the content, but to the way something is written or told, and the social and historical conditions surrounding writing and telling. Discourse can be treated as heterogeneous networkings, technologies of cultural production (of a particular kind) which enable and are the conditions within which statements may be made, texts constituted, interpretations made, knowledges developed, even people constituted as subjectivities. Discourse may consist of people, buildings, institutions, rules, values, desires, concepts, machines and instruments. These are arranged according to systems and criteria of inclusion and exclusion, whereby some people are admitted, others excluded, some statements qualified as legitimate candidates for assessment, others judged as not worthy of comment. There are patterns of authority (committees and hierarchies, for example) and systems of sanctioning, accreditation and legitimation (degrees, procedures of reference and refereeing, personal experiences, career paths). Discourses include media of dissemination and involve forms of rhetoric. Archives (physical or memory-based) are built up, providing reference and precedents. Metanarratives, grand systems of narrative, theory or explanation, often approaching myth, lie in the background and provide general orientation, framework and legitimation.

Discourses may vary and clash in close proximity. In a factory the discourse of the workforce may differ considerably from that of the management. Academic archaeology probably includes several discourses: Near Eastern and classical archaeology being distinct from Anglo-American processual archaeology. The discourse of commercial excavation is different again. (...)

Archaeological poetics

An awareness of discourse implies an attention to technique, to style, to the way archaeology designs and produces its pasts. This is the project of an *archaeological poetics* (Shanks and Tilley 1989; Shanks 1992; Tilley 1993) and involves a shift from validation to signification, from anchoring our accounts in the past itself (divorced somehow from our efforts in the present to make sense of it) to the ways we make sense of the past by working through artefacts. (...)

Some concerns of an archaeological poetics include narrative; rhetoric; rhizomatics; quotation and illustration.

Narrative – telling stories – is a basic human way of making sense of the world as particular details are given sense by incorporating them into story forms. The following are components of narrative (Cohan and Shires 1988; Ricoeur 1989; Rimmon-Kenan 1983; White 1973, 1987): story (a temporal sequence), plot (the causation and reasoning behind the story), allegory (metaphor, the story and plot may stand for something else), arrangement of parts (this need not necessarily be a linear sequence of events, there may be temporal slips and changes of pace, condensation and focus on key points), agency (the medium through which the story is told) and point of view (given to the reader). Archaeological narrative is often very predictable. Arrangement is usually linear or analytical, the agency is anonymous or impersonal powers, and the point of view is academic, white, Anglo-American, middle-class. Little experiment is encouraged even though it might considerably improve archaeological writing and attend more to the interests of *different* audiences (an essential component of narrative after all).

Archaeology almost of necessity has to quote because so much of the past is destroyed in excavation. Quotation here refers to bits of 'reality' brought into the picture in the form of photographs or lists of actual objects lodged in a museum (quotation is thus distinct from referencing or citation of other texts). In archaeology this is usually to witness and legitimate the writing. Quotation is to do with collage and montage – direct quotation, literal repetition of something taken out of its context and placed in another. Collage is of essential importance to museum display. Objects need not only credit a statement with concrete validity, but also be used for their heterogeneity, treated in terms of their autonomy from what is written about them, overflowing the words. This aesthetic principle is familiar from art museums and books but can be greatly extended.

The field of rhetoric is coextensive with all communicative and expressive acts (Shanks 1994). Classically it comprises the following: *Inventio* (the discovery of ideas and arguments. Here are included modes of creative generation covering the history of ideas, historiography, the sociology of knowledge, and also interdisciplinary connections); *Dispositio* (the arrangement of ideas into sequences and narratives. Logical and aesthetic links may be considered); *Elocutio* (forms of expression and figures of speech, stylistic treatment. This may be divided into *aptum* – appropriateness to subject matter and context (for example, is a line drawing appropriate?); *puritas* – correctness of expression (according, or not, to rules of discourse and the discipline); *perspicuitas* – the comprehensibility of expression (clarity and density); *ornatus* – the adornment of expression. Tropes or figures of speech provide a great insight into varieties of text structure within *elocutio*. Here are included strategies such as antithesis and irony (figures of contrast), metaphor (identity in difference), metonymy. These particularly would seem to be very relevant to archaeology in its translation of material pasts into a different medium, text and image. Another issue is that of humour; mention has already been made of the importance of pleasure as a constitutive principle in interpretation); *Memoria* (the techniques of storage and the retrieval of speech or text); *Pronunciatio* (delivery, gestures and setting. Included here are the design and delivery of lectures and television programmes, books and publishing projects, museum displays).

Illustration may be treated simply as a visual appendage to a written text, not intended to add anything to verbal description, for example – simply exemplifying. It may approximate to quotation, a photograph witnessing what is written. But illustration can also perform a summarising function, particularly in the form of diagrams. (...) Illustration or graphic representation can draw together things, establishing and mobilising connections which are made all the more effective by being visible at a glance in one place. Thought is hereby guided, possibly even conditioned (Lynch and Woolgar 1990). Latour (1990) has argued that graphic representation can perform a key role in scientific controversy by performing this function. (...)

Tilley (1993) has remarked upon the paradox that what we now term interpretive archaeology hardly exists, yet all archaeology is interpretive. The number of empirical studies which are self-consciously postprocessual or interpretive (in the senses outlined here) is growing, and the range of issues discussed in this volume attests to the wide applicability of the concept of interpretation, but it is less important that archaeologists adopt the label. We are simply proposing that archaeologists, whatever their claims, always have done and can do no other than interpret the past. This places archaeology in symmetry with those in the past who are studied, and with those who are not archaeologists but who try to make sense of the material past. They, too, interpreted and interpret their world, engaging in cultural production. Foregrounding the interpretive character of archaeology deprives archaeologists of an authority which would lie in their restricted access to scientific method, abstract truth and the objectivity of the past. But they can potentially offer to others their skill in crafting and interpreting material pasts, cherishing their creative responsibilities.

References

Bhaskar, R. (1979) *The Possibility of Naturalism*, Hassocks: Harvester Press.

Binford, L. (1977) 'General introduction', in *For Theory Building in Archaeology*, London: Academic Press.

Cohan, S. and Shires, L.S. (1988) *Telling Stories: Theoretical Analysis of Narrative Fiction*, London: Routledge.

Conkey, M. (1990) 'Experimenting with style in archaeology: some historical and theoretical issues', in M. Conkey and C. Hastorf (eds) *The Uses of Style in Archaeology*, Cambridge: Cambridge University Press.

Connerton, P. (ed.) (1976) *Critical Sociology*, Harmondsworth: Penguin.

Foucault, M. (1972) *The Archaeology of Knowledge*, London: Tavistock.

Foucault, M. (1979) *The History of Sexuality*, Vol. 1, *An Introduction*, Harmondsworth: Penguin.

Foucault, M. (1981) 'The order of discourse', in Young, R. (ed.) *Untying the Text*, London: Routledge & Kegan Paul.

Foucault, M. (1984a) *Histoire de la sexualité*, Vol. 2, *L'Usage des plaisirs*, Paris: Gallimard.

Foucault, M. (1984b) *Histoire de la sexualité*, Vol. 3, *Le Souci de soi*, Paris: Gallimard.

Giddens, A. (1984) *The Constitution of Society: Outline of the Theory of Structuration*, Cambridge: Polity Press.

Hebdige, D. (1979) *Subculture: The Meaning of Style*, London: Methuen.

Held, D. (1980) *Introduction to Critical Theory: Horkheimer to Habermas*, London: Hutchinson.

Hodder, I. (ed.) (1982) *Symbolic and Structural Archaeology*, Cambridge: Cambridge University Press.

Hodder, I. (1985) 'Postprocessual archaeology', in M. Schiffer (ed.) *Advances in Archaeological Method and Theory*, London: Academic Press.

Hodder, I. (1986) *Reading the Past; Current Approaches to Interpretation in Archaeology*, Cambridge: Cambridge University Press.

Hodder, I. (ed.) (1987) *The Archaeology of Contextual Meanings*, Cambridge: Cambridge University Press.

Kellner, D. (1989) *Critical Theory, Marxism and Modernity*, Cambridge: Polity Press.

Latour, B. (1988) *The Pasteurization of France*, Cambridge, MA: Harvard University Press.

Latour, B. (1990) 'Drawing things together', in Lynch, M. and Woolgar, S. (eds) *Representation in Scientific Practice*, Cambridge, MA: MIT Press.

Leone, M., Potter, P. and Shackel, P. (1987) 'Toward a critical archaeology', *Current Anthropology*, 28: 283–302.

Lynch, M. and Woolgar, S. (eds) (1990) *Representation in Scientific Practice*, Cambridge, MA: MIT Press.

Macdonell, D. (1986) *Theories of Discourse: An Introduction*, Oxford: Blackwell.

Nietzsche, F. (1967) *The Genealogy of Morals*, trans. W. Kaufmann, New York: Random House.

Olsen, B. (1986) 'Norwegian archaeology and the people without (pre)history: or, how to create a myth of a uniform past', *Archaeological Review from Cambridge*, 5: 25–42.

Pearson, M. (1994) 'Theatre/archaeology', *The Drama Review*, Summer.

Renfrew, C. (1989) Comments on 'Archaeology into the 1990s', *Norwegian Archaeological Review*, 22: 33–41.

Renfrew, C. and Bahn, P. (1991) *Archaeology: Theories, Methods, and Practice*, London: Thames & Hudson.

Ricoeur, P. (1989) *Time and Narrative*, Vol. 3, Chicago: University of Chicago Press.

Rimmon-Kenan, S. (1983) *Narrative Fiction: Contemporary Poetics*, London: Methuen.

Shanks, M. (1992) *Experiencing the Past: On the Character of Archaeology*, London: Routledge.

Shanks, M. (1994) 'The archaeological imagination: creativity, rhetoric and archaeological futures', in Kuna, M. and Venclova, N. (eds) *Whither Archaeology? Archaeology in the End of the Millennium*, Prague.

Shanks, M. and McGuire, R. (1991) 'The craft of archaeology', paper delivered at the Society for American Archaeology Meetings, New Orleans.

Shanks, M. and Tilley, C. (1987a) *Re-Constructing Archaeology*, Cambridge: Cambridge University Press.

Shanks, M. and Tilley, C. (1987b) *Social Theory and Archaeology*, Oxford: Polity Press.

Shanks, M. and Tilley, C. (1989) 'Archaeology into the 1990s', *Norwegian Archaeological Review*, 22: 1–12.

Tilley, C. (1989) 'Discourse and power: the genre of the Cambridge inaugural lecture', in Miller, D., Rowlands, M. and Tilley, C. (eds) *Domination and Resistance*, London: Unwin Hyman.

Tilley, C. (1990a) 'Michel Foucault: towards an archaeology of archaeology', in Tilley, C. (ed.) *Reading Material Culture*, Oxford: Blackwell.

Tilley, C. (1990b) 'On modernity and archaeological discourse', in Bapty, I. and Yates, T. (eds) *Archaeology after Structuralism*, London: Routledge.

Tilley, C. (ed.) (1993) *Interpretative Archaeology*, London: Berg.

Trigger, B. (1989a) *A History of Archaeological Thought*, Cambridge: Cambridge University Press.

Trigger, B. (1989b) 'Hyperrelativism, responsibility and the social sciences', *Canadian Review of Sociology and Anthropology*, 26: 776–97.

Watson, P. (1990) 'The razor's edge: symbolic-structuralist archaeology and the expansion of archaeological inference', *American Anthropologist*, 92: 613–21.

White, H. (1973) *Metahistory*, Baltimore, MD: Johns Hopkins University Press.

White, H. (1987) *The Content of the Form: Narrative Discourse and Historical Representation*, Baltimore, MD: Johns Hopkins University Press.

Willey, G.R. and Sabloff, J.A. (1980) *A History of American Archaeology*, San Francisco, CA: Freeman.

Yoffee, N. and Sherratt, A. (eds) (1993) *Archaeological Theory: Who Sets the Agenda?*, Cambridge: Cambridge University Press.

Edited extract from Shanks, M. and Hodder, I. (1995) 'Processual, postprocessual and interpretive archaeologies', in Hodder, I., Shanks, M., Alexandri, A., Buchli, V., Carman, J., Last, J. and Lucas, G. (eds) *Interpreting Archaeology*, London: Routledge, 3–29. Ian Hodder is Professor at Stanford University, California, and author of numerous books on archaeological theory and practice. This collaboration with Michael Shanks arose from a Cambridge conference in 1991 which brought together a diverse audience to debate the interpretation of the material past.

Chapter 13

Artefacts and the meaning of things

Daniel Miller

I MAGINE WE DECIDE TO ESTABLISH a museum of contemporary material culture in order to preserve for posterity the artefacts of today. A comprehensive collecting policy is intended. It will not be very long before the farcical nature of this scheme becomes apparent. Some things, such as houses and ships, are too big, some things, such as candy floss and daisy chains, too ephemeral. Is a softwood plantation a natural or an artefactual form? Do we start with industrially produced goods and, if so, do we include every brand of car door mirrors and shampoo, and if a company proclaims a change in the product is this a new artefact or not? What about self-made artefacts, those that children have made at school, or that individuals have knitted on the bus? Clearly we cannot create such a museum, although we may observe the extraordinary variety of exhibitions that might be put on, featuring collections of anything from matchboxes to garden gnomes.

To acknowledge the problems faced by such a proposal, however, is liable to produce a rather uneasy feeling that we live in a world that has gone beyond our capacities of ordering. As Simmel (1968: 43–4) argued at the turn of the century, to be continually faced with objects which we cannot assimilate is one of the key problems of the modern age. We constantly strive for such assimilation. That is, artefacts appear as given concrete forms, but human societies have always striven – through their construction, alteration, consumption and application of meaning – to make them internal to, and in part definitional of, themselves. In many ways it is the very physical nature of artefacts, at once the product of human desires, yet in themselves inanimate, which will always render them ambiguous as regards the dualism between persons and non-persons. It is intrinsic to their nature as social things.

This problem has constituted a kind of meta-context for the study of anthropology. Anthropologists have generally come from societies which are experiencing a massive increase in the quantity of material culture, whether these societies are industrial nations or developing countries with rapidly increasing importation of consumer goods in exchange for primary products. The general sense of an infinitude of new varieties of things and the new flux of fashion and transience may itself be the prime source of this feeling that artefacts are threatening to us. There is a continual unease about being what is colloquially termed 'materialistic'. An underlying question has therefore been to understand the manner by which persons come to identify with objects or even to become undifferentiated from them.

When the phrase the 'meaning of things' is used in anthropology it tends to implicate something beyond the narrow questions of semanticity by which artefacts, like words, might have sense and reference. Rather, the notion of meaning tends to incorporate a sense of 'meaningful' closer to the term 'significance'. When we think of buildings, foods, clothes and other artefacts we automatically concern ourselves with meaning in the sense of asking what does this building or drink mean to us and for us? Is this an artefact I identify with as conforming to my 'taste' or 'style', or do I think of it as relating primarily to some other person or group? Is it a suitable present for . . . ? Is it a suitable environment to be inhabited by . . . ? Is it an appropriate symbol of . . . ? And so forth. Artefacts are very different from words, and when we talk about the meaning of things we are primarily concerned with questions of 'being' rather than questions of 'reference'. Artefacts are a means by which we give form to, and come to an understanding of, ourselves, others, or abstractions such as the nation or the modern. It is in this broad sense that their very materiality becomes problematic, and it is this problematic which I shall take as the central theme of this article.

This point is not always acknowledged in anthropology, since the primary concern has tended to be with the meaning of artefacts for others, in particular for those living in relatively small-scale communities with a relatively limited and clearly defined array of artefacts. But here, as in so much of anthropology, the very interest in what have tended to be presented as small, closed systems can be fully understood only in relation to, and often in contrast with, the preoccupations of the societies from which the anthropologists have come and for whom they write, societies in which simplicity in the relation to objects is consigned to remote places or far-off times. Therefore, to understand the meaning of things for anthropology, both ends of this polarity have to be considered. On the one hand anthropologists can call on their experience of living and participating in small communities, where to study the meaning of things is almost always to assume that such artefacts are 'full' of meaning, often integrating various otherwise disparate elements of cultural life. On the other hand all contemporary anthropologists, as members of their own societies, also relate to objects, for example by going shopping. Whether selecting car seat covers, ice cream flavours or a new novel to read, we are constantly aware that the choice threatens to be problematic, that we might find ourselves delaying others as we strive, internally torn between choices on a menu. The problem lies less in the time expended than in the awareness that it is very hard to justify, to find criteria which would lend importance to such decisions and therefore make sense of this activity as a substantial element in our lives. We feel that to be unable to choose the appropriate birthday card in a shop is symptomatic of a new banality. Modern mass material culture has made us all feel silly at different times, and it is this which makes the study of material culture such a serious pursuit.

The concept of the artefact is best defined in the broadest terms. There is lit-tle point in attempting to distinguish systematically between a natural world and an artefactual one, except when we are concerned with the ways in which terms such as 'natural' may have particular consequences or entailments, as when a com-modity in the shops is labelled 'natural' simply because a single ingredient, such as a chemical dye, has been deleted, or when something as apparently natural as radi-ation is taken to be antithetical to true 'nature'. It is not only in industrial soci-eties that virtually all objects encountered are artefactual. If we remove ourselves to the South Pacific, for example to a Polynesian outlier within the Solomon Islands, then at first glance we might seem to encounter a dense natural forest environ-ment within which villages represent clearings. This, however, would be to ignore the highly developed arboriculture which over several centuries has removed vir-tually all trees which are not of direct economic value to the inhabitants, to leave an environment which is in fact entirely the product of cultivation. Plants and animals are natural species, but is not a lap-dog produced by selective breeding over genera-tions an animated artefact — still more a bonsai tree? Even when it comes to those objects such as the sea or snow which we do not control, we still interact with them as classified and therefore structured sets of forms, which are experienced through such human ordering. Snow for the Inuit out hunting is only in the most trivial sense the same thing as snow experienced by a London youth at Christmas.

It would be similarly pointless to attempt to define material culture as the out-come of specific desires or to differentiate the products of intention from those of history — artefacts which are made deliberately as opposed to those which come down to us as given forms. Since intentions themselves have their source in sub-jects who are inevitably situated historically, the argument would always tend to circularity, because we would find that the artefacts we have received in turn influence the artefacts we choose to make. Few contemporary inhabitants of Sweden wear the clothes fashionable in the eighteenth century, but this is not the result of some calculative decision. The micro-element of conscious decision between perceived possibilities can be attributed to intentionality, but the alternatives from which we choose, and the strategies which inform our taste in objects, are usually derived from larger historical forces.

If material culture is not defined in relation to its artificiality or intentionality, what alternative basis can be found? It seems most reasonable to take it as a sub-set of culture, so that a theory of artefacts as material culture would be derived from a more general theory of culture. If culture is understood not in the narrow sense of some particular element of the human environment, but in the more gen-eral sense of the process through which human groups construct themselves and are socialized, then material culture becomes an aspect of objectification, consist-ing in the material forms taken by this cultural process. Hence to study material culture is to consider the implications of the materiality of form for the cultural process.

This sense of material culture as a form of being-in-the-world becomes clearer when we consider the process of socialization. From quite early on, the infant born in one cultural context becomes recognizably distinct in manners and outlook from an infant socialized in another setting. Much of this results from the micro-routines of daily life, in which we become oriented to and by the spaces, the objects and the small but significant distinctions in object forms through which we form our classifications and habits. In turn these create our expectations, which allow much of the world to become quickly absorbed as a 'taken-for-granted' context for our lives. In this sense our cultural identity is not merely embodied but literally 'objectified' (Bourdieu 1977).

This suggests a starting point for examining the cultural process, which lies in the manner by which we order things and are ordered by things. Subsequently two further problems arise: first, the implications of the very materiality of things, and second, the dualism by which we tend to think of things as being opposed to persons.

The order of things (1): ordering things

In this section my central concern is both with elucidating dominant principles by which arrays of artefacts are ordered and with showing how these are derived by means of different methodologies developed for the study of material culture. Both historians and anthropologists have argued that particular societies or particular historical periods have tended to emphasize particular principles of classification. Foucault, for example, divides European history into separate 'epistemes' based on the dominant principle of classification employed in each. He argues that with the rise of natural history, sight became dominant over smell and touch (1970: 132–3), while forms of resemblance and affinity were similarly demoted as against other principles of order. With the rise of the sciences it was not enough to assume that a root which happened to have a shape reminiscent of the human body was therefore likely, when eaten, to have an effect upon the body. Rather, from systematic collections of natural objects, such as butterflies or rock forms, patterns of affinity were sought which could then be analysed in conjunction with consistent theories of their connectivity.

The order of things is also culturally constructed. Strathern (1988: 268–305) has argued that in traditional Melanesian societies transformative principles are stressed, rather than those of either affinity or theory. An object is always perceived in terms of its ability to transform into or elicit another object: a tool is the potential creator of garden crops, a boy is a potential man, a shell necklace may attract another form of valuable. Objects are thus viewed less in themselves than for their place in an exchange or ritual which will have an effect. In some cases it is forbidden to eat or consume that which you have yourself produced, because to do so prevents the object from becoming part of an exchange (e.g. Munn 1986: 49–60) or some other process through which it may act on the world in a transformative capacity. Hence one's sense of any given thing is one in which other things are always implicated.

When we set out to represent a set of objects, the dimensions by which an order is constructed either explicitly or implicitly give meaning to the array of forms. In nineteenth-century museums, for example, objects such as musical instruments or arrows were often organized into a sequence, from the most simple to the most sophisticated. What was illustrated, but equally taken as 'demonstrated', was the sense in which material culture has 'evolved' from primitive forms to the refinements of advanced civilization by direct analogy with what were assumed to be the principles of biological science. Ethnographers might then search for the 'missing link' in the guise of some tribal form which would show how one stage in this process gave way to the next (Steadman 1979: 74–102). This principle, by which museums tend to reflect wider changes in attitudes towards classification, continues to operate today. In the 1980s, when the desire for the holistic emerged with new force in areas as diverse as alternative medicine and 'whole' foods sold in the supermarket, an ethnographic exhibition of, for example, South Asian peasant life would have attempted to provide an image of the village as it was lived in, allowing the visitor almost to breathe the dust and smell the odours which belonged to the original context of the artefacts displayed (though it was the smell of spices rather than that of urine or garbage which seemed to survive this change of setting). Often, virtually all the detailed labelling characteristic of earlier exhibition forms was removed, so as to leave no barrier to the sense of entering into a whole and natural social environment.

If the meaning of objects derives from the orders into which they are incorporated, then the same artefact may change its implications simply by being introduced into some new order. Gilsenan (1982: 192–214) writes about the construction of old towns or the old quarters of towns in the Middle East which are often visited today by tourists who view them as picturesque remains. Clearly at one time such areas were themselves new, and for a long period they were merely the ordinary form of urban environment, but once the point is reached at which much of the rest of the town has been rebuilt in a new style, the remaining areas may be redesignated as the 'old' city and gain thereby an aura of being quaint or traditional, the ideal haunt for tourists: a dark, obscure and fossilized form. This is not, as some have assumed, a new type of change. A very similar process occurred two millennia earlier when the same areas with which Gilsensan is concerned were Hellenized or Romanized. As with modern colonialism, the Greek sector of the city may well have appeared modern and as the inevitable outcome of historical change which rendered the original, non-Hellenized sector of, for example, Jerusalem quaint, barbaric or merely scruffy.

At least one major paradigm in anthropology, that of structuralism, has made the ordering of things central to its understanding of human culture. Although the 'things' in question were often non-material, such as myths or kinship rules, structuralist studies of the internal logic of symbolic systems – linked as they were to semiotic studies of the relations between symbols and their external referents – led to many refinements in the study of cultures as cosmologies whose sense of order and integrity emerged in large part through the logical ordering of concrete objects. Two examples may serve as illustrations. The first is Lévi-Strauss's own study (1982: 93) of the masks used by the Indians of the American Northwest Coast, in which these figure as material equivalents of myths. Like myths, they would undergo inversion, either in their physical attributes or in the symbolic interpretation of their material form, at the boundaries between different tribal groups. Thus the Xwexwe mask of the Kwakiutl, with its bulging eyes, protruding jaws and tongue, is the inverse transformation of their Dzonkwa mask, which has sunken eyes, hollow cheeks, and no tongue, but is the same as the mask called Swaihwe of the neighbouring Salish. Here the objects of one society are seen to derive their meanings not only from their relations of opposition one with another, but from the ways in which this system of relations undergoes partial inversion as it crosses the boundaries with neighbouring societies. It is as though the meanings of British foods only become clear when they are seen as systematic inversions of French culinary symbolism

While anthropological structuralism was much influenced by the linguistic theory of de Saussure, many other studies of the order embodied in artefacts were inspired by the subsequent and equally influential linguistics of Chomsky (e.g. Faris 1972). In Chomsky's 'generative grammars' we were able to see how systems of rules which are never explicit are applied through language to determine what combinations of sounds form meaningful sequences rather than unintelligible juxtapositions. Each grammar is specific to a particular group of speakers.

For my second illustrative example I draw on the work of Glassie (1975), who has applied similar ideas to a study of historical folk housing in Middle Virginia. Noting the repetition in geometric form and combinations of elements, Glassie argues that rules are being systematically applied. As with language, these are not conscious, and there are no professional architects. Rather, these 'rules' determined the normative order which generated buildings with which the people of the time felt comfortable, and which were acceptable in their general aesthetics. Overall, he argues that nine subdivided rule-sets can account for the generation of all the culturally acceptable vernacular buildings that are found. These include such micro-elements as 'fenestration of the façade' or 'the fireplace must be central to the wall on which it is located' (Glassie 1975: 29). The analysis is a dynamic one which reveals how, around the middle of the eighteenth century, a major change occurred by which chimneys and central halls became incorporated into the main building, and a new concern with symmetry appeared along with a homogenization of the exterior around a more conspicuously ordered façade associated with the Georgian style.

This historical study may be brought up to date by ethnographic work being carried out in the nearby area of coastal North Carolina (Forrest 1988, especially 192–203). As in other recent studies, the tendency has been to move away from the tight and rather formal methods of strict structural analysis and to allow a more flexible, contextual and interpretive dimension, while still examining patterns which link different sets of artefacts. In this case the aesthetics of house outlines are linked to interior decoration, including items such as quilts or the recipes used for home cooking. The aesthetics of the home interior are compared with the decoration of the church and contrasted to objects used outside the home and associated with men, such as the duck decoys used in sports. The ethnography allows the physical and spatial forms to be presented in the context of the aesthetics of smell and taste, and of more general sensual appreciation. An overall 'message' is seen to emerge consistent with the more explicit messages of the church. This is directed particularly to men, who, after spending much of their life outside the home milieu, often working at some distance from the community and associated with a more material-transactional ethos, are then encouraged to return to the fold of religion and domestic life as reflected in a more incorporative aesthetic and practice. At this stage, however, we have moved from a focus on the ordering of things to the manner by which we might be said to be ordered by things.

The order of things (2): ordered by things

In the above studies the patterning found in material culture is essentially a reflection of a dominant mode of classification imposed either by the anthropologist as analyst or by the group being studied (in practice, usually some amalgamation of the two). The other side of the coin, however, lies in the impact the taxonomic order of things has upon those who are socialized into that environment. The original Portuguese title of Gilberto Freyre's classic work on the early development of Brazilian society is *Casa-Grande e Senzala* – that is, *The Big House and the Slave Quarters*. Within this work the author constantly attempts to evoke the manner by which social relations are established by reference to this spatial context, the setting for a sensual and languid life in the hammock, where to have to use one's legs was to risk a degrading comparison with slaves and plebeians (Freyre 1986: 429). The development of particular behaviours in relation to sexuality and sadism is closely tied to the way their normality is enshrined in a spatial nexus defined by the architectural forms and the institutions they represented and literally channelled into particular relations.

There has recently been a return to this kind of more impressionistic anthropology in which such material paraphernalia as clothing forms or baroque façades are understood as core elements in evoking a sense of 'atmosphere' in which certain social relations and activities develop and become normative. In industrial societies commercial classifications often clarify such relations. Objects made by the London-based firm Heal's in the late nineteenth century clearly constructed systematic stylistic distinctions contrasting the furnishing appropriate for servants against that appropriate for the mistress (Forty 1986: 85). This distinction was given symbolic form in every decorative detail and may be set alongside that ubiquitous Victorian phrase of people 'knowing their place'. Forty (1986: 156–81) examines the development of concepts of hygiene and cleanliness, and activities such as constant dusting, promoted on the grounds of their being based on important discoveries in medical science but then elevated to something rather more in the formation of the modern role of the housewife. 'Disorder and lack of cleanliness should cause a sort of suffering in the mistress of the house. Put in these terms the condition of total cleanliness was comparable to a religious state of grace, and just as unattainable' (Forty 1986: 169). The decline in this obsession with dusting has not led to a perceptible rise in poor health, but the point made by Forty is not just that the concept of cleanliness was central to changes in gender relations but that it was literally enshrined in a wide array of new furnishing forms, colours, textures and designs which constituted the acceptable standard of interior decoration. Cleanliness was transformed into beauty.

In some societies such ordering principles appear to be all-encompassing. South Asian caste society is usually described not only as hierarchically ordered by caste but also as deriving all forms of classification from hierarchy, so that even different woods or metals are seen as high or low. All object and material classifications evoke social distinctions, such that aluminium vessels are seen as more suitable for lower-caste use than brass vessels, one wood is more appropriate to high-caste ritual use than another, and so forth. It is commonly argued that to be brought up in such an environment, in which all things declare the ubiquity of a particular ordering principle, will result in a perception of the world which takes this principle as second nature, close to the concept of habit, an order accepted without any conscious thought or consideration as to the way things might otherwise be. Many of those authors who have concentrated on the place of material culture in socialization have tended to emphasize the way in which ordinary objects can have this effect without appearing to do so (e.g. Bourdieu 1977). However, recent work suggests that we have tended to exaggerate the homogeneity of such meaning, and to ignore the degree of contradiction and ambivalence.

The effect of artefacts in creating a taken-for-granted meaning which is thereby less likely to be challenged than a more explicit set of principles has come under recent scrutiny with the impact of feminism. A vast number of ordinary commercial objects are 'gendered' according to what appear to be consistent patterns. For example, where objects are destined for males it is more likely that the machine parts will be exposed to view. When typewriters switched from being mainly associated with male clerks to being used largely by female secretaries the keys were enclosed; likewise when the motor scooter was developed as a female equivalent to the male motorbike it not only enclosed the engine but took its lines from the familiar children's scooter (Hebdige 1988: 84). Although individual instances of such practices are easy to locate, as in the dichotomy between playing with dolls and trains, it is the overwhelming ubiquity of this trend and the realization that there are many other more subtle manifestations of distinction which frustrate those who desire to end what is regarded as an asymmetrical division. The debate is complicated by the sense of deliberate commercial involvement in creating meanings as images for artefacts in a world of commodities, and by the existence of professionals such as advertisers whose job it is to give meaning to artefacts. It gives rise to the question, however, as to how this situation may be compared with instances from non-industrial societies where similar symbolic schemes operate to 'gender' village material culture without deliberate recourse to any such mechanisms.

From here it is a small step to the study of ideology using material culture (Larrain 1979; Miller and Tilley 1984). This tends to be based upon two assumptions. The first is that certain interest groups in a society have more influence to create the world of artefacts in such a manner that they embody the ordering principles established by those same interests. The second is that people who are brought up surrounded by artefacts which embody such ordering principles will tend to understand the world in accordance with this order, with the result that dominated groups will tend to have some difficulty in understanding the nature of their own interests, since these are not given concrete form in the world they inhabit. Since higher-caste Indians dominate the spatial order of villages and the forms of village goods, these spatial orders and material forms will embody a caste view of the world which reproduces the interests of these same higher castes. This view of ideology as misrecognition or false consciousness has certainly been challenged, but central to its credibility is the notion that ordinary artefacts have a considerable impact in ordering people. It may be noted that this approach does not presuppose deliberate manipulation by dominant groups, merely that those with power will anyway tend to construct the world according to the perspectives from which they view it.

What are the implications for groups of people who are living within a world which largely manifests the ideals and values of others? For anthropologists this question presents itself most acutely in terms of a fragmentation of what had previously appeared as a relatively simple opposition between *our* kinds of material culture and *theirs*, which I introduced at the beginning of this article. In the contemporary world, the ethnographer who travels to highland New Guinea or goes to study shamans in Brazil is likely to have the uncomfortable experience of finding people who will ask questions about the latest shifts in popular music styles or the characters of a soap opera on national television. The study of material culture today takes place under conditions in which multinational firms have a presence in virtually every country, and where the same chocolate milk drink, brand of blue jeans, paperback books, gift perfumes and videos are readily available. Once again people who did not initially see material culture as of primary importance are faced with such overwhelming visible changes that certain questions simply force themselves into the foreground. If these are the material forms being employed today, at the very least the problem arises of whether it makes any difference to *this* kinship system if the dowry has to include a fridge, or to *that* ritual if a plastic doll figures in it prominently. More importantly for the study of the significance of image construction, what are the implications of photography or film, which as a medium allows ordinary villagers access to visual images which had previously been reserved for deities? Finally, does a quantitative increase in material culture bring about a qualitative change for the society concerned?

The initial reaction to these changes has tended to be to see them as the harbinger of the end of anthropology as we have known it, since they spell the end of the simple or isolated society, and the end of the authentic 'unspoiled' humanity which for so long has provided a foil for the industrial world. Homogenization of material culture is thus taken as symptomatic of the homogenization of culture itself. This process is often called Americanization, since the United States is viewed as a symbol for mass consumption in general. Similarly the quantitative increase in goods is taken to represent an immediate fall into alienation, and the ensuing problems are generalized as those of 'modernity'. Furthermore, since these goods are made in metropolitan societies by multinational corporations, their spread is assumed to be tantamount to a form of actual control over the peoples who now become subject to the goods and thus subservient to the values and authorities from which they emanate. Yet, in recent years, anthropologists have increasingly realized that the societies represented in their ethnographies were never so isolated, ahistorical, functional or in some sense authentic as they had often been portrayed to be. If New Guinea societies could adopt such radical innovations as the sweet potato prior to colonial contact, was it reasonable to argue that a Melanesian group which had proved to be entrepreneurially adept at harnessing the possibilities of high coffee prices was necessarily less traditional or authentic than the group which was better known as reacting to new possibilities through cargo cults? Given this broad context, however, it is becoming clear that questions about the meaning of artefacts are increasingly tied up with larger issues about whether the world is literally becoming more or less meaningful, and about how far artefacts marketed with a homogenizing global meaning are given specific local meanings in the contexts in which they are consumed.

The materiality of artefacts

The importance of considering the materiality and specificity of the world of artefacts should now be clear. A discussion of the way in which we order things and are in turn ordered by things certainly makes 'things' sound very orderly. In practice, however, artefacts may relate more to a multiplicity of meanings and identities, and the relations between form and meaning may be complex and ambiguous. The ingenuity displayed by human societies in investing the world with meaning is one of the abiding lessons of anthropology, and it is very difficult therefore to insist that artefacts always *do* this or *are* that. It is, however, possible to argue that objects, by their nature, tend to lend themselves to certain kinds of cultural appropriation. In constructing such an argument around the intrinsic potential of artefacts, their very physicality must play a major part.

The specificity of artefacts is considered here first by way of a critical account of that approach which centres on the meaning of artefacts in the narrower sense based on an analogy with language. From this there follows a concern with the differences between the artefactual and linguistic domains. While in linguistics the study of semantics (reference) and syntax (grammar) has tended to predominate over the study of pragmatics (context), we may expect an anthropological approach which is sensitive to the relativity of context to emphasize pragmatics.

We have already seen that approaches to material culture have often been profoundly influenced by ideas derived from the study of language. Both structuralist techniques for examining the internal relations and oppositions between objects, understood as parts of relatively closed systems, and the complementary techniques of semiotics which examine the reference of objects as signs, have been applied to artefacts. To make the analogy with language work, however, artefacts have tended to be detached from their physical nature and functional context and to be treated as relatively arbitrary signs formed through the application of contrast, making them potential meaningful units which could then be combined to produce something resembling a text. The influence of linguistics continues in the framework of trends in poststructuralist analysis, which has tended to focus upon the hidden agenda of messages, the dominant myths which are promulgated through language. Influential writers in this tradition, from Barthes (1973) to Baudrillard (1981), have emphasized the use of mundane artefacts as carriers of these myths, which they have seen it as their task to expose to scrutiny.

The linguistic analogy has proved very fruitful in demonstrating the symbolic malleability and power of artefacts; but it also has its limitations. Artefacts are not words, and the differences between them may provide further clues as to what artefacts really are. Langer (1942: 90–3) long ago pointed out that language always works through sequences of sounds, and that as examples of what she called 'discursive' forms, linguistic utterances *unfold* as meaning. By contrast, objects are typically what she termed 'presentational' forms – that is, they present themselves with all their aspects at one time. Compared with words, artefacts much less often have clear propositional content, and the patterns and distinctions found may not necessarily correspond to units of meaning. Although certain anthropologists have claimed to be able to reveal grammar-like structures in objects, these are generally much looser and do not have the same necessity as grammar in language. Clearly objects relate to wider perceptual functions than do words. Remarkably subtle distinctions can be evoked through smell, taste, touch and most especially sight; by comparison, language may appear as a clumsy vehicle for the conveyance of difference. Try to describe in words the difference in smell between two kinds of fish, or the shape of two different shirts! This subtlety can also be seen in the extremes of personal identification. The problem of choosing between hundreds of pairs of shoes is most often caused less because we are spoilt for choice, and more because of the extraordinary feeling that despite the diversity not one of these pairs is quite right for us. To recall such a familiar experience helps us to acknowledge the subtleties in the way we differentiate between objects as meaningful forms and so to resolve the anthropological puzzle of why, say, one particular representation of a crocodile was an acceptable totemic representation while another, apparently almost identical to the first, had to be discarded.

The central difference lies in the physicality of objects, however. Earlier it was suggested there is little to be gained through attempting to impose a rigorous distinction between the artefactual world and the natural world; later on it was suggested that objects operate with particular effectiveness as ideology, making the taxonomic orders of a particular culture appear to the individual as second nature. These two observations are clearly connected. Objects often appear as more 'natural' than words, in that we come across them in the main as already existing things, unlike at least spoken language, which is produced in front of us. This quality of artefacts helps, as it were, to entrance us, to cause us to forget that they are indeed artefacts, embodiments of cultural codes, rather than simply the natural environment within which we live. Artefacts and their physicality tend to become implicated in a wide variety of similar ambiguities. In English there is a strong sense of instrumental function, and it is commonly by their functions that artefacts are semantically labelled – e.g. 'frying pan' or 'hammer'. Nevertheless, for most ordinary artefacts it is extremely difficult to determine any clear boundary between functionally based and purely decorative aspects of form. Most pots have as their functional role the act of containing some substance, but the diversity of shape is only relatively loosely related to the range of needs for particular kinds of containment (Miller 1985: 51–74): If decoration communicates symbolically, can this be said to be its function? This ambiguity reinforces that between the natural and the artefactual, because the relation between form and function is generally taken to be 'natural', while other elements of form are more evidently expressive of a deliberate ordering. In all such cases, objects appear to orient us in the world, but in a way that remains largely implicit.

In a sense artefacts have a certain 'humility' in that they are reticent about revealing their power to determine what is socially conceivable. Curiously, it is precisely their physicality which makes them at once so concrete and evident, but at the same time causes them to be assimilated into unconscious and unquestioned knowledge. When viewing a work of art, it is often the frame which determines our perception of the quality of the content (that is, it cues us in to the fact that we are about to have an aesthetic experience), when the contained item, left to itself, might well have failed to evoke the 'proper' response. In a similar fashion, 'subtle' cosmetics are intended to enhance the attractiveness of the face without drawing attention to themselves. Thus artefacts may be most effective in determining our perception when they express a sense of humility in which they avoid becoming the direct focus of our attention. Many artefacts, whether house decorations or daily clothing, incline to this position on the borders of our perception rather than, as with the picture itself, capturing the focus of our gaze. They most often attract our attention when we feel there is either something new or something wrong about them.

Ethnographic findings seem to have an almost perverse tendency to refute any generalization produced by anthropological theory. Clearly words are capable of having any of the effects and properties which have here been associated with objects. As Derrida's (1977) work has shown, the difference in relative physicality between written and oral language may be of enormous significance. Equally, objects may occupy almost any of the propositional niches utilized by words. Thus the argument presented above has to be seen as one of tendencies rather than absolutes. However, although a particular society may refuse to exploit a given potential, the physical properties of artefacts nevertheless lend themselves to their being used to construct this sense of a frame, which does not have to pass through consciousness in order constantly to reconstruct the context of our experience of the world.

The specificity of artefacts

Apart from these general qualities of artefacts, which arise from their physical materiality, they also have many qualities which are important for understanding their specific place in particular social contexts. Each of these qualities may become a focus within material culture studies, but for purposes of illustration only one, that of temporality, is discussed in any detail here. Artefacts are manufactured objects which may reveal in their form the technology used, but may equally seek to hide it. Items such as craft products may be conspicuously hand-made to highlight the contrast with industrial goods; alternatively, the stoneworker may seek to emulate the prestige of the blacksmith by using techniques which are inefficient when applied to stone but create a similar style, which in that particular context underwrites status. Again the instrumental function of an object may be exploited symbolically, or buried under decorative ornament. Artefacts may establish an individualistic relation, as with the emblem of a ruler or the prized blue jeans of a teenager, or they may stand for a wider social group such as a nation state. An object may confer added prestige through its having been imported from a considerable distance, through being rare or made from a rare raw material. An object may derive its specific meaning as part of an emergent style or order, such as a particular ceramic style in ancient China or a style of cathedral building seen as quintessentially Gothic.

The point to bear in mind is that all of these potential symbolic elements are exploitations of the specific nature of artefacts: they are manufactured, come from a particular place and are used in particular ways. Size itself can be expressive, as in monumentality or, at the other extreme, in the concept of the 'petite', where small is also feminine. The vast symbolic potential to be drawn from exploiting the attributes of things is limited only by the ingenuity of a particular social group. In order to provide more substantial illustration of this symbolic potential and the resourcefulness of cultures in exploiting it, I now turn, in what follows, to consider the temporality of artefacts. Temporality is intrinsic to objects in the sense that there is always a period of time between their creation and the moment they are being considered, but this temporal quality may be either entirely inconsequential or, as with an heirloom, the element which endows the object with meaning.

Things, persons and time

To examine the relationship between the meaning of artefacts and temporality, three situations will be explored. In the first, the artefact, or at least that which the artefact represents, outlasts persons and thus becomes the vehicle by which persons attempt to transcend their own temporal limits. In the second situation there is some temporal equivalence between persons and artefacts which tends to give rise to issues of representation. In the third, artefacts are regarded as relatively ephemeral compared with persons, and the focus is then on the manner in which identity is carried along by the flood of transforming things. By drawing examples from various cultural contexts I do not mean to suggest their likeness; on the contrary, what is revealed is the very diverse manner in which the same relation between time and artefact is constructed and used in the manifold contexts of different human groups.

Longevity

All people initially experience the world as something given by history rather than something they create. The child struggles to control, often vicariously through play, at least some elements of the encountered world, but this desire is constantly frustrated by ever-expanding vistas of the massiveness of this already created world. Among the items encountered are those which children may be taught to treat with special respect because they are icons of identity, commonly tokens of the longevity of their culture and of cross-generational continuity – a heritage which must never be lost because it has always existed. For example, in many Australian Aboriginal groups the male youth is presented at puberty with the sacred objects which have come down from the ancestors of the Dreamtime (the period in which the world was first created). The identity of an Indian peasant may be focused upon a piece of land that has been owned by the family for generations. The Jew may be constantly reminded of ritual knowledge enshrined in books which only exist because each generation has maintained them in the face of persecution. In all such cases the mere fact of the previous existence of things confers responsibility at the same moment that it bestows identity. Just as persons know themselves through identification with their clan totem or with the boundary stones of their land, so it is now their duty to ensure preservation through to the next generation.

Monuments are, in general, very large material forms built specifically to embody such a notion of transcending the generations – for example to symbolize the enduring nature of a 'thousand-year Reich'. But the same notion may equally be embodied in a simple ancestral shrine. Such objects may also fix the corporate entity on which identity and responsibility should fall. In the case of a national monument such as the Eiffel Tower, it is the nation state; in the case of the burial place of a deceased relative established through geomancy, future connections are determined by specific genealogical rules. With monuments it is the quality of size which is exploited, with burials it is spatial fixity. It need not be the case that these are ideological notions foisted by small elites on the population at large; the enormous heritage industry which has developed in most industrial societies includes countless small local museums or historical shrines to industrialization, as well as engaging many groups from all classes of society in archaeological excavations amounting to a collective act of self-consecration. This does presuppose, however, that a historical identity has already been established and rendered conventional.

An irony of this process is that whereas the material objects may actually transcend the generations, the corporate groups with which they are associated are themselves likely to change. Stonehenge is now a symbol of Britain, but was probably established initially by some tribal grouping in the Wessex region, and in the intervening period has undergone many changes in its symbolic appeal. Different groups may struggle over who built Great Zimbabwe, or who should retain the Elgin marbles from the Parthenon, aware that there is much more at stake than simple historical veracity or quality of conservation. Both Constantinople and Rome have been fought over at different historical periods for their ability to confer imperial legitimacy, and the Saudi authorities who possess Mecca spatially may nevertheless find themselves confronted by conflicting spiritual claims from, for example, the Iranian *haj*. On a smaller scale, disputes may arise over access by different castes to a village temple in India. Such conflict becomes particularly poignant in the conflicting claims to rights over cemeteries lodged by archaeologists and the descendants of those buried therein. The former try to incorporate the dead in the collective heritage, the latter treat them as their specific ancestral legacy.

Weiner (1985) has noted that for Polynesian peoples such as the Maori there may develop a special category of objects termed *taonga*, which are rendered inalienable precisely because they come to evoke the ancestral past. For example, items made of nephrite may come to have individual names and 'biographies' which are held to bear witness to events at which they were present, or to owners who are now deceased (Weiner 1985: 217–18). She refers to the case of a nephrite adze which was lost for seven generations but recognized on its rediscovery in 1877 when the stories associated with it were retold. Such valuables are often imbued with special meaning by virtue of the rich symbolic nexus which ties in their semantic or decorative properties with cosmological ideas relating to such events as birth, death and renewal.

Temporal identity

The second form of relationship between artefacts and persons is derived from a temporal equivalence in which objects stand for the particular states of persons at that time, so that a change in the material attributes of the person is indicative of a change in the person him- or herself. This is the relationship which commonly most concerns anthropologists, because their technique of participant observation tends to freeze the relationship between persons and artefacts in one frame of time, within which the logic of the relationship may be studied. For example, the project of Mass Observation led by the anthropologist Tom Harrison attempted to study and characterize Britain in the years before the Second World War. In one of the best-known studies the team attempted to deal with that key British institution, the pub, in Worktown. The interest was not directly in material culture but in understanding class, and the social implications of the pub as an institution. However, in order to accomplish this task a further element of material culture, clothing, became a key index. Considerable effort went into the differentiation of caps, bowler hats, ties, and so forth, and many statements fix the sociological variables in sartorial form; for example: 'caps are a working class badge, scarves around the neck instead of collar and tie usually indicate middle and lower (unskilled and semi-skilled) working class – but they are not necessarily invariable indications' (Mass Observation 1987: 144). So we are informed that for their clientele of beerhouse vaults between week-night and Saturday, the proportion of caps goes down from 92 to 80 per cent while that of bowlers goes up from 0 to 6 per cent. This is set against the observation that, contrary to expectations, Sundays show less of a move to respectable clothing than Saturdays. This, in turn, starts a chain of analysis leading to an important discussion of the relationship between the place of religion and of drinking for the inhabitants of the town (Mass Observation 1987: 140–67), according to which a change in an individual's dress sense becomes the instrument for signifying a desire to change his or her social position.

Similarly, in the anthropology of South Asia the focus of most ethnographic attention has been the institution of caste, and initially the study of food preparation, transaction and ingestion was developed simply because it seemed to provide the best set of indicators for an 'objective' study of caste hierarchy that would complement verbal accounts. It was argued that if you examined who actually accepted particular kinds of food from whom, then this would provide a picture of caste hierarchy in practice. Increasingly, however, it was appreciated that – partly because Hinduism has a much more sustained philosophy of the direct relationship between that which is ingested and the resultant qualities of the person ingesting – the study of food has to become integral to the understanding of caste as much more than a simple system of sociological categorization. A classification is not just made manifest through its correlation with material forms, but the experience of a particular identity and sense of being is created through the very sensual qualities involved in preparing and ingesting foodstuffs (compare Marriot 1968 with Marriot 1976). In moving from meaning to the meaningful, from cognitive to sensual expression, what is involved is not only the anthropological task of 'translating' another culture through widening the power of evocation, but a more profound appreciation of the manner by which culture reveals itself as a constitutive process.

Since my concern in this section is neither with the longevity nor with the transience of artefacts, but rather with their ability to relate to the larger cultural project of the moment, it is appropriate to consider the possibility of using changes in the materials as a means of investigating cultural change. Shanks and Tilley (1986: 172–240), for example, have investigated the different approaches taken to alcoholism by the Swedish and British states, as indicated in the designs of beer cans. Their work exemplifies an emphasis on the precise forms of the material artefacts themselves, which are then related to the wider contexts of their production. One hundred and twenty beer cans, half from each country, were subjected to a formidable analysis including 45 variables such as forms of lettering or whether or not there was a design band around the top of the can. Detailed accounts were then provided of representational designs, names and other features on the can, and these in turn were related to a systematic analysis of advertisements, articles in newspapers about alcoholism, and so forth. Overall the differences in design and the manner in which alcohol is marketed were related to the distinction traced by the authors over the last century according to which the Swedish state has tended to take a more interventionist stance influenced by earlier prohibitionist tendencies, which, as Shanks and Tilley (1986: 191–8) put it (following Foucault), were linked to a desire to discipline its population. In Britain, by contrast, the state took a more *laissez-faire* but also more fiscally minded approach, emphasizing the possibilities for raising income through taxation.

Shanks and Tilley's work is directed to archaeologists, who are as much concerned as are anthropologists with questions of the meaning of artefacts. The task of the archaeologist is to reconstruct past societies on the basis of their material remains, and this in turn must depend a good deal on how the relationship between persons and artefacts is understood. In the past the tendency has been to invert the social-anthropological bias by making persons merely representations of the movements of things. Thus prehistorians documented such movements as 'the invasion of the black burnished pottery folk', or the rise of the 'jade axe peoples'. This was eventually opened out to encompass a more general concern with reconstructing the internal structure of ancient societies. Often the key sources of information for this were burials. If the grave goods buried with the deceased were highly differentiated, the society was supposed to be hierarchical; if less differentiated, it was supposed to be egalitarian. If one brooch signalled a commoner and two brooches a chief, then three brooches indicated a regional lord.

The problem with this approach may be clarified by means of a contemporary analogy. British society today includes vast differences in wealth and social status, but this would certainly not be evident from a visit to the cemeteries, where gravestones are used to express a belief about equality in death and where the most common concern of mourners is to avoid ostentation. Archaeologists are thus increasingly coming to realize that their interpretations of the nature of ancient societies are dependent upon developing a more sophisticated and less mechanical approach to the meaning of the artefacts which they uncover (e.g. Hodder 1986).

Transience

Transience, as also longevity, is a potential property of the relationship between persons and things, but its cultural significance may vary considerably. It is usually assumed that a concern with the ephemeral nature of artefacts is a peculiar condition of modernity, but, as with most other characteristics of being modern, there is no a priori reason to suppose that there are not, or have not been, other societies which have focused upon this quality of objects as having profound implications for the nature of their world. Kuechler (1988) has pointed out, with respect to the Malangan wooden funerary carvings of New Ireland, that although these are now incorporated as art objects in museums around the world, the major

consideration in their original use in rituals associated with death was that they would
rot away, and in this context even the smells associated with this process of deterioration were of central importance in the cosmology of the people concerned.

On the island of Trinidad certain sections of the community are generally regarded
as having a particular penchant for style (Miller 1994). Considerable effort and expense
may be directed towards originality in constructing effective displays. Here it is
the very transient quality of industrial goods which is the focus of concern. Although
international fashions are exploited, the mere following of fashion is left to the more
conservative elements in the community, since style demands a more creative appropriation and juxtaposition of items. Individuals involved in this pursuit of style are
often also characterized as reacting against those institutional and structural mechanisms which would otherwise place them in more stable and more hierarchical
frameworks. There may be an unwillingness to associate closely with any occupation or social role. Many of the familiar structural forms of kinship may be denied,
for example through recognizing little sense of obligation towards persons simply
on the basis of some genealogical connection, preferring pragmatic and dyadic forms
of social association.

The use of material culture in transitory modes in which no lasting or affective relationship is built up with any particular objects is clearly related to the search
for autonomy and independence in these other arenas. The particular mode may
well be related to a strongly expressed concern for freedom whose historical roots
may go back to the experience of slavery and indentured labour of the ancestors
of many of those concerned. It has certainly been affected by the rise of industrialization and mass consumption, in this case paid for largely by profits from an
oil-based economy. Indeed, mass consumption may be taking over from kinship as
the main vehicle by which this historical project of freedom may be objectified.

In such circumstances there are considerable advantages to be gained from moving away from a medium such as kinship where transience is generally condemned
by those whose models of proper family relations are developed elsewhere. By concentrating instead on the medium of fashion, the sense of style which is created
may be positively expressed and blessed by international canons which favour
creativity in this expressive field. Thus what locally may be the same cultural project, that is of creating an experience of transience as freedom, is either condemned
or envied, depending upon whether a social or a material medium is used to express
it. Style, far from being superficial, has here become the central instrument by which
identity is constructed without its being made subservient to social institutional structures. Within the same society there is an opposing tendency associated with highly
structured kinship and emphasis on intergenerational continuity. In this case the
accumulation of property and goods, and the control over resources which goes
with it, is seen to provide an alternative route to freedom from control by others,
and thereby to emancipation.

An analysis such as that presented above assumes that people are able to appropriate and transform the products of international manufacture, in this case largely
because tendencies in economic development happen to have been pre-empted
by tendencies in the development of local culture. In many other contexts it seems
that the capacity of transience to demolish received structures is not matched
by the possibilities of appropriation, and the result is closer to the experience of

alienation so often observed in the rise and spread of mass and transient material culture. Unfortunately, anthropologists have so far paid very little attention to the analysis of industrial material culture and mass consumption, and the articulation between macro-economic shifts and the local elaboration of cultural projects is little understood. Such issues are of considerable importance today, particularly because it is becoming increasingly evident that in much of the developing world, expenditure patterns have moved swiftly towards prioritizing objects such as televisions and new forms of clothing, often at the expense of those priorities proposed by international agencies, such as achieving adequate levels of nutrition and shelter. We are nowadays confronted with images of decaying slums festooned with cars and television aerials.

Embodiment and objectification: against a dualism of artefact and persons

So far in this article we have considered the idea that the meaning of artefacts goes beyond the narrow cognitive questions of sense and reference, we have examined the dialectical interplay between ordering objects and being ordered by them, we have explored the implications of their physicality and their differences from the words of language, and we have discussed their symbolic qualities in regard to the factor of time. To conclude, I now lift the argument onto a slightly more abstract level to challenge the most basic of the assumptions underwriting consideration of these questions: that we are dealing with the relations between two quite separate kinds of entities, namely persons and things.

For a long time anthropologists have assumed that a pristine level of 'social relations' furnishes the authentic foundation for what they are supposed to be studying. The theoretical rationale for this approach was provided by Durkheim, and the study of kinship provided its ethnographic substance. Thus whatever cultural domain was being investigated was ultimately treated as symbolic of underlying social relations. The meanings of artefacts were always seen to lie in their positioning within such symbolic systems. When the term 'constituting' became fashionable in the literature, it seemed to grant a more active role to these cultural forms than the more passive-sounding notion of 'symbolizing', and this reflected a move from a simple 'social' anthropology towards a sense of 'cultural' anthropology in which social forms are created by the same media that express them. An example of this approach was presented in the previous section, where the use of fashion was seen to be in some sense equivalent to kinship in expressing and constructing a historically situated cultural project. Recently, further attempts have been made to erode the asymmetry in the relationship between social relations and cultural forms.

In theoretical writings which have come to be known as 'postmodernist' or 'poststructuralist' (e.g. Foucault 1970) the demise of this act of reference to social relations was in one sense welcomed, since it was suggested that the idea of a pure humanity or individual person was a fiction of relatively recent times which virtually deified the human in order to fill the void left by a secular rejection of the divine (e.g. Barthes 1977: 142–8, Foucault 1977: 113–18). However, the trend was also seen as a negative one in that it was said to reflect a new era of mass commodities in which objects refer mainly to lifestyles comprising the association with other sets of objects, and have lost the ability to relate 'authentically' to any cultural project (e.g. Baudrillard 1981).

One area in which anthropologists have been most effective in establishing an image of culture which is not based on a dualistic opposition of persons and artefacts is in the literature on gifts and gift exchange, as established originally by Mauss and subsequently developed mainly in writings on Melanesia and the Pacific. In his essay of 1925 on *The Gift*, Mauss (1954) argued that the gift had to be returned because it carried with it a sense of the inalienable – that is, something which could never really be given away. This something involved, among other elements, the sense that the object retained attributes of the person by whom it was given, and, furthermore, the object was seen to embody a relationship which exists between persons by virtue of their mutual obligation to give and return gifts. This also helped to account for the observation that persons might be exchanged as gifts in a manner which did not diminish their sense of humanity or value, since to be so exchanged (as, for example, with the 'gift' of a bride in marriage) is not to be reduced to some less exalted, thing-like status. In recent anthropological literature, especially on Melanesian societies, the subtleties of such processes have been much further elaborated (e.g. Strathern 1988).

Unfortunately, Mauss also established a means by which this new understanding could be incorporated into a romantic primitivism, according to which small-scale societies could be seen as having a totalizing vision which repudiates any simple distinction between persons and things. These societies were then contrasted with those which were based on commodity exchange and which, following Marx, were seen to have gone to the other extreme in not only creating this fundamental dualism but also establishing institutions in which persons achieve a sense of humanity only to lose it through being reduced to thing-like status.

As I noted at the beginning of this article, these concerns have been paramount in establishing the framework within which scholars have considered the question of the meaning of artefacts. For example, Durkheim's writings on – and concern with – mass consumption (Williams 1982: 322–42) help us to understand why he developed a 'social' rather than a 'cultural' approach. This may also explain why anthropologists, who have successfully elucidated how objects like canoes or spears may be caught up in complex networks of symbolic meaning connecting diverse domains within small-scale societies, nevertheless tend to join the postmodernists in dismissing the possibility of a similarly complex exegesis of industrial artefacts.

There have, however, been some recent attempts to soften this dualism between persons and objects, or between gifts and commodities. Appadurai (1986: 3–63), for example, has attempted to do this by examining the literature on exchange, while Miller (1987) explores the manner in which the notion of objectification might be used to overcome a dualistic or reductionist approach to material culture. Ironically, while writers on postmodernism discover that artefacts no longer seem to make reference to 'people', this may in part be because commodities as well as gifts have the capacity to construct cultural projects wherein there is no simple dichotomy between things and persons. Indeed, anthropologists have exaggerated the totalizing holism of small-scale social groups, often ignoring contradictions and feelings of alienation, while on the other hand failing to see the strategies by which people in industrial societies attempt to appropriate their own material culture.

It may be preferable in all cases to resist the assumption, which is given in the experience of ethnography, that we are dealing with an already established set of objects whose social meaning has to be (retrospectively) determined. For, in reality, such objects only come into being through prior acts of construction, and in the process of their manufacture they manifest a particular system of categorization. Likewise, persons only come into being, with the particular cultural identities that they have, through a process of socialization involving these same material taxonomies. The process does not stop with socialization, however, for material forms remain as one of the key media through which people conduct their constant struggles over identity and confront the contradictions and ambiguities that face them in their daily lives. To go beyond a dualistic approach means recognizing that the continual process by which meaning is given to things is the same process by which meaning is given to lives.

References

Appadurai, A. (1986) 'Introduction', in Appadurai, A. (ed.) *The Social Life of Things*, Cambridge: Cambridge University Press.

Barthes, R. (1973) *Mythologies*, London: Paladin.

Barthes, R. (1977) *Image, Music, Text*, London: Fontana.

Baudrillard, J. (1981) *For a Critique of the Political Economy of the Sign*, St Louis, MO: Telos Press.

Bourdieu, P. (1977) *Outline of a Theory of Practice*, Cambridge: Cambridge University Press.

Derrida, J. (1977) *Of Grammatology*, Baltimore, MD: Johns Hopkins University Press.

Faris, J. (1972) *Nuba Personal Art*, London: Duckworth.

Forrest, J. (1988) *Lord I'm Coming Home*, Ithaca, NY: Cornell University Press.

Forty, A. (1986) *Objects of Desire*, London: Thames & Hudson.

Foucault, M. (1970) *The Order of Things*, London: Tavistock.

Foucault, M. (1977) *Language, Counter-Memory, Practice*, Ithaca, NY: Cornell University Press.

Freyre, G. (1986) *The Masters and the Slaves*, Berkeley, CA: University of California Press.

Gilsenan, M. (1982) *Recognizing Islam*, London: Croom Helm.

Glassie, H. (1975) *Folk Housing in Middle Virginia*, Knoxville, TN: University of Tennessee Press.

Hebdige, D. (1988) *Hiding in the Light*, London: Routledge.

Hodder, I. (1986) *Reading the Past*, Cambridge: Cambridge University Press.

Kuechler, S. (1988) 'Malangan: objects, sacrifice and the production of memory', *American Ethnologist* 15(4): 625–37.

Langer, S. (1942) *Philosophy in a New Key*, Cambridge, MA: Harvard University Press.

Larrain, J. (1979) *The Concept of Ideology*, London: Hutchinson.

Lévi-Strauss, C. (1982) *The Way of the Masks*, Seattle: University of Washington Press.

Marriot, M. (1968) 'Caste ranking and food transactions: a matrix analysis', in Singer, M. and Cohn, B. (eds) *Structure and Change in Indian Society*, Chicago: Aldine.

Marriot, M. (1976) 'Hindu transactions: diversity without dualism', in Kapferer, B. (ed.) *Transactions and Meaning: Directions in the Analysis of Exchange and Symbolic Behaviour*, Philadelphia, PA: Institute for the Study of Human Issues.

Mass Observation (1987) *The Pub and the People*, London: Century Hutchinson.

Mauss, M. (1954) *The Gift*, London: Cohen & West.

Miller, D. (1985) *Artefacts as Categories*, Cambridge: Cambridge University Press.

Miller, D. (1987) *Material Culture and Mass Consumption*, Oxford: Blackwell.

Miller, D. (1994) *Modernity: An Ethnographic Approach*, Oxford: Berg.

Miller, D. and Tilley, C. (eds) (1984) *Ideology, Power and Prehistory*, Cambridge: Cambridge University Press.

Munn, N. (1986) *The Fame of Gawa*, Cambridge: Cambridge University Press.

Shanks, M. and Tilley, C. (1986) *Re-constructing Archaeology*, Cambridge: Cambridge University Press.

Simmel, G. (1968) *The Conflict in Modern Culture and Other Essays*, New York: New York Teachers College Press.

Steadman, P. (1979) *The Evolution of Designs*, Cambridge: Cambridge University Press.

Strathern, M. (1988) *The Gender of the Gift*, Berkeley, CA: University of California Press.

Weiner, A. (1985) 'Inalienable wealth', *American Ethnologist* 12(2): 210–27.

Williams, R. (1982) *Dream Worlds*, Berkeley, CA: University of California Press.

First published as Miller, D. (1994) 'Artefacts and the meaning of things', in Ingold, T. (ed.) *Companion Encyclopedia of Anthropology*, London: Routledge, 396–419. Daniel Miller is Professor of Material Culture at University College London. His books include *The Dialectics of Shopping*, *Car Cultures*, *Consumption: Critical Concepts* (4 vols), *Home Possessions: Material Culture Behind Closed Doors*, *The Sari* and *Materiality*.

PART THREE

The Consumed World

Introduction to Part Three

Simon J. Knell

THIS COLLECTION OF READINGS is concerned with consumption – in its broadest sense the utilisation of resources. Here the resource is cultural objects and ideas, which we consume in exhibited narratives, knowledge, aesthetics and so on. This is precisely the focus of Pierre Bourdieu's highly influential *Distinction: A Social Critique of the Judgement of Taste*. In the edited extract from this book republished here, Bourdieu gets to that critical moment where he reveals a fundamental distinction between the tastes of the working and middle classes. He shows that works of art, for example, are rejected in increasing numbers according to the limitations of one's education. His powerful arguments raised fundamental questions about the authority and legitimising role of the museum, when it came to culture, revealing that the museum was inevitably self-perpetuating in its middle-class values and tastes, and for this reason politically charged. For Weil – as he revealed in the previous section – Bourdieu was a step too far. This conversation regarding art and the art world continues in two further chapters by Derrick Chong and Jonathan Vickery. In a rich literature, Chong's chapter usefully summarises aspects of the art world from his own particular interest in art world economics. The study provides a good starting point for anyone wishing to look beyond the aesthetics, art history and criticism. Vickery, like Weil and Chong, ponders a question most clearly articulated by Marcel Duchamp in 1916 when he exhibited his 'readymades'. For Vickery, the subject is Carl Andre's artistically arranged bricks which became a popular subject of derision. Vickery is wide-ranging in his attempts to understand how such things become art, and in doing so foregrounds the need to understand art world organisation, within which the museum plays a key role.

From the consumption of art, it is a rather small step to appreciate the purchase an image-enhancing commodity of a quite different type. Brian McVeigh's delightful study of Hello Kitty, elegantly and succinctly explores commodification, market manipulation, and consumption. It is useful to museums for revealing relationships between object and identity, in this case the commodification of innocence and cuteness; a materialisation of the values located in target markets which is then sold back to those markets which in turn inevitably consolidates and reinforces these values. Here the object becomes far more cynical than usually understood by museums. Here, too, there is a complex relationship between production and consumption, and the role of objects in the social world. It suggests, as other studies also show, that consumption cannot be understood as a true reflection of taste – there are many other factors at play here. Miller raised some of these issues in an earlier article, and Colin Campbell does so here. For the museum, Campbell's questions concern the symbolic conclusions one might draw from an individual's consumption patterns. This is important for the museum wishing to collect and interpret contemporary society and raises the questions regarding the generalising of groups in post-industrial society, which takes interpretation away from objectivity or reality.

The extract from Annette Weiner's paper discusses notions of keeping while giving in non-Western societies. It reveals a complexity of object–human relationship that long challenged Western understanding, and is still debated by anthropologists. It stands as an example, in a rich literature, which permits us to question some of our presumptions regarding consumption. Here, for example, there is no (or not always an) evaluation of relative worth. My own extract, places this world of exchange within the museum at the time when museums in Britain really took off. Here the objects aren't armshells, there is no circulation, though one might well see some keeping while giving. More important is the reciprocity inherent in the act of donation which proved so critical to binding society at a time of social upheaval. If museums were engaged in an empirical project – which they were – then that empiricism relied upon subjective and socialised processes involving the very same objects. This section ends with a modern counterpart to the story I tell here. In her short chapter Virginia Morell is discussing the same subject – fossils – and reveals that the political implications of consumption and social competition, and the creation of legitimising hegemonies have not disappeared from this science. These involve political actions which could fundamentally reshape the material world in terms of society's engagement with it. There is much published on pillaging of cultural remains but this presents a rather different picture, one where arguments for control are rather less clear-cut.

Chapter 14

The aristocracy of culture

Pierre Bourdieu

The aesthetic disposition

A NY LEGITIMATE WORK TENDS in fact to impose the norms of its own perception and tacitly defines as the only legitimate mode of perception the one which brings into play a certain disposition and a certain competence. Recognizing this fact does not mean constituting a particular mode of perception as an essence, thereby falling into the illusion which is the basis of recognition of artistic legitimacy. It does mean taking note of the fact that all agents, whether they like it or not, whether or not they have the means of conforming to them, find themselves objectively measured by those norms. At the same time it becomes possible to establish whether these dispositions and competences are gifts of nature, as the charismatic ideology of the relation to the work of art would have it, or products of learning, and to bring to light the hidden conditions of the miracle of the unequal class distribution of the capacity for inspired encounters with works of art and high culture in general.

Every essentialist analysis of the aesthetic disposition, the only socially accepted 'right' way of approaching the objects socially designated as works of art, that is, as both demanding and deserving to be approached with a specifically aesthetic intention capable of recognizing and constituting them as works of art, is bound to fail. Refusing to take account of the collective and individual genesis of this product of history which must be endlessly 're-produced' by education, it is unable to reconstruct its sole raison d'être, that is, the historical reason which underlies the arbitrary necessity of the institution. If the work of art is indeed, as Panofsky says, that which 'demands to be experienced aesthetically', and if any object, natural or artificial, can be perceived aesthetically, how can one escape the conclusion that it is the aesthetic intention which 'makes the work of art', or, to transpose a formula of Saussure's, that it is the aesthetic point of view that creates the aesthetic object? To get out of this vicious circle, Panofsky has to endow the work of art with an 'intention', in the Scholastic sense. A purely 'practical' perception contradicts this objective intention, just as an aesthetic perception would in a sense be a practical negation of the objective intention of a signal, a red light for example, which requires a 'practical' response: braking. Thus, within the class of worked-upon objects, themselves defined in opposition to natural objects, the class of art objects would be defined by the fact that it demands to be perceived aesthetically, i.e. in terms of form rather than function. But how can such a definition be made operational? Panofsky himself observes that it is virtually impossible to determine scientifically at what moment a worked-upon object becomes an art object, that is, at what moment form takes over from function: 'If I write to a friend to invite him to dinner, my letter is primarily a communication. But the more I shift the emphasis to the form of my script, the more nearly does it become a work of literature or poetry' (Panofsky 1955: 12).

Does this mean that the demarcation line between the world of technical objects and the world of aesthetic objects depends on the 'intention' of the producer of those objects? In fact, this 'intention' is itself the product of the social norms and conventions which combine to define the always uncertain and historically chang-ing frontier between simple technical objects and objets d'art: 'Classical tastes', Panofsky observes, 'demanded that private letters, legal speeches and the shields of heroes should be "artistic" . . . while modern taste demands that architecture and ash trays should be "functional"' (Panofsky 1955: 13).

But the apprehension and appreciation of the work also depend on the beholder's intention, which is itself a function of the conventional norms governing the rela-tion to the work of art in a certain historical and social situation and also of the beholder's capacity to conform to those norms, i.e. his artistic training. To break out of this circle one only has to observe that the ideal of 'pure' perception of a work of art qua work of art is the product of the enunciation and systematization of the principles of specifically aesthetic legitimacy which accompany the consti-tuting of a relatively autonomous artistic field. The aesthetic mode of perception in the 'pure' form which it has now assumed corresponds to a particular state of the mode of artistic production. An art which, like all Post-Impressionist painting, for example, is the product of an artistic intention which asserts the *absolute primacy of form over function*, of the mode of representation over the object represented, *categorically* demands a purely aesthetic disposition which earlier art demanded only conditionally. The demiurgic ambition of the artist, capable of applying to *any* object the pure intention of an artistic effort which is an end in itself, calls for unlimited receptiveness on the part of an aesthete capable of applying the specifically aesthetic intention to any object, whether or not it has been produced with aesthetic intention.

This demand is objectified in the art museum; there the aesthetic disposition becomes an institution. Nothing more totally manifests and achieves the autono-mizing of aesthetic activity vis-à-vis extra-aesthetic interests or functions than the art museum's juxtaposition of works. Though originally subordinated to quite dif-ferent or even incompatible functions (crucifix and fetish, Pietà and still life), these juxtaposed works tacitly demand attention to form rather than function, technique rather than theme, and, being constructed in styles that are mutually exclusive but all equally necessary, they are a practical challenge to the expectation of realistic representation as defined by the arbitrary canons of an everyday aesthetic, and so lead naturally from stylistic relativism to the neutralization of the very function of representation. Objects previously treated as collectors' curios or historical and ethnographic documents have achieved the status of works of art, thereby materializing the omnipotence of the aesthetic gaze and making it difficult to ignore the fact that – if it is not to be merely an arbitrary and therefore suspect affirmation of this absolute power – artistic contemplation now has to include a degree of erudition which is liable to damage the illusion of immediate illumination that is an essential element of pure pleasure.

Pure taste and 'barbarous' taste

In short, never perhaps has more been asked of the spectator, who is now required to 're-produce' the primary operation whereby the artist (with the complicity of his whole intellectual field) produced this new fetish (Bourdieu 1971, 1975, 1980). But never perhaps has he been given so much in return. The naive exhibitionism of 'conspicuous consumption', which seeks distinction in the crude display of ill-mastered luxury, is nothing compared to the unique capacity of the pure gaze, a quasi-creative power which sets the aesthete apart from the common herd by a radical difference which seems to be inscribed in 'persons'. One only has to read Ortega y Gasset to see the reinforcement the charismatic ideology derives from art, which is 'essentially unpopular, indeed, anti-popular' and from the 'curious sociological effect' it produces by dividing the public into two 'antagonistic castes', 'those who understand and those who do not'. 'This implies', Ortega goes on, 'that some possess an organ of understanding which others have been denied; that these are two distinct varieties of the human species. The new art is not for everyone, like Romantic art, but destined for an especially gifted minority.' And he ascribes to the 'humiliation' and 'obscure sense of inferiority' inspired by 'this art of privilege, sensuous nobility, instinctive aristocracy', the irritation it arouses in the mass, 'unworthy of artistic sacraments': 'For a century and a half, the "people", the mass, have claimed to be the whole of society. The music of Stravinsky or the plays of Pirandello have the sociological power of obliging them to see themselves as they are, as the "common people", a mere ingredient among others in the social structure, the inert material of the historical process, a secondary factor in the spiritual cosmos. By contrast, the young art helps the "best" to know and recognize one another in the greyness of the multitude and to learn their mission, which is to be few in number and to have to fight against the multitude' (Ortega y Gasset [1925] 1966).

And to show that the self-legitimating imagination of the 'happy few' has no limits, one only has to quote a recent text by Suzanne Langer, who is presented as 'one of the world's most influential philosophers': 'In the past, the masses did not have access to art; music, painting, and even books, were pleasures reserved for the rich. It might have been supposed that the poor, the "common people", would have enjoyed them equally, if they had had the chance. But now that everyone can read, go to museums, listen to great music, at least on the radio, the judgement of the masses about these things has become a reality and through this it has become clear that great art is not a direct sensuous pleasure. Otherwise, like

cookies or cocktails, it would flatter uneducated taste as much as cultured taste'
(Langer 1968: 183).

It should not be thought that the relationship of distinction (which may or may
not imply the conscious intention of distinguishing oneself from common people)
is only an incidental component in the aesthetic disposition. The pure gaze implies
a break with the ordinary attitude towards the world which, as such, is a social
break. One can agree with Ortega y Gasset when he attributes to modern art –
which merely takes to its extreme conclusions an intention implicit in art since the
Renaissance – a systematic refusal of all that is 'human', by which he means the
passions, emotions and feelings which *ordinary* people put into their *ordinary* existence, and consequently all the themes and objects capable of evoking them: 'People
like a play when they are able to take an interest in the human destinies put before
them', in which 'they participate as if they were real-life events' (Ortega y Gasset
1966: 356–7). Rejecting the 'human' clearly means rejecting what is generic, i.e.
common, 'easy' and immediately accessible, starting with everything that reduces
the aesthetic animal to pure and simple animality, to palpable pleasure or sensual
desire. The interest in the content of the representation which leads people to call
'beautiful' the representation of beautiful things, especially those which speak most
immediately to the senses and the sensibility, is rejected in favour of the indifference and distance which refuse to subordinate judgement of the representation to
the nature of the object represented. It can be seen that it is not so easy to describe
the 'pure' gaze without also describing the naive gaze which it defines itself against,
and vice versa; and that there is 'no *neutral*, impartial, 'pure' description of either
of these opposing visions (which does not mean that one has to subscribe to aesthetic relativism, when it is so obvious that the 'popular aesthetic' is defined in
relation to 'high' aesthetics and that reference to legitimate art and its negative judgement on 'popular' taste never ceases to haunt the popular experience of beauty).
Refusal or privation? It is as dangerous to attribute the coherence of a systematic
aesthetic to the objectively aesthetic commitments of ordinary people as it is to
adopt, albeit unconsciously, the strictly negative conception of ordinary vision which
is the basis of every 'high' aesthetic.

The popular 'aesthetic'

Everything takes place as if the 'popular aesthetic' were based on the affirmation
of continuity between art and life, which implies the subordination of form to function, or, one might say, on a refusal of the refusal which is the starting point
of the high aesthetic, i.e. the clear-cut separation of ordinary dispositions from
the specifically aesthetic disposition. The hostility of the working class and of the
middle-class fractions least rich in cultural capital towards every kind of formal experimentation asserts itself both in the theatre and in painting, or still more clearly,
because they have less legitimacy, in photography and the cinema. In the theatre
as in the cinema, the popular audience delights in plots that proceed logically and
chronologically towards a happy end, and 'identifies' better with simply drawn
situations and characters than with ambiguous and symbolic figures and actions or
the enigmatic problems of the theatre of cruelty, not to mention the suspended

animation of Beckettian heroes or the bland absurdities of Pinteresque dialogue. Their reluctance or refusal springs not just from lack of familiarity but from a deep-rooted demand for participation, which formal experiment systematically disappoints, especially when, refusing to offer the 'vulgar' attractions of an art of illusion, the theatrical fiction denounces itself, as in all forms of 'play within a play'. Pirandello supplies the paradigm here, in plays in which the actors are actors unable to act — *Six Characters in Search of an Author, Comme ci (ou comme ça)* or *Ce soir on improvise* — and Jean Genet supplies the formula in the Prologue to *The Blacks*: 'We shall have the politeness, which you have taught us, to make communication impossible. The distance initially between us we shall increase, by our splendid gestures, our manners and our insolence, for we are also actors.' The desire to enter into the game, identifying with the characters' joys and sufferings, worrying about their fate, espousing their hopes and ideals, living their life, is based on a form of *investment*, a sort of deliberate 'naivety', ingenuousness, good-natured credulity ('We're here to enjoy ourselves'), which tends to accept formal experiments and specifically artistic effects only to the extent that they can be forgotten and do not get in the way of the substance of the work.

The cultural divide which associates each class of works with its public means that it is not easy to obtain working-class people's first-hand judgements on formalist innovations in modern art. However, television, which brings certain performances of 'high' art into the home, or certain cultural institutions (such as the Beaubourg Centre or the Maisons de la culture), which briefly bring a working-class public into contact with high art and sometimes avant-garde works, create what are virtually experimental situations, neither more nor less artificial or unreal than those necessarily produced by any survey on legitimate culture in a working-class milieu. One then observes the confusion, sometimes almost a sort of panic mingled with revolt, that is induced by some exhibits — I am thinking of Ben's heap of coal, on view at Beaubourg shortly after it opened — whose parodic intention, entirely defined in terms of an artistic field and its relatively autonomous history, is seen as a sort of aggression, affront to common sense and sensible people. Likewise, when formal experimentation insinuates itself into their familiar entertainments (e.g. TV variety shows with sophisticated technical effects, such as those by Jean-Christophe Averty) working-class viewers protest, not only because they do not feel the need for these fancy games, but because they sometimes understand that they derive their necessity from the logic of a field of production which excludes them precisely by these games: 'I don't like those cut-up things at all, where you see a head, then a nose, then a leg . . . First you see a singer all drawn out, three metres tall, then the next minute he's got arms two metres long. Do you find that funny? Oh, I just don't like it, it's stupid, I don't see the point of distorting things' (a baker, Grenoble).

Formal refinement — which, in literature or the theatre, leads to obscurity — is, in the eyes of the working-class public, one sign of what is sometimes felt to be a desire to keep the uninitiated at arm's length, or, as one respondent said about certain cultural programmes on TV, to speak to other initiates 'over the viewers' heads'. It is part of the paraphernalia which always announces the sacred character, separate and separating, of high culture — the icy solemnity of the great museums, the grandiose luxury of the opera-houses and major theatres, the decor and decorum of concert-halls. Everything takes place as if the working-class audience vaguely grasped what is implied in conspicuous formality, both in art and in life, i.e. a sort of censorship of the expressive content which explodes in the express- iveness of popular language, and by the same token, a distancing, inherent in the calculated coldness of all formal exploration, a refusal to communicate concealed at the heart of the communication itself, both in an art which takes back and refuses what it seems to deliver and in bourgeois politeness, whose impeccable formalism is a permanent warning against the temptation of familiarity. Conversely, popular entertainment secures the spectator's participation in the show and collective par- ticipation in the festivity which it occasions. If circus and melodrama (which are recreated by some sporting spectacles such as wrestling and, to a lesser extent, box- ing and all forms of team games, such as those which have been televised) are more 'popular' than entertainments like dancing or theatre, this is not merely because, being less formalized (compare, for example, acrobatics with dancing) and less euphem- ized, they offer more direct, more immediate satisfactions. It is also because, through the collective festivity they give rise to and the array of spectacular delights they offer (I am thinking also of the music-hall, light opera or the big feature film) – fabulous sets, glittering costumes, exciting music, lively action, enthusiastic actors – like all forms of the comic and especially those working through satire or parody of the 'great' (mimics, chansonniers, etc.), they satisfy the taste for and sense of revelry, the plain speaking and hearty laughter which liberate by setting the social world head over heels, overturning conventions and proprieties.

Aesthetic distancing

This popular reaction is the very opposite of the detachment of the aesthete, who, as is seen whenever he appropriates one of the objects of popular taste (e.g. Westerns or strip cartoons), introduces a distance, a gap – the measure of his distant dis- tinction – vis-à-vis 'first-degree' perception, by displacing the interest from the 'content', characters, plot, etc., to the form, to the specifically artistic effects which are only appreciated relationally, through a comparison with other works which is incompatible with immersion in the singularity of the work immediately given. Detachment, disinterestedness, indifference – aesthetic theory has so often presented these as the only way to recognize the work of art for what it is, autonomous, selb- ständig, that one ends up forgetting that they really mean disinvestment, detach- ment, indifference, in other words, the refusal to invest oneself and take things seriously. Worldly-wise readers of Rousseau's Lettre sur les spectacles, who have long been aware that there is nothing more naive and vulgar than to invest too much passion in the things of the mind or to expect too much seriousness of them, tend- ing to assume that intellectual creativity is opposed to oral integrity or political consistency, have no answer to Virginia Woolf when she criticizes the novels of Wells, Galsworthy and Bennett because 'they leave one with a strange sense of incom- pleteness and dissatisfaction' and the feeling that it is 'necessary to do something – to join a society, or, more desperately, to write a cheque', in contrast to works like Tristram Shandy or Pride and Prejudice, which, being perfectly 'self-contained', 'leave one with no desire to do anything, except indeed to read the book again, and to understand it better' (Woolf 1966).

But the refusal of any sort of involvement, any 'vulgar' surrender to easy seduction and collective enthusiasm, which is, indirectly at least, the origin of the taste
for formal complexity and objectless representations, is perhaps most clearly seen
in reactions to paintings. Thus one finds that the higher the level of education the
greater is the proportion of respondents who, when asked whether a series of objects
would make beautiful photographs, refuse the ordinary objects of popular admiration – a first communion, a sunset or a landscape – as 'vulgar' or 'ugly', or reject
them as 'trivial', silly, a bit 'wet', or, in Ortega y Gasset's terms, naively 'human';
and the greater is the proportion who assert the autonomy of the representation
with respect to the thing represented by declaring that a beautiful photograph, and
a fortiori a beautiful painting, can be made from objects socially designated as meaningless – a metal frame, the bark of a tree, and especially cabbages, a trivial object
par excellence – or as ugly and repulsive – such as a car crash, a butcher's stall
(chosen for the Rembrandt allusion) or a snake (for the Boileau reference) – or
as misplaced – e.g. a pregnant woman.

Thus, nothing more rigorously distinguishes the different classes than the disposition objectively demanded by the legitimate consumption of legitimate works,
the aptitude for taking a specifically aesthetic point of view on objects already constituted aesthetically – and therefore put forward for the admiration of those who
have learned to recognize the signs of the admirable – and the even rarer capacity
to constitute aesthetically objects that are ordinary or even 'common' (because they
are appropriated, aesthetically or otherwise, by the 'common people') or to apply
the principles of a 'pure' aesthetic in the most everyday choices of everyday life,
in cooking, dress or decoration, for example.

Statistical enquiry is indispensable in order to establish beyond dispute the social
conditions of possibility (which will have to be made more explicit) of the 'pure'
disposition. However, because it inevitably looks like a scholastic test intended to
measure the respondents against a norm tacitly regarded as absolute, it may fail to
capture the meanings which this disposition and the whole attitude to the world
expressed in it have for the different social classes. What the logic of the test would
lead one to describe as a deficiency (and that is what it is, from the standpoint of
the norms defining legitimate perception of works of art) is *also* a refusal which
stems from a denunciation of the arbitrary or ostentatious gratuitousness of stylistic
exercises or purely formalistic experiments. A certain 'aesthetic', which maintains
that a photograph is justified by the object.

The anti-Kantian 'aesthetic'

It is no accident that, when one sets about reconstructing its logic, the popular
'aesthetic' appears as the negative opposite of the Kantian aesthetic, and that the
popular ethos implicitly answers each proposition of the 'Analytic of the Beautiful'
with a thesis contradicting it. In order to apprehend what makes the specificity of
aesthetic judgement, Kant ingeniously distinguished 'that which pleases' from 'that
which gratifies', and, more generally, strove to separate 'disinterestedness', the sole
guarantee of the specifically aesthetic quality of contemplation, from 'the interest
of the senses', which defines 'the agreeable', and from 'the interest of Reason',

which defines 'the Good'. By contrast, working-class people, who expect every image to fulfil a function, if only that of a sign, refer, often explicitly, to norms of morality or agreeableness in all their judgements. Thus the photograph of a dead soldier provokes judgements which, whether positive or negative, are always responses to the reality of the thing represented or to the functions the representation could serve, the horror of war or the denunciation of the horrors of war which the photographer is supposed to produce simply by showing that horror. Similarly, popular naturalism recognizes beauty in the image of a beautiful thing or, more rarely, in a beautiful image of a beautiful thing: 'Now, that's good, it's almost symmetrical. And she's a beautiful woman. A beautiful woman always looks good in a photo.' The Parisian manual worker echoes the plain-speaking of Hippias the Sophist: 'I'll tell him what beauty is and I'm not likely to be refuted by him! The fact is, Socrates, to be frank, a beautiful woman, that's what beauty is!' (Plato, *Greater Hippias*, 287e).

This 'aesthetic', which subordinates the form and the very existence of the image to its function, is necessarily pluralistic and conditional. The insistence with which the respondents point out the limits and conditions of validity of their judgements, distinguishing, for each photograph, the possible uses or audiences, or, more precisely, the possible use for each audience ('As a news photo, it's not bad', 'All right, if it's for showing to kids') shows that they reject the idea that a photograph can please 'universally'. 'A photo of a pregnant woman is all right for me, not for other people', said a white-collar worker, who has to use his concern for propriety as a way of expressing anxiety about what is 'presentable' and therefore entitled to demand admiration. Because the image is always judged by reference to the function it fulfils for the person who looks at it or which he thinks it could fulfil for other classes of beholders, aesthetic judgement naturally takes the form of a hypothetical judgement implicitly based on recognition of 'genres', the perfection and scope of which are defined by a *concept*. Almost three-quarters of the judgements expressed begin with an 'if', and the effort to recognize culminates in classification into a genre, or, which amounts to the same thing, in the attribution of a social use, the different genres being defined in terms of their use and their users ('It's a publicity photo', 'It's a pure document', 'It's a laboratory photo', 'It's a competition photo', 'It's an educational photo', etc.). And photographs of nudes are almost always received with comments that reduce them to the stereotype of their social function: 'All right in Pigalle', 'It's the sort of photos they keep under the counter.' It is not surprising that this 'aesthetic', which bases appreciation on informative, tangible or moral interest, can only refuse images of the trivial, or, which amounts to the same thing in terms of this logic, the triviality of the image: judgement never gives the image of the object autonomy with respect to the object of the image. Of all the characteristics proper to the image, only colour (which Kant regarded as less pure than form) can prevent rejection of photographs of trivial things. Nothing is more alien to popular consciousness than the idea of an aesthetic pleasure that, to put it in Kantian terms, is independent of the charming of the senses. Thus judgements on the photographs most strongly rejected on grounds of futility (pebbles, bark, wave) almost always end with the reservation that 'in colour, it might be pretty'; and some respondents even manage to formulate the maxim governing their attitude, when they declare that 'if the colours are good, a colour photograph is always beautiful.' In short, Kant is indeed referring to popular taste when he writes:

'Taste that requires an added element of charm and emotion for its delight, not to speak of adopting this as the measure of its approval, has not yet emerged from barbarism' (Kant 1952: 65).

Refusal of the meaningless (*insignifiant*) image, which has neither sense nor interest, or of the ambiguous image means refusing to treat it as a finality without purpose, as an image signifying itself, and therefore having no other referent than itself. The value of a photograph is measured by the interest of the information it conveys, and by the clarity with which it fulfils this informative function, in short, its legibility, which itself varies with the legibility of its intention or function, the judgement it provokes being more or less favourable depending on the expressive adequacy of the signifier to the signified. It therefore contains the expectation of the title or caption which, by declaring the signifying intention, makes it possible to judge whether the realization signifies or illustrates it adequately. If formal explorations, in avant-garde theatre or non-figurative painting, or simply classical music, are disconcerting to working-class people, this is partly because they feel incapable of understanding what these things must signify, insofar as they are signs. Hence the uninitiated may experience as inadequate and unworthy a satisfaction that cannot be grounded in a meaning transcendent to the object. Not knowing what the 'intention' is, they feel incapable of distinguishing a tour de force from clumsiness, telling a 'sincere' formal device from cynical imposture.

But formal refinement is also that which, by foregrounding form, i.e. the artist, his specific interests, his technical problems, his effects, his allusions and echoes, throws the thing itself into the background and precludes direct communion with the beauty of the world – a beautiful child, a beautiful girl, a beautiful animal or a beautiful landscape. The representation is expected to be a feast for the eyes and, like still life, to 'stir up memories and anticipations of feasts enjoyed and feasts to come' (Gombrich 1963: 104). Nothing is more opposed to the celebration of the beauty and joy of the world that is looked for in the work of art, 'a choice which praises', than the devices of cubist or abstract painting, which are perceived and unanimously denounced as aggressions against the thing represented, against the natural order and especially the human form. In short, however perfectly it performs its representative function, the work is only seen as fully justified if the thing represented is worthy of being represented, if the representative function is subordinated to a higher function, such as that of capturing and exalting a reality that is worthy of being made eternal. Such is the basis of the 'barbarous taste' to which the most antithetical forms of the dominant aesthetic always refer negatively and which only recognizes realist representation, in other words, a respectful, humble, submissive representation of objects designated by their beauty or their social importance.

References

Bourdieu, P. (1971) 'Disposition esthétique et compétence artistique', *Les Temps Modernes*, 295: 1345–78.

Bourdieu, P. (1975) 'L'invention de la vie d'artiste', *Actes*, 2: 67–93.

Bourdieu, P. (1980) 'The production of belief', *Media, Culture and Society*, 2: 261–93.

Gombrich, E.H. (1963) *Meditations on a Hobby Horse*, London; Phaidon.
Kant, I. (1952 [1790]) *Critique of Judgement*, London: Oxford University Press.
Langer, S.K. (1968) 'On significance in music', in Jacobus, L.A. (ed.) *Aesthetics and the Arts*, New York: McGraw-Hill, 182–212.
Ortega y Gasset, J. (1966 [1925]) 'La deshumanización del arte', *Obras Completas, III*, Madrid: Revista de Occidente, 355–6.
Panofsky, E. (1955) *Meaning in the Visual Arts*, New York: Doubleday Anchor Books.
Woolf, V. (1966) 'Mr and Mrs Brown', *Collected Essays I*, London: Hogarth Press, 326–7.

Edited extract from Bourdieu, P. (1984) *Distinction: A Social Critique of the Judgement of Taste*, Cambridge, MA: Harvard University Press, 28–44. Pierre Bourdieu (1930–2002) was one of the most influential sociologists of the late twentieth century. His other books include *Outline of a Theory of Practice*, *The Love of Art: European Art Museums and Their Public*, *Photography: A Middle-Brow Art* and *Rules of Art: Genesis and Structure of the Literary Field*.

Chapter 15

Stakeholder relationships in the market for contemporary art

Derrick Chong

Business art is the step that comes after Art . . . good business is the best art.

(Andy Warhol 1975: 92)

A CLASSICAL VIEW of the industrial economy as 'production-distribution con-sumption' is not unhelpful in appreciating the world of so-called high art. Marcel Duchamp (1973: 47), as much as any informed commentator, recognized that the artist (creator) and spectator (consumer) were embedded as part of a circular process: 'In the final analysis, the artist may shout from all the rooftops that he is a genius; he will have to wait for the verdict of the spectator in order that his declarations take a social value and that, finally, posterity includes him in the primers of art history.' Complementing this 'flow-of-exchanges' outlook, one can turn to the role of relationships, as artist and critic Martha Rosler (1997: 20–1, n.1) does, in articulating the various stakeholders (also called actors or players) constituting the '*high* art world':

> I am taking the art world as the changing international group of com-mercial and non-profit galleries, museums, study centers, and associated venues and the individuals who own, run, direct, and toil in them; the critics, reviewers, and historians, and their publications, who supply the studies, rationales, publicity, and explanations; the connoisseurs and collectors who form the nucleus of sales and appreciation; plus the artists living and recently dead who supply the goods.

Within this system, several points can be noted. First, there are indications that networks of cooperation exist such that works of art are joint products of all stake-holders who cooperate; of course, this emphasis on a complex set of relationships runs counter to the dominant tradition of emphasizing the individual artist as unique creator of a work (Becker 1982; Wolff 1981). Second, the marketing effects of intermediaries help to refine market taste. Systems vary in the kind of intermediaries such as curators, critics, dealers and arts institutions, who handle the movement of work and money between artist and audiences (of spectators and collectors), and in the immediacy of the communication and influence between the two groups (Becker 1982). These intermediary stakeholders play a role in the cross-valuation and certification of works of art. Third, economies of agglomeration are important. A threshold market size is necessary. A core–periphery relationship structure is created with an identifiable acme of success. City centres can represent geographical clustering of productive activity. New York has grown in stature since the end of the Second World War, with European entrepôts located in Paris, London and Berlin. Clusters form and change within cities. During the 1990s New York's SoHo gave way to Chelsea; and in London, Hoxton emerged as an alternative to London's West End dealers with Cork Street falling even further behind. The influence of dealers, curators and critics is subject to varying life cycles. The aesthetic ranking of museums of modern art may be less volatile compared to the reputation of individual contemporary arts venues (like ICAs, Kunsthalles, or artist-run centres) that rely on programming temporary exhibitions. Large-scale, international art fairs like the Venice Bienniale and Dokumenta afford high visibility to artists and are complemented by an increasing global list (e.g. São Paolo, Prague, Toronto, Shanghai, Lisbon, Istanbul and Chicago). Fourth, there is a blurring of private–public relationships in the way stakeholders manage their networks. Numerous relationships operate at the same time. Contemporary artists seek to exhibit at state-funded institutions as a means to validate their work, which can lead to higher prices charged by their commercial dealers. Dealers sell to private clients (individuals and corporation) and public institutions – indeed one might argue that large-scale conceptual art is only suited to public collections. Individuals working freelance find that they can wear different hats spanning the private–public divide: curating a temporary exhibition at a public institution, writing reviews for an arts magazine, and offering advice to buyers as a consultant to a commercial dealer. Each can raise ethical issues for the individual actors. Fifth, a hierarchy of effects is discernible: high, middle and low art is a common tripartite classification system to indicate the existence of markers of taste (e.g. Bourdieu 1984; Wolff 1981), and linked sub-markets (e.g. Throsby 1994). Indeed the 'pyramid' structure represents an important way to represent facets of the art world. Sixth, contemporary art relies, by definition, on a temporal marker. Many art museums, for example, classify art works created within the last 30 years as 'contemporary'. The best of contemporary art, then, enters the canon as 'modern' art. Seventh, there is an unlimited supply of contemporary art of varying 'quality'. This invites change within the system, which is to suggest that entrepreneurial activity can allow neophyte players of artists, dealers, critics and collectors to take root and prosper; moreover, change means that new core players can displace over time some established players falling from power.

In teasing out implications that flow from the citations of Duchamp and Rosler, this chapter seeks to examine the networks and institutional structures as posited by prominent commentators from two strands of writing: sociology of the arts (e.g. Bourdieu 1984; Becker 1982; Moulin 1987; Wolff 1981) and cultural economics (e.g. Frey and Pommerehne 1989; Grampp 1989; Throsby 1994; Frey 2000; Towse

2000). A central interest is to reflect the relationships between the various stakeholders and their role in helping us to better understand forces shaping the contemporary art world. (...)

Consuming art: addiction or cultivation of taste

(...) The sociological approach to understanding the predisposition to arts consumption, as advanced by Pierre Bourdieu, is at odds with the standard Kantian view in which the purity of aesthetic contemplation derives from disinterested pleasure. Bourdieu's pioneering investigations challenged the myth of innate taste: it set out to define the social conditions which made Kant's experience – the beautiful is that which pleases without concept – and the people for whom it is possible (namely art lovers and so-called people of taste). Arts consumption – visiting art museums let alone buying 'original' art – is closely linked to level of education (whether measured by qualifications or length of schooling) and social origins. Thus, according to Bourdieu, a work of art has meaning and interest only for someone who possesses the requisite cultural competence.

Successful mastery of the code to gain artistic competence requires the use of the scarce resource: time. First, the economic means to invest in educational time must exist. Second, as the development of cultural practice and artistic production has become more complex in its coding, there is the requirement that one is competent with a wider and wider range of cultural references. Much contemporary art is self-referential so that one needs to devote more and more time to it in order to remain competent. For example, how does one separate a work of art from non-art, the ready-made from commodity? Arthur Danto's analysis of Andy Warhol's *Brillo Boxes* (1964) is an instructive reminder:

> What in the end makes the difference between a Brillo box and a work of art consisting of a Brillo box is a certain theory of art. It is the theory that takes it up into the world of art, and keeps it from collapsing into the real object which it is (in a sense of *is* other than that of artistic identification). Of course, without the theory, one is unlikely to see it as art, and in order to see it as part of the artworld, one must have mastered a good deal of artistic theory as well as a considerable amount of the history of recent New York painting. (Danto 1964: 581; italics in the original)

He continues, 'It is the role of artistic theories, these days as always, to make the artworld, and art, possible' (Danto 1964: 581). According to Danto, the atmosphere of interpretation is needed. Knowledge of the history of art serves to help make conceptual links to objects already deemed art. Aesthetic theory is needed to justify such a linkage. Moreover, the art world stands at the ready with a willingness to shift with the times to accommodate new languages and ideas.

Gaining cultural competence can also be achieved by using money to recruit advisors who can supplement one's own taste and time constraints. This echoes a cultural economics position: 'One of the reasons why an interest in the arts is limited to a relatively few people is that only a few have made the investment in taste or learning which the interest requires, and that is because the investment is worthwhile to only a few' (Grampp 1989: 58). The few who do make an investment may enjoy a flow of social dividends: 'Art is a sign of affluence; it belongs to the good life; it is part of the furnishings which the world gives to the rich and beautiful. But a work also suggests a cultural authority, a form of dignity, even of wisdom, which is superior to any vulgar material interest; an oil painting belongs to cultural heritage; it is a reminder of what it means to be a cultivated European' (Berger 1972: 135). A 'high' art object offers a gloss that glitters. It remains a superb symbolic good.

The value of art

Art provides satisfaction – utility in the case of economists – in the same sense that any object that is desired provides it:

> Works of art are economic goods, their value can be measured by the market, and the sellers and buyers of art – the people who create and benefit from it – are people who try to get as much as they can from what they have. In a word or two, the activity of art is a maximizing activity. Without that assumption, economics has no place in the study of art or of anything else. (Grampp 1989: 8)

This is to suggest the transformation of aesthetic value into economic value. At one level, the artist is integrated into society's economy (Moulin 1987). Moreover, cultural economists view fine art as offering two types of value: art as investment and art as consumption. In the former, art is viewed in terms of a financial rate of return; in the latter, art offers an aesthetic yield (or psychic return). Most collectors seek to balance satisfaction on both fronts. Art can appreciate in monetary value, while it is enjoyed from an aesthetic perspective: 'Part of the pleasure of collecting lies in risk and competition. Collectors gamble on paintings and artists the way racing enthusiasts gamble on horses or market enthusiasts on stocks . . . It is an elite recreation, a game in which the losers are presumably those without culture or artistic flair' (Moulin 1987: 82). Speculators represent an interesting category of collector: they highlight some of the nuances of art collecting. First, pure speculators have an 'aesthetic yield' of zero as they receive no pleasure from holding art. 'The financial rate of return on an art object should, in equilibrium, be *lower* than that in other markets with similar risk' (Frey 2000: 166). Second, the successful speculator needs to know something of the value of works of art: 'Speculation, whatever its objects, is amusing. Because good taste and good investment go hand in hand, the speculator qualifies as a connoisseur by the profit he earns' (Moulin 1987: 99). (...)

Stakeholders

'The art market is the place where, by some secret alchemy, the cultural good becomes a commodity' (Moulin 1987: 3). The institutional approach views the art world as a social and economic network, with more incentives to be connected to the network than disincentives to remain disconnected (Becker 1982). Artists serve as producers; collectors and spectators serve as consumers. From the exchange process of 'production-distribution-consumption', 'today's contemporary art scene places marketing and distribution at the forefront' (Cowen 1998: 121). This means that players in the contemporary art market, operating as dealers, critics or curators, have significant roles as intermediaries; moreover, institutions displaying contemporary art also influence taste among non-specialist audiences.

Artists

So-called 'Young British Artists' (YBAs) of the 1990s, centred in London, offer some instructive pointers. Gilbert and George, from an earlier generation of British artists, served as role models and Goldsmiths College at the University of London, served as a prominent training ground for some of the lead YBAs. The influence of Michael Craig-Martin, a conceptual artist who has served as a trustee of the Tate Gallery, is viewed as crucial; Craig-Martin and Jon Thompson, another educator at Goldsmiths, are often cited as progenitors to the YBAs, and particular attention is devoted to the importance of the now-famous 'Freeze' exhibition of 1988, organized by the then Goldsmiths' student Damien Hirst.

Exploiting the marketing potential associated with 'celebrity', successful creators can accrue fame and money earlier in their careers. (This is not unlike the situation in popular music and mass spectator sports.) The case of Hirst is illustrative of the required entrepreneurial qualities. For a brief period during the late 1990s, he was involved with a fashionable restaurant venture called Pharmacy – situated in an old chemist's shop in London's Notting Hill – that was designed to exploit references to the artist's work. Not unlike the owners of luxury brands (e.g. Prada, Gucci, etc.), artists could be shrewder in exploiting marketing segmentation and price discrimination, such as by creating separate bodies of work that can be sold at lower prices to the less wealthy. Hirst's spin paintings, for example, represent a recent example of product line extension. At the bottom of the 'fine' art market, there are firms that publish 'limited edition prints' by recognizable contemporary artists.

Spectators/collectors

Should the artist be leading the spectator? Audience reception to 'new' art can be one of bafflement and bewilderment; one may even be troubled by certain shifts – the destruction of values one still cherishes – as they occur in contemporary art. Who, then, is the intended spectator? There is a suggestion that as art turns in on itself, the audience becomes more specialized even if occasional 'blockbusters' of contemporary art invite the curious. For example, does the large scale of some contemporary works of art seek specialized consumption in the form of approval from institutional collectors like museums and corporations?

The individual collector might be viewed as an engaged and sophisticated spectator, someone situated at an advanced level of arts consumption. The individual collector serves as buyer and seller of art. An important duality exists for such art connoisseurs: 'The same person cannot be an ignorant buyer and a shrewd seller' (Grampp 1989: 28–9). Charles Saatchi, adman *par excellence*, has served as an entrepreneurial collector of contemporary art, including an appetite for work by British artists. (His collecting activity is pronounced given that it takes place in a country where the state has become the chief patron.) In interview with Lisa Jardine, she notes the relationship between Saatchi's career in advertising and his taste in contemporary art:

> From the beginning he 'felt' pretty confident with visual images and their manipulation and that made him relaxed about saying what he liked and following that up with purchasing. He acknowledges that some people consider his advertising man's eyes a weakness. It is true that he instinctively picks the kind of work that plays vigorously on rapid audience reception, and that he has a preference for artists who are likely [to be] aware about the interaction between themselves, their work and the gallery goer. (Jardine 1997)

In this way, Saatchi is not unlike other collectors, who desire to differentiate themselves from peers (Moulin 1987: 85). Moreover, the establishment of the Saatchi Gallery at County Hall – a private museum of indeterminate tenancy situated near Tate Modern – is an indication of a serious preoccupation with collecting contemporary art (approaching what Peggy Guggenheim achieved in Venice).

Collectors with the money and the acquired esoteric taste in contemporary art necessary to be enlightened in how to spend it (Becker 1982: 104) have come under the critical gaze of cultural commentators:

> Today, an increasingly large fraction of owners and upper management throughout the world graduate from the best schools. Although they may not be great intellectuals, those who dominate the economic world, the owners of industry and commerce, are no longer the narrow-minded bourgeois of the nineteenth century. In the nineteenth century, artists such as Baudelaire and Flaubert could oppose the 'bourgeois' as ignorant or dim-witted philistines. Today's owners are, often, very refined people, at least in terms of social strategies of manipulation, but also in the realm of art, which easily becomes part of the bourgeois style of life, even if it is a product of the heretical raptures and veritable symbols revolutions. (Bourdieu and Haacke 1995: 41)

In extreme cases, a major collector of art can be likened to the fat boy in a canoe: when he moves, all the others need to change their position.

Institutional exhibition venues

The Royal Academy, a temporary exhibition venue in London under the curatorial direction of its exhibitions secretary, Norman Rosenthal, has hosted a trio of shows – 'Sensation: young British artists from the Saatchi collection' (1997), 'Apocalypse: beauty and horror in contemporary art' (2000), and 'The Galleries Show' (2002) – that were interpreted as promoting a particular perspective of contemporary art practice. In some respects, Rosenthal represents the role of the curator as the *creator* of the exhibition, that is on a par with the artists on display.

Dominant members of the 'Sensation' exhibition can, as they approach early middle age, be viewed entering the canon of British art. That (Sir) Nicholas Serota, director of the Tate since 1988, has been an ardent supporter of YBAs is of interest, particularly as he views taste formation as an essential role of the national collections:

> I think that the collections, if they are doing their job, will establish taste. There are plenty of examples going back to the nineteenth century that demonstrate how the National Gallery established taste, particularly in terms of collecting early quattrocento painting. You could say the same is true of the Tate at certain moments, for example when it collected minimal art in the 1970s. This was regarded as an affront by some parts of the popular press at the time, but I don't think there is any doubt that it was the right thing for the Tate to bring that work into this collection. (Serota 2003: 52)

One can see that Serota associates YBAs of the 1990s with minimalist art production of the 1970s. He continues on the role of making critical judgements:

> Museums have to make selections. Choices are made all the time, and you can't duck those choices. They establish the frame through which we look at the very recent past. Later generations can make corrections, and that may be more or less expensive to do; generally more expensive, because we have failed to collect some of those things that have become regarded as important. But you can't evade the responsibility of taking a View. (Serota 2003: 52)

Dealers

A shift away from traditional forms of patronage (e.g. church, royalty and aristocrats) to the public sale of works by contemporary artists to members of the well-to-do or affluent middle classes helps to account for the rise of commercial art dealers (Alsop 1982; Becker 1982; Shubik in Towse 2000). Art dealing remains an unregulated market – vis-à-vis other occupations or the selling of financial instruments – such that art dealers are self-selected. The current period is marked by dealers behaving as entrepreneurs, which is to suggest that self-promotion and innovation are important in being a successful market agent (Moulin 1987; Cowen 1998). Yet the social cachet associated with art means that there are class differences from other types of selling. Even in contemporary art, it is not uncommon to meet dealers from 'privileged' backgrounds (including sources of private wealth as a form of income support). Dealers can make direct acquisitions of art, or sell works on consignment by artists. The former requires capital outlay to buy works (on the primary or secondary markets) and managing risk, but all capital gains accrue to the dealer. The latter operates on a commission basis (50–50 is not untypical) between the dealer and artist based on the sales price. Such (primary market) dealers enter into contract with artists (producers of works), which the dealer turns into commercial properties. Leading dealers like Jay Jopling (White Cube), Sadie Coles (Sadie Coles HQ), Anthony D'Offay, or Nicholas Logsdail (Lisson) can become as well known as the artists they exhibit.

Critics

The critic serves as a communications link between artist and public. Critics come in different forms, including those with training such as art historians, curators and artists. Journals like *Artforum* and *October* represent one end of the field, writing in a specialist language to a restricted coterie who can understand it. The most common category, focusing on the wider general audience, is the newspaper journalist, who can be viewed as a 'poor relation' of the family of art (Moulin 1987: 69). Indeed one might argue that too often the journalist-as-critic serves a public relations role, with limited critical reviewing, which has devalued criticism and robbed it of its usefulness. It is suggested that a gap exists in the middle ground.

Of course, there are critics who view the contemporary situation as one of declining morals. Moreover, they protest that an insular contemporary art system exists that exploits public funding: a handful of dealers represent featured artists at leading publicly-funded venues of contemporary art in London (e.g. ICA, Serpentine, Whitechapel and Hayward) and others within the UK (e.g. Modern Art Oxford, Cornerhouse (Manchester), Baltic (Gateshead-Newcastle), Arnolfini (Bristol), and Ikon (Birmingham)). These critics contend that there is a presumed bias in favour of institutionalized conceptual art. In particular, the shortlist for the Turner Prize, established in 1984 by the Tate as an annual prize to recognize a contemporary British artist, is scrutinized for representation. What artistic styles are on display? Who are the dealers of the artists? Where did the artists study?

Power relations

Exchanges in the arts sector form a complex network that can be interpreted as a combination of different principal–agent relationships (Trimarchi in Towse 2000: 373). Cooperation is emphasized in art-world networks (Becker 1982). In an ideal network situation, maximizing the overall value of the relationship would be a key objective. Yet competition is an economic reality as differing interests and conflicting goals can be observed among the various stakeholders. Three prominent relationships are examined: dealer–artist; dealer–collector; and collector–artist. What these relationships share in common is an emphasis on 'face-to-face' exchanges, which is a direct acknowledgment of an art scene, namely the 'performance' elements of the art world (Rosler 1997).

Dealer–artist relations

It has been suggested that the dealer–artist relationship always involves a struggle for power (Moulin 1987: 60). Loyalty is possible if their careers advance together. However, there is the common perception that relationships between dealers and artists, apart from the case of 'superstar' artists, tend to tip the balance of power to the dealer, who acts as an important gatekeeper (by selecting, representing and promoting artists in his 'stable').

In the early 1970s, New York lawyer Bob Projansky drafted a three-page agreement based on Seth Siegelaub's discussions and correspondence with people involved in the day-to-day workings of the international art market. 'The artist's reserved rights to transfer and sale request agreement' was signed to offer the artist certain economic benefits and aesthetic control: 15 per cent of any increase in the value of each work each time it is transferred in the future; a record of who owns each work at any given time; the right to be notified when the work is to be exhibited, so the artist can advise on or veto the proposed exhibition of his/her work; the right to borrow the work for exhibition two months every five years (at no cost to the owner); the right to be consulted if repairs become necessary; half of any rental income to be paid to the owner for the use of the work at exhibitions, if there is any; all reproduction rights in the work; and the economic benefits to accrue to the artist for life, plus the life of the surviving spouse (if any) plus 21 years (Projansky and Siegelaub 1971).

The role of the dealer is acknowledged to be central to the success of the agreement as 'he is going to be very important in getting people to sign the contract when he sells your work' because 'your dealer knows all the ins and outs that go down in the business of the art world'. This emphasizes the 'gatekeeper' role of the dealer. However, it is less clear what incentives exist to encourage dealers to participate, as Projansky and Siegelaub's proposed agreement would be viewed by many prospective buyers as an additional transaction cost.

Projansky and Siegelaub acknowledged that the proposed agreement would alter the existing relationship between artist and dealer. The agreement would start with primary market transactions and then carry over to all subsequent secondary market transactions. Owners of art would face new obligations. Projansky and Siegelaub's lead point – 15 per cent of any increase in the value of each work each time it is transferred in the future – serves as a form of capital gains tax payable to the artist by the seller. Enforcement is a major obstacle in secondary markets without a regulated system of collecting royalties like *droit de suite* in France. Buyers might well ask for a reduced purchase price to account for a prospective capital gains tax when the work is resold.

Re-reading Projansky and Siegelaub's agreement three decades later, it is still the case that (visual) artists do not recoup all the intellectual property rights due to them. Yet there are means that artists have adopted, using their artistic output, in the absence of royalties from secondary market transactions. For example, by retaining a small portion of one's own output throughout different stages of an artistic career, these works would later enter the marketplace as primary sales at a time when other works trade in secondary markets at higher prices. Reciprocal trading of works of art with peer artists would enable a 'diversified' portfolio (collection) to be established.

Dealer–collector relations

Contemporary art dealers, it is suggested, can take an attitude that the dealer makes the customer-as-collector (Moulin 1987: 63). This assumes that certain conditions exist in the primary market for contemporary art. Customers are engaged in ambiguous purchase decisions and do not have adequate information; at the same time, the buying task is complex and repeat business is possible. The dealer has the resources (e.g. personal qualities, product alternatives, and negotiable terms of sale) to engage in adaptive sales behaviour. The dealer has an incentive to adapt his or her behaviour to better present his or her products as a solution to the buyer's problems. As such, the level of conflict can be low as the dealer anticipates future relationships with the buyer. Moreover, a collector may seek to forge a special relationship with 'in-demand' dealers to gain access to popular artists and potential discounts.

A more competitive dynamic is present if the balance of negotiating power shifts. A powerful dealer can tie up the work of art of a particular artist, essentially acting as a monopsonist in dealing with the artist and as a monopolist in dealing with buyers (Throsby 1994: 5). This works best under certain conditions: a successful artist who produces few works each year; and a (restrictive) resale agreement that a dealer can persuade buyers to sign. In the resale agreement the buyer agrees to offer the work back to the dealer when he or she wants to sell it. It is difficult to enforce the agreement, but a dealer can blacklist a buyer who breaks it.

Collector–artist relations

There is a strong case that 'distribution has a crucial effect on reputation' (Becker 1982: 95). Artists who are not distributed are not known to audiences. At the same time, an artist without a good reputation will not be distributed. This circular argument replicates the exchange process as it operates in the contemporary art market. As such, what is the value of the dealer-as-intermediary? Projansky and Siegelaub (1971) were supportive of the dealer's role in strengthening collector–artist relationships. Dealers can articulate benefits to art owners: chief was 'a certified history and provenance of the work'; the others, such as the establishment of 'a non-exploitative, one-to-one relationship' and 'recognition that the artist maintains a moral relationship to the work' appear more idealistic.

Disintermediation questions the costs associated with intermediaries vis-à-vis the value they provide to the overall exchange relationship. The so-called direct selling model bypasses intermediaries between producer (artist) and end consumer (collector). How would exchange relationships establish and develop between artist and collector in the absence of a dealer? An artist would need to have acquired a sufficient reputation not to require the promotional value afforded by a dealer. The artist would be saving the cost of the commission paid to the dealer. A collector would need strong access networks to works of art comparable to the wares offered by a good dealer. Degree shows at leading art schools allow a unique opportunity for artists to sell direct to collectors: relationships may be established. Dealers are absent from the buying–selling exchange, yet their presence is noticeable as they scout for new artistic talent.

There are cases of collectors gaining potential market power over contemporary artists. For example, a collector can gain significant market share by buying the entire degree show (i.e. primary market) output of selected artists. Any collector with a significant share of an artist's output can influence the artist's reputation. Subsequent works of the artist may attract a premium to recognize inclusion in a major private collection. Market power can also operate in the opposite way. A collector 'off-loading' works of an artist (in the secondary market) can damage the artist's reputation; of course the collector is also cognizant not to indicate that particular artists are no longer favoured, as this would have a depressing impact on the collector' sales prices.

Concluding remarks

The sociological and economic approaches can be viewed as complementary in helping one to better appreciate the contemporary art world. In examining stakeholder relationships in contemporary art, aesthetic concerns are of secondary significance. Social conditions, such as education and social class which help to explain the consumption of the arts are prime concerns for sociologists of the arts. A great deal of research on understanding how one gains cultural competence follows the work of Bourdieu. At the same time, cultural economists, by applying economic thinking to the arts, are better at articulating the value of art, namely assessing art as an investment vehicle (offering a financial return and aesthetic yield). Investing in contemporary art, which can represent a more speculative market (than for Old Masters), as reputations and prices are subject to fluctuation, remain underresearched.

Cooperation is highlighted as crucial to network systems in the contemporary art world, from production (artists) to consumption (spectators and collectors) with intermediaries (critics, curators, collectors) playing a role in valuating and certificating works of art. Competition, the flip side of cooperation, also makes an appearance: economic spoils accrue to some stakeholders more than others. A pyramid system exists with 'talent' and 'celebrity' being important not just for artists but also for other stakeholders such as curators, critics, dealers and collectors.

The relative bargaining power of stakeholders in what can be described as one-to-one relationships (artist–dealer, dealer–collector, or collector–artist) can lead to varying levels of cooperation and competition. The role of the dealer, as an important intermediary between artists and collectors, is exposed. What value does the dealer offer? This needs to be viewed in terms of what artists and collectors can do on their own. At the same time, there is inter-firm rivalry among contemporary art dealers: competitive positioning occurs as dealers seek to be viewed as more innovative than rivals; and securing attractive resources in the form of artists and collector networks is necessary if the dealer is to be a successful market agent.

Within a relatively short period of time, namely 20–30 years, contemporary art becomes 'modern' or fades from art historical significance. As YBAs of the 1990s start to enter permanent collections of museums of modern art, it will be interesting to assess the impact of the 'Sensation' exhibition in 2012. In doing so, we may also be evaluating the impact of Charles Saatchi's 'eye' on the permanent collections of Tate Modern and Tate Britain. Collectors of contemporary art, who are buying on personal taste, can have an impact on shaping the permanent collections of museums of modern art, which may represent national views of taste through donations of works.

References

Alsop, J. (1982) *The Rare Art Traditions: The History of Art Collecting and its Linked Phenomenon*, Bollinger Series 27, New York: Harper and Row.

Ashenfelter, O. and Graddy, K. (2002) 'Art auctions: a survey of empirical studies', NBER Working Paper No. 8997.

Baumol, W. (1986) 'Unnatural value: or art investment as floating crap game', *American Economic Review*, 76 (May): 10–14.

Becker, H. (1982) *Art Worlds*, Berkeley, CA: University of California Press.

Berger, J. (1972) *Ways of Seeing*, London: BBC and Harmondsworth: Penguin Books.

Bourdieu, P. (1984 [1979]) *Distinction: A Social Critique of the Judgement of Taste*, London: Routledge & Kegan Paul.

Bourdieu, P. and Haacke, H. (1995) *Free Exchange*, Cambridge: Polity.

Cowen, T. (1998) *In Praise of Commercial Culture*, Cambridge, MA: Harvard University Press.

Danto, A. (1964) 'The artworld', *Journal of Philosophy*, 61 (October): 571–84.

Duchamp, M. (1973 [1957]) 'The creative act', reprinted in Battcok, G. (ed.), *The New Art*, New York: E.P. Dutton, 46–8.

Frey, B. (2000) *Arts and Economics: Analysis and Cultural Policy*, Berlin: Springer-Verlag.

Frey, B. and Pommerehne, W. (1989) *Muses and Markets: Explorations in the Economics of Art*, Oxford: Basil Blackwell.

Grampp, W. (1989) *Pricing the Priceless: Art, Artists and Economics*, New York: Basic Books.

Jardine, L. (1997) 'How one man decides what is good art', interview with Charles Saatchi, *Daily Telegraph*, 19 November.

Moulin, R. (1987 [1967]) *The French Art Market: A Sociological View*. New Brunswick, NJ: Rutgers University Press.

Projansky, B. and Siegelaub, S. (1971) 'The artist's reserved rights transfer and sale agreement', Mimeograph copy.

Rosen, S. (1981) 'The economics of superstars', *American Economic Review*, 7 (December): 845–58.

Rosler, M. (1997) 'Money, power and contemporary art', *Art Bulletin*, LXX (March): 20–4.

Serota, N. (2003) 'The way forward', in *Art Nation: Celebrating 100 Years of the National Art Collections Fund*, London: Cultureshock Media and NACF, 52–7.

Throsby, D. (1994) 'The production and consumption of the arts: a view of cultural economics', *Journal of Economic Literature* 32 (March): 1–29.

Towse, R. (ed.) (2000) *A Handbook of Cultural Economics*, Cheltenham and Northampton, MA: Edward Elgar.

Warhol, A. (1975) *The Philosophy of Andy Warhol from A to B and Back Again*, London: Michael Dempsey in association with Cassell.

Wolff, J. (1981) *The Social Production of Art*, London: Macmillan.

First published as Chong, D. (2005) 'Stakeholder relationships in the market for contemporary art', in Robertson, I. (ed.) *Understanding International Art Markets and Management*, London: Routledge, 84–102. Derrick Chong is Senior Lecturer in Marketing at Royal Holloway, University of London. He is a specialist in arts administration with a particular interest in art business organizations.

Chapter 16

Organising art
Constructing aesthetic value

Jonathan Vickery

T HIS ESSAY BROADLY CONCERNS the relation between the concept of art and the study of organisation. The terms 'art' and 'organisation' usually come together in one of four ways. First, art is a form of organised production: from the workshops of the medieval era to the modern studio, artists have always created art within a system of co-ordinated labour; second, art is created to be displayed, disseminated and often sold: 'the art world' is a network of interrelated organisations devoted to that task; third, non-art world organisations collect art and participate in the process of artistic production; for example, many large corporations and pension funds have expensive art collections, and also sponsor artistic events or initiate artistic projects through patronising individual artists; and lastly, art is not merely a collection of interesting objects, but a mode of thought, a multi-media discourse investigating the nature of visual reality; all kinds of cultural and academic organisations are devoted to studying and researching art for this reason.

All forms of art organisation involve management systems, whether managing materials, arts funding distribution, or managing knowledge. It may seem obvious that the study of management organisations will have something to contribute to our knowledge of art production and the various activities which make up the art world, like corporate patronage or the private art markets. My argument in this essay, however, is that the study of organisation goes to the heart of the central problematic of contemporary art, and that central problematic is the nature of aesthetic value.

One cannot use the term 'work of art' without a presupposition of value. The very term 'work of art' is itself an appellation of value, not merely an annunciation of an object's identity. It is less obvious, however, determining what it is that constitutes aesthetic value and how value is identified or certified. Aesthetic value, even at the dawn of the modern era, was conceived in opposition to the instrumental rationality of bureaucratic systems and rational organisation of all kinds. Friedrich Schiller's (1795) *On the Aesthetic Education of Man* proclaimed art as a restorative force in a society that is becoming increasingly bureaucratised and functions according to the 'fragmentary specialisation of human powers' (Schiller, 1982: 43). In our present society, where the management systems of commercial corporations have formed a template to which all social institutions must conform – from art museums to universities – there is unsurprisingly still some faith in the restorative-therapeutic power of art. Even today, we assume art has a deep affective and thus intrinsic value and these values are ends in themselves, that is, broadly existential values. For example, art is champion of a reflective, contemplative mode of life (over goal-oriented, achievement-driven forms of motivation); art elevates subject-ive experience and individual perception (over scientific objectivity and impersonal specialised knowledge); art promotes both community or shared values and experi-ence (against the 'individualisation' and atomisation of modem capitalism society), and art embodies authentic expressive individuality (against the homogenisation of corporate culture) (Albrecht 1968: 390).

In what follows I will outline common conceptions of aesthetic value, argue for the centrality of the concept of value in the validation and criticism of con-temporary art, and outline the way value is principally a matter for organisational analysis. I will do this via a case-study of an object forever celebrated by the con-temporary art world: the 'Tate Bricks'.

Art as non-art

In 1972 the Tate Gallery purchased a work of art from the John Weber Gallery in New York (Tate Gallery 1975: 73–5). The work was made by the American 'min-imalist' sculptor Carl Andre: it comprised 150 firebricks in rectangular formation set without a plinth on a gallery floor and was entitled *Equivalent VIII*. This work usually provokes three categories of question from critics and the general public alike: The first concerns *identity*: Is this object art? If so, what kind of art? The sec-ond category concerns *meaning*: what does this object mean, or signify? Is the artist making a statement? The third category concerns *value*: Is this object significant? What does it say about the nature of art? What kind of artistic or aesthetic value does it have? I will be pointing out the way the first and second categories of ques-tion have, in the contemporary art world, become entirely submerged in the last. In any case, the first two questions are somewhat anachronistic, as Andre's bricks (and minimal art in general) has assumed a privileged place in the official surveys and critical histories of contemporary art.

Andre's bricks had been exhibited by the Tate twice without incident before a journalist happened to use them in a provocative newspaper article on concep-tual art in 1976. Public derision and over 70 articles about 'the Tate Bricks' emerged in journals, newspapers and magazines over the following 12 months. In a time of severe Government cuts in public spending, £2297 of 'tax payers' money' was used to buy a pile of bricks (Spalding 1998: 182). The Director of the Tate Gallery forbade his staff to talk to the Press, and he remained rather reticent in his response to the public attacks. As is characteristic of the Tate's institutional protocol, public debate was allowed to continue without a defence of self-justification, except for a few scholarly articles and further exhibitions on 'conceptual art'. The Tate tacitly chose to retain professional judgement, rather than polemic, as the ground of their decisions regarding acquisition policy.

It is worth considering a few factual details. Firstly, *Equivalent VIII* was, as the title indicates, just part 'VIII' of an eight-part work, a work originally exhibited *in toto* at the Tibor de Nagy Gallery in New York in 1966. For the artist, the sculptural 'qualities' of the original work were generated by the sequential spacing and formal variation of the separate pieces placed together in a gallery space of particular dimensions. Does *Equivalent VIII* – as one part – constitute a single work of art? Andre himself was party to the purchase, and in this he overruled the initial organisational motivations of his own activity, and the aesthetic investment in that organisation. (Consequently, on the level of interpretation, considering the artist's 'creative intention' becomes nugatory.) Secondly, Andre informed the Tate shortly after the purchase, that the *Equivalent VIII* they had bought was not the 'original' work of art. The original only existed for the duration of the Tibor de Nagy exhibition – the original and unsold work of bricks was returned to the Long Island City Brickworks. Andre obtained a refund.

Is the *Equivalent VIII* – made of replacement bricks (in fact, firebricks and not sand-lime bricks like the original) – a fake? A forgery? Can an artist forge an identical copy of one of his own artworks? Can works of art be re-created? Was this the institutionalisation of intellectual gullibility? Oddly perhaps, these questions were rarely asked at the time; the initial protests related rather to the categories of identity and meaning: Is it art? What does it mean/what is the artist saying? One of the tabloid newspaper protests was by Keith Waterhouse in the *Daily Mirror* on the 19 February, 1976. He stated, 'Bricks are not works of art. Bricks are bricks. You can build walls with them or chuck them through jewellers' windows, but you cannot stack them two deep and call it sculpture'.

Waterhouse, however, did not have the same complaint against contemporary sculptor Anthony Caro, who used steel girders and aluminium pipes. Caro's girders and pipes were juxtaposed, joined and painted; they testified to a certain species of creative organisation having taken place and related to certain formal and spatial concerns of the practice of sculpture. Andre's bricks, for Waterhouse, were simply assembled bricks, untouched by the processes of creative transformation. Assembling bricks in a gallery may be a novel idea, but where was creative transformation, art's determining characteristic? Without any qualities one could identify as either sculptural or artistic, conventional processes of interpretation or artistic appreciation are rendered inoperable; the active function of the viewer is truncated. For Waterhouse the spectator becomes a passive consumer of an art world spectacle whose only claim to significance is art world provocation.

Again, the conceptual orientation of this discussion is anachronistic. The battle over the artistic validity of minimal art has been won. What needs to be looked at more closely, however, is how the original objections and questions concerning the categories of identity and meaning have become irrelevant, submerged in the concept of value. Firstly, what is aesthetic value?

Models of value

There are three broadly conceived ways of investigating art, all of which appeal to a distinct category of aesthetic value. These categories are three modes of organisation, all of which have to some degree provided a source of inquiry for management and organisation studies. They can be described as the following: (1) *material organisation*: the technical or material construction of the work of art: the physical structure towards which the viewer's perceptual activity is directed; (2) *aesthetic organisation*: the composition, artistic techniques, or aesthetic qualities of the object's material organisation; and (3) *hermeneutic organisation*: art's interpreted meaning, which is always configured within or in relation to existing systems of thought or institutional practice. This tripartite character of art bears an analogical reference to the basic structure of any organisation or corporation: the physical infrastructure of the organisation as institution, the routes or modes of activity, transaction and interaction facilitated by that infrastructure, and the network of meaning-laden activities of the corporate, and more broadly, socio-cultural, context.

Category (1), *material*, involves an analysis of the technology of the artwork's material construction. Art is primarily a form of material technology, and from every cultural epoch new aesthetic possibilities are engendered by technical innovation, whether oils to bind pigment, a portable blowtorch for welding metal, or complex chemical compounds to pickle dead animals; moreover, the use of material technology is always subject to economics, both the economics of art production (material expenses, facilities, patronage, etc.) and the economics of art's location (transportation, display, maintenance, etc.). The order of value we can identify in this category is *technical innovation* (often judged by degree according to the extent to which it transforms artistic practice through 'influence'). For example, Picasso's (1930–31) *Head of a Woman* in the Tate Collection is not an outstanding composition nor of significant conceptual meaning, but finds a significant role in art historical narratives for pioneering the use of welded metal, and in doing so ostensibly extended the expressive potential of the medium of sculpture. Andre's bricks hardly strike one as similarly technically innovative (or in retrospect, particularly influential).

Category (2), *aesthetic*, would identify the artistic conventions according to which such technical innovations are used to create a 'composition'. In a sense this category attempts to identify the uniqueness of the 'work of art as a non-utilitarian form of manufacturing' – an artistic composition with its unique conventions (which in turn demonstrates 'artistic' quality). 'Categories of artistic' quality are defined in terms of the work's pictorial form/shape, line/contour, colour, space, light/dark and surface/texture. The concept of *the medium* is given to mean way the materials and technical methods of construction appear when mediated by such conventions. The medium is not simply the materials, but the materials in application according to the conventions of painting, or of sculpture, etc. The mode of value we can identify in this category is *stylistic innovation*: the way materials and techniques of construction generate a new and expressive pictorial language. Again, style, expression, artistic convention and formal vocabulary are not concepts relevant to the bricks.

Category (3), *hermeneutic*, encompasses a broad range of concerns. Literally referring to the methods of interpretation available to the viewer (the way the object is made to yield a meaning that extends beyond its visual appearance), the subject matter of this category ranges from the compositional *content* of an artwork – symbols, iconography, metaphors, allusions, associations, narrative, and so on –

to its socio-cultural and political *contexts*. These contexts can be categorised as: (A) the contexts of production: the social milieu of the artist, the demands of the market or patronage, the location, and all the other ways the social, economic or political circumstances act as determining factors on the way the form and content of the work is constructed; and (B) the contexts of reception: the intellectual milieu of the artist, the circulation of influential ideas, professional networks of activity, criticism and art historical assessment, and other social, economic or political circumstances acting as determining factors on the way the form and content of the work is subsequently understood. This latter category has many temporal registers, as a work of art's 'reception' is something that changes through every cultural epoch, can be continuous and incremental over time, or occur as periodic trends or debates provoked by specific circumstances. The kind of value we can identify in the category of the hermeneutic is, broadly, *cultural significance* – the way in which the modes of meaning and experience generated by the work of art extend beyond the confines of the physical object, its immediate location and its specialist audience.

A general sociology of art's 'cultural significance' might be organised around the following typology. This typology will allow us to consider the concept of value at its most extensive (in and against the art world selective appropriation of its many manifestations). It comprises: (a) *intellectual* significance (the function of the object for analysis, history writing, intellectual enlightenment, object of philosophical con-templation, etc.); (b) *historical* significance (art maintains continuity with historical development of a national culture and plays a role in the formation of national iden-tity; promotes knowledge and concern for heritage and historical property; artis-tic influence; public impact or acclaim; popularity); (c) *social* significance (its impact on society, on a person's character or behaviour; art as collective interaction); and (d) *political* significance (art as socially demonstrative use of personal freedom; extend-ing arenas of socially acceptable individual expression, extending the powers of the individual to represent or challenge the norms of the collective; art as political education or propaganda).

Each of these individual categories of value might have sub-categories. For example, *social* significance could comprise the following: (I) *innovation*: promotes research and development of ideas; provides a well of creative activity for indus-try to draw upon (especially the 'creative industries'); (II) *environment*: improves quality of life through the creative transformation of urban-surrounds; creates the conditions for a renewed sense of social or communal identity; (III) *interaction*: pro-motes social involvement, interaction and thus social responsibility; can create a sense of occasion, atmosphere and social well-being important for promoting social cohesion; (IV) *education*: improves capacity for thought and creative expression in the individual; promotes self-development; broadens intellectual horizons; improves social skills and interpersonal skills; and (V) *economics*: can provide cost-effective forms of employment; can be the spring-board for new creativity-based businesses; can cross-subsidise the education sector and provide a range of services for media broadcasting.

The purpose of this lengthy conspectus is to underscore the expansive nature of 'value'. Accepting such an expansive concept does have its costs, involving the paradox that appallingly 'bad' art can achieve cultural significance if circumstances are favourable. But 'bad' according to what criteria? Generally, organisation studies uses art as an intellectual resource, and only art that has achieved categories (a) and (b) significance (*intellectual* and *historical*) art that has at some stage been institutionally endorsed by the art world. It usually does so on the supposition that these categories testify to a work of art's intrinsic value – it is bearer of a truly alternative and fecund order of rationality – while the latter two categories (c) and (d) are merely concerned with art's functional value or instrumental use according to other, non-art criteria.

As I noted earlier, however, in the contemporary art world (as exemplified by the bricks) characteristics intrinsic to the work of art – technical construction and stylistic or compositional convention – have been evacuated as sources of value. Moreover, the hermeneutics of reception have almost wholly supplanted the hermeneutics of production. For example, three of the most common arguments in defence of *Equivalent VIII* have been the following: (i) the bricks (and minimal art in general) were a pivotal moment in a far-reaching debate on the nature of abstract art and modernist formalism, emanating from New York between 1962–68; the basic terms of this debate were instrumental in the emergence of postmodernism in art; (ii) minimal art was a powerful symbol of resistance against modernist hegemony in the art world; Andre's *Equivalent VIII* has become a trophy for all those who favour experimentation unfettered by conventions of style, historical precedents, and institutionalised forms of viewing; and (iii) minimal art works like the bricks are an important touchstone for speculation on the ontology of art or the historical evolution of our concept of art, generating a significant route of theoretical speculation (Colpitt 1990: 101–32).

An outline of the various theoretical trajectories of (iii), the last and most influential argument, could look like this: The bricks 'comment' on the way the institution of the art museum has detrimentally severed our experience of art from our experience of everyday life. They 'question' the nature of creativity and its concomitant concepts of originality and genius. They exemplify something essential to the concept of art – the minimal conditions needed for an object to attain an identity as art. Or, they stand as a symbol of the bankruptcy of modem art *in toto*: the historical trajectory of modem art was predicated on the intellectual fecundity and aesthetic efficacy of stylistic innovation, a motivation which has revealed its own absurdity in that innovation was revealed to be little more than the dissolution of all aesthetic content through progressive abstraction – *Equivalent VIII* is the logic of modernism fulfilled. We might point out that minimal art *circa* 1964–68 was part of the reception of Marcel Duchamp's 'readymades', and can be understood as a series of responses to their aesthetic implications. The bricks are thus 'meta-art': art that reflects on its own aesthetic-historical conditions of (im)possibility.

Mapping the conceptual terrain of art world responses to the bricks is certainly wearisome; it is important, however, in order to substantiate an important general observation. All these above arguments amount to saying that the bricks maintain a sufficient and necessary aesthetic value for the object to attain to an identity of art because of their role or function in art world discourse. A conception of aesthetic value as *intrinsic* to the object has been supplanted by a conception of value of what is *extrinsic*. Value grounded in the artistic specificity of the work has been replaced by value emerging from the object's discursive function. Furthermore, the hermeneutics of reception as articulated by these dominant arguments has been shorn of any direct set of connections between the work of art and socio-cultural context; the 'art world' wholly stands in for 'context'. The strength of the object's function in art world discourse alone is the measure of its cultural significance.

Our problem is that there is only an arbitrary relation between the physical object itself and the institutional discourse, or between the intrinsic specificity of the work of art and the extrinsic arena wherein it is ascribed aesthetic value. Andre could have used planks of wood or car batteries.

How could one defend the bricks from the charge that they are only an arbitrary cipher for institutional discourse?

Value as aesthetic experience

While I have just emphasised the arguments for aesthetic value appealing to institutional discourse, there are at least three species of argument in support of minimal art which have *ostensibly* privileged the object itself as a locus of value. All three maintain that the artwork, primarily through the kind of aesthetic experience it generates, conveys meaning and convinces us of its intrinsic value. The first can be adequately represented in terms of the commentary on *Equivalent VIII* to be found in the recent *Tate Modern: The Handbook*. It states:

> *Equivalent VIII* was one of eight works exhibited together as a group in 1966. All the works were made from the same quantity of the same materials. Each individual work, however, was arranged into a different rectangular shape. Thus each was equivalent to but not exactly the same as every other work. In addition, variations in colour, texture and surface wear were visible among the components of each individual. Each brick is thus equivalent to but not the same as every other work. Clearly we would not normally notice such apparently slight variations. But perhaps this is the point: when the materials Andre uses are taken out of their normal context, we begin to look at them rather differently. Where we assume there is sameness, we find difference. Furthermore, Andre's work invites us to look at these non-artistic materials such as bricks or steel with the same kind of attention that we might normally reserve for, say, bronze or marble. That is to say, such work invites us to look at all materials – expensive or cheap, exotic or plain, artistic or non-artistic – as if they were equivalent. (Tate Gallery 2000: 114)

This statement admits that the very title 'Equivalent' indicated that specific qualities of *Equivalent VIII* were sustained only within a comparative relation to seven other works; this fact is then elided in favour of a comparison between the individual bricks themselves – the different 'variations in colour, texture and surface wear'. As they are different bricks altogether from the original artwork (firebricks and not sand-lime bricks), *Equivalent VIII* is not even an original fragment which could be defended as a metaphor or metonymy for a now non-extant whole. Nevertheless, the Tate's rationale is clear: the basic empirical distinction between de-contextualised identical objects engenders a unique perceptual of visual attentiveness. An otherwise trivial series of empirical observations on the difference between bricks finds an intrinsic value as a meditation on the ontology of difference. This mode of heightened awareness is possible with our relation to all materials, or all aspects of everyday life. The implication is that art revives our repressed or depleted powers of perceptual awareness, enlivening or transforming our basic perception of the natural world around us. Echoes of Derridean deconstruction are imaginary; this is a common art world variant of romantic modernism that emerged around the time of Schiller. Art is a kind of cognitive therapy – a cultural palliative for the destructive effects of the harsh world of social and economic rationalisation.

What is telling is the logic of this aesthetic encounter: for this sustained contemplation of the object-hood of ordinary objects to take place, the object must be framed within an institutional context which itself is encoded in such a way as to allow an unconscious presupposition of the object's identity and meaning.

Our second species of argument is somewhat more radical and usefully described using philosopher George Dickie's (2001: 77) term 'dis-value'. 'Dis-value' is not a *lack* of value, but an experience of its inversion, or at least an inversion of artistic characteristics that are usually associated with aesthetic value. Like Duchamp's (1917) *Fountain* (a urinal placed upside-down on a sculpture plinth), *Equivalent VIII* inverts conventional artistic practice and thus arrests or disrupts our perceptual expectations. This disruption offers a moment of reflection whereby two related thoughts emerge: (1) commonplace objects have aesthetic content; a urinal, for example, when inverted and placed on a pedestal, quickly loses its identity as a vulgar piece of utility plumbing and invokes an uncanny visual fascination; and (2) the location of viewing (usually a historic art museum or gallery) is encoded with viewing conventions (instituted by practices like placing objects on pedestals), which themselves ascribe an object an intrinsic 'value'. These viewing conventions, we may surmise, do not indicate inherent value in the object, but embody the proclivities and aspirations of a certain kind of sensibility; they further the legitimisation of class-based modes of 'taste' (and which, to extend the argument, colonise, conceal or repress the more socially expansive and subversive power of 'the aesthetic'). The artist's use of 'dis-value' thus finds significance as a moment of resistance against the hegemonic norms of traditional museum culture and its social substrate. It defines art less by its sensory qualities than its power of 'critical intervention' in the circuits of meaning and value that construct our historical conception of art (Paz 1975: 84–9).

However, evidently, dis-value is a symbolic negation of that to which it is beholden. It does not lay claim to an independent value outside the values it rejects; it has no purchase outside the immediate confines of art world institutions, institutions encoded with traditional artistic conventions and a sensibility which they embody. The traditional concept of the work of art remains implicit within the object. In the present day, traditional aesthetic values no longer govern institutional policy, and the objects once characterised by dis-value inevitably appeal either to a longing nostalgia for the avant-garde, or they cease to shock and collapse back into a variant of romantic modernism: sensible stimulation by peculiar objects.

Our third line of argument is adequately represented by Rosalind Krauss's early defence of minimal art (Krauss 1973: 43–53). For Krauss, minimal art has cognitive significance in that our experience (as subject) of the artwork (as object) rehearses a fundamental epistemological problematic – how the subject acquires objective knowledge of the physical world. The object's very arbitrariness strategically upsets our usual expectations and perceptual habits, and presents the possibility of another mode of meaning altogether. For minimal art, 'meaning' is not internal to the work of art, embodied in composition and originating in the mind of the artist; it has no 'artistic' conventions, detail or incident that would even prompt us to consider the possibility of intrinsic content. Rather, for any meaning to exist at all, that meaning must be actively created within our reflective apprehension of it. This mode of apprehension does not fixate us on the object's physical qualities, by the very *conventions of viewing* by which we perceive objects per se – the modes of perception that structure the viewing process.

The minimal art object has no significance outside the spatio-temporal site of the aesthetic encounter; within this site, however, it performs a critical function. For Krauss, we are prone to rationalise works of art, repressing the moment of the aesthetic encounter, denying the object its aesthetic specificity. We do this either by explaining it in terms of inherited concepts like 'style', 'convention' or 'technique', or by inserting it in an order of precedents within established historical narratives, or by identifying the way an expressive composition embodies the psychological intention of the artist. Our conventions of viewing are governed by this impulse to rationalise, or find meaning in terms of a logical chain of pre-formed concepts. This cognitive impulse, for Krauss, is consonant with the epistemology of Cartesian rationalism (itself symptomatic the rationalisation of human society and the atrophy of our aesthetic experience of nature).

Minimal art, for Krauss, strips art of anything that would facilitate this rationalisation; it supplants the hegemony of the mind with the body; minimal art demands that the body reassert its cognitive function as the driver in our knowledge of the sensory world. In other words, it appeals to a model of knowledge-acquisition consonant with phenomenology. Krauss (1995: 217) observes that with Carl Andre's first floor pieces in 1966 (arrangements of flat metal tiles) 'sculpture had been reduced to just this single defining property: space understood as a pure directional axis, its horizontal extension bodied forth by the continuity of the floor'. In Krauss's terms, *Equivalent VIII* 'vectors' the axis along which our bodies travel through space, offering us a specific reflective consideration of one of the fundamental elements of our perceptual experience of the world around us.

The 'value' of minimal art in this scheme of things is speculative-philosophical. Krauss's argument for aesthetic value maintains a compelling weight, but any object could be awarded both an identity and value for demonstrating a tenet of some academic philosophy or other. *Equivalent VIII*, it can be argued, demonstrates a central truth of phenomenology. But why would we need an artwork to demonstrate a philosophical commonplace? Something already philosophically comprehended? We find ourselves again faced with the specific object (intrinsic value) subsumed in a generic theory issuing from art world discourse (extrinsic value) – the relation between them being arbitrary. In short, *Equivalent VIII* has no aesthetic autonomy from the art world, its identity is derivative. Ironic perhaps, but

Krauss's aesthetic experience is merely empirical experience 'rationalised' by art world theory.

Institutional politics

So far I have attempted to show how all major arguments defending *Equivalent VIII* involve some kind of appeal to institutional context, an appeal that makes their validating account of the work insubstantial. In this penultimate section I wish to enlarge on the character of this institutional context. One of the most pervasive theories of aesthetic value to date directly appeals to context in general, and is known as 'the institutional theory of art', alternately 'the art world theory of art.' Sociologically, the 'art world' should not be conflated with the term 'institution of art' (as usually happens in art world criticism and theory). Art as a social 'institution' extends to the broad socio-cultural dissemination of art-knowledge and experience as a set of visual references, cognitive reflexes and general knowledge learned in the domestic environment, school and social interaction generally. For sociologists like Bourdieu (1989), this institution is primarily (though not exclusively) national in character, and whose structure is understood most accurately in terms of the way sensibility has been used as a mode of socialisation and aspiration for economic classes. The art world, conversely, is a concrete network of professionals, public and private organisations and commercial businesses. It can be defined in terms of institutions/organisations that create and exhibit art, and those which facilitate that activity and disseminate both objects and exhibitions. As with our previous conspectus of value, it is important to remind ourselves of the extensive character of the art world, as against the small and select networks of galleries and dealers through which the art world defines itself. The art world as organisational structure can be defined in terms of the 'core' activities of art production and exhibition, and the 'supplementary' activities of facilitating production or exhibition and aiding the dissemination of art and art discourse.

1   Core activities:
   (A)   *production of* art: artists and their studios, collectives and workshops, associations, clubs and societies; and
   (B)   *exhibition of* art: galleries: (i) public – national, regional, metropolitan; (ii) commercial; (iii) temporary – public or private; (iv) country houses, heritage sites and culture parks.
2   Supplementary activities:
   (A)   *facilitation of production* and *exhibition*: arts boards, arts councils, charitable funding bodies; art schools and other educational institutions; auction houses; art societies and civic organisations; arts managers, arts agencies and promotional agents (including consultants, advertising and public relations agencies); arts services (insurance, accounting and legal advice; conservation, manufacturers, transportation; photographers; printers; packers and shippers); and
   (B)   *dissemination of* art and art *discourse*: competitions; fairs and festivals; commercial and academic publishers; arts libraries; arts magazines;

specialist arts journals (general and academic); internet; film and television production.

Ironically, the two most influential theories of art that attempted to conceptualise art's art world function did not emerge from the sociology of art or sociology of institutions, but analytical philosophy; they are George Dickie's 'institutional theory of art' and Arthur Danto's theory of 'the artworld'. They have (wrongly) been held responsible for the wholesale acceptance of Duchamp's 'readymade' (such as the urinal or the bottle rack) as the establishment of an a priori principle for creative practice. Minimalist Donald Judd articulated this principle when he stated, 'If someone says his work is art, it's art' (Meyer 2001: 221). In a series of articles between 1969 and 1974, George Dickie observed that the identity of the art object was no longer *created* from a mediation of historic artistic conventions but was *conferred* upon the work by a representative of the 'institution of art', in most cases the artist. Dickie (2001: 55), in an updated version of his theory, holds that contemporary art can only be defined in terms of the following five propositions:

> *Proposition 1*: An artist is a person who participates with understanding in the making of a work of art.

> *Proposition 2*: A work of art is an artefact of a kind created to be presented to an artworld public.

> *Proposition 3*: A public is a set of persons the members of which are prepared in some degree to understand.

> *Proposition 4*: The artworld is the totality of all artworld systems.

> *Proposition 5*: An artworld system is a framework for the presentation of a work of art by an artist to an artworld public.

Propositions 1 and 2 are truisms, at the same time a key phrase, such as 'participates with understanding', without extensive clarification is surely vacuous. Proposition 4 is surely a tautology; and again in Proposition 5 the terms 'system' and 'framework' need sociological clarification for them to maintain substantive content. Dickie excises aesthetic specificity from his definition of the object; the terms 'art' and 'artworld' could be substituted for any luxury commodity and its market or network of enthusiasts. Dickie's definition is merely a simple conceptual schema of commodity production, distribution and consumption. It presupposes what is in question: an object with a unique aesthetic identity, which embodies or is the occasion for aesthetic value.

It was Arthur Danto's (1964) essay, 'The Artworld', that offered the original institutional theory of art. He stated:

> What in the end makes the difference between a Brillo box and a work of art consisting of a Brillo box is a certain theory of art. It is the theory that takes it up into the world of art, and keeps it from collapsing into the real object which it is (in a sense of *is* other than that of artistic identification). Of course, without the theory, one is unlikely to see it as art, and in order to see it as part of the artworld, one must have

mastered a good deal of artistic theory as well as a considerable amount
of the history of recent New York painting. (Danto 1964: 581)

We 'see' the *Brillo Box* as art because of a series of related concepts that structure
our perceptual apprehension of the object. Danto's reference to one city – New
York – is interesting; one wonders how 'local' art's identity, and value, can be.
Danto in a later article revised his suggestion that 'a certain theory' of art simply
conferred art identity on a non-art object (avoiding trivial implications of the
nominalism – 'art is anything I say is art' – to which Dickie's definition of art is
vulnerable). Rather, artworks like Warhol's *Brillo Box* emerge from a circuit of
'theories' or interpretative processes – exhibitions, debates, philosophy, history-
writing, and reflection on other artworks – and gain an identity through participation in this circuit. The *Brillo Box* has an intrinsic semantic value for Danto, in that
the individual object bears visual reference to certain conceptual issues (debates,
theories) internal to art's current development. That is, the art work itself is a visual
act of interpretation – a speculative reflection on the concept of art and the function of that concept within art world activities (Danto 1974).

Danto attempts to acknowledge the intrinsic specificity of individual art works as
well as the institutional function through which (and only which) they have their being.
His emphasis on the visual specificity and semantic content of the art object was an
attempt to articulate a non-arbitrary relation between the intrinsic and extrinsic spheres
of value (art object and art world). However, Danto's conception of the 'artworld'
still remained indeterminate. In a series of lectures in the early 1990s he re-defined
the art world as 'the discourse of reasons'. Danto (1992: 40) states: 'the discourse of
reasons is the art world construed institutionally'. The art world as a concrete network of organisations and actors for Danto is dissolved in the discursive character
of art as an institution. And art has no identity or value apart from discourse. The
object has no certifiable specificity apart from its discursive function. In fact, it is
this function (what discourse does to an object) that constitutes aesthetic experience.

Danto's theory is rich and holds many nuances I must ignore here: I am attempting to isolate his central assertion. My point must be prefaced by a simple empirical observation: only *certain* sectors of the art world have the power to participate
in 'discourse' in a way that has any implication whatever for the concept of art –
and discourse is not merely criticism or theoretical speculation, but frameworks of
endorsement, legitimisation and expectation, which themselves are inseparable from
the function of organisational structures. Only certain works of art, and certain ideas
or theories, construct the discursive framework that is called, 'the art world' at
any given time and place. Danto refers to 'the discourse of reasons' as art's conditions of possibility, not assuming that discourse (as he conceives it) has conditions
of possibility, institutional conditions of possibility which have something to do with
a social network of organisations and their actors.

Danto criticised Dickie for defining the art world as some kind of empower-
ing cultural elite, in terms of power and institutions; and rightly so: to describe
the art world simply in terms of bosses in large institutions, or conspiracies among
powerful dealers and critics, all making arbitrary decisions on the nature of art,
misrepresents the art world. The art world is indeed discourse. However, Danto
mystifies the character of discourse, concealing its organisational nature – the way

artworks find an identity in the first instance only in and through organisational structures and policies, patronage and professional protocols, whose guiding objectives are often inimical to the intellectual quest for the nature of art or the 'truth' of aesthetic experience. Moreover, we are left with no real indication of the complex internal life of *esoteric* or intra-communal value (the corporate values of the organisational network that makes up the art world, within and often distinct from the aesthetic values that they promote) and the relation between these and *exoteric* or extra-communal value (socio-cultural values in general). What is the value-structure of the art world (as embodied in the operations of the different species of organisation, with their individual and often historic mandates, contemporary fiscal and political pressures, and individual careers and opportunities for professional self-advancement)? What is the value of art world 'values' anyhow? What cultural function does the art world (and its art) maintain?

For Pierre Bourdieu, discourse in the art world functions as part of a 'linguistic market': terms of distinction, description, critique and classification – the lexicon of Danto's 'discourse of reasons' – exist only for those able to appropriate them. The art world is a 'field' of forces – a sphere where essential conditions of legitimacy are sought via a struggle for certain positions, positions of restricted access and professional authority. Within this field, individuals and institutions strive to increase their cultural capital (signified by their relation or position within the field), but only do so within the logic of that field – the structure of the socio-cultural space, which is as concrete as it is intellectual (Bourdieu 1993). I would say that anyone with even a minor experience of participation in the art world would say that Bourdieu's assertions are empirically quite evident.

Moreover, Bourdieu opens up another way of conceiving the relation between art's identity, meaning and value in the internal logic of art world: identity and meaning are never wholly submerged in 'value', but denote certain dimensions of the relation between art and art world. Art's identity functions as *taste* (modes of judgement and discrimination that attain to a level of collective credibility, and in turn constitutes a person's ability to mediate collective modes of authority); art's meaning functions in terms of *aesthetic distinctions* (sensibility expressive terminology, which delimits the subject's range of professional activity); and art's value functions as *cultural capital* (the modes of interaction between organisational structures and their individual actors involving decision-making power within the economy of symbolic goods). Importantly, cultural capital is not hermetic – like a fictional art world currency of concepts and objects, of value only to their own members. The fields of power within which cultural capital is created is co-extensive and often structurally homologous with the broader fields of social and political power through which it exists. For art's concepts and objects only maintain a genuine cultural significance if they bear a sustainable relation to the fields of power within which the art world itself is sustained (Bourdieu 1989).

Bourdieu's conceptualisation of discourse as organisational power offers the possibility of conceptualising the relation between the physical object of the work of art and institutional discourse as something other than intellectually arbitrary. It offers a structure that begins to unpack the concealed relation between the individual work of art and its discursive relation to that organisational network called the art world. A Bourdieu-analysis would show, among other things, the way definitions of art – like those of Dickie and Danto – are not purely 'reasons' or speculative propositions creating a purely reflective frame of reference. Their function in the art world is substantial (one might want to say ideological). The production and regulation of definitions is an activity within the art world that all institutions and their members attempt to participate in.

Definitions of art, for example, are the template through which acquisition and exhibition policy is formulated. On a basic sociological level, what our public institutions exhibit are henceforth considered *de facto* 'exemplary works of art' that engender attitudes, reference points, conceptions or frameworks of understanding, which maintain a determining impact on the nature of: (1) public museums' acquisitions policies; (2) the art education system; (3) the subjects of art criticism and art historical narratives; and (4) the pricing system of the private art market. And that in turn creates the framework of further practice for the current or next generation of artists. Considerable 'cultural capital' is at stake in our defining aesthetic value. Definitions are both schemes of validation and modes of legitimisation, and because they are, they generally need to be malleable to be institutionally useful. Dickie's is a case in point: it maintains sufficient conceptual clarity, yet contains chronic semantic vagueness. Danto's embodies strategic ambiguities, among other things inadvertently concealing his own personal legitimising power in the contemporary New York art world.

Organising art

To conclude: *Equivalent VIII* has maintained the status of an exemplary work of art within the art world for the last 25 years. As a test-case it is not long before we find that the art world's justifications of works of art usually involve a circular appeal to its own authority. What has emerged from our discussion is that most variants of aesthetic value are not recognised by the art world, and the ones that are, are constructed within a complex of unexplained and seemingly arbitrary relationships – between the specific work of art and the institutional discourse or 'theory', between the art world discourse and the art world as organisational system, between the art world elite and the rest of the art world, and between the art world and the broader context of social culture. *Equivalent VIII* is a severe case, but it is the boundaries of institutional practice that usually throw into relief institutional norms. What has concerned us is how exemplary forms of contemporary art find an identity and meaning as art only by virtue of possessing aesthetic 'value', and value is the extent of its usefulness to a small but powerful organisational network of institutions and professionals extending their own fictive discourse of cultural legitimisation.

Bourdieu provided an example of a way of opening up the monotonous dichotomy of 'art–art world'. Bourdieu, however, has a limited scope for our investigation, in that his concept of art and aesthetics is largely anachronistic, largely based on pre-1960s art forms. His work shares a limitation with traditional sociological accounts of art patronage and institutional practice, as they by and large need a categorical distinction between a work of art and its contexts in order to identify structural symmetries between art production and commodity production, art exchange and commodity exchange, artistic conventions and social conventions, aesthetic experience and social experience, and so on. The art world problem, as I have attempted to demonstrate, is complex in the sense that both work of art and institutional activity have become categorically indistinct on the level of their only salient realm of meaning: aesthetic value. Moreover, Bourdieu is limited on both the internal workings of institutions and organisations, and on the nature of contemporary intellectual networks.

I began this essay with the assertion that an organisational analysis is central to an investigation of aesthetic value. Both art and art world are constructed in and through the agendas, strategic choices and protocols of physical institutions as well as discourse and professional networks: their relationship involves a complex and changing relation between language, administrative structures and organisational activity. Any serious investigation of contemporary art needs an organisation analysis of aesthetic value. Such an analysis would map the organisational field, observing discrete and overt alliances, associations, and organisational interaction, and register the circuits of power that travel through the various hierarchies within the diversity of institution or organisation. It would observe the institutional determinations that converge to facilitate a coherent 'discourse of reasons', a discourse that acts to repress, censor, prohibit and stall as much as reveal and promote current movements of creative production. It would track the generation, transference and monopolisation of cultural capital, and the way the accumulation of capital is relative to the strategic choices available to individual organisations. A systematic organisational study of contemporary art is yet to fully emerge.

References

Albrecht, M.C. (1968) 'Art as an institution', *American Sociological Review*, 33: 383–97.

Bourdieu, P. (1989) *Distinction: A Social Critique of the Judgement of Taste*, London: Routledge.

Bourdieu, P. (1993) *The Field of Cultural Production: Essays on Art and Literature*, Cambridge: Polity Press.

Colpitt, F. (1990) *Minimal Art: The Critical Perspective*, Seattle: University of Washington Press.

Danto, A. (1964) 'The artworld', *Journal of Philosophy*, 61: 571–84.

Danto, A. (1974) 'The transfiguration of the commonplace', *Journal of Aesthetics and Art Criticism*, 33: 139–48.

Danto, A. (1992) 'The artworld revisited', *Beyond the Brillo Box: The Visual Arts in a Post-historical Perspective*, New York: Farrar, Straus, Giroux, 33–53.

Dickie, G. (2001) *Art and Value*, Oxford: Blackwell.

Krauss, R. (1973) 'Sense and sensibility: reflections on post '60s sculpture', *Artforum*, 12(3): 43–53.

Krauss, R. (1995) 'Theory of painting', in Field, R. (ed.) *Mel Bochner: Thought Made Visible, 1966–1973*, New Haven, CT: Yale University Art Gallery, 217–22.

Meyer, J. (2001) *Minimalism: Art and Polemics in the Sixties*, New Haven, CT: Yale University Press.

Paz, O. (1975) 'The ready-made', in Masheck, J. (ed.) *Marcel Duchamp in Perspective*, New Jersey: Prentice Hall.

Schiller, F. (1982) *On the Aesthetic Education of Man*, Oxford: Clarendon Press.

Spalding, F. (1998) *The Tate: A History*, London: Tate Gallery Publishing.

Tate Gallery (1975) *The Tate Gallery 1972–4 Biennial Report and Illustrated Catalogue of Acquisitions*, London: Tate Gallery.

Tate Gallery (2000) *Tate Modern: The Handbook*, London: Tate Gallery.

First published as Vickery, J. (2006) 'Organising art: constructing aesthetic value' *Culture and Organization*, 12: 51–63. Jonathan Vickery is located at the Centre for Cultural Policy Studies, University of Warwick, UK, where his research focuses on design and contemporary communication.

Chapter 17

How Hello Kitty commodifies the cute, cool and camp

Brian J. McVeigh

IN JAPAN, Mickey Mouse is being pursued by a cat. By many accounts she is an even more innocent, innocuous, and cute creature. She goes by the name of Hello Kitty. Currently, this kitten queen of cuteness with tiny eyes and a large, marshmallow-shaped head seems to pop up everywhere in Japan. At the risk of sounding conspiratorial, Hello Kitty is not as innocent as she appears, and it is her very innocuousness that conceals her power. Her efficacy, influence, and impact derive from her plainness, simplicity, and artlessness – a contagion of consumerism grounded in her looks of sincerity, openness, and innocence. Her quietude generates dynamism, a feverish activity of consumption spun from a placid disposition that lacks even a smile. Indeed, some attribute Hello Kitty's distinctive charm to the simplicity of her visage, referred to as 'Zen cuteness' (Fox 1998). As one woman put it, 'Her expressionless face (*muhyôjô*) is unexpectedly cute.'

Hello Kitty comes to life at the nexus between the drive for capital accumulation of a corporation, a daily aesthetic of cuteness and campiness (an artificiality of manner or appearance, appreciated for its humour or triteness), and the consumerist desires of individuals. In Japanese, her name is pronounced *harôkitî* or sometimes *kitî-chan* ('*chan*' is a diminutive), and written in Roman letters – to add a foreign, exotic flavour – or in the angular syllabary of Japanese (*katakana*) rather than the cursive syllabary (*hiragana*), since the former highlights its novelty. Hello Kitty is the best known product of Sanrio, a Tokyo-based company founded in 1960 by Tsuji Shintarô. Sanrio's profits are enormous, totalling ¥120 billion in 1998 (Aoki, 1997; 'Kitty bankbook', 1998; Saito, 1998). In 1999, that equals approximately one billion US dollars (US$1.00 = ¥120).

Like other items of material culture, Hello Kitty has a useful lesson: how purchasing and collecting practices establish a discourse about matters apparently unrelated to the commodity consumed, i.e. respondents frequently judged those interested in Hello Kitty within a framework of unhindered/freedom/self-autonomy versus coercion/control/compulsion. For my purposes, the former set of terms is associated with what I call 'consumutopia', while the latter, as we shall see, are connected to 'control', a less positive, more critical view of social relations. I will order my arguments, then, within a framework of consumutopia and control. I first investigate certain aspects of 'consumutopia' (Jameson 1979; Morris-Suzuki 1988), a sort of counter-presence to mundane reality fuelled by late capitalism, pop culture industry (Kogawa 1988: 54–5; Nakanishi 1997a; and White 1994), and consumerist desire. Then, I examine what individuals have to say about Hello Kitty, which, in addition to being a stuffed doll, appears in many other forms, including countless images and icons.

Before proceeding, a few words about other lessons Hello Kitty has for us concerning the vagaries of fashion. She teaches us the need to focus not just on different tastes within a certain 'society' (however this term may be defined), but also on diverse attitudes within the same individual. Such intra-subjective diversity is expressed, at least in the case of Hello Kitty, in two ways. The first is visible across generations. Through its marketing of Hello Kitty, Sanrio has made a concentrated effort to tie together within a single individual different modes of self-presentation that chronologically correspond to girlhood, female adolescence, and womanhood: 'cute', 'cool', and 'camp'. That is, as an individual matures, appeals to nostalgia encourage a reconnection with the past by buying certain products united by one leitmotif; *same* commodity, *same* individual, *different* ages/tastes/styles/desires. Obviously, such a strategy may reap enormous profits.

A second type of intra-subjective diversity concerns ambivalent ideas held by the same individual about an item of pop culture synchronically (rather than chronologically). A notable number of individuals pointed out to me that though they do not really care for Hello Kitty, they feel they must act as if they do and 'take advantage of a ride (*binjô*, i.e. an opportunity)' in order to fit in. Thus, from a company's perspective, successfully pushing trendy products in the market does not require full participation or commitment from aficionados. But it does require partial participation, i.e. 'everyone is doing it, so I should, too'. Indeed, many of those who were critical of Hello Kitty would possess (or wear) her goods. Not a few exchanges with respondents went like this: 'So, since you dislike her so much, you don't buy any of her products, right?' Answer: 'Well, I don't like her, but perhaps I like her a little. I do have a Hello Kitty key chain and stationery.'

Most would agree that there is often a disconnect between media reports, mass communication hype, and a general belief about the large role played by a pop culture fad *and* what many individuals actually think. The idea that media can magnify a phenomenon out of proportion is not terribly insightful and is certainly not a novel point, but I hope to draw attention to the way in which an icon/product of popular culture/industry such as Hello Kitty teaches us how the purchasing and collecting practices of a group of people, refracted through the mass media (TV, newspapers, comics) and reflected off the surfaces of public space (advertising copy, signs, interiors of post offices, etc.), manufacture a massive field of desire (e.g. pursuit of being cute, cool, feminine, in-group status, nostalgia). But this field of desire contains sentiments that are ambiguous, and items such as Hello Kitty seem to indicate that we need to take into account how different levels of devotion vary within the same individual.

The characteristics of 'consumutopia'

The literature on postmodernist conceptions of 'Utopia' is too extensive to treat here, but Falk's exegesis will suffice:

> There is no human culture without mythical visions of a state devoid of any lack, of the Paradise Lost or the Kingdom of Heaven to come. These Utopias located in indefinite Otherness (*u-topos*), the models of the Good World, are primarily negations of the existing reality – either as simple inversions of scarce life, the carnivalistic 'Land of Cockaygne' characterized by abundance and endless pleasure, or as elaborated depictions of Perfect Order in which well-being, virtue and justice are finally realized. (1994: 129–30)

Unlike ancient and mythological conceptions, the 'good state of being' in modern times is associated with Enlightenment projects (specifically, the idea of progress) and located in the 'attainable temporal world':

> But what is really new in the pursuit of happiness of modern (consumer) society is that the Utopian project is reduced in scale to the *individual*, into a modern mode of self building aiming at completion within the boundaries of one's own self and one's own life, and that this is done primarily by means of goods as the building blocks. (Falk 1994: 130, emphasis in original)

If we define 'Utopia' as a condition, place, or situation of social or political perfection, we can describe 'consumutopia' as a joint endeavour between capitalist producers and product consumers to establish sites, practices, or spaces of 'perfect consumption'. These sites, practices, or spaces are idealized and fantasized, thereby making consumutopia a state/place in which individuals cheerfully consume and a happy fit between steadfast supply and desirous demand occurs. Certain developments of modernity, such as mass society, mass culture, markets and marketing strategies, the culture industry, and modern communication technologies, are prerequisites of a consumutopia. However, we should note that particular historical trajectories, cultural contexts, and social conditions shape consumutopias. Of course, being an ideal condition, situation, or place, there is no actual consumutopia. However, there are definitely serious attempts toward constructing one, and needless to say, Hello Kitty is not the only character turned into a line of products that illustrates the workings of consumutopia (though her commercial success certainly exemplifies consumutopia).

What are the traits of consumutopia? There are many ways to answer this question depending on the particular consumutopia in question, but for my present purposes I list five: (1) unifying leitmotif; (2) accessibility; (3) ubiquity; (4) projectability; and (5) contagious desire. Below I explicate and illustrate these traits with examples from the consumutopia of Hello Kitty.

Unifying leitmotif

Perhaps the most basic trait of consumutopia is the production of an endless variety of products – different shapes and colours, diverse functions, and numerous designs – that nevertheless possess some unifying theme, emblem or motif. Of course, it can be quite profitable for a business if it can successfully market an array of products that rides a unifying leitmotif. Here it should be noted a unifying leitmotif resonates deeply with the bourgeoisie obsession with rationalization and order, i.e. matching the motifs, colours, and shapes of one's possessions, effects, and environment.

Hello Kitty exemplifies a unifying leitmotif, and seems to be an example of Sanrio's determination to 'paint' a vast number of daily goods with images rather than just merely manufacturing similar knick-knacks. As one woman explained it, 'Though her face [Hello Kitty's] is always the same, she has many goods of various styles (*bariêshon no sutairu no gudzu*) that just make me want to collect them all.' By one count, there are 15,000 Hello Kitty products (Herskovitz 1999). (By another count, Ono (1998) suggests there are 4000 Hello Kitty products, half of which are aimed at adults.) Sanrio receives 3 percent in royalties every time a company sells a product bearing a Sanrio character (Yamazaki 1999), and one-third of its profits comes from licensing fees (Ono 1998). Sanrio spends ¥1.5 billion annually on documenting and protecting its copyrights (Yamazaki 1999). From Sanrio's perspective, then, Hello Kitty has good reason to appear on and in stickers, coffee mugs, glasses, calculators, blankets, notebooks, phone cards, cameras, pocketbooks, watches, towels, pillows, toothbrushes, lunch boxes, pens, pencils, garbage pails, golf bags, boxer shorts, safes, luggage, scooters, and at Dai-Ichi Kangyô Bank, bankbooks and cash cards. There are Hello Kitty-shaped toys, handbags, and appliances such as telephones and televisions. A section in a typical shopping catalogue is called 'Hello Kitty's Happy Life' and advertises spatulas, sets of dishes, pans, pots, bowls and cups, a tea kettle, coffee maker, shaved ice machine, hair dryer, cookie mould, toaster, toaster oven (the latter two cook Hello Kitty's image onto bread or other foods), and waffle maker (which makes Hello Kitty-shaped waffles). Daihatsu Motor Co. even manufactures the 'Hello Kitty car', a small, white passenger vehicle with 'Hello Kitty wheel covers' and a choice of pink or blue 'Hello Kitty seats'. Hello Kitty also appears on packages of local specialties across the country, such as Nagahama Ramen of Kyûshû and Yatsuhashi sweets of Kyoto ('Cat Icon has Merchandisers Clawing in Big Revenues', 1998).

One can partake of the boons of Hello Kitty consumutopia without alerting others to one's dedication. Many Hello Kitty products for women – dresses, skirts, hats, etc. – look quite ordinary except for an inconspicuous Hello Kitty image placed somewhere on them, perhaps indicating the ambiguous feelings some individuals have toward Hello Kitty. This is true for a line called 'Super Hello Kitty' that features clothing and items that only have small Hello Kitty emblems (men's ties, socks, shoes, sandals, wallets, sunglasses, pens, pocketbooks, etc.).

Other clothes for women are less shy about their origins in Hello Kitty consumutopia. For example, the backside of bikinis and halter tops have Hello Kitty's image boldly printed on them. Even 'traditional' clothes such as kimonos are adorned with Hello Kitty's image.

Sometimes there is a deeper level than a unifying leitmotif that an array of products shares, a sort of fundamental aesthetic of the everyday, and in the case of Hello Kitty products this would be *kawaisa* (cuteness). I have investigated elsewhere how in Japan 'cuteness' operates symbolically as a daily aesthetic and qualifies as a standard attribute, rather than as a mere fad (McVeigh 1996, 1997a, forthcoming; see also Kinsella 1995, 1997; Masubuchi 1994). Therefore, Hello Kitty embodies and makes visible the trafficking in socio-semantics legitimated by a key aesthetic experience, and each representation of Hello Kitty acts as a transmitter that reflects, refracts, and reverberates a host of complex messages about affection and authority, harmony and hierarchy, and admiration and attachment.

Sanrio uses cuteness as its company's marketing motif, though it is always on the look out for more specific manifestations and variations of this theme and attempts to follow fashion trends (for example, *kawaî* can sometimes be glossed as 'cool'). Thus, Yamaguchi Yôko, a Sanrio employee who has been in charge of Hello Kitty since 1980, goes to Harajuku, a shopping and hang-out mecca in Tokyo for the younger generation, and talks to young girls in order to discover their interests. In 1995 she 'learned that high school students were opting for clothes that were cuter and more feminine. Kitty's ribbon was coloured and replaced with a flower in some cases' (Masuda 1998).

Here I would like to suggest that another fundamental aesthetic characterizes products such as Hello Kitty: campiness. I will have more to say about this aesthetic later as it relates to expressions of femininity, but here it suffices to say that such campiness resonates with the theatricalized ambience of much of Japanese social life (McVeigh 1997b).

It must be stressed that not all women like Hello Kitty or things cute (I can still remember the slightly embarrassed face of the female bank teller as she asked me which kind of Hello Kitty bankbook I wanted). Some characterize women who purchase Hello Kitty objects as 'wanting to be kids forever'; 'not wanting to grow up'; or 'emotionally undeveloped'. But we must choose our adjectives carefully, because women who collect Hello Kitty articles are not necessarily interested in things cute, but rather have a predisposition towards what is better described as camp, and this campiness, for older female Hello-Kitty aficionados, is tied to a type of femininity that highlights cultural desirables such as sincerity, kindness (*yasashisa*), and sensitivity to the feelings of others (*omoiyari*), the latter being a norm heavily emphasized in different spheres (see Lebra 1984; McVeigh 1997b, 1998). What we have is not immaturity, *naiveté*, or regression, but theatricalized innocence, accessorized cheerfulness, and affected youthfulness. According to one social psychologist, 'Owning things with cartoon characters on them shows one's childlike nature . . . It is proof of one's youthfulness, which is now considered a positive attribute' (Yamazaki 1999). And for many women, Hello Kitty is a celebration not of childishness but of the childlike, a hope that in spite of a gloomy, harried, and harassing world in which they are forced to outmanoeuvre others, they are still light-hearted, spirited, buoyant, and ingenuous. Hello Kitty allows an individual to express a direct emotional impact in a social world that usually privileges indirect messages and circumlocution. Hello Kitty is for those who want to believe that in their hearts of hearts they are innocent, and that ironically, despite the campiness of Hello Kitty, artlessness will win over artifice and the actual over the artificial.

Ubiquity

If products can be seen and sold everywhere, both consumers and producers view their respective positions as advantageous. Or if the perception that a product is everywhere can be successfully manufactured, then at least the producers can benefit from profits generated by novelty (see 'Contagious desire' later). There are different degrees of ubiquity, and for a variety of practical reasons not all products obtain the magical status of omnipresence. But Hello Kitty comes close. From a company's point of view, Hello Kitty is an ideal product since it crosses generational lines; for young girls it is 'cute', for teenagers it is 'cool' (*kûru* or *torendî*), and for women in their twenties and older it is best described as camp. She is everywhere, and her omnipresence – which cannot be understood without appreciating Japan's powerful and ubiquitous daily aesthetic of cuteness (*kawaisa*) – exemplifies the notion of simulacrum, i.e. copies of copies of the same commodified image with no apparent original (Baudrillard 1983).

Bill Hensley, Sanrio's marketing manager in southern San Francisco, explained that 'We're the leader in the retail-first strategy of creating characters to be on products.' 'Retail first' means having characters debut on products, rather than using characters who start their lives in books, comics strips, cartoons, or films and then move onto products. Thus, 'Sanrio's characters begin their existence right off as retail products, without the benefit of prior celebrity' (Fox 1998). Though she is in stiff competition from other creatures (e.g. Mickey Mouse, Minnie Mouse, Doraemon, Pingu, Moomin), as of this writing Hello Kitty is the most popular and best known character in Japan's commercial and consumerist landscape. She can be seen in spaces both private (personal possession) and public (displayed in stores and post offices), and of course, she appears in countless avatars in objects of material culture.

Hello Kitty is ubiquitous in other senses. As already noted, Hello Kitty and her products are popular not just among young girls, but also among women of all ages:

> Sanrio began researching designs aimed at the adult consumers about 10 years ago when demographers began talking about the shrinking of Japan's younger generation. One reason for the spread of character-based products is the meticulously-laid business strategies of the companies producing them. (Yamazaki 1999)

Sanrio's homework paid off, and sales of Hello Kitty items 'more than doubled in the past three years' among female office workers and housewives (Masuda 1998). But Hello Kitty has received some help in the popular media, whose style of reporting on such matters often borders on a type of boosterism for capitalist consumerism. Supposedly she became very popular among female office workers and housewives when entertainment idol Kahara Tomomi (now 24 years old) announced her fascination with the kitten character on television. An endorsement from 46-year-old singer Koyanagi Rumiko, who displayed her Hello Kitty products on TV, also increased sales (Ono 1998).

Though Hello Kitty is more popular among girls, young women, female teenagers, and mothers, some young men do buy her products, and there are plans to target males for the next line of Hello Kitty products (Hello Kitty has recently been seen accompanied by a male counterpart called Dear Daniel who is also a cat).

Hello Kitty's powers of transformation are so powerful that she can take on different incarnations. For example, there is Mermaid Kitty (*Mâmeido no kitî*), Bee Kitty (*Hachi no kitî*), and Koala Kitty (*Koara no kitî*). The latter is known as a 'transforming stuffed animal' (*henshin nuigurumi*), i.e. a stuffed animal disguised as another stuffed animal (cute, so cute, it self-duplicates). There is also Hello Kitty Angel and a totally white Kitty that rides a unicorn.

Accessibility

Products that are ubiquitous, needless to say, are everywhere to be seen, are easily obtainable, can be conveniently bought, and have, of course, a better chance of satisfying a consumer's desires and generating profits.

Hello Kitty makes regular appearances (along with other Sanrio characters) at Sanrio Pyûrorando (or if in Roman letters, Sanrio Puroland) and other amusement parks. She is in fact everywhere, and some companies have adopted her to attract attention: on the cover of the catalogue for services at the Takano Yuri Beauty Clinic she wears a pink dress and says 'Hello Kitty has become a softened Day Spa character'. A karaoke lounge has adopted the Hello Kitty theme to boost business:

> Each of the lounge's 11 rooms boasts a different version of Sanrio Co.'s cat character. Pictures of Hello Kitty in Chinese dress, as an angel flying through the heavens, or clad in a kimono, have schoolgirls and young office ladies squealing with delight [and] devoted lovers of the icon are treated to more images on the video screen between songs, and the bathrooms feature Kitty toilet paper and towels. ('Cat icon has merchandisers clawing in big revenues', 1998)

Hello Kitty's very presence, then, is a force to be reckoned with; her appearance on countless surfaces a mighty enforcement of a daily aesthetic of cuteness and campiness; her occupancy of public space an ascendancy of the commercial; her residence in stores, banks, and post offices (where she is used to advertise services) a state-sanctioned operation of modern economics.

Accessibility is aided through publications such as *Kitty Goods Collection* (1999), which advertises itself as the 'newest Kitty catalogue' (*saishin kitî katarogu*). This catalogue promotes and discusses the latest Little Kitty's goods (*Kitî-chan no gudzu*). Sometimes discussions in the catalogue are quite detailed; one feature compares the small differences between Japanese-made and American-made versions of Hello Kitty. *Kitty Goods Collection* (1999) also provides the names, addresses, and phone numbers of overseas stores that carry Hello Kitty items.

Projectability

Imagine a product on which an individual can project his or her wishes, fantasies and pleasures. If properly marketed, such a product could be quite profitable. Now consider Hello Kitty, whose appearance is simplicity itself: three dots for eyes and a nose, no mouth, three lines for whiskers on either side of her face, and a huge forehead that grants her a decidedly infantile appearance. 'Her big head and little body makes her funny', according to one young woman. Near her left ear she dons a pink or red ribbon or sometimes a flower. Such a lack of embellishment provides carte blanche for whatever an individual feels, and it is this very impreciseness, inde-terminateness, and vagueness that works to the advantage of the business concerns behind Hello Kitty: her plainness characterizes her as a cryptic symbol waiting to be interpreted and filled in with meanings. Thus, she functions as a mirror that reflects whatever image, desire or fantasy an individual brings to it. Her mood is ambiguous; neither happy, sad nor agitated, thus ready to absorb and reflect back to her admirers whatever they are feeling on a certain day. Sanrio spokesperson Yoneyama Kazuhide explains that Hello Kitty's mouthless countenance is part of her appeal: 'Without the mouth, it is easier for the person looking at Hello Kitty to project their feelings onto the character . . . The person can be happy or sad together with Hello Kitty' (Herskovitz 1999). Such projectability applies to other characters: 'Sanrio believes that because its characters are not tied into a definitive story line or movie plot, children can project their own feelings and emotions onto the characters' (Fox 1998). Characters hopefully develop a life of their own. Indeed, there are books written to help one understand the 'inner heart of characters' (*kyarakutâ no naishin*).

In a certain sense, projectability resonates with individuality. As is well known, capitalist forces do not simply foist knick-knacks on the masses, and we must give credit to the individual consumer who, after all, chooses to purchase certain incarnations of Hello Kitty but not others (or chooses not to buy Hello Kitty at all). Furthermore, a young girl does not buy a Hello Kitty doll for the same rea-sons that a mother buys a Hello Kitty toaster, and a teenager does not buy a Hello Kitty key chain for the same reasons that a middle-aged woman buys Hello Kitty bath towels. There is a considerable amount of individualistic (*koseiteki*) style and decision-making to collecting Hello Kitty products, and much of this individual-istic style is expressed across generations. As one woman put it, the rich 'variety' (*baraetî*) of Hello Kitty goods allows young girls to 'have a feeling of solidarity (*rentaikan*) while being able to let others have a peek at their individuality (*kosei*)' (cf. McVeigh 1999).

Contagious desire

The last trait of consumutopia is the most intangible and thus difficult to describe and define. It concerns the assembling not of the product itself, but rather the manufacture of a generalized sentiment of desire, aspiration, longing, craving, even euphoria, for the product. Ideally, a corporation somehow initiates a craze, passion, and mania for its product, but usually such heightened interest, fixation, and excitement is very difficult to maintain for long. However, even if a certain 'contagious sentiment' can be manufactured (via peer groups, covetousness, effect-ive advertising, etc.), some fetishization may result which produces a mystique.

The secret of administering a consumutopia is to maintain a delicate balance between a unifying leitmotif (a trait of consumutopia noted earlier) and product variety. Producers and manufacturers must try their hardest to keep at bay monotony, a sense of sameness, ennui, and satiation, while maintaining a unifying leitmotif of the product line. After all, the ultimate aim of corporations is not to satisfy the wants of consumers but to instil dissatisfaction and incite desire.

Besides manufacturing a vast line of goods, another way to spread sentiments of desire and demand is to spin a fantasy world around a product that consumers can enter. Thus, Hello Kitty has her own world. Her birthday is 1 November 1974 and she lives in London. She has the 'weight of three apples' and is characterized as *akarui* (cheerful, lively) and *yôki* (bright), two key themes found in Japanese pop culture, advertising, everyday aesthetics, and idealized as an essential component of 'human relations' (*ningen kankei*). Not surprisingly, Hello Kitty likes 'small cute things, candy, stars, goldfish, etc.', and is described as 'A very energetic little girl, Kitty loves to play outdoors, in the park or forest. But you can also find her happily practicing on the piano or baking a cake, too!' She is a third grader who likes travelling, reading, eating, and making cookies, and has adventures at school. Hello Kitty has a family: papa (described as hardworking, dependable, absent-minded, with a sense of humour); mama (who is very kind and loving, takes care of her house, and is famous for her apple pie); grandpa (who is smart, paints, and likes to tell stories); and grandma (who likes to embroider in her rocking chair). Hello Kitty also has a twin sister, Mimi, who wears a yellow ribbon over her right ear to distinguish her from her sister.

The special world of Hello Kitty is appreciated by aficionados. For instance, one woman in her early twenties explained that many people like Hello Kitty because she offers them a chance 'to get away from the harshness of reality' (*genjitsu*). They buy something cute (*kawaî*) like Hello Kitty and enter a world that is *higenjitsu teki* (unreal, fantastic). Fans and collectors of Hello Kitty are called 'Kittilers' (there are Hello Kitty fan clubs all over the world, see Herskovitz 1999) and they seem ready to fulfil the dreams of Sanrio by engaging in a 'collecting that focuses on things that can be used every day' (*Kitty Goods Collection*, 1999). *Kitty Goods Collection* features 'super collectors' creation of space' (*chô shûshûka kûkan sôzô*); examples of children who have amassed mountains of Hello Kitty goods or people who have designed room-sized micro-consumutopias especially for their out-of-control Kitty collections.

Here it might be mentioned that Sanrio has a whole range of cute creatures and little critters that qualify as Hello Kitty's friends. They include: Bad Badtz Maru (a bad-attitude grinning penguin with spiked feathers); Chococat (a chocolate-coloured cat); Keroppoi (a sprite, goggle-eyed frog); Kuririn (a perky hamster); Monchichi (a monkey whose friend is Monta); Pinkuru Corisu (a pink female squirrel of royal heritage from Pinkuru Planet); Little Star Twins (Kiki and Lala, sisters from a star with mystical powers); My Melody (a mouse-like creature whose brother is named Rhythm); Picke Bicke (a mouse that imitates other animals and was born in Sanrio Puroland); Patty and Jimmy (children from Kansas); Pippo (a curious pig that likes to tell stories); Pochacco (a soccer-playing Golden Retriever puppy that likes pudding and has a friend called Muffin); Spottie Dottie (a female Dalmatian who is a fashion-expert and wears a large pink ribbon; her father was chief fire dog with the New York City fire department); Tuxedo Sam (a penguin from Antarctica that has two brothers, Tam and Ham, and was educated in England); Pekkle (an aquatically-challenged duck from Australia that wants to be a lifeguard).

If a corporation is lucky they will receive free advertising from those infected with contagious sentiment who have uses for a product line (or its representation) that is not directly connected to profit-making endeavours of the corporation. For instance, in order 'to make children happy', a farmer created a 20-m Hello Kitty image using 3000 colourful kale plants in Hyôgo Prefecture ('Veggie art', 1999). And in Tokyo, cab-driver Fukuoka Tôru, in order to appeal to women and children, 'has packed the interior of the car with goods bearing the Kitty character'. He wants them to enjoy their trip in his 'dream world'. Some high school girls in the area believe that they will receive good luck if they spot the 'Kitty taxi' ('Kitty kitsch draws fares to custom cab', 1999).

Hello Kitty and 'control'

Several recurrent themes appeared in discussions with individuals about Hello Kitty. These themes say more about what many Japanese think concerning individual freedom/societal constraints and how they view themselves as consumers of pop culture than Hello Kitty per se. Moreover, as indicated later, there is a fair amount of 'we-Japanese-are-this-way' self-stereotyping in what many had to say.

Accounting for the popularity of Hello Kitty

What was the response to the query 'why is Hello Kitty so popular?' Initially, among men and women in their twenties to forties, most engaged in circular reasoning: 'She is popular because many people like her'; 'She is popular because she is always on TV and in the media'. A majority responded that her popularity is due to her 'cuteness'. 'What, then, is "cute"?' I would ask. The usual answer would run along the lines of 'Hello Kitty's appearance'.

   After cuteness, probably the most important reason cited to account for Hello Kitty's popularity is the feelings of nostalgia (*natsukashî*) she evokes. Nostalgia involves what McCracken calls 'displaced meaning', which 'consists in cultural meaning that has deliberately been removed from the daily life of a community and relocated in a distant cultural dynamism' (1988: 104). Individuals 'prefer to displace their ideals, removing them from the "here and now" to the relative safety of another time or place' (McCracken 1988: 108). Certain objects of material culture come 'to concretize a much larger set of attitudes, relationships, and circumstances, all of which are summoned to memory and rehearsed in fantasy when the individual calls the object to mind' (McCracken 1988: 110). Such objects 'become a bridge to displaced meaning and an idealized version of life as it should be lived' (McCracken 1988: 110). Here I should note that in Japan the role of 'nostalgia advertisements' (*nosutarujî kôkoku*) and 'nostalgia products' (*nosutarujî shôhin*) is explicitly recognized, and Hello Kitty has been around since 1974, so that her popularity can be at least partially accounted for by memories of women now in their twenties and thirties (cf. Herskovitz 1999). The 'nostalgiazation' of Hello Kitty for purposes of profit appears to start early in the individual's life-cycle: 'I remember once when I was very young I was made fun of when I brought a Hello Kitty lunch box to school. So, years later, I was very surprised to see my classmates collect Hello Kitty goods, even though at the time they were teenagers, about 16 or 17 years old' (woman in her early twenties).

Hello Kitty is also closely associated with sentiments of 'intimacy', 'familiarity', and 'friendship' (*shitashimi*). Other common terms that surfaced were 'affection' (*aichaku*), 'sense of comradeship' (*nakama ishiki*), 'feeling of unity' (*ittai-kan*), and 'sense of security' (*anshinkan*). (See Nakanishi's 1997b '*Yasashî—omoshiroi—kawaî*' — 'Kind, Interesting and Cute', for a treatment of some of the themes covered here). I was told that her friendly facial expression 'puts people at ease'. She 'relaxes' or 'calms people down' (*nagomu*). 'She frees me from troublesome thoughts.' Others noted that she is a *karafuru kyarakutâ* (colourful character) and that the 'colours of Kitty goods have a warm feeling'. One young woman explained that 'Sanrio uses colours that stand out, like pink and red. That's why she's attractive.'

'Real' feelings toward Hello Kitty

What surprised me when discussing Hello Kitty with individuals was how few claimed they liked her (though some said they had no particular feelings one way or another). Indeed, most young adults I spoke with clearly claimed that they do not like her at all. Moreover, there was a good amount of cynicism and scepticism in what many had to say. According to one person, 'I have my doubts that so many people can really like something so trite.' Some described Hello Kitty fans as 'childish' (*kodomo-ppoi*). 'They look like children with their little toys,' quipped one woman in her mid-twenties. A young man explained that he likes Hello Kitty but does not like being told what to buy and felt unhappy with what he perceived as Sanrio's profiteering. The theme of being forced to buy things – or *maindo kontorôru* (mind control), in the words of one young man – was a topic that repeatedly came up. 'I resent being made a *tâgetto* (target) of corporations'. Another young woman said that 'People buy the newest Little Kitty, and then again they have to buy another new Little Kitty. This is why I hate this system that makes us buy things one after another.' One young man stated that '*Kitî-chan* is cute and being so popular, I guess she's cool. However, unlike walking yourself, it [her popularity] is like a train. You can only go along the tracks to a place that's been decided.' One female university student explained that Hello Kitty is 'too popular' (*hayarisugiru*) for her taste.

Interestingly, the negative attitude toward Hello Kitty was often extended to criticism of a 'Japanese-like' (*nihon teki*) trait of group behaviour, a 'follow-the-leader' propensity, and how Japanese blindly follow trends. The Hello Kitty boom, in many people's estimation, illustrates how overly sensitive Japanese are to the whims of fashion. Many pointed out that though they do not care much for Hello Kitty, they felt they must pretend they do. If not, they become *fuan* (anxious, insecure, uneasy) and only feel *anshin* (at ease) after they go along with the trend. 'Even if they don't like Hello Kitty, they don't want to be out of fashion. So they must buy her goods. They are also proud of all the different things they carry around with them.' According to one young woman, 'If I see other people with certain things, then I don't want those things. However, if other people have something, many Japanese feel they have to get it for themselves.' A woman in her late twenties said that 'Japanese do not like to be conspicuous. If they stand out, they worry about being shunned by those around them. In such a country, if Kitty is popular, everyone runs off to buy her. Young people are especially sensitive to what's fashionable (*ryûkô*).' Another woman said that buying Hello Kitty items provides a sense of solidarity (*rentaikan*) and security (*anshinkan*) for young people since such purchases marks them as members of a group.

Hello Kitty fans lack a self

Others went beyond the notion that Hello Kitty aficionados march too quickly to the beat of the drum and claimed that they actually lack a sense of self-worth. Many explained that individuals who like Hello Kitty lack their own identity (*aidentîtî*); have lost their 'individuality' (*kosei*); need to acquire their 'own style' (*jibun no sutairu* or *jibun-teki*). These are people who have lost a sense of *jûnin-to-iro* (to each his/her own; literally, 'ten people, ten colours') and cannot obtain 'self-satisfaction' (*jiko manzoku*) on their own, and 'because they do not have self-identity (literally, self-likeness)' (*jibun-rashisa ga nai kara*) must rely on superficial, silly, and immature props. According to one female student, Hello Kitty is a sign that 'Japanese are gradually becoming infantilized' (*yôjika shite iru*). They 'can't express themselves' (*jibun o hyôgen dekinai; jiko hyôgen ga dekinai*) without meaningless knick-knacks. One female university student was of the opinion that 'if we don't consider the individuality of each person and if we don't firmly have our individual consciousness (*kosei no ishiki*), then the number of mechanical people (*kikai teki na ningen*) will increase.' Some pointed out that this loss of self is particularly strong among Japan's youth. 'They have lost their ability (*nôryoku*) to do anything.' Another student said that 'It is the young people who play but don't study and can't express themselves that are hurting Japan. Hello Kitty is just one example of this.' Some were particularly negative in their appraisal of Hello Kitty fans: 'Because they are people who can't express their own will (*jibun no ishi o hyôgen dekinai*), they are offensive, have a bad character, do stupid things, and can't get along with others. So they try to confirm their own existence (*jibun no sonzai o tashikameyô toshite iru*) [through Hello Kitty]'. Also, they can't decide anything for themselves and have no common sense (*jôshiki*, i.e. 'manners').

In spite of the many individuals who linked the Hello Kitty boom to a loss of self and personal identity, there were a few that had an opposite view and told me that Hello Kitty actually represents an independent spirit which is seen in her enigmatic facial expression: 'Little Kitty doesn't have a smile and she acts on her own. She suits the people of modern times. I think that though modern people must face their superiors with an ingratiating smile (*aisowarai*), something that is hard to do, Little Kitty doesn't exert herself doing such things, and she shows her true self' (male university student). Another male university student said that 'She doesn't follow group behaviour (*gurûpu kôdô*), and acts on her own, so she really stands out (*medatsu*).' One individual saw a virtuous aspect to Hello Kitty as an art form unique to Japan: 'Japan has lost its culture, like Nô and Kabuki, which are out of date and anyway are disappearing. But Hello Kitty is cute (*kawaî*), and though some people like her while others don't, everyone buys her goods. This means that people have a strong sense of themselves and this is a good thing.' It might also be added that some saw the Hello Kitty boom (*kitî-chan no bûmu*) and the proliferation of Little Kitty goods (*kitî-chan no gudzu*) as a much-needed boost to Japan's recession-plagued economy.

Conclusion: Hello Kitty as an indicator of individual/society relations

Though respondents talked about Hello Kitty's tangible, observable, and 'cute' attributes, many judged their peers' interest in Hello Kitty as evidence of their lack of independence and autonomy. Too much devotion to Hello Kitty, then, indicates one has fallen prey to the power of society (specifically demonstrated by too much group behaviour, fear of standing out, conformity, and loss of self). And for many individuals, there are too many people who are overly sensitive to fashion trends. But as someone who has lived in Japan for almost twelve years and taught in universities for eight years, I find these assertions that Japanese are afraid to be different and that a salient number of Japan's young people readily conform to the whims of fads and fashion unconvincing. Certainly, in Japan group pressures are present (as in any society) and many people do follow the latest pop cultural developments, but there are, of course, many spheres of social life in which Japanese do not conform and they do freely express themselves. The notion that they are easily bossed around by corporate culture smacks too much of a stereotype.

Why, then, (1) do individuals apparently believe that a large number of people are too group-oriented and have become slaves to corporate culture? And (2) why does an innocuous item of material culture prompt (as would, one imagines, other similar items of material culture) a rather pointed discussion about self/ collectivity relations?

Any attempt to answer the first question readily rounds up the usual suspect of the media. But media hype can only partially account for such massive belief. I contend that the use of somewhat stereotypical 'national character' attributes to account for consumer behaviour is noteworthy, e.g. Japanese purchase Hello Kitty goods because of their 'group consciousness' (*shûdan ishiki*); they 'conform too easily'; they have 'lost their identity' (*shutaisei*). Japan, after all, is a place where, to use the cliché, 'the nail that sticks out gets hammered down'. Whether such clichés are true or not is, in a sense, beside the point for my present purposes. What is significant is how such beliefs, mobilized to account for some phenomenon, end up reinforcing descriptions and definitions of ethnocultural identity that are in themselves suspect.

The second question is, admittedly, far more difficult to answer. But I offer a suggestion: there are certain social settings in which expressions of self are not always welcomed (e.g. exam-centred classrooms in middle and high school, factory floors, and offices). When individuals centre a discussion about self/collectivity dynamics on a character from consumutopia perhaps it is because they perceive it to be a bit safer than doing so in education-examination and employment sites. It is not that serious discussions — concerning, for example, management/labour, state/ individual, male/female relations — do not occur in schools and work places; they certainly do. The point is that borrowing characters from cartoon land to make one's case seems somehow less threatening, and here I want to return to McCracken's notion of how certain items of material culture can displace meaning (1988). But here I do not mean the displacement of meaning in the temporal sense (Utopias of an idealized past or a fantastic future), but rather in spatial terms: the appropriation of Hello Kitty as a symbolic lightning rod that collects electrical currents from other territories of social life (e.g. socializing and labouring sites). Indeed, as an eminently cute icon of popular culture, Hello Kitty resonates powerfully with a tendency to aesthetically 'soften' controversial, sensitive, or troublesome issues (as well as warnings, street signs, and corporate images; see McVeigh 1996, forthcoming). This phenomenon abounds in Japan. Some examples:

- In order to soften its image as a state institution whose mission is violence, Japan's Self-Defence Forces give out stickers of infantilized, cute cartoon soldiers for recruiting purposes (it also uses the smiling faces of little girls and frolicking puppies in some of its recruiting posters). The two main *imêji kyarakutâ* (image characters) of the Self-Defence Forces are Prince Pickles (*Pikurusu ôji*) and Little Parsley (*Paseri-chan*).
- A 55-minute documentary about the Aum Shinrikyô trial ('Kyôzo no Kamisama – Asahara Hôtei Manga') has 'cute cuddly images'. Journalist Yichiro Aonuma, the documentary's creator, explained that by depicting the cult members (who were responsible for the Tokyo subway sarin attack and other murders) as cartoon characters, he 'emphasizes the tragic fact that many innocent lives were taken by the cult' ('Documentary Animation: Aum Shinrikyô Trial', 1998).
- At over 200 Sanrio outlets there are application forms for Dai-Ichi Kangyô Bank credit cards: 'If the image of banks is forbidding, so is that of the item perhaps most frequently found in their vaults. Cash, after all, is typically described as "cold" and "hard", not "warm" and "soft" ' (Bailey 1999). Thus the need for Hello Kitty to convince people of the 'softness' of the banking industry.
- The mouse-like Pipo-chan, the mascot of the police, was recently seen in the form of individuals dressed as the character handing out pamphlets warning pedestrians about molesters (*chikan*) in Tokyo train stations.
- Residents of Katsushika Ward in Tokyo recently received a colourful flyer about traffic safety that details actual accident deaths using cartoon characters. From one corner of the flyer snarls *Mamoru-kun* – or if loosely translated, 'Obedience Kid' (i.e. obey traffic rules) – who can only be described as a deranged pink Bugs Bunny wearing a brown toupee.

Hello Kitty is more than just a representation expressing herself through various objects of material culture. She is an icon for the everyday, an idol for the masses, an image for modernity (i.e. capitalism, consumerism, state projects and programs), a symbol that allows meaning displacement, or 'a kind of epistemological immunity for ideas' (McCracken 1988: 109). Hello Kitty teaches us that what we have in our daily life is not a stern Big Brother from the monolithic state office of propaganda demanding blind obedience, but rather countless little sisters – or more accurately in the case of Hello Kitty, little critters – dispatched by corporate culture who kindly persuade (but not necessarily convince us) to consume. There is no conspiracy here to control the masses through hedonistic consumption, but there is an ideology – or a set of ideologies to be more exact – of capital accumulation, profit-making, and expanding market share, all given a powerful aesthetic spin. As one young woman said, 'I wonder what kind of thing will appear next. I'm waiting to see if it will it be as popular as *Kitî-chan*'. Or as one young man sarcastically commented, 'I'm now looking forward to what kind of character will become popular next.'

References

Aoki, N. (1997) 'Hello Kitty has girls purring, craze targets older women with TVs, toasters, cars', *Japan Times*, 27 December, 3.

Bailey, J. (1999) 'Progress behind the scenes', *Tokyo Weekender*, 30(7): 7.

Baudrillard, J. (1983) *Simulations*, New York: Semiotext(e).

'Cat Icon has merchandisers clawing in big revenues' (1998) *Daily Yomiuri*, 14 May, 18.

'Documentary animation: Aum Shinrikyo trial' (1998) *Asahi Evening News*, 11 November, 9.

Falk, P. (1994) *The Consuming Body*, London: Sage.

Fox, D. (1998) 'Hello Kitty items a global rage in "Zen cuteness"', *Japan Times*, 30 April, 15.

Herskovitz, J. (1999) 'Itty-bitty merchandise hawker leads Sanrio's world conquest', *Japan Times*, 5 February, 3.

Ivy, M. (1993) 'Formations of mass culture', in Gordon, A. (ed.) *Postwar Japan as History*, Berkeley, CA: University of California Press, 239–58.

Jameson, F. (1979) 'Reification and utopia in mass culture', *Social Text*, 1(winter): 130–48.

Kinsella, S. (1995) 'Cuties in Japan', in Skov, L. and Moeran, B. (eds) *Women, Media, and Consumption in Japan*, Honolulu: University of Hawaii Press, 220–54.

Kinsella, S. (1997) 'Comments on McVeigh', *Journal of Material Culture*, 2(3): 383–5.

'Kitty bankbook' (1998) *Daily Yomiuri*, 2 April, 18.

Kitty Goods Collection (1999) Sanrio, Vol. 6 (July 20).

'Kitty kitsch draws fares to custom cab' (1999) *Asahi Evening News*, 18 April, 6.

Kogawa, T. (1988) 'New trends in Japanese popular culture', in McCormack, G. and Sugimoto, Y. (eds) *The Japanese Trajectory: Modernization and Beyond*, Cambridge: Cambridge University Press, 54–66.

Lebra, T.S. (1984) *Japanese Women*, Honolulu: University of Hawaii Press.

Masubuchi, S. (1994) *Kawaî shôkôgun (The Cute Syndrome)*, Tokyo: Nihon Hôsô Shuppan Kyôkai.

Masuda, Y. (1998) 'Small, cheap, quirky – formula for fast sellers in slow times', *Asahi Evening News*, 26 May, 5.

McCracken, G. (1988) *Culture and Consumption*, Bloomington and Indianapolis: Indiana University Press.

McVeigh, B. (1996) 'Commodifying affection, authority and gender in the everyday objects of Japan', *Journal of Material Culture*, 1(3): 291–312.

McVeigh, B. (1997a) 'Reply to Kinsella', *Journal of Material Culture*, 2(3): 385–7.

McVeigh, B. (1997b) *Life in a Japanese Women's Junior College: Learning to Be Ladylike*, London: Routledge.

McVeigh, B. (1998) *The Nature of the Japanese State: Rationality and Rituality*, London: Routledge.

McVeigh, B. (1999) 'What cuteness, cleanliness and consumerism say about the "Group Model" in Japan', paper presented at Anthropology of Japan in Japan 1999 Annual Meeting. The Institute of Comparative Culture, Sophia University, 9 May.

McVeigh, B. (2000) *Wearing Ideology: State, Schooling and Self-Presentation in Japan*, Oxford: Berg.

Morris-Suzuki, T. (1988) *Beyond Computopia: Information, Automation and Democracy in Japan*, London: Kegan Paul International.

Nakanishi, S. (1997a) *Kodomotachi no sabukaruchyâ daikenkyû* (*Great Research on Children's Subculture*), Tokyo: Rôdô Junpô.

Nakanishi, S. (1997b) '*Yasashî–omoshiroi–kawaî*' ('Kind, interesting and cute'), in Nakanishi Shintarô (ed.) *Kodomotachi no sabukaruchyâ daikenkyû* (*Great Research on Children's Subculture*), Tokyo: Rôdô Junpô, 82–121.

Ono, Y. (1998) 'From cars to karaoke, Kitty-mania places its grip on Japanese adults', *The Wall Street Journal*, 15 December, 1–3.

Saito, S. (1998) 'Kitty comes to the rescue', *Daily Yomiuri*, 25 March, 13.

'Veggie art' (1999) *Asahi Evening News*, 17 December, 4.

White, M. (1994) *The Material Child: Coming of Age in Japan and America*, Berkeley, CA: University of California Press.

Yamazaki, T. (1999) 'Money in the Kitty', *Look Japan*, February, 39.

First published as McVeigh, B.J. (2000) 'How Hello Kitty commodifies the cute, cool and camp', *Journal of Material Culture*, 5(2), 225–45. Brian McVeigh is Associate Professor at Tôyô Gakuen University. His books include *Wearing Ideology: State, Schooling, and Self-Presentation in Japan*, *The Nature of the Japanese State: Rationality and Rituality*, *Life in a Japanese Women's Junior College: Learning to Be Ladylike*, and *Spirits, Selves, and Subjectivity in a Japanese New Religion: The Cultural Psychology of Belief in Sûkyô Mahikari*.

Chapter 18

The sociology of consumption

Colin Campbell

CONSUMER GOODS MAY serve to fulfil a wide range of personal and social functions. Fairly obviously, they commonly serve to satisfy needs or indulge wants and desires. In addition they may serve to compensate the individual for feelings of inferiority, insecurity or loss, or to symbolise achievement, success or power. They also commonly serve to communicate social distinctions or reinforce relationships of superiority and inferiority between individuals or groups. They can also, on some occasions, express attitudes or states of mind, or communicate specific messages from one person to another. Finally they may be instrumental in creating or confirming an individual's sense of self or personal identity. All these possibilities have been canvassed in the wide variety of theories that can be said to have a bearing on consumption. Yet it is noticeable that in contemporary sociological discussions not all these perspectives are equally represented. Generally we may say that special emphasis tends to be placed on those theories that relate consumption to issues of identity and, within this, to those that represent consumption as an activity which conveys information about the consumer's identity to those who witness it. Indeed, we can be more specific still and identify theories that represent the consumer as actually preoccupied with conveying specific 'meanings' or 'messages' about his or her identity (or 'lifestyle') to others, as those currently predominant within the discipline.

In general this would seem to be because sociologists have been persuaded that modern industrial societies have evolved in such a way that individuals are presented, effectively for the first time, with the possibility of choosing their identity by varying their pattern of consumption. What is commonly argued is that changes in production techniques associated with post-Fordism, together with ever-greater differentiation in the identification and targeting of market sectors, have led to a significant move away from mass consumption and towards an ever-wider diversity of consumption patterns. Quoting from Stuart and Elizabeth Ewen's book, *Channels of Desire*, Mike Featherstone suggests that such changes can be summed up in t phrases 'Today there is no fashion: there are only *fashions*', 'No rules, only choice 'Everyone can be anyone' (Featherstone 1991: 83, italics in original). Thus, in co trast to the comparative fixity of a hierarchical system of social status groups, the claim is that there is now a completely 'open' system, one in which an individual is free self-consciously to choose to manifest any of the multitude of lifestyles on offer; and 'lifestyle', is the key term in such theories. Very much 'in vogue' as Featherstone suggests, it is usually employed to connote

> individuality, self-expression, and a stylistic self-consciousness. One's
> body, clothes, speech, leisure pastimes, eating and drinking preferences,
> home, car, choice of holidays, etc., are to be regarded as indicators of
> the individuality of taste and sense of style of the owner/consumer.
> (Featherstone 1991: 83)

Thus, because of the wide range and character of goods and services currently on offer in the marketplace, and consequently the considerable choice which this presents to consumers, individuals are regarded as free to select an identity for themselves. The consumption pattern that they select, whether represented by their choice of car or clothes, house, furnishings or leisure-time pursuits, can therefore be regarded as indicative not simply of their 'self-identity', but of how they wish others to regard them. Indeed, because George Herbert Mead's thesis concerning the dependence of self-images upon the attitudes of others is generally presumed to be valid, changing one's consumption habits in order to indicate a new identity to others is presumed to be the only way in which consumers can effectively adopt a new one for themselves.

Now, in part, this tendency to assume that the members of modern (or postmodern) society can be more adequately categorised, not on the basis of old production-style criteria such as occupation, educational qualifications or income, but rather by 'lifestyle', has gained considerable impetus because of recent developments in the fields of advertising and marketing. These professions now typically class people on consumption criteria, often employing what Gardner and Sheppard (1989: 217) refer to as 'psychographic techniques', that is 'a way of looking at future market segments by attitudes and lifestyle'. Market researchers increasingly make use of geo-demographic databases to construct profiles of 'consumer types' based on different 'lifestyles'. These profiles may include types such as 'working-class stay at homes', 'young upwardly-mobile' and 'well-off-retired', or the 'co-op, club and colliery', and 'families in the sky' (see Flowers 1993). Or the categories may focus on attitudes and values toward contemporary issues, such as conservation and the environment, with the consequent identification of different varieties of 'greens' (see Gardner and Sheppard 1989: 224). In general one may say that marketers have moved over the past ten to twenty years from categorising people by class and purchasing power, firstly to demographics and life-stages, and then increasingly to consumption patterns and 'lifestyle'. However, it was probably with the appearance of the 'yuppie' that the wider public first became aware of this change (see Burnett and Bush 1986; Hammond 1986). This move has culminated in advertisers abandoning the old socio-economic classifications of A, B, C1, C2, D in favour of lifestyle categories, on the grounds that 'It is now misleading to relate lifestyles simply to income or occupation' (Tharpar 1994). In the light of these developments, there must be a strong suspicion that sociologists, in accepting that it is valid to change from using older 'objective' criteria such as occupation or income to these newer 'subjective' ones, are merely following a fashion, effectively taking their cue from the advertisers and market researchers, rather than modifying their views as a consequence of their own research findings.

However, there may well be good reasons for believing that it is unwise of sociologists to build theories of modern consumer behaviour around the concept of 'lifestyle'. For whilst lifestyle-based categories may be of value in the context of marketing and advertising, there is little evidence to suggest their sociological significance. In the first place it is important to note that even the marketing 'lifestyle' categories are still commonly built around discriminators – such as age, marital status, employment status, or stage of the life-cycle – which are 'objective' criteria and not simply features of a consumption pattern. For, not surprisingly, market researchers are well aware that age, employment status and life-cycle position are major factors influencing disposable income and hence purchasing power. Consequently it is still rare for individuals to be categorised on lifestyle variables alone. Second, when more 'subjective' factors are taken into account, as for example in the development of categories of 'green' consumer, the criteria employed relate more to differences in people's values than to differences in taste. This is clearly critical because although individuals may easily develop new tastes, there is much evidence to suggest that the values that people hold do not change much through-out their lifetime. Both these considerations suggest that the majority of consumers are not actually in a position freely to adopt a new lifestyle (or identity) simply by the expedient of changing their consumption patterns; either because of the lim-itations imposed by their objective circumstances or because to do so would require them to undergo the equivalent of a 'conversion' experience.

In the light of this conclusion it is easy to understand why so much emphasis is placed upon 'youth' in those theories which present consumption as guided by a desire to adopt a 'lifestyle' (see, for example, Langman 1992: 59–61). For not only is 'youth' (especially perhaps adolescence) necessarily a life-cycle stage in which experimentation with identity is a central concern, but it is also a stage when individuals generally have little in the way of regular, fixed financial com-mitments. Very often lacking a career, if not permanent employment, as well as dependants, property-maintenance payments or mortgages, youth is in an ideal position to 'play' with identities. In addition, they are more likely than 'adults' to be in need of reassurance concerning their identity from their peers, and con-sequently to engage in the 'other-directed' activities of 'viewing and being seen'. However, it is still necessary to note that, even here, the identities on offer fre-quently consist of merely one or two subcultural alternatives which are themselves set within clear class boundaries; ones which are experienced by the individual as both objective and subjective (that is internalised values) constraints on their choice. This would suggest that it is unwise to treat the identity-experimentation charac-teristic of youth as if it were in fact typical of the conduct of modern consumers as a whole. This danger may be most apparent when generalisations are made on the basis of studies of working-class or lower-middle-class youth, but there is a similar danger of treating the attitudes and practices of certain sections of the affluent middle class, for example yuppies, or the *nouveaux riches*, as if they too were typical of consumers as a whole.

But there are yet deeper problems with the 'lifestyle' or 'consumption as indicative of identity choice' thesis; ones that surround the suggestion that consumption carries distinct meanings, in the form of 'messages' about identity, to those in a position to witness it. Veblen was the first theorist to suggest that an act of consumption might carry such a message and he was very explicit about what it might be. He considered that it indicated something about the consumer's 'pecuniary strength'. In other words, observers, because of their knowledge of how much things cost, would be able to assess an individual's wealth (and hence in Veblen's terms, social status) from the purchased goods which they displayed. This thesis is problematic enough given that people's knowledge of the price of goods is far from perfect, whilst the casual observer is often not in a position to judge the 'expensiveness' of items that are conspicuously displayed. Yet modern theories generally presume that consumer goods carry more complex messages than this one, and what is more, they assume that consumer and observer share a common understanding of the 'language' in which they are conveyed. Both must be judged highly dubious assumptions.

It has become almost routine for theorists to employ a communicative act or expressive paradigm when focusing on consumption; with the consequence that consumer actions are not viewed as real events involving the allocation or use of material resources (or even as transactions in which money is exchanged for goods and services) so much as symbolic acts or signs: acts which do not so much 'do something' as 'say something', or more properly, perhaps, 'do something through saying something'. This communicative act paradigm – in which talk or language more generally is the model for all action – is one common to theorists as diverse in other ways as Veblen, Goffman, Bourdieu, Barthes and Baudrillard. Now in one sense the perception that individuals may employ material objects to send messages to others and thus to symbolise or express an existing social relationship or to mark a new one, is something of a platitude in the social sciences. Indeed, it is easy to illustrate this perspective by reference to inheritance practices, the giving of dowries, indeed gift-giving in general, or to 'hosting' (that is, entertaining) and the like. One can indeed 'say it with flowers' (and with other things); that is to say, convey love, affection, gratitude, or the like (the precise message depending on the circumstances surrounding the gift) to one or more other people (see, for example, Corrigan 1989). However, in these instances not only is it the case that actual objects are transferred to specific targeted others, but such acts are themselves usually clearly situated in time and space, something which helps to determine their 'meaning'. By contrast, sending a message to largely unknown and generally unspecified others merely by a process of displaying or using goods, and often without the assistance of specifically designated display situations, is a rather different matter.

There are several important distinctions which often become confused when the 'meaning' of goods is under discussion. The first concerns the difference between the fact that actions are intelligible and the assumption that they have an agreed meaning; the second concerns the confusion between possessing a meaning and constituting a message; and the third, the confusion between receiving a message and intending to send one. Now one could reasonably claim that most actions that individuals perform are usually intelligible to other fully socialised members of the same culture. Consequently it is rare for anyone to be completely mystified by the goods that others have purchased or by the way that they are being utilised. This is not the same, however, as claiming that all, or even most members of that society would be in a position to agree on what 'meaning' should be attributed to the fact that a particular individual has purchased a pair of blue jeans or chooses to wear them to go shopping. For such conduct does not possess a given meaning in contemporary British society, in the way, for example, that a bride wearing a white dress on her wedding day has a given and widely understood meaning. This is not to say that blue jeans do not carry a range of associations and indeed market researchers devote a good deal of time and effort to discovering precisely what these might be. But this does not mean that the activity of wearing them can be compared in any way with uttering a word or even giving a hand signal. For in this case, there is simply no commonly agreed code (let alone a 'language') which would allow any such 'message' to be decoded.

This is not to deny that cultural categories or even cultural principles cannot be 'encoded' in clothes or indeed in goods generally. The anthropological evidence here is strong (see, in particular, Bogatyrev 1971; McCracken 1985). Yet the case is more easily made for traditional or non-literate societies than it is for modern, complex industrial ones. Here, as McCracken's research has shown, the more that individuals try to employ clothing as a language, that is by making their own combinations of items to construct a personal 'ensemble', the less successful it is as a means of communication (McCracken 1988: 55–70). What is more, the essentially fixed nature of a person's appearance renders any 'dialogue' or 'conversation' through clothes an impossibility. Typically, individuals 'read' clothing as if it were a single Gestalt, whilst they employ a very limited range of nouns and adjectives to categorise those portrayed. No attempts are made to 'read' outfits in a linear sense or to detect novel messages. Indeed, only when individuals wear conventional 'outfits' of the kind that correspond to existing social stereotypes (such as 'housewife', 'businessman' or 'hippie') can a 'language code' be read at all.

What is more, the fact that one individual may be able to perceive some 'meaning' (in the sense of clues about 'identity') in the consumption activities of another does not imply either that other observers would discern similar 'meanings' in that activity, or that the meanings discerned correspond to those the consumer intended to convey (if indeed they intended to convey any) through their conduct. In fact, there is a considerable gulf between the wide range of possible meanings which an observer might claim that they can discern in the consumption activities of an individual and the very limited and highly general messages which any individual can possibly hope to succeed in conveying consciously and deliberately to others solely by means of their deployment of consumer goods. Thus despite the many claims that there is a 'language' of goods, especially of clothes (see in particular Lurie 1981), this metaphor, as Davis (1992) has argued most forcibly, is deeply misleading.

None of this should be taken as implying that the material objects that individuals possess or display are not implicated in the creation or maintenance of their sense of self, for there is ample evidence that this is indeed the case (Dittmar 1992).

But this is most obviously true in a developmental and particularistic sense, as in the case of a child's cuddly toy or comfort blanket, a bride's wedding ring, a teenager's first car, or an old person's family album. Such objects have meaning to their owners because of the part that they have played (or still play) in their life experiences. Such meanings as these, however, are usually invisible to others (or at least they are to strangers). To assume, therefore, that the casual observer can 'read' the consumer goods that an individual possesses in such a way as to reveal the nature of a person's identity is necessarily to override or ignore this dimension. What is typically put in its place is a categorisation which is necessarily both highly general, far from all-embracing, very speculative and (since consumers are not usually subject to interrogation by observers about their consumption habits) not open to falsification. All of this suggests ample ground for scepticism concerning the general claim that the activity of consuming should be viewed as an endeavour by individuals to indicate a chosen 'lifestyle' to others. The central problem here (and it goes back at least as far as Veblen, although it is most apparent in Goffman) is the tendency of sociologists to apply a communication act paradigm to conduct that is essentially instrumental, and consequently 'read backwards' from the presumed (that is imputed by the sociologist) existence of a message to the presumed intention to send one. Consumption is then seen as involving an 'attempt' by the consumer to 'adopt a lifestyle' or 'create an identity' when there are few grounds for any such assumption.

References

Bogatyrev, P. (1971) *The Functions of Folk Costume in Moravian Slovakia*, trans. R.G. Crum, The Hague: Mouton.

Burnett, J. and Bush, A. (1986) 'Profiling the Yuppie', *Journal of Advertising Research*, April.

Corrigan, P. (1989) 'Gender and the gift: the case of the family clothing economy', *Sociology*, 23, 4.

Davis, F. (1992) *Fashion, Culture and Identity*, Chicago: University of Chicago Press.

Dittmar, H. (1992) *The Social Psychology of Material Possessions: To Have Is to Be*, Hemel Hempstead: Harvester Wheatsheaf.

Featherstone, M. (1991) *Consumer Culture and Postmodernism*, London: Sage.

Gardner, C. and Sheppard, J. (1989) *Consuming Passion: The Rise of Retail Culture*, London: Unwin Hyman.

Flowers, S. (1993) 'Information overload', *The Guardian*, 10 Nov.

Hammond, J.L. (1986) 'Yuppies', *Public Opinion Quarterly*, 50.

Langman, L. (1992) 'Neon cages: shopping for subjectivity', in Shields, R. (ed.) *Lifestyle Shopping: The Subject of Consumption*, London: Routledge.

Lurie, A. (1981) *The Language of Clothes*, New York: Random House.

McCracken, Grant (1985) 'Dress colour at the court of Elizabeth I: an essay in historical anthropology', *Canadian Review of Sociology and Anthropology*, 22, 4.

McCracken, Grant (1988) *Culture and Consumption: New Approaches to the Symbolic Character of Consumer Goods and Activities*, Bloomington, IN: Indiana University Press.

Tharpar, N. (1994) 'Advertisers usher in classless society', *Independent on Sunday*, 6 March.

Edited extract from Campbell, C. (1995) 'The sociology of consumption', in Miller, D. (ed.) *Acknowledging Consumption: A Review of New Studies*, London: Routledge, 96–126. Professor Colin Campbell of the University of York, UK, has published widely on consumption and consumerism. His books include *Culture, Identity and Consumption* (with Livia Barbossa), *The Shopping Experience* (with Pasi Falk), *The Myth of Social Action* and *The Romantic Ethic and the Spirit of Modern Consumerism*.

Chapter 19

Inalienable wealth

Annette B. Weiner

I N *ESSAI SUR LE DON*, Marcel Mauss noted that things such as Samoan fine mats, Northwest Coast coppers, Maori cloaks, and nephrite weapons remained attached to their original owners even when they circulated among other people. Mauss referred to these particular objects as '*immeuble*' (in the English translation of *Essai*, 'indestructible'), in the sense that they were inalienable [that is, non-transferable] wealth that could not be detached from their origins. He illustrated that the cultural meanings of such wealth made these objects different from those that lacked the value of inalienability. What gives Mauss's concept of inalienable wealth its profundity is that it forces us to consider the way value is created in objects that should remain out of circulation.

Weiner, in her book *Inalienable Possessions: The Paradox of Keeping-While-Giving*, helps clarify what is meant here. It is not a matter of giving gifts and those receiving them acquiring indebtedness, as in the case of gifts, but rather it is about objects which are in effect loaned to be later returned: 'At issue is not how one gift elicits a return, but rather which possessions the members of a group are able to keep through generations, even if they must loan them for a time to others . . . Often these possessions are on loan to people born into other matrilineages, a prominent way of temporarily making kin of non-kin. Later, these inalienable possessions must be reclaimed, often by people in the next generations who had nothing to do with the original giving . . . So although the circulation of inalienable possessions permits the reproduction of an expanded network of kin through time, such acts always carry the potential for loss and the chance of betrayal' (Weiner 1992: 26). If the object is destroyed then the giver/loaner will aim to replace it.

Much like the Elgin Marbles or the horses of San Marcos, whatever happens to these objects, they are perceived to belong in an inherent way to their original owners. Inalienable possessions are imbued with affective qualities that are expressions of the value an object has when it is kept by its owners and inherited within the same family or descent group. Age adds value, as does the ability to keep the object against all the exigencies that might force a person or a group to release it to others. The primary value of inalienability, however, is expressed through the power these objects have to define who one is in an historical sense. The object acts as a vehicle for bringing past time into the present, so that the histories of ancestors, titles, or mythological events become an intimate part of a person's present identity. To lose this claim to the past is to lose part of who one is in the present. In its inalienability, the object must be seen as more than an economic resource and more than an affirmation of social relations.

Inalienable wealth takes on important priorities in societies where ranking occurs. Persons and groups need to demonstrate continually who they are in relation to others, and their identities must be attached to those ancestral connections that figure significantly in their statuses, ranks, or titles. To be able to keep certain objects that document these connections attests to one's power to hold oneself or one's group intact. For to give up these objects is to lose one's claim to the past as a working part of one's identity in the present.

In this essay, I explore in some detail Mauss's classification of things 'immeuble' and, of necessity, I enter the long-standing debates on what Mauss and the Maori meant by the *hau*, the spirit thought by the Maori to reside in persons and things. Lévi-Strauss (1950: xxxvii) insisted that Mauss's phenomenological approach kept him preoccupied with ethnographic data and prevented him from recognizing the structural features of reciprocity. For Lévi-Strauss, the *hau* was merely the Maori point of view and understanding the 'native' meaning could not expose the structural features of exchange. Yet, when the ethnographic record is explored in depth, the data reveal the Maori *hau* as the example par excellence substantiating the dynamics entailed in keeping while giving. I elaborate these points by using historical data from the New Zealand Maori to document the meaning and use of Maori valuables that in Mauss's terms are 'immeuble'. In my analysis the object, rather than the act of reciprocity, plays the dominant role. My concern is to show how a narrow understanding of the nature of things has led to rigid preconceptions in anthropology about the nature of exchange.

In the closing paragraph of *The Elementary Structures of Kinship*, Lévi-Strauss (1969: 497) described what he considered the universal dream expressed in an Andaman Island myth of 'a world in which one might *keep to oneself*' and escape from the 'law of exchange'. The Andaman view, however, represents a reality that many societies achieve to some degree. Keeping things instead of giving them away is essential if one is to retain some measure of one's social identity in the face of potential loss and the constant need to give away what is most valued. For example, in many societies in Papua New Guinea where the degree of individual and group political power remains diffuse, stones and/or the bones of ancestors are believed to 'anchor' a clan or a lineage to a particular locality, physically securing its identity and ancestral rights (see especially, Young 1983; Weiner 1982a). In those societies in Oceania where the notion of sacredness gives rise to social and political separateness between some individuals, objects other than stones and bones, perceived to have attachments to lineage or chiefly identities, may move in exchange among people. What we find in these cases is a range of solutions to the inherent problem of how one can keep while giving.

For example, in the Trobriand Islands, certain objects, lineage names, shell body decorations, and rights to land may be exchanged among individuals for years or even generations. Yet these things never lose their identity and attachment to the lineage that originally owned them. At some future time, these things should be returned to the original owners or their descendants. A lineage, or actually the person who controls lineage activities, gives up part of its resources, creating through the giving the sociability inherent in exchange, while simultaneously assuring the *replacement* for lineage members of those resources once given. As I describe more fully elsewhere (see Weiner 1980), in the Trobriands the processes of replacement are directly tied to the life cycle of individuals, for most things are reclaimed by the original giver or his descendants when the receiver dies. From this perspective, replacement is central to attaining some measure of keeping-while-giving.

Other societies, however, keep some things out of circulation on a more permanent basis and these things take on heightened qualities of sacredness. In societies with divine rulers, the ruler and her or his things must be separated from ordinary people. Although divine rulers give things to their subjects, they also keep some things out of circulation. Crown jewels and other objects of divine association are perceived to be as sacred as the office itself, and equally inalienable. In the great kingdoms of ancient Egypt, the ultimate in keeping to oneself was achieved by royal marriages between brothers and sisters. (…)

Therefore, we find two classes of inalienable possessions: those that should never circulate and those that under certain circumstances may be given to others either on loan, as copies, or in return for another object of the same kind. In the latter case, the affective qualities constituting the giver's social and political identity remain embedded in the objects so that when given to others the objects create an emotional lien upon the receivers.

In any situation, however, loss of an object, through warfare or theft, diminishes one's ancestral identity as a social or political force in the present, although even a tiny piece of the object may be enough to perpetuate one's identity with the past. All effort is made to retain some part of possessions that mark out who a person is in relation to the past. (…)

In all these cases, from Trobrianders to Egyptian rulers to Australian aborigines, things kept to oneself carry the affective qualities of sacredness that constitute the social self in relation to a past and future that, out of all the myriad possibilities, create a totality of ancestral identities. The immaterial characteristics that inalienable objects absorb, such as one's mythical or sacred origin, one's antecedents through past generations, and one's hierarchical position vis à vis others, give to these objects a force that carries beyond the social or political exigencies of the moment. An individual becomes more than she or he is because the self is enlarged and enhanced by the power of the past. In linking persons with things, the things are made into more than their own materiality, for the things themselves stand as the means through which individual mortality is transcended, ensuring some measure of the person's or group's immortality. Whether such objects remain hidden away as sacred possessions, or circulate among other people or whether the objects actually return to their original owners in one generation, in six generations, or never, the fact that they remain attached, that they belong to 'the capital stock of substance belonging to a family' (Granet 1975: 89) makes keeping them the primary element in the creation of value.

Mauss's legacy

In *Essai sur le Don*, Mauss described objects as embedded with 'a spiritual matter, comprising men and things' that created the obligation to give, to receive and to repay:

> one gives away what is in reality a part of one's nature and substance, while to receive something is to receive a part of someone's spiritual essence . . . The thing given is not inert. It is alive and often personified, and strives to bring to its original clan and homeland some equivalent to take its place. (Mauss 1954: 10)

Mauss found the ethnographic key to this view in a brief Maori text which described the concept of the *hau*, thought by the Maori to be the vital essence of life found in human beings, in land, and in things. Because the *hau* is connected through people to land and things, things take on the power of personification. Mauss's critics found this view of the 'gift' mystical and inappropriate for a rational understanding of exchange. Yet Mauss's formulation was based on comparative ethnographic reports. His first example was from Samoa where he noted that two kinds of objects were used in exchange. Fine mats (*'ie tōga*) presented by a woman's kin to her husband's kin at marriage are also exchanged at births and deaths. Another kind of wealth ('oloa), consisting of expendables such as food and traditionally produced and Western manufactured goods are given by the man's relatives to his wife's relatives at marriage. Mauss, in noting these sets of exchanges, labelled fine mats and 'oloa, respectively, 'feminine' and 'masculine' property. Mauss argued that fine mats, given in marriage by the woman's side, were 'more closely bound up with the land, the clan, the family and the person' than the other property called 'oloa (Mauss 1923–24: 157).

Mauss (1923–24: 156) called fine mats *'immeuble'*, a word used in French medieval legal codes to refer to landed estate, fixed, real property. In contrast, 'oloa was called *'meuble'*, personal property, chattel, things that could be confiscated. What Mauss emphasized in making this discrimination was that fine mats were more valued and were held in higher esteem than things called 'oloa and that the former things were associated with women and the regeneration of some fundamental aspect of kinship identity.

Although in the first pages of *Essai sur le Don*, Mauss called attention to significant differences between inalienable and alienable wealth, his insights have not been recognized by others who continue to analyze exchanges of fine mats and 'oloa as balanced reciprocity (see for example, Shore 1982: 203–5). Yet fine mats differ considerably from 'oloa in substance and meaning. Some of the most highly valued fine mats are from 100 to 200 years old. Fine mats take on a history in their circulation and specially prized fine mats possess specific titles and secret stories of origin which belong to the histories of certain high titles. Even with the contemporary cash economy in both American and Western Samoa, fine mats still are presented in exchanges associated with births, marriages, deaths, and the taking of chiefly titles. (...)

The New Zealand Maori case reexamined

Following the Samoan example of fine mats ('*ie tōga*), Mauss briefly surveyed other parts of Polynesia. The most important parallel was with the Maori *taonga* (valuable).

> In the Maori, Tahitian, Tongan and Mangarevan languages it [*taonga*] *denotes everything which may be rightly considered property*, which makes a man rich, powerful or influential, and which can be exchanged or used as compensation: that is to say, such objects of value as emblems, charms, mats and sacred idols . . . *The taonga are, at any rate with the Maori, closely attached to the individual, the clan and the land; they are the vehicle of their mana — magical, religious and spiritual power.* (Mauss 1954: 7–8; emphasis mine)

Cognates of *taonga* and '*ie tōga* occur in many Polynesian languages. The reference is to valued property, including barkcloth and mats. For example, in Tahitian, *taoa* means property or goods and in ancient Tahiti, barkcloth was among the most valued wealth objects. In Tonga, *tooga* refers to fine mats and in Mangareva, *toga* is the word for a cloak made from the paper mulberry tree. Yet such 'cloth' wealth seldom is given prominence by anthropologists as a valued resource.

In my earlier research on Trobriand exchange (Weiner 1976) I examined the economic importance of bundles of dried banana leaves, an object of exchange ignored by Malinowski and other early writers. More recently (Weiner 1982b), I illustrated that these bundles of banana leaves are not isolated, exotic objects. From a comparative perspective, they are elementary forms of 'cloth' wealth related to barkcloth, fine mats, and cloaks found throughout Polynesia. In these latter cases, not only are forms of cloth of economic significance, but such wealth has sacred value as it becomes the documentation for the histories of mythical and ancestral connections. In turning to the Maori material, these similarities become extremely important because their woven cloaks, often called mats in the early literature, are one of the two primary traditional wealth objects. The other class of *taonga* includes nephrite weapons and ornaments.

Among Robert Hertz's papers, Mauss found a reference to a Maori text which, he said, illuminated the relationship between Samoan fine mats and the Maori *taonga* and gave 'the key to the whole problem' (Mauss 1954: 8). The text was translated by Elsdon Best (1909: 439) from his noted Maori informant, Tamati Ranapiri. Based on the Maori text, Mauss developed his argument that the *hau*, the spirit of the thing given, was the force embedded in an object that demanded a return.

In the Maori text, Ranapiri described a series of exchanges in which the return for a valuable that had passed from A to B to C would go from C through B and back to A. With some changes in Best's text, Mauss quoted the following brief passage in which Ranapiri explained the meaning of the *hau*:

> I shall tell you about *hau*. *Hau* is not the wind. Not at all. Suppose you
> have some particular object, *taonga*, and you give it to me; you give it
> to me without a price. We do not bargain over it. Now I give this thing
> to a third person who after a time decides to give me something in repay-
> ment for it (*utu*), and he makes me a present of something (*taonga*).
> Now this *taonga* I received from him is the spirit (*hau*) of the *taonga* I
> received from you and which I passed on to him. The *taonga* which I
> receive on account of the *taonga* that came from you, I must return to
> you. It would not be right on my part to keep these *taonga* whether
> they were desirable or not. I must give them to you since they are the
> *hau* of the *taonga* which you gave me. If I were to keep this second *taonga*
> for myself I might become ill or even die. Such is *hau*, the *hau* of per-
> sonal property, the *hau* of the *taonga*, the *hau* of the forest. Enough on
> that subject. (Mauss 1954: 89)

(...) When a *taonga* is given to someone, either the original or a replacement must
return whether it is given to the second, the third, or the tenth person. The *taonga*
carries the 'semblance' (*aahua*) of the person in the form of the *hau*. The *taonga*
given should return, but the *hau* can be detached from the object so that another
taonga may carry the original 'semblance'. In this way, a replacement for the *taonga*
is created through the returning *hau*.

Mauss (1954: 10) was correct: 'the thing given is not inert. It is alive and often
personified'. For *taonga* are 'to some extent parts of persons' (Mauss 1954: 11) in
the sense that the *taonga* is the material document of its owner's ancestral past and
is itself the carrier of the *hau*. The stone and cloth valuables believed to contain
the same life force, the *hau*, as do humans, are not only the agents of individuals,
but through their collective histories the valuables become the proof of a group's
immortality. To lose a *taonga* forever is a material admission of one's own mortality and a sign of the weakening of a tribe's identity and power.

Keeping-while-giving

Anne Salmond (1984: 120), in describing the way nephrite *taonga* bind tribal groups
together wrote, 'The alchemy of *taonga* was to bring about a fusion of men [and
women] and ancestors and a collapse of distance in space-time'. As John White
recounted in 1888:

> in the old custom it was proper for such men [chiefs] to exchange such
> weapons, because they represented the descent lines which held them
> in keeping. A prized greenstone weapon was kept for a time by the descend-
> ants in one line of descent, and then they carried it and presented it to
> those in another line of descent from the tribal ancestor who first made
> it. (quoted and translated by Salmond 1984: 119)

From these examples, we can see that Ranapiri's text was not enigmatic, nor was
Mauss's interpretation of the *hau* mystical. The opposition in anthropological

interpretation between a spiritual explanation and a material explanation has been falsely constructed. The *hau* attached to objects embodies the relation of the person to a sacred world of spiritual force. The ethnography shows us that the *hau* must be given following birth and is lost at death, and that it must be replaced continually in people and things, thereby making people and things more than they are. As the agent of replacement, the *hau* is a force against loss, securing a group's individual strengths and identities against the demands of others.

The *taonga* also attends to the problem of loss and the expansion of self, but from an historical perspective. By bringing one's ancestral and mythical histories into the present, the *taonga* endows present actions with greater force. If Mauss's (1979) essay on the role and place of the person is read in conjunction with *Essai sur le Don*, the relationship between persons and things inalienable becomes more explicit. For example, in his discussion of Zuni rituals and ancestral names, Mauss (1979: 68–9) called attention to the importance of understanding that the person had to be seen in relation to his or her past. 'What is at stake . . . is more than the privilege and authority of the chief of the clan; it is the very existence both of the latter and of the ancestors'. The clan is constituted by persons, who play particular roles in social life, but the purpose of these roles is 'to symbolize, each in its own portion, the pre-figured totality of the clan' (Mauss 1979: 65).

An individual's role in social life is fragmentary unless attached to something of permanence. The history of the past, equally fragmentary, is concentrated in an object that, in its material substance, defies destruction. Thus, keeping an object defined as inalienable adds to the value of one's past, making the past a powerful resource for the present and the future. The dynamics surrounding keeping-while-giving are attempts to give the fragmentary aspect of social life a wholeness that ultimately achieves the semblance of immortality, thereby adding new force to each generation.

The dilemma of the situation is apparent, loss, decay, death, and defeat shatter the semblance of wholeness and the vision of immortality. The *hau* can be lost; the *taonga* can be taken away. Therefore, the value created through keeping must be seen in relation to the constant threats and needs of giving. Replacement allows the keeping of things while giving things to others. For replacement allows a person to retain some part of inalienable possessions or some degree of inalienability. The need to exchange with others is inherently dangerous because a person not only gives away material things, but a measure of her *or* his own identity.

Keeping, giving, and replacement are the three fundamental processes through which persons play out the dynamics of social exchange. Keeping, however, is primary as the means for achieving wealth that not only expresses a person's or a group's identity, but concentrates that identity into a symbol of immortality. Thus, true inalienability is extremely difficult to attain. Taking account of inalienable wealth in a range of societies, we find various solutions to the problem of keeping-while-giving. For future research, differentiating how these solutions accommodate the degree of ranking and the nature of kinship and gender relations in these societies should give us important comparative insights. What seems clearly established, however, is that the creation and possession of wealth that has the qualities of inalienability is a major step in sustaining marked, hierarchical relations between individuals and groups. As this wealth stands for the totality of a person's social history in relation to her or his clan or lineage, it seems no accident that the objects are made from cloth and the material amplifications of human bones. Susanne Langer (1953: 73) wrote that in art it is necessary to have '*visual substitutes* for the things that are normally known by touch, movement or inference'. With inalienable wealth, we also find '*visual substitutes*' for history, ancestors, and the immortality of human life.

References

Best, E. (1909) 'Maori forest lore', *Trans. New Zealand Institute*, 42: 433–81.

Granet, M. (1975 [1922]) *The Religion of the Chinese People*, New York: Harper & Row.

Langer, S.K. (1953) *Feeling and Form: A Theory of Art*, New York: Charles Scribner's Sons.

Lévi-Strauss, C. (1950) 'Introduction à l'œuvre de Marcel Mauss', in Mauss, M. *Sociologie et Anthropologie*, Paris: Presses Universitaires de France, ix–liii.

Lévi-Strauss, C. (1969) *The Elementary Structures of Kinship*, Boston: Beacon Press.

Mauss, M. (1923–24) *Essai sur le Don: Forme et Raison de l'Échange dans les Sociétés Archaïques*, Année Sociologique, Nouvelle Série 1.

Mauss, M. (1954) *The Gift*, Glencoe, IL: Free Press.

Mauss, M. (1979) *Sociology and Psychology: Essays by Marcel Mauss*, London: Routledge & Kegan Paul.

Salmond, A. (1984) 'Nga nuarahi o te ao maori: pathways in the maori world', in Mead, S.M. (ed.) *Te Maori: Maori Art from New Zealand Collections*, New York: Harry N. Abrams Inc.

Shore, B. (1982) *Sala'ilua: A Samoan Mystery*, New York: Columbia University Press.

Weiner, A.B. (1976) *Women of Value, Men of Renown: New Perspectives in Trobriand Exchange*, Austin, TX: University of Texas Press.

Weiner, A.B. (1980) 'Reproduction: a replacement for reciprocity', *American Ethnologist*, 7(1): 71–85.

Weiner, A.B. (1982a) 'Sexuality among the anthropologists, reproduction among the informants', *Social Analysis*, 12: 52–65.

Weiner, A.B. (1982b) 'Plus précieux que l'or: relations et échanges entre hommes et femmes dans les sociétés d'Océanie', *Annales*, 37(2): 222–45.

Weiner, A.B. (1992) *Inalienable Possessions: The Paradox of Keeping-While-Giving*, Berkeley, CA: University of California Press.

Young, M. (1983) *Magicians of Manumanua: Living Myth in Kalauna*, Berkeley, CA: University of California Press.

Edited extract from Weiner, A.B. (1985) 'Inalienable wealth', *American Ethnologist*, 12: 210–27. Annette Weiner (1933–97), a distinguished cultural anthropologist and former Professor at New York University, published a number of important works including *Women of Value, Men of Renown: New Perspectives in Trobriand Exchange*, *The Trobrianders of Papua New Guinea*, and *Cloth and Human Experience* (with Jane Schneider) and *Inalienable Possessions: The Paradox of Keeping-While-Giving*.

Chapter 20

Consuming fossils and museums in early nineteenth-century England

Simon J. Knell

The establishment of [philosophical societies] in numerous . . . towns, within the last few years, forms undoubtedly one of the most distinguishing characteristics of the spirit of the age in which we live.

(Hull Literary and Philosophical Society, 1825, *Annual Report* 1/2)

IN THE 1820S, philosophical societies were established in towns and cities across England, and formed the basis for that rich provincial museum infrastructure that remains a distinctive feature of the country today. In the north, in Yorkshire – the largest county – the movement found its greatest realisation. In a simultaneous explosion of interest – Leeds (1818), Bradford (1822), Hull (1822), Sheffield (1822), York (1822), Whitby (1822), Wakefield (1826) and Scarborough (1827) – each town consolidated its emergent civic identity in an act of museum making which as a first step sought to preserve local collections from the avaricious attentions of its neighbours.

In these societies and museums, geology became the central recreation. It was then rising to the heights of social and intellectual fashion as it was affordable, universally available, politically and religiously neutral (in a time of revolutionary concerns), easily preserved and built from the extraordinary remains of animals of mythological proportions. The Yorkshire public was suddenly being exposed to a much deeper past which linked a history of Norman churches and legendary kings, to a time when hyenas and elephants roamed the local hills, and back still further to a time of tropical ferns and giant monsters. Geology could also claim practical value from the discoveries of engineer and mineral surveyor, William Smith, who, in the late eighteenth century, found that rocks had a natural order and that each contained its own peculiar fossils. However, the task of realising the full potential of Smith's discovery still remained unfinished when Smith arrived in Yorkshire at that moment when the philosophical societies were being born. Possessing unique knowledge, Smith, with his eloquent ward and nephew John Phillips, gave evangelising lectures to the county's societies, and utterly transformed them. The rich fossil wealth of the region, so long admired but hardly exploited, was in that moment altered. It now had immense cultural value – fossils were now objects of new knowledge, not simply records of the Biblical Flood or, mythology, or folklore. Most famed of all was the small coastal town of Whitby known for its snakestone ammonites, and its extinct fossil reptiles: the dolphin-like ichthyosaurs, the oldest known crocodiles and the most extraordinary of all animals, living or dead, the long-necked plesiosaurs. However, most of these still lay in the cliffs; there were no public displays.

So while antiquities and art remained locked up in the estates of the rich await-ing the emergence of art history, archaeology, and the proven possibilities of the public museum, and natural history found itself dealing with fugitive materials, geology had its heyday and became that critical intellectual key, amongst many other keys (economic growth, urban renewal, individualism, social inequality, etc.) that permitted the English museum a birth. The consumption of fossils, then, lay at the heart of these societies, their social relations played out utilising the petrified remains of an alien world.

The collections formed in these museums were to be an encapsulation of know-ledge and not the idle curiosities of avarice so frequently observed in the posses-sion of contemporary private collectors. While the cabinet had long been established as an educational tool and cultural symbol, many private collections showed little sign of any intellectual process. So often the obsession was with collecting, not with knowledge: 'The best way, perhaps, to become thoroughly familiar with an object is to possess it, and the desire to possess is likely to develop into a collecting mania' (Sheppard 1916: 1). 'It is the chase, not the quarry, that counts; the pursuit of the unattainable, the discovery of the unexpected, with all its vicissitudes of success and failure' (Sir Robert Witt quoted by Hermann 1972: 22). This was so even in many of the most noted collections of the time.

For others, collecting was more selective. Indeed selectivity was the key to its effectiveness. Here the aesthetics of the collection, suffused with intimations of science or knowledge, bestowed a cultured image upon its possessor. And because geology, amongst all the sciences, had a strong link to an obscure and exotic mater-ial culture, it too could signify taste, that vital determinant of the cultured. Such a collection was in the possession of James Johnson of Hotwells, Bristol. Re-nowned during his lifetime, it was the source of specimens for Bristol philosophical society member William Conybeare's pioneering work on marine reptiles, and James Sowerby's *Mineral Conchology*, and was later to be used in Oxford professor, William Buckland's Bridgewater Treatise. Being a frequent buyer of the celebrated Lyme Regis collector Mary Anning's specimens, Johnson had acquired a considerable collection of marine reptiles before they became fashionable and had sent informa-tion on them to Georges Cuvier in Paris, then the world's most distinguished anatomist. His was amongst the collections that another Bristol savant, George Cumberland, in 1826, recommended visitors to the region to see, on the under-standing that the 'collection of fossils is very extensive, though not at all arranged, and deficient in many things'.

When in 1829, John Phillips, then curator at the York society and his Bristol counterpart, Johann Miller, saw it, Phillips noted that this collection of fine saur-ians (reptiles), crinoids (sea lilies) and other fossils was only 'a show collection and not an illustrative solution'. Phillips had been brought up to expect collections to be illustrative of knowledge – three-dimensional explanations or demonstrations. His uncle's collection in London was just this: 'Each separate stratum recognised by Smith had one or more shelves sloping to represent the dip as he knew them in the typical ground of the Dunkerton Valley, near Bath, where he first studied them' (Anon. 1874: 510). Phillips derived his use of collections as research and teaching devices directly from Smith who had used his own collection to explain the significance of his ideas. The unassuming Smith was the archetypal museum geologist who effectively invented the geological museum as a tool for contemporary geological research. Johnson's collection was a resource to be exploited. In the hands of others it made science, but exhibited at his home it made entirely different statements about its possessor, his intellect and sophistication.

There were certainly exceptions. Collections that were well organised and named as best as was possible. Many collectors had no choice but to invent their own names as no alternative terminology was available. Indeed, the substance of these collections was at a point of invention and language could only follow; collections were used in a formative sense, not as mere reference to proven knowledge. Progressively expectations of collections increased but collectors were often handicapped by the poor state of development of the science locally. Their collections were only to be transformed with the arrival of a local treatise which explained local stratigraphy and named local fossils.

The Yorkshire Philosophical Society (YPS) in York made frequent reference to the value of collections and museums, distancing itself from the private collector who coloured contemporary opinion: 'the naturalist by whom they are formed, is sometimes suspected of claiming the dignity of a science, for pursuits little higher than the amusements of children. If the object of a collector be no more than to accumulate and to display, he is indeed very idly employed' (YPS (1828) *Annual Report for 1827*). The society was to 'acquire' and 'diffuse a more perfect knowledge of the works of creation': a 'rational', and therefore fashionable, objective which placed the museum and collection at the centre of its activities. In the hands of these philosophers the collection was to become a medium for the acquisition and diffusion of knowledge; a three-dimensional encyclopaedia of hard evidence from which philosophers (the term 'scientist' was not in popular use at this time) could derive the principles and language for scientific discourse. And combined into formidable scientific institutions the philosophers collected on an entirely new scale: 'the advantages of Institutions like this, in preserving for the benefit of science those large fossil specimens, which being too bulky for cabinets or private collections, would be in danger of being altogether lost or destroyed' (Whitby Literary and Philosophical Society (1834) *Annual Report*, 12). (Taylor and Torrens (1987: 145), for example, note fossil dealer Mary Anning's complaint that an extraordinary ichthyosaur in a three metre long case was too large for a private collection; the wonder of the fossil itself was secondary when faced with commercial reality.) But how were these societies to acquire this material? Without it they could not function, and while they initially concentrated on gathering in existing private collections, the number of these available was extremely limited.

The York society, so well placed for travel to the four corners of the county, was, unfortunately, some distance from the major natural repositories of fossils. It had soon realised that it would need to rely upon a network – 'the combined obser-vation of many individuals' (YPS Minutes of General Meetings, 6 January 1823). However, the philosophical world had considerable distrust of the inferences and potential naivety of such observations. Few provincial observers were sufficiently well versed in geology to produce information of any reliability. Anyone, though, could collect fossils and send them to a central museum for scientific interpreta-tion. Such specimens became the principal means of data collection – literally hard facts! From the outset the York philosophers sought to instil rational and informat-ive investigation. Specimens sent to the museum were to be accompanied by informa-tion on the nature of the stratum and its position with respect to other strata. However, novices who found such things difficult were told to pay particular atten-tion to points of junction between different clearly defined strata. These precise and yet simple collecting instructions were published in the local newspapers. In York, the collections that resulted were fed into the inductive machine to be regurgitated as interpretations of local geological phenomena. In Scarborough and Whitby the discourse on such subjects had its own particular philosophical bias.

If the York society was to achieve its hoped-for understanding of the county's geology, it needed collectors on the spot as new material became available and before it could be acquired by rivals or sold on. For the coastal societies of Whitby and Scarborough this was not a problem. Their ambitions were to be met from their own small hinterland, over which they might attempt to hold dominion. The key to the success of each philosophical society's collecting strategy, then, lay first and foremost in the personnel it could attract into its membership. This allegiance was invariably built upon local attachment to a town, city or county. Each society devel-oped its own mechanisms for encouraging this sense of attachment and the highly ambitious society in York provides a useful model through which to investigate these mechanisms. Its collections were, after all, to be built on that same spirit of mutual co-operation that was also to fund its building; on the face of it, co-operation built on rank, honour and patronage. In this the York society was as typical as any other.

Far from being derived from a single social stratum – the new and the dis-senting middle classes – the York society was a microcosm of the county's middle and upper class elite. This had been possible not only through the city's elevated position as the 'capital' of the county but also through a strong and well-connected leadership, here in the form of its president, William Vernon, a son of the arch-bishop of York. The most successful societies were invariably dominated by the ambitions of one man. A stamp of credibility was added by the association of a group of noblemen who acted largely as non-participatory patrons. Depending on its size, a society might also acquire a complement of scientific *literati*. A further group of individuals established themselves as parish representatives or outpost observers both inside and outside the main collecting region. Existing collectors were also brought into the fold, or patronised, depending on gender and social sta-tus. These 'useful' people – the collectors and literati – were often acquired through the gift of honorary memberships, which both honoured and made the honoured indebted. The essential social elite – essential at least in the case of the York society – participated out of duty and patronage, though one can also see a reflexive rela-tionship between the gift of participation and the self-ennoblement embodied in that act. Professional men, merchants and the more affluent sectors of the local middle classes made up the bulk of the membership and exploited their own personal networks for society ends. Finally, there were the curators, servants of the society, whose primary duty was to give the museum its intellectual edge.

Social interactions between these groups reflected society as a whole; internally honour and patronage in one form or another, rather than sterling, became the currency with which to win or buy favours, and through which the collections would grow. In this role they were universally recognised, particularly as science remained almost entirely a private enterprise: 'In a poor country this is at least a cheap way of advancing science' (David Brewster (1830) quoted by Morrell and Thackray 1984: 24). The Yorkshire Philosophical Society, then, was built from the top down. A power base of the social and scientific elite gave the society the status necessary to attract lowlier members. In this it was probably not untypical of societies forming across Britain though the social, cultural and political make-up of towns and cities had become increasingly diverse with the progress of industry and commerce. Such stratification was not always as apparent as it was in York, nor were all societies so drawn by the determination to collect. But even in those towns, such as Leeds, where the society outwardly proclaimed an avoidance of servile patronage, the same structural elements were in place. Only here patronage was internalised within the class. The city had long been dominated by wealthy mercantile interests and inevitably it was these, rather than the county's landed establishment, which formed a leading element in the society's governance (Morris 1990: 233, 238).

On touring Yorkshire in the 1820s, Richard Phillips reflected that three quarters of the population formed the working classes and were largely shunned by all others. A further ten per cent were an 'aristocracy of mere craft and position' which had arisen in the current generation and aspired to join the professional group. Fifteen per cent were professional men – 'poor and proud, or rich and lordly'. These formed the core of the new societies. The professionals aspired to the status of the largely insular local aristocracy, who made up a further one per cent of the populace and whom they 'aped' (Richard Phillips, in White 1988: 86).

Social elevation

The York society's links into the county establishment also gave it a lobbying force within parliament and government; provincial scientific interests were, potentially, to influence national support for science. By association, the philosophers' pursuits were given a cultured and sophisticated complexion. In a country indoctrinated with the importance and validity of rank such associations would attract social climbers into the membership. By this means the society gained a most useful marketing tool. Like other assemblies, the Yorkshire Philosophical Society became an entry point for those nouveaux riches of trade, manufacture and the professions, who wished to mix with the county establishment. The rise of 'new men' had long been 'a distinctive feature of English History', upon which the gentry and the social stability of the past were founded – as Daniel Defoe noted in an earlier century, 'trade in England makes gentlemen' (Perkin 1969: 57). The philosophical society gave access to the elite, a means of proclaiming one's status and a chance to satisfy 'an appetite for gentlemanly pursuit' rather than simply and more obviously 'an appetite for natural knowledge' (Thackray 1974: 678–80; Shapin 1991: 313; Cannon 1978: 218; Orange 1971: 321). In this age of accumulating wealth, the door to the gentry was open; 'a man could call himself what he thought he could carry off' (English 1990: 4); 'In the middle classes we note an almost universal unfixedness of position. Every man is rising or falling or hoping that he shall rise, or fearing that he shall sink' (W.J. Fox (1835) quoted in Gash 1979: 24; Altick 1973: 18). Although many made their fortunes, the period was a difficult one economically. The merchant classes in Bristol and Leeds, for example, frequently opted out of their business ventures when profits waned, sometimes to live the life of the gentleman (Wilson 1971: 111–35; Neve 1983: 183; Perkin 1969: 213ff). In adopting traditional values, those who rose inevitably changed to take on the airs of the class within which they wished to be subsumed; snobbery was an expectation of transition (Bulwer-Lytton 1830: I: 16).

On comparing late eighteenth-century models of the provincial learned society with earlier examples, Porter (1977: 133–5) noted that 'for the first time, it was the science itself which achieved sufficient cohesion, attraction and importance as to be its own social glue' and overcome differences in 'wealth, occupations, professions, in education, in religion'. He cites the Newcastle Literary and Philosophical Society and the Royal Geological Society of Cornwall as illustrating 'how a range of enthusiasts, highly disparate in terms of rank, class and profession, could be brought together . . . as a result of a shared concern with geology'. But rather than being moved to the background, certain of these key attributes were exploited for their exclusivity so as to create a honey pot to attract an audience of participants in the society's scientific and educational enterprise. In similar fashion the relatively lowly Whitby Literary and Philosophical Society sought the support of those locals of 'respectability and property' (Anon 1827); which by implication was conferred upon those who joined.

Within the urban elite political persuasion did not always dominate relations and cultural bridges were possible; a shared conservatism could act as a bond in a period of change, and seems to have done so in Leeds and Bristol. In the unstable world of local politics support for a philosophical society could have all kinds of advantages. Property qualifications for serving in local government excluded around 97 per cent of the population (Garrard 1983: 13 and Perkin 1969: 41). Nepotism and religious qualification restricted this still further. The local elite really was an elite. Whether the mercantile dynasties of Leeds or the county gentry of York, they had near absolute control over local institutions. Those of dissenting faiths made up a considerable proportion of the provincial middle classes but were excluded from the English universities, local government, the army and navy, and so on. By 1820 dissenters made up 30 per cent of the population (Gash 1979: 63); dissent was threatening to become more popular than the state religion. Often well-educated and wealthy, they were an important intellectual component in the local community – Perkin (1969: 72) suggests 50 per cent of principal inventors were dissenters; their position within society gave 'added piquancy . . . to material success and social emulation' (Orange 1973). However, they were not excluded from the philosophical societies, which embodied a much wider social, religious and political make-up. As such these societies became places where it was hoped local politics could be defused (Cooter 1984: 70), where bridges could be built between established wealth and new wealth, between the politics of stability and the politics of change, between the religion of the state and the religion of the people. This was to be achieved not by making these subjects central to the affairs of the society, as they were in so many other institutions, but rather by removing them, in an overt sense, from its discourse.

Political allegiances were important in the local community but not more so than perceptions of wealth (Garrard 1983: 23). Alliances both in politics and marriage were built across traditional class boundaries, making for complex readings of the local scene (Bulwer-Lytton 1830: I: 25). Society meetings became mechanisms for cross-fertilisation so that patronage could be appropriately placed amongst friends (Perkin 1969: 45). The societies formed a medium to adjust middle-class structures – as much to allow the nouveaux riches to enter the middle-class fold, as for the gentlemen of established families to bring them into this fold and thus retain control.

The social mechanism which these societies manipulated relied upon a 'uniformity of upper-class taste' (Wilson 1971: 213) dictated by the aristocracy but which filtered down to the lesser gentry and the middle classes. It was not simply a matter of taste but the very manner of wealth that the middle classes wished to imitate. Thus there was a desire to patronise. 'Charitable and other social endeavours' had political significance and as such had to be public events: 'For what was important was not merely that an individual should be a substantial businessman, or an active philanthropist, but that he should personally be seen to be such by a large, attentive and admiring audience' (Garrard 1983: 26). Even if the core of philosophical societies were not 'marginal men', as was the case in Leeds, they would none-the-less need a forum within which to prove the point. An embodiment of 'That eternal vying with each other; that spirit of show; that lust of imitation which characterise our countrymen and countrywomen' (Bulwer-Lytton 1830: I: 27). The landed gentry made up nearly 50 per cent of the York society's membership.

In the first months of its existence, then, the Yorkshire Philosophical Society had established a power base which would act as a magnet to men of science, collectors, and others interested in this new social phenomenon. Vernon Harcourt was later to build a similar infrastructure for the British Association for the Advancement of Science. On its first meeting, held in York in September 1831, Roderick Murchison remarked, in his presidential address to the Geological Society of London in February 1832, that its importance lay not least in 'bringing the working men of science into communication with individuals of rank and property'.

The Yorkshire Philosophical Society established a complex and structured membership in order to create a sustainable institution capable of meeting society objectives. Key amongst these objectives was the desire to construct a collection as a resource and cultural statement. From our retrospective view it might appear that building respectable collections was, for these institutions, just a matter of time – they were expected to exist into 'future ages'. Patience, however, was not a viable collecting strategy. It was soon apparent that a museum's reputation lay not in its collecting programme or intentions but in what it possessed. The main objective was to create a functioning scientific institution. To further science, and provide display, lecture and identification services, an institution needed a collection. Without this it could not operate, or indeed, attract the army of observers and collectors so essential to its plans. The philosophers needed an immediate solution to the collecting problem.

Viewing the natural world as a finite resource, they envisaged a process which was essentially one of transporting specimens from the field into the cabinet. With effort the fossil realm could simply be gathered up. While acquisition was to continue throughout the life of these institutions this was, in part, to satisfy the social motives and bonds bound up in the act of donation, and also a recognition of the impossibility of drawing boundaries to collecting. While many participants were collectors or knew collectors, the size, nature and socio-political make-up of these corporate bodies provided opportunities for collecting in new ways and on a new scale.

These institutions saw no limits to growth, and the immediacy of the collecting problem meant acquisition at the maximum possible rate. Their annual reports, in the early years, generally placed geological items at the head of the list of topics for review. And rather than review research successes, or the highlights of their lecture programme, they chose to chronicle donations received giving the most important additional emphasis in the main preamble. In its first two years the Yorkshire Philosophical Society gathered 4500 fossils, and although Phillips considered this a small collection, it was seen by the society's council as a great achievement.

The culture of the gift

When Vernon first came to consider how his institution could rapidly build the necessary fossil resource he called upon the expertise of his former Oxford University mentor and friend William Buckland. Undoubtedly the quickest way to secure a museum was simply to draw in existing private collections; all philosophical societies did this in their early years. Buckland had no doubts concerning the power of honorary membership in making this possible. As he told Vernon on 29 December 1822, 'There is a very fine collection at Scarborough belonging to Mr Hinderwell, an elderly gentleman, which would at once set you up if he could be induced to bequeath it to you, or transfer it immediately wh[ich] w[oul]d be much better', adding, 'by all means make him a Member'. At the next meeting they did just that.

Hinderwell, however, was unwilling to donate his collection. As a historian connected entirely with Scarborough he had no reason to give allegiance to its city neighbour. Hinderwell was not part of the city or county clan. However, the York society proceeded with an honorary membership anyway, hoping perhaps to win by attrition. In the meantime Vernon actively sought intelligence regarding other collections which their owners might wish to donate, perhaps with an additional bribe, or sell. In 1823, for example, he discovered from the artist John Bird in Whitby that a Mr W. Wetherall had left Whitby to reside in Ripon, to the north of York, and had taken his collection with him. Bird had never thought to attempt to acquire it, but enquired on behalf of Vernon and obtained for the York society the promise of a donation.

However, acquisition of ready-made collections was never likely to be the key to the collecting problem nor would it satisfy the focused research objectives of the York philosophers. Instead, all societies relied upon an entirely new (at least in local circles) collecting mechanism, that of 'selfless' donation. The York society would 'congratulate' itself on the 'zeal' of its supporters, and 'the spirit of research which it has awakened'. They found 'no reason to regret the rule which they have laid down to themselves, of relying, for the augmentation of the Geological part of the Museum, chiefly on the individual exertions of the Members of the society, and the liberality of those who are willing to contribute to its objects.' Of the 9183 geological specimens in the collections at the end of 1826, 89 per cent had been donated (YPS (1825/1827) *Annual Reports for 1824 and 1826*). Private collectors, who relied upon their own fieldwork or the fullness of their purses, could hardly compete with these collective enterprises.

In the fee structure, initially discussed by the York society's founders, a five guinea admission (joining) fee was to be used as the basis for a purchase fund. Objects bought with this money were to remain the property of those who paid the fee. Alternatively, new members might gain admission by donating objects to the value of five guineas. All specimens were to be ticketed with the name of the donor and returned to him if the society dissolved (YPS Minutes of General Meetings, 14 December 1822). These were obviously nervous first steps. The new societies were uncertain of the potential of donation but need not have concerned themselves; this fitted very well with the social mechanisms which underpinned their operation.

Take William Danby, for example. He was typical of the wealthy gentlemen who supported the York society, a 'liberal and disinterested patron of natural science', an author and cultivator of the arts who also invested heavily in paintings which he displayed at his Swinton Park home. Here he also created a mock Stonehenge. What motivated such men to participate and were they really so disinterested? When Danby donated the remains of a fossil elephant tusk from Harswell in the south of the county it was he who was recorded in the annual report, not the finder or his agent. His wealth, status and time for leisure enabled him to acquire specimens and most importantly give them in his own name. Although they were then possessed by the new institution they always retained an attachment to the giver and as such remained as much a statement about him as about anything else: 'the thing given is not inert. It is alive and often personified' (Mauss (1954) quoted by Weiner 1985: 223). He was not, in fact, entirely disinterested, and was no doubt aware of the benefits of attaching his name to something which in the hands of the society might achieve celebrity. At very least it enhanced his reputation as knowledgeable patron. And as has been noted elsewhere, it was important that such acts of patronage were visible; only then could their social and political potential be exploited. As an act of benefaction and patronage, a donation placed the institution in a position sub-servient to the giver. Donation was claimed as a right by the giver, and gifts were rarely refused. Refusal could establish a cancer in such a closely inter-linked and often politicised network. To the donor the gesture was often more important than the gift: the donor hoped to reap a social reward from the act; the institution in return gained another building block towards its scientific and cultural reputation. Such objects simultaneously performed plural functions: fact, cultural artefact, gift, prestige symbol and so on.

The exchange culture adopted by the nineteenth-century philosophical societies was much like that associated with 'primitive', 'archaic' or 'clan-based' cultures in Papua New Guinea and elsewhere. These patterns of exchange, explored by Marcel Mauss, have in recent years drawn a resurgence of interest. Mauss compared Western ownership of private property, where a person has alienable rights of ownership, with clan-based economies, where there is no private property, and consequently no alienable rights over things. The distinction is between the exchange of commodities where a price is paid and ownership is transferred, and the exchange of gifts where it is not. Thus gifts 'are never completely separated from the men who exchange them'; an 'indissoluble bond' existed between 'a thing' and its 'original owner' (Gregory 1982: 18). In accepting gifts, a society gained possession but its rights of ownership were reduced. Theoretically, donors could ask for the return of specimens. If material was no longer needed (through duplication or the arrival of better examples) it was sometimes possible to return it to the donor or dispose of it following consultation. Purchased objects were much more malleable.

While they received no payment as such, donors were given the return gift of notice whether in society reports, on museum labels, in the name of the collection or even the naming of the object. Such return gifts may have been the equal of the original donation, but in many cases they were not and so the society remained indebted to the individual. In the gift-giving culture of Papua New Guinea, status is achieved by having others indebted to you. To infer similar processes in the philosophical societies is to infer a 'clan-based' culture – a middle-class unity which cut across political and social divides. Here too the gift became a cultural mechanism, symbolic of and cementing, in one respect, a close bond. But in another respect it became a means of claiming social status. The gift, by being given to the society, was given to the group. That group, which may have been formalised as joint shareholders in the enterprise, then became indebted to the giver. Gregory discusses concentric circles of exchange around the core of the clan, as the circles increase away from the centre the bonds are weaker. Marx determined that, at the boundaries of communities, transactions take the form of commodity exchange where a price is paid (Gregory 1982: 12). This too is seen, for example, at the interface between society men and the artisan collectors.

Collectors were particularly keen to reap the rewards which might arise from the use of their material in scientific publication. Theirs were claims of scientific discovery. Even if they had not been present in the field at the point of collection, they had still been able to distinguish the worth of the specimens held in their cabinets. Often they were able to provide data which linked the cabinet specimen to its field context – small but vital information for those assembling the geological jigsaw.

The need to credit collectors is seen in the reprinting of early society reports. Understandably, the first report of each philosophical society was produced in small numbers and rapidly went out of print. But so that donors should see their gifts acknowledged, the York society republished the donation list of the first report in the second. They chose to do this rather than extol their mission statement which later members might also have missed. Donors expected to see their names emblazoned on labels and in the annual report. Here they were patronised with superlatives. In an era when language was uncontrolled in advertising, it should be no surprise to find it in museum reports. Donations were 'fine', 'important', 'beautiful', 'rare', 'valuable' and so on. These adjectives were a linguistic payment, flattering the donor and advertising the increasingly significant collections.

Fossils as commodities

In Whitby there was an awareness than acquisitions might involve purchase but the society knew it could sell on what it did not need. Its motivation continued to be promotional:

> The amazing number of 660 visitors entered since last anniversary, attests the pleasing fact, that the Whitby Museum has lost nothing of its interest in the eyes of strangers, who view with delight those fine specimens of Organic Remains, which so particularly distinguish this Institution from all others. Your Council would respectfully urge, the propriety of purchasing chiefly any new fossil specimens which may be found on the immediate coast and neighbourhood, as they consider those the most valuable and interesting parts of the collection. (Whitby Literary and Philosophical Society (1829) *Annual Report*, 7)

Whitby society men George Young and Richard Ripley's contacts with local collectors gave them access to all that was found; they could simply pick what they wanted. With shelves groaning under the weight of the collections, they still complained of incomplete local series and continued to draw up lists of desiderata (Whitby and Literary Philosophical Society (1839) *Annual Report*, 17).

Many members of these societies, including Vernon, often purchased their donations from dealers; they simply went shopping for presents. The new social need to give presents to these institutions bolstered the supplementary income derived from selling fossils among the impoverished labouring classes of the coastal towns. Each coastal locality had its gaggle of workers scouring the coast for its natural products which could be sold or used in some way. Fossils were simply added to the list. During the summer fieldwork season, philosophers regularly toured the coast picking up what they could. They perhaps experienced the excitement of the hunt, feeling that they were pursuing philosophical ends, but not all had the skill, patience or local knowledge to find fine specimens. The summer months were, and still are, not the time for the true fossil enthusiast, as the best material reveals itself in the cliff falls brought down by the winter's stormy seas and torrential rain storms. These specimens were gathered up by jet workers, and others, and retained for future sale to tourists or 'strangers' when they flocked to the coast during the summer, or sold on to middlemen and women who specialised in such materials.

Ripley knew that he could sell on what he did not want. The societies also found dealing a useful adjunct to their activities; they had no scruples about selling the poorer duplicates, and indeed all societies saw this as a legitimate way of raising income. In some cases the duplicate might be a poorer specimen yet which may have been at the heart of an original discovery. The practice of selling duplicates had long existed in private collecting circles, and there was no reason not to expect it in society museums. [These practices of selling and dealing are dealt with elsewhere in this book.]

Conclusion

In their early years the philosophical societies discovered for themselves both the means to collect and an understanding of its implications. In a material sense they were responsive to contemporary issues in geology, and their collections formed an encyclopaedic record of discovery. The need for a collection was such that the societies collected as rapidly as possible, exploiting as many avenues to specimens as could be found. The collection was essential to progress. It performed a social function, bonding members and shareholders. It was also a mechanism to acquire recognition and status. As gifts and commodities, fossils existed in two different social worlds, each giving them different cultural meanings. Societies tried to direct, if not control, collection growth, and in the process became effective dealers. By this means, a process of distillation took place within these collections – particularly those of the coastal societies – which resulted in a progressive improvement in the quality of material as less aesthetic or complete items were sold as duplicates. The criteria used in this process of distillation were essentially those of the cabinet rather than those of science. Value was placed on aesthetics and rarity. But ultimately these collections became too large for the available resources. From cultural symbols they metamorphosed into historical burdens which contributed to the decline of these societies.

Curators sought to maintain order and reason in the collections so as to maintain the status of the gifts received. Some were required to use their collecting and connoisseurship skills to generate income through dealing but their most critical role was in giving collections the aura of science. A few, and none more so than John Phillips, were central to a process of constructing knowledge from collections. This was a process which placed the collection and the field in close harmony but also, for Phillips and others, placed the collector and dealer between nature and its understanding. As a result the fieldcraft of geology became not simply the province of the hammer and notebook but also of the purse and the manipulation of collectors' personal agendas.

References

Altick, R.D. (1973) *Victorian People and Ideas*, New York: Norton.
Anon. (1827) 'Whitby Museum', *Whitby Panorama*, 1: 251–2.
Anon. (1874) 'John Phillips', *Nature*, 30 April: 510–15.
Bulwer-Lytton, E. (1830) *England and the English* (2 volumes, facsimile reprint 1970), Shannon: Irish University Press.
Cannon, S.F. (1978) *Science in Culture: The Early Victorian Period*, New York: Dawson and Science History Publications.
Cooter, R. (1984) *The Cultural Meaning of Popular Science: Phrenology and the Organisation of Consent in Nineteenth-Century Britain*, Cambridge: Cambridge University Press.

English, B. (1990) *The Great Landowners of East Yorkshire*, London: Harvester Wheatsheaf.

Garrard, J. (1983) *Leadership and Power in Victorian Industrial Towns 1830–80*, Manchester: Manchester University Press,.

Gash, N. (1979) *Aristocracy and People: Britain 1815–1865*, London: Arnold.

Gregory, C.A. (1982) *Gifts and Commodities*, London: Academic Press.

Hermann, F. (1972) *The English Collectors*, London: Chatto and Windus.

Morrell, J.B. and Thackray, A. (1984) *Gentlemen of Science: Early Correspondence of the British Association for the Advancement of Science*, Camden 4th Series, London: Royal Historical Society.

Morris, R.J. (1990) *Class, Sect and Party: The Making of the British Middle Class, Leeds 1820–1850*, Manchester: Manchester University Press.

Neve, M. (1983) 'Science in a commercial city: Bristol 1820–60', in Inkster, I. and Morrell, J.B. (eds) *Metropolis and Province: Science in British Culture 1780–1850*, London: Hutchinson, 179–204.

Orange, A.D. (1973) 'The British Association for the Advancement of Science: the provincial background', *Science Studies*, 1: 315–29.

Perkin, H. (1969) *Origins of Modern Society*, London: Routledge,

Porter, R. (1977) *The Making of Geology: Earth Science in Britain, 1660–1815,* Cambridge: Cambridge University Press.

Shapin, S. (1991) ' "A scholar and a gentleman": the problematic identity of the scientific practitioner in early modern England', *History of Science*, 29, 279–327.

Sheppard, T. (1916) *Yorkshire's Contribution to Science*, London: Brown.

Taylor, M.A. and Torrens, H.S. (1987) 'Saleswoman to a new science: Mary Anning and the fossil fish Squaloraja from the Lias of Lyme Regis', *Proc. Dorset Nat. Hist. and Arch. Soc.*, 108: 135–48.

Thackray, A. (1974) 'Natural knowledge in cultural context: the Manchester model', *Amer. Hist. Rev.*, 79: 672–709.

Weiner, A.B. (1985) 'Inalienable wealth', *American Ethnologist*, 12: 210–27.

White, A. (1988) 'Class, culture and control: the Sheffield Athenaeum movement and the middle class 1847–64', in Wolff, J. and Seed, J. (eds) *The Culture of Capital: Art, Power and the Nineteenth-century Middle Class*, Manchester: Manchester University Press, 83–115.

Wilson, R.G. (1971) *Gentlemen Merchants: The Merchant Community in Leeds 1700–1830*, Manchester: Manchester University Press.

Edited and adapted extract from Knell, S.J. (2000) *The Culture of English Geology, 1815–1851: A Science Revealed Through Its Collecting*, Aldershot: Ashgate. The book explores in considerable detail the ways in which the births of the English provincial museum and the new science of geology – in which Britain played such an important role – were intimately related, bound together by the values, processes, and social conditions of collecting.

Chapter 21

Dustup in the bone pile
Academics v. collectors

Virginia Morell

T HE SOCIETY OF VERTEBRATE PALEONTOLOGISTS (SVP) used to be an awfully open-minded, tolerant group. In fact, back in the 1960s, to prove his point that 'any S.O.B with an interest in old bones', could become a member, US Geological Survey paleontologist G. Edward Lewis nominated his dog for membership. (The canine was duly elected.) But times have changed, and the once superegalitarian society now finds itself divided by a bitter debate over whether a certain group should be ushered out: commercial fossil collectors who violate the SVP's ethics. That issue has provoked the next president of the society into resigning even before being anointed at the society's annual meeting, set to begin on 28 October in Toronto. Everybody in the world of palaeontology is expecting the issue of commercial collecting to cause fireworks at the meeting. 'It's liable to be a lot like the shoot-out at the OK Corral', warns Michael Woodburne, a geologist at the University of California, Riverside, and a member of the SVP executive committee.

The immediate cause for the resignation of president-elect Clayton Ray, a paleontologist at the Museum of Natural History at the Smithsonian Institution, was a resolution passed by the executive committee in June calling for the 'consideration for expulsion from the society of any commercial dealers who engage in unauthorized fossil collecting on public lands'. Ray, who has worked closely with commercial collectors, believes the resolution is too dogmatic and the executive committee had not considered it in a 'democratic enough fashion'.

And that resolution isn't the only contentious issue related to commercial collecting that the members of the society will be called on to discuss. Another is a bill introduced in the Senate by Democratic Senator Max Baucus of Montana that would forbid commercial enterprises from gathering fossils on federal land – now prohibited by a tangled web of regulations but not strictly forbidden by federal law. The commercial operators argue that even the present regulations are unconstitutional and that the proposed law would further infringe on their rights.

Like scattered signs on the surface of the earth that signal a buried cache of dinosaur bones, the society's resolution and Baucus' bill are surface manifestations of an enmity that has disrupted the once-amicable relations between professional paleontologists and those who collect old bones for profit [note in the UK dealers are often referred to, confusingly, as 'professional collectors']. The researchers complain that they are being driven away from choice sites — and out of the market — by a fad that has made dinosaur relics as desirable in the world of collectibles as paintings by Van Gogh. The result, say the academics, is that the public is losing choice pieces of its prehistoric heritage — data needed to understand such things as what the consequences of greenhouse warming might be. The commercial collectors, on the other hand, argue that they're just as entitled to the fossils as anyone else, and that they and their clients get real pleasure out of their collections, whereas any bone that becomes an academic find is likely to wind up at the back of some dusty museum drawer. They also fear that protective legislation for fossils on public land might one day be extended to private lands, as is the case in the dinosaur-rich province of Alberta, where all fossils belong to the government.

Although their numbers in the SVP are small (some 40 of 1500 members), many commercial collectors are coming to Toronto to wage war. 'We didn't start this battle', says John Kramer, who owns a commercial enterprise in Golden, Minnesota, called the Potomac Museum Group and is president of the American Association of Paleontological Suppliers, an organization representing commercial fossil dealers. 'It's the academic palaeontologists who've drawn the line; they've made it us versus them. Some of them think we're nothing but the devil's own brew', he adds. 'It's their mission to outlaw all commercial collectors. We can't ignore that kind of rhetoric — it's a call to arms.'

But in their zeal to fend off the academics, the commercial collectors have been broadcasting inflammatory rhetoric of their own. Peter Larson, president of another commercial venture, the Black Hills Institute of Geological Research in Hill City, South Dakota, has labelled Baucus' bill 'The Governmental Paleontologist Welfare Act' — words calculated to raise academic hackles. And in flyers distributed to amateur fossil collectors (who number at least 200,000), Larson has stated that the bill will limit their access to public lands — and could even lead to criminal charges if they or their children chance to pick up a fossil. (In fact, the bill applies only to commercial collecting and makes special provisions for amateurs to collect on public land.)

'It's a pack of lies that the bill will mess up amateurs',' fumes Jack Horner, head of paleontology at the Museum of the Rockies in Bozeman, Montana, and the recipient of a MacArthur Grant for his discoveries and interpretations of dinosaur nesting sites. 'Larson's words remind me of the creationists. Just like them, he takes everything out of context and exaggerates and misinterprets all for his own advantage', says Horner.

The old-bone game hasn't always been so heated. Like warm-blooded and cold-blooded species inhabiting an ancient landscape, academics and commercial collectors once coexisted quite nicely. Many great collections of vertebrate fossils (including the dinosaurs at the American Museum of Natural History in New York) were started by wealthy individuals who funded expeditions and paid top dollar for the best specimens. Commercial collectors have also been key suppliers of fossils to schools and, because they are able to work in the field year round, are often responsible for some of the most stunning discoveries. (Peter Larson's group, for example, in 1990 found the most complete skeleton of a *Tyrannosaurus rex* – a specimen dubbed 'Sue', now in the hands of the U.S. government, that is the subject of a complex legal battle over ownership.) In many cases, commercial collectors also readily donate their rare finds to museums and universities. But, like species competing for shrinking resources as the climate turns colder, relations between the two groups have turned savage in the past decade.

Some academic palaeontologists blame the change on a surge of popular interest in dinosaurs and the desire of Europeans and Japanese for specimens of their own; others on the taste of interior decorators or the advice of investment counsellors. Whatever the cause, the fossil market is booming. 'Twenty years ago you might see a skull of an oreodont [a hoofed relative of camels and pigs that lived 35 million years ago] for sale at a gas station near the Badlands for $25 or $30', says Michael Voorhies, curator of vertebrate paleontology at the University of Nebraska's State Museum in Lincoln. 'Today, skulls of anything go for hundreds if not thousands of dollars.' Fossils of everything from 150 million-year-old shrimp to bags of fossilized dinosaur eggshell to complete skeletons of mastodons and stegosaurs are marketed at gem and mineral shows and through catalogues – for breathtaking prices.

Last spring, at the world's largest fossil event, Tucson Week in Tucson, Arizona, fossilized shrimp were fetching $800 apiece, while the skeleton of a triceratops was being offered for $990,000, and a bog-preserved 11,600-year-old mastodon was on the block for a cool 1.5 million greenbacks. Investment-minded collectors can keep track of their fossils' value by reading the quarterly *Fossil Index*, a newsletter published by the commercial venture Prehistoric Journeys in Santa Barbara, California. The *Index* carries articles such as 'Investing in Fossils during 1992', along with cheery quotes from *The Wall Street Journal:* 'There's only one way fossil values can go . . . and that's up!'

This burgeoning trade alarms academic palaeontologists who worry that fat prices tempt commercial collectors to work on public lands, where they aren't supposed to be. (In a very few cases, permits are issued to commercial collectors to work on federal lands, but the fossils found this way cannot be sold.) Because the amount of public land in the fossil-rich west is so vast – national parks, monuments, forest service, Bureau of Land Management (BLM), and state properties are all included in this designation – and the number of rangers are so few, land managers cannot possibly patrol their entire domain. For example, the Badlands National Park in South Dakota employs four permanent and three seasonal rangers to oversee 243,000 acres. Consequently, nearly every academic paleontologist and land manager has a horror story to tell about sites being vandalized and specimens stolen.

'To me, fossils are sacred objects that should not be bought and sold', says Voorhies. 'So when I came on one of my sites [on BLM land] and saw that the fossils had just been chopped out of the wall with the intent of selling them to who knows . . . well, I just wanted to weep.'

Poaching of fossils on public land has become such a problem that the rangers themselves are baffled by how best to control it. 'Fossils are being dynamited, drilled, and removed by the ton', says Bart Fitzgerald, a special agent with the Utah BLM State Office in Salt Lake City. 'Unfortunately, we're about 20 or more years behind in getting a sense of what's really going on.' Only two weeks ago Lee Spencer, the Utah State palaeontologist for the BLM, discovered several miles of dinosaur deposits that had been so badly damaged they 'looked like a bombing range.' And the current laws don't carry nearly as much bite as a *Tyrannosaurus*: one man convicted of collecting and selling fossils from Badlands National Park was fined a trifling $50 – even though he had sold a fossilized turtle from the park for $35,000. Baucus' bill would up the charge to a year in prison and a $10,000 fine.

That's a change many academic paleontologists would welcome, since they argue that public lands should be protected by federal legislation and set aside for science, just as archaeological sites are. Commercial operators counter that the academics are an 'elite group who don't want a fossil touched until they've removed it, written a paper and gotten their notoriety, and stuck the fossil in a drawer', as Barry James, the owner of Prehistoric Journeys, says.

But the scientists counter that their concerns are more substantial than adding another specimen to museum collections. 'The days of being a stamp collector are long over', explains Ted Fremd, the palaeontologist at the John Day National Monument in Oregon. 'We work in multidisciplinary teams now to excavate a site, because we want to understand the paleoecology of the past – who was living with whom; what plants were there; what were the soils like? Commercial collectors don't take the time to do this – there's no money in it. So, while they may be making important discoveries in terms of finding the biggest dinosaur, they are not engaged in hypothesis testing, in truly trying to understand the past. The specimens they find only end up decorating somebody's shelf.'

Adds Charles Repenning, palaeontologist emeritus at the USGS in Denver, 'What's missing in this debate is an understanding of why fossils are important. They are important in reconstructing geologic time – and without that you can't predict what will be the results of the greenhouse effect, or the effects of deforestation on timber, or the suitability of sites for radioactive waste storage.' Fossils in museums, he adds, may entertain the public, but that is not the main purpose of palaeontology. 'Its purpose is to determine what and when events have happened in the past so that the future may be better evaluated.'

The academics far outnumber the commercial collectors in the SVP, but whether the hardliners' desire to discipline the commercial types will prevail in Toronto remains to be seen. William Clemens, the University of California, Berkeley, palaeontologist who replaced Clayton Ray as president-elect, urges tolerance. 'I think we all have to recognize that there is a diversity of viewpoints on this issue', he says. 'All of us – professionals, commercial and amateur collectors – share the common ground of an interest in prehistoric life . . . We need to find a way to cooperate so that we get the maximum benefit from fossils, particularly those which come from public land. Hopefully, we can achieve that and then get on with the science.' If that happens, perhaps palaeontologists will be able to stop throwing the dirt and start digging it once again.

First published as Morell, V. (1992) 'Dustup in the bone pile: academics v. collectors', *Science*, 258: 391–2. Virginia Morell is a science writer.

The Transient World

Introduction to Part Four

Simon J. Knell

T HIS SECTION OPENS WITH a dispute over bones which is fundamentally
different to the one affecting palaeontologists discussed in Chapter 21. Here,
I include an extract from Andrew Gulliford's history of the exploitation of Native
American human remains in the run up to, and immediately after the passing of
the Native American Graves Protection and Repatriation Act (NAGPRA) in 1990.
This continues coverage in this book of a debate begun for us by Berlo and Phillips.
It is further continued by Alan Trachtenberg. Gulliford's history charts a period
during which 'objects' were utterly transformed but often without any firm or concrete conclusion. By this means Native Americans moved closer to their ancestral past and a continuity of values and beliefs. In contrast, the descendants of
the white settlers – heroic pioneers of the West – were asked to seek historical
and cultural separation from the values of their forebears. This was seen in the
exhibition, *The West as America*, which soon found itself a site of contestation.
Among those drawn to it was Trachtenberg who masterfully unpicks the exhibition's ideology from its historiography and material culture. Here iconic objects
(paintings) appear to be in a state of flux, their nationalistic status compromised
as curators turned them into depictions of a shameful past. In one respect,
Trachtenberg's analysis is about placing intellectual rigour over subjective polit-
icization, but he also shows that the very notion of the West has a particular
sensitivity to the past, a willingness to let go, to move on.

In Edward Bruner's and Eric Gable and Richard Handler's chapters there is
an attempt to understand the nature of history at two of the most visited historical
heritage attractions in the United States: New Salem and Colonial Williamsburg.
There is a direct link here to Trachtenberg's and Gulliford's historical narratives
as both attempt to understand histories which have been distorted and misrepresented. Bruner's and Gable and Handler's pieces have much in common but
also, as the latter two authors argue, rather different conclusions: 'What Bruner

observed at New Salem and what we observed at Colonial Williamsburg are essentially the same phenomena. Yet we interpret them in almost opposite ways.' Arguments here again return us to questioning reality, notions of authenticity and tradition, and issues of objectivity – which might be contrasted with Shanks and Hodder's readings. Things museums often perceive as concrete are here demonstrated to be in flux.

Tradition and authenticity are also in Sandra Dudley's mind as she studies the Karenni, where women's clothes were found to have specific but clearly relative meaning. Identities were bound up in their clothing and yet came under constant assault as new refugees were exposed to the social expectations of existing refugees, camp workers and a pervasive missionary atmosphere which perpetuated a nineteenth-century view – not far removed from Gulliford's study – of Christianity being synonymous with civilisation. Dudley never lets herself get swept up in the politics as to do so would simply undermine the strength of her conclusions. However, one cannot help but see the same insidious and deeply regrettable altering of people and things.

In Glen Collins's snapshot of post-9/11 New York, the curator's professional desire for empirical rationality is mixed with an emotional response; a sense of needing to act but not knowing why or how. In terms of the transience of the material world, this is about loss and transitory opportunity, notions of the historical and worthy, and issues of identity and remembrance. In a moment it seemed the world had changed, and in that moment not only had the objects the curators collected changed – and would continue to change – but now innocent objects elsewhere in the world became suspicious. Objects are woven into the same complex social fabric; in an objective sense they are real things but their meaning and legitimate interpretation are in a flux of overlapping experiences, sacrifices, decisions. Even during the course of their collecting project the relationship of individuals to the objects changed. At first, they were compelled, but later they could rationalize – yet still the objects remained unbelievably powerful. Over time these objects will continue to change, moving from contemporary to historical and, perhaps, as they do so, the personal will diminish as the national and iconic grows.

The final three chapters return to the museum to consider loss and change there. Phil Doughty's diatribe shook up the UK's museum profession in the early 1980s, and kick-started a renewed process of professionalisation. Driven by a new and expanding museum generation which had met its inheritance and saw it (subjectively – though rationally) with the idealism of a new era, this also marked a change of perception and interpretation. Now old fossils became heroic remains, and geologists an abused 'Other'. In time, however, the specificity of Doughty's argument became lost as the British government and employers began to homogenise these concerns into a generalized solution involving 'collection care' and 'museum education'. Consequently, the intellectual bedrock of the museum – the specialist provincial curator which Doughty sought to reinvigorate – found itself in a state of erosion. Once again objects were changed, and they would continue to change as museums responded to their changing contexts.

Environmentalist Valerius Geist raises rather different concerns, though equally resting upon the subjectivity of interpretation – here in the world of scientific nomenclature. What something is called and why – key museum operations – can have a tremendous effect on its survival. As Geist shows, there is considerable complexity here, and with each decision collections change, and our view of living animals, and indeed of the landscape, changes. All these things are related and they rest in large degree upon decisions made in the museum. And while Geist is concerned with animals, his argument could just as well be applied to paintings, archaeological remains, and so on. Finally, this section ends with Pere Alberch's article written at that moment when world governments appeared to be taking the global environment seriously for the first time. At that moment, the Victoriana of the natural history museum escaped its past and claimed a social relevance lost long ago. For Alberch and his contemporaries, the museum's collections had changed, and they now stood at the forefront of a morally-just environmentalism. However, later this virtue would be questioned as the project seemed contaminated by an association with multinational pharmaceutical companies who were cutting their way through the rainforest in search of commercial materials, colonialists of a new kind in search of twentieth-century gold.

Chapter 22

Bones of contention
The repatriation of Native American human remains

Andrew Gulliford

O F ALL THE CULTURAL RESOURCE issues affecting Indian tribes today, none is more complicated than the return and reburial of human remains. Some tribes seek to rebury all their ancestors on tribal lands. Other Native Americans are not interested in having bones in museums reburied, but they are keenly interested in claiming unidentified remains found on public land for various reasons, including the assertion of expanded territorial boundaries, the settlement of land claims suits, and as a means to tribal recognition. This essay explores the history of the collection of Native American skeletons and explains the unintended efforts of recent legislation which was passed to help return Indian remains to tribal hands. For public historians working with tribal peoples these are vital issues which must be understood both in a historical context and in terms of how Indians today perceive their relationship to contemporary archaeologists, anthropologists, historical researchers and museum curators.

During the nineteenth century, no Indian society was left unmolested in the race systematically to collect and classify human remains from all American aboriginal cultures. The same nineteenth-century mindset that saw tribal peoples as 'savages' saw their human remains as appropriate for scientific inquiry rather than continuous respect. As Indians were being killed on battlefields and forced onto reservations native bones were often collected and examined, and then placed in long-term permanent storage in hundreds of private collections or in the US Army Medical College.

In 1988, the American Association of Museums reported to the Senate Select Committee of Indian Affairs that 163 museums held 43,306 Native America skeletal remains. The Smithsonian Institution alone held 18,600 American Indian and Alaskan native remains and thousands of burial artefacts. Indian activist Susan Shown Harjo explained that Indians are 'further dehumanized by being exhibited alongside mastodons and dinosaurs and other extinct creatures' (Vizenor 1990: 62). For most of America's native peoples, no other issue has touched a more sensitive chord than these disrespectful nineteenth-century collecting practices. For that reason, the repatriation of human remains to their tribes of origin for reburial is one of the most important cultural resource issues today.

Many Indians seek to rescue their human remains from what they believe to have been dubious and prolonged scientific research. As Curtis M. Hinsley notes, 'the painful and immensely complex matter of repatriation of bones and burial goods has become an issue extending beyond proprietorship per se; indeed, the debate is ultimately not over control of bones at all, but over control of narrative: the stories of peoples who went before and how those peoples (and their descendants) are to be currently represented and treated.' Hinsley (1994) writes, 'The heart of the matter, as always lies in the negotiation between power and respect.' How to research and handle these delicate human remains issues is a fundamental challenge for public historians but one that will offer enormous satisfaction both for historians and tribal leaders as old injustices are finally corrected.

As early as 1972, anthropologists and Indian people had cooperated in the reburial of Narragansett remains (Simmons 1989). In the late 1980s, major protests by Native Americans and the national exposure of commercial grave-robbing incidents like the devastation of Slack Farm in Kentucky brought repatriation to the forefront of public discourse. Sympathy and understanding for Native American issues prompted Congress in 1989 to pass the National Museum of the American Indian (NMAI) Act to create an Indian museum in the last space available on the mall in Washington, D.C. The NMAI Act helped solidify a constituency which pushed for a broad national law to redress a century of Indian grave robbing.

After years of intense wrangling and dissension among college professors, archaeologists, museum directors, and native tribes, Congress passed the Native American Graves Protection and Repatriation Act (NAGPRA) in 1990. NAGPRA required all museums and facilities receiving federal funds to inventory human remains and associated burial goods in their collections and to notify modern tribal descendants by November 1995. The burden of notification was placed upon the museums, and native peoples were allowed to choose which materials, if any, they wished to consider for repatriation. The bill represented a major victory for Indian peoples, a significant piece of human rights legislation that permits the living to reassert control over their own dead.

At issue has been not just the interests of science versus the interests of descendants, but also, as many Indians see it, 'the rights of the dead themselves, toward whom the living bear responsibility' (King 1993). Cultural resources consultant Thomas King explains, 'The living are responsible for the dead, and the dead – often seen not as being really "dead" but transformed and still powerful – must be treated with respect.' In testimony prepared for the U.S. Senate, University of Colorado anthropologist Deward Walker explained: 'Everywhere in Native North America one encounters a great religious importance attached to the dead who are believed to have a continuing influence on the lives of their descendants and other survivors.' Walker continued: 'Given proper rituals and proper respect, [the dead] are believed to provide assistance in curing illnesses, in determining the future, in guaranteeing the outcome of risky events, and in other general ways helping make the lives of the living more secure.'

A century ago, this issue of reverence for the dead underscored much Indian opposition to removal or to the sale of Indian lands, but scientific theories of the nineteenth century supported non-white inferiority and denied Indians their human-ity. Public history research has demonstrated those racist paradigms. Independent scholar Robert Bieder, writing as a consultant for the Native American Rights Fund, a legal advocacy group in Boulder, Colorado, noted prevalent attitudes in the second and third decades of the nineteenth century, 'that neither Africans nor Indians could ever advance beyond their allegedly low mental states and must either be kept in slavery or exterminated (or allowed to pass into extinction) in order to make room for progress'. Providing scientific 'proofs' of non-white inferiority became an international undertaking linking the science of craniology with 'the politics of colonial exploitation' (Bieder 1990: 5).

Contemporaneous with the idea of a rigid racial hierarchy was the belief that each race had a uniquely shaped skull. In 1823, Samuel Morton the founder of physical anthropology in America began to teach at the Philadelphia Hospital and Pennsylvania College, where he actively solicited skulls to add to his collections. The appropriation of human specimens enabled Morton to publish his *Crania Americana* in 1839, in which he showed that Caucasians had a brain capacity of 87 cubic inches, whereas American Indian skulls, from 147 samples, had a capacity of only 82 cubic inches. He concluded that small cranial size correlated with intellectual inferiority, and a reviewer of the book took Morton's statements as proof of racial inferiority (Bieder 1990: 10–11).

Collecting skulls continued as a hobby of gentlemen. (…) Indian skulls had a dollar value, and amateur scientists or philosophers collected Indian skulls and relics much as one would collect butterflies or categorize types of birds. (…)

This process of acquiring Indian skulls for scientific study eventually became institutionalized. On May 21, 1862, Surgeon General William A. Hammond estab-lished the Army Medical Museum. He ordered all medical officers 'diligently to collect, and to forward to the office of the Surgeon General, all specimens of morbid anatomy, surgical or medical, which may be regarded as valuable . . . These objects should be accompanied by short explanatory notes.' As an added induce-ment the Surgeon General stated 'Each specimen in the collection will have appended the name of the medical officer by whom it was prepared.' Two years later at the infamous dawn massacre at Sand Greek, Colorado, Colonel John M. Chivington and his drunken troops killed innocent women and children and then cut off their heads for shipment to Washington, D.C.

In January 1865, Harvard University zoologist Louis Agassiz reminded Sec-retary of War Edwin Stanton that he had promised to 'let me have the bodies of some Indians; if any should die at this time . . . all that would be necessary . . . would be to forward the body express in a box . . . In case the weather was not very cold . . . direct the surgeon in charge to inject through the carotids a solution of arsenate of soda.' Agassiz added, 'I should like one or two handsome fellows entire and the heads of two or three more' (Bieder 1990: 16).

Three years later, on January 13, 1868, an additional request went out from the U.S. Army 'urging upon the medical officers . . . the importance of collecting for the Army Medical Museum specimens of Indian crania and of Indian weapons and utensils, so far as they may be able to procure them'. (…)

Collectors also looted ancient and prehistoric burials. Warren K. Moorehead shipped hundreds of Indian remains to Chicago for the 1893 World's Columbian Exposition, an unabashed celebration of the triumph of American civilization. Many of these bones and artefacts became the property of the Field Museum of Natural History. Nineteenth-century competition for collections pitted the Peabody Museum of Harvard against the Smithsonian Institution while several institutions contended for control of burial mounds. The sharpest competition erupted between the Field Museum and New York City's American Museum of Natural History over access to Northwest Coast skeletons and artefacts. These had become highly profitable for collectors, with skulls fetching $5 each and complete skeletons $20 apiece (Bieder 1990: 31; Cole 1995: 102–64). (…)

By 1898, the Army Medical Museum donated over 2,000 crania to the US National Museum where most of the skulls and skeletons remained in storage in the National Museum of Natural History of the Smithsonian Institution. Although native peoples represent less than 1% of today's American population and they were an equally small percentage a century ago, native peoples represented 54.4% of the Smithsonian's collection of 34,000 human specimens. Blacks represented 5.1% of the collections and whites 20%. (…)

In June of 1986, the Skokomish Tribe of Shelton, Washington, passed resolution No. 86–31 stating that 'the necessary time for holding these human remains for scientific inquiry has expired' and 'the practice of keeping Native American skeletons for further study is in conflict with our tribe's cultural and moral beliefs, and is in total disregard to the rights, dignity, and respect that all human beings in the United States of America enjoy under the Constitution.' (…)

In 1987, in the middle of this controversy, Secretary of the Smithsonian Institution Robert McCormick Adams asked the U.S. Senate for support of a National Museum of the American Indian authorization bill. Attorney Walter Echo-Hawk of the Native American Rights Foundation in Boulder, Colorado, favoured a new Indian museum, but he complained of 'the deplorable fact that the Smithsonian is America's largest Indian graveyard, in possession of almost 19,000 dead Indian bodies'. In Senate testimony Echo-Hawk explained. 'It is therefore critical, as a matter of moral consistency that the founding principles of the proposed museum, as well as its enabling legislation, cause the Museum to be built as "a living memorial" to the Nation's First Citizens – and not be built upon a foundation of tens of thousands of dead bodies and over the sensibilities of the nearest living next of kin.'

Secretary Adams admitted that skeletons in the Smithsonian's collection had been acquired under unscrupulous circumstances. He stated, 'Some officers were excessive in their zeal to collect, robbing fresh graves or forwarding battlefield finds and the remains of Indians who died while Army prisoners.' He was not willing, however, to repatriate the human remains of 'individuals who cannot be directly identified'. An archaeologist himself, Adams argued for 'the claims of science', explaining that the Smithsonian's collection existed 'to enable scientists to learn about human adaptations and biology by studying living and past populations'. (…)

By the late 1980s, a few universities and museums acquiesced and realized that it was past time to relinquish their collections of human remains. The Museum of New Mexico in Santa Fe drafted its own repatriation policy for the return of tribal human remains and grave goods, as did the Arizona State Museum in Tucson. In 1989, Stanford University agreed to return 550 Indian bodies to the Ohlone-Costanoan tribe of California for reburial because the remains came from the tribe's historic areas. (...)

In Minnesota the state legislature appropriated $90,000 over three years to study skeletons at a cost of $500 to $1,000 each, prior to the University of Minnesota relinquishing 150 human remains to the Devil's Lake Sioux and another 1,000 remains excavated from diverse Indian burial mounds. In 1989, Seattle University returned 150 boxes of bones to Indian tribes in Washington State, and Omaha Indians received artefacts and human remains both from the University of Nebraska-Lincoln and from Harvard University's Peabody Museum.

Then in August 1989, at a special meeting between Indian tribes and Smithsonian representatives including Secretary Robert Adams, an agreement was reached for the return of human remains and burial artefacts from the Smithsonian itself, provided they could be linked with 'reasonable certainty' to present-day tribes. By that date, twenty-two states had passed laws against disturbing unmarked Indian grave sites. In November of 1989, President George Bush signed into law the National Museum of the American Indian Act which established a new Indian museum as part of the Smithsonian Institution complex and mandated that the Smithsonian return human remains and associated and unassociated funerary objects to culturally affiliated Indian tribes. Tribal members considered the Smithsonian concession a major victory for Indian rights, including the right of the dead to remain buried. Under Secretary Adams' direction, the Smithsonian organized a Repatriation Office to begin the long and complicated task of returning human remains and grave goods.

Finally, in October of 1990, President George Bush signed into law the Native American Graves Protection and Repatriation Act, providing sanctity for unmarked graves on public land and the return of human remains and associated grave goods to their tribes of origin from any museum receiving federal funds.

A century after the theft of Blackfeet bones, Curly Bear Wagner, Cultural Coordinator for the Blackfeet tribe, and John 'Buster' Yellow Kidney, a spiritual leader of the tribe, travelled to the Field Museum in Chicago to arrange for their ancestors' reburial. In 1991 Yellow Kidney commented that returning remains to their rightful place has stirred a hot bed of political controversy 'both on and off the reservation' and that 'tribes are experiencing infighting and squabbling among themselves'. Some tribal members want human remains to come home so that the dead may rest in peace. Others fear that the dead may harass the living or that human remains may have been mixed up and the wrong bones will be returned. Tribal members do not want accidentally to 'bury the bones of their historic enemies on tribal soil.' (...)

Earlier the Blackfeet had sought the return of human remains from the Smithsonian Institution. Scientific research on the skeletal remains had proven to be an asset because positive genetic links could be made between living Blackfeet and human remains in the collection. An excellent example of cooperation between the Smithsonian and Indians involved returning to the Blackfeet fifteen skulls stolen in 1892 and sent to the Army Medical College. Secretary Robert Adams noted that the skulls had been collected 'in an inappropriate manner', but he also added that the Blackfeet wanted positive identifications, because 'in 1892 there were open hostilities between themselves and many of their Indian neighbors, and to bury

Blackfeet remains next to those of enemies would result in an undesirable mixing of spirits'. The identified remains have been returned and reburied in Montana and a monument erected on the Blackfeet reservation.

To their surprise, scientists are finding that Indian peoples are also interested in their ancestry and prehistoric past. Excavated or discovered human remains can be removed for scientific study and analyzed provided no destructive techniques are used on the bones and they are returned for reburial within a reasonable time of a year or two. Indians generally do not oppose legitimate scientific research; they oppose the unnecessary warehousing of their dead. (...)

Some tribes and native peoples are uninterested in the repatriation of human remains and fear the consequences if skeletal material is returned. There is no consensus on reburial issues among the nation's over 500 federally registered tribes. The Eastern Shoshone on the Wind River Reservation in Wyoming do not want their ancestors repatriated because they doubt that the museum provenience (record-keeping) of the bones is accurate. The California Chumash are not interested in the responsibility of reburial and neither are the Zuni, who feel that because bones have left their home area they have lost their cultural identity. The Navajo are also not interested in repatriation. When Seminoles in Florida found out that 1,200 pounds of bones had been dug up by a developer, they asked for assistance from other American Indian leaders, and members of the Sioux and Seminole tribes helped bury the bones on the Pine Ridge Reservation near Wounded Knee, South Dakota.

After more than a century of exploitation, a national consensus has emerged granting tribal people hegemony over their dead. Across the nation, the return of human remains has added to a renewed spirit of cautious optimism among Indian peoples. Human remains on public display have been removed or closed from view at Mesa Verde National Park in Colorado, the Allen County Museum in Ohio, Wickliffe Mounds in Kentucky and Dickson Mounds Museum and State Park in Illinois. But the successes of the Native American Graves Protection Act of 1990 and the Smithsonian's Repatriation Office, officially established in 1991 although effective before then, have not been without their consequences.

Indians have been overwhelmed with paperwork from museums, and few tribes have adequate staff or facilities to process the immense flow of formal letters and computer-generated inventories which may weigh several pounds. Tribes question who should answer all of the enquiries they are receiving and which tribal members should seek repatriation of associated funerary remains and sacred objects. Deep divisions have developed within tribes over who has the authority to speak about repatriation issues, and tribal cultural committees have found themselves embroiled in squabbles among Indian bands split between two or more reservations. Native American families argue over ancient artefacts and worry about the repercussions of bringing home human remains and the belongings of the dead.

According to Native American consultant, Kenny Frost, those who have been the most troubled are the medicine men and women responsible for assessing human remains. Frost states, 'One of my friends at the Standing Rock Reservation in South Dakota has been handling human remains. Those medicine men are being separated by tribal members and being treated as if they are spirits.' He explains, 'They are not being accepted as a living person on this side but rather as a person from the spiritworld. They are shunned by their own people.' Some of the medicine men want to stop handling human remains altogether. Frost believes it is an 'emotional drain, particularly in handling the crania of small children and women with evidence of bullet holes and trauma to the head [which] were collected by U.S. Army surgeons'. Medicine men who bring human remains home for reburial must themselves undergo cleansing ceremonies. For smaller tribes, the psychological effects of revisiting a bitter frontier past can trouble everyone.

An equally thorny issue involves Indian tribes not seeking repatriation of skeletal remains in museums, but instead claiming skeletons found on public land as their descendants and thus pressing for an extension of land claims. Although these Indians are unwilling to have scientific DNA studies conducted to see if the human remains really are their genetic ancestors, they argue that because of cultural affiliation and oral traditions about their tribal origins, human remains found on public lands are their ancestors and tribal land claims should be reopened. This issue is especially acute in the Southwest among the Navajo, Hopi, Zuni, Ute, and Pueblo peoples, where tribal rivalries continue. The dead are being used as pawns in land claim cases and political disputes. The Navajo, for instance, are not interested in repatriation and reburial of human remains, but they are very interested in claiming skeletal remains as evidence to extend their aboriginal territory. Ultimately, public historians will get involved in these delicate questions over interpreting tribal pasts.

In Colorado, notification of human remains found on public land must go out to fourteen different tribes who at one time or another hunted or gathered within what is now the political boundaries of the state of Colorado. The legal complexities of complying with NAGPRA are enormous and include respectful repatriation and reburial of Indian remains for which there are no known descendants. (...)

As for science, physical anthropology, and archaeology, a century after wholesale looting of Indian graves, a quiet truce has been negotiated. Although the recent 1996 meeting of the Society of American Archaeology was attended by over 2,500 anthropologists and archaeologists and only two dozen Indians, the dialogue has begun over how to conduct scientific investigations. Kenny Frost, who was invited to the meeting by Washington University in St. Louis, explains, 'If scientists approach Indian tribes in regards to testing human remains in a manner that will benefit mankind, then tribes are somewhat willing to agree to testing if the benefits are there and the remains are returned for repatriation at a later date.' Frost adds that scientists can have longer than a year to do their studies if they 'work diligently on the remains and show cause why the remains should be kept for additional study'.

The long-term storage of Native American human remains begun in the nineteenth century is over. Now tribal cultural officers, anthropologists, public historians, archaeologists, and tribal historians can work together. Such collaboration will succeed if they maintain an atmosphere of mutual respect. A century ago scientists thought there was much to learn about Native Americans and indigenous peoples as a 'vanishing race.' A century later there is even more to learn from living members of vital native cultures.

References

Bieder, R.E. (1990) *A Brief Historical Survey of the Expropriation of American Indian Remains*, Bloomington, IN: Robert E. Bieder and Native American Rights Fund.

Cole, D. (1995) *Captured Heritage: The Scramble for Northwest Coast Artifacts*, Norman, OK: University of Oklahoma Press.

Hinsley, C.M. (1994) *The Smithsonian and the American Indian: Making a Moral Anthropology in Victorian America*, Washington, DC: Smithsonian Institution Press.

King, T.F. (1993) 'Beyond Bulletin 38: comments on the Traditional Cultural Properties Symposium', in Parker, P.L. (ed.) *Traditional Cultural Properties: What You Do and How We Think*, CRM 16.

Simmons, W. (1989) *The Narragansett*, New York: Chelsea House.

Vizenor, G. (1990) *Crossbloods*, Minneapolis: University of Minnesota Press.

Edited extract from Gulliford, A. (1996) 'Bones of contention: the repatriation of Native American human remains', *The Public Historian*, 18(4): 119–43. Andrew Gulliford is currently Director of Special Projects at Fort Lewis College and a public historian with interests in museum work, historic preservation and cultural resource management. He is well known for his work on the protection of Native American cultural artefacts on federal lands and on tribal museum and repatriation issues associated with the Native American Graves Protection and Repatriation Act.

Chapter 23

Contesting the West

Alan Trachtenberg

I F FOR NOTHING ELSE, the revisionist exhibition of paintings and other images of the American West at the National Museum of American Art in Washington, D.C., deserves credit for the commotion it has raised among self-styled guardians of the American past. 'The West as America' drew protests from indignant conservative reviewers, from outraged congressmen who never bothered to see the show and from the former head of the Library of Congress, historian Daniel Boorstin, whose books celebrate America as a society artfully fumbling along without serious problems. And, judging by the comments in the visitors' book, quite a few of the unsuspecting folk who trekked their way through the image-and-text-laden galleries also took offence at the unexpected messages of the show's wall labels.

The organizers of the show may have winced at the various accusations levelled at them, which included just about everything short of treason, but they shouldn't have been surprised. They might have expected that their efforts to dismantle the cherished belief in the 'winning of the West' as America's epic, and western art as its sublime portrayal, would draw blood. After all, the myth of Manifest Destiny is along with the landing of Columbus, Plymouth Rock and Thanksgiving, the Battle of the Alamo and the 'War Between the States', one of the foundation myths of American nationalism. Manifest Destiny was the belief, popular in the 1840s and '50s that the United States was impelled by providence to expand its territory westward. You don't mess with such sacred subjects in the galleries of the government-funded Smithsonian Institution with impunity.

Art works have played a central role in forming national myths. When we think of emblematic national events, what comes to mind are nineteenth-century American history paintings, works whose fame derives less from their status as serious art than from their endless reproduction in high school history books. Can we think of the signing of the Declaration of Independence without recalling John Trumbull's painting? Can we envisage Daniel Boone crossing the Cumberland Gap without the aid of George Caleb Bingham? Can we imagine the Old West without seeing before us Charles Russell's vision of cowboys and Indians? If we add to these countless lesser works – engravings in periodicals, illustrations in books, photographs in old albums, stereo cards and picture postcards – we can reconstruct a graphic equivalent to the nation's official version of its past, the past as depicted in the giant murals of the Capitol rotunda, for example, or in statehouses throughout that country.

Whether people believe that the past actually looked like these depictions matters less than the fact that such images call up whole narratives deeply etched in our collective memory by scores of movies, billboards, commercials and textbook illustrations. Paintings and other modes of visual art ritualize our sense and idea of the past, of American nationality. Just look at *Time* magazine's Fourth of July cover story. 'Whose America?' (July 8, 1991), and you will see, once again, details taken from the usual famous paintings dished up as examples of the history now under revision in the name of multiculturalism.

In 'The West as America' wall labels were used to suggest that such overtly nationalistic images ought not to be taken as the gospel truth. This is a message one would think unnecessary for viewers of any sophistication. Ironically, however, the outrage prompted by the show precisely confirms the curators' assumption that some beliefs about art history and nationality lie too deep merely to prod – they must be blasted, jolted, even at the risk of offending.

To be sure, some viewers left the show grateful for enlightenment. Remarks in the visitors' book suggest that many were made aware of expansionist and racist ideologies disguised as exotica in George Catlin's portraits of Indians, as natural beauty and adventure in the grandiose canvases of Albert Bierstadt and as down-home work and play in Bingham's genre scenes. The appreciative comments were outnumbered about three to one, however. True believers reacted with pain, disbelief and anger at seeing adventure and settlement recast as expansion and conquest: with the terms reversed and revalued, pride became an occasion for shame.

No one should be upset by all the fuss. For the organizers, it's a sign of success, in a manner of speaking. Of course, the melodrama might turn ugly if Senator Ted Stevens makes good on his threat to investigate Smithsonian policies and funding. But planners of the show have stirred up genuine controversy about American art and its relation to nationalism, and that is all to the good.

It would be unfortunate, however, if the commotion deflected attention from the exhibition's fundamental revisionary aims, the most important of which was to interrogate the role of art within nationalist ideology. While the exhibition did not foreground nationalism as such, its deflation of western myths inevitably broached questions about the cultural basis for establishing and fostering a particular version of national identity.

How, exactly, 'did the exhibition threaten the sacred grounds of nationalism'? Principally, it suggested that nineteenth-century territorial expansion, justified at the time as the fulfilment of Manifest Destiny, included military conquest and outright theft of lands from native peoples. It also pointed out that this imperial aggression was justified by an ideology that described Indians as 'savages' – inferior peoples whose only hope lay in adopting the white man's ways; otherwise, extinction. Equally important was the belief that the continent's breadth virtually invited the push to the Pacific shore as inevitable, good and natural.

Even at the time of the American Revolution and the Early Republic, ideas and images of the western lands had teased the imagination of white Americans. As Yale professor of history Howard Lamar points out in his superb historical essay in the exhibition catalogue, the West has been a screen for many projected ideals. One was that because of free land in the West, America would be different from Old World societies, exempt from the hold of the past and especially from the grinding class conflicts of Europe. Did not the seemingly virgin lands beyond the Mississippi beckon European settlers to turn themselves into freeholders and the plains into a garden where the annoying facts of history and strife need not interfere with happy labour and abundant rewards? People like James Madison in the Revolutionary period and Horace Greeley two generations later argued that free lands in the West would serve as a safety valve against the social upheavals that afflicted the festering cities of Europe.

Springing from the Puritan belief in a covenant promising a New Jerusalem in America, this idea of American exemption – often called 'Exceptionalism' – has been evoked to explain why socialism and other revolutionary movements have failed to gain a foothold in the US. By virtue of its fluid opportunities and upward mobility, the argument goes, America escapes from the economic analysis of Karl Marx and others who argued that capitalism breeds inevitable social crisis. Throughout the nineteenth century, the seemingly inexhaustible lands west of the Appalachians and the Mississippi were cited by advocates of expansion as a warranty or perpetual exemption from Old World evils.

In 1893, when the census bureau announced that the frontier had closed, that it was no longer a discernible line on the American land, the historian Frederick Jackson Turner delivered his famous paper on 'The Significance of the Frontier in American History'. This powerfully influential essay lamented the end of a process Turner saw as fundamental to American national identity, the process of discarding the past and setting of one's face to the future. According to Turner, everything unique about Americans – their individualism, ingenuity, impatience with the past and hope for the future – derived from the existence of the frontier. It was on the frontier that Europeans became American; the frontier was the formative experience of the nation. Now, in 1893, the progressive Turner argued pointedly, Americans must redirect their frontier energies to solving the new problems of cities and social conflict; they must learn to replace rugged individualism with a collective outlook. This plea for a redirection of thought is often overlooked, however; by both critics and admirers of Turner, whose thesis is best known for the support it lends to the continuing myth of the frontier and American Exceptionalism.

'The West as America' originated in a revisionary movement among historians. The new western historians want to replace the myth of national character propagated by Turner with a more complex and conflicted picture of the actual life in the western regions. They point out, for example, that Turner's version of national traits is entirely masculine, derived from the presumed experience of white male pioneers and settlers; the very different experiences of women on the frontier are not represented in his picture. In Turner's account, the white male in buckskin serves as the typical American.

The masculine appeal of this vision helps explain its tenacious hold on popular culture both here and abroad. It also explains why the western myth has proven so vulnerable to ridicule. Since the antiwar protests of the 1960s, icons of western manhood like the Marlboro man and John Wayne have suffered some tarnishing. To be sure, the reign of Ronald Reagan, himself a cowboy-manqué, restored some of the glamour. And Hollywood obligingly continues to update the image of western manhood with blasts of gunfire and ever-escalating male aggression. But the fact is that at least since Vietnam, the American West has been a subject of contested meaning. And never before has the conflict of interpretation been sharper or more public than now.

'The West as America' extended recent popular scepticism, not only toward the role of art in constructing and maintaining the inherited image of the West, but toward the historiography as well. For example, the show argued that western expansion was less a natural evolutionary process than an economic process driven in part by needs of the marketplace – by the search for raw materials and new fields for capital investment – and pushed forward by the ambitions of businessmen and their political spokesmen. The organizers of the exhibition share with the new western historians and with popular satirists the desire to correct the historical record and to see the West and its art in a fresh perspective, free from the distortions of self-congratulatory myth and chauvinist ideology.

We might in fact, question whether the exhibition went far enough. To be sure, the project's agenda did represent something new in the historiography and exhibition of American art, a belated turn toward critical historicism in a field long held in check by a bland but stubborn filiopiety in the guise of connoisseurship. Wanting to dispel myths curator William Treuttner and his colleagues called upon recent interdisciplinary cultural studies (which is another demystifying enterprise based on a historicist hermeneutics of suspicion). Cultural studies assumes that discursive meanings are never given but are constructed within and by means of precise historical and material conditions. It also assumes that such constructions arise out of contest and everyday frontier life, natural scenery and turn-of-the-century inventions of the Old West. Unfortunately, however, there was a substantial gap between Treuttner's intention and the actual appearance of the show; the structure simply didn't work as intended. Instead of provoking critical responses, the themes created nothing more than conventional spaces for canvases by Bierstadt, Moran, Bingham, Remington, Russell, Leutze and lesser academic painters. Here and there were a few naïve works in oil and a scattering or works on paper, but popular and 'dissenting' material was confined to a very subordinate role.

The exhibition established an intellectual basis for an alternative perspective on the West but did not deliver any real evidence of that view. What was missing was the effort to construct a different way of thinking about the nation itself, one which would take diversity and multiplicity as much into account as distortion and ideological rhetoric. One would have expected the curators to support their argument with any number of alternative art works – vernacular art by Native Americans, for example, or graphics by some of the many ardent opponents of the Mexican War. Also interesting would have been examples of art produced by working cowboys and homesteaders, blacks on the range or Hispanics to the Southwest and California. Indeed, the Wobblies, who did silver and copper mining in the Far West during the first two decades of this century produced a fascinating body of graphics which might have disrupted the otherwise conventional panorama of high art. As it was, studio paintings predominated. In fact, the centrality accorded these studio paintings raised serious doubts about the organizers' willingness to break with the curatorial conventions they ostensibly deplored.

Too often the curators simply repudiated official art, instead of reaching beyond it to a positive alternative vision. And too often that repudiation seemed more a sign of up-to-date moral fervour than the beginning of an exploration of the social uses of art.

It is surprising, in light of their intentions, that the organizers of 'The West as America' had relatively little to say about how the meanings they wanted to question got established in the first place, how interpretations were put into circulation, how paintings communicated their messages and whether those messages were always taken to be univocal. There was little information about modes of production and distribution of art works, and no analysis of patterns of reception and response or other contextual specifics about the art itself. Here, again, the incorporation of documents such as letters or memoirs and popular graphics might have helped viewers to understand better the process by which paintings enter the discursive channels of a culture.

The organizers of the show wanted to historicize, and they were certainly right in asking, for example, why an outpouring of historical paintings should have occurred at mid-century, the years of the Mexican War and the heating up of expansionist rhetoric, particularly on the part of slaveholders seeking western lands. But in their compulsion to demystify, to expose virtually every displayed work as serving a hegemonic function, the curators tended to deprive viewers of a potentially far more complex view. By a strange twist of intention, they tended to replicate – through reversal – the very beliefs and attitudes they wanted to repudiate. Their demythologizing process led to a simplistic, negative version of the West, a remythologizing of the subject construed in much the same way, only now as the focus of all that is wrong with America.

Take the exhibition's title itself: 'The West as America'. The layered implications of these deceptively simple words compress the rhetorical gambit of the exhibition. We start with an apparently innocent given – the West – as the source of the nation's originality, the crucial element in understanding America's true past. Then we learn from the wall texts that 'the West' is no more than a construction, an ideological fiction disguising run-of-the-mill rapacity and greed and racial oppression. As the show unfolds, it transforms both of its terms – 'West' and 'America' – into occasions for lament. This, in itself, is not an unworthy end, considering all there is to mourn in shattered native cultures and depredations against the earth. But it is still a limited goal and something of an easy shot.

There seemed to be a lament for something else as well, a rather vague, naive hope that art could be (or ought to be) free of contrivance, fiction, even myth and ideology. The opening wall text carried a note of surprise and outrage, warning the visitor that these 'grand compositions suffused with light, color, and factual detail . . . are carefully staged fictions, constructed from both supposition and fact. Their role was to justify the hardship and conflict of nation-building.' Doesn't this convey an innocent wish for a transparent, sincere, honest art – everything the exhibited works were not? And doesn't this desire run parallel to the dream of a virtuous, morally correct America, all that, according to the exhibition, the actual history of the West shows to be false?

The show conveyed the impression that there is a much different western experience to be known simply by supplying facts about slaughtered Indians and land grabs to go alongside the idealized landscapes and portraits. In the same vein, to show what painters left out of their pictures, the exhibition deployed photographs next to paintings here and there, as though the camera lens were a more faithful transcriber of historical truth. The naiveté of this approach glares at us, given the fact that the extraordinary place of photographs themselves within the visual culture and ideological representation of the West goes unexamined in the exhibition. How photographs brought home to the rest of the country the ideology of nationalism attached to western scenes deserves attention in itself.

Even the conventional art on display might have served to foster a different kind of critical seeing, not merely a simplistic inversion of values in the name of the 'real' facts of western history. There are ways of looking at a canvas such as Bingham's *The Puzzled Witness* (1874) and noting that the picture of justice in practice is less celebratory than may seem the case at first glance. By clothing, posture, gesture and facial expression, the artist portrays a social realm divided by social class and implicitly raises doubts about the impartiality of the law – doubts the wall label takes it upon itself to hammer home to the viewer, instead of explaining how the message can be read in the picture.

Well represented in the exhibition – one of the show's delights in fact – Bingham's genre paintings on the whole are treated too much at face value, too little explored for ambiguities and nuance. Nevertheless, here and elsewhere in the show, by looking closely at the best of the works, we can detect fractures in the hegemonic vision and see, on the contrary, representations of contradiction, ambivalence, anxiety about the very coherence of the vision. By admitting doubts and fluxions of belief, the show might have produced a more complex and challenging historical account of the very same material.

One of the chief implications of the exhibition was that the art distorts or denies historical fact – that we cannot expect to find 'truth' or 'reality' in art itself. We were also warned that we ought not to trust the report of our own eyes. Indeed, the opening wall text proclaimed, 'Seeing is not believing':

> History, many people believe, is an objective reading of the past. *An Artist's Studio* by John Ferguson Weir on display adjacent to this wall panel asserts that the past can be accurately reconstructed by an artist working with selected texts, props, and images. And yet history, like the people who make it, is inevitably subject to personal bias . . . The paintings in this gallery and those that follow should not be seen as a record of time and place. More often than not, they are contrived views, meant to answer the hopes and desires of people facing a seemingly unlimited and mostly unsettled portion of the nation.

Much was made of the wall texts in reviews of the show – their tendentious and didactic tone, their outright gaffes and, in a few egregious instances, their painfully obvious misreadings. Although the wall labels provided considerable information about social facts excluded from the canvases, the show's heavy reliance on such labels in the first place indicated something amiss in its basic design. Visitors were not, on the whole, explicitly encouraged to look at the exhibited works in relation to one another or to think about differences between high and popular arts or between official and dissenting views. Instead, the wall labels provided answers to questions that the art itself or the juxtaposition of works on the wall did not overtly pose.

Those wall texts that were sermonizing might be forgiven as badly executed pedagogy. But several astonishing misinterpretations of art works both in the wall labels and in the catalogue beg for correctives, or at least additional explanation. The wall text nearest to Thomas Moran's *Ponce de León in Florida, 1514*, for instance, suggested the following: 'Ready to claim future riches are Ponce de León's men, whose martial order reveals that they, not the reclining Indians, possess the resources to wrest from the land its vast potential.' Yet look at that poor Spanish soldier at center-right, edging nervously toward the thicket, ready to turn tail at the first twitch of a branch. The Indians, meanwhile, sit very much at ease on their own turf. Here, the problem appears to stem from the wish to fit everything into the contours of a thesis, even where ragged edges must be trimmed.

Similarly, in the exhibition's catalogue, Treuttner writes that Joshua Shaw's *Coming of the White Man* (1850) shows the arrival of Columbus's ships against a rising sun whose light is 'accepted by Indians . . . as if it were a dazzling (Christian) prophecy'. Yet anyone can see that the figures on the ledge at the centre of the canvas cringe in terror and the tiny native on the beach flees for his life.

Later, Treuttner writes that Emanuel Leutze's *The Storming of the Teocalli by Cortez and His Troops* (1848) 'acknowledges a more militant spirit in which the might of Christianity prevails against a dark and bloodthirsty foe (a judgment Leutze's contemporaries would have applied to the Plains Indians)'. But just who are dark and bloodthirsty in Leutze's picture? The imagery tells a quite different story from Treuttner's: fierce, black-clad Spanish warriors with steely armor, guns and swords attack half-naked Indians (including women and children) who use wooden clubs to defend themselves against marauders who cast living babies from the parapet and loot the fallen of their jewellery. If the canvas must be read as a morality play, there can be no doubt who are the villains and who the victims. The catalogue text exactly reverses what the eye perceives.

If Treuttner and the other authors of the catalogue had paid more attention to Howard Lamar's essay, they would have recognized that nineteenth-century meanings ascribed to the West were in fact less neatly categorizable, more complex and conflicted, than the writers assume. To begin with, rather than a monolithic West, Lamar identifies several distinct regions (the Great Plains, the Southwest, the Rockies, the Far West), later conflated into one. In actuality, even as it was being conquered and settled, the West represented many ideas, images and social and economic policies, and its different regions gave birth to various versions of the western myth.

Lamar makes the compelling point that a common thread linking the several versions of the West was violence, not just of whites against Indians and Mexicans (and vice versa), but also, battles among whites with conflicting interests. The West was not immune to its own kind of class warfare, even if the antagonists shared skin color and went by the names of outlaws or cattle ranchers or wheat farmers or, indeed, Populists. Sections of the West served as battlegrounds over slavery; John Brown in 'Bleeding Kansas' is as much a western story as Custer at the Little Big Horn. So were the Rockefeller thugs assaulting striking silver miners at

Ludlow. Not all of these are Lamar's examples, but they fit his description of the West as an idea wrapped in controversy and conflict.

Although the catalogue authors make frequent reference to the 'recent scholarship' of the new western historiography, most stick to identifying iconography rather than analyzing form. Fearful of the twin monsters of formalism and aestheticism, the curators and catalogue authors (with certain exceptions) abjure any consideration of aesthetic form — as if it doesn't matter whether the Art is good or bad, how it achieves its effects or by what formal means it conveys its messages. Both foolish and self-defeating, this avoidance weakens the exhibition's revisionary statement. To think about art as ideology, must we deny art-as-art? If we learn that a painting of a historical scene is a constructed fiction, is there no more need to think about that painting's materials of construction, or the wide-ranging meanings conveyed by its actual, pictorial form? The flight from form leaves us with a subject empty at its centre: art without art.

Also missing from these essays, as from the exhibition itself, is any account of how social interests, the very ground of ideology, operate culturally. Typically, cultural studies seeks to interpret social acts as displaced signs or class interests. In 'The West as America', in place of a discursive theory of art and social class, of subjectivity and ideology, we have art abjectly serving the paymaster. A typical example cited in the catalogue is John Gast's *American Progress* (1872), a flagrantly commercial invocation of Manifest Destiny commissioned by the publicist George A. Crofutt to promote his series of western guidebooks. The ultimate culprits, according to the show's revisionist tale of good guys and bad guys, are the wealthy and self-interested: patrons, more or less greedy, predatory and prone to believe in the divine goodness of their mission — and their profits. But where does this leave the more serious painters like Bierstadt, Bingham and Remington, whose relationship to social issues and to their patrons was considerably more complicated?

In the other outstanding essay in this catalogue, Alex Nemerov attempts to pose just this sort of question. His subject is Remington and his turn-of-the-century colleagues, the group of artists who actually invented the popular imagery of the Old West. Nemerov concedes Remington's personal nastiness — his hatred of Jews, blacks and Injuns — but takes his art seriously nevertheless. Alone among the catalogue's essayists, Nemerov raises the issue of class in connection with the consciousness incarnated in these art works and attempts to factor that issue into a formal reading of them and an understanding of their meaning.

Nemerov tends to indulge himself with a familiar kind of deconstructive hermeneutical gymnastics, but on the whole he writes with genuine regard for the object before his eyes, for craft and imagistic complexity as much as ideology. He has important things to say about the displaced social symbolism of Remington's paintings of sun-baked and grizzly-bearded white cowboys or soldiers encircled and outnumbered by red savages; he points out that such images echo scenes of immigrant workers threatening soldiers and police during the fierce labour confrontations of the 1980s. Nemerov also writes astutely about the highly nuanced formal elements in Remington's extraordinary nocturnes.

Nemerov's vacillation between an ideological and a formalist criticism gives his essay particular heuristic value. Willing to talk about paint, about canvas, about the materiality of the artwork and of its status, as cultural artefact, he makes

illuminating incursions into Remington's painted world. He provides perceptive exposi-
tions of his brushstrokes, the artist's use of raw canvas, even the deployment of
his signature, in the spirit of Michael Fried's dissection of Thomas Eakins. But how
does this material formalism connect with what Nemerov regards as Remington's
social criticism? About *Fight for the Water Hole* (1903), Nemerov asks whether the
painting 'borrows its imagery – a group of outnumbered whites desperately defending themselves against the "strike" of a racial enemy – from the urban world where
Remington lived'. Behind this question and throughout Nemerov's essay is a theory
of art as symbolic action. Such a theoretical base is lacking in the rote inversion of
the meaning of paintings, often blind to the actual work that the curators deployed
throughout the show.

How might we view art as rhetoric and art as form in the same critical discourse? The question itself indicates the need for resolution of the dilemma latent
in the exhibition's title. To counter in a constructive way the popular myth of the
West takes more than disbelief. We need to be given alternative visions of the historical West, the West that belonged to an expanding society divided along many
fault lines: between free and slave states, between social classes impelled by conflicting or opposing interests and between urban East and frontier West. The myth of
the West helped make the nation seem unified, a single whole entity. The representation of the West in nineteenth-century art served to incorporate the western
regions not only geopolitically but emotionally and ideologically, as the core
element of national identity.

The project of re-evaluating that art needs is to take more seriously its own
radical premises and not settle for demystification alone. Exhibitions such as 'The
West as America' provide much-needed opportunities for examining alternative
traditions and, in particular, for testing against historical fact the ideological claims
(nationalist, racist, sexist) that paintings often embody. The meaning of the past,
of historical facts, even of the word 'America' itself, has been a subject of controversy and contest throughout American history, and those conflicts seem to have
sharpened recently. The organizers of this show deserve praise for posing difficult
questions just at a time when old answers are disintegrating before new realities.

The media's anxiety over 'Whose America?' may augur trouble ahead. But considering the potent role of art in ritualizing nationalist myths, it seems that art communities have it in their hands to restore to view the visual evidence of different
histories and dissenting meanings and, in the process, to revive critical intelligence
in the public discussion of culture. 'The West as America' takes an important step
in this direction, and it is therefore valuable as much for its intrinsic flaws as for
its audacity, courage and flagrant challenge to officialdom.

First published as Trachtenberg, A. (1991) 'Contesting the West', *Art in America*,
79(9): 118–23. Alan Trachtenberg is Professor Emeritus of American Studies and
English at Yale University. His books include *Reading American Photographs: Images
as History*, *The Incorporation of America: Culture and Society in the Gilded Age* and *Shades
of Hiawatha: Staging Indians, Making Americans, 1890–1930*.

Chapter 24

Abraham Lincoln as authentic reproduction

A critique of postmodernism

Edward M. Bruner

New Salem

NEW SALEM HISTORIC SITE is a reconstructed village and outdoor museum in Illinois where Abraham Lincoln lived in the 1830s (Thomas 1934). Most Americans know that Abraham Lincoln was U.S. president during the Civil War, that he freed the slaves, and that he was assassinated in 1865. Arguably the greatest American folk hero, Lincoln's life is an embodiment of the American success ideology. Abraham Lincoln came to New Salem at the age of 22, and he lived there between 1831 and 1837. In his own words, Lincoln arrived as 'a piece of floating driftwood', 'a friendless, uneducated penniless boy', and by hard work and strength of character this humble backwoodsman left New Salem to become a lawyer and politician in the state capital. An Illinois Historic Preservation Agency hand-out distributed at the park, entitled 'Lincoln's New Salem' (n.d.), says, 'The six years Lincoln spent in New Salem formed a turning point in his career. From the gangling youngster who came to the village in 1831 with no definite objectives, he became a man of purpose as he embarked on a career of law and statesmanship.' The same theme appears in Sandburg's (1954: 743) famous biography, where he calls New Salem 'Lincoln's Alma Mater' and refers to the site as Lincoln's 'nour-ishing mother' (Sandburg 1954: 55). Implicit in the story is the 'frontier hypo-thesis' of Frederick Jackson Turner, which suggests that, just as the United States was formed by overcoming the obstacles of the wilderness, so too Lincoln was formed by overcoming the hardships of frontier life. Also implicit is the notion that America is an open society, that the American dream of success can be achieved by anyone willing to work hard by day and study by night. New Salem, then, is a national shrine, a site of America's civil religion, because it was the locality that gave birth to the adult Lincoln. New Salem was the site of transformation, and Lincoln's story is the story of America, the rags-to-riches, log-cabin-to-White-House American myth.

The premier tourist attraction in Illinois, drawing over a half million visitors a year, New Salem Village is located in a 640-acre park that also contains a campground and picnic areas. The site is a public facility owned by the state of Illinois. The village consists of 23 log houses, and in most of the houses there are interpreters in period dress who greet the tourists, discuss aspects of life in the 1830s, tell about the original residents of the house, and answer the tourists' questions. It is third-person interpretation, although in practice it sometimes slips into first person. The site features craft demonstrations, including blacksmithing and cooking, carding, spinning and dyeing of wool, and the making of candles, soap, brooms, shoes, and spoons. New Salem is one of a number of reconstructed prairie villages in the Midwest, and indeed, Baudrillard and Eco are correct: there are many reconstructed historic sites in America (Anderson 1984).

Authenticity, copies, and originals

Ada Louise Huxtable (1992: 24) writes that 'It is hard to think of a more dangerous, anomalous, and shoddy perversion of language and meaning than the term "authentic reproduction"'. She is writing about Colonial Williamsburg, but the term is used at many other historic sites. New Salem is one of the sites that describes itself in its own brochures as an 'authentic reproduction'. We ask, What does this mean? Rather than give a general answer to the question, I turn first to the discourse produced by museum professionals, by the staff and the interpreters at New Salem, to learn how the term *authentic reproduction* is used. As anthropologists know, the meaning of any expression is not a property inherent in the wording or in the dictionary, but rather is dependent on the perceptions and practices of those who use the expression.

By *authentic reproduction*, the museum professionals acknowledge that New Salem is a reproduction, not an original; but they want that reproduction to be authentic in the sense of giving the appearance of being like the 1830s. Most aim for what Taylor and Johnson (1993) call 'historical verisimilitude', to make the 1990s New Salem resemble the 1830s New Salem. *Authentic* in this sense means credible and convincing, and this is the objective of most museum professionals, to produce a historic site believable to the public, to achieve mimetic credibility. This is the first meaning of *authenticity*.

Some museum professionals go further, and speak as if the 1990s New Salem not only resembles the original but is a complete and immaculate simulation, one that is historically accurate and true to the 1830s. This is the second meaning of *authenticity*. In the first meaning, based on verisimilitude, a *1990s* person would walk into the village and say, 'This looks like the 1830s', as it would conform to what he or she expected the village to be. In the second meaning, based on genuineness, an *1830s* person would say, 'This looks like 1830s New Salem', as the village would appear true in substance, or real. I found that museum professionals use *authenticity* primarily in the first sense, but sometimes in the second. Handler and Saxton (1988: 242) write that for all living-history practitioners, authenticity is an exact isomorphism, the second meaning; but I found at New Salem this was so only for some practitioners, some of the time. In order to achieve authenticity, museum professionals rely on historical scholarship, on such sources as archae-ological research, deeds, court documents, diaries, letters, newspaper accounts, recorded statements and memories of older settlers, and comparative evidence of other 1830s villages in the Midwest, as these sources are interpreted by scholars and experts.

There are at least two other meanings of *authenticity*. In the third sense, it means original, as opposed to a copy; but in this sense, no reproduction could be authentic, by definition. New Salem Historic Site, however, claims to have some original objects and one original building, so the aura of authenticity pervades the 1990s site, as if the lustre of the few originals had rubbed off on the reproductions. In the fourth sense, *authenticity* means duly authorized, certified, or legally valid; in this sense New Salem is authentic, as it is the authoritative reproduction of New Salem, the one legitimized by the state of Illinois. There is only one officially reconstructed New Salem, the one approved by the state government. This is a fascinating mean-ing because, in this sense, the issue of authenticity merges into the notion of author-ity. The more fundamental question to ask here is not if an object or site is authentic, but rather who has the authority to authenticate, which is a matter of power – or, to put it another way, who has the right to tell the *story* of the site. This question emerged late in the 19th century when the term *authenticity* first appeared in New Salem discourse.

After William Randolph Hearst purchased the site in 1906 and donated the land to the local Chautauqua Association, the movement to reconstruct New Salem appeared poised to achieve its objective, for a reconstructed New Salem had become a real possibility. The question emerged, What did the 1830s New Salem look like? The village had been abandoned in 1839 and, by 1906, the site was simply a barren plot of ground on the top of a hill with no remaining buildings or markers. Local historians, journalists, politicians, entrepreneurs, businesspeople, the descendants of the original settlers, and residents in the surrounding Menard County who had an interest in the reconstruction all voiced their views and their interests. Authen-ticity committees were formed. This concern with authenticity began even before any museum professionals or scholars became involved in the reconstruction. Questions surfaced, such as: Where should the buildings be located? Should they be built with one story or two? What were the details of construction? Which material objects should be in which houses?

From the late 19th century to the present, experts gave different answers to these questions, reflecting their own understandings and concerns. Even before it was given to Illinois in 1919, the reconstructed New Salem was a contested site. The layers of contestation – scholarly versus popular views of Abraham Lincoln, various descendants of the original settlers defending their family names, New Salem as a public park versus as a historic site, the Lincoln message versus craft activities, and historical versus business interests – have hovered over New Salem as the dark clouds of a thunderstorm engulf the Illinois prairie (Bruner 1993b).

Because of conflicting interests and the struggle over meaning at New Salem, the fourth sense of *authenticity* – who has the authority and the power to authen-ticate – is always present in the background, at least for museum professionals, insiders, locals, and scholars, and at times of open dissent becomes even more pro-minent. However, most tourists are not aware of authenticity in this fourth sense, unless a particular dispute over interpretation becomes a public issue. The museum staff rely on the authority of professional and local historians, but frequently the scholars do not agree. Because the state of Illinois owns the site and provides the funding, some (e.g. Wallace 1981) might expect the site to reflect the interests of the dominant classes and the elite; but the administrators at New Salem report that in practice state officials will rarely interfere, and then only when an issue has become openly politicized. The problem is not one of the establishment versus the people, but rather one of multiple competing voices, even within what may appear to be such homogeneous blocks as the scholars, the people, the locals, or the establishment. There are many different views, and the question is, Who has the authority to decide which version of history will be accepted as the correct or authentic one (Bruner 1993a)? The issue of who constructs history is a familiar one in this age of multiculturalism.

In summary thus far, we have identified four meanings of *authenticity* based on verisimilitude, genuineness, originality, and authority. Museum professionals at New Salem accept the first and strive for a New Salem that resembles the 1830s and is credible to the visitors; they occasionally lapse into the second and speak of an accurate simulation; they tend to ignore the third as New Salem is an acknowledged reproduction, except for a few originals; and they cannot avoid the fourth, the question of authority. The problem with the term *authenticity*, in the literature and in fieldwork, is that one never knows except by analysis of the context which meaning is salient in any given instance. My aim was to understand the different meanings of *authenticity* as employed in social practice rather than to accept at face value the usually unexamined dichotomy between what is and what is not authentic.

The staff at New Salem use the term *authenticity* consciously and frequently, and they want to work toward the approximation of a believable simulation, if not an accurate one, in part because their reputations and their professional identities depend on it. They are defined by others and define themselves as experts on the 1830s. We may then ask, Have the museum professionals achieved authenticity at New Salem in either the first or second senses? Is New Salem either a credible simulation or true to the 1830s original? How well do the museum professionals achieve their objectives? I begin with some trivial examples and then move to deeper levels, from the explicit to the implicit, as we penetrate the unexamined and the taken-for-granted.

The site

One day the superintendent saw a gasoline can exposed to public view in the cooper shop, and he requested that in the future it be hidden from the visitors. If the gasoline can was needed, he said, it could be retained, but it should not be visible. On another occasion, one of the interpreters constructed a flower bed outside the Sam Hill house, as after the construction of a new road there was a patch of ground that got muddy in the rain and the tourists tracked mud into the house. When the assistant superintendent saw the flowers she said they looked 'ridiculous' and were not 'authentic', as there were no flower beds in the 1830s, and she promptly replaced the flowers with less obtrusive wood shavings. Although one could raise questions about the shavings, in these two cases items considered inappropriate, a gasoline can and flowers, were simply replaced or removed from the tourist view. Authenticity in either the first sense of believable or the second as genuine cannot be taken for granted; there is backsliding, and the site needs constant monitoring and editing.

At New Salem there are many conscious compromises to authenticity. Some are necessary for the creation or longevity of the site, while others (most) are designed to make the visitors' experience more enjoyable. These compromises are the little white lies of historical reconstruction. They make the reconstructed New Salem better than the original, at least for contemporary tourists.

Here are examples. Gutters are constructed on the log cabins to channel rainwater. In the past the animals would roam free, but now they are fenced in so that animal waste is not scattered throughout the village and so that visitors are protected. There are fences, made to look as if they were original, that are designed to direct the flow of tourist traffic. Unobtrusive restrooms have been built with drinking fountains on the side, a convenience not found in the 1830s. Along the path, benches have been erected so that the visitors may sit and rest. The road is now paved so that when it rains the tourists do not have to walk in the mud. The schoolhouse in the 1830s was located 1.5 miles away from the village, but it has been reconstructed inside the compound for the convenience of the visitors. The carding mill is supposedly operated entirely by animal power, by oxen moving in a circle, but it has a hidden motor. The Rutledge Tavern and the first Berry-Lincoln Store have electric heaters placed so that they cannot be seen by the tourists. The caulking between the logs on the sides of the cabins is now made of cement, but in the 1830s cement had not yet been invented. There is a disguised security gate around the entire village to protect against vandalism, as well as a security system and alarm boxes, which the tourists never see. At one time New Salem provided self-guided commentaries from recording devices, which have since been removed; but there are still small wires sticking out from some of the houses. As the houses are old, they periodically need renovation. In one case over 50 percent of a house was renovated, and the state building codes required that a ramp be built for persons who use wheelchairs. A flagstone ramp was constructed as required, but is kept covered up with leaves and dirt so that it will be less conspicuous. At New Salem the lawn is now mowed. I asked the superintendent if they mowed in the 1830s and he replied that they probably did not, adding that if you do not mow your lawn in central Illinois now you are not regarded as a good citizen. Many more such examples of conscious compromises to a believable or precise replication could be presented, but more subtle factors are at work, to which I now turn.

The houses at the 1990s New Salem represent the original 1830s houses, thus they are weathered to look old so that they will be more credible, as the original houses existed 160 years ago. The 1830s houses, however, actually looked much newer, as the village of New Salem was founded in 1829 and abandoned by 1839, a period of only ten years. The 1830s houses were not occupied long enough to look aged, hence the 1990s houses at New Salem appear older than the originals. This example shows that there is a tension between the first and second meanings of *authenticity*. To the degree that the houses look old and weathered, they are more credible to the visitors but are a less accurate reproduction of the 1830s. The houses also look more respectable than those of the original village, as all are substantial log houses and there are no cabins, shacks, or flimsy structures, which may well have existed in the 1830s village. Thus 1990s New Salem presents a more suburban version of history, and this is built into the construction of the houses and the site. Again, it makes the site more believable to 1990s tourists, but less true to the 1830s original.

In the 1830s, over the ten years of occupation, the surrounding trees were cut down to obtain lumber for building and for firewood; but in the reconstructed New Salem, the trees have been allowed to grow and hence the foliage is more dense and lush. In the 1990s the thick stand of trees at New Salem gives the village a much more rural and rustic appearance than in the 1830s.

The interpreters are in period dress, but they have a special problem with eyeglasses. The volunteers and the staff do wear their own eyeglasses, which they need, but some have bought small round 'granny' glasses, as these are somehow thought to look more 'old-fashioned'. The costumes in general present a dilemma, as no one really knows about the dress of the original occupants of New Salem. There are no specific records about attire.

A June 19, 1936, newspaper account from the *Peoria Journal* reads as follows: 'Four guides at the village wear jeans jackets and trousers, linsey-woolsey shirts and leather boots as part of their costumes, to portray the role of the original residents'. Although jeans, wool shirts, and boots may have been an acceptable version of 1830s dress for the 1930s, this is no longer the case in the 1990s, as most students and many visitors themselves now wear jeans. There has to be some difference in attire to distinguish between the tourists and those who play the parts of the original residents. What was proper 1830s dress in 1930 is not proper in 1990; in terms of the concepts developed in this essay, what was considered authentic in the sense of credible in one historical era has changed in the course of 60 years. Standards change, and what any era considers authentic moves in and out of consciousness. The museum professionals at historic sites realize that they need to be aware of the public's sense of what is believable – a complex problem, because there are many publics; because some persons are more aware, knowledgeable, or sceptical than others; and because the professional's and the public's view are not independent, for each shapes and is shaped by the other, in dialogic interplay.

When I initiated research at New Salem in 1988, there was little discussion of the interpreters' costumes; but this changed during the summer of 1990. At that time some of the staff made the criticism that too many interpreters dressed the same, that all the costumes seemed to be derived from the television series 'Little House on the Prairie', that everyone wore work clothing, and that they all looked like farmers. As the accuracy of the costumes was called into question, an internal dialogue began among the staff about authenticity. As Lionel Trilling (1972) notes, authenticity becomes an issue only after a doubt arises.

The debate about clothing reminded me somewhat of Victor Turner's concept of social drama, and illustrates the constructivist process at work in showing how the culture at New Salem is continually reinvented. At first the style of clothing was simply accepted and was neither examined nor discussed. The critique of clothing practices emerged as an abrupt breach, as a rupture of accepted custom, leading to a period of doubt, wide discussion, and a mounting crisis. Alternative clothing styles were explored, and experts were consulted. New dress patterns were devised and the issue was at least temporarily resolved. The dispute was less about what genuinely existed in the 1830s New Salem, which no one knew, and more about the issue of credibility, about what was currently acceptable 1830s dress. In all probability, the issue will arise again in the future and the cycle will be repeated.

During the discussion about clothing, someone made the point that costumes should reflect class distinctions. It was argued that as the residents of the Sam Hill house were rich, as Hill was a successful merchant, and those of the Burner house were poor, they should have different costumes. Current views of class disparities were projected into the past. Thus the interpreters at the Hill house, for example, were to wear upper-class clothing, and those at the poorer Burner house were to wear working-class dress – except for Mrs Hinsley. She was a volunteer interpreter assigned to the Caliher house, known to be a poor 1830s family. In the new vision, Mrs Hinsley was expected to wear poor work clothing; but she was interested in clothing, had nice outfits of her own design, wanted to dress well, and wore what was considered to be inappropriate 'rich' clothing. Mrs Hinsley was a point of resistance, and no one could change her. She expressed her own individuality in dress.

Authenticity is a struggle. From the point of view of the professional staff, who have the goal of making New Salem a believable or genuine reproduction, one constantly has to be aware of possible inauthenticities. But there are even more fundamental problems, as the inauthentic is built into the fabric of New Salem, into the details of construction, and into the social practices of production of the site.

Each log house is named for its most prominent resident, and when the visitors come, the interpreters tell the story of the occupants of that particular house. For example, there are the Rutledge Tavern, the Onstot house, the Hill house, and so forth. Many of the buildings in the 1830s, however, were occupied by a series of families, and the Onstots lived in three different residences, as did others. The first Berry-Lincoln store was only a store for a few months, but because of the importance of Abraham Lincoln and the widely known story that he was a shopkeeper, the Berry-Lincoln name has been given to the residence. The consequence is to fix history, to solidify and to simplify it.

Although the focus is on a single resident family for each dwelling, the story told about that particular family is one of transitoriness, of when the family arrived, what they did at New Salem, and when they departed. Although these narrative histories are not necessarily inaccurate, they would not appear to be the stories that 1830s residents would have told about themselves, at least not in their finality, for at the end of each story the family leaves the community, providing an absolute ending. Each narrative contains a complete cycle of transition, beginning with when the family came and ending when it left. Clearly, such stories could not have been told until at least 1839, after the village had been abandoned. This retrospective perspective serves to reinforce the master narrative of New Salem, the transition of Abraham Lincoln from common labourer to educated lawyer and politician, in preparation for his life work of leading the nation in the Civil War and saving the Union. If New Salem is seen as a site of transformation for its hero Abraham Lincoln, then the individual stories of each family replicate the larger narrative structure.

Not only is each house given the name of only one former resident, but in each house there is only a single interpreter, a concession to a limited state budget. The visitors move from house to house, serially, and in each house the interpreter provides information about one or another aspect of life in the 1830s. There are no groups talking and visiting together, no scenes of surrounding farmers coming with their families to town to sell grain, to repair tools, to see a doctor, to buy supplies, or to pick up their mail at the post office. New Salem is thus presented as a village of autonomous homes and isolated individuals, without any sense of group or community activity, with the consequence that the 1990s representation provides a distorted view of 1830s life. There are special events at New Salem, like craft or quilt shows, but even then the visitors move serially through the display booths, visiting them in sequence. The result is that 1830s life is devoid of its group character and is presented much more like 1990s suburban life in America, where neighbours live in their individual homes and are socially isolated from one another.

Taylor and Johnson (1993) note that New Salem does not have any interpreters representing the frontier toughs, 'Clary's Grove boys', and the carousing, gambling, cockfighting, hard drinkers who were part of 1830s pioneer life in New Salem. The roughnecks have been left out of history. This concession to middle-class sensibilities is similar to Colonial Williamsburg ignoring blacks, the 'other half' of Williamsburg life (Gable et al. 1992), at least until recently. There is, however, no current movement to represent the frontier roughnecks in New Salem.

New Salem is an outdoor museum, and like all museums, the way it is apprehended by the visitors is primarily visual. The tourists do hear about the 1830s from the interpreters inside the homes, generally in the form of oral narratives, and there is conversation, but as the tourists walk about the village their mode of perception is mainly visual. Basically, they look. They almost never hear two or more interpreters talking to each other. However, the 1830s may well have been more of an oral than a visual culture, characterized by the exchange of information, by talking, gossiping, and telling. As this dimension is less dominant in the 1990s New Salem, the way the village was experienced and the sensory mode through which it was perceived in the two eras may be fundamentally different.

As we can see, it is impossible to make a historic reproduction accurate in every regard, especially with limited knowledge and resources; the best one can hope for is a representation that the tourists are willing to accept. Even if the log houses of the 1990s prairie village were an exact physical replica of the original 1830s, in every detail, the question could then be raised: How does one make authentic the sensory mode of experiencing and indeed the very meaning of the site?

There are truly momentous differences between the 1830s and the 1990s. One difference, almost too obvious to mention, is that most persons in the 1990s New Salem are tourists, while in the 1830s there were no tourists, although there were visitors, travellers, and traders. Also, the 1990s New Salem is an idealized community that leaves out the conflict, tension, and dirt of the 1830s. New Salem in the 1990s is presented as an idyllic, peaceful, harmonious village.

The craft activities in New Salem in the 1830s were considered to be the most modern and advanced technology of the time, designed for efficiency and survival, but in the 1990s the same handicrafts represent nostalgia for an earlier period when material culture was made by hand and was locally produced. The meaning of *craft* was completely different in the two historical eras. In the 1830s New Salem was a commercial trading centre, and when Lincoln migrated there he probably thought he was moving to an urban centre; but in the 1990s New Salem, for many, is rural, isolated, self-contained, rustic, and folk-like (cf. Whisnant 1983), in opposition to the commercialism, materialism, and fragmentation of 20th-century America.

The 1990s New Salem features Abraham Lincoln – indeed, the site is called Lincoln's New Salem, or as an official in the state tourist bureau told me, 'What we sell in Illinois is Lincoln' – but Abraham Lincoln was not that prominent in the 1830s village. Lincoln left New Salem in 1837, and by 1839 the village was abandoned when the county seat was moved to another location. Thereafter, from 1839 to 1860, New Salem was unmarked and effectively out of history. Then, in 1860, when Lincoln became the presidential nominee of the Republican party, campaign biographers and politicians constructed the political image of Abraham Lincoln as Honest Abe, the rail-splitter, the common man of the prairies, the man of humble origin who stood in opposition to the Eastern establishment. In fact, in 1860 Lincoln was a corporate lawyer in Springfield, a man of wealth and power, who had married into a socially prominent family. After Lincoln was assassinated in 1865, he became the martyred leader, the Christ figure who gave his life so the nation might live, who was sacrificed for the Union. Thus arose the mythic Lincoln, the great American folk hero, celebrated in novels, songs, poems, plays, biographies, and textbooks, known by every schoolchild in America.

In 1897 local residents formed a Chautauqua Association to reconstruct New Salem, 60 years after Lincoln had left the village. The interest in restoration arose after most of the original settlers who had known Lincoln had passed away. Possibly the movement to restore the site was an effort to preserve the memory of a way of life fast disappearing, as the old pioneers who had first settled the land were dying off. The oral traditions about Abraham Lincoln were recorded in a number of books (Herndon and Weik 1889; Onstot 1902; and Reep 1927) long after Lincoln had lived in New Salem. The Old Salem Lincoln League gathered the elders together to tell their stories in 1918, after the village of New Salem had already been abandoned for 79 years. The present-day New Salem was reconstructed during the 1930s, a full century after the old village had been occupied. The point is that the present-day restoration of the 1830s New Salem attempts to reconstruct the historical and the mythic Lincoln, but this history and myth did not yet exist in the 1830s, for it emerged only after 1865, a disjuncture illustrative of the many built-in paradoxes, ambiguities, and ironies at this historic site.

Two stores

The challenge in this anthropological analysis is to transcend the opposition between the authentic and the inauthentic. In considering the 1830s and the 1990s, there is no need to prioritize, to define one as better than, more real than, more basic than, or more authentic than the other, nor does such a qualitative comparison typically occur to visitors at historic sites. There is the 1830s New Salem and there is the 1990s New Salem. The 1830s village was historically prior, it came first, whereas the 1990s New Salem came later and conforms to 1990s sensibilities, allowing visitors to attribute their own meanings to the site. The point may seem obvious, but the implications will be developed by examining two New Salem stores.

The first Berry-Lincoln store, where Lincoln worked in the 1830s as a store-keeper, has been reconstructed as a store selling souvenirs to the visitors, unlike other reconstructed stores in New Salem such as the second Berry-Lincoln, the Hill-McNeil, and Offutt's, which do not have items for sale. The first Berry-Lincoln store is operated by the New Salem Lincoln League for profit, with volunteer sales-persons in period dress. It is quite successful and the proceeds are used to support the activities of the site. When the store first began, the New Salem Lincoln League formed an authenticity committee to check on each item sold; but these early efforts met with limited success. They eventually hired a professional manager for the store who had an eye on the bottom line. The new manager selected inventory that sold, and the authenticity committee no longer met.

It will be instructive to examine the inventory of the Berry-Lincoln store. It has become a craft shop, with many handmade items, including pottery, baskets, quilts, rugs, stuffed dolls, brooms, large wooden ladles, copper pots, products of the carding shop such as small barrels and tubs, pattern books of early American clothing, coonskin caps, and candles. I was told that many tourists come asking for objects made in the craft shops of New Salem, but my observation was that they did a brisk business in all items, and that the shop was frequently crowded with tourists. When I asked the volunteer if their inventory was representative of the items sold in the 1830s store, the answer was that they want everything they sell to be 'authentic to the era', which means that it could have been made in the 1830s. This is authenticity in the sense of credibility. When I inquired if tourists ask for authentic items, the reply was that the question rarely comes up.

The setting is a log cabin; the storekeepers are dressed in 1830s clothing; the objects sold look 'old fashioned', 'country', or 'folk'; and my interviews suggest that the tourists accept it as such. To the degree that the museum professionals are successful in adhering to the goal of creating a credible reproduction based on verisimil-itude – that is, a historic site believable to the visitors – the probability will be greater that the tourists will be satisfied with what they find at the site. It is import-ant to note that the discussion has turned from the museum professionals to the tourists. It would be a mistake to assume that the distinctions made in this essay about the concept of authenticity used by museum professionals would necessarily be the same distinctions made by the tourists. Museum professionals are the pro-ducers, whereas tourists are the consumers, and they do not approach the site in the same way. Tourists know, of course, that the objects they purchase are not from the 1830s and that many are not even reproductions of 1830s objects, and they may realize that no store in the 1830s ever had an inventory like the present first Berry-Lincoln store. They are buying souvenirs, mementos of their trip to New Salem, gifts for those back home, and not necessarily 'authentic' objects or even objects that are 'authentic reproductions'.

We have no direct knowledge of the inventory of the first Berry-Lincoln store in the 1830s at New Salem, as no records have been found; but we do know that other stores in the prairies at that time period stocked items such as varnish, shellac, paint ingredients, dyes, spectacles, spices, knives, axes, tools, pens and ink, hardware, thread, buttons, needles, jewellery, liquor, china, books, textiles, hats, window glass, tin pans, nails, gunpowder, door locks and hinges, and foodstuffs such as coffee, tea, sugar, flour, rice, cheese, and molasses (Atherton 1939; Kwedar *et al.* 1980). There were fashionable goods from Eastern wholesalers, manufactured items, and products from Europe. Tourists in the 1990s are not interested in these 1830s items, or if they are, the items are better purchased elsewhere than in the New Salem craft shop.

Given the inventories of the 1830s and the 1990s stores, we can see clearly that each of the first Berry-Lincoln stores stocked items that met the needs of their respective clientele. The older store sold items necessary for the survival of the 1830s prairie pioneers, while the contemporary store with its handmade crafts sells souvenirs to the 1990s tourists. Each store is meaningful in its era, and I do not see what we gain by privileging one at the expense of the other. It is the post-modernists and the social theorists who make judgmental evaluations, as I will show in the next section.

Discussion

My argument about authenticity and reproductions is different than the postmod-ern one presented by Baudrillard and Eco and is also different than the position taken by such theorists as MacCannell (1976) (not MacCannell 1992) and Handler (Handler (1986) and Handler and Saxton (1988), not of Handler and Linnekin (1984) and not of the Colonial Williamsburg research conducted with Eric Gable) in their writings about tourism, authenticity, and historic sites. I begin by framing my argu-ment in terms of the postmodernist vision, then turn to MacCannell and Handler, then develop some of the implications of my constructivist perspective.

For Baudrillard and Eco, the simulacrum becomes the true, the copy becomes the original or even better than the original. In postmodern hyperreality, all we have is pure simulacra, for origins are lost, or are not recoverable, or never existed, or there was no original reality. As Baudrillard (1983: 48) says, 'it is always a false problem to want to restore the truth beneath the simulacrum'. This is the post-modern condition, one specific to our electronic era, argues Baudrillard. I argue that this is the human condition, for all cultures continually invent and reinvent themselves. In the 1830s during the development of New Salem, there was a prior image, the cultural knowledge of how other prairie villages in central Illinois were built in the 1820s. We could say that the 1830s village was a copy based on a model of 1820s villages, adapted to the conditions of the 1830s, modified in accordance with the particular situation of the New Salem locality, and subject to whatever creative modifications were devised by the New Salem residents. We all enter society in the middle, and culture is always in process (Turner and Bruner 1986).

This perspective, which I have been advocating for the past few decades (e.g. Bruner 1973, 1984, 1993a), has sometimes been known as the constructivist position. Recently it has been called the 'invention of culture' tradition, and has produced important studies (e.g. Babcock 1990; Borofsky 1987; Handler and Linnekin 1984; Hanson 1989; Hobsbawn and Ranger 1983; Hymes 1975; Wagner 1975). But the roots of the perspective are really very old, going back to Wilhelm Dilthey,

John Dewey, George Herbert Mead, and the American pragmatists; to the writings in the 1920s of the great Russian literary scholar Mikhail Bakhtin; to Roland Barthes and the poststructuralists; and to performance theory (cf. Bauman 1992).

The constructivist view that culture is emergent, always alive and in process is widely accepted today (Lavie *et al.* 1993). This is not the place to present an intellectual history of the perspective or to discuss its variations, but what all proponents have in common is the view that the meaning of the text is not inherent in the text but emerges from how people read or experience the text. All share the view that socialization is at best an imperfect mechanism for cultural transmission, and that each new performance or expression of cultural heritage is a copy in that it always looks back to a prior performance, but each is also an original in that it adapts to new circumstances and conditions. As Handler and Linnekin (1984: 288) argue, 'All genuine traditions are spurious . . . all spurious traditions are genuine'; or as Geertz (1986: 380) says, 'It is the copying that originates'. We could say that the 1990s New Salem is an original because each reproduction in the process of emerging constructs its own original – or better yet, as I advocate in this essay, we could just abandon the distinction.

In our era both the 1830s New Salem and the 1990s New Salem are continually being constructed in an endless process of production and reproduction. All we have of the 1830s now are a few artefacts, archaeological remains, old records, stories, and mental models of the old prairie village, models that may exist vividly in the imagination of the public and the historians, but that are ever-changing. We are continually reconstructing the 1830s New Salem, rewriting history to fit the era, just as we rewrite Abraham Lincoln (e.g. Basler 1935). The 20th-century New Salem has changed many times and has been totally rebuilt at least twice. An earlier effort to restore the village in 1918 was razed to the ground in 1932, and a second restoration occurred in stages during the 1930s. Periodically, the log houses receive additions and modifications, as do the interiors. In the 1990s, a new visitor and orientation centre was opened, the location of the store was moved, and a restaurant at the entrance to the park was built.

It is not just that the 1990s and the 1830s New Salem are always in process of construction, but that the 1990s New Salem influences our conception of the 1830s. In other words, what is called the copy changes our view of the original, a problem that haunts Taussig's (1993) book on *Mimesis and Alterity*. Academic historians would agree that the 1990s New Salem, by its very presence, overemphasizes the importance of New Salem on the early Abraham Lincoln, to the neglect of the formative influences of the earlier Indiana years and the time spent at Vandalia. Lincoln was 22 years old when he arrived at New Salem, already an adult, and his truly formative adolescent years were spent elsewhere. The historian Mark E. Neeley (1982: 222) suggests that New Salem as a tourist attraction may have served to inflate the importance of the New Salem years in Lincoln biographies. Thus a 20th-century touristic representation may have distorted the discourse of professional historians, and hence our understanding of the 1830s.

In their work on authenticity, hyperreality, and the simulacrum, Baudrillard, Eco, MacCannell, and Handler all are making a critique of the culture of the West and of America. MacCannell (1976) makes the claim that tourists are so dissatisfied with their own culture that they seek authentic experiences elsewhere. MacCannell's work was rooted in the 1960s and repeated the old 19th-century critique of Western civilization, of alienated man in search of self.

Handler and Saxton (1988: 243) have a similar position. They write, 'For living-history practitioners, as for many of us, everyday experience is "unreal", or inauthentic, hence alienating. Practitioners seek to regain an authentic world, and to realize themselves in the process, through simulation of historical worlds'. For MacCannell, tourists seek authenticity in another place, in a tourist site; for Handler and Saxton, it is in another time period, in a historic site. Authenticity for Handler (1986) has to do with our 'true, self', and for him and Saxton (1988: 243), 'an authentic experience . . . is one in which individuals feel themselves to be in touch both with a "real" world and with their "real" selves', which assumes that our every-day worlds are not experienced as real or authentic. In the work of MacCannell and Handler and Saxton, the quest for authenticity is doomed, or as they point out, it is a failed quest, because the very search destroys the authenticity of the object, which before the quest was presumed to be pristine and untouched. These authors thus assume an original pure state, an authentic culture in the third sense, like the ethnographic present, before contact. It is as if history begins with tourism, which then pollutes the world.

MacCannell and Handler say that tourists are looking for authenticity, but it may be these contemporary intellectuals who are the ones looking for authenticity, and who have projected onto the tourists their own view of themselves. The museum professionals who say that a historic site is an authentic reproduction use *authenticity* in the first and second senses, not the third. The question is, who are the ones seeking authenticity? Trilling's (1972) insight again is that authenticity emerges to consciousness when a doubt arises. Those in the early 20th century in central Illinois who found themselves in the predicament of having to reconstruct an 1830s New Salem without adequate knowledge became concerned with authenticity. In our era, anthropologists, museum curators, historians, serious collectors, and art dealers as well as some tourists acknowledge that they are seeking authenticity. I agree with Appadurai (1986: 44—45) that authenticity today is becoming a matter of the politics of connoisseurship, of the political economy of taste, and of status discrimination; beyond that, I would claim, it is a matter of power, of who has the right to authenticate.

The concept of authority serves as a corrective to misuses of the term *authenticity*, because in raising the issue of who authenticates, the nature of the discussion is changed. No longer is authenticity a property inherent in an object, forever fixed in time; it is seen as a struggle, a social process, in which competing interests argue for their own interpretation of history. Culture is seen as contested, emergent, and constructed, and agency and desire become part of the discourse. When actors use the term *authenticity*, ethnographers may then ask what segment of society has raised a doubt, what is no longer taken for granted, what are the societal struggles, and what are the cultural issues at work. These are ethnographic questions, empirical questions, requiring investigation and research. Grand theorizing gives way to ethnography.

There are two fundamental problems with the essentialist vocabulary of originals and copies, of the authentic and the inauthentic. One is that, despite claims to the contrary, there frequently is an implicit original, an authenticity in the third sense. For the postmodernists the original is Europe and America is a satellite. Baudrillard (1988: 5, 10, 28, 7) says that he knew all about America 'when I was still in Paris', claims that America 'was born of a rift with the Old World', asserts that 'the truth of America can only be seen by a European', and contends that America is 'the only remaining primitive society'. If for the postmodernists the original is civilized Europe, then for MacCannell and Handler the original is before alienation, the pure state, located elsewhere, around the bend, beneath or behind the touristic or the historic site.

The second problem with essentialist vocabulary is that there is a built-in judgmental bias that regards one side of the dichotomy as better so that the other side becomes denigrated. It usually implies that originals are better than copies or, as the postmodernists Baudrillard and Eco say, the exact opposite, which is still the inverse of the same binary logic. The consequence of the project of Baudrillard, Eco, and MacCannell (and Boorstin 1961) is to diminish historical sites like New Salem because they are seen as inauthentic, as pseudo, as surface, as plastic, as simulacra, as hyperreality, even as fakes. It also implies that copies are based on originals, but from a constructivist perspective, the process may not be that simple. Sometimes an object is constructed in the contemporary era and then an older form is somehow 'discovered' as a hypothetical original to add historic depth and legitimacy. To label one form a copy highlights the features that are similar to the supposed original, and may not adequately take account of the differences or of the variations in the societal context within which the originals and the copies were produced. The vocabulary of origins and reproductions and of the authenticity and the inauthentic may not adequately acknowledge that both are constructions of the present.

Conclusion

Let us turn to my speculations about the tourists. If the tourists are not buying into scripts of postmodern hyperreality or authenticity, then what are they buying at New Salem? In their writings, Baudrillard and Eco make grand generalizations about America, without nuances. They use homogenizing monolithic language when they write about Americans, and they do not differentiate among the many kinds of tourists of historic sites. They fail to recognize the constructed nature of the meanings of historic sites.

In the view argued here, the meanings of New Salem Historic Site for tourists are constructed in the performance of the site, as visitors move through the village and as they interact with the interpreters. Experiencing the site gives rise to meanings that might not have been predicted before the visit, so that the site in this sense is generative. It is not that all meaning is individual and idiosyncratic — for of course there are cultural patterns, as I will demonstrate but meanings are generated in a social context. An ethnographic perspective is needed to examine the social organizational settings within which New Salem is experienced. Baudrillard and Eco reflect none of this complexity.

For example, many visitors to theme parks come as family groups, not as isolated individuals, so that the family becomes the basic social unit for processing the touristic experience, and as such the visit frequently assumes an educational focus (Willis 1993). At New Salem, especially when school is in session, busloads of schoolchildren arrive with their teachers on class outings to the site. One day there were forty different bus loads of schoolchildren at New Salem, and the educational function was quite explicit. Another time a group of immigrants from Chicago, taking their citizenship training class, spent a hurried two hours rushing through New Salem. In these cases, parents or teachers or immigration officials were explaining the meaning of New Salem, emphasizing the role of Abraham Lincoln in American history. The recipients of the knowledge had come to New Salem as children, students, or learners.

I have shared the New Salem experience with a troop of 7- and 8-year-old girl scouts, on an all-day outing with their scout leader, supported by a few parent volunteers, and the main attraction appeared to be cooking beef stew for lunch on a wood-burning fireplace. It seemed to take hours for the stew to cook, everyone was hungry, and the conversation centred on the life of the early pioneers who settled in central Illinois, and particularly on the difficulty of that life. This was a recurrent theme among many of the visitors.

One farmer from Illinois entered a log house where one of the interpreters was spinning wool. The farmer stated that when he was a child there was a spinning wheel in his home very similar to the one at New Salem, and he recalled images of his grandmother sitting at the spinning wheel telling stories about her early life on a family farm in the prairies. That experience of New Salem was very evocative, but many tourists make associations between what they see at the site and their personal lives. The meaning of New Salem is emergent in the social context of the visitor's experience of the site.

A judge told me how he loved to come to New Salem very early on snowy winter mornings so that he could walk, in solitude, on the same hallowed ground that Abraham Lincoln had walked. The judge had practiced law in the same district as had Lincoln. He had a bronze bust of Lincoln in his office, he had played the part of Lincoln in local theatrical productions, he was tall and thin, he physically resembled Lincoln, and clearly he had made a personally meaningful identification.

Visitors to New Salem include Lincoln buffs, antique collectors, retired people making their way through the theme parks of America, sophisticated urbanites from Chicago on a visit to the 'rural' hinterlands, and university professors entertaining foreign visitors. It is indeed a varied audience. Tourists are not monolithic, and neither is the meaning of the site. There are many New Salems (Bodnar 1992). Tourists construct a past that is meaningful to them and that relates to their lives and experiences, and this is the way that meanings are constructed at historic sites.

What encourages the local production of meaning is the format of dialogic interaction between the interpreter and small groups of tourists who move from house to house. As the interpreter tells about Lincoln or about the 1830s village or about the history of the original residents, the tourists have an opportunity to ask questions and to interact with the interpreter. Although the tourists have received the main message of the museum professionals, of New Salem as the site of Lincoln's transformation presented to them in the orientation video and the brochures, their relationship to the interpreters has a more personal and immediate quality. The interpreters, too, have received the official messages of the site, primarily in training sessions and in manuals, but they frequently depart from the official scripts and move off in their own directions. The tourists, as we have seen, bring their own concerns and interests to the interaction. The result is a very open format, more like a discussion than a lecture, one that allows for improvisation and that facilitates the constructivist process.

I found many instances of a playful quality to the interaction, whereas much of the literature emphasizes the seriousness of the tourist quest and experience. The interaction between interpretive guides and visitors at historic sites may be oriented to enjoyment as much as to discovery of historic fact. For example, one time on the reconstructed Mayflower in Plymouth, which does first-person interpretation, I saw a woman guide in period dress. She told me that it was a long and arduous journey across the ocean, that she had lost her husband on the voyage, and that she felt so lonely in this vast new country. Then she looked me straight in the eye and winked, and I could not tell if it was a 1620s wink or a 1990s wink. On numerous occasions, interpreters at New Salem will engage in light banter and joking behaviour with the visitors. A woman storekeeper in period dress will say to the assembled tourists, 'What have you come to purchase today?' Such an inquiry, an example of slippage from third to first person, will lead to humorous conversation about the goods sold in the store or the 1830s prices, noting how low they were compared to today's prices. In these settings, many tourists play with time frames and experiment with alternative realities; it is a good way to learn about the past. Visits to historic sites have a strong entertainment and playful quality.

In the course of my fieldwork, I often remained in one location and noted how the topic of conversation changed with the arrival of each new group of tourists. Also, I followed some groups from house to house, and noted how the discourse and even the roles changed as persons moved through the village. The roles of tourist and interpreter are not fixed. A mother who had been a tourist began to explain New Salem to her children, and at that point she was in a sense becoming an interpreter, switching roles. Subjectivities and motives change, even within one individual, even during the course of a single visit.

Although individuals construct their own meanings, I found there were clearly recurring patterns and generalizations that emerged. In reporting on what I learned about the meaning of New Salem to the tourists, I acknowledge that my findings are hypotheses and that they are my own constructions of meaning, open to further study and testing. In addition to learning about the past and enjoying the historic site, I found the following three major themes.

First, some tourists to New Salem are consuming nostalgia, the hand-crafted and the locally produced, in opposition to machine age materialism. Many tourists to New Salem view the village with a sense of nostalgia for a vanished past, for an imagined time when life was more natural, purer, and simpler – in effect a Midwest equivalent of the Garden of Eden. Many see in New Salem the image of early pioneer life in the prairies, a return to the first settlers in central Illinois. For these tourists, New Salem is an Illinois origin myth, a prairie pastoral.

Second, as visitors walk through the village they are also buying the idea of progress, of how far we have advanced, for the one question that the interpreters repeatedly ask is: Would you like to live back in the 1830s, when life was so hard?

The answer is invariably no. The theme of progress is prominent in New Salem discourse. The emphasis is on the contrast between the hardships of the 1830s and the conveniences of the 1990s. The two themes mentioned thus far are not in conflict, because where the first focuses on the simplicity of life in the past, the second focuses on the severity of that life. In the first, technology is seen as evil; in the second, as progress. Many visitors hold both views simultaneously. In their imagination, they yearn for a simpler life. But they are not alienated beings; they want modern 1990s conveniences, and they would not be willing to give up their 1990s lives in exchange for the 1830s.

Finally, many tourists are also buying a commemoration of traditional America, of honest values, good neighbours, hard work, virtue and generosity, the success ideology, and the sense of community in small-town America. The tourists are seeking in New Salem a discourse that enables them to better reflect on their lives in the 1990s. New Salem and similar sites enact an ideology, recreate an origin myth, keep history alive, attach tourists to a mythical collective consciousness, and commodify the past. The particular pasts that tourists create/imagine at historic sites may never have existed. But historic sites like New Salem do provide visitors with the raw material (experiences) to construct a sense of identity, meaning, attachment, and stability. In the America of Baudrillard and Eco, copies refer only to themselves, no origin myths pertain, and no collective reality is invoked. This, however, is an America of their own imaginations and not an America of everyday practices.

Following Zipes (1979), New Salem can be read in two different ways. There is the pessimistic view (Haraway 1984; Wallace 1981), which sees museums and historic sites as exploitative, as strengthening the ruling classes, as deceit, as false consciousness, as manipulation of the imagination of already alienated beings. Or there is the optimistic view, which focuses on the utopian potential for transformation, offers hope for a better life, says people can take charge of their lives and change themselves and their culture. The story of Abraham Lincoln is, as Zipes writes (1979: 119), the 'folk tale motif of the swineherd who becomes a prince', but there is revolutionary potential in this fantasy, for it can be heroic and can lead to greater – not less – contact with social life. In this respect, fantasy, art, and historic sites have a similar function.

In postmodern writings, contemporary American tourist attractions tend to be described in ways that replicate elements of the theory of postmodernism, emphasizing the inauthentic constructed nature of the sites, their appeal to the masses, their imitation of the past, and their efforts to present a perfected version of themselves. This is a narrow and distorted view that fails to account for the popularity and frequency of such sites on the American landscape, that begs the question of the meaning of the sites to the participants, and that by its denigration of popular American culture and mass tourist sites imposes an elitist politics blind to its own assumptions.

References

Anderson, J. (1984) *Time Machines: The World of Living History*, Nashville, TN: American Association for State and Local History.

Appadurai, A. (ed.) (1986) *The Social Life of Things: Commodities in Cultural Perspective*, Cambridge: Cambridge University Press.

Atherton, L.B. (1939) *The Pioneer Merchant in Mid-America*, New York: Da Capo Press.

Babcock, B. (1990) 'By way of introduction', Inventing the Southwest, Special Issue, *Journal of the Southwest*, 32(4): 383–437.

Basler, R.P. (1935) *The Lincoln Legend: A Study of Changing Conceptions*, Boston: Houghton Mifflin.

Baudrillard, J. (1983) *Simulations*, New York: Semiotext(e).

Baudrillard, J. (1988) *America*, London: Verso.

Bauman, R. (1992) 'Performance', in Bauman, R. (ed.) *Folklore, Cultural Performances, and Popular Entertainments*, New York: Oxford University Press, 41–9.

Bodnar, J. (1992) *Remaking America: Public Memory, Commemoration, and Patriotism in the Twentieth Century*, Princeton, NJ: Princeton University Press.

Boorstin, D. (1961) *The Image: A Guide to Pseudo-Events in America*, New York: Harper Row.

Borofsky, R. (1987) *Making History: Pukapukan and Anthropological Constructions of Knowledge*, Cambridge: Cambridge University Press.

Bruner, E.M. (1973) 'The missing tins of chicken: a symbolic interactionist approach to culture change', *Ethos*, 1(2): 219–38.

Bruner, E.M. (ed.) (1984) *Text, Play and Story: The Construction and Reconstruction of Self and Society*, 1983 Proceedings of the American Ethnological Society. Washington, DC: American Anthropological Association.

Bruner, E.M. (1993a) 'Epilogue: creative persona and the problem of authenticity', in Lavie, S., Narayan, K. and Rosaldo, R. (eds) *Creativity/Anthropology*, Ithaca, NY: Cornell University Press.

Bruner, E.M. (1993b) 'New Salem as a contested site', *Museum Anthropology*, 17(3): 14–25.

Gable, E., Handler, R. and Lawson, A. (1992) 'On the uses of relativism: fact, conjecture, and Black and White histories at Colonial Williamsburg', *American Ethnologist*, 19(4): 791–805.

Geertz, C. (1986) 'Making experience, authoring selves', in Turner, V. and Bruner, E.M. (eds) *The Anthropology of Experience*, Urbana, IL: University of Illinois Press, 373–80.

Handler, R. (1986) 'Authenticity', *Anthropology Today*, 2(1): 2–4.

Handler, R. and Linnekin, J. (1984) 'Tradition, genuine or spurious', *Journal of American Folklore*, 97(385): 273–90.

Handler, R. and Saxton, W. (1988) 'Dyssimulation: reflexivity, narrative, and the quest for authenticity in "Living"', *Cultural Anthropology*, 3(3): 242–60.

Hanson, A. (1989) 'The making of the Maori: cultural invention and its logic', *American Anthropologist*, 91(4): 890–902.

Haraway, D. (1984) 'Teddy bear patriarchy: taxidermy in the Garden of Eden, New York City, 1908–1936', *Social Text*, 11: 20–64.

Herndon, W.H. and Weik, J.W. (1889) *Herndon's Lincoln: The Story of a Great Life*, Chicago: Belford, Clarke.

Hobsbawn, E. and Ranger, T. (eds) (1983) *The Invention of Tradition*, Cambridge: Cambridge University Press.

Huxtable, A.L. (1992) 'Inventing American reality', *The New York Review of Books*, December 3: 24–9.

Hymes, D. (1975) 'Folklore's nature and the sun's myth', *Journal of American Folklore*, 88: 345–369.

Kwedar, M.F., Patterson, J.A. and Allen, J.R. (1980) 'Interpreting 1830s storekeeping in New Salem, Illinois', Report submitted to the National Endowment for the Humanities, July 1.

Lavie, S., Narayan, K. and Rosaldo, R. (eds) (1993) *Creativity/Anthropology*, Ithaca, NY: Cornell University Press.

MacCannell, D. (1976) *The Tourist: A New Theory of the Leisure Class*, New York: Schocken.

MacCannell, D. (1992) *Empty Meeting Ground: The Tourist Papers*, London: Routledge.

Neeley, M.E., Jr. (1982) *The Abraham Lincoln Encyclopedia*, New York: McGraw-Hill.

Onstot, T. G. (1902) *Pioneers of Menard and Mason Counties*, Forest City, IL: T. G. Onstot.

Reep, T.P. (1927) *Lincoln at New Salem*, Chicago: Old Salem Lincoln League.

Sandburg, C. (1954) *Abraham Lincoln: The Prairie Years and the War Years*, San Diego: Harcourt Brace Jovanovich.

Taussig, M. (1993) *Mimesis and Alterity: A Particular History of the Senses*, New York: Routledge.

Taylor, R.S. and Johnson, M.L. (1993) 'Inventing Lincoln's New Salem: the reconstruction of a pioneer village', unpublished MS.

Thomas, B.P. (1934) *Lincoln's New Salem*, Springfield, IL: Abraham Lincoln Association.

Trilling, L. (1972) *Sincerity and Authenticity*, Cambridge, MA: Harvard University Press.

Turner, V. and Bruner, E.M. (eds) (1986) *The Anthropology of Experience*, Urbana, IL: University of Illinois Press.

Wagner, R. (1975) *The Invention of Culture*, Englewood Cliffs, NJ: Prentice-Hall.

Wallace, M. (1981) 'Visiting the past: history museums in the United States', *Radical History Review*, 25: 63–96.

Whisnant, D. (1983) *All That is Native and Fine: The Politics of Culture in an Appalachian Region*, Chapel Hill, NC: University of North Carolina Press.

Willis, S. (ed.) (1993) 'The world according to Disney', *Special Issue of South Atlantic Quarterly*, 92(1).

Zipes, J. (1979) *Breaking the Magic Spell: Radical Theories of Folk and Fairy Tales*, Austin, TX: University of Texas Press.

Edited version of Bruner, E.M. (1994) 'Abraham Lincoln as authentic reproduction: a critique of postmodernism', *American Anthropologist*, 96 (New Series): 397–415. Edward Bruner is Professor Emeritus at the Department of Anthropology, University of Illinois, Urbana-Champaign. This article captures well his desire to interrogate the processes and sites of tourism. Among his recent books is *Culture on Tour: Ethnographies of Travel* which deals with many of these interests in greater detail.

Chapter 25

After authenticity at an American heritage site

Eric Gable and Richard Handler

A N ENDURING IMAGE of modernist anxiety is that the world we inhabit is no longer authentic – that it has become fake, plastic, a kitschy imitation. Anxiety, so the common wisdom has it, goes hand in hand with desire. We may have lost authenticity, but we want to find it again, and will pay what it costs (within reason) to get it. This image of 'authenticity lost' has also been at the centre of much 'countermodern' cultural critique, and it has given anthropology a kind of romantic aura – a longing for a lost authenticity. Thus it often seems that the scholarly study of late modern or postmodern culture is a study of a reverse alchemy. What was once golden is now plastic.

Lately cultural critics claim to have shed their romanticism. Countermodern romanticism is no longer an unacknowledged scholarly motive, but an object of study, even an object of derision. However, as several scholars have noted, most recently Edward Bruner (1994) in an article appearing in this journal, it often seems that cultural critics do not go beyond the assertion that the world is empty, that outward appearances are facades, that everything is somehow constructed. In part, this is because one standard assumption among such critics is that those in power benefit from the prevailing definition of the authentic. They need the authority of authenticity to legitimate their power. Moreover, many of the critics assume that the public at large, the more or less disenfranchised masses of consumers, are co-opted into buying, say, a pedigree or an experience to make up for what they have been taught is the emptiness of their daily lives. The critic's dream is that once already anxious natives are exposed to the constructedness of authenticity, they will stop buying it. As a result, much of current cultural criticism involves exposing the authentic as construction. If the real past is revealed to be a present-day invention, if the natural fact is revealed to be a cultural convention, then the ruling order will topple and the masses will be freed from the yoke of anxious desire.

Museums – and especially heritage museums – play a peculiar role in all of this, for they are perfect topoi upon which to enact such critiques, even as they are also outgrowths of precisely the kind of countermodern anxiety that is the enduring basis for cultural critique. Heritage is one form of cultural salvage. A 'lost world' or a world about to be lost is in need of 'preservation', and the museum or heritage site bills itself as the best institution to perform this function. Heritage museums become publicly recognized repositories of the physical remains and, in some senses, the 'auras' of the really 'real'. As such, they are arbiters of a marketable authenticity. They are also objective manifestations of cultural, ethnic, or national identity, which outside the museum is often perceived as threatened by collapse and decay. Yet preservation entails artful fakery. Reconstruction, as it were, is the best evidence for the validity of a constructivist paradigm. Critics of this or that version of authenticity have before them in a heritage site ample evidence from which to build their deconstructive arguments.

In this essay, we would like to explore what happens to a heritage site 'after authenticity' – where the pursuit of an elusive authenticity remains a goal even as it generates public statements intended to call into question the epistemology of authenticity. Colonial Williamsburg – a place that fashions itself as one of the most ambitious and extensive reconstruction projects ever undertaken – intends to be experienced as an objective correlate of an American national 'identity.' Because Colonial Williamsburg makes such claims for itself, it has throughout its history also been subject to critiques of its authenticity by those who wish to undermine its authority to speak as the voice of an all-encompassing America. Moreover, in the past 20 years, the professional historians who ostensibly set the pedagogic agenda at Colonial Williamsburg have become increasingly articulate on-site critics of the epistemological underpinnings of authenticity as they promulgate, at this particular site, a historiography currently popular in history museums at large and in the academy.

The question that frames our essay is, What happens to authenticity when the public are both openly sceptical about the capacity of the powers that be at Colonial Williamsburg to make definitive judgments about authenticity and also openly sceptical about authenticity itself as a foundational value? We will argue that the vernacular concept of authenticity changes very little, that it shows a remarkable resilience, in a sense, because it is under threat. This is because one crucial way that Colonial Williamsburg maintains its authority is by selective or managed admissions of failure to discern what is fact, fancy, real, or fake. This attention to the management of impressions allows for the dream of authenticity to remain viable even in an environment in which all available empirical evidence could easily be perceived as supporting constructivist paradigms or alternatively as undermining authenticity-based claims to truth or value. When constructivist paradigms flourish, as they currently do at sites such as Colonial Williamsburg, they do so not in the service of a critique of the status quo but in defense (to borrow from Durkheim) of what come to be perceived as socially 'necessary illusions.' While we draw our examples from research we carried out at Colonial Williamsburg from 1990 to 1993, the arguments are applicable to heritage sites in general and ultimately to the way constructivist paradigms are deflected or domesticated in the American vernacular in the 'post-authentic' age.

Colonial Williamsburg: the ethnographic setting

Colonial Williamsburg's central district, the Historic Area, which covers 173 acres and includes over 500 buildings, is an inherently ambiguous object of authenticity. Of this collection of buildings, 88 are said to be original and the rest are advertised as reconstructions. These buildings range in size from large public buildings, such as the Governor's Palace and the Capitol, to the dozens of outbuildings dotting the backyards of the stores and residences of the museum-city's streets. Outside the Historic Area are three major museums (devoted to folk art, decorative arts, and archaeology) and a James River plantation called Carter's Grove. The museum was founded in 1926 with the backing of John D. Rockefeller Jr. and is today owned and operated by the non-profit Colonial Williamsburg Foundation. The foundation has a for-profit subsidiary, Colonial Williamsburg Hotel Properties, Inc., which operates several hotels and restaurants, with the profits used to support the museum. The foundation employs well over 3,000 people, and about a million people visit it each year. It had an annual budget of close to $130 million and an endowment of close to $200 million in 1989 (Colonial Williamsburg 1989: 21–27).

The history that Colonial Williamsburg teaches has changed over the decades. In the past two decades, a crucial shift has occurred. The museum's patriotic, celebratory story of the American founding has been challenged by a new generation of historians hired at Colonial Williamsburg beginning in the late 1970s. These historians were profoundly influenced by the 'new social history' that had developed in academic history departments in response to the social turmoil of the 1960s. When they came to Colonial Williamsburg, they wanted to revive what they saw as a moribund cultural institution by making it tell a new story, one that included the total colonial community. In other words, to the story of the colonial elites, which the museum had always told, the new historians wanted to add stories about the masses, the middle classes, the tradesmen, the lower classes, and, crucially, the African American slaves. They wanted to depict the total social life of the community in order to emphasize inequality, oppression, and exploitation. The new story of the American Revolution was to be one of complicated social, political, and economic motivations and relationships, not simply a glorious triumph of democratic principles.

Moreover, the new historians at Colonial Williamsburg were explicitly constructivists. Not only did they wish to replace a patriotic history with one that was more critical, they wanted to teach the public that history making itself was not simply a matter of facts and truth. It was, instead, a process shot through with hidden cultural assumptions and ideological agendas. Indeed, when we began our research at Colonial Williamsburg, we were particularly interested in the ways that constructivist theory operated and how it fared in the face of an entrenched objectivist historiography that celebrated the authenticity of the site and the truth of the history it embodied. As we shall see, the relationship of authenticity to credibility speaks to a kind of compromise between constructivism and objectivism, a compromise that allows business to continue as usual at mainstream institutions such as Colonial Williamsburg – an institution on the cutting edge of the way heritage is packaged and produced and at the same time typical.

Authenticity, credibility, and the tourist market

Despite the fact that Colonial Williamsburg's historians espouse a constructivist epistemology, the daily discourse that one hears on the site stresses the museum's commitment to total authenticity, that is, to historical truth in every detail. To understand why the institution is willing to live with this contradiction, we need to examine how Colonial Williamsburg tries to position itself in the tourist marketplace. Ironically, but perhaps not surprisingly, Disneyland is a dominant presence, both symbolically and literally in that market (Kratz and Karp 1993). One of the first things that staff members told us when we began our field study is that Colonial Williamsburg 'isn't some historical Disneyland.' Instead, they asserted, it was a 'serious educational institution.' Colonial Williamsburg differs from Disneyland, in the view of the museum's staff, because it presents 'the real past' rather than one that is made up. It strives for historical accuracy. In so doing, it is constrained by 'documented facts' and by historiographical methods of interpretation and presentation. By contrast, theme parks like Disneyland can make up whatever imaginary past, present, or future they wish, since they purvey amusement and fantasy, not education and history. In sum, Colonial Williamsburg is real, while Disneyland is fake.

Interestingly, the Disney corporation accepts this division of the labor of cultural representation. Late in 1993, Disney announced plans to build an American history theme park in northern Virginia. Though Colonial Williamsburg's administrators must have been worried by the possibility of head-to-head competition with Disney, they put on a brave face, as the headlines in local newspapers announced, 'Williamsburg hopes Disney park will draw interest to the real thing.' Moreover, that Disney was clearly distinguished from 'the real thing' was taken as a given throughout the 'history-based tourism industry.' As a spokesperson for Monticello, the 'historic house' of Thomas Jefferson, put it, 'It will be interesting for people to get the Disney experience and then . . . to come here and get the real thing.' Disney executives, too, spoke the same language, at least to the press: 'Colonial Williamsburg has the same thing the Smithsonian and the Manassas battlefield have: real history. We can do everything we want, but we can't create that'.

Despite the fact that the Disney corporation publicly accepts the 'reality' of the historical presentations at Colonial Williamsburg, the museum's critics often do not. An example of their critique appeared recently in the *New York Review of Books*, in the form of an attack on contemporary architecture by critic Ada Louise Huxtable. Huxtable's essay opened with a tirade against Colonial Williamsburg, which she saw as 'predating and preparing the way for the new world order of Disney Enterprises', an order that systematically fosters 'the replacement of reality with selective fantasy'. According to Huxtable, Colonial Williamsburg 'has perverted the way we think', for it has taught Americans

> to prefer – and believe in – a sanitized and selective version of the past, to deny the diversity and eloquence of change and continuity, to ignore the actual deposits of history and humanity that make our cities vehicles of a special kind of art and experience, the gritty accumulations of the best and worst we have produced. This record has the wonder and distinction of being the real thing. (Huxtable 1992: 24–25)

These remarks epitomize an enduring critique of Colonial Williamsburg. Many of the museum's critics have said that it is literally too clean – that it does not include the filth and stench that would have been commonplace in an 18th-century colonial town. Many of these critics also find that Colonial Williamsburg is metaphorically too clean; it avoids historical unpleasantness like slavery, disease, and class oppression in favour of a rosy picture of an elegant, harmonious past. This, of course, is exactly what similarly positioned critics say of Disneyland. Indeed, from the perspective of the people who take this critical stance, Colonial Williamsburg is all too much like Disneyland. Both produce the kinds of tidy, over-sanitized products they do because they are big, middle-of-the-road 'corporate worlds' who sell entertainment rather than education.

Credibility armor

Colonial Williamsburg has suffered the too-clean critique almost from the moment of its founding (Kopper 1986: 165). That critique – which labels Colonial Williamsburg a fake like Disneyland instead of an authentic historic site – strikes at the museum's very conception of itself. Indeed, because authenticity is what Colonial Williamsburg sells to its public, the institution's claims to authenticity become a point of vulnerability. This is especially true for the foundation's professional intelligentsia – its historians, curators, and the like – for they are in many respects the peers of Huxtable and the others who snipe at them from the ivory tower. But the too-clean critique extends to the public at large, and so a defense against this critique becomes the business of the institution as a whole, especially on the 'front line' where interpreters meet the public.

Every day hundreds of people visit Colonial Williamsburg, an institution whose mission is to show the public what colonial Virginia 'was really like.' Foundation staff know that in every crowd there are individuals casting a cold and critical eye on the museum's claim to present that reality. In these circumstances, Colonial Williamsburg staff work hard not only to present an authentic site but to maintain the institution's reputation for authenticity. Moreover, maintaining an image of authenticity means protecting Colonial Williamsburg's chosen institutional identity – that of a serious history museum, not a theme park. As one interpreter put it, 'It is important to discuss facts because each facility wants to be accurate and to present to our customers and visitors the best historical interpretation possible and to retain its authentic reputation' (see Bruner 1994: 401).

'Reputation' is something that pertains to the self or to the institution as a corporate personality, yet it is made and maintained vis-à-vis others. As Colonial Williamsburg staff see it, 'the museum's' reputation for authenticity is on the line every day, and every one of the myriad historical details it exhibits is both a witness to institutional authenticity and a window of vulnerability. When we asked a manager who was working on increasing the accuracy of the museum's costumes to explain the 'educational payoff' of attention to historical detail, he responded by talking about reputation rather than pedagogy:

> The clothing is just as important as creating an accurate interior, creating any sort of accuracy. Any time you have a break in your

credibility, then everything that is credible is lost, or it's called into question. If you have someone who comes in, and they happen to see plastic buttons, or someone wearing obvious knee socks, instead of proper hosiery, then to me that's saying, well, that's not accurate. I wonder if the way that tea service is laid out is accurate? I wonder if the fact that that garden's laid out the way it is, I wonder if that's accurate? You start to lose it. That's why it's so important that our interpreters have the ability to take things that are less than accurate and get people to start thinking beyond them. And catching people, anticipating problems of credibility. Now if we can catch them up, by using better tools, better floor arrangements, better costumes, better gardens, then that's one less chink in our credibility armor that we have to worry about.

Colonial Williamsburg defends its credibility every day on the streets of the reconstructed capital, but its defenses are not perfect. Mistakes happen, visitors complain. In Colonial Williamsburg's corporate archives is a revealing record of how such complaints are resolved – files containing letters from disappointed visitors, along with the foundation's responses to them. These files record an ongoing effort to put the best spin it can on these criticisms by invoking Colonial Williamsburg's unwavering fidelity to authenticity.

For example, an elderly couple wrote that their most recent visit had turned into 'a long disappointing day' because they 'found many things that did not fit the Williamsburg we've known over the past 20 years.' They complained that the 'lovingly truly preserved past of our America' was being marred by the presence of employees with nail polish, plastic earrings, and tennis shoes. Charles Longsworth, president of the Colonial Williamsburg Foundation, replied, February 20th 1987:

> You brought a sharp eye with you on your recent visit to Colonial Williamsburg. You caught a few of our interpretive staff with their authenticity and courtesy down. You may be sure that each of the violations you cite of courtesy standards and 18th-century apparel and appearance is being addressed by the supervisors of the violators. Your standards are ours, and we strive to see them honored by all employees. Being human, we sometimes fail, but our efforts to achieve authenticity and friendliness have been and will continue to be unflagging.

Phrases such as 'reputation' and 'credibility armor', and the image of being caught with one's authenticity (pants?) down, suggest the pervasive insecurity that, apparently, accompanies Colonial Williamsburg's claims to possess the really real. Even the foundation's professional historians, who espouse a relativistic or constructivist philosophy of history, experience this embattled concern for reputation. An architectural historian, for example, told us what he characterized as a humorous story about an encounter he had with a visitor early in his career at Williamsburg. The visitor came up to him and said that Colonial Williamsburg did not have a single padlock on the reconstructed buildings that was genuinely 18th-century in design. In response to this criticism, the historian spent a day tracking down all the information he could find on the locks in the reconstruction. Then he went to a museum famous for its collection of early American artefacts 'to study the 24 or so 18th-century padlocks they had'. He made drawings of those. Next, he told us, he 'developed a rough typology – I think there were four recognizable styles of padlock, and the visitor was right, none of ours were like these.' As a result, the historian wrote the visitor thanking him and promising that while Colonial Williamsburg could not afford to change all the old locks, 'on every subsequent project' they would make more faithful reproductions.

The historian prefaced his humorous story by explaining that he and his colleagues sweat the details so that 'you aren't a joke' in the eyes of the public. His humorous portrayal of himself as an insecure ferret let loose on the problem of padlocks – because veracity in every detail is Colonial Williamsburg's hallmark and because he doesn't want to be a joke – reflects an abiding institutional concern, for the visitor who points out flaws in the mimetic portrait of the past Colonial Williamsburg professes to create is a stock character in many stories employees tell about their encounters with the visitors. He is, as one supervisor of frontline interpreters told us, like 'a magpie' that weaves odd trinkets – tinfoil, some colored yarn – into its nest. A human magpie at places such as Colonial Williamsburg is someone who collects, indeed is obsessed with, a certain category of obscure historical facts.

Frontline employees are, if anything, more sensitive to the threat of the magpie than are backstage personnel like research historians. To these employees at Colonial Williamsburg, the magpie is an embarrassing nuisance who may be hiding among every flock of tourists, threatening to reveal the guide's ignorance (and knock the guide off his or her storyline) with a pointed query about some object or some theme about which the guide will have no clue.

Magpies threaten individual reputations during brief encounters at particular sites; and they also threaten institutional reputations. When the architectural historian says that it is a point of honour that Colonial Williamsburg get the details right, it is in part to protect his reputation, but also to protect the institution's reputation. Veracity, authenticity, or getting the facts right is a deep value at Colonial Williamsburg and it has a double quality. People like the architectural historian sweat the details, in part, because they too are like magpies. The architectural historian used to tell us how he loved the detective work involved in tracking down just such stray facts. But he and his colleagues also get the facts right so that they won't be exposed as a joke in public. The institution rewards employees for responding to the magpie's trivial or tangential queries because this keeps the credibility armor nicely burnished.

Constructivist ploys in defense of objectivist authenticity

Credibility armor is important because those who work at Colonial Williamsburg assume (and often have such assumptions confirmed) that the public is concerned with authenticity. Every claim to possess or represent the 'real' at least implies a claim to possess or represent the knowledge and authority to decide what's real and what isn't. Furthermore, Colonial Williamsburg employees expect that a significant number of their public are always somewhat sceptical of such claims to authority, especially those made on behalf of large corporate institutions like Colonial

Williamsburg. As one of the foundation's historians put it, during a workshop we led concerning historical relativism and African American history,

> I think there are a lot of interpreters who share with many of our visitors this suspicion, that, in fact, there are official histories, and that this institution has been in the past, and may still be . . . either consciously or unconsciously purveying an official history. Which is simply to say, a history that somebody knows to be wrong, but has good reasons for wanting to promote anyway, either because if we tell the real story we'll turn off visitors, or we'll open up questions of racial antipathy which a well-behaved place — which Americans, good citizens — don't want to [hear] . . . So there are lots of reasons why an institution like ours — particularly a slick institution like ours — is likely to have a hidden agenda. Which is only to say that there are probably lots and lots of people who don't know they're relativists, but fear that history is something that is concocted.

People, in sum, are oftentimes predisposed to think (unkindly) of Colonial Williamsburg as a 'slick institution' manufacturing facades and cover-ups rather than the authentic truth. Faced with such scepticism, and with the more sophisticated critiques of the intelligentsia, Colonial Williamsburg routinely deploys what might be called a proactive attitude, trying to defuse criticisms by anticipating them. Sometimes this takes the form of teaching visitors about 'mistakes' the foundation has made in its depiction of the past. For example, on one tour that we took, the interpreter explained that in an earlier era in the museum's history all the clapboard outbuildings had been kept freshly painted and the woodwork had been of the highest quality. At that time, she explained, 'We assumed that every building on the property would be as neat as every other.' But now, she continued, researchers know better: 'Only the front's important, that's your first impression, so buildings out back are going to be rougher.' As a result, outbuildings were being painted less frequently and allowed to wear unevenly. Thus, as we looked at the crisp, white clapboard in front of us, we were asked to imagine more shabbily painted outbuildings elsewhere.

Another proactive ploy is to point out the purposeful artifice of the museum-city, a place meant to recreate an 18th-century reality but one that also, of necessity, must negotiate 20th-century realities. For example, many buildings in the Historic Area are used either as office space or as residences for foundation employees. In such cases, 20th-century elements must be 'disguised.' 'The rules say you can't show anything 20th-century,' one interpreter explained. 'No anachronisms! That means no television antennas . . . no Christmas lights.' Other interpreters told us that garages were made to look like stables, central air-conditioning was allowed because it did not have to be visible, and garbage cans could be hidden behind hedges. When we came across these artfully disguised elements, they were duly pointed out to us. As we paused, on one occasion, to marvel at 200-year-old boxwoods, we were reminded that 'we also have wonderful things like fire hydrants, trash cans, and soda machines that we try to hide'. As we continued our stroll beneath some tall trees, our guide added that 'if you look up in trees this time of year you see things that look like an upside-down bucket, and it's a light. You don't find them in the summer because of the leaves'.

A third ploy for parrying criticisms entails blaming the visitors for inauthenticities. The best example of this ploy concerns trees (cf. Bruner 1994: 402; Gable and Handler 1993). The streets of the Historic Area are shaded by tall and stately oaks and other deciduous trees. Inevitably, interpreters would call our attention to these beautiful and obviously old trees and remark that they would not have been there in the colonial era. They would go on to explain that the foundation would never cut down those trees because, despite its commitment to authenticity, it had also to consider visitor comfort. Without the shady trees, the streets in summer ('when most of our visitors come') would be unbearable. In pointing to the trees, our guide on one occasion enjoined us to 'keep in mind that many changes have been made to the-town itself, things we have done to make it basically more comfortable for . . . 20th-century people.' As on many tours, he advised us to look past or through these anachronisms in order to imagine the real past. It was as if the foundation was trying to shape the visitor's appreciation of the landscape in such a way as to confirm that, yes, the town is artificial, but Colonial Williamsburg could not be as accurate as it wished to be because the visitors' needs precluded it.

These rhetorical tactics might be seen as a kind of 'impression management' – constructivism deployed in the defense of objectivism. Interpreters point out repeatedly (and indeed they are trained to do so) that history changes constantly, that what is believed to be true at one moment is discovered to be inauthentic later on, and that the business of history making involves all sorts of compromises. Yet these constructivist confessions, as it were, stem ultimately from a concern for maintaining Colonial Williamsburg's reputation as an arbiter of authenticity. Constructivist caveats shore up the assertion that the foundation aims for authenticity in every detail. As we discovered in interviews with visitors, its public by and large expects that, but some are also inclined to doubt the museum's honesty. Cognizant of that doubt, the museum repeatedly highlights not only the authenticity of its exhibits but the details that fall short of total authenticity. Employed to manage impressions, these admissions of small errors are expected to bolster the public's faith that the institution is diligently working toward its larger goal: to re-create the past in its totality, that is, with complete authenticity.

But Colonial Williamsburg recognizes that there are some elements of its public for whom authenticity if authenticity is defined as fidelity to objective truth is anathema. In interviewing them, we occasionally encountered such visitors. An elderly widow stands out, perhaps because she was among the first visitors we talked to. She had been coming to Colonial Williamsburg for over 30 years and always stayed in the Williamsburg Inn, a five-star hotel famous for its slightly rusticated elegance. Explaining to us that she was one of the foundation's regular donors (we never asked her how much she was accustomed to giving), she admitted that she was somewhat chagrined by the 'recent', as she put it, preoccupation with refashioning the town as it 'really was'. Christmas, she told us, was her favorite time to visit, precisely because of the 'festive decorations', although, she emphasized, they were not true to the 18th century. 'Would Williamsburg do away with these anachronisms?', she worried aloud.

For the widow, the recent move toward greater truth was threatening to ruin what lay at the heart of Williamsburg's appeal. It was a place, she reminded us, where she, an old woman, could still stroll the streets at night. She explained Colonial Williamsburg's appeal by way of a vignette having to do with an early stay at the inn. She had been eating in the luxurious dining room and, desiring sugar for her coffee, was about to dip her spoon into a large pewter cup in front of her when a liveried black waiter quickly bent over, moved the cup, and spooned sugar from a smaller container into her coffee. The first container, she elaborated, was salt. Apparently, in colonial times, she added, they served salt in what today might look like a sugar bowl. But it wasn't the inn's attention to that little piece of authenticity that she wanted us to see through her eyes. Rather, it was the black waiter's silent skill. Ever attentive, waiting unobtrusively but alertly in the background, he'd anticipated her faux pas and resolved her problem without calling attention to her mistake. Skilled waiters like that, she emphasized, could not be reproduced, or faked, or trained. They embodied for her the essence of what Colonial Williamsburg used to stand for before 'that new word, "authenticity"', had become such a concern.

Visitors such as the widow are not significant characters in the imaginary public Colonial Williamsburg employees created and re-created in daily conversations. Nevertheless, it is entirely plausible that people such as the widow played a larger (if not explicitly recognized) role in the way Williamsburg's higher-ups imagined their *donating* public — a close to 50,000-strong subgroup that Colonial Williamsburg was increasingly relying on for the gifts and grants that would enable the museum to preserve itself.

To this public, the powers that be at Colonial Williamsburg employed what could be characterized as a constructivist historiography, but in the service of the status quo, as celebration, not critique. Consider President Longsworth's annual report for the years 1980 and 1981 — a report that introduces Colonial Williamsburg's donating public to the new social history and reassures them that old celebratory history will not be erased as a result.

Longsworth's report is in the form of a history of shifts in the major ideas — couched as consumer preferences — that guided the foundation. In short, it is a constructivist history. It begins with the aesthetic motives of the customers — 'visitors came here . . . to see buildings and furnishings.' Later, in 'the days of the cold war . . . interpretation was fired by a sense of duty to inspire and encourage patriotism, to imbue visitors with a perception of the preciousness and fragility of personal freedom.' In Longsworth's (1982: 6–7) historical sketch, the new social history 'reflected the dominant characteristics of the 1960s: suspicion and distrust of leaders and a concomitantly populist view of the world.'

Longsworth notes that the new social history 'inevitably caused a strong reaction from those whose commitment to the patriots as the source of inspiration was steadfast'. And while he avers that it is 'the tension of these differences of view that . . . creates a lively learning environment', the tenor of his report is to defend the patriots against the new social historians. He does so by embracing a constructivist historiography:

It would be easy and perhaps popular to embrace social history with passionate abandon and forsake the patriots, retaining their memory as

symbolic of an outworn and naive view of America's past. But I know
of no one who advocates such a course. One needs to retain always
a cautious view of any claim of exclusive access to the true history.
I believe one must accept the puzzlement, confusion, ambiguity, and
uncertainty that characterizes scholarship – the search for truth.
(Longsworth 1982: 8)

Longsworth recognizes that the 'reasonable and dispassionate interpretation of evidence' is fogged by 'some ideological base'. But, given that history cannot escape
ideology, Colonial Williamsburg should 'maintain an ideological blend rather than
develop a pure strain'. Ultimately this ideological blend of the 'dramatic, inspir-
ing story that never loses its significance' and the new social history is good for
Colonial Williamsburg as an institution. It is a strategy that guarantees survival,
for it gives the public what it wants, or, at least, what Colonial Williamsburg has
gotten them used to: 'An organization such as this has by its longevity and its
success created certain expectations. They may not be blunted summarily by a generation of scholars or administrators who have discovered the new historiography'
(Longsworth 1982: 8–9).

Because the foundation must cater to the desires of a market that it has, in a
sense, created, Longsworth (1982: 9–10) concludes that 'we shall . . . continue
to do what we do.' As proof he cites the 60 percent increase in the collections
budget and the construction of the De Witt Wallace Decorative Arts Gallery – meant
to house a collection of colonial era 'masterworks', which, according to the social
historians' canons of authenticity, could no longer be displayed in the well-
appointed homes of the reconstructed village because they were neither made nor
used in Williamsburg itself.

Longsworth (who left the presidency in 1992, remaining at Colonial
Williamsburg as chairman of the board) has consistently used constructivist
rhetoric to promote the preservation of a certain patriotism linked to
a certain aesthetic. In a preface to Philip Kopper's sumptuous coffee-
table history of the site, he argues that Colonial Williamsburg makes
myths 'because of America's need for myth'. 'It is easy', he writes, 'to
dismiss Williamsburg as a purveyor of patriotism,' but, he argues, 'the
stimulus provided by patriotic feeling will be a vital tonic to the body
politic.' He goes on to assert that Colonial Williamsburg 'is constantly
changing, as it stands its iconographic ground' – that 'the recreation of
our usable past' is a necessary social process. In concluding, he notes
how the old idea that Colonial Williamsburg would be 'finished' rather
than an ongoing enterprise of great vigour and complexity seems naive
today. But, I suppose, it also seemed naive, or at least highly unlikely
to many, that the dream of a new nation would ever be realized. So,
out of our dreams we find reality and in myth our dreams are forged.
(Longsworth 1986: 6–7)

Here Longsworth invokes a 'usable' past – a self-conscious, ongoing invention of
history – in the twin service of national identity and corporate survival.

The uses of constructivism

In a challenging essay that recently appeared in this journal, Edward Bruner uses similar observations from his fieldwork at New Salem, Illinois – a site associated with Abraham Lincoln – to suggest that authenticity from the native point of view is evidence of a home-grown cultural constructivism. He shows that authenticity has several meanings for the staff and visitors at New Salem, one of which is 'historical verisimilitude.' As Bruner (1994: 399) puts it, *'authentic* in this sense means credible and convincing, and this is the objective of most museum professionals, to produce a historic site believable to the public, to achieve mimetic credibility'. 'Some museum professionals go further,' Bruner (1994: 399) continues, and this entails a second native meaning of authenticity – to 'speak as if the 1990s New Salem not only resembles the original but is a complete and immaculate simulation, one that is historically accurate and true to the 1830s'. Bruner elaborates upon the distinction between the former and latter senses:

> In the first meaning, based on verisimilitude, a 1990s person would walk into the village and say, 'This looks like the 1830s,' as it would conform to what he or she expected the village to be. In the second meaning, based on genuineness, an *1830s* person would say, 'This looks like 1830s New Salem,' as the village would appear true in substance, or real. I found that museum professionals use *authenticity* primarily in the first sense, but sometimes in the second. (Bruner 1994: 399)

The important point for Bruner is that insiders at the site are well aware that what they are producing is not a perfect copy, but something that is credible to an audience. The implication is that the natives (and here Bruner is referring especially to the professional staff at New Salem) do not confuse the reproduction with the real. Instead, they are aware that what they are creating is 'verisimilitude' – something that will convince an audience or be congenial to an audience's sensibilities.

Bruner takes this a step further. Just as professionals are not preoccupied with recreating the real thing, so, too, are visitors to the site less concerned with this kind of absolute authenticity:

> The tourists are seeking in New Salem a discourse that enables them to better reflect on their lives in the 1990s. New Salem and similar sites enact an ideology, recreate an origin myth, keep history alive, attach tourists to a mythical collective consciousness, and commodify the past. The particular pasts that tourists create/imagine at historic sites may never have existed. But historic sites like New Salem do provide visitors with the raw material . . . to construct a sense of identity, meaning, attachment, and stability. (Bruner 1994: 411)

Bruner concludes his essay by noting that 'New Salem can be read in two different ways' – from a pessimistic view or an optimistic one. The pessimists see such sites 'as exploitative, as strengthening the ruling classes, as deceit, as false consciousness, as manipulation of the imagination of already alienated beings.' Bruner counts

himself among the optimists who focus on the ways the site offers 'the utopian potential for transformation, offers hope for a better life, says people can take charge of
their lives and change themselves and their culture.'

According to Bruner (1994: 410), visitors and employees alike 'take charge' of
the way they consume and produce culture. He emphasizes that visitors and guides
'bring their own interests and concerns to the interaction'. He describes these interactions as 'playful', as 'improvisation'. The upshot, for Bruner (1994: 411), is that
Americans 'seeking . . . a discourse that enables them to better reflect on their lives
in the 1990s' can and do find such a discourse at New Salem.

Having made these ethnographic observations, Bruner wishes to link native notions
of authenticity to anthropological theories of culture. Bruner is a constructivist. He
asserts that the production of authenticity-as-verisimilitude is no more or less than
a clear manifestation of what culture everywhere and always is — an invention (in
many instances based on an attempt at replication). As such it is a benign fact. It
is benign, too, because it allows natives to play with an invented past and revivify
certain enduring ideals relevant to their present and future.

What Bruner observed at New Salem and what we observed at Colonial
Williamsburg are essentially the same phenomena. Yet we interpret them in almost
opposite ways. Let us examine the ways our interpretations differ, and what this
implies for theories of cultural production at (what some natives at least like to
claim are) 'shrines' to an American identity.

Perhaps most significantly, we have different attitudes toward our respective sites.
If Bruner celebrates the native preoccupation with authenticity-as-verisimilitude
as a benign sign of a universal human tendency to construct culture (and, in the
American case, to be aware that they are doing so), then we criticize authenticity-
as-impression-management as a symptom of an ongoing preoccupation in American
culture with a certain kind of past. For us, it is bad enough that this kind of
authenticity allows an airbrushed past to become exactly the kind of mythological
standard middle-class Americans aspire to. What disturbs us just as much is that
authenticity-as-impression-management is one of an array of practices (both intentional and unintentional) that effectively enervate constructivist insights at a place
whose built environment is living proof, as it were, of the power of constructivist
theory as a model for what history, as narrated or embodied or objectified memory,
really is.

We, like Bruner, are constructivists. Along with Bruner, we would even go
so far as to say that constructivist theory has been the bread and butter of most
cultural anthropologists for a long time. For us, the pervasiveness of constructivist theory raises some ethnographic questions when an anthropologist studies
American culture, particularly at sites such as New Salem and Colonial Williamsburg.
The first question is whether constructivism is also a native theory in the sense
that it is part of the commonsense baggage of people who are not professional
anthropologists.

When we began our research at Colonial Williamsburg, we were interested
in the ways constructivist theory operated on the ground. At first, it seemed to
us that native discussions of authenticity-as-impression-management revealed commonsense understandings of constructivist theories of culture. But authenticity-
as-impression-management turned out to have less to do with teaching about

constructivist historiography than with protecting or shoring up a threatened reputation. To talk of verisimilitude as credibility armor, to sweat the details so you're
not a joke in public in a reconstructed place that was 'always changing because new
facts are found', but that was nonetheless always being criticized by powerful outsiders for producing a bowdlerized past – this was, we decided, a tactic meant to
protect the dream of authenticity as perfect copy.

As we have argued elsewhere (Gable and Handler 1994), Colonial Williamsburg
is a shrine to a 'naive objectivism'. One of the ways that the priesthood of this
shrine protects this cherished paradigm is by judicious legerdemain in the service
of public relations. So, one way that we differ from Bruner is that we would argue
that a Kuhnian paradigm shift has not occurred at Colonial Williamsburg. The site's
authority – its reputation, if you will – depends on the public enactment of fidelity
to an essentialist authenticity, not on constructivism.

This does not mean, however, that there are no spaces on Colonial Williamsburg's
rhetorical terrain for native versions of constructivist notions as Bruner describes
them. Ironically, just as the new social history began to make headway, advocates
of the older, more celebratory history were able to use constructivist rhetoric
against the new social history in order to repackage celebratory history and reassert
its claims to ultimate authority. Longsworth's defense of the status quo reminds us
of what philosophers have occasionally pointed out (cf. Hiley 1988), but what
we, in the midst of the 'culture wars', perhaps overlook. You can be a constructivist and a conservative. Longsworth does this in a speech we quoted above. If
all is relative, then why not 'continue to do what we do' – while, in effect, rela-
belling it?

This kind of constructivism has the added benefit of insulating the particular
social actors (or institutions) from their own personal scepticism. Longsworth
does not have to personally believe in the authenticity of the reconstructed
Williamsburg. Instead, he simply has to be convinced that myths, if they contain
morally uplifting messages, are salutary. In this way, a conservative constructivism
protects an obviously empirically false image of the past, because it is a 'necessary
illusion' of the same kind Durkheim, personally an atheist, posited for religion.
We might add that in America, conservative constructivism has usually been tinged
with a wilful optimism. If we all believe, or 'think positive' as one euphemism has
it, then it will come true. Or more cynically still, if we pretend to believe, or, in
our role as leaders, if we ensure that 'they', the herd, the mass, believe, then it
will come true. It is this kind of constructivism that lends itself to conservatism in
its political and cultural sense.

This, then, is a chief way that constructivist notions thrive at Colonial
Williamsburg. Authorities such as President Longsworth use constructivist arguments to justify supporting good myths over bad facts, or authenticity as a model
for, rather than a model of, a reality. They do so, as often as not, in the name of
consumer preference. They do so in order to protect what they take to be universal ideals and values, and, nowadays, they do so against the implied background
of a society under siege – a society threatened by postmodern plague. When they
lay claim to being the enlightened arbiters of universal values – servants and guides
to the public – they import what to us are self-serving visions about how the world
should look.

This is the reason why we are more pessimistic than Bruner about the ways Americans construct identities for themselves at shrines such as Colonial Williamsburg and New Salem. It is not that we are essentialists — that we see such sites as unreal or inauthentic. Rather, we are ultimately less sanguine than Bruner that what goes on there is a universal form of cultural construction. Natives exhibit what to us is a kind of divided consciousness. On the one hand, they continue to be preoccupied with the past as the last refuge of the really real. On the other hand, some of them, at least, allow for the possibility that the really real is myth. Yet, according to them, it is 'myth' that, if institutions such as Colonial Williamsburg and the American nation itself are to survive and prosper, people must believe.

References

Bruner, E.M. (1994) 'Abraham Lincoln as authentic reproduction: a critique of post-modernism', *American Anthropologist*, 96: 397–415.

Colonial Williamsburg (1989) *Annual Report*, Williamsburg: Colonial Williamsburg Foundation.

Gable, E. and Handler, R. (1993) 'Colonialist anthropology at Colonial Williamsburg', *Museum Anthropology*, 17(3): 26–31.

Gable, E. and Handler, R. (1994) 'The authority of documents at some American history museums', *Journal of American History*, 81(1): 119–36.

Hiley, D.R. (1988) *Philosophy in Question: Essays on a Pyrrhonian Theme*, Chicago: University of Chicago Press.

Huxtable, A.L. (1992) 'Inventing American reality', *New York Review of Books*, 39(20): 24–9.

Kopper, P. (1986) *Colonial Williamsburg*, New York: Harry N. Abrams.

Kratz, C.A. and Karp, I. (1993) 'Wonder and worth: Disney museums in world showcase', *Museum Anthropology*, 17(3): 32–42.

Longsworth, C.R. (1982) 'Communicating the past to the present, in *Communicating the Past to the Present: Report on the Colonial Williamsburg Foundation with a Summary of the Years 1980 and 1981*, Williamsburg: Colonial Williamsburg Foundation, 5–10.

Longsworth, C.R. (1986) 'Foreword' to Kopper, P., *Colonial Williamsburg*, New York: Harry N. Abrams.

This article was first published as Gable, E. and Handler, R. (1996) 'After authenticity at an American heritage site', *American Anthropologist*, 98: 568–78. Eric E. Gable is Associate Professor of Anthropology at the University of Mary Washington in Virginia. Richard Handler is Professor and Associate Dean at the University of Virginia. They collaborated on this same subject in a monograph entitled *New History in an Old Museum: Creating the Past in Colonial Williamsburg*.

Chapter 26

Diversity, identity and modernity in exile
'Traditional' Karenni clothing

Sandra Dudley

T HIS CHAPTER, based on long-term anthropological field research, concerns forms of so-called 'traditional' Karenni clothing and the meanings and values associated with them in exile. Dress, I argue, plays an important role in the ongoing forging and changing of Karenni cultural and political identities.

Clothing – especially women's – is an aspect of 'tradition' that in the refugee camps is important in the processes concerned with what it means to be a modern Karenni person and what it means to become and be a Karenni refugee. These processes and the clothing itself are highly politicised, embedded in webs of myth, history and nationalist aspiration. Here, I consider both the clothing of newly arrived refugees and its meanings for different sectors of the refugee population, and other interpretations of 'traditional' clothing in the camps.

I focus on women's dress. The basic forms of male dress in the camps show a greater variety, with men wearing shorts, skirt-cloths, or trousers. Women dress far more 'traditionally' (this may mean different things to different sectors of the population) than do men. Indeed, amongst the Karenni as elsewhere in the world, women seem 'charged more than men with upholding a group's culture and identity' (Wilson and Frederiksen 1995: 4). Ideas about 'Karenni-ness' and sub-Karenni ethnicities are expressed through appropriate women's clothes worn especially at religious, national and traditional occasions. But the significance of women's dress lies not only in its ability to signal ethnic similarity and distinction; it lies too in the preservation of prevailing morality. Female clothing is caught up in processes by which those with most power in determining political and communal agendas seek both to uphold morality and to strengthen national identity.

Karenni refugees

The subjects of this chapter are refugees from Kayah (Karenni) State now living in refugee camps near the Burmese border in northwest Thailand, under the auspices of the Karenni National Progressive Party (KNPP). Karenni refugees are highly diverse in ethnicity, language, level of education, religion, awareness of the wider world, political aspirations, and the experience of displacement itself. Exile has brought together people who all originate in Kayah State but who are otherwise disparate. Some have elements of shared history, ethnicity and language, but all had 'less direct contact with and influence upon each other' prior to their relocation to refugee camps. Nonetheless, they all call themselves 'Karenni'. What 'Karenni' actually means, however, depends upon whom one talks to; this term is itself diverse and changing, variously defined in terms of ethnicity, territoriality and history. There are at least eleven ethnic groups and associated languages in the camps, all originating in Karenni State and all referring to themselves as 'Karenni', but simultaneously describing themselves as ethnically distinct. Identities are multiple. Most refugees who have been in the camps for some time, emphasise that while they are, for example, Kayan, they are of course 'Karenni'; they then add that 'we are all Karenni, we are the same family'.

In the camps, people's lives, the things that give meaning to their lives, their sense of belonging to a particular group, and the labels they give themselves, are all in a state of flux. From within this fluid, heterogeneous population is emerging a pan-Karenni national identity for which there was no real precedent before independence from the British in 1948 (Lehman 1967). This continual redefining of what it means to be Karenni involves self-conscious appropriations and rejections of elements of tradition, on the one hand so as to bring together disparate Karenni groups and, on the other, so as to reinforce the differences between the Karenni and other, non-Karenni communities. Some sectors of the Karenni population are more dominant than others in these processes, attempting to create and enforce what they see as a modern, desirable Karenni identity. These dominant groups come from the longer-staying refugee community and comprise relatively well-educated, Christian individuals in the highest levels of the social and political hierarchy.

The first significant numbers of Karenni came to Thailand in 1989, but some political leaders have been in Thailand for thirty years or more. Indeed, a number of today's Karenni adolescents were born in Thailand and have never been to Karenni State. Yet, many others have become refugees very recently, particularly in and after June 1996, when the Burmese army enforced widespread relocations of villages inside Karenni State. These recent arrivals doubled the total Karenni refugee population from around 5,500 to nearly 11,000 by March 1997 (by the year 2000, numbers stood at almost 20,000). Ethnically Kayah, they came from very remote hill villages between the Pon and Salween Rivers. They differed from the pre-existing refugee population in religious and curative practices, dialect, education, female dress, and awareness of the wider world. Most claimed never to have seen motor vehicles or foreigners before, or even women of their own ethnic group who did not dress as they did. Most of their villages had not yet received Christian missionaries, and most follow 'traditional' Kayah religion and curative practices rather than Christianity. Furthermore, unlike their ethnic cousins amongst the longer-staying refugee community, almost all of these people had little if any awareness of the KNPP's nationalist agenda. Once in the camps, they suddenly found themselves in the midst of the politicised moulding of a pan-Karenni national identity, a process over which their lack of education and political awareness gave them little influence.

It was evident that for these new arrivals the three things particularly emblematic of who they were and had been, were their main occupation of farming, the clothing traditionally worn by women, and the annual *ka-thow-bòw* festival and its associated beliefs and practices. Here, I turn to women's clothing, a distinctive element of culture that for the recent arrivals represents and reproduces the essence of who they are.

The traditional dress of new arrivals

All the newly arrived women wore home-made clothing that exposed their knees, lower thighs, back, and often one breast. The marked distinction between this and the ubiquitous T-shirts (always with brassieres underneath) and *longyi* worn by women in the pre-existing Karenni refugee community both indicated and generated some important differences between new and old refugees concerning ideas of history, morality, and what it means to be 'Kayah' and 'Karenni'. Once the women were in the camps, this 'traditional' dress also became subject to changes that were a direct cause of distress to the new arrivals.

I use 'traditional' in describing the clothing worn by the newly arrived female refugees for two reasons. Firstly, this clothing is regarded as 'traditional' by the pre-existing refugees and by the new arrivals themselves, although what each group means by 'traditional' differs. And secondly, archive photographs and early descriptions by missionaries, colonial officers and others, indicate that this kind of costume has indeed been the customary dress of Kayah women for a long time, and certainly for much longer than the so-called 'national costume' favoured in the camps (see the section on 'national dress' below).

'Tradition' and value: the meanings of female dress for new refugees

Briefly, the new refugees' female dress consists of: a skirt and head-cloth both always home-made of home-grown cotton; a breast-cloth usually made of commercial fabric; a fabric belt-cum-purse; a string of old silver British India one rupee coins worn as a belt, sash or necklace; necklaces of glass beads; large silver ear ornaments; and a great number of black, lacquered, 2-ply cotton rings worn around and just below the knee. It is important that the full dress, with the occasional exception of the head-cloth, is worn at all times. Other than the head-cloth, no items, including jewellery, are removed, even at night. The silver functions not only as ornament, but also as family wealth and as an heirloom for safe-keeping and passing on to the next generation. In general, the clothes and jewellery worn by a Kayah woman are an extension of herself, with which she signifies her identity on a number of levels: as a Kayah woman, as a woman of a certain age and marital status, and perhaps as a woman from a particular village. This dress is more than a repository and expression of the identity of its wearer alone. Both women and men are proud of the women's weaving and clothes, and invariably describe them as 'more beautiful' and 'more comfortable' than the ubiquitous T-shirts and skirt-cloths worn by other women in the camps. Recently arrived women do not appear to feel stigmatised now that they are living amongst their Kayah cousins who wear a less traditional style of dress, although a few have encountered problems. Four years after arrival, the overwhelming majority continues to wear only traditional clothing.

Together with farming and the annual *ka-thow-bòw* festival, women's dress was one of the most significant topics of conversation among the new refugees when they first arrived in 1996. It was also the focus point for anxiety about leaving the village and becoming a refugee. There was much distress amongst women *and* men about the women's present inability – due to lack of cotton or money to buy it – to continue weaving. That is, distress did not pertain solely to the desire to continue wearing these clothes; it directly related also to the desire to continue *making* them. Like farming, this is an occupation intrinsic to being Kayah and to the meaning of women's lives. The *process* of weaving, like the process of farming, is as important to the integrity of Kayah culture as its end-products. Weaving is simultaneously connected to what has been left behind and the painful nature of the leaving-behind process itself. Also, like traditional festivals, it is one of the things refugees prioritise in their desire to make their current situation more familiar. It is both a symbol of the past and an important factor in trying to make the present more bearable and familiar.

Female dress symbolises the past for new refugees in a positive and short-term sense. It stands as a reminder of 'home' and of everyday life in the recent, village-based past. Furthermore, this connection of female dress with the recent past is intrinsic to the process of becoming a refugee. As soon as they arrive in a camp, see large numbers of other people wearing T-shirts and *longyi*, and realise the impossibility of growing or purchasing cotton in this new environment, Kayah refugees immediately begin to express anxiety about the likelihood of women not being able to continue to wear their existing style of clothing. This is not necessarily the same, however, as immediately seeing female dress as 'traditional', in the sense either of how things have always been done or in the sense of how they always used to be done.

Nevertheless, within a short time of the new refugees coming to the camps, both the pre-existing and the new refugee communities had indeed come to regard this female dress as 'traditional'. However, the values and meanings each group ascribes to female dress in particular and to 'tradition' in general, vary. For the recent arrivals, their clothing is beautiful and for both women and men is the most immediate signifier of their identity as Kayah; immediately on arrival in a refugee camp in Thailand, it was the only tangible remaining sign of what and who they were and had been. It is an obvious visual marker of difference between these Kayah and others, from which derive self- and other-defined ideas of who they are. This difference only becomes important after the Kayah have become refugees, as in their villages difference in female dress is not important. There, most if not all women wear similar clothes (it was simply the way women dressed) and most villagers, male or female, rarely if ever, encounter non-local Karenni women who dress otherwise. On arrival in the camps, however, this immediately changes, as the new refugees are suddenly exposed to large numbers of *longyi*-clad women on a daily basis. Such exposure and the associated awareness of difference combine with the attitudes and comments of pre-existing refugees (see below) to stimulate a rationalisation by new refugees of why their women dress as they do. They begin to explain it in terms of 'as things have always been done', 'as our mothers and grand-mothers did before us', or 'because, long ago, the old man [i.e. wise ancestor] told us to'. I suggest that the shift in self-perception and its presentation, shown by these Kayah after they have become refugees, can in some sense be defined as them coming to regard themselves as 'traditional' when compared to other Kayah and non-Kayah Karenni. This shift is subtle, operating on the level of how existing ideas of identity are rationalised, rather than on the level of changing identity itself. Nonetheless, what is essentially a raising of consciousness facilitated by a change of context has impact not only on the Kayah's experience of refugeeness, but also on ways in which they increasingly become aware of their place in a wider, Karenni 'nation'.

Attitudes of the pre-existing refugee community

Longer-staying Karenni refugees all discussed the new arrivals in similar, double-edged terms. On the one hand, they were Karenni people, 'the same as us', whose treatment by the Burmese army and subsequently awful journeys through the jungle to the border were seen as a tragedy to be shared and grieved over by *all* Karenni people; they were brethren, united by misfortune, a common geographical origin, a common enemy, and for some a common language or ethnic origin. On the other hand, longer-staying refugees also talked continually of the differences between the new arrivals and themselves. The focal point was always female dress, which was, like many aspects of the culture of the new arrivals, described by other Karenni as 'traditional'. They talked of the new arrivals as *defined* by wearing clothes and adher-ing to religious and curative practices worn and practised long ago by all Kayah people, but now by only a few who had stayed with their old-fashioned ways because of their geographical remoteness and — as the longer stayers saw it — unfortunate lack of exposure, thus far, to education, Christianity and modernity.

This indicates a possible paradox in pre-existing Karenni refugee attitudes to the new arrivals. It seems as if the second Karenni view of the new arrivals as 'different' and highly 'traditional' in some way conflicts with the concurrent view that the new arrivals are 'the same as us'. Yet, notions of difference do not neces-sarily contradict the idea of the recent arrivals belonging to the Karenni family as a whole. It is rather that these new refugees are seen by other Karenni to be the most traditional members of the Karenni family, in some ways representative of its past, of threads common to the fabric from which all Karenni or, at the very least all Kayah, are cut. It is this perception of the newly arrived Kayah as the epitome of 'tradition' that is the essence of the contradictions in the attitudes of longer-staying Karenni.

The perception of tradition and the consequently contradictory attitudes of the longer-staying refugees are derived from the obvious visual stimulus of female dress. Some longer-staying refugees, particularly young adults who have been in Thailand most or all of their lives, or who have come to Thailand from places of origin out-side Karenni State, prior to 1996 had never seen traditionally-dressed Kayah women *en masse*. Others, including other young adults, come from villages where most women, including their own mothers, used to wear such clothes (and perhaps still do, if they remain inside Karenni State). Most longer-stayers I knew fell somewhere between these two extremes, having seen traditionally-dressed Kayah women before, but not in such large numbers as began to arrive in 1996. The excitement engendered in some of my Karenni friends by the new arrivals was not dissimilar to the excitement I felt myself; where we differed, however, was in the meanings we attributed to the traditional dress.

On my way to the new arrivals' camp for the first time, I stayed overnight in another camp with the family of Klaw Reh, my companion and translator. Klaw Reh's older brother, a relatively senior member of the Karenni political community, himself ethnically Kayah, was concerned that I would be shocked when I first saw the new arrivals. 'They are very, errm, *natural*', he said, laughing nervously. He wanted to forewarn me of the semi-nudity of the new refugees, with women's knees, lower thighs and, worst of all, breasts on show. He was worried not about my sensibilities alone, but also that I may judge the new arrivals harshly. By extension, I might also then judge all Kayah and ultimately all Karenni people in a similar manner.

From the beginning then, the new arrivals' clothing has been a complex issue for members of the largely Christian, pre-existing refugee population. They regard it as a 'traditional' form symbolic of the ethnic and historical roots of contemporary Karenni culture, yet it also represents to them backwardness, lack of education, poor hygiene and, above all, an unchristian immodesty on the part of the women. In this sense, it is for them a metaphor for the negative aspects of a past without the apparent moral and practical benefits of Christianity and modernity. Furthermore, the pre-existing refugee population immediately began also to act intentionally and unintentionally to influence the experience and self-perceptions of the new arrivals. At the most basic level, this involved comments being made to new arrivals and in their hearing about the revealing nature of the women's clothing. For example, on first arrival many of the women wore their breast-cloths in such a way that one breast was exposed, but within a short time as a result of comments made they had begun to wear the breast-cloth more self-consciously, ensuring that both breasts were covered. Particularly influential amongst those who made such comments were the refugee staff of the camp clinic and the Camp Committee. More specifically, certain groups within the longer-staying refugee community made a deliberate decision to 'help' the new arrivals. Residents of one camp, for example, organised their own collection of used clothing within the camp, for donation to the new refugees. Such donated clothing included items for children and men, but also T-shirts and *longyi* for women. Even if these longer-staying refugees did not deliberately intend their donations to alter the way these new female refugees dressed, the effect of the composition of their donations (as of course with other donations made by international organisations) was to reinforce the fact that newly arrived women had to change their mode of dress if the particular clothes in which they had arrived were eventually to fall apart (as many women's did).

Even more significantly, soon after the first, large waves of arrivals in 1996 the Karenni Border Catholic Association held an extraordinary meeting of its officers in order to plan systematic missionary activity amongst the new refugees. These evangelists and the initiative for their work all came from within the existing Karenni refugee community itself. They included a number of ethnic Kayah, but were dominated by Kayans. Certainly, the main objective was not to persuade women to wear different style of clothing; rather, it was to convert people to Christianity and at the same time, to the value of education. However, in practice, for the dominant, longer-staying Karenni refugee community, ideas of Christianity, education, female propriety, and what it means to be a modern Karenni person, are all intertwined. Most Christian Karenni would consider that a side-effect of Christianity is its 'civilising' influence, including encouraging women to cover themselves decently. There is little separation of a biblically derived Christian morality on the one hand, and an historically derived, Victorian morality repressive of women and originating with the nineteenth-century American and European missionaries, on the other.

More general issues raised by this mesh of ideas of Christianity, propriety, modernity and education cannot be discussed here; suffice to say that these ideas were no more separable for those planning missionary work with the new arrivals than for any other Christian member of the pre-existing population. Most members of this population, and certainly its leadership and educated youth sectors, whether Catholic missionaries or not, found it hard to separate such ideas in their attitudes towards and interaction with the new refugees. Even in 1998, two years on, members of the longer-staying community continued to hold onto their ideas about the 'traditional' Kayah. Paw, for example, a young woman who had herself conducted human rights interviews with the new refugees back in 1996, giggled in horror with her friends about how, when these refugees first came to the camp, 'They didn't even know how to *wash!* They had to be taught how to keep themselves *clean!*'

Such attitudes are complex, not least because of their co-existence with feelings of fraternal sympathy. What matters here, is that they are always associated with traditional Kayah female dress. As a visual fact it stimulates these attitudes, and is returned to repeatedly in the ways in which the pre-existing refugee community thinks of its traditional Kayah cousins. Ideas about the new arrivals' cleanliness – or lack of – are intimately bound up with traditional dress (not least because it is well known that this dress is never removed, even at night and even when washing). Similarly bound up with dress are notions (often pitying) about the new refugees' unawareness of Christian soteriology and what are believed to be Christian ideas about propriety and decency. By extension, there is pity too for their ignorance of the modern world, how to live in it, and how to deal with its politics. In sum then, female dress is central to a set of existential processes whereby pre-existing refugees make moral judgements about their newly arrived cousins (Dudley 1999). Such attitudes, together with those of outsiders, gave to the new refugees an impression of the camp as an area apart, a place of mixed messages. In the face of such confusion, rather than turning their back on this clothing, the new arrivals instead clung tighter to it, its significance in their everyday conversation and concerns growing, rather than diminishing with time.

'Traditional' clothing in the camps

Amongst the longer-staying refugee population, the particular kinds of *longyi* worn by men and women with their T-shirts are usually varied and personal. Women's are generally either woven commercially in Malaysia or Thailand and printed at source with designs mimicking traditional Malay and Indonesian *batik* patterns, or are more traditional-style cloths made by women on back-strap or non-automated frame looms in the camps. The first type is ubiquitous in markets throughout Southeast Asia. The second type, however, is important in what I call 'transitional' dress.

On Sundays, during festivals, and on other special occasions, many people choose to dress in what they refer to as 'traditional' or 'national' dress. Many women also wear this style of clothing or at least a 'traditional' hand-woven *longyi* rather than a Malaysian or Indonesian printed one on an everyday basis, particularly in the cold season (hand-woven *longyi* being thicker and warmer).

Nonetheless, these transitional types of clothing are not worn daily by large numbers of people on the kind of scale on which recent arrivals wear their traditional Kayah costume. Furthermore, with the exception of so-called 'Paku' cloths (i.e. cloths identified as belonging to the Paku Karen Karenni sub-group, further discussed below), the skirt-cloths in these types of so-called 'traditional' outfits are notably absent from early archive photographs and museum collections. Indeed, I suggest that these clothes represent a mid-point on a continuum between, on the one hand, increasingly 'Burmese' (this is a contentious term for the Karenni) and 'universal' sorts of dress and, on the other, highly 'traditional' clothing worn by recently arrived refugee women. It is because of its location midway along the continuum that I refer to this style of dress as 'transitional' (Dudley 2001).

There are a number of different sorts of the transitional skirt-cloths hand-woven in the camps, differentially characterised as 'traditional' to and by various Karenni groups. Other than the so-called 'Karenni national' cloths (see below), the most common types are 'Paku (Karen)' and 'Padaung' cloths. Women make these on continuous warp back-strap looms, using yarn purchased ready-spun and ready-dyed in Mae Hong Son market or in a camp shop. They may be made by the eventual wearer herself, or subsequently sold. They are often worn as everyday wear with T-shirts, but they are also worn on occasions that are more formal. Both types are predominantly black, with thin coloured stripes near the top and bottom of the skirt, and stripes and subtle patterning in the central portion.

The characterisation of these two types of cloth as 'Padaung' and 'Paku' is not mine, but that of my informants. They describe each type of cloth as being the traditional, typical type for each of these two ethnic groups. Yet, this neat labelling does not necessarily fit with a complex ethnographic reality. 'Padaung' here refers to all Kayan, each of the self-defined sub-groups of which actually has its own traditional cloths that do not correlate to the type described as 'Padaung' in the camps. Indeed, some Kayan informants said the cloths described as 'Padaung', and thus implied to be in some way representative of and traditional to all Kayan groups, were in fact typical only to Kayan Kang-Ngan, and inside Karenni State were to be found mainly in two particular villages near the state capital of Loikaw.

National dress as transition and transformation: Karenni 'national' cloths

I have indicated that traditional Kayah clothing is a female repository and expression of Kayah (and a form of Karenni) identity. At the same time, the diverse Karenni community as it exists in its refugee context, is continually developing a highly politicised sense of 'Karenni-ness', a national identity dependent on real and imagined shared pasts. Yet, traditional Kayah women's dress, an obvious marker of the legacies of the past and of difference between Karenni and non-Karenni, is not directly appropriated as a symbol in this process. This is because it is emblematic of aspects of the past not wanted in dominant groups' formulations of 'Karenni-ness'.

Instead, a transformation of traditional Kayah dress has become a metaphor for an emerging pan-Karenni national identity. Female school students and others, on occasions of annual festivals and ceremonies, wear what they describe as 'traditional' Karenni/Kayah dress, but which bears little resemblance to the clothes worn by the recently arrived refugee women. It comprises a striped, red *longyi* reaching to mid-calf length, a similar cloak, a white or pale pink blouse, and a white sash. In colour and patterning the skirt-cloth and cloak are clearly related to the skirt- and head-cloth worn by newly arrived refugees. There are two important differences to this wider form of dress, however. Firstly, it does not expose the amounts of female flesh seen with the 'traditional' version. And secondly, it is considered 'national Karenni', not 'Kayah', dress, not only by Kayah members of the longer-staying refugee population, but by all that population's other members too. Seng and Wass (1993: 229), writing about Palestinian wedding dress in the USA, similarly explore 'how the concept of tradition has changed, like the garments, over time, and how that change is linked to a search for national identity'. They point out that contrary to outsiders' understandings of 'tradition' as implying an unchanged form, 'the ["insiders"] definition of what is traditional involves a selective process, for as long as an object contains certain determined elements it may still be considered as "traditional". Both process and definition are dynamic'. For longer-staying Karenni refugees, the 'certain determined elements' include colour and patterning on the skirt-cloth and cloak.

This form of dress was developed by members of the growing national movement after 1948, and is a transformation of 'tradition' which includes elements of traditional Kayah dress. Like promulgations of 'tradition' discussed by Knauft (1997) in the cases of Melanesia and the Amazon, it 'actively appropriates aspects of perceived modernity in reconstruction of indigenous identity'. In this case, the appropriated 'aspects of perceived modernity' concern propriety, with women becoming more covered up. Furthermore, concurrently with ideas about dress, notions of proper feminine behaviour are also transformed. For example, young, unmarried, traditional Kayah girls joke about their breast-cloth (which usually only covers one breast), saying their boyfriends can have the exposed breast now, but they have to wait until marriage to get their hands on the other one. Such sexual banter is in sharp contrast to the self-consciously demure way in which most other refugee Karenni girls behave. Increasing nationalism, here accompanied by increasing Christianity, seems also to imply increasing conservatism, especially with respect to women and their sexuality. In this case, it is female dress that undergoes the most obvious conservative transformation.

Friedman (1992: 338) suggests that an engagement with modernity frequently implies devaluation of local culture. In the case of traditional Kayah female dress, an essentially *female* signification and reinforcement of cultural identity has in its untransmuted, traditional form, been devalued and ultimately rejected by the mainly male groups that dominate contemporary ideas of 'Karenni-ness'. For these dominant groups, transformation of traditional female dress represents continuation of a body of tradition that identifies Karenni people as having a distinct and glorious history, and emergence as a modern, Christian, educated and united people. The continuation and transformation of tradition are part of a set of processes aimed at ensuring Karenni identity remains Karenni, and at keeping Karenni people clearly distinct from others.

But transformation of female dress is only one of a number of ways in which Karenni groups to different extents use past- and future-oriented ideas of self, community and belonging, both to give meaning to their present displaced state, and to attempt to re-define identity and control a set of realistic and semi-mythical futures. For the new arrivals in their first months in the camp, in the initial and distressing stages of becoming a Karenni refugee, the only way they could give meaning to this experience was to tighten their grip on the visual markers of self that they had brought with them, particularly women's clothing, grasping firmly the most emblematic aspects of traditional Kayah culture and village life. As time has passed, the new arrivals have been drawn into the constant re-assessment and re-negotiation of identity experienced by all members of the Karenni refugee community.

Traditional dress, like festivals, exemplifies not only the complexities involved in emic interpretations of 'tradition', but also the extent of the elite's role in continuity and change in the context of Karenni nationalism. Clothing especially demonstrates too that actors other than the elite also have an important part to play in the ascription of identities, i.e. they 'are involved in *making* classifications as well as in simply following them . . . [they are] making decisions, choosing to some extent their own self-image, playing with identities and recognising the role of clothes in image construction and interpretation' (Tarlo 1996: 7–8). In a process by which Karenni identity is self-consciously, and reasonably successfully, strengthening and remoulding itself, elements of 'tradition' are selectively appropriated, transformed or rejected. This is part of a general process in which clothing, annual festivals, and other aspects of real and imagined shared pasts articulate political aspirations and revolutionary ideologies. Ideas of the past and the future combine to define a Karenni nationalism and national identity which rise above and are inclusive of all the related but distinct ethnic identities. Clothing plays an important part in this process.

References

Dudley, S. (1999) '"Traditional" culture and refugee welfare in north-west Thailand', *Forced Migration Review*, 6: 5–8.

Dudley, S. (2001) 'Displacement and identity: Karenni refugees in Thailand', unpublished DPhil. thesis, University of Oxford.

Friedman, J. (1992) 'Narcissism, roots, and postmodernity: the constitution of selfhood in global crisis', in Lash, S. and Friedman, J. (eds) *Modernity and Identity*, Oxford: Basil Blackwell.

Knauft, B.M. (1997) 'Gender identity, political economy and modernity in Melanesia and Amazonia', *Journal of the Royal Anthropological Institute*, 3(2): 233–59.

Lehman, F.K. (1967) 'Burma: Kayah society as a function of the Shan-Burma-Karen context', in Steward, J.H. (ed.) *Contemporary Change in Traditional Societies II: Asian Rural Societies*, Urbana, IL: University of Illinois Press, 1–104.

Seng, Y.J. and Wass, B. (1993) 'Traditional Palestinian wedding dress as a symbol of nationalism', in Eicher, J.B. (ed.) *Dress and Ethnicity*, Oxford: Berg.

Tarlo, E. (1996) *Clothing Matters: Dress and Identity in India*, London: Hurst.

Wilson, F. and Frederiksen, B.F. (eds) (1995) *Ethnicity, Gender and the Subversion of Nalionalism*, London: Frank Cass & Co.

First published as Dudley, S. (2002) 'Diversity, identity and modernity in exile: "traditional" Karenni clothing', in Green, A. and Burton, T.R. (eds) *Burma: Art and Archaeology*, London: British Museum, 143–51. Sandra Dudley is Programme Director for Interpretive Studies in the Department of Museum Studies at the University of Leicester. She is a specialist in material culture and exile.

Chapter 27

Tangible reminders of Sept. 11th

Glenn Collins

THE FLOWER-BEDECKED MOUNTAIN BIKE believed to have been abandoned by a missing World Trade Center messenger. A crushed firefighter's helmet from ground zero. The twisted shield from a police officer who perished. And the bent squeegee handle used to escape from a North Tower elevator. These objects of disaster will soon be on view at, respectively, the New York Historical Society, the New York City Fire Museum, the New York City Police Museum and the National Museum of American History of the Smithsonian Institution. And many more will be exhibited at these and a dozen other institutions from New York to New Orleans.

Over the last 12 months, historians, curators and archivists collected these artefacts, mindful of the urgencies that shaped their selection. 'There were no guidelines', said Dr Sarah M. Henry, Vice President for Programs at the Museum of the City of New York. 'From the beginning, there were impassioned calls to collect artefacts, but there was also institutional squeamishness at not being like ambulance chasers. We asked, was it ghoulish, or in some way unseemly, to proceed?' Some historians, like Kenneth T. Jackson, President of the New York Historical Society, began collecting almost immediately. A vestryman at St Paul's Chapel near ground zero, Dr Jackson found himself gathering paper and debris, most notably a blasted window blind from the trade center that had lodged in a churchyard tree. It will be part of the society's exhibition beginning Tuesday of 30 of the hundreds of objects it collected. 'These objects have been touched by history', said Dr Jackson, who directed his staff to respond immediately to the terrorist attacks. 'They have the power to speak to people, because the artefacts witnessed the event and its aftermath.'

Other institutions, however, were tentative about the collecting impulse, a sensitive topic that became an issue at an emotional three-hour meeting at the Museum of the City of New York held scarcely three weeks after the tragedy. Some

70 curatorial and archival professionals from more than 30 institutions attended. 'Many of the museums at that meeting had not been that collaborative or cooperative, so it was really important to get things on the table', said James B. Gardner, Associate Director for Curatorial Affairs at the National Museum of American History. Recalling the tone of the meeting, Mark A. Schaming, Director of Exhibitions at the New York State Museum in Albany, said: 'I felt we had to collect, and move quickly. But it was difficult to even talk about the whole thing. And it was hard to bring yourself to say what you wanted preserved.' Already, outdoor shrines and memorials were being damaged by the elements. 'But it was our clear conviction that it was not up to us to take anything down', Dr Henry said. 'History requires preservation, but that doesn't trump other things, like the need for public displays of mourning and grief.'

At the New Jersey Historical Society in Newark, the collection technique was to spread the word among community organizations and in the media, said Sally Yerkovich, the Society's President. She pointed out that 25 per cent of those who died in the trade center lived in New Jersey. The response was gratifying. For example, a school group near Holmdel, N.J., where several students had lost parents, donated the six-foot-high plywood letters – painted white and spelling out 'AMERICA UNITED' – that it had erected at the side of the Garden State Parkway.

Near ground zero, New York Historical Society staff members made field visits to firehouses, St. Paul's Chapel and Nino's restaurant, where recovery workers sought refuge. 'We offered our services as volunteers, and we surely wanted to help', said Jan Seidler Ramirez, Director of the Society's museum division. Ultimately the personal relationships that were developed in that way became crucial when the rescue workers began asking for help in maintaining and preserving objects and shrines that had by now acquired the aspect of the sacred. From the start, curators realized that 'the objects we collected were special and powerful', Dr Ramirez said. 'Very humble objects constructed of humble materials became priceless. People's hands were shaking as they gave them to us. They were conduits to the event, allowing people to personalize the experience.'

Almost immediately the private non-profit institutions, already suffering from personnel and space shortages, found their workload staggering. At the New York Historical Society, 'we weren't at our desks a lot', Dr Ramirez said, adding, 'We conducted business by walking with cell phones in our hands.' Eager benefactors began swelling their collections. 'In mid-October we had collected enough to fill a shelf', said Amy A. Weinstein, curator of the Society's twentieth- and twenty-first-century collections. 'Then we filled a corner of a room. Then a storage container. Then it went everywhere.'

But ground zero was initially a lockdown area, off limits to most curatorial collecting. The logistics of collecting there, as well as the legality, were fraught. Ownership was contested, and the site was divided into jurisdictional zones run by different law-enforcement agencies. The curators who managed to get in were stunned to discover how little had survived. 'I was astonished and overwhelmed at how destroyed everything was', Mr Schaming said. Voorsanger & Associates Architects were sanctioned by the Port Authority of New York and New Jersey, owner of the World Trade Center, to collect artefacts for a future memorial. But items that might not be pristine enough to be memorial material could still be immensely valuable,

Dr Henry said. 'The hardest thing to recapture for future generations', she said, 'is the fabric of everyday life. We kept telling people that museums might be interested in stuff that looked like garbage.'

Fresh Kills, the 175-acre municipal landfill on Staten Island, became the ground zero repository. And in early January curators from the Historical Society, the Museum of the City of New York, the Fire Museum and the New York State Museum were permitted entry to the Fresh Kills operation, where 1,000 workers sifted debris down to objects the size of a dime. 'Getting artefacts was like pulling teeth', Dr Ramirez said. There was a certain amount of suspicion, since 'we were trying to keep the media out, and we didn't want souvenir hunters to get these materials on our watch', recalled an F.B.I. special agent, Richard B. Marx, who headed F.B.I. operations at Fresh Kills. 'We were so lost in the task of recovering the victims that we couldn't see the history around us', he said. And since victims' family members were often escorted through the site by the F.B.I., interaction with curators could be both limited and awkward. 'You can't tell a relative looking for a loved one, I'm going to stop and pick up this item now for a museum', Agent Marx said.

Trust developed slowly at Fresh Kills, often 'after we did a lot of schmoozing', Ms. Weinstein said. She added, 'The literal fact at Fresh Kills was that if we didn't save it then, it was gone for good.' Some of the Historical Society's artefacts, like the door from a 78th Precinct van, were rescued from the car crusher at the last minute. Access was everything. Mr Schaming won frequent admission to Fresh Kills thanks to Gov. George E. Pataki, who also asked the National Guard to transport recovery objects on flatbed trucks sent from upstate. The artefacts were decontaminated at a prison, then brought to Albany. As a result Mr Schaming's exhibition of more than 40 artefacts has some remarkable, and remarkably large, objects, including an entire fire truck – which was severely damaged in the collapse – from Engine Company 6, which lost four firefighters.

The New York City Police Museum was invited to Fresh Kills by the Police Department and did locate artefacts there, but it also received many items in its exhibition from 'the families of the 23', said Katherine Adamenko, curator of special exhibitions at the Police Museum, referring to the police officers who died. Theoretically the New York City Fire Museum had access to artefacts, 'but many of our Fire Department contacts were lost on Sept. 11', said Peter Rothenberg, curator of the museum, 'and for those who survived, saving things was hardly a priority in dealing with the tragedy.' Ultimately, he said, 'we were the recipient of contributions of artefacts, for which we were very grateful.' In a time when access was all, 'we shared our contacts in the F.B.I. – names and phone numbers – with Sarah and Mark', said Dr Gardner, project director for the Smithsonian exhibition opening Wednesday in Washington. It will include some 50 items from ground zero, the Pentagon and the Pennsylvania crash site of the fourth hijacked plane.

After the Voorsanger firm, the Smithsonian was often the collection leader, thanks to its federal scope, its budget and its law-enforcement contacts. 'Some felt the artefacts should stay in the state, but the Smithsonian is America's museum', Mr Schaming said. 'It was an attack on America that happened in New York. And in Washington, they had the Pentagon.' The difficulty for recovery managers was that 'there were so many institutions coming to us that wanted a piece of the buildings

– from the city archives to the museums – that we couldn't stop every few minutes and talk to them', Agent Marx said, adding, 'so they realized early on that their best effort was to work together, to get materials and then divide them up at a later date.'

Sharing was instinctual. 'Mark and I were on the phone every day', Dr Henry said of Mr Schaming. 'They used their trucks to pick up our stuff.' Mr Schaming gave Dr Yerkovich of the New Jersey Historical Society a patch from a Port Authority worker found in the rubble that will appear in the society's exhibition opening Wednesday. And the New York State Museum itself 'deferred to the Fire Museum people when there were Fire Department objects to be collected', Mr Schaming said. For many, Fresh Kills was an alternative universe. 'Nothing in art history school ever prepared us for this', Ms Weinstein said. Dr Henry said, 'I was an academic historian, and I never thought I would be up to my ankles in toxic mud and picking up shards of people's lives and then throwing away my clothing when I got home.'

At Fresh Kills access suddenly changed for the better in March, six months after the attacks. Recovery workers 'began to realize that the process would have an end, that they could walk away from it', Dr Jackson said. 'We didn't want the work that we did there to be forgotten', Agent Marx recalled. 'We wanted future generations to know what the agents and detectives did up there.' Subsequently, in considering their inventory of materials, there was institutional soul-searching as objects were selected. The New York Historical Society chose to leave out 'artefacts that we did not want sensationalized', Dr Ramirez said, including aluminium aircraft pieces from the hijacked planes. But the Smithsonian has decided to display jetliner fragments. 'We had misgivings at first', Dr Gardner said. 'Then there was the recognition that without the fragments, it was hard to represent the memory of those folks who were in the planes.'

Even now, as they toil to perfect their exhibitions, curators are struck by the power of the artefacts. 'Touching these things is still very emotional', said Ms Adamenko at the Police Museum, referring to the many objects contributed by families of officers who perished, including the officers' damaged service weapons, handcuffs and shields. 'It's such an honor to have these things', Ms Adamenko said. 'I can't talk about them without having tears in my eyes.'

First published as Collins, G. (2002) 'Tangible reminders of Sept. 11th', *The New York Times*, September 5. Glenn Collins is a journalist well known for his contributions to the *New York Times*.

Chapter 28

On the rocks

Philip S. Doughty

THE MUSEUMS ASSOCIATION, in conference, deals with a wide range of topics. In the last ten years it has considered education in museums, museum ethics, museums in relation to their communities, finance, interrelationships within the profession, museums as record centres, managing museums, government employment schemes and museums, and museums as tourist attractions. But what about museums as specimen repositories? It is, after all, why they exist. Is there no concern about museums as material research centres – about the problems concerning the modern caring curator?

In a decade at Conference, the Association has not directly addressed itself once to the central concern of museums, the curatorial care of the specimens they hold. The outside world has looked on in benign satisfaction, sympathising with the latest art appeal but accepting, because the institutions concerned appear to, that generally the world of museums is basically sound, the garden is lovely. But, as more dedicated curators meet and compare notes, there is a rising voice of concern, a realization that all in the garden is far from satisfactory.

In fact this Association has something of a reputation for training curators, declaring them Associates, and then ignoring them unless they emerge as directors on Council. The voice of the mature curator is rarely heard, and despite a number of proposals for injecting informed curatorial opinion into the deliberations of Council the political representatives have much preferred schemes that left their power base intact.

But the Association has paid a price for preserving such imbalance. It still has scant recognition in the national museums, where the curatorial power-base chiefly lies and over the last decade we have witnessed the growth of a movement of specialist curatorial groups outside the Association. They have no difficulty attracting membership from the national museums, the local authority museums and the universities and they speak with a curatorial authority which cannot be matched inside the Association, and which is now impossible to ignore. But the main price paid for the want of curatorial opinion in the top ranks of influential museum bodies, and in any ranks of politics, has been in the museums themselves, and very largely the local authority museums and the universities.

It might be useful to compare the requirements of just one of these new groups, the Geological Curators' Group, against the performance of the Museums Association, now so close to its centenary. The Geological Curators Group was formed in 1974 and quickly attracted members expressing the same kind of very basic unmet needs. Most urgent was a forum within which specialist curators could meet to express and exchange views. There was none, and no urgency on the part of the major museological agencies to provide one. Inexperienced and non-specialist curators wanted advice on curatorial standards, but there was no curatorial standard written in the practical language so much needed. The requirement seen by established curators to advise on the deployment of collections was thwarted by the information vacuum relating to geological specialists and specialist collecting areas in UK museums. The only worthwhile list of collections was a partial document arising out of an amateur and private interest. Published in 1940, it mentions fewer than 10 per cent of collections we know to exist. In fact, for a major specialist science strongly represented in museums, the degree of ignorance in which it found itself operating was a damning stricture on a museum establishment which arose to support the 'amateur' curators of the first four decades of this century and which has found evolution in recent time increasingly difficult in the face of a rapidly increasing and specialized curatorial demand. I would contend that evolution has been difficult mainly because experienced curatorial voice has not been central in the power structure of the Association, and the services it offers are of little relevance to the working curator.

In these circumstances it was decided that nothing further could be achieved until some basic information was available, and the Group embarked on a postal questionnaire survey to determine some of the fundamental facts relating to geology in UK museums. The full form of the report on this exercise will be published by the Geological Society of London later this year.

Every museum authority, within this Association's definition of a museum, was approached, and eventually a 98 per cent return on questionnaires was reached giving real potency to the results. It emerged that half the authorities in the UK own geology collections, and among other things information was sought on collection size, content, contained collections, specialist interests, key specimens, the nature of original data, the volume and variety of museum documentation, the nature of storage, storage furniture, accessibility of material, its arrangement, the systems used, specimen condition and staffing. The statistics will appear in the report but what follows from them is likely to be of much wider professional interest since the situation discovered may not be unique to geology.

The report reveals a frightening picture of the material heritage of the science of geology in the museums of the UK. It exposes a situation of disorder, neglect, mismanagement and decay on an unsuspected scale, with a mere handful of curators, lacking any professional cohesion, struggling, in general ineffectually, in the face of impossible odds. The odds are represented by some 20–30 million geological specimens housed in a little under 300 museums spread widely throughout the UK.

Only 46 of these museums employ full-time geological staff. Primitive curatorial arrangements exist for a further 51, but they do not involve professional geologists. A staggering 65 per cent of geological collections have no formal curatorial arrangements of any kind, and about half the nation's major collections outside the national museums fall into this group. This mass of geological material, perhaps the most important single national geological resource in the world, should be a source of pride and a spring of scientific stimulation to the whole nation. Almost all of it is in public ownership in the Institute of Geological Sciences [now British Geological Survey], the British Museum (Natural History) [the Natural History Museum], other national museums, the local authority museums and the university museums. In reality it does not exist as a national resource at all and with over half the museums admitting that they have dirty material and a third that parts of their collections are in decay, it seems highly unlikely that much of it will survive to become part of one. It exists as hundreds, perhaps thousands, of collections isolated geographically, professionally and organizationally, and in terms of public awareness almost all of these collections might not exist. Undoubtedly very large parts of the heritage remain, but the condition of the specimens, and equally important, of the information relating to them, is endangered in almost all directions.

A lack of curatorial care appears to be the fundamental factor in all these ills. Without informed curation the physical state of specimens may not be maintained. Delicate minerals and fossils are frequently mishandled, damaged and bruised, reducing their scientific and financial worth. Dirt is allowed to penetrate material which is unavoidably damaged in the cleaning process; specimens are stored in environments lacking even the crudest atmospheric control, laying them open to chemical and biological attack. The survey shows that most original information about specimens is in the form of labels on or with specimens and in poor storage conditions chemically unstable papers disintegrate, pigments fade, and fungal attack can render the best quality labels worthless. Without this documentation specimens become almost useless scientifically and the interests and aspirations of the collector and the community he sought to serve are betrayed.

Against this background one particular category of fossil material is so important that it must be isolated for discussion. Type specimens are of such overriding scientific significance that any museum which is a repository for them has, in effect, committed itself to the ultimate curatorial obligation and the highest academic standards. The type concept is complex and hedged in by internationally agreed rules, but stated simply it says that any specimen or group of specimens which are discovered to be new to science and which are named, described and published for the first time achieve type status. They assume paramount importance as name bearers and become the standards of comparison for all similar material subsequently discovered anywhere in the world. Since the classification of all fossil and living organisms is based on the species concept, which is rooted in type specimens, it can be appreciated that deterioration, damage or loss of type material is an irreparable loss to the whole of the science. It usually leads to disputes which can never be fully resolved.

The report shows that of the 64 museums which are type repositories, only 29 have curatorial staff. There are therefore 35 museums with fossil type material and no informed curatorial staff. The museums in this situation are not professionally equipped to discharge their responsibilities to the scientific community and quite how they learn, and meet, their basic curatorial obligations is difficult to comprehend. There are undoubtedly geological Rembrandts decaying in our museums alongside the hosts of lesser collections.

Perhaps of all the museums in the report the group which might be expected to recognize its scientific responsibilities is the university museums. The whole basis of science relates to truths demonstrated by experiment or facts related to observation and one would expect the high centres of learning to be the first to recognize and expound this principle and consequently to be in the forefront of curatorial care. The reality by no means bears this out. Thirty-eight university geology departments and related institutions are included in the survey. Among them are some of the most professional museums encountered, but they also include some of the worst and the great majority fail to meet basic standards. Despite large and usually important collections, fewer than half have curators, and of these most bear the title as a secondary responsibility to a lectureship or a technical position. Since, presumably, those responsible are aware of the implications of their actions the onus is placed on the donor or the researcher to ensure the survival of his most important material, or the body granting the research funds, particularly if it is in the public sphere. It is certain that some action needs to be taken to ensure the survival of published and research material in university departments whether or not they consider themselves to be museums.

It is literally true that not a single person knows the variety, quality and significance of even the geological collections housed by the UK museums. The appendixes to the survey listing over 800 collections hint at what might be available, but it is certain that the list represents only a fraction of collections known to exist, and there are bound to be many others. The reasons for this ignorance are twofold. There is insufficient documentation of the collections which do have geological curators, and there is no central agency whose concern it is to maintain and update documentation of the rest and centrally collate a record. The basically unsound situation of geological documentation, as treated in the report, still masks the problem of the quality of existing museum records. The only investigation of them, unfortunately unpublished, indicates that most do not even meet basic stocktaking requirements, and almost all fall far short of the simplest academic needs. The figures in the report should be seen in this setting. New standards of documentation are now emerging from the work of the Museums Documentation Association, but even the small numbers of geological records appearing from the museums working this scheme are not uniform. Although most are scientifically valuable, if no standardization of record structure and terminology is achieved, the resulting ambiguities will lead to new generations of problems for future curators. Professional skill is the only basis of sound work and, regardless of mechanisms, the only worthwhile museums record is that written by a qualified and experienced geologist with developed curatorial skills.

Proper scientific records are of little use if the material itself is not available when it is needed. The situation also commonly arises in UK museums where primary documentation cannot even proceed because the material is inaccessible. The simplest of logistical problems are involved here yet clearly the report shows that solutions have not been found. The reasons are evident to almost all curators and relate to the provision of storage space and suitable storage furniture. Storage space is a problem in almost all museums, and storage space meeting the atmospheric requirements of geological specimens is rarely met. Suitable geological furniture is sparse, and even drawered cabinets, the most convenient of all structures, often fail to meet geological requirements. Cardboard box and packing case storage, of which there is a considerable amount, is symptomatic of the general geological malaise and should be squarely branded as unacceptable. If there was ever a case for secure, robust and durable furniture it must surely apply to museum storage where curatorial obligations are known to extend into the indefinite future. The ideal solutions to the problems are in this case the most economical in the long term.

The failure of owning authorities to comprehend the nature, value and uses of their museums has led museum staff into an attitude of mind, frequently not consciously registered, in which they have come to regard the collection almost as their private preserve to work, or to ignore, as they choose. This situation can only be a consequence of bankruptcy of purpose, one of the worst forms of mismanagement. It lays the owning authorities open to accusations of indifference to their collections to the point of exposing them to risk, and in extremity of passively supervising their destruction. At a time when three authorities have very recently been made aware of crises affecting their own property, and have done nothing, it is hardly an overstatement of the case.

If a director or curator fails to assert the importance of collections, then management problems are compounded. Pressures from local government committees, whose political composition makes them intrinsically unstable and transient, are acceded to. Understandably, such bodies press for exhibitions, displays, demonstrations, lectures, educational involvement and similar short-term activities where an injection of resources can be seen to yield 'results' within a political term of office. But museums cannot perform their essential role on such a time scale, and the compiling of collections, their housing, their cataloguing and the essential scholastic work which accompanies them should be recognized as the long-term fundamental work from which all else derives. That is not to deny the service aspects of a museum's programme of activity, but good displays can only be based on good collections, and good collections can only result from curatorial discernment, expert care and sound scholarship.

The present plight of geology in museums has arisen despite the 91 years of existence of this Association; the 49 years of effort of the Standing Commission on Museums and Galleries (SCMG) and the more recent accession of the area museums councils and their area services. Their credibility in curatorial terms is now exposed, and its restoration depends on right policy, real influence and a measure of power.

The area councils are central to funding in the Drew Report of the SCMG, *Framework for a System for Museums* (1979), and so deserve some consideration. The area museum councils are often held up as the salvation of the underdog, and this may well be true in the field of technical services, but they have proved to be little more than tokens at disciplinary level. It could hardly be otherwise. They were simply not conceived on a scale, nor do they have the appropriate power or curatorial expertise, to make a significant impression on the major areas of neglect. Furthermore their chairmen and committees are drawn from the very same local authorities responsible for the condition of many of the museums in the report. A solution of the problems outlined here is certainly beyond the scope of the area services as presently organized, and beyond the vision of them in the Drew Report.

Government recognition of the place of science in the cultural life of the nation is still awaited. That the scientific content of the heritage is overlorded by a Minister for the Arts is not merely an etymological quibble. This nation, which lives on its scientific attainment and the associated technologies, last year spent £61 million, and this year will be spending £70 million through the Arts Council of Great Britain on the arts, very largely on the performing arts, in areas of interest only to a minority of the population. The history of government involvement with the arts relates very closely to personalities within parliament, and the lack of a vociferous support for a public representation of scientific culture is sorely felt and by comparison long overdue, particularly when, as at present, scientists are misrepresented as remote, self-interested beings pursuing pure science regardless of the threat to humanity. There is a world of difference between the Natural Environmental Research Council's Grant which Mr St John Stevas [Minister for the Arts in the Thatcher government until 1981] cannot touch, and the Arts Council of Great Britain's Grant which he can, as they affect the community, and the consequences of this uneven treatment of the public face of science should be examined in the DES [Department of Education and Science] as a matter of urgency.

It would be a mistake to assume that the appointment of a large number of geological curators in the appropriate places would solve the problems of geology in museums. Sixty per cent of the museums in the survey said they needed help, and a significant number of them already have geological staff. Geology is now so complex, and the specialised collections in our museums so demanding, that only experts in particular groups of geological material can help. The overwhelming need is for an integrated national museum service capable of handling all curatorial problems regardless of how or where they arise. That presupposes a central authority able to view the problems of geology at the national level and to plan resources accordingly.

Certain facts are inescapable in the light of the survey, but the most important is that the permissive legislation relating to museums allows authorities to establish them without even rudimentary safeguards for collections. Government by exhortation simply has not worked in this area. The legislation needs to be re-examined as a matter of urgency. Although geology highlights this situation dramatically, it is only one of a range of museum interests suffering similarly, though probably less glaringly, and the solution is one which must apply to the whole museum field.

The following recommendations, if carried through, would establish a framework within which a national museum service might be brought into being.

1   Legislation defining museums, their functions and responsibilities, based on national, local authority and university institutions should be introduced.

2   Minimum standards of curatorial care should be determined to include the environment, furniture organization, documentation and conservation, of museum collections, and their staffing, and written into the same Bill.

3   An organization should be established either as an agency of DES or directly controlled by them, with a brief to establish the contents of all UK museums,

the prevailing conditions in museums in relation to paragraph 2 of these recommendations, and to frame a national plan for museums accordingly.

4   It is imperative that the Council of such an organization should include among its membership prominent practising curators at least in proportion to the administrators appointed. Without such a balance the reality of the professional situation could remain as remote, and the decisions taken as unreal, as at present.

5   A small full-time secretariat working in close collaboration with specialist panels of professional advisers should be able to take, and act on, decisions requiring special expertise without the necessity for a larger bureaucracy.

It is an incontrovertible fact that there will be no significant improvement in the museums situation without legislation placing well-defined responsibilities on the authorities which maintain or create them. To do nothing would not maintain a *status quo*. There is no stability in the present situation: outside the national museums there is rapid deterioration and decay on a grand scale.

When this recession is over there may be an opportunity to provide a national service at the academic level which, with a little vision and adventurous planning, could make a reality of those much-mouthed ideals of personal enrichment and spiritual fulfilment so often linked with museums and which are now almost discredited political platitudes. The possibilities in its realization may even exceed our boldest vision, but as organized curators we shall first need to be able to speak with authority on the situation which exists in museums now, with the facts and the figures, and, as with all political cases, we shall have to be patient, relentless and prepared to fight on for however long it takes to convert an unanswerable case into positive, corrective action.

First published as Doughty, P.S. (1980) 'On the rocks', *Museums Association Conference Proceedings*, 1980: 12–14. Philip Doughty was at the time Keeper of Geology at the Ulster Museum in Belfast, and later directed science programmes at the museum. Now retired, Philip Doughty is widely regarded for his significant contribution to the professionalisation of museum practice in the UK.

Chapter 29

Endangered species and the law

Valerius Geist

T HE SCIENCE OF TAXONOMY may be thought of by many as an arcane subject, innocent of the problems of the real world. But when taxa became included
in conservation laws, this innocence vanished. Endangered species acts, wildlife management laws and the Convention on International Trade in Endangered Species
(CITES) – essential, if imperfect, tools for conservation – label species and subspecies with formal taxonomic names. Such taxa, elevated to legal status, became
subject to legal action. That may place biologists, accustomed to privacy, anonymous peer review and uncertainty in knowledge, in the witness stand, subject to
hostile cross-examination. In one Canadian court case I was questioned for 24 hours
on the taxonomy of red deer (*Cervus elaphas* Linnaeus, 1758). The case led to fines
of $25,000 for the defendant, who argued that by crossing two (invalid) subspecies
listed in legislation he had created a new form of life, and that laws controlling
commerce in wildlife did not apply to his creations.

Implications

It is not the image of scientists squirming in witness chairs that merits attention,
rather the fact that courts and solicitors' offices are allowed to rule on taxonomy.
Judges may now decide on matters such as the definition of species or subspecies,
the criteria for establishing taxa, which taxa are valid, and which populations can
be legally protected. The implications for conservation, but also for biology in
general, are profound and worrying.

Collectors, scientific or otherwise, are playing risky games taking chances on
taxonomic uncertainties, for taxonomic mislabelling may now be a breach of law.
That is no trivial matter if it leads to stiff fines or imprisonment, in particular if
it brands the perpetrator a criminal. Even without such draconian consequences,

the repercussions may be serious enough, as shown by the 'Chinese argali' case. Argalis (*Ovis ammon* Linnaeus, 1766) are giant sheep from central Asia, one of which, the Tibetan argali (*O. a. hodgsoni* Blyth, 1840), is on the endangered list of the US Endangered Species Act. Four argali rams, shot in April 1988 by four US hunters in Ganzu Province, China, for a payment of $100,000, were confiscated by agents of the US Fish and Wildlife Service upon entry to San Francisco. The hunters had been accompanied by an employee of the service, who was on temporary loan to the Smithsonian Institution. The trophies were labelled merely as *O. ammon* on the export permit. The sheep were subsequently identified as Tibetan argalis by four experts, but this was disputed by the hunters.

Although the case was eventually settled out of court, it had wide repercussions. It led to hundreds of thousands of dollars in attorney fees, a Grand Jury investigation, a flurry of diplomatic activity between the United States and China, embarrassing publicity, serious rifts within the US Fish and Wildlife Service and within the International Union for the Conservation of Nature over policy, several international meetings on caprid conservation and formal taxonomic and status reviews. The case embroiled two secretaries of the interior, five senators, two congressmen, affected even Secretary of State James Baker, and led to frantic activity to 'de-fang' the Endangered Species Act by some hunters' organizations. Pressure was exerted on scientists acting as expert witnesses to change their testimony, and they were maligned or blackmailed. Nearly four years afterwards, the affair is not yet over.

Species identity

The use of alloenzymes and mitochondrial DNA analysis has thrown doubt on the identity of some species named in conservation legislation. Eastern timber wolves (*Canis lupus* Linnaeus, 1785) and the red wolf (*C. rufus* Audubon and Bachman, 1851) may carry the mitochondrial DNA of coyotes (*C. latrans* Say, 1823) (Lehman *et al.* 1991; Wayne and Jenks 1991), whereas Florida panthers (*Felis concolor coryi* Bangs, 1896) carry genes of pumas from central America because of a release of hybrids decades ago. These cases have generated concern since the US Solicitor's office of the Department of the Interior ruled that hybrids are not protected by the Endangered Species Act (O'Brien and Mayr 1991; Gittleman and Pimm 1991; Rennie 1991). Although I agree with O'Brien and Mayr (1991) that the hybrid policy should be carefully applied on a case-by-case basis, and that hybridization need not be a tragedy for conservation, the unresolved question is whether the courts, rather than other specialists, will concur with their view. Moreover, to succeed in court, there needs to be agreement on the criteria to use when applying the 'hybrid policy'. As I discuss below, one such criterion should be the success of hybrids as tested in their natural habitat.

Taxonomic flaws may have severe consequences for conservation, and Canada's 'wood bison' (*Bison bison 'athabascae'* Rhoads, 1897) are a case in point. These bison are enshrined as a formal subspecies in legislation, and have been subject to a longstanding, well-publicized national conservation effort. Recently, a consortium of agencies led by Agriculture Canada (including the interagency organization in charge of 'wood bison' conservation), proposed that the bison of Wood Buffalo National Park, as carriers of bovine brucellosis and tuberculosis, be eliminated and replaced with disease-free 'wood bison'. A federal review panel agreed with the consortium.

The proposal sparked controversy even beyond Canada's borders. The park bison are derived from about 1,500 native bison and 6,673 (diseased) southern-plains bison moved to the park in 1925. The 'wood bison' are captive off-spring from bison captured in the northern part of the park that were once thought to have escaped hybridization. If 'wood' and 'plains' bison are valid subspecies, then the park bison are hybrids and, as such, the consortium argues, are not worthy of conservation. Not only was the taxon *athabascae* based on an inadequate second-hand description of a single specimen and subsequently on worthless taxonomic methods, but when the animals were properly fed, the characteristic hair coat of 'wood bison' transforms into that of 'plains bison' within about a year.

Wood bison are, consequently, not a taxon, but an ecotype (and an artefact of captivity at that) (Geist 1991a). Genetic analysis shows that 'wood bison' herds differ no more from plains bison herds than one from another. The designation of 'hybrid' for the park bison is thus false on taxonomic and genetic grounds. The species *B. bison* Linnaeus, 1758 has no subspecies, and that turns official con-servation policy on its head. The park bison, still under selection pressure from predators, are not the worthless hybrids defined by officialdom, but are the most diverse, naturally tested gene pool remaining of the species *B. bison*. Replacing them with an inbred 'wood bison' ecotype, untested for decades by predators, would not only confuse phenotype with genotype, but would undermine the essence of conservation.

Clearly, taxonomy is important in a tangible sense. Yet worthless taxonomic methods, ignorance about the biology of taxonomic criteria, failure to review original and foreign-language literature, faulty curation, tampering with museum specimens and labels, and artistic licence in illustrating taxa not only cast doubt on standards of scholarship in taxonomy (Geist 1991b), but reduce the effectiveness of science in providing urgently needed legal protection to various forms of life. Already the American Society of Zoological Parks and Aquaria has expressed doubt about formal taxonomy, and is focusing instead on 'genetically significant' popula-tions as subjects of conservation. But this is no substitute, in my view, for an improved, formal taxonomy.

A fatal flaw in much large-mammal taxonomy is the use of comparative morphometrics as a taxonomic tool. Comparative morphometrics of crania or skeletons of free-living populations can no more be used to measure taxonomic (genetic) differences than a rubber band can be, used to measure distance. Every set of comparable measurements conceals genetic, epistatic, environmental and statistical variation. That is, the gross variation is a mixture of different types of variation, within which the genetic variance is undefined. It remains indefinable, despite various approximations. Comparative morphometrics as a taxonomic tool is logically flawed. It confuses phenotype with genotype, analogy with homology, ecotype with taxon, and does not reveal the taxonomic and evolutionary differ-ences between the populations compared. It reveals only differences, the origins of which remain obscure.

This flaw is not uncommon in other fields of biology (Hirsch 1981) when quantitative comparisons between populations are used to bolster evolutionary analysis. Such comparisons are futile if the proportion of variance attributable to heredity is unknowable. The closer the relationship between populations of a given form, the more speculative must be the conclusions about evolutionary relationships, because large phenotypic differences can arise from closely related genotypes in different environments. Taxonomic or evolutionary differences in close relatives should be studied experimentally, provided different variables affecting ontogeny are subject to effective control.

Taxa determination

In the absence of quantitative factors that are firmly (experimentally) based on genetic expression, what criteria might one use for determining taxa at the species and sub-species levels? The 'biological species concept' defines the species level in sexually reproducing organisms by using incompatibility of reproduction as an objective distinguishing criterion. Undoubtedly, this is a good and sufficient criterion in many cases, particularly in species-rich communities with much sympatry [when two species live in the same geographical area]. But this criterion, narrowly interpreted as the absence of hybridization in captivity by some (Haltenorth 1963), is biologically flawed. This is painfully evident in the case of ruminants in the palaearctic and nearctic biogeographical domains, as widely differing forms hybridize readily in captivity, and the hybrids grow into adults under human care. But survival into adulthood is unlikely in natural conditions, where the hybrids are frequently exposed to predation. For instance, we found that hybrids of white-tailed (*Odocoileus virginianus* Boddaert, 1785) and mule deer (*O. hemionus* Rafinesque, 1817), which may develop in captivity into truly magnificent specimens, suffer from severe deficiencies when it comes to tactics and strategies of predator avoidance. The parent species have quite different means of escaping predators, whereas hybrids have non-functioning mixtures of parental escape behaviours, plus inefficient locomotion. Escape strategies and tactics are, evidently, under close genetic control.

Is the current attempt to classify sika (*Cervus nippon* Temminck, 1837) and red deer into hybrid populations in several European localities (Bartoš *et al.* 1981; Bartoš and Žirovnický 1981, 1982), an artefact of the absence of predators? In Manchuria, where both forms are sympatric, the populations remain distinct despite an occasional hybrid. Reproductive compatibility does not necessarily define a species, and sika and red deer differ in anti-predator strategies. Applying the conventional biological species concept would include in the same species hybrids that are not viable in nature. Viability of between-population hybrids under natural conditions of predation appears to be a better criterion for 'species'. It is a severe test, for even hybrids between subspecies may show loss of viability. This is suggested, for instance, by narrow hybrid zones, by ecological separation between some subspecies of Asiatic red deer, and by some difficulties in the hybridization of European red deer and North American wapiti.

Taxonomy without an understanding of ecology may have little relevance. Yet obtaining such understanding is difficult or even impossible today because of the widespread destruction of natural environments and the concomitant holding of large mammals in small populations in predator-free, artificial environments. The criterion of viability in natural environments will become increasingly difficult to test in the field, though experimental exposure of hybrids to predators, for instance, may be helpful. Consequently, species could be defined heuristically, as the next level of dissimilarity above the subspecies level, a practice adopted by those studying caprid biology (Nadler *et al.* 1973).

Although O'Brien and May (1991) defined subspecies geographically, this should be a fall-back criterion at best, as geographical origin has to be accepted on faith. For conservation laws to function effectively, one needs to be able to establish the geographical original of specimens by factors intrinsic to the specimen. How could one spot that a protected species or subspecies was being imported without recourse to the label stating its origin?

The nuptial hair coat of reproductively active adults is an old, widely used taxonomic criterion for subspecies, but only in some lineages. Circumstantial evidence suggests that nuptial hair patterns are under close genetic control in almost all cases. Bison appear to be unique among large mammals, as the structure of their hair coat varies environmentally, just as do antlers in deer. The nuptial coat of adult mammals as a taxonomic criterion delineating subspecies can be applied accurately only with an understanding of sex, age and seasonal differences, as well as some knowledge of the effects of transplants to different environments.

Uniting populations with the same nuptial 'uniform' into one subspecies greatly reduces splintering of species based on meaningless morphometric differences. But it may obscure real genetic differences in ecological adaptations between populations which deserve to be recognized formally. This is difficult to accomplish, with few exceptions. One such exception is the bighorn sheep (*Ovis canadensis* Shaw, 1803) of North America. Although the 'uniform' is nearly the same in all sheep of this species, there are differences based on ecology, such as the short hair-coat, large ears and long tooth rows of sheep adapted to hot deserts. Some species, however, such as bears, cougar or white-tailed deer, are amenable neither to sub specific distinctions by nuptial dress, as they look much the same no matter where they live, nor to differences in morphology based on differences in ecological adaptations.

White-tailed deer, an ancient and very successful species, have a distribution from just short of the Arctic Circle in Canada, to 18 degrees south of the Equator in Peru. Although they differ in such social features as presence or size of the metatarsal gland, or the relative size of the tail, or in ecological adaptations such as differences in the shedding patterns of the seasonal hair coats, these differences are overshadowed by the great uniformity in nuptial dress. Differences in size and antler morphology are not taxonomically meaningful, because these features vary greatly with environmental quality and seasonal factors. Yet, although remarkably uniform in external appearance, white-tailed deer in South America differ more genetically from white-tailed deer in North America than do white-tailed deer from black-tailed deer in North America. White-tails also differ genetically between regions, without these differences reflecting conventional 'taxonomic' differences (Smith *et al.* in Halls 1985). A white-tailed deer's geographical origin cannot be determined from its morphology, as can be done with reasonable accuracy for black-tailed deer, wild sheep, ibex or even red deer.

Species definition

How then does one define useful taxonomic units within such a species? Should one define subspecies genetically? That may be necessary, but it has pitfalls, as the Canadian bison controversy reveals. Genetic analysis shows that different plains bison populations differ somewhat and are, roughly, equidistant from one another. All plains bison arose at the turn of the century from the same stock based on about 90 bison captured between 1873 and 1886. The differences between herds appear to be meaningless captivity effects, generated in part by the founder effect and subsequent drift in small herds. A further reduction in genetic diversity should arise in tiny founder herds when the dominant bull displaces others from breeding and, after breeding several cohorts of daughters, is displaced in turn by his larger sons. His sons go on to breed from their mother, aunts, sisters, daughters, cousins and so on. The male-dominance effect in small founder herds thus promises to narrow and distort genetic differences.

Should differences that arise from random factors and captivity effects be part of taxonomic nomenclature? One could generate 'subspecies' *ad infinitum* with every founding herd. We assume that the genetic differences between taxa are linked to adaptations to natural environments, otherwise taxonomy does not reflect the natural order of life. We must be careful to ensure that this order is not drowned out by the 'genetic noise' of man-made artefacts.

Clearly, the taxonomy of large mammals needs to be rethought. Taxonomy has gained greatly in importance since the advent of conservation legislation, and must be freed from neglect by proper funding and by intelligent practitioners. The dismantling of museum collections is not only tragic, but irresponsible, now that the specimens have gained legal significance. Without good collections and good taxonomists, signatories to international conservation conventions cannot adequately manage conservation within their own borders, let alone live up to their international obligations.

References

Bartoš, L., Hyánek, J. and Žirovnický, J. (1981) 'Hybridization between red and sika deer. I. Craniological analysis', *Zool. Anzeiger*, 207: 260–70.

Bartoš, L. and Žirovnický, J. (1981) 'Hybridization between red and sika deer. II. Phenotype analysis', *Zool. Anzeiger*, 207: 271–87.

Bartoš, L. and Žirovnický, J. (1982) 'Hybridization between red and sika deer. III. Interspecific behaviour', *Zool. Anzeiger*, 208: 20–36.

Geist, V. (1991a) 'Phantom subspecies: the wood bison *Bison bison "athabascae"* Rhoads 1897 is not a valid taxon, but an ecotype', *Arctic*, 44: 287–300.

Geist, V. (1991b) 'On taxonomy of giant sheep (Ovis ammon Linneaus, 1766)', *Canadian Journal of Zoology*, 69: 706–23.

Gittleman, J.L. and Pimm, S.L. (1991) 'Crying wolf in North America', *Nature*, 351: 524–25.

Halls, L. (ed.) (1985) *White-tailed Deer*, Harrisburgh: Stackpole, 119–28.

Haltenorth, T. (1963) *Handbuch der Zoologie*, 1(18): 1–67.

Hirsch, J. (1981) 'To "unfrock the charlatans"', *Sage Race Relations Abstracts*, 6: 1–65.

Lehman, N., Eisenhawer, A., Hansen, K., Mech, L.D., Peterson, R.O., Gogan, P.J.P. and Wayne, R.K. (1991) 'Introgression of coyote mitochondrial DNA into sympatric north American gray wolf populations', *Evolution*, 45: 104–19.

Nadler, C.F., Korobitsina, K.V., Hoffmann, R.S. and Vorontsov, N.N. (1973) 'Cytogenic differentiation, geographic distribution and domestication in palaearctic sheep (*Ovis*)', *Zeit f. Saugetierkunde*, 38: 109–25.

O'Brien, S.J. and Mayr, E. (1991) 'Bureaucratic mischief: recognizing endangered species and subspecies', *Science* 251: 1187–8.

Rennie, J. (1991) 'Howls of dismay: if red wolves are coyotes, they could lose protection', *Scientific American*, 256(4): 18–20.

Wayne, R.K. and Jenks, S.M. (1991) 'Mitochondrial DNA analysis implying extensive hybridization of the endangered red wolf *Canis rufus*', *Nature*, 351: 565–8.

First published as Geist, V. (1992) 'Endangered species and the law', *Nature*, 357: 274–6. Valerius Geist is Professor Emeritus of Environmental Science at the University of Calgary, and a specialist in human and large mammal biology and the environment. He was appointed the first director of the Environmental Science programme at the University in 1971.

Chapter 30

Museums, collections and biodiversity inventories

Pere Alberch

R ECENT YEARS HAVE WITNESSED an increased awareness on the part of the media and the general public that we live on a planet that is a relative unknown to us. Current estimates suggest that the 1.4–1.8 million species of living organisms described by scientists represent less than 15% of the actual number (Raven and Wilson 1992; Stork 1994).

This surprising fact has found its echo among politicians, who at the 'Earth Summit', held in 1992 in Rio de Janeiro, introduced (under the auspices of the United Nations) the 'Convention on Biological Diversity', which is currently in the process of being endorsed by most countries. Among other issues, such as technology transfer and patent rights on biotechnological products, the Convention on Biological Diversity binds the signing parties to undertake a survey of the species of plants and animals living within the political boundaries of the country as well as setting aside enough protected areas to allow the preservation and sustainable use of their national flora and fauna.

This is a lofty and commendable goal and it is very positive that politicians have realized the potential economic importance attached to biodiversity. A key question now is: can such an inventory of biological diversity be done within a reasonable time? Habitat destruction is occurring rapidly and, consequently, many species disappear before we know they ever existed. It has taken science, since Linnaeus, 200 years to describe 1.4–1.8 million species.

Currently, description rates across all taxa are remarkably low, averaging 13,078 per year for the period 1978–1987 (Hammond 1992). Stork (1994) estimates, in my view quite optimistically, that it would take a minimum of 90–120 years to describe all species at present rates. Wilson (in Wilson and Peters 1988) has suggested that it would take 25,000 taxonomist lifetimes to complete the task. In any case, the timeframe is clearly unacceptable given the urgency of the task.

In contrast with the widely accepted view that inventorying biodiversity is an urgent and deserving task, natural history museums — reservoirs of data on biological diversity as well as centres of taxonomic expertise — continue to suffer from an image problem. They are often perceived as intellectually stagnant, even anachronistic, institutions. The reasons for this misperception are mainly historical.

Descendants of the cabinets of curiosities, natural history museums first appeared in the 18th century in most cultured capitals of Europe. At that time museums were progressive scientific institutions. As Foucault (1966) persuasively argues, museum displays and collections were a reflection of a novel view of the natural world — the Linnaean concept that there exists an intrinsic order in nature. In the 19th century, and particularly with the advent of the Darwinian theory of evolution, museums began to miss the train of progress. How could one integrate a dynamic view of nature within the static framework of museum collections? Slowly, museums were becoming 'museums of themselves'. In the face of change, and shrinking budgets, museum curators often have become more and more self-centred and isolated from society, revelling in past splendours and on the importance of their collections (while bitterly complaining about the insensibility and ignorance of the science policymakers who deny them the necessary funding to adequately support their institutions).

Natural history museums are at a turning point in their history. They can now play a central and critical role in the development of research leading towards the understanding, conservation and sustainable use of biodiversity. To achieve this goal, however, they must radically change their mode of operation and public image, to clearly define goals, objectives and new research strategies. If museums are unable to meet the challenge, other institutions will be created *de novo* to fill the niche. The Instituto Nacional de Biodiversidad (lNBio) of Costa Rica is an example of the latter (see below).

I am convinced of the urgency of the task and the need to react quickly. Museums cannot be dominated by the philosophy of inward-looking curators, working leisurely on their taxa of choice all their lives. As Raven and Wilson point out, 'if taxonomy is to play the role foreordained by the biodiversity crisis, its practitioners need to formulate an explicitly stated mission with a timetable and cost estimate'.

When confronted with a changing view of nature — from order to dynamics, from description of objects to elucidation of processes — museums have undergone an identity crisis that has resulted in a progressive dilution of their research objectives. Museums should remain faithful to their identity. The collections are the museum's 'soul' and *raison d'être*. Collections are also a unique research tool in comparative biology. Therefore, whatever the research strategy that a museum wishes to develop, it cannot ignore the existence of such a unique resource. Consequently, museum-based research must emphasize disciplines that have a comparative component and that make use of the collections to some degree. Biodiversity studies are at the core of such philosophy. Therefore, museums, and allied institutions such as herbaria and botanical gardens, are uniquely qualified to play a role in any multidisciplinary approach to the biodiversity crisis.

INBio: a success story

The Instituto Nacional de Biodiversidad de Costa Rica (lNBio) is a non-profit-making public-interest organization, established in 1989 (Gámez 1991). The brain-child of a molecular biologist, Rodrigo Gámez, and an ecologist, Daniel Janzen, INBio is a novel way of using a country's biodiversity for education and economic development. The first and foremost goal of the institution is to create a relatively complete inventory of Costa Rica's biodiversity within a decade. This amounts to a total of over 500,000 species of animals and plants (including fungi, viruses, bacteria, etc.).

To achieve this ambitious goal, INBio has developed a heterodox approach to the problem. The most unusual is, perhaps, the figure of the 'parataxonomist'. Parataxonomists are selected among country people (e.g. farmers, national park rangers, housewives, etc.). In general, they have a primary school level of edu-cation. They receive a six-month basic training in collection and preparation of biological samples, taxonomy and park administration. They work full-time with an adequate salary, which would be low for a person with a university degree but well above salaries obtained by people with similar levels of education. The parataxonomists are stationed at biodiversity offices located in a network over the country's con-served wildlands. They spend 17 days a month in the field and seven days at INBio headquarters. There, they receive feedback and advice when they revise the collected material with the taxonomists at INBio.

The role of the parataxonomist is important in a social as well as in a scientific context. Their residence in the field allows adequate in-depth temporal and spatial surveying. Their in-job training raises their awareness of their natural surround-ings. This is transmitted to their social milieu where natural diversity is suddenly perceived both as a source of curiosity and an intellectual challenge, as well as a means of obtaining a respectable source of income.

The taxonomists at INBio are university educated but, in general, do not hold a PhD degree. They are generalists rather than experts on specific taxonomic groups. They act as liaisons between the parataxonomists and the internationally-based experts that identify difficult material and describe new species.

The collections (currently only plants and arthropods are being collected) that are assembled by the 'parataxonomists' are organized at INBio headquarters and the data entered into a computer. The specimen labels are bar-coded to make com-puterized information reading more efficient. In collaboration with companies in the field of information technology, INBio is devising software packages that would allow the ecological and taxonomic data to be integrated into land management and conservation.

INBio has actively, and aggressively, searched new uses of the information com-piled. A tangible first step was achieved when it signed an agreement with the phar-maceutical company Merck. In what is probably the first joint venture between a multinational biotechnology company and a country that is a reservoir of biodiversity, Merck made an initial investment of $1 million to INBio. In exchange, INBio will collect samples of plants and animals to be examined for new chemicals to be used as pharmaceutical drugs. If this 'biochemical prospecting' leads to marketable prod-ucts then there are arrangements for sharing the royalties. The potential revenues through such type of agreement are enormous. Therefore, it is not surprising that the INBio experience is being closely followed by many tropical countries. INBio is showing that a well-managed biodiversity survey can result in tangible social and economic benefits.

Collections

Museum people must convince our peers in other scientific disciplines that museums can carry out 21st century research – in particular, that the biological collections that are stored in museums are essential tools for research. They certainly deserve the same support and recognition as any other database of biological diversity (e.g. banks of gene sequences). In my view, there are three interrelated reasons why natural history collections have not been properly appreciated, and consequently underfunded: (1) loose compilation criteria; (2) absence of unified data standards; and (3) failure to identify new potential users.

Natural history collections have grown in a largely haphazard manner, contingent on the personal interests and preferences of the successive curators. Therefore, data have been organized mainly to serve the interests of the collector. It is not unusual to hear zealous field biologists talking about 'their collections', even if the material has been gathered while on the museum's payroll and the collections trip sponsored by a government funding agency. As a result, collections around the world (and this assertion includes major institutions) are not organized along the same criteria, do not share the same data standards and the information associated with most of them has not been computerized. Such factors make the information hard to retrieve and to use most effectively.

Finally, museums need to confront the fact that they are 'service providers' to an outside user community. But, who are the users? Data on biodiversity is essential for conservation and public education programs, as well as applied purposes such as 'chemical prospecting' – the search for new natural products. Museums should look beyond traditional uses of the collections and organize the information associated with them accordingly. INBio in Costa Rica is an excellent example of collections being assembled to fulfil the needs of a multi-user community.

The need for creating networks and standardizing practices among museums, under the auspices of international funding, is underscored by the fact that the building of reference collections, such as the ones currently existing in Europe, Australia and North America, is a slow and very expensive endeavour. Therefore, these institutions are likely to remain the primary centres of information in the near future. It is advisable and cost efficient, and also a duty to developing countries, to make the information stored in the major museums readily available to researchers in distant countries through the use of modern technology.

Taxonomic expertise

Biodiversity surveys generate enormous numbers of specimens to be processed and identified. A large percentage of these specimens corresponds to species unknown to science that can only be described by a professional taxonomist with experience in the relevant group. For example, the entomological expedition of the Natural History Museum (London) to Sulawesi in 1985 collected 1690 species of Hemiptera [true bugs] of which 62% were new to science (Stork 1994). Closer to home, the Museo Nacional de Ciencias Naturales (Madrid) coordinates a comprehensive survey of the fauna of the Iberian Peninsula. As part of this project, a recent oceanographic collecting trip along the Southern coast of Spain yielded 25000 specimens, mostly invertebrates. They comprised about 800 species; of them, at least 96 were new to science (M.A. Ramos, pers. commun.).

The existence of large numbers of rare and undescribed species is a major problem in comprehensive national surveys. INBio experience supports this contention. INBio's 'army' of parataxonomists does an excellent job in surveying both spatially and temporally different regions of Costa Rica. Huge collections are assembled and preliminarily sorted by technical staff in INBio headquarters. The common species are not a problem, but the process slows down with the rare or undescribed species.

Since it is impossible for INBio, or for any other single institution, to train local experts in every group, it must rely on a worldwide network of external experts. These experts do the work mostly on a voluntary basis and consequently their assistance to INBio is subordinated to other professional demands. To avoid these shortcomings, and to provide an effective and comprehensive taxonomic assistance international collaboration is required. For example, the natural history museums of London and Madrid are spearheading an initiative, hopefully funded by the EC, that would assemble a group of European institutions, and of expert taxonomists, to provide INBio with assistance in the identification of material as well as training of specialized personnel. The experience could then be extended to other countries such as Indonesia and Kenya that are beginning to develop biodiversity institutes. The purpose of this international collaboration benefits all parties involved. Tropical countries gain access to taxonomic expertise and to reference collections. European institutions have the opportunity to recycle a workforce of taxonomists that often are underemployed.

In this global problem, we suffer from a lack of global planning. For example, as emphasized by Gaston and May (1992), the distribution of taxonomists is ill-matched to the species richness of taxa and to the jobs remaining to be done for different groups (e.g. too many vertebrate taxonomists, not enough fungi specialists). To palliate this problem we must resort to international collaboration. Worldwide databases of taxonomists need to be compiled. An example along these lines is DIRTAX, a computerized database of all taxonomists in Spain, which contains addresses, taxonomic and geographic areas of expertise, etc. (Bello, Becerra and G-Valdecasas 1992). Similar databases for other countries probably exist; if not, they should be compiled. The objective is to have access to a worldwide database of taxonomic expertise. This would allow us to identify areas in which training is redundant and others in which it is needed. Optimally, experts should be 'on-call' for identification of new material sent to them from the various national surveys. Here again we need to operate at a global scale. Planning, and setting priorities, must be clearly established to ensure efficiency and avoid undue duplication of effort.

Finally, even if we had a worldwide 'corps' of experts to determine new taxa, we also need appropriate information technology which would allow routine identification of material by non-experts. This again would facilitate a more efficient use of personnel and resources. The technology is available. I am most familiar with the effort of the Dutch foundation ETI (Expert-Centre for Taxonomic Identification) who are developing, in CD-ROM format, user-friendly software that allows one to identify taxa using an approach that includes an abundance of diagrams, drawings, photographs and even moving images (Schalk 1992). Such interactive systems will become an indispensable tool in biodiversity inventories.

Conclusions

Taxonomy, in spite of its devotion to orderliness and nomenclatural zeal, has done a poor job at coordination and planning. Driven by individual initiatives and personal preferences we find ourselves in a position in which we do not even know how many species have been described (estimates range from 1.4 to 1.8 million) – even less an adequate assessment of the task that lies ahead. We need more computerized databases amenable to constant updating instead of, say, lavishly published taxonomic monographs.

Recent years have witnessed a renewed recognition for taxonomy and its practitioners. But the same spotlight forces us to review the standard working methodology: it is too slow and does not readily respond to the needs of outside users, such as applied scientists, policymakers or, even, private companies. The solution must include international collaboration, use of tools from modern information technology and, most importantly, the establishment of priorities. Efforts to increase the degree of coordination in biodiversity studies are underway in several countries. The United States, in response to this need, is in the process of creating a 'Biological Survey', an ambitious institution that will fund and coordinate biodiversity studies (e.g. Reichhardt 1993). At a more modest level, but adequately funded, the Spanish national science funding agencies decided, over five years ago, to channel all support for research on taxonomy and faunal surveys through three national-level projects: Flora Ibérica, Fauna Ibérica and Flora Micológica. As the names suggest, the goal is to compile a complete biodiversity survey of the Iberian Peninsula. Such a financing structure allows for some degree of coordination. For example, at this time the project Fauna Ibérica, managed by the Museo Nacional de Ciencias Naturales, funds and coordinates the activities of over 80 taxonomists (working in universities, research centres or as private specialists) all over the country.

At the international level, museums and allied institutions must organize into networks to implement a change in working methods. This is necessary both in terms of developing more efficient approaches to a global challenge as well as in devising a strategy to lobby international funding agencies. Obviously, a respectable amount of money is needed to carry out the proposed inventory and analysis of biodiversity. However, the level of funding needed to map out the biodiversity of this planet is not superior to that already allocated to study the human genome or in the construction of ever more powerful particle accelerators, not to speak of space exploration. I mention these examples to emphasize that the financial request is not utopian and the knowledge of our natural surroundings is as important as deciphering the organization of our genome or the structure of the atom.

If taxonomists, and the institutions that house them, have not been able to muster support, it is because they lack the image of progress and modernity that physicists and molecular biologists have so successfully conveyed. To change the image we must propose new approaches, and most importantly, set deadlines. But, even if we had the money, we need to deliver. Large natural history museums are often too engrossed in their own distinguished past and traditions. If they continue in this frame of mind, unable to rise to the new challenges, they will indeed turn into museums of themselves.

References

Bello, E., Becerra, I.M. and G.-Valdecasas, A. (1992) 'Counting on taxonomy', *Nature*, 357: 531.

Foucault, M. (1966) *Les Mots et les Choses*, Paris: Gallimard.

Gámez, R. (1991) 'Biodiversity conservation through facilitation of its sustainable use: Costa Rica's National Biodiversity Institute', *Trends, Ecology and Evolution*, 6: 377–8.

Gaston, K.I. and May, R.M. (1992) 'The taxonomy of taxonomists', *Nature*, 356: 281–2.

Hammond, P.M. (1992) 'Species inventory', in Groombridge, B. (ed.) *Global Biodiversity: Status of the Earth's Living Resources*, London: Chapman & Hall, 17–39.

Raven, P.H. and Wilson, E.O. (1992) 'A fifty-year plan for biodiversity surveys', *Science*, 258: 1099–100.

Reichhardt, T. (1993) 'Clinton announces package of environmental reforms', *Nature*, 362: 779.

Schalk, P.H. (1992) *Systematics Goes Multimedia: Computerized Biological Knowledge*, Amsterdam: Expertise Centre for Taxonomic Identification.

Stork, N.E. (1994) 'Inventories of biodiversity: more than a question of numbers', in Forey, P.L. Humphries, C.J. and Vane-Wright, R.I. (eds) *Systematics and Conservation Evaluation*, Oxford: Clarendon Press, 81–100.

Wilson, E.O. and Peters, M.P. (eds) (1988) *Biodiversity*, Washington, DC: National Academy Press, 3–18.

First published as Alberch, P. (1993) 'Museums, collections and biodiversity inventories', *Trends in Ecology and Evolution*, 8(10): 372–5. Pere Alberch (1954–98) was Director and then Research Professor at the National Museum of Natural Sciences in Madrid. A passionate evolutionist, he made important contributions to the understanding of biodiversity.

Index